D0984304

LOEB CLASSICAL LIBRARY

FOUNDED BY JAMES LOEB 1911

EDITED BY

JEFFREY HENDERSON

POLYBIUS

I

LCL 128

POLYBIUS

THE HISTORIES

BOOKS 1–2

TRANSLATED BY
W. R. PATON

REVISED BY
FRANK W. WALBANK
AND
CHRISTIAN HABICHT

HARVARD UNIVERSITY PRESS
CAMBRIDGE, MASSACHUSETTS
LONDON, ENGLAND
2010

First published 1922

Revised 2010

LOEB CLASSICAL LIBRARY® is a registered trademark
of the President and Fellows of Harvard College

Library of Congress Control Number 2009937799
CIP data available from the Library of Congress

ISBN 978-0-674-99637-3

*Composed in ZephGreek and ZephText by
Technologies 'N Typography, Merrimac, Massachusetts.
Printed on acid-free paper and bound by
The Maple-Vail Book Manufacturing Group*

CONTENTS

PREFACE TO THE SECOND EDITION   vii

INTRODUCTION   xi

BIBLIOGRAPHY   xxix

THE HISTORIES

     Book I   2

     Book II   262

INDEX   459

PREFACE TO THE
SECOND EDITION

The Loeb Polybius, first published in 1922, contains the
Büttner-Wobst text, still standard today, and an excellent
translation by W. R. Paton, but it was never properly completed: Paton died suddenly in 1921 while still at work
on the project, leaving a draft that included indexes but
no introduction and scant explanatory notes. The general
editors, deeming the draft sufficiently advanced to be serviceable, decided not to search for another scholar to revise and complete the edition but made it ready for publication more or less as it was, with a minimal introduction
supplied by H. J. Edwards, C.B.

So matters stood until 1964, when Frank W. Walbank,
the ideal candidate to revise Paton's edition, agreed to do
so concurrently with work on his great *Historical Commentary on Polybius* (Oxford 1957–79). By 1968, as he embarked on the third volume of the *Commentary*, Walbank
had begun to annotate the edition, entering changes to
be made both in the text and translation. But further delay was in store: in the early 1970s, when the Library and
its publishers entered a difficult era of restructuring and
reorganization, the Paton revision was put indefinitely
on hold, and there would be no further communication

with Walbank about the project for another twenty-five years.

In 1993, when the Library's fortunes had revived, Zeph Stewart, executive trustee, contacted Walbank about the status of the revision. Walbank replied that he had completed his annotations in the mid-1980s, and although he was no longer inclined to complete the revision himself, he was happy to make his annotations available to someone the Library might recruit for the task. After still further delays and some false starts, in 2007 Christian Habicht reviewed Walbank's annotations and, concluding that they were ready to incorporate with little change, agreed to perform the remaining tasks of revision: to supply explanatory notes and a new introduction, and to revise the indexes, bringing everything up to date with current scholarship. He also acted on Walbank's recommendation that fragments referring to a book number should be integrated in the text. Meanwhile, S. Douglas Olson agreed to prepare an edition of the remaining fragments, which will appear in the final volume.

Frank Walbank, who died on 23 October 2008, just short of his ninety-ninth birthday, was pleased that the revision was finally going forward in such capable hands, though it is unfortunate that he will miss the publication of this, the latest of his many signal contributions to classical scholarship.

On behalf of the Library I wish to express thanks to Ernst Badian, Glen W. Bowersock, and Christopher P. Jones for advice and good offices along the way; to Dr. Dorothy J. Thompson, Walbank's daughter and executor, for readiness to provide information, useful documents, and general encouragement; and to Julia Bernheim, Habicht's assistant at the Institute for Advanced Study for more than twenty years, whose service to this project has been invaluable.

JJH
July 2009

INTRODUCTION

Together with Thucydides and Tacitus, Polybius ranks among the outstanding historians of antiquity. While he does not equal these two in sheer intellectual power, his work makes up for this slight deficiency by the broad range and uniqueness of its content. What he tells is nothing less than the story of Rome's surge, within the short span of some fifty years, to undisputed rule over the Mediterranean world. The author witnessed the later stages of this process as an interested observer, once in a while even as an active participant. For his task he benefitted from close personal connections to some of the leading Roman figures instrumental in bringing about Rome's dominion. His work covers the time during which the Republic first annexed territories overseas that were to become its first provinces: Sicily in 241, Sardinia with Corsica in 227, Hispania in 197, Macedonia in 148, Achaea (added to Macedonia) in 146.* A little later he also witnessed the acquisition of two others, Asia in 129 and Gallia Narbonensis in 121. Polybius originally intended to end his report with the defeat of King Perseus of Macedonia in 168, but then continued down to the year 146, which saw the destruction of both Carthage and Corinth. With this addition, the de-

* All dates in this work refer to years B.C., unless otherwise stated.

xi

tailed treatment covers seventy-four years, from 220 to 146. A less detailed forerunner of what was to follow dealt with the decades from 264 to 221, with narratives about the First Punic War and the First Roman expedition to Illyria as its main topics.

Life

The author was born into a prominent family of the Arcadian town of Megalopolis, a member of the Achaean Confederacy in or very close to 200, just before the Achaeans switched their alliance from King Philip V of Macedonia to his Roman enemies. He may have died, aged eighty-two years, in 118 or shortly thereafter. His father, Lycortas, was among the leading Achaean politicians and saw his son, as soon as he reached the qualifying age in 170, elected as hipparch, commander of the League's cavalry. While in office, 170/69, during the war of the Romans against King Perseus, Polybius played a minor role which involved delicate dealings with the Roman generals in command. He seemed on his way to a brilliant career when the end of the war brought it to an abrupt close. Like many others, he was suspected of lacking in his pro-Roman commitment; he was deported to Italy with one thousand other Achaeans. None was ever formally charged or convicted, but those who lived long enough had to wait seventeen years before they were finally permitted to go home. It was Polybius' good fortune that he was not only allowed to remain in Rome and move freely about, but that he became acquainted with Scipio Aemilianus and soon became his close friend. He was the son of Lucius Aemilius Paullus but adopted into the family of Scipio Africanus. It was his destiny to destroy Carthage, and when this happened, Polybius was at his side.

Polybius' presence at Rome placed him in an ideal position to gather the information that he needed for his task. His contacts included other members of the Roman nobility, such as the elder Cato, and also kings, princes, and pretenders visiting the Senate, foreign ambassadors, hostages such as the prince Demetrius of Syria, as well as other detainees from various parts of the ancient world. Many became his sources for particular events, in which they had often played a significant role. He had the freedom to associate with Prince Demetrius and with ambassadors from the court in Alexandria. He could go hunting with members of the Roman nobility and even played a very active role in helping Demetrius escape to Syria, where he successfully claimed the throne that was rightfully his: the story of that escape (31.11–15) illustrates all of this.

It was also as a detainee that Polybius came to know much more of the world than he would otherwise have. Before his deportation he knew the Peloponnese and most of Greece proper very well and had come to see Macedonia during the war against King Perseus. Most of what he saw beyond—a great deal of the Mediterranean—came in his status as a detainee of Rome. He made the passage through the Alps once crossed by Hannibal with his army (3.45.12) and left a vivid description of them (2.14–15), as well as a classic account of the Po (2.16. 6–15). He saw Gaul, Africa, Spain, the Atlantic, and Africa (3.59.7) and visited Locri in southern Italy more than once (12. 5.1). He made most of these journeys in the company of Scipio or another of the Roman nobles. Soon after the destruction of Carthage in 146, Scipio sent him with a squadron of the

Roman fleet to explore the African coast (34.15.7). Later that year he finally returned home. He found Achaea in a deplorable state, soon after the lost war against the Romans and the destruction of Corinth. He then used his influence with the Romans and his talents trying "to appease the anger of the ruling power" (38.4.7). When "a certain Roman" attempted to have the numerous statues of Philopoemen removed, Polybius persuaded Mummius and the ten legates attached to him to let them stand. The Achaeans thanked him by awarding him a statue (39.3.1–3 and 11). When the Romans left Greece in the spring of 145, they gave Polybius the authority to interpret the new constitution and the new laws to the cities and to clear up matters at which people were in doubt (39.5.1–2). The former detainee of the Romans had become their representative in his country, and his career, so suddenly halted earlier, was now given a conciliatory conclusion by the same Romans who had precluded its natural course.

Virtually nothing is heard of him after that, but he probably was with Scipio once again in 134/3, when Scipio finally brought the war in Spain to an end at Numantia. Polybius had an older brother, Thearidas, who was spared deportation to Italy and is mentioned as active in Achaean politics in the years 159/8 and 147/6 (32.7.1 and 38.10.1). The historian never mentions a wife or children, but a single sentence makes it almost certain that he was married and a father (12.25h.5).

The Work

In the period that his work covers, Rome had to deal not only with the Carthaginians but also with the Gauls in

Italy and the Illyrians on the Balkans, with King Philip V of Macedonia, who allied himself with Hannibal, and then with Antiochus III the Great of the vast Seleucid Empire. The Third Macedonian War against King Perseus followed. Long before that, in the course of the Punic Wars, Rome had also become involved in Spain and, following the conquest of Egypt by Antiochus IV of Syria, in the affairs of the Ptolemies and of the Jews. Since he covers all these different spheres, Polybius rightly insists that his approach is universal, as distinct from the monographs of historians content to write about narrower, particular topics. Nor did he doubt that his approach is superior to theirs.

Polybius had no doubt that it was Rome's aim to dominate the known world, and he recognized that Scipio's victory over Hannibal in 202 put that goal within reach. The event happened a little more than a decade after Rome's darkest day, the defeat at Cannae in 216. According to Polybius, it was the strength of the Roman constitution that allowed the Republic not only to survive but to triumph in the end. Polybius' assessment of that constitution, to which Book Six is devoted, follows logically immediately after that disaster.

The *Histories* were not Polybius' first venture as a writer. When he had just grown into manhood, he was selected to carry the urn with the ashes of the Achaean hero Philopoemen to his public funeral; he then composed a description of his life in a style resembling a panegyric. It was certainly at Rome that he conceived the idea of writing his main work. It was aimed at Roman readers (6.11.3; 31.22.8), a clear sign that educated Romans were able to read Greek, but the author also had a Greek audience in mind (10.4.9). Unfortunately, his *Histories* is only partly preserved. Only the first five books are complete, amounting to more than a third of what is still extant. In addition, longer or shorter excerpts made in the tenth century, as well as quotations from his *Histories* found in other writers, are preserved from the other books. From Book 37 just one insignificant fragment survives, and nothing at all from Books 17 and 40. For much of the lost parts a good and fairly full idea of their contents can be gained from other writers who followed Polybius, principally Livy, who in his Books 31 to 45 depends largely on him and mostly translated his text word for word into Latin.

As for the date of composition, not a single sentence in the preserved parts of the work can be shown to have been written before 167, the date of the author's confinement at Rome. Moreover, even the early books contain elements clearly written between 167 and 146 (2.37.7–11) or after 146 (3.4.12–5.6). As early as 3.32 Polybius refers to the total of forty books as already written. The latest recognizable dates point to after 138 (18.41), to 129 at the earliest (31.28.13 and 38.21.3), and to ca. 118 (3.39. 8). Late dates in the early books are most likely later additions to a narrative written much earlier. It is natural to assume that the research for such a vast work and the time required to execute it would have consumed several decades.

Sources

For events happening before his starting date of 264 Polybius used earlier historians such as Ephorus, Theopompus, Timaeus, and Calisthenes wherever needed to complement what he knew from memory. For the Punic Wars he regards the Roman Fabius Pictor and the Greek

Philinus as the best authorities, whereas he condemns
Sosylus, who accompanied Hannibal on his campaign, as
untrustworthy. Since several generations of the Scipiones
played large roles in the two later Punic Wars, family tradition would have come to Polybius through his friend Scipio
Aemilianus. Gaius Laelius, a lifelong companion of the elder Scipio Africanus, obviously contributed much for the
years of the Hannibalic War. For Greek affairs in the third
century, the memoirs of Aratus, the leading statesman of
Achaea for almost forty years, seem to have been the most
important source, complemented by Phylarchus, whom
Polybius accused of bias toward the Spartan King Cleomenes, the adversary of Aratus. Polybius' father, Lycortas, was in close contact with Philopoemen, the dominant
figure after the death or Aratus, and the son must have
learned from him much about the events of his time. At
the time of Philopoemen's death, Polybius had reached
the age where he himself closely followed major develop-
ments. At Rome, finally, he found, as noted, a plethora
of important actors whom he interviewed regarding the
events in which they had been or were still involved.

Use of Documents

The most reliable parts of the work are the numerous
documents that Polybius inserted into his narrative, some
word for word, such as the alliance between Philip V and
Hannibal (7.9), a copy of which had fallen early into Roman hands, or several of Rome's peace treaties, as well as
others in a more or less detailed summary form. There is
near-general agreement that he had access to archives at
Rome and at Rhodes and to the documents of the Achaean

League. In particular he searched for international treaties, and to a substantial degree it is thanks to him that so many of these can now be found in the second and third volumes of *Die Staatsverträge des Altertums*, where they are discussed together with other evidence wherever it exists.

Speeches

As was the custom of Greek historians, Polybius included speeches in his narrative. The question for him, as for other historians, is whether or to what degree the speeches resembled what was actually said in a given situation, or whether they were, in substance, inventions of the author himself attempting to capture the speakers' intentions. In this respect Polybius, severely criticizes Timaeus, who, he says, simply invented the speeches by making the speakers say what in his opinion they *ought* to have said, so that his speeches are labeled pure fiction, whereas the true historian's task was to find out and report what was actually said: τὰ κατ' ἀλήθειαν λεχθέντα (36.1.7) or οἱ κατ' ἀλήθειαν εἰρημένοι λόγοι (12.25b.l). As to the speeches inserted by Polybius, opinions differ widely and differ, within his work, from one case to the other. For example, when in the summer of 189 King Eumenes and ambassadors from Rhodes were heard in the Senate on the question of how the new order for Asia Minor ceded by King Antiochus ought to look, both sides are given long speeches (21.19.1–21.11 and 21.22.5–23.12 respectively). Polybius probably had been given various reports from oral witnesses of what had been said on that occasion, and these may have included essential elements of the actual speeches. But nothing could come even close to a transcript. Some scholars, such as E. Bikerman, regard both speeches as compositions of Polybius and as his interpretation of the divergent interests of both parties. Other scholars, among them M. Gelzer and F. W. Walbank, put greater stock in the reliability of these and other speeches, such as the one by the Aetolian Agelaus on the eve of the peace concluded in 217 at Naupactus. Agelaus spoke, referring to the Romans and the Carthaginians, of "the cloud in the West" dangerously hanging over Greece. In general, not much argues for the basic genuineness of the speeches, so that in most cases it is doubtful that Polybius came close to reproducing what had actually been said. But of course judgment will vary from case to case, and in the end remain personal and subjective.

Historical Causality

Polybius' aim is not simply to narrate events as they occurred. He always probes into their causality and sharply distinguishes between causes, pretexts, and beginnings (3.6, repeated 22.18). For the Hannibalic War he names three different causes of unequal weight: first, Hamilcar's bitterness after the defeat in the First Punic War (3.9.6); second, the loss of Sardinia (3.10.3); and third, Carthage's success in Spain (3.10.6). The first two would be incentives for Carthage to renew the war; the third, however, is clearly different, providing a Roman motive, although Polybius does not say so. His way of thinking leads him to construct causalities of doubtful validity, for instance his assertion that the main cause for the Third Macedonian War was Philip's bitterness after his defeat in 197 and his treatment at the hands of Rome in the 180s, and that he passed these feelings on to his successor Perseus (22.18). It is nevertheless quite clear that the Senate wanted this war and not Perseus, who did his utmost to avoid it. Similarly, Hamilcar implanted his hatred of Rome onto his son Hannibal at an early age (3.10.7–12.6). It follows that from the beginning Hannibal had no other goal than to make war on Rome, which then leads Polybius to argue that he had a careful plan to invade Italy, and that to this end he sought early connections to the Gauls living in areas leading to and through the Alps (3.34). But in fact all indications seem to show that the plan to invade Italy, and to do so by crossing the Alps, was an improvisation resulting from the news that war had been declared at Carthage (see nn. on 3.34).

Polybius' Views On the Historian's Task

Polybius states that the historian has no higher duty than to stick to the truth. For the sake of truth he must not shrink from accusing his friends or praising his enemies (1.14). In a given instance he indeed does not hesitate to criticize his idol Philopoemen (22.19.1) or his own father, Lycortas (22.9. 12; 23.15.1), whom he nevertheless considers the equal of Philopoemen. Conversely, he admits that King Philip V, whom he so often bitterly accuses of defying divine and human laws, overcame political and personal misfortunes to become the most moderate of men (25.3). He credits Perseus with excellent beginnings and as showing true royal dignity in his first years (25.8) but later condemns him as a coward (29.17–18). While he admires the path of the Romans to world dominion and is convinced

of their superiority, he does not hesitate to give their enemies credit whenever they prove to be worthy opponents.
Among the Carthaginians these are not only the leading
figures Hamilcar and Hannibal but also such minor commanders as Himilco (1.42, 45). He depicts the Senate of
Carthage in 256 as displaying manly and noble dignity in a
seemingly hopeless situation (1.31).

Historians who err deserve to be pardoned, but not
those who deliberately deviate from the truth (12.12.4).
He finds Philinus and Fabius Pictor lacking in impartiality,
but says that he does not accuse them of intentional falsehood, only of being too favorably inclined to one side,
Philinus toward the Carthaginians, Fabius toward the
Romans. He directs similar criticism at the Rhodian historians Zeno and Antisthenes in connection with their reports on the battle of Lade in 200 (16.14–16). He is much
harsher in his condemnation of others: unnamed authors
who praised even severe outrages of Philip V as commend-
able achievements (8.8), Theopompus for his irrational
treatment of Philip II (8.11–13), and in particular Timaeus
(in large parts of Book 12), whom he accuses of all possible professional sins, almost the least of which is sloppy
research. Attentive readers will see for themselves that
Polybius, for the Punic wars, seems in general very fair to
both sides, while in other instances he is not free of the
faults he castigates in others: his criticism of Callisthenes
(on military matters) and his verdict of Timoleon, the pro-
tector of the Greeks in Sicily against the Carthaginians (for
which role Timaeus eulogized him), are downright mean
(nn. on 12.17.2 and 12.23. 4).

Polybius also shows his preferences and animosities
fairly often: against the Aetolians (4.62), the Boeotians (20.

4), and the Athenians, when their leaders put Athenian interests above those of the Achaeans (5.106.6–8). His fellow Achaeans, on the other hand, mostly receive good marks, except for the period after 167, when Callicrates wielded power and his opponents were detained in Italy. He puts the blame for the catastrophe of the confederacy in 146 squarely on its corrupt and irresponsible leaders, without ascribing to the Romans a share in what happened. On the Roman side too he is not always impartial, but shows bias against three of the consuls of 218, 217, and 216, all of whom, incidentally, were losers in battles against Hannibal (3.70.3. 80.3; 110.3). Given his warm friendship with Scipio Aemilianus, it is no wonder that not only this man, but also earlier members of the family into which he was adopted, receive much praise, in particular Scipio Africanus maior. Though most of this praise might seem well deserved, Polybius overstepped the limit when he lauded his treacherous nightly attack on the camp of Hasdrubal and Syphax (n. on 14.2.11) and even counted it as "the most splendid" of his exploits (14.5.15). Ironically, he has anonymous defenders of Roman actions saying, "Their particular merit, on which they prided themselves, is that they conducted their wars in a simple and noble manner, employing neither night attacks nor ambushes, disapproving of every kind of deceit and fraud, and considering that nothing but direct and open attacks were legitimate for them" (36.9.9).

Reliability

Errors are unavoidable in such a voluminous work as his, the more so wherever the author depends on the testimony of others. Most often they are simple errors of fact: a consulship is misdated by a year (1.52.5), a consul is given the wrong praenomen (2.11.1), or a sculptor named Hypatodorus is erroneously called Hecatodorus (4.78.5). There are inexact data for the Euphrates (9.43.4), for the highest mountains in Sicily (1.55.7), and for the foundation date of Brundisium (10.1.9). Other errors refer to events of the past: Polybius should have known that Hermocrates of Syracuse had been dead for several years when the battle of Aegospotami was fought (12.25k.11), that Attalus I was not the first to have a new Athenian tribe created and named in his honor (16.25.8), and that Quintus Fabius, appointed dictator in 217 after the battle of Trasimene, did not earn but had inherited the name of Maximus (3.87.6). These are minor mistakes due to ignorance and therefore pardonable, as he himself says (12.12.4). It is more serious that Polybius did not know (at least not at the time he wrote it) that a consul was not allowed to march with his army through the city of Rome (3.68.12). Mistaken is also his statement that all magistrates ceased to hold office once a dictator was appointed (3.87.8): in fact they continued to serve. More surprising is a series of wrong statements about some of the Scipiones (10.4.1–5.8), given Polybius' familiarity with them and with their friend Gaius Laelius. None of this, however, justifies the verdict that Polybius was not thorough and careful in his research; he certainly deserves high marks for accuracy.

Polybius' Views on Writing History

True history is for Polybius political history or history of events: πραγματικὴ ἱστορία, as he calls it. It consists of three parts: the study of the evidence, a geographical survey of the areas treated, and the account of political activity (12.25e.1). Studies in the library are not sufficient (e.4). He who undertakes the writing of history must have personal experience in politics, government, and military affairs. A man so qualified will be able to write history from which his readers can learn, provided he sticks to the truth and is not satisfied with simple statements of facts but enquires into their causes. Facts are interesting but do not illuminate. Insight into their causes, however, bears fruit, because if transposed to similar circumstances of one's own time, it provides the means to foresee what may happen, to take precautions, or to absorb lessons from the examples shown of good and evil. In this way history can teach what to emulate and what to avoid, as it places before our eyes professional or ethical excellence on the one hand, mistakes and injustices on the other.

From his own military experience Polybius expands more fully on one of the points he has made. He mentions among the skills a commander must possess astronomy and geometry in particular (9.14.5; 26a). He then gives four instances in which known generals failed on certain occasions by not having fully paid attention to what the moment required (9.17–19). From the perspective of his role as cavalry commander, he criticizes Callisthenes' description of movements during Alexander's victory over Darius at Issus and flatly states that they were not possible, given the location and the numbers involved (12.17–18).

Tyche

It is Polybius' opinion that the historian must look for the causes of major events, that these can be known, and therefore that people can learn from history. There is, however, one major obstacle to this reasoning: Tyche (Fortune), a divine being that can overthrow every rational calculation: "Fortune, who always defeats our reckoning by some novel stroke" (29.21.5). She is an irrational element making herself felt in capricious ways, thereby nullifying causality. When and how she may intervene can never be predicted, but her interventions can also have a rational aim, as 15.20.5–7 shows: it is Tyche who punishes two seasoned kings who conspired to rob a minor orphaned king of his paternal realm. This makes Polybius exclaim that those who have reasons to blame Tyche will be reconciled to her when learning of that punishment, for which Tyche chose the Romans as her instrument. In a similar reversal, she saw to it that on the very day on which the statues of Callicrates were removed from the public places in Achaea, those of his antipode Lycortas were once again erected (36.13.1–2).

Tyche, although unpredictable, can still follow a rational plan. It is she who brought about the surge of Rome to world dominion (1.4.1; 1.4.4), a statement contradicting other passages, in which Polybius ascribes that surge to the rational planning and resolve of the Romans (3.2.6; 15.10.2). One has to conclude that he lacked the analytical acumen that would have pointed out the incompatibility of both assertions. Reflecting on the events of 168, the author says that Tyche endowed the Macedonians with the whole wealth of Persia, but then made it clear that she had but lent them these blessings until she decided otherwise (29.21.6). The Athenian Demetrius of Phalerum, blessed with unique foresight, had foretold the end of the Macedonian monarchy more than a century before it happened. No one believed him at the time, and no one would have believed, fifty years before it happened, that the Persian Empire could fall (29.21.1–9). The consul Regulus of 256 provides Polybius (1.31–34) with a striking example that one cannot trust Tyche, especially when one enjoys success (1.35.2–3).

Style

From ancient to modern times, Polybius got and still receives lower marks for his style than for the contents of his narrative. He writes in a plain, straightforward manner, without embellishments. It is the style of Hellenistic documents, of the decrees of the cities and the letters of the kings. Always serious in pursuing his task and eager to bring home his point that people can learn from history, he often assumes the tone of a teacher, and a somewhat pedantic teacher at that. Even so, he can narrate engagingly, as can best seen from the long and fascinating story of the rebel Achaeus (7.15–18 and 8.15–34), which no one can read without being overcome by emotion. But whereas Polybius seems to view Achaeus' tragedy with some empathy, he is shockingly indifferent to the misfortunes of Greeks such as the Rhodians Deinon and Polyaratus, the victims of a merciless manhunt in 168 (30.7–9), since after the defeat of King Perseus it was considered a crime for them to have favored his side in their community.

A peculiarity of Polybius' style is his fondness for proverbs. Proverbs sometimes occur in a dense sequence, as for instance "Justice has an eye" and "A fool who slays the sire and leaves the sons alive" (both in 23.10), or in book 38.16, which contains three proverbs. Also characteristic of his style are about a dozen succinct notes on famous persons, usually on the occasion of their deaths. Three such men died during the year 183/2 and receive obituary notes from Polybius in three successive chapters of Book 23: Philopoemen (12), Hannibal (13), and Scipio Africanus maior (14); Polybius admired all three. Strikingly different are some bad notices, which occur for Sosibius, the chancellor of Ptolemy IV, "a dexterous instrument of evil" (15.15.1), for Pharnaces, who "surpassed all previous kings in his contempt for laws" (27.17), and for Prusias II, "a coward . . . , effeminate in body and mind" (36.15.2). Among others who receive notices of praise are Hannibal's brother Hasdrubal, who did not want to survive his defeat at the Metaurus River (11.2), Attalus I (18.41), the Galatian chieftain Ortiagon (23.22), Eumenes II (31.8), Massinissa (36.16), and Ptolemy VI (39.7). Unique is the eulogy of Queen Apollonis of Pergamum, the mother of four sons, all famous for the harmony prevailing among them, and of whom two became kings (22.20).

Reception

For the period that his work covers and for the events he described, Polybius remained the undisputed authority. He was very widely read. No attempt was made to replace his work. Posidonius and Strabo were two prominent historians who began where he had ended. Later authors who followed him more or less closely include Livy on the Roman side, Diodorus, Appianus, Pausanias, Cassius Dio, and others among Greek authors. Polybius may have shared parts of his work with contemporaries before publication: it has been assumed, for instance, that Marcus Porcius Cato, whom Polybius visited in 150, may have known something of it (cf. K. Ziegler, *RE* Polybius 1453, commenting on 35. 6). Another passage suggests that Polybius has received some critical reactions (38. 5.1). He himself reports that he addressed the Rhodian historian Zeno by letter and made him aware of mistakes he had made concerning the topography of Laconia. Zeno replied courteously, accepting the criticism, and added that he was unable to make changes, as he had already published his work (16.20.4–7). Such an exchange between two historians in antiquity is very rarely attested; it may recall the correspondence between Tacitus and Pliny the Younger on the eruption of Mount vesuvius in AD 79, when Tacitus, approaching the moment in which he would have to discuss the event in his *Histories*, wanted to learn more about the death of Pliny's uncle in that catastrophe.

Despite its great popularity, the *Histories* has not survived in its entirety. Only the first five books are completely preserved; for the following, mainly excerpts remained, made by order of the emperor Constantinus Porphyrogennetus in the tenth century. At that time Books 17, 19, 37, and 40 had already been lost. The authors who used Polybius, usually without quoting him, are of great assistance in attempts to reconstruct the contents of the lost books and parts of the work.

Readers will find a more comprehensive and still very useful introduction to the author and his *Histories* in Konrad Ziegler's article "Polybios," *RE* 21 (1952) 1440–1578, and another valuable summary is F. W. Walbank, *A Historical Commentary on Polybius*, I (Oxford 1957) 1–37.

SELECT BIBLIOGRAPHY

Aalders, G. J. D. *Die Theorie der gemischten Verfassung im Altertum*. Amsterdam 1968.

Accame, S. *Il dominio Romano in Grecia dalla guerra acaica ad Augusto*. Rome 1946.

Ager, S. A. *Interstate Arbitration in the Greek World, 337–90 B.C.* Berkeley 1996.

Allen, R. E. *The Attalid Kingdom: A Constitutional History*. Oxford 1983.

Astin, A.E. *Scipio Aemilianus*. Oxford 1967.

———. *Cato the Censor*. Oxford 1978.

Aymard, A. *Les premiers rapports de Rome et de la Conféderation achaienne (198–189 av. J.-C.)*. Bordeaux 1938.

Badian, E. *Titus Quinctius Flamininus: Philhellenism and Realpolitik*. Cincinnati 1970.

Bagnall, R. S. *The Administration of the Ptolemaic Possessions Outside Egypt*. Leiden 1976.

Bar-Kochva, B. *The Seleucid Army: Organization and Tactics in the Great Campaigns*. Cambridge 1976.

Bastien, J.-L. *Le triomphe romain et son utilisation politique*. Rome 2007.

Bastini, A. *Der Achäische Bund als hellenische Mittelmacht. Geschichte des achäischen Koinon in der Symmachie mit Rom*. Frankfurt am Main 1987.

SELECT BIBLIOGRAPHY

Beard, M. *The Roman Triumph*. Cambridge, MA 2007.

Behrwald, R. *Der Lykische Bund*. Bonn 2000.

Beloch, K. J., *Griechische Geschichte*² IV 1–2. Berlin 1925–1927.

Bernhardt, R. *Imperium und Eleutheria: Die römische Politik gegenüber den freien Städten des griechischen Ostens*. Diss. Hamburg 1971.

Berve, H. *König Hieron II*. Abh. Bayr. Akad. 1959.

———. *Die Tyrannis bei den Griechen*. 2 vols. Munich 1967.

Bikerman, E. *Institutions des Séleucides*. Paris 1938.

Brink, C. O. and Walbank, F. W. "The Construction of the Sixth Book of Polybius." *CQ* 48 (1954) 97–122.

Cabanes, P. *Les Illyriens de Bardylis à Genthios (IVe–IIe siècles avant J.-C.)*. Paris 1988.

Cartledge, P.-E. Spawforth. *Hellenistic and Roman Sparta: A Tale of Two Cities*. London 1989.

Champion, C. *Cultural Politics in Polybius's "Histories."* Berkeley 2004.

Chaniotis, A. *Die Verträge zwischen kretischen Poleis in der hellenistischen Zeit*. Stuttgart 1996.

——— *War in the Hellenistic Period*. Malden, MA 2005.

Cohen, G. M. *The Hellenistic Settlements in Europe, the Islands, and Asia Minor*. Berkeley, CA 1995.

———. *The Hellenistic Settlements in Syria, the Red Sea Basin, and North Africa*. Berkeley 2006.

Coskun, A., ed. *Roms auswärtige Freunde in der späten Republik und im frühen Prinzipat*. Göttingen 2005.

Dahlheim, W. *Struktur und Entwicklung des römischen Völkerrechts im 3. und 2. Jahrhundert v. Chr*. Munich 1968.

Dany, O. *Akarnanien im Hellenismus*. Munich 1999.

De Sanctis, G. *Storia dei Romani, III 1–2.*[2] Florence 1967–1968; *IV 1–3*. Florence 1953–1969.

Deininger, J. *Der politische Widerstand gegen Rom in Griechenland 217–86 v. Chr*. Berlin 1971.

Derow, P. "Polybius, Rome, and the East." *JRS* 69 (1979) 1–15.

Dreyer, B. *Die römische Nobilitätsherrschaft und Antiochos III. (205–188 v. Chr.)*. Hennef 2007.

Eckstein, A. M. *Moral Vision in the "Histories" of Polybius*. Berkeley 1994.

Ehling, K. *Untersuchungen zur Geschichte der späten Seleukiden (164–63 v. Chr): Vom Tode des Antiochos IV bis zur Einrichtung der Provinz Syria unter Pompeius*. Stuttgart 2008.

Eisen, F. *Polybios-Interpretationen*. Heidelberg 1966.

Errington, R. M. *Philopoemen*. Oxford 1969.

Erskine, A. ed. *A Companion to the Hellenistic World*. Malden, MA 2003.

Ferrary, J.-L. *Philhellénisme et impérialisme. Aspects idéologiques de la conquête romaine du monde hellénistique, de la seconde guerre de Macédoine à la guerre contre Mithridate*. Rome 1988.

Feyel, M. *Contribution à l'épigraphie béotienne*. Le Puy 1942.

Flacelière, R. *Les Aitoliens à Delphes*. Paris 1937.

Foucault, J. A. *Recherches sur la langue et le style de Polybe*. Paris 1972.

Franke, P. R. *Die antiken Münzen von Epirus*. 2 vols. Wiesbaden 1961.

Fraser, P. M. *Ptolemaic Alexandria*. 3 vols. Oxford 1972.

Fraser, P. M. - G. E. Bean. *The Rhodian Peraea and Islands*. Oxford 1954.

Gabba, E. ed. *Polybe. Neuf exposés suivis de discussions*. Entretiens 20. Geneva 1973.

Gabrielsen, V. ed. *Hellenistic Rhodes: Politics, Culture, and Society*. Aarhus 1999.

Gauthier, Ph. *Les cités grecques et leurs bienfaiteurs (IVe–Ier siècle avant J.-C.)*. Paris 1985.

Gelzer, M. *Über die Arbeitsweise des Polybios*. Heidelberg 1956.

Giovannini, A. *Untersuchungen über die Natur und die Anfänge der bundesstaatlichen Sympolitie in Griechenland*. Gottingen 1971.

Green, P. *Alexander to Actium. The Historic Evolution of the Hellenistic Age*. Berkeley, CA 1990.

Gruen, E.S. *The Hellenistic World and the Coming of Rome*. 2 vols. Berkeley, CA 1984.

Haake, M. *Der Philosoph in der Stadt*. Munich 2007.

Habicht, C. *Athènes hellènistique*, traduit de l' allemand par M. et D. Knoepfler.[2] Paris 2006.

———. *Gottmenschentum und griechische Städte*.[2] Munich 1970.

———. *The Hellenistic Monarchies: Selected Papers*. Ann Arbor 2006.

Hammond, N. G. L. *Epirus: The Geography, the Ancient Remains, the History and the Topography of Epirus and Adjacent Areas*. Oxford 1967.

Hammond, N. G. L. - F. W. Walbank. *A History of Macedonia*, vol. 3: *336–167* B.C. Oxford 1988.

Hansen, E. V. *The Attalids of Pergamon*.[2] Ithaca, NY 1970.

Harter-Uibopuu, K. *Das zwischenstaatliche Schiedsverfahren im Achäischen Koinon*. Köln 1998.

Hatzopoulos M. *L' organisation de l' armée macédonienne sous les Antigonides*. Athens 2001.

———. *Macedonian Institutions under the Kings*. 2 vols. Athens 1996.

Heuss, A. *Stadt und Herrscher des Hellenismus in ihren staats- und völkerrechtlichen Beziehungen*. Leipzig 1937.

Hölbl, G. *Geschichte des Ptolemäererreiches. Politik, Ideologie und religiöse Kultur von Alexander dem Grossen bis zur römischen Eroberung*. Darmstadt 1994.

Holleaux, M. *Études d' épigraphie et d' histoire grecques*. ed. L. Robert. 6 vols. Paris 1938–1968.

———. *Rome, la Grèce et les monarchies hellénistiques au IIIe siècle av. J.-C*. Paris 1921.

Hopp, J. *Untersuchungen zur Geschichte der letzten Attaliden*. Munich 1977.

Huss, W. *Agypten in hellenistischer Zeit, 332–30 v. Chr.* Munich 2001.

Kahrstedt, U. vol. 3 of Meltzer's *Geschichte der Karthager*. Berlin 1913.

Kallet-Marx, R. *Hegemony to Empire. The Developmen of the Roman Imperium in the East from 148 to 62 B.C.* Berkeley 1995.

Kobes, J. *Kleine Könige. Untersuchungen zu den Lokaldynasten im hellenistischen Kleinasien (323–185 v. Chr.)*. St. Katharinen 1996.

Laronde, A. *Cyrène et la Libye*. Paris 1987.

Larsen, J. A. O. *Greek Federal States: Their Institutions and History*. Oxford 1968.

Launey, M. *Recherches sur les armées hellénistiques*. 2 vols. Paris 1949–1950.

Le Bohec, S. *Antigone Dôsôn roi de Macédoine*. Nancy 1993.

Lefèvre, F. *L' Amphictionie pyléo-delphique. Histoire et Institutions*. Paris 1998.

Lehmann, G. A. *Untersuchungen zur historischen Glaubwürdigkeit des Polybios*. Münster 1967.

Lévêque, P. *Pyrrhos*. Paris 1957.

Ma, J. *Antiochos III and the Cities of Western Asia Minor*. Oxford 2000 (paperback ed. 2002).

Magnetto, A. *Gli Arbitrati Interstatali Greci*, II *(Dal 337 al 196 A.C.)*. Pisa 1997.

Mason, H. J. *Greek Terms for Roman Institutions: A Lexicon and Analysis*. Toronto 1974.

Mastrocinque, A. *La Caria e la Ionia meridionale in epoca ellenistica*. Rome 1979.

Mauersberger, A. et al. *Polybios-Lexikon*. Berlin 1956–2004.

Meister, K. *Historische Kritik bei Polybios*. Wiesbaden 1975.

Meloni, P. *Perseo e la fine della monarchia macedone*. Cagliari 1953.

Meltzer, O. *Geschichte der Karthager*, 1 Berlin 1879, 2 Berlin 1896 (for vol. 3 see Kahrstedt).

Mioni, E. *Polibio*. Padova 1949.

Mittag, P. F. *Antiochos IV. Epiphanes. Eine politische Biographie*. Berlin 2006.

Moore, J. M. *The Manuscript Tradition of Polybius*. Cambridge 1965.

Moretti, L. *Olympionikai, i vincitori negli antichi agoni olimpici*. Mem. accad. Lincei 1957.

SELECT BIBLIOGRAPHY

Mørkholm, O. *Antiochos IV of Syria*. Copenhagen 1966.

Nachtergael, G. *Les Galates en Grèce et les Sotéria de Delphes*. Brussels 1977.

Nadig, P. *Zwischen König und Karikatur. Das Bild Ptolemaios' VIII. im Spannungsfeld der Überlieferung*. Munich 2007.

Narain, A. K. *The Indo-Greeks*. Oxford 1957.

Niese, B. *Geschichte der griechischen und makedonischen Staaten seit der Schlacht bei Chaeroneia*. 3 vols. Gotha 1893–1903.

Nissen, H. *Kritische Untersuchungen über die Quellen der vierten und fünften Dekade des Livius*. Berlin 1863.

Nottmeyer, H. *Polybios und das Ende des Achaierbundes. Untersuchungen zu den römisch-achaiischen Beziehungen, ca. 180–146*. Munich 1995.

Oberhummer, E. *Akarnanien, Ambrakien, Amphilochien, Leukas im Altertum*. Munich 1887.

Olshausen, E. *Prosopographie der hellenistischen Königsgesandten*. Leuven 1974.

O'Neil, J. L. "'The Political Elites of the Achaean and Aetolian Leagues," *Ancient Society* 15–17 (1984–86) 33–61.

Otto, W. *Zur Geschichte der Zeit des 6. Ptolemäers*. Abh. Bayr. Akad. 1934.

Palm, J. *Polybios und der Kanzleistil*. Lund 1957.

Pape, M. *Griechische Kunstwerke aus Kriegsbeute und ihre öffentliche Aufstellung in Rom*. Diss. Hamburg 1975.

Paschidis, P. *Between City and King*. Athens 2008.

Pédech, P. *La méthode historique de Polybe*. Paris 1964.

Petzold, K.-E. *Studien zur Methode des Polybios und zu ihrer historischen Auswertung*. Munich 1969.

SELECT BIBLIOGRAPHY

Pritchett, W. K. *The Greek State at War*. 5 vols. Berkeley 1971–1991.

———. *Studies in Ancient Greek Topography*. 6 vols. Berkeley 1965–1989.

Radt, W. Pergamon. *Geschichte und Bauten einer antiken Metropole*. Darmstadt 1999.

Rigsby, K. J. *Asylia. Territorial Inviolability in the Hellenistic World*. Berkeley 1996.

Rizakis, A.D. *Achaïe*. 3 vols. Athens 1995–2008.

Robert, L. and Robert, J. *La Carie, II*. Paris 1954.

Robert, L. *Hellenica, recueil d' épigraphie, de numismatique et d' antiquités grecques*. 13 vols. Paris 1940–1965.

———. *Opera Minora Selecta*. 7 vols. Amsterdam 1969–1990.

Roesch, P. *Études Béotiennes*. Paris 1982.

Roussel, P. *Délos colonie Athénienne (1916). Réimpression augmentée*. Paris 1987.

Ryffel, H. Μεταβολὴ Πολιτειῶν. *Der Wandel der Staatsverfassungen*. Bern 1949.

Sánchez, P. *L'Amphictionie des Pyles et de Delphes*. Stuttgart 2001.

Savalli-Lestrade, I. *Les "Philoi" Royaux dans l' Asie Hellénistique*. Geneva 1998.

Schmitt, H. H. *Rom und Rhodos*. Munich 1957.

———. *Untersuchungen zur Geschichte Antiochos des Grossen und seiner Zeit*. Wiesbaden 1964.

Scholten J. B. *The-Politics of Plunder. Aitolians and their Koinon in the Early Hellenistic Era, 279–217* B.C. Berkeley 2000.

Schulten, A. *Numantia: Die Ergebnisse der Ausgrabungen 1905–1912*. 2 vols. Munich 1914; 1927.

SELECT BIBLIOGRAPHY

Schwertfeger, Th. *Der Achaiische Bund von 146 bis 27 v. Chr.* Munich 1974.

Sherwin-White, S. *Ancient Cos. An Historical Study from the Dorian Settlement to the Imperial Period.* Göttingen 1978.

Shimron, B. *Late Sparta: The Spartan Revolution 243–146 B.C.* Buffalo 1972.

Stähelin, F. *Geschichte der kleinasiatischen Galater.*[2] Leipzig 1907.

Stählin, F. *Das hellenische Thessalien.* Stuttgart 1924.

Stiewe, K. and Holzberg, N., eds. *Polybios. Wege der Forschung.* Darmstadt 1982.

Tataki, A. B. *Macedonians Abroad.* Athens 1998.

Texier, J. G. *Nabis.* Paris 1975.

Thissen, H.-J. *Studien zum Raphiadekret.* Meisenheim am Glan 1966.

Thornton, J. "Polibio e Roma. Tendenze negli studi degli ultimi anni," *Studi Romani* 52 (2004) 108–139; 508–525.

Touloumakos, J. *Der Einfluss Roms auf die Staatsform der griechischen Stadtstaaten des Festlandes und der Inseln im ersten und zweiten Jhdt. v. Chr.* Diss Göttingen 1967.

Tracy, St. V. *Athenian Letter Cutters of 229 to 86 B.C.* Berkeley 1990.

Urban, R. *Wachstum und Krise des Achäischen Bundes.* Wiesbaden 1979.

Veisse, A.-E. "Les révoltes égyptiennes," *Studia Hellenistica* 41. Leuven 2004.

Versnel, H. S. *Triumphus: An Inquiry into the Origin, Development and Meaning of the Roman Triumph.* Leiden 1970.

Virgilio, B. *Gli Attalidi di Pergamo: Fama, Eredità, Memoria. Studi Ellenistici* 5. Pisa 1993.

———. "Polibio, il mondo ellenistico e Roma," *Studi Ellenistici* 20 (2008) 315–345.

Vitucci, G. *Il regno di Bitinia*. Rome 1953.

van Effenterre, H. *La Crète et le monde grec de Platon à Polybe*. Paris 1948.

von Staden, H. *Herophilos. The Art of Medicine in Early Alexandria*. Cambridge 1989.

WC = Walbank's *Commentary*.

Walbank, F. W. *Aratos of Sicyon*. Cambridge 1933.

———. *Philip V of Macedon*. Cambridge 1940.

———. "Polybius on the Roman Constitution," *CQ* 37 (1943) 73–89.

———. *A Historical Commentary on Polybius*. 3 vols. Oxford 1957–1979.

———. *Polybius*. Berkeley 1972.

———. *Polybius, Rome, and the Hellenistic World; Essays and Reflections*. Cambridge 2002.

Welwei, K.-W. *Könige und Königtum im Urteil des Polybios*. Diss. Cologne 1963.

Wiemer, H-U. Krieg, *Handel und Piraterie. Untersuchungen zur Geschichte des hellenistischen Rhodos*. Berlin 2000.

Will, Ed. *Histoire politique du monde hellénistique (323–30 av. J.-C.).*² 2 vols. Nancy 1979–1982; new ed. in 1 vol. Paris 2003.

Zahrnt, M. "Die Überlieferung über den Ersten Illyrischen Krieg," *Hermes* 136 (2008) 391–414.

Ziegler, K. "Polybios." *RE* XXI.2 (1952) 1440–1578.

THE HISTORIES OF POLYBIUS

BOOKS 1–2

ΙΣΤΟΡΙΩΝ ΠΡΩΤΗ

1. Εἰ μὲν τοῖς πρὸ ἡμῶν ἀναγράφουσι τὰς πράξεις παραλελεῖφθαι συνέβαινε τὸν ὑπὲρ αὐτῆς τῆς ἱστορίας ἔπαινον, ἴσως ἀναγκαῖον ἦν τὸ προτρέπεσθαι πάντας πρὸς τὴν αἵρεσιν καὶ παραδοχὴν τῶν τοιούτων ὑπομνημάτων διὰ τὸ μηδεμίαν ἑτοιμοτέραν εἶναι τοῖς ἀνθρώποις διόρθωσιν τῆς τῶν προγεγενημένων

2 πράξεων ἐπιστήμης. ἐπεὶ δ' οὐ τινὲς οὐδ' ἐπὶ ποσόν, ἀλλὰ πάντες ὡς ἔπος εἰπεῖν ἀρχῇ καὶ τέλει κέχρηνται τούτῳ, φάσκοντες ἀληθινωτάτην μὲν εἶναι παιδείαν καὶ γυμνασίαν πρὸς τὰς πολιτικὰς πράξεις τὴν ἐκ τῆς ἱστορίας μάθησιν, ἐναργεστάτην δὲ καὶ μόνην διδάσκαλον τοῦ δύνασθαι τὰς τῆς τύχης μεταβολὰς γενναίως ὑποφέρειν τὴν τῶν ἀλλοτρίων περιπετειῶν

3 ὑπόμνησιν, δῆλον ὡς οὐδενὶ μὲν ἂν δόξαι καθήκειν περὶ τῶν καλῶς καὶ πολλοῖς εἰρημένων ταυτολογεῖν,

4 ἥκιστα δ' ἡμῖν. αὐτὸ γὰρ τὸ παράδοξον τῶν πράξεων, ὑπὲρ ὧν προῃρήμεθα γράφειν, ἱκανόν ἐστι προκαλέσασθαι καὶ παρορμῆσαι πάντα καὶ νέον καὶ

5 πρεσβύτερον πρὸς τὴν ἔντευξιν τῆς πραγματείας. τίς

BOOK I

1. Had previous chroniclers neglected to speak in praise of History in general, it might perhaps have been necessary for me to recommend everyone to choose for study and welcome such treatises as the present, since men have no more ready corrective of conduct than knowledge of the past. But all historians, one may say without exception, and in no halfhearted manner, but making this the beginning and end of their labor, have impressed on us that the soundest education and training for a life of active politics is the study of History, and that the surest and indeed the only method of learning how to bear bravely the vicissitudes of fortune, is to recall the calamities of others. Evidently therefore no one, and least of all myself, would think it his duty at this day to repeat what has been so well and so often said. For the very element of unexpectedness in the events I have chosen as my theme will be sufficient to challenge and incite everyone, young and old alike, to peruse my systematic history. For who is so indifferent or

γὰρ οὕτως ὑπάρχει φαῦλος ἢ ῥᾴθυμος ἀνθρώπων ὃς
οὐκ ἂν βούλοιτο γνῶναι πῶς καὶ τίνι γένει πολιτείας
ἐπικρατηθέντα σχεδὸν ἅπαντα τὰ κατὰ τὴν οἰκου-
μένην ἐν οὐχ ὅλοις πεντήκοντα καὶ τρισὶν ἔτεσιν ὑπὸ
μίαν ἀρχὴν ἔπεσε τὴν Ῥωμαίων, ὃ πρότερον οὐχ
6 εὑρίσκεται γεγονός, τίς δὲ πάλιν οὕτως ἐκπαθὴς πρός
τι τῶν ἄλλων θεαμάτων ἢ μαθημάτων ὃς προυργιαίτερον ἄν τι ποιήσαιτο τῆσδε τῆς ἐμπειρίας;

2. Ὡς δ᾽ ἔστι παράδοξον καὶ μέγα τὸ περὶ τὴν
ἡμετέραν ὑπόθεσιν θεώρημα γένοιτ᾽ ἂν οὕτως μάλιστ᾽
ἐμφανές, εἰ τὰς ἐλλογιμωτάτας τῶν προγεγενημένων
δυναστειῶν, περὶ ἃς οἱ συγγραφεῖς τοὺς πλείστους
διατέθεινται λόγους, παραβάλοιμεν καὶ συγκρίναιμεν
2 πρὸς τὴν Ῥωμαίων ὑπεροχήν. εἰσὶ δ᾽ αἱ τῆς παρα-
βολῆς ἄξιαι καὶ συγκρίσεως αὗται. Πέρσαι κατά
τινας καιροὺς μεγάλην ἀρχὴν κατεκτήσαντο καὶ δυ-
ναστείαν· ἀλλ᾽ ὁσάκις ἐτόλμησαν ὑπερβῆναι τοὺς τῆς
Ἀσίας ὅρους, οὐ μόνον ὑπὲρ τῆς ἀρχῆς, ἀλλὰ καὶ περὶ
3 σφῶν ἐκινδύνευσαν. Λακεδαιμόνιοι πολλοὺς ἀμ-
φισβητήσαντες χρόνους ὑπὲρ τῆς τῶν Ἑλλήνων ἡγεμονίας, ἐπειδή ποτ᾽ ἐκράτησαν, μόλις ἔτη δώδεκα
4 κατεῖχον αὐτὴν ἀδήριτον. Μακεδόνες τῆς μὲν Εὐρώπης ἦρξαν ἀπὸ τῶν κατὰ τὸν Ἀδρίαν τόπων ἕως ἐπὶ
τὸν Ἴστρον ποταμόν, ὃ βραχὺ παντελῶς ἂν φανείη
5 μέρος τῆς προειρημένης χώρας. μετὰ δὲ ταῦτα προσέλαβον τὴν τῆς Ἀσίας ἀρχήν, καταλύσαντες τὴν τῶν
Περσῶν δυναστείαν. ἀλλ᾽ ὅμως οὗτοι, πλείστων
δόξαντες καὶ τόπων καὶ πραγμάτων γενέσθαι κύριοι,

4

indolent as not to wish to know by what means and under what system of polity the Romans in less than fifty-three years (220–167) succeeded in subjecting nearly the whole inhabited world to their sole government—a thing unique in history? Or who again is there so passionately devoted to other spectacles or studies as to regard anything as of greater moment than the acquisition of this knowledge?

2. How striking and grand is the spectacle presented by the period with which I purpose to deal, will be most clearly apparent if we set beside and compare with the Roman dominion the most famous empires of the past, those which have formed the chief theme of historians. Those worthy of being thus set beside it and compared are these. The Persians for a certain period possessed a great rule and dominion, but so often as they ventured to overstep the boundaries of Asia they imperiled not only the security of this empire, but their own existence.[1] The Lacedaemonians, after having for many years disputed the hegemony of Greece, at length attained it but to hold it uncontested for scarce twelve years (405–394). The Macedonian rule in Europe extended but from the Adriatic region to the Danube, which would appear a quite insignificant portion of the continent. Subsequently, by overthrowing (334–330) the Persian empire they became supreme in Asia also. But though their empire was now regarded as the greatest geographically and politically that

[1] In Egypt and Greece.

5

τὸ πολὺ μέρος ἀκμὴν ἀπέλιπον τῆς οἰκουμένης ἀλλό-
6 τριον. Σικελίας μὲν γὰρ καὶ Σαρδοῦς καὶ Λιβύης οὐδ᾽
ἐπεβάλοντο καθάπαξ ἀμφισβητεῖν, τῆς δ᾽ Εὐρώπης
τὰ μαχιμώτατα γένη τῶν προσεσπερίων ἐθνῶν
7 ἰσχνῶς εἰπεῖν οὐδ᾽ ἐγίνωσκον. Ῥωμαῖοί γε μὴν οὐ
τινὰ μέρη, σχεδὸν δὲ πᾶσαν πεποιημένοι τὴν οἰκου-
μένην ὑπήκοον αὑτοῖς, [ἀνυπόστα]τον μὲν τοῖς [νῦν
ὑπάρχου]σιν, ἀνυπέ[ρβλητον δὲ] τοῖς ἐπιγι[νομένοις
ὑπερ]οχὴν κα[τέλιπον τῆς αὑτῶν] δυναστ[είας. περὶ
τοῦ] μὲν τ<ὰ> ὅλα διὰ τ[ί ὑπερεῖχον ἐκ τῆς γρα]φῆς
8 ἐξέσται σαφέστερον κατανοεῖν· ὁμοίως δὲ καὶ περὶ
τοῦ πόσα καὶ πηλίκα συμβάλλεσθαι πέφυκε τοῖς
φιλομαθοῦσιν ὁ τῆς πραγματικῆς ἱστορίας τρόπος.

3. Ἄρξει δὲ τῆς πραγματείας ἡμῖν τῶν μὲν χρόνων
ὀλυμπιὰς ἑκατοστὴ καὶ τετταρακοστή, τῶν δὲ πράξεων παρὰ μὲν τοῖς Ἕλλησιν ὁ προσαγορευθεὶς συμμα-
χικὸς πόλεμος, ὃν πρῶτον ἐξήνεγκε μετ᾽ Ἀχαιῶν πρὸς
Αἰτωλοὺς Φίλιππος, Δημητρίου μὲν υἱός, πατὴρ δὲ
Περσέως, παρὰ δὲ τοῖς τὴν Ἀσίαν κατοικοῦσιν ὁ περὶ
Κοίλης Συρίας, ὃν Ἀντίοχος καὶ Πτολεμαῖος ὁ Φιλο-
2 πάτωρ ἐπολέμησαν πρὸς ἀλλήλους· ἐν δὲ τοῖς κατὰ
τὴν Ἰταλίαν καὶ Λιβύην τόποις ὁ συστὰς Ῥωμαίοις
καὶ Καρχηδονίοις, ὃν οἱ πλεῖστοι προσαγορεύουσιν
Ἀννιβιακόν. ταῦτα δ᾽ ἔστι συνεχῆ τοῖς τελευταίοις
3 τῆς παρ᾽ Ἀράτου Σικυωνίου συντάξεως. ἐν μὲν οὖν
τοῖς πρὸ τούτων χρόνοις ὡς ἂν εἰ σποράδας εἶναι
συνέβαινε τὰς τῆς οἰκουμένης πράξεις, διὰ τὸ καὶ

had ever existed, they left the larger part of the inhabited world as yet outside it. For they never even made a single attempt to dispute possession of Sicily, Sardinia, or Libya, and the most warlike nations of Western Europe were, to speak the simple truth, unknown to them. But the Romans have subjected to their rule not portions, but the whole of the world, leaving behind for those living irresistible, for those to come insurpassable prominence of their rule. As for the reasons why they excelled in everything, these will become clearer from what I have written, and it will also be seen how many and how great advantages accrue to the student from the systematic treatment of history.

3. The date from which I propose to begin my history is the 140th Olympiad,[2] and the events are the following: (1) in Greece the so-called Social War, the first waged against the Aetolians by the Achaeans in league with and under the leadership of Philip of Macedon, the son of Demetrius and father of Perseus, (2) in Asia the war for Coele-Syria between Antiochus and Ptolemy Philopator, (3) in Italy, Libya, and the adjacent regions, the war between Rome and Carthage, usually known as the Hannibalic War. These events immediately succeed those related at the end of the work of Aratus of Sicyon.[3] Previously the doings of the world had been, so to say, dispersed, as they were held to-

219–217 B.C.

219–216 B.C.

220–201 B.C.

[2] Reckoning by Olympiads was introduced by the 4th/3rd c. historian Timaeus (5. 1); Ol. 1. 1 = 776/75, so that Ol. 140, 1–4 = 220/19–216/5.

[3] The remains of Aratus' work, ending in 221/1: *FGrH* 231.

κατὰ τὰς ἐπιβολάς, ἔτι δὲ καὶ τὰς συντελείας αὐτῶν
ὁμοίως δὲ καὶ κατὰ τοὺς τόπους ἀπέχειν ἕκαστα τῶν
4 πεπραγμένων. ἀπὸ δὲ τούτων τῶν καιρῶν οἷον εἰ
σωματοειδῆ συμβαίνει γίνεσθαι τὴν ἱστορίαν, συμ-
πλέκεσθαί τε τὰς Ἰταλικὰς καὶ Λιβυκὰς πράξεις ταῖς
τε κατὰ τὴν Ἀσίαν καὶ ταῖς Ἑλληνικαῖς καὶ πρὸς ἓν
5 γίνεσθαι τέλος τὴν ἀναφορὰν ἁπάντων. διὸ καὶ τὴν
ἀρχὴν τῆς αὐτῶν πραγματείας ἀπὸ τούτων πεποιή-
6 μεθα τῶν καιρῶν. Τῷ γὰρ προειρημένῳ πολέμῳ κρατήσαντες Ῥωμαῖοι Καρχηδονίων, καὶ νομίσαντες τὸ
κυριώτατον καὶ μέγιστον μέρος αὐτοῖς ἠνύσθαι πρὸς
τὴν τῶν ὅλων ἐπιβολήν, οὕτως καὶ τότε πρῶτον ἐθάρ-
σησαν ἐπὶ τὰ λοιπὰ τὰς χεῖρας ἐκτείνειν καὶ περαι-
οῦσθαι μετὰ δυνάμεως εἴς τε τὴν Ἑλλάδα καὶ τοὺς
κατὰ τὴν Ἀσίαν τόπους.

7 Εἰ μὲν οὖν ἡμῖν ἦν συνήθη καὶ γνώριμα τὰ πολιτεύματα τὰ περὶ τῆς τῶν ὅλων ἀρχῆς ἀμφισβητή-
σαντα, ἴσως οὐδὲν ἂν ἡμᾶς ἔδει περὶ τῶν πρὸ τοῦ
γράφειν, ἀπὸ ποίας προθέσεως ἢ δυνάμεως ὁρμηθέντες ἐνεχείρησαν τοῖς τοιούτοις καὶ τηλικούτοις
8 ἔργοις. ἐπεὶ δ᾽ οὔτε τοῦ Ῥωμαίων οὔτε τοῦ Καρχηδονίων πολιτεύματος πρόχειρός ἐστι τοῖς πολλοῖς τῶν
Ἑλλήνων ἡ προγεγενημένη δύναμις οὐδ᾽ αἱ πράξεις
αὐτῶν, ἀναγκαῖον ὑπελάβομεν εἶναι συντάξασθαι
9 ταύτην καὶ τὴν ἑξῆς βύβλον πρὸ τῆς ἱστορίας, ἵνα
μηδεὶς ἐπιστὰς ἐπ᾽ αὐτὴν τὴν τῶν πραγμάτων ἐξήγησιν τότε διαπορῇ καὶ ζητῇ ποίοις διαβουλίοις ἢ ποίαις
δυνάμεσι καὶ χορηγίαις χρησάμενοι Ῥωμαῖοι πρὸς

gether by no unity of initiative, results, or locality; but ever since this date history has been an organic whole, and the affairs of Italy and Libya have been interlinked with those of Greece and Asia, all leading up to one end. And this is my reason for beginning their systematic history from that date. For it was owing to their defeat of the Carthaginians in the Hannibalic War that the Romans, feeling that the chief and most essential step in their scheme of universal aggression had now been taken, were first emboldened to reach out their hands to grasp the rest[4] and to cross with an army to Greece (in 200) and the continent of Asia (in 190).

Now were we Greeks well acquainted with the two states which disputed the empire of the world, it would not perhaps have been necessary for me to deal at all with their previous history, or to narrate what purpose guided them, and on what sources of strength they relied, in entering upon such a vast undertaking. But as neither the former power nor the earlier history of Rome and Carthage is familiar to most of us Greeks, I thought it necessary to prefix this Book and the next to the actual history, in order that no one after becoming engrossed in the narrative proper may find himself at a loss, and ask by what counsel and trusting to what power and resources the Romans embarked on

[4] P. sees Rome aiming at world domination and emboldened by the victory over Hannibal; a similar statement in 3. 9–10.

ταύτας ὥρμησαν τὰς ἐπιβολάς, δι᾽ ὧν καὶ τῆς γῆς καὶ
τῆς θαλάττης τῆς καθ᾽ ἡμᾶς ἐγένοντο πάσης ἐγκρα-
10 τεῖς, ἀλλ᾽ ἐκ τούτων τῶν βύβλων καὶ τῆς ἐν ταύταις
προκατασκευῆς δῆλον ᾗ τοῖς ἐντυγχάνουσιν ὅτι καὶ
λίαν εὐλόγοις ἀφορμαῖς χρησάμενοι πρός τε τὴν
ἐπίνοιαν ὥρμησαν καὶ πρὸς τὴν συντέλειαν ἐξίκοντο
τῆς τῶν ὅλων ἀρχῆς καὶ δυναστείας.

4. τὸ γὰρ τῆς ἡμετέρας πραγματείας ἴδιον καὶ τὸ
θαυμάσιον τῶν καθ᾽ ἡμᾶς καιρῶν τοῦτ᾽ ἔστιν, ὅτι
καθάπερ ἡ τύχη σχεδὸν ἅπαντα τὰ τῆς οἰκουμένης
πράγματα πρὸς ἓν ἔκλινε μέρος καὶ πάντα νεύειν
ἠνάγκασε πρὸς ἕνα καὶ τὸν αὐτὸν σκοπόν, οὕτως καὶ
2 ⟨δεῖ⟩ διὰ τῆς ἱστορίας ὑπὸ μίαν σύνοψιν ἀγαγεῖν τοῖς
ἐντυγχάνουσι τὸν χειρισμὸν τῆς τύχης, ᾧ κέχρηται
πρὸς τὴν τῶν ὅλων πραγμάτων συντέλειαν. καὶ γὰρ
τὸ προκαλεσάμενον ἡμᾶς καὶ παρορμῆσαν πρὸς τὴν
ἐπιβολὴν τῆς ἱστορίας μάλιστα τοῦτο γέγονε· σὺν δὲ
τούτῳ καὶ τὸ μηδένα τῶν καθ᾽ ἡμᾶς ἐπιβεβλῆσθαι τῇ
τῶν καθόλου πραγμάτων συντάξει· πολὺ γὰρ ἂν ἧτ-
3 τον ἔγωγε πρὸς τοῦτο τὸ μέρος ἐφιλοτιμήθην. νῦν δ᾽
ὁρῶν τοὺς μὲν κατὰ μέρος πολέμους καί τινας τῶν
ἅμα τούτοις πράξεων καὶ πλείους πραγματευομένους,
τὴν δὲ καθόλου καὶ συλλήβδην οἰκονομίαν τῶν γεγονότων, πότε καὶ πόθεν ὡρμήθη καὶ πῶς ἔσχε τὴν
συντέλειαν, ταύτην οὐδ᾽ ἐπιβαλόμενον οὐδένα βασα-
4 νίζειν, ὅσον γε καὶ ἡμᾶς εἰδέναι, παντελῶς ὑπέλαβον
ἀναγκαῖον εἶναι τὸ μὴ παραλιπεῖν μηδ᾽ ἐᾶσαι παρ-
ελθεῖν ἀνεπιστάτως τὸ κάλλιστον ἅμα κὠφελιμώτα-

that enterprise which has made them lords over land and sea in the present age; but that from these Books and the preliminary sketch[5] in them, it may be clear to readers that they had quite adequate grounds for conceiving the ambition of a world empire and adequate means for achieving their purpose.

4. For what gives my work its peculiar quality, and what is most remarkable in the present age, is this. Fortune[6] has guided almost all the affairs of the world in one direction and has forced them to incline toward one and the same end; a historian should likewise bring before his readers under one synoptical view the operations by which she has accomplished her general purpose. Indeed it was this chiefly that invited and encouraged me to undertake my task; and secondarily the fact that none of my contemporaries have undertaken to write a general history, in which case I should have been much less eager to take this in hand. As it is, I observe[7] that while several modern writers deal with particular wars and certain matters connected with them, no one, as far as I am aware, has even attempted to inquire critically when and whence the general and comprehensive scheme of events originated and how it led up to the end. I therefore thought it quite necessary not to leave unnoticed or allow to pass into oblivion this, the

5 The contents of Books 1 and 2, down to 221.

6 The role of *Tyche* (Fortune) is central to Polybius' historical thinking: see e. g. *RE* Polybios 1532–1543 (K. Ziegler).

7 P. contrasts his universal approach with partial works of others and claims to be the first to take all interconnected events into consideration; see also 3. 32. 1–10.

5 τον ἐπιτήδευμα τῆς τύχης. πολλὰ γὰρ αὕτη καινοποι-
οῦσα καὶ συνεχῶς ἐναγωνιζομένη τοῖς τῶν ἀνθρώπων
βίοις οὐδέπω τοιόνδ᾽ ἁπλῶς οὔτ᾽ εἰργάσατ᾽ ἔργον οὔτ᾽
ἠγωνίσατ᾽ ἀγώνισμα, οἷον τὸ καθ᾽ ἡμᾶς. ὅπερ ἐκ μὲν
6 τῶν κατὰ μέρος γραφόντων τὰς ἱστορίας οὐχ οἷόν τε
συνιδεῖν, εἰ μὴ καὶ τὰς ἐπιφανεστάτας πόλεις τις κατὰ
μίαν ἑκάστην ἐπελθὼν ἢ καὶ νὴ Δία γεγραμμένας
χωρὶς ἀλλήλων θεασάμενος εὐθέως ὑπολαμβάνει
κατανενοηκέναι καὶ τὸ τῆς ὅλης οἰκουμένης σχῆμα
7 καὶ τὴν σύμπασαν αὐτῆς θέσιν καὶ τάξιν· ὅπερ ἐστὶν
οὐδαμῶς εἰκός. καθόλου μὲν γὰρ ἔμοιγε δοκοῦσιν οἱ
πεπεισμένοι διὰ τῆς κατὰ μέρος ἱστορίας μετρίως
συνόψεσθαι τὰ ὅλα παραπλήσιόν τι πάσχειν, ὡς ἂν εἴ
τινες ἐμψύχου καὶ καλοῦ σώματος γεγονότος διερριμ-
μένα τὰ μέρη θεώμενοι νομίζοιεν ἱκανῶς αὐτόπται
γίνεσθαι τῆς ἐνεργείας αὐτοῦ τοῦ ζῴου καὶ καλλονῆς.
8 εἰ γάρ τις αὐτίκα μάλα συνθεὶς καὶ τέλειον αὖθις
ἀπεργασάμενος τὸ ζῷον τῷ τ᾽ εἴδει καὶ τῇ τῆς ψυχῆς
εὐπρεπείᾳ, κἄπειτα πάλιν ἐπιδεικνύοι τοῖς αὐτοῖς ἐκείνοις, ταχέως ἂν οἶμαι πάντας αὐτοὺς ὁμολογήσειν
διότι καὶ λίαν πολύ τι τῆς ἀληθείας ἀπελείποντο
πρόσθεν καὶ παραπλήσιοι τοῖς ὀνειρώττουσιν ἦσαν.
9 ἔννοιαν μὲν γὰρ λαβεῖν ἀπὸ μέρους τῶν ὅλων δυνατόν, ἐπιστήμην δὲ καὶ γνώμην ἀτρεκῆ σχεῖν ἀδύνα-
10 τον. διὸ παντελῶς βραχύ τι νομιστέον συμβάλλεσθαι
τὴν κατὰ μέρος ἱστορίαν πρὸς τὴν τῶν ὅλων ἐμπειρίαν
11 ρίαν καὶ πίστιν. ἐκ μέντοι γε τῆς ἁπάντων πρὸς
ἄλληλα συμπλοκῆς καὶ παραθέσεως, ἔτι δ᾽ ὁμοιότη-

achievement of Fortune most excellent and profitable to contemplate. For though she is ever producing something new and ever playing a part in the lives of men, she has not in a single instance ever accomplished such a work, ever achieved such a triumph, as in our own times. We can no more hope to perceive this from histories dealing with particular events than to get at once a notion of the form of the whole world, its disposition and order, by visiting, each in turn, the most famous cities, or indeed by looking at separate pictures of each: a result by no means likely. He indeed who believes that by studying isolated histories he can acquire a fairly just view of history as a whole, is, as it seems to me, much in the case of one, who, after having looked at the dissevered limbs of an animal once alive and beautiful, fancies he has been as good as an eyewitness of the creature itself in all its action and grace. For could anyone put the creature together on the spot, restoring its form and the comeliness of life, and then show it to the same man, I think he would quickly avow that he was formerly very far away from the truth and more like one in a dream. For we can get some idea of a whole from a part, but never knowledge or exact opinion. Special histories therefore contribute very little to the knowledge of the whole and conviction of its truth. It is only indeed by study of the interconnection of all the particulars, their resem-

τος καὶ διαφορᾶς, μόνως ἄν τις ἐφίκοιτο καὶ δυνηθείη κατοπτεύσας ἅμα καὶ τὸ χρήσιμον καὶ τὸ τερπνὸν ἐκ τῆς ἱστορίας ἀναλαβεῖν.

5. Ὑποθησόμεθα δὲ ταύτης ἀρχὴν τῆς βύβλου τὴν πρώτην διάβασιν ἐξ Ἰταλίας Ῥωμαίων. αὕτη δ' ἔστι συνεχὴς μὲν τοῖς ἀφ' ὧν Τίμαιος ἀπέλιπε, πίπτει δὲ κατὰ τὴν ἐνάτην καὶ εἰκοστὴν πρὸς ταῖς ἑκατὸν ὀλυμ-
2 πιάδα. διὸ καὶ ῥητέον ἂν εἴη πῶς καὶ πότε συστη-σάμενοι τὰ κατὰ τὴν Ἰταλίαν, καὶ τίσιν ἀφορμαῖς μετὰ ταῦτα χρησάμενοι, διαβαίνειν ὥρμησαν εἰς Σι-κελίαν· ταύτῃ γὰρ τῇ γῇ πρῶτον ἐπέβησαν τῶν ἐκτὸς
3 τόπων τῆς Ἰταλίας. καὶ ῥητέον αὐτὴν τὴν τῆς δια-βάσεως αἰτίαν ψιλῶς, ἵνα μὴ τῆς αἰτίας αἰτίαν ἐπιζη-τούσης ἀνυπόστατος ἡ τῆς ὅλης ὑποθέσεως ἀρχὴ
4 γένηται καὶ θεωρία. ληπτέον δὲ καὶ τοῖς καιροῖς ὁμολογουμένην καὶ γνωριζομένην ἀρχὴν παρ' ἅπασι, καὶ τοῖς πράγμασι δυναμένην αὐτὴν ἐξ αὑτῆς θεω-ρεῖσθαι, κἂν δέῃ τοῖς χρόνοις βραχὺ προσαναδρα-μόντας κεφαλαιώδη τῶν μεταξὺ πράξεων ποιήσασθαι
5 τὴν ἀνάμνησιν. τῆς γὰρ ἀρχῆς ἀγνοουμένης ἢ καὶ νὴ Δί' ἀμφισβητουμένης οὐδὲ τῶν ἑξῆς οὐδὲν οἷόν τε παραδοχῆς ἀξιωθῆναι καὶ πίστεως· ὅταν δ' ἡ περὶ ταύτης ὁμολογουμένη παρασκευασθῇ δόξα, τότ' ἤδη καὶ πᾶς ὁ συνεχὴς λόγος ἀποδοχῆς τυγχάνει παρὰ τοῖς ἀκούουσιν.

6. Ἔτος μὲν οὖν ἐνειστήκει μετὰ μὲν τὴν ἐν Αἰγὸς ποταμοῖς ναυμαχίαν ἐννεακαιδέκατον, πρὸ δὲ τῆς ἐν
2 Λεύκτροις μάχης ἑκκαιδέκατον, ἐν ᾧ Λακεδαιμόνιοι

blances and differences, that we are enabled at least to make a general survey, and thus derive both benefit and pleasure from history.

5. I shall adopt as the starting point of this Book the first occasion on which the Romans crossed the sea from Italy. This follows immediately on the close of Timaeus' History[8] and took place in the 129th Olympiad. Thus we must first state how and when the Romans established their position in Italy, and with the aid of what resources they afterward crossed to Sicily, the first country outside Italy where they set foot. The actual cause of their crossing must be stated without comment; for if I were to seek the cause of the cause and so on, my whole work would have no clear starting point and principle. The starting point must be a date generally agreed upon and recognized, and one self-apparent from the events, even if this involves my going back a little in point of date and giving a summary of intervening occurrences. For if there is any ignorance or indeed any dispute as to what are the facts from which the work opens, it is impossible that what follows should meet with acceptance or credence; but once we produce in our readers a general agreement on this point they will give ear to all the subsequent narrative.

6. It was, therefore, the nineteenth year after the battle of Aegospotami and the sixteenth before that of Leuctra, the year in which the Spartans ratified the peace known as

264–261
B.C.

387–386
B.C.

8 *FGrH* 566; the *Histories* ended with the death of Agathocles in 289, but Timaeus continued with an account of Pyrrhus.

μὲν τὴν ἐπ' Ἀνταλκίδου λεγομένην εἰρήνην πρὸς βασιλέα τῶν Περσῶν ἐκύρωσαν καὶ πρεσβύτερος Διο-
νύσιος τῇ περὶ τὸν Ἑλλέπορον ποταμὸν μάχῃ νενι-
κηκὼς τοὺς κατὰ τὴν Ἰταλίαν Ἕλληνας ἐπολιόρκει
Ῥήγιον, Γαλάται δὲ κατὰ κράτος ἑλόντες αὐτὴν τὴν
3 Ῥώμην κατεῖχον πλὴν τοῦ Καπετωλίου. πρὸς οὓς
ποιησάμενοι Ῥωμαῖοι σπονδὰς καὶ διαλύσεις εὐδοκουμένας Γαλάταις, καὶ γενόμενοι πάλιν ἀνελπίστως
τῆς πατρίδος ἐγκρατεῖς, καὶ λαβόντες οἷον ἀρχὴν τῆς
συναυξήσεως, ἐπολέμουν ἐν τοῖς ἑξῆς χρόνοις πρὸς
4 τοὺς ἀστυγείτονας. γενόμενοι δ' ἐγκρατεῖς ἁπάντων
τῶν Λατίνων διά τε τὴν ἀνδρείαν καὶ τὴν ἐν ταῖς
μάχαις ἐπιτυχίαν, μετὰ ταῦτ' ἐπολέμουν Τυρρηνοῖς,
ἔπειτα Κελτοῖς, ἑξῆς δὲ Σαυνίταις, τοῖς πρός τε τὰς
ἀνατολὰς καὶ τὰς ἄρκτους συντερμονοῦσι τῇ τῶν
5 Λατίνων χώρᾳ. μετὰ δέ τινα χρόνον Ταραντίνων διὰ
τὴν εἰς τοὺς πρεσβευτὰς Ῥωμαίων ἀσέλγειαν καὶ τὸν
διὰ ταῦτα φόβον ἐπισπασαμένων Πύρρον τῷ πρότερον ἔτει τῆς τῶν Γαλατῶν ἐφόδου τῶν τε περὶ
6 Δελφοὺς φθαρέντων καὶ περαιωθέντων εἰς τὴν Ἀσίαν,
Ῥωμαῖοι Τυρρηνοὺς μὲν καὶ Σαυνίτας ὑφ' αὑτοὺς
πεποιημένοι, τοὺς δὲ κατὰ τὴν Ἰταλίαν Κελτοὺς πολ-
λαῖς μάχαις ἤδη νενικηκότες, τότε πρῶτον ἐπὶ τὰ
λοιπὰ μέρη τῆς Ἰταλίας ὥρμησαν, οὐχ ὡς ὑπὲρ ὀθνεί-
ων, ἐπὶ δὲ τὸ πλεῖον ὡς ὑπὲρ ἰδίων ἤδη καὶ καθηκόντων σφίσι πολεμήσοντες, ἀθληταὶ γεγονότες ἀληθι-

---

9 General, then tyrant of Syracuse and ruler of Sicily, born

that of Antalcidas with the King of Persia, that in which also Dionysius the Elder,[9] after defeating the Italiot Greeks in the battle at the river Elleporos, was besieging Rhegium, and that in which the Gauls, after taking Rome itself by assault, occupied the whole of that city except the Capitol. The Romans, after making a truce on conditions satisfactory to the Gauls and being thus contrary to their expectation reinstated in their home and as it were now started on the road of aggrandizement, continued in the following years to wage war on their neighbors. After subduing (in 338) all the Latins by their valor and the fortune of war, they fought first against the Etruscans, then against the Celts,[10] and next against the Samnites,[11] whose territory was conterminous with that of the Latins on the East and North. After some time the Tarentines, fearing the consequences of their insolence to the Roman envoys, begged for the intervention of Pyrrhus (in 280). (This was in the year preceding the expedition of those Gauls who met with the reverse at Delphi[12] and who crossed to Asia.) The Romans had ere this reduced the Etruscans and Samnites and had vanquished the Italian Celts in many battles, and they now for the first time attacked the rest of Italy not as if it were a foreign country, but as if it rightfully belonged to them. Their struggle with the Samnites and

in 430, died in 367: H. Berve, *Die Tyrannis bei den Griechen* (München 1967) 1. 222–260.

[10] Peace with the tribe of the *Boii* in 284 after a century of fighting since the sack of Rome in 387. [11] Decades of war between Rome and the Samnites began in 327.

[12] In 279: see G. Nachtergael, *Les Galates en Grèce et les Sôtéria de Delphes* (Brussels 1977).

νοὶ τῶν κατὰ τὸν πόλεμον ἔργων ἐκ τῶν πρὸς τοὺς
7 Σαυνίτας καὶ Κελτοὺς ἀγώνων. ὑποστάντες δὲ γενναίως τὸν πόλεμον τοῦτον, καὶ τὸ τελευταῖον τάς τε
δυνάμεις καὶ Πύρρον ἐκβαλόντες ἐκ τῆς Ἰταλίας,
αὖθις ἐπολέμουν καὶ κατεστρέφοντο τοὺς κοινωνή-
8 σαντας Πύρρῳ τῶν πραγμάτων. γενόμενοι δὲ παραδόξως ἁπάντων ἐγκρατεῖς, καὶ ποιησάμενοι τοὺς τὴν
Ἰταλίαν οἰκοῦντας ὑφ' αὑτοὺς πλὴν Κελτῶν, μετὰ
ταῦτα πολιορκεῖν ἐνεχείρησαν τοὺς τότε κατέχοντας
τὸ Ῥήγιον Ῥωμαίους.

7. Ἴδιον γάρ τι συνέβη καὶ παραπλήσιον ἑκατέ-
ραις ταῖς περὶ τὸν πορθμὸν ἐκτισμέναις πόλεσιν· εἰσὶ
2 δ' αὗται Μεσσήνη καὶ Ῥήγιον. Μεσσήνην μὲν γὰρ οὐ
πολλοῖς ἀνώτερον χρόνοις τῶν νῦν λεγομένων καιρῶν
Καμπανοὶ παρ' Ἀγαθοκλεῖ μισθοφοροῦντες, καὶ πάλαι περὶ τὸ κάλλος καὶ τὴν λοιπὴν εὐδαιμονίαν τῆς
πόλεως ὀφθαλμιῶντες, ἅμα τῷ λαβεῖν καιρὸν εὐθὺς
3 ἐπεχείρησαν παρασπονδεῖν· παρεισελθόντες δ' ὡς φί-
λιοι, καὶ κατασχόντες τὴν πόλιν, οὓς μὲν ἐξέβαλον
4 τῶν πολιτῶν, οὓς δ' ἀπέσφαξαν. πράξαντες δὲ ταῦτα,
τὰς μὲν γυναῖκας καὶ τὰ τέκνα τῶν ἠκληρηκότων, ὥς
ποθ' ἡ τύχη διένειμε παρ' αὐτὸν τὸν τῆς παρανομίας
καιρὸν ἑκάστοις, οὕτως ἔσχον· τοὺς δὲ λοιποὺς βίους
5 καὶ τὴν χώραν μετὰ ταῦτα διελόμενοι κατεῖχον. ταχὺ
δὲ καὶ ῥᾳδίως καλῆς χώρας καὶ πόλεως ἐγκρατεῖς
γενόμενοι, παρὰ πόδας εὗρον μιμητὰς τῆς πράξεως.
6 Ῥηγῖνοι γάρ, καθ' ὃν καιρὸν Πύρρος εἰς Ἰταλίαν

Celts had made them veritable masters in the art of war, and after bravely supporting this war with Pyrrhus and finally expelling himself and his army from Italy (in 275), they continued to fight with and subdue those who had sided with him. When, with extraordinary good fortune, they had reduced all these peoples and had made all the inhabitants of Italy their subjects excepting the Celts, they undertook the siege of Rhegium now held by certain of their compatriots.

7. For very much the same fortune befell the two cities on the Straits, Messene and Rhegium. Certain Campanians[13] serving as mercenaries under Agathocles[14] had long cast covetous eyes on the beauty and prosperity of Messene; and not long before the events I am speaking of they availed themselves of the first opportunity to capture it by treachery. After being admitted as friends and occupying the city, they first expelled or massacred the citizens and then took possession of the wives and families of the dispossessed victims, just as chance assigned them each at the time of the outrage.[15] They next divided among themselves the land and all other property. Having thus possessed themselves so quickly and easily of a fine city and territory, they were not long in finding imitators of their exploit. For the people of Rhegium, when Pyrrhus crossed

[13] The so-called Mamertines; see 8. 1.

[14] Tyrant, then king of Syracuse, fought the Carthaginians in Africa; see Berve (6. 1), 1. 441–447. [15] A century earlier, Aen. Tact. had warned the cities to guard against such events (*De obsidione toleranda* 12–13); see D. Whitehead, *Aineias the Tactician: How to Survive Under Siege* (Oxford 1990) 12–13 and 58–59. Other such cases in P. are 2.5.4 and 2. 7. 12.

19

ἐπεραιοῦτο, καταπλαγεῖς γενόμενοι τὴν ἔφοδον αὐτοῦ, δεδιότες δὲ καὶ Καρχηδονίους θαλαττοκρατοῦντας, ἐπεσπάσαντο φυλακὴν ἅμα καὶ βοήθειαν παρὰ Ῥω-
7 μαίων. οἱ δ᾽ εἰσελθόντες χρόνον μέν τινα διετήρουν τὴν πόλιν καὶ τὴν ἑαυτῶν πίστιν, ὄντες τετρακισχίλιοι
8 τὸν ἀριθμόν, ὧν ἡγεῖτο Δέκιος Καμπανός· τέλος δὲ ζηλώσαντες τοὺς Μαμερτίνους, ἅμα δὲ καὶ συνεργοὺς λαβόντες αὐτούς, παρεσπόνδησαν τοὺς Ῥηγίνους, ἐκπαθεῖς ὄντες ἐπί τε τῇ τῆς πόλεως εὐκαιρίᾳ καὶ τῇ τῶν Ῥηγίνων περὶ τοὺς ἰδίους βίους εὐδαιμονίᾳ· καὶ τοὺς μὲν ἐκβαλόντες, τοὺς δ᾽ ἀποσφάξαντες τῶν πολιτῶν, τὸν αὐτὸν τρόπον τοῖς Καμπανοῖς κατέσχον τὴν πό-
9 λιν. οἱ δὲ Ῥωμαῖοι βαρέως μὲν ἔφερον τὸ γεγονός· οὐ μὴν εἶχόν γε ποιεῖν οὐδὲν διὰ τὸ συνέχεσθαι τοῖς
10 προειρημένοις πολέμοις. ἐπεὶ δ᾽ ἀπὸ τούτων ἐγένοντο, συγκλείσαντες αὐτοὺς ἐπολιόρκουν τὸ Ῥήγιον, καθάπερ ἐπάνω προεῖπον. κρατήσαντες δὲ τοὺς μὲν πλεί-
11 στους ἐν αὐτῇ τῇ καταλήψει διέφθειραν, ἐκθύμως ἀμυνομένους διὰ τὸ προορᾶσθαι τὸ μέλλον, ζωγρίᾳ δ᾽ ἐκυρίευσαν πλειόνων ἢ τριακοσίων. ὧν ἀναπεμφθέν-
12 των εἰς τὴν Ῥώμην, οἱ στρατηγοὶ προαγαγόντες εἰς τὴν ἀγορὰν καὶ μαστιγώσαντες ἅπαντας κατὰ τὸ παρ᾽ αὐτοῖς ἔθος ἐπελέκισαν, βουλόμενοι διὰ τῆς εἰς ἐκείνους τιμωρίας, καθ᾽ ὅσον οἷοί τ᾽ ἦσαν, διορθοῦσθαι
13 παρὰ τοῖς συμμάχοις τὴν αὑτῶν πίστιν. τὴν δὲ χώραν καὶ τὴν πόλιν παραχρῆμα τοῖς Ῥηγίνοις ἀπέδοσαν.

8. Οἱ δὲ Μαμερτῖνοι, τοῦτο γὰρ τοὔνομα κυριεύσαντες οἱ Καμπανοὶ τῆς Μεσσήνης προσηγόρευσαν

to Italy, dreading an attack by him and fearing also the Carthaginians who commanded the sea, begged from the Romans a garrison and support. The force which came, four thousand in number and under the command of Decius, a Campanian, kept the city and their faith for some time, but at length, anxious to rival the Mamertines and with their cooperation, playing the people of Rhegium false, and eagerly coveting a city so favorably situated and containing so much private wealth, expelled or massacred the citizens and possessed themselves of the city in the same manner as the Campanians had done. The Romans were highly displeased, yet could do nothing at the time, as they were occupied with the wars I have already mentioned. But when they had a free hand they shut up the culprits in the city and proceeded to lay siege to it as I have stated above. When Rhegium fell, most of the besieged were slain in the actual assault, having defended themselves desperately, as they knew what awaited them, but more than three hundred were captured. When they were sent to Rome the Consuls had them all conducted to the forum and there, according to the Roman custom, scourged and beheaded;[16] their object being to recover as far as possible by this punishment their reputation for good faith with the allies. The city and territory of Rhegium they at once restored to the citizens.

271 B.C.

8. The Mamertines (for this was the name adopted by the Campanians after their seizure of Messene), as long

[16] The earliest and most common form of capital punishment in Rome; see Mommsen, *Strafr.* 916–918, and E. Levy, *Die römische Kapitalstrafe*, Sitz. Heidelberg 1930–1931 = *Kl. Schr.* 2 (Cologne 1963) 325–378.

σφᾶς αὐτούς, ἕως μὲν συνεχρῶντο τῇ τῶν Ῥωμαίων
συμμαχίᾳ τῶν τὸ Ῥήγιον κατασχόντων, οὐ μόνον τῆς
ἑαυτῶν πόλεως καὶ χώρας ἀσφαλῶς κατεκράτουν,
ἀλλὰ καὶ περὶ τῆς συνορούσης οὐχ ὡς ἔτυχε παρ-
ηνώχλουν τοῖς τε Καρχηδονίοις καὶ τοῖς Συρακοσίοις,
2 καὶ πολλὰ μέρη τῆς Σικελίας ἐφορολόγουν. ἐπεὶ δ'
ἐστερήθησαν τῆς προειρημένης ἐπικουρίας, συγκλει-
σθέντων τῶν τὸ Ῥήγιον κατεχόντων εἰς τὴν πολιορκίαν, παρὰ πόδας ὑπὸ τῶν Συρακοσίων αὐτοὶ πάλιν
συνεδιώχθησαν εἰς τὴν πόλιν διά τινας τοιαύτας αἰτί-
3 ας. χρόνοις οὐ πολλοῖς πρότερον αἱ δυνάμεις τῶν
Συρακοσίων διενεχθεῖσαι πρὸς τοὺς ἐν τῇ πόλει, καὶ
διατρίβουσαι περὶ τὴν Μεργάνην, κατέστησαν ἐξ
αὐτῶν ἄρχοντας, Ἀρτεμίδωρόν τε καὶ τὸν μετὰ ταῦτα
βασιλεύσαντα τῶν Συρακοσίων Ἱέρωνα, νέον μὲν
ὄντα κομιδῇ, πρὸς δέ τι γένος εὐφυῆ βασιλικῆς καὶ
4 πραγματικῆς οἰκονομίας. ὁ δὲ παραλαβὼν τὴν ἀρχὴν
καὶ παρεισελθὼν εἰς τὴν πόλιν διά τινων οἰκείων καὶ
κύριος γενόμενος τῶν ἀντιπολιτευομένων, οὕτως ἐχρήσατο πράως καὶ μεγαλοψύχως τοῖς πράγμασιν, ὥστε
τοὺς Συρακοσίους, καίπερ οὐδαμῶς εὐδοκουμένους ἐπὶ
ταῖς τῶν στρατιωτῶν ἀρχαιρεσίαις, τότε πάντας ὁμοθυμαδὸν εὐδοκῆσαι στρατηγὸν αὐτῶν ὑπάρχειν Ἱέρω-
5 να. ὃς ἐκ τῶν πρώτων ἐπινοημάτων εὐθέως δῆλος ἦν
τοῖς ὀρθῶς σκοπουμένοις μειζόνων ὀρεγόμενος ἐλπίδων ἢ κατὰ τὴν στρατηγίαν.

9. θεωρῶν γὰρ τοὺς Συρακοσίους, ἐπειδὰν ἐκπέμ-
ψωσι τὰς δυνάμεις καὶ τοὺς ἄρχοντας μετὰ τῶν

as they enjoyed the alliance of the Romans together with the Campanians who had occupied Rhegium, not only remained in secure possession of their own city and territory but caused no little trouble to the Carthaginians and Syracusans about the adjacent territories, levying tribute from many parts of Sicily. When, however, they were deprived of this support, the captors of Rhegium being now closely invested, they were at once in their turn driven to take refuge in their city by the Syracusans owing to the following causes. Not long before the Syracusan army had quarreled with those in the city. They were then posted near Mergane[17] and appointed two magistrates chosen from their own body, Artemidorus and Hiero,[18] who was subsequently king of Syracuse. He was still quite young but because of his royal descent qualified to be a ruler and statesman of a kind. Having accepted the command, he gained admittance to the city through certain relatives, and after overpowering the opposite party, administered affairs with such mildness and magnanimity that the Syracusans, though by no means inclined to approve camp elections, on this occasion unanimously accepted him as their general. From his first measures it was evident at once to all capable of judging that his ambition was not limited to military command.

275 B.C.

9. For observing that the Syracusans, every time they dispatch their forces on an expedition accompanied by

17 Unknown, but hardly the same as Morgantina, as suggested by A. Vallone; see R. Stilwell, *AJA* 71 (1967) 250.   18 Berve (6. 1), 462–471; 733–735. That Hiero really was connected to the family of the Deinomenids is disputed (see 7. 8. 1 and WC 2. 41), and the chronology of his early years is very uncertain.

23

δυνάμεων, αὐτοὺς ἐν αὑτοῖς στασιάζοντας καὶ καινο-
2 τομοῦντας αἰεί τι, τὸν δὲ Λεπτίνην εἰδὼς καὶ τῇ προστασίᾳ καὶ τῇ πίστει πολὺ διαφέροντα τῶν ἄλλων
πολιτῶν, εὐδοκιμοῦντα δὲ καὶ παρὰ τῷ πλήθει διαφερόντως, συνάπτεται κηδείαν πρὸς αὐτόν, βουλόμενος οἷον ἐφεδρείαν ἀπολιπεῖν ἐν τῇ πόλει τοῦτον, ὅτ᾽
3 αὐτὸν ἐξιέναι δέοι μετὰ τῶν δυνάμεων ἐπὶ τὰς πράξεις.
γήμας δὲ τὴν θυγατέρα τοῦ προειρημένου, καὶ συνθεωρῶν τοὺς ἀρχαίους μισθοφόρους καχέκτας ὄντας
καὶ κινητικούς, ἐξάγει στρατείαν ὡς ἐπὶ τοὺς βαρ-
4 βάρους τοὺς τὴν Μεσσήνην κατασχόντας. ἀντιστρα-
τοπεδεύσας δὲ περὶ Κεντόριπα, καὶ παραταξάμενος
περὶ τὸν Κυαμόσωρον ποταμόν, τοὺς μὲν πολιτικοὺς
ἱππεῖς καὶ πεζοὺς αὐτὸς ἐν ἀποστήματι συνεῖχεν, ὡς
κατ᾽ ἄλλον τόπον τοῖς πολεμίοις συμμίξων, τοὺς δὲ
ξένους προβαλόμενος εἴασε πάντας ὑπὸ τῶν βαρ-
5 βάρων διαφθαρῆναι· κατὰ δὲ τὸν τῆς ἐκείνων τροπῆς
καιρὸν ἀσφαλῶς αὐτὸς ἀπεχώρησε μετὰ τῶν πολιτῶν
6 εἰς τὰς Συρακούσας. συντελεσάμενος δὲ τὸ προκείμενον πραγματικῶς, καὶ παρῃρηκὼς πᾶν τὸ κινητικὸν
καὶ στασιῶδες τῆς δυνάμεως, ξενολογήσας δι᾽ αὑτοῦ
πλῆθος ἱκανὸν μισθοφόρων, ἀσφαλῶς ἤδη τὰ κατὰ
7 τὴν ἀρχὴν διεξῆγε. θεωρῶν δὲ τοὺς βαρβάρους ἐκ τοῦ
προτερήματος θρασέως καὶ προπετῶς ἀναστρεφομένους, καθοπλίσας καὶ γυμνάσας ἐνεργῶς τὰς πολιτικὰς δυνάμεις ἐξῆγε, καὶ συμβάλλει τοῖς πολεμίοις ἐν
τῷ Μυλαίῳ πεδίῳ περὶ τὸν Λογγανὸν καλούμενον
8 ποταμόν. τροπὴν δὲ ποιήσας αὐτῶν ἰσχυράν, καὶ τῶν

24

their supreme magistrates, begin quarreling among themselves and introducing continual changes, and knowing that Leptines[19] had a wider circle of dependents and enjoyed more credit than any other burgher and had an especially high name among the common people, he allied himself with him by marriage, so that whenever he had to take the field himself he might leave him behind as a sort of reserve force. He married, then, the daughter[20] of this Leptines, and finding that the veteran mercenaries were disaffected and turbulent, he marched out in force professedly against the foreigners who had occupied Messene. He pitched camp opposite Centuripa and offered battle near the river Cyamosorus.[21] He held back the citizen cavalry and infantry at a distance under his personal command as if he meant to attack on another side, but advancing the mercenaries he allowed them all to be cut up by the Campanians. During their rout he himself retired safely to Syracuse with the citizens. Having thus efficiently accomplished his purpose and purged the army of its turbulent and seditious element, he himself enlisted a considerable number of mercenaries and henceforth continued to rule in safety. Observing that the Mamertines, owing to their success, were behaving in a bold and reckless manner, he efficiently armed and trained the urban levies and leading them out engaged the enemy in the Mylaean plain near the river Longanus,[22] and inflicted a severe defeat on

19 RE Leptines 2073–2074 (Th. Lenschau).

20 Philistis, on record as queen on coins and, together with the king, in SIG 429 from Syracuse.

21 Fiume Salso.

22 The river west of Mylae; the date of the battle is disputed.

ἡγεμόνων ἐγκρατὴς γενόμενος ζωγρίᾳ, τὴν μὲν τῶν
βαρβάρων κατέπαυσε τόλμαν, αὐτὸς δὲ παραγενόμενος εἰς τὰς Συρακούσας βασιλεὺς ὑπὸ πάντων προσ-
ηγορεύθη τῶν συμμάχων.

10. Οἱ δὲ Μαμερτῖνοι, πρότερον μὲν ἐστερημένοι
τῆς ἐπικουρίας τῆς ἐκ τοῦ Ῥηγίου, καθάπερ ἀνώτερον
εἶπον, τότε δὲ τοῖς ἰδίοις πράγμασιν ἐπταικότες ὁλοσχερῶς διὰ τὰς νῦν ῥηθείσας αἰτίας, οἱ μὲν ἐπὶ
Καρχηδονίους κατέφευγον, καὶ τούτοις ἐνεχείριζον
2 σφᾶς αὐτοὺς καὶ τὴν ἄκραν, οἱ δὲ πρὸς Ῥωμαίους
ἐπρέσβευον, παραδιδόντες τὴν πόλιν καὶ δεόμενοι
βοηθῆσειν σφίσιν αὐτοῖς ὁμοφύλοις ὑπάρχουσι. Ῥω-
3 μαῖοι δὲ πολὺν μὲν χρόνον ἠπόρησαν διὰ τὸ δοκεῖν
4 ἐξόφθαλμον εἶναι τὴν ἀλογίαν τῆς βοηθείας. τὸ γὰρ
μικρῷ πρότερον τοὺς ἰδίους πολίτας μετὰ τῆς μεγίστης ἀνῃρηκότας τιμωρίας, ὅτι Ῥηγίνους παρεσπόνδησαν, παραχρῆμα Μαμερτίνοις βοηθεῖν ζητεῖν τοῖς
τὰ παραπλήσια πεποιηκόσιν οὐ μόνον εἰς τὴν Μεσσηνίων, ἀλλὰ καὶ τὴν Ῥηγίνων πόλιν, δυσαπολόγη-
5 τον εἶχε τὴν ἁμαρτίαν. οὐ μὴν ἀγνοοῦντές γε τούτων
οὐδέν, θεωροῦντες δὲ τοὺς Καρχηδονίους οὐ μόνον τὰ
κατὰ τὴν Λιβύην, ἀλλὰ καὶ τῆς Ἰβηρίας ὑπήκοα
πολλὰ μέρη πεποιημένους, ἔτι δὲ τῶν νήσων ἁπασῶν
ἐγκρατεῖς ὑπάρχοντας τῶν κατὰ τὸ Σαρδόνιον καὶ
Τυρρηνικὸν πέλαγος, ἠγωνίων, εἰ Σικελίας ἔτι κυριεύ-
6 σαιεν, μὴ λίαν βαρεῖς καὶ φοβεροὶ γείτονες αὐτοῖς
ὑπάρχοιεν, κύκλῳ σφᾶς περιέχοντες καὶ πᾶσι τοῖς τῆς
7 Ἰταλίας μέρεσιν ἐπικείμενοι. διότι δὲ ταχέως ὑφ' αὐ-

them, capturing their leaders. This put an end to the audacity of the Mamertines, and on his return to Syracuse he was with one voice proclaimed king by all the allies.

10. The Mamertines had previously, as I above narrated, lost their support from Rhegium and had now suffered complete disaster at home for the reasons I have just stated. Some of them appealed to the Carthaginians, proposing to put themselves and the citadel into their hands, while others sent an embassy to Rome, offering to surrender the city and begging for assistance as a kindred people. The Romans were long at a loss,[23] the succor demanded being so obviously unjustifiable. For they had just inflicted on their own fellow citizens the highest penalty for their treachery to the people of Rhegium, and now to try to help the Mamertines, who had been guilty of like offense not only at Messene but at Rhegium also, was a piece of injustice very difficult to excuse. But fully aware as they were of this, they yet saw that the Carthaginians[24] had not only reduced Libya to subjection, but a great part of Spain besides, and that they were also in possession of all the is lands in the Sardinian and Tyrrhenian Seas. They were therefore in great apprehension lest, if they also became masters of Sicily, they would be most troublesome and dangerous neighbors, hemming them in on all sides and threatening every part of Italy. That they would soon be su-

[23] See the discussion in WC 1. 57–58, who accepts Gelzer's conclusion that P.'s account reproduces Fabius Pictor and is substantially reliable.

[24] On the extent of Carthage's influence in the western Mediterranean at the time, see WC 1. 59.

τοὺς ποιήσονται τὴν Σικελίαν, μὴ τυχόντων ἐπικουρίας τῶν Μαμερτίνων, προφανὲς ἦν. κρατήσαντες γὰρ
8 ἐγχειριζομένης αὐτοῖς τῆς Μεσσήνης ἔμελλον ἐν ὀλίγῳ χρόνῳ τὰς Συρακούσας ἐπανελέσθαι διὰ τὸ πάσης
9 σχεδὸν δεσπόζειν τῆς ἄλλης Σικελίας. ὃ προορώμενοι
Ῥωμαῖοι, καὶ νομίζοντες ἀναγκαῖον εἶναι σφίσι τὸ μὴ
προέσθαι τὴν Μεσσήνην, μηδ' ἐᾶσαι Καρχηδονίους
οἷον εἰ γεφυρῶσαι τὴν εἰς Ἰταλίαν αὐτοῖς διάβασιν,
11. πολὺν μὲν χρόνον ἐβουλεύσαντο, καὶ τὸ μὲν
συνέδριον οὐδ' εἰς τέλος ἐκύρωσε τὴν γνώμην διὰ τὰς
ἄρτι ῥηθείσας αἰτίας. ἐδόκει γὰρ τὰ περὶ τὴν ἀλογίαν
τῆς τοῖς Μαμερτίνοις ἐπικουρίας ἰσορροπεῖν τοῖς ἐκ
2 τῆς βοηθείας συμφέρουσιν. οἱ δὲ πολλοί, τετρυμένοι
μὲν ὑπὸ τῶν προγεγονότων πολέμων καὶ προσδεό-
μενοι παντοδαπῆς ἐπανορθώσεως, ἅμα δὲ τοῖς ἄρτι
ῥηθεῖσι περὶ τοῦ κοινῇ συμφέρειν τὸν πόλεμον καὶ
κατ' ἰδίαν ἑκάστοις ὠφελείας προδήλους καὶ μεγάλας
3 ὑποδεικνυόντων τῶν στρατηγῶν, ἔκριναν βοηθεῖν. κυ-
ρωθέντος δὲ τοῦ δόγματος ὑπὸ τοῦ δήμου, προχειρισάμενοι τὸν ἕτερον τῶν ὑπάτων στρατηγὸν Ἄππιον
Κλαύδιον ἐξαπέστειλαν, κελεύσαντες βοηθεῖν καὶ
4 διαβαίνειν εἰς Μεσσήνην. οἱ δὲ Μαμερτῖνοι τὸν μὲν
τῶν Καρχηδονίων στρατηγόν, ἤδη κατέχοντα τὴν
ἄκραν, ἐξέβαλον, τὰ μὲν καταπληξάμενοι, τὰ δὲ
παραλογισάμενοι· τὸν δ' Ἄππιον ἐπεσπῶντο, καὶ τού-
5 τῳ τὴν πόλιν ἐνεχείριζον. Καρχηδόνιοι δὲ τὸν μὲν
στρατηγὸν αὐτῶν ἀνεσταύρωσαν, νομίσαντες αὐτὸν
ἀβούλως, ἅμα δ' ἀνάνδρως, προέσθαι τὴν ἀκρόπολιν·

preme in Sicily, if the Mamertines were not helped, was evident; for once Messene had fallen into their hands, they would shortly subdue Syracuse also, as they were absolute lords of almost all the rest of Sicily.[25] The Romans, foreseeing this and viewing it as a necessity for themselves not to abandon Messene and thus allow the Carthaginians as it were to build a bridge for crossing over to Italy, debated the matter for long.

11. The Senate[26] did not sanction the proposal at all, considering that the objection on the score of inconsistency was equal in weight to the advantage to be derived from intervention. The commons, however, worn out as they were by the recent wars and in need of any and every kind of restorative, listened readily to the consuls, who, besides giving the reasons above stated for the general advantageousness of the war, pointed out the great benefit in the way of plunder which each and every one would evidently derive from it. They were therefore in favor of sending help; and when the measure had been passed by the people they appointed to the command one of the Consuls, Appius Claudius, who was ordered to cross to Messene. The Mamertines, partly by menace and partly by 264 B.C. stratagem, dislodged the Carthaginian commander, who was already established in the citadel, and then invited Appius to enter, placing the city in his hands. The Carthaginians crucified their general, thinking him guilty of a lack both of judgment and of courage in abandoning the

---

[25] Carthage was in control of the island's western part, including Agrigentum (once Pyrrhus had left). [26] As the Senate was unable to decide on the request of the Mamertines, the people, following the lead of the consuls, accepted it in 264 (*StV* 478).

6 αὐτοὶ δὲ τῇ μὲν ναυτικῇ δυνάμει περὶ Πελωριάδα
στρατοπεδεύσαντες, τῷ δὲ πεζῷ στρατεύματι περὶ τὰς
Σύνεις καλουμένας, ἐνεργῶς προσέκειντο τῇ Μεσ-
7 σήνῃ. κατὰ δὲ τὸν καιρὸν τοῦτον Ἱέρων, νομίσας
εὐφυῶς ἔχειν τὰ παρόντα πρὸς τὸ τοὺς βαρβάρους
τοὺς τὴν Μεσσήνην κατέχοντας ὁλοσχερῶς ἐκβαλεῖν
ἐκ τῆς Σικελίας, τίθεται πρὸς τοὺς Καρχηδονίους
συνθήκας. καὶ μετὰ ταῦτ᾽ ἀναζεύξας ἐκ τῶν Συρα-
8 κουσῶν ἐποιεῖτο τὴν πορείαν ἐπὶ τὴν προειρημένην
πόλιν· καταστρατοπεδεύσας δ᾽ ἐκ θατέρου μέρους
περὶ τὸ Χαλκιδικὸν ὄρος καλούμενον ἀπέκλεισε καὶ
ταύτης τῆς ἐξόδου τοὺς ἐν τῇ πόλει. ὁ δὲ στρατηγὸς
9 τῶν Ῥωμαίων Ἄππιος νυκτὸς καὶ παραβόλως περαι-
10 ωθεὶς τὸν πορθμὸν ἧκεν εἰς τὴν Μεσσήνην. ὁρῶν δὲ
πανταχόθεν ἐνεργῶς προσηρεικότας τοὺς πολεμίους,
καὶ συλλογισάμενος ἅμα μὲν αἰσχράν, ἅμα δ᾽ ἐπι-
11 σφαλῆ γίνεσθαι τὴν πολιορκίαν αὐτῷ, τῆς τε γῆς τῶν
πολεμίων ἐπικρατούντων καὶ τῆς θαλάττης, τὸ μὲν
πρῶτον διεπρεσβεύετο πρὸς ἀμφοτέρους, βουλόμενος
12 ἐξελέσθαι τοῦ πολέμου τοὺς Μαμερτίνους· οὐδενὸς δὲ
προσέχοντος αὐτῷ, τέλος ἐπαναγκαζόμενος ἔκρινε
13 διακινδυνεύειν καὶ πρῶτον ἐγχειρεῖν τοῖς Συρακοσίοις. ἐξαγαγὼν δὲ τὴν δύναμιν παρέταξε πρὸς μάχην,
ἑτοίμως εἰς τὸν ἀγῶνα συγκαταβάντος αὐτῷ καὶ τοῦ
14 τῶν Συρακοσίων βασιλέως· ἐπὶ πολὺν δὲ χρόνον δια-
γωνισάμενος ἐπεκράτησε τῶν πολεμίων, καὶ κατεδί-
15 ωξε τοὺς ὑπεναντίους ἕως εἰς τὸν χάρακα πάντας.
Ἄππιος μὲν οὖν σκυλεύσας τοὺς νεκροὺς ἐπανῆλθε

citadel. Acting for themselves they stationed their fleet in the neighborhood of Cape Pelorias,[27] and with their land forces pressed Messene close in the direction of Sunes. Hiero now, thinking that present circumstances were favorable for expelling from Sicily entirely the foreigners who occupied Messene, made an alliance[28] with the Carthaginians, and quitting Syracuse with his army marched toward that city. Pitching his camp near the Chalcidian mountain on the side opposite to the Carthaginians he cut off this means of exit from the city as well. Appius, the Roman consul, at the same time succeeded at great risk in crossing the Straits by night and entering the city. Finding that the enemy had strictly invested Messene on all sides and regarding it as both inglorious and perilous for himself to be besieged, as they commanded both land and sea, he at first tried to negotiate with both, desiring to deliver the Mamertines from the war. But when neither paid any attention to him, he decided perforce to risk an engagement and in the first place to attack the Syracusans. Leading out his forces he drew them up in order of battle, the king of Syracuse readily accepting the challenge. After a prolonged struggle Appius was victorious and drove the whole hostile force back to their camp. After despoiling the dead

27 Capo di Faro, some twelve kilometers northeast of Messina.
28 Not in *StV*.

πάλιν εἰς τὴν Μεσσήνην. ὁ δ᾽ Ἱέρων, ὀττευσάμενός τι περὶ τῶν ὅλων πραγμάτων, ἐπιγενομένης τῆς νυκτὸς ἀνεχώρησε κατὰ σπουδὴν εἰς τὰς Συρακούσας.

12. τῇ δὲ κατὰ πόδας ἡμέρᾳ γνοὺς Ἄππιος τὴν ἀπόλυσιν τῶν προειρημένων, καὶ γενόμενος εὐθαρσής, ἔκρινε μὴ μέλλειν, ἀλλ᾽ ἐγχειρεῖν τοῖς Καρ-

2 χηδονίοις. παραγγείλας οὖν τοῖς στρατιώταις ἐν ὥρᾳ γίνεσθαι τὴν θεραπείαν, ἅμα τῷ φωτὶ τὴν ἔξοδον

3 ἐποιεῖτο. συμβαλὼν δὲ τοῖς ὑπεναντίοις πολλοὺς μὲν αὐτῶν ἀπέκτεινε, τοὺς δὲ λοιποὺς ἠνάγκασε φυγεῖν

4 προτροπάδην εἰς τὰς παρακειμένας πόλεις. χρησάμενος δὲ τοῖς εὐτυχήμασι τούτοις καὶ λύσας τὴν πολιορκίαν, λοιπὸν ἐπιπορευόμενος ἀδεῶς ἐπόρθει τήν τε τῶν Συρακοσίων καὶ τὴν τῶν συμμαχούντων αὐτοῖς χώραν, οὐδενὸς ἀντιποιουμένου τῶν ὑπαίθρων· τὸ δὲ τελευταῖον προσκαθίσας αὐτὰς ἐπεβάλετο πολιορκεῖν τὰς Συρακούσας.

5 Ἡ μὲν οὖν πρώτη Ῥωμαίων ἐκ τῆς Ἰταλίας διάβασις μετὰ δυνάμεως ἥδε καὶ διὰ ταῦτα καὶ κατὰ

6 τούτους ἐγένετο τοὺς καιρούς, ἣν οἰκειοτάτην κρίναντες ἀρχὴν εἶναι τῆς ὅλης προθέσεως, ἀπὸ ταύτης ἐποιησάμεθα τὴν ἐπίστασιν, ἀναδραμόντες ἔτι τοῖς χρόνοις, τοῦ μηδὲν ἀπόρημα καταλιπεῖν ὑπὲρ τῶν

7 κατὰ τὰς αἰτίας ἀποδείξεων. Τῷ γὰρ πῶς καὶ πότε πταίσαντες αὐτῇ τῇ πατρίδι Ῥωμαῖοι τῆς ἐπὶ τὸ βέλτιον ἤρξαντο προκοπῆς, καὶ πότε πάλιν καὶ πῶς κρατήσαντες τῶν κατὰ τὴν Ἰταλίαν τοῖς ἐκτὸς ἐπιχειρεῖν ἐπεβάλοντο πράγμασιν ἀναγκαῖον ὑπελάβο-

he returned to Messene. Hiero, divining the final issue of the whole conflict, retreated in haste after nightfall to Syracuse.

12. On the following day Appius, learning of the result of this action and encouraged thereby, decided not to delay but to attack the Carthaginians. He ordered his troops to be in readiness early and sallied forth[29] at break of day. Engaging the enemy he slew many of them and compelled the rest to retreat in disorder to the neighboring cities. Having raised the siege by these successes, he advanced fearlessly, devastating the territory of the Syracusans and of their allies, no one disputing the open country with him. Finally he sat down before Syracuse and commenced to besiege it.

Such then was the occasion and motive of this the first crossing of the Romans from Italy with an armed force, an event which I take to be the most natural starting point of this whole work. I have therefore made it my serious base, but went also somewhat further back in order to leave no possible obscurity in my explanations of the causes. To follow out this previous history—how and when the Romans after the disaster to Rome itself began their progress to better fortunes, and again how and when after conquering Italy they entered on the path of foreign enterprise—

[29] Beginning of the war, as the Romans open hostilities.

μεν εἶναι παρακολουθῆσαι τοῖς μέλλουσι καὶ τὸ κεφά-
8 λαιον αὐτῶν τῆς νῦν ὑπεροχῆς δεόντως συνόψεσθαι.
διόπερ οὐ χρὴ θαυμάζειν οὐδ' ἐν τοῖς ἑξῆς, ἐάν που
προσανατρέχωμεν τοῖς χρόνοις περὶ τῶν ἐπιφανεστά-
9 των πολιτευμάτων. τοῦτο γὰρ ποιήσομεν χάριν τοῦ
λαμβάνειν ἀρχὰς τοιαύτας, ἐξ ὧν ἔσται σαφῶς κατανοεῖν ἐκ τίνων ἕκαστοι καὶ πότε καὶ πῶς ὁρμηθέντες
εἰς ταύτας παρεγένοντο τὰς διαθέσεις, ἐν αἷς ὑπάρχουσι νῦν. ὃ δὴ καὶ περὶ Ῥωμαίων ἄρτι πεποιήκαμεν.

13. Ἀφεμένους δὲ τούτων λέγειν ὥρα περὶ τῶν
προκειμένων, ἐπὶ βραχὺ καὶ κεφαλαιωδῶς προεκθε-
2 μένους τὰς ἐν τῇ προκατασκευῇ πράξεις. ὧν εἰσι
πρῶται κατὰ τὴν τάξιν αἱ γενόμεναι Ῥωμαίοις καὶ
3 Καρχηδονίοις ἐν τῷ περὶ Σικελίας πολέμῳ. ταύταις
συνεχὴς ὁ Λιβυκὸς πόλεμος· ᾧ συνάπτει τὰ κατ' Ἰβηρίαν Ἀμίλκα, μετὰ δὲ τοῦτον Ἀσδρούβᾳ πραχθέντα
4 καὶ Καρχηδονίοις. οἷς ἐγένετο κατὰ τὸν αὐτὸν καιρὸν
ἡ πρώτη Ῥωμαίων διάβασις εἰς τὴν Ἰλλυρίδα καὶ
ταῦτα τὰ μέρη τῆς Εὐρώπης, ἐπὶ δὲ τοῖς προειρη-
5 μένοις οἱ πρὸς τοὺς ἐν Ἰταλίᾳ Κελτοὺς ἀγῶνες. τούτοις δὲ κατὰ τὸν αὐτὸν καιρὸν παρὰ τοῖς Ἕλλησιν ὁ
Κλεομενικὸς καλούμενος ἐνηργεῖτο πόλεμος, εἰς ὃν
καὶ τὴν καταστροφὴν ἐποιησάμεθα τῆς ὅλης κατασκευῆς καὶ τῆς δευτέρας βύβλου.

6 Τὸ μὲν οὖν ἐξαριθμεῖσθαι τὰ κατὰ μέρος ὑπὲρ τῶν
προειρημένων πράξεων οὐδὲν οὔθ' ἡμῖν ἀναγκαῖον
7 οὔτε τοῖς ἀκούουσι χρήσιμον. οὐ γὰρ ἱστορεῖν ὑπὲρ
αὐτῶν προτιθέμεθα, μνησθῆναι δὲ κεφαλαιωδῶς προ-

seemed to me necessary for anyone who hopes to gain a proper general survey of their present supremacy. My readers need not therefore be surprised if, even in the further course of this work, I occasionally give them in addition some of the earlier history of the most famous states; for I shall do so in order to take such a starting point as will make it clear in the sequel from what origins and how and when they severally reached their present position. This is exactly what I have just done about the Romans.

13. Enough of such explanations. It is now time[30] to come to my subject after a brief summary of the events included in these introductory Books. To take them in order we have first the incidents of the war between Rome and Carthage for Sicily. Next follows the war in Libya and next the achievements of the Carthaginians in Spain under Hamilcar and afterward under Hasdrubal. At the same time occurred the first crossing of the Romans to Illyria and these parts of Europe, and subsequently to the preceding events their struggle with the Italian Celts. Contemporary with this the so-called Cleomenic war was proceeding in Greece, and with this war I wind up my Introduction as a whole and my second Book.[31]

Now to recount all these events in detail is neither incumbent on me nor would it be useful to my readers; for it is not my purpose to write their history but to mention

[30] P. has reached the point at which all that follows is anchored.

[31] Books 1 and 2 cover the years 264 through 220 in some detail, but still are but a summary introducing the actual history (13. 7).

αιρούμεθα χάριν τῆς προκατασκευῆς τῶν μελλουσῶν
ὑφ' ἡμῶν ἱστορεῖσθαι πράξεων. διόπερ ἐπὶ κεφαλαίων
8 ψαύοντες κατὰ τὸ συνεχὲς τῶν προειρημένων πειρασόμεθα συνάψαι τὴν τελευτὴν τῆς προκατασκευῆς τῇ
9 τῆς ἡμετέρας ἱστορίας ἀρχῇ καὶ προθέσει. τοῦτον γὰρ
τὸν τρόπον συνεχοῦς γινομένης τῆς διηγήσεως, ἡμεῖς
τε δόξομεν εὐλόγως ἐφάπτεσθαι τῶν ἤδη προϊστο-
ρημένων ἑτέροις, τοῖς τε φιλομαθοῦσιν ἐκ τῆς τοιαύτης οἰκονομίας εὐμαθῆ καὶ ῥᾳδίαν ἐπὶ τὰ μέλλοντα
10 ῥηθήσεσθαι παρασκευάσομεν τὴν ἔφοδον. βραχὺ δ'
ἐπιμελέστερον πειρασόμεθα διελθεῖν ὑπὲρ τοῦ πρώτου
συστάντος πολέμου Ῥωμαίοις καὶ Καρχηδονίοις περὶ
11 Σικελίας. οὔτε γὰρ πολυχρονιώτερον τούτου πόλεμον
εὑρεῖν ῥᾴδιον οὔτε παρασκευὰς ὁλοσχερεστέρας οὔτε
συνεχεστέρας πράξεις οὔτε πλείους ἀγῶνας οὔτε περιπετείας μείζους τῶν ἐν τῷ προειρημένῳ πολέμῳ συμ-
12 βάντων ἑκατέροις. αὐτά τε τὰ πολιτεύματα κατ' ἐκείνους τοὺς καιροὺς ἀκμὴν ἀκέραια μὲν ἦν τοῖς
ἐθισμοῖς, μέτρια δὲ ταῖς τύχαις, πάρισα δὲ ταῖς δυ-
13 νάμεσι. διὸ καὶ τοῖς βουλομένοις καλῶς συνθεάσασθαι τὴν ἑκατέρου τοῦ πολιτεύματος ἰδιότητα καὶ
δύναμιν οὐχ οὕτως ἐκ τῶν ἐπιγενομένων πολέμων ὡς
ἐκ τούτου ποιητέον τὴν σύγκρισιν.

14. Οὐχ ἧττον δὲ τῶν προειρημένων παρωξύνθην
ἐπιστῆσαι τούτῳ τῷ πολέμῳ καὶ διὰ τὸ τοὺς ἐμπει-
ρότατα δοκοῦντας γράφειν ὑπὲρ αὐτοῦ, Φιλῖνον καὶ
Φάβιον, μὴ δεόντως ἡμῖν ἀπηγγελκέναι τὴν ἀλή-
2 θειαν. ἑκόντας μὲν οὖν ἐψεῦσθαι τοὺς ἄνδρας οὐχ

them summarily as introductory to the events which are my real theme. I shall therefore attempt by such summary treatment of them in their proper order to fit in the end of the Introduction to the beginning of the actual History. Thus there will be no break in the narrative and it will be seen that I have been justified in touching on events which have been previously narrated by others, while this arrangement will render the approach to what follows intelligible and easy for students. I shall, however, attempt to narrate somewhat more carefully the first war between Rome and Carthage for the possession of Sicily; since it is not easy to name any war which lasted longer, nor one which exhibited on both sides more extensive preparations, more unintermittent activity, more battles, and greater changes of fortune. The two states were also at this period still uncorrupted in morals, receiving but modest help from fortune, and equal in strength, so that a better estimate of the peculiar qualities and gifts of each can be formed by comparing their conduct in this war than in any subsequent one.

14. An equally powerful motive with me for paying particular attention to this war is that, to my mind, the truth has not been adequately stated by those historians who are reputed to be the best authorities on it, Philinus[32] and Fabius.[33] I do not indeed accuse them of intentional false-

[32] Greek historian of the First Punic War, from Agrigentum; *FGrH* 174. [33] Quintus Fabius Pictor, the first Roman historian, writing in Greek, however (*FGrH* 809). His work, beginning with the mythical origins of Rome, was used by P. for the First and Second Punic Wars. A copy is recorded as being in the library at Taormina in the 2nd century (*SEG* 26. 1123). In 216, after the Roman defeat at Cannae, Fabius was sent to consult the oracle at Delphi.

ὑπολαμβάνω, στοχαζόμενος ἐκ τοῦ βίου καὶ τῆς αἱρέσεως αὐτῶν· δοκοῦσι δέ μοι πεπονθέναι τι παρα-
3 πλήσιον τοῖς ἐρῶσι. διὰ γὰρ τὴν αἵρεσιν καὶ τὴν ὅλην
εὔνοιαν Φιλίνῳ μὲν πάντα δοκοῦσιν οἱ Καρχηδόνιοι
πεπρᾶχθαι φρονίμως, καλῶς, ἀνδρωδῶς, οἱ δὲ Ῥωμαῖ-
4 οι τἀναντία, Φαβίῳ δὲ τοὔμπαλιν τούτων. ἐν μὲν οὖν
τῷ λοιπῷ βίῳ τὴν τοιαύτην ἐπιείκειαν ἴσως οὐκ ἄν τις
ἐκβάλλοι· καὶ γὰρ φιλόφιλον εἶναι δεῖ τὸν ἀγαθὸν
ἄνδρα καὶ φιλόπατριν καὶ συμμισεῖν τοῖς φίλοις τοὺς
5 ἐχθροὺς καὶ συναγαπᾶν τοὺς φίλους· ὅταν δὲ τὸ τῆς
ἱστορίας ἦθος ἀναλαμβάνῃ τις, ἐπιλαθέσθαι χρὴ
πάντων τῶν τοιούτων, καὶ πολλάκις μὲν εὐλογεῖν καὶ
κοσμεῖν τοῖς μεγίστοις ἐπαίνοις τοὺς ἐχθρούς, ὅταν αἱ
πράξεις ἀπαιτῶσι τοῦτο, πολλάκις δ᾽ ἐλέγχειν καὶ
ψέγειν ἐπονειδίστως τοὺς ἀναγκαιοτάτους, ὅταν αἱ
6 τῶν ἐπιτηδευμάτων ἁμαρτίαι τοῦθ᾽ ὑποδεικνύωσιν.
ὥσπερ γὰρ ζῴου τῶν ὄψεων ἀφαιρεθεισῶν ἀχρειοῦται
τὸ ὅλον, οὕτως ἐξ ἱστορίας ἀναιρεθείσης τῆς ἀληθείας
7 τὸ καταλειπόμενον αὐτῆς ἀνωφελὲς γίνεται διήγημα.
διόπερ οὔτε τῶν φίλων κατηγορεῖν οὔτε τοὺς ἐχθροὺς
ἐπαινεῖν ὀκνητέον, οὔτε δὲ τοὺς αὐτοὺς ψέγειν, ποτὲ δ᾽
ἐγκωμιάζειν εὐλαβητέον, ἐπειδὴ τοὺς ἐν πράγμασιν
ἀναστρεφομένους οὔτ᾽ εὐστοχεῖν αἰεὶ δυνατὸν οὔθ᾽
8 ἁμαρτάνειν συνεχῶς εἰκός. ἀποστάντας οὖν τῶν πραττόντων αὐτοῖς τοῖς πραττομένοις ἐφαρμοστέον τὰς
πρεπούσας ἀποφάσεις καὶ διαλήψεις ἐν τοῖς ὑπο-
9 μνήμασιν·

38

hood, in view of their character and principles, but they seem to me to have been much in the case of lovers; for owing to his convictions and constant partiality Philinus will have it that the Carthaginians in every case acted wisely, well, and bravely, and the Romans otherwise, while Fabius takes the precisely opposite view. In other relations of life we should not perhaps exclude all such favoritism;[34] for a good man should love his friends and his country, he should share the hatreds and attachments of his friends; but he who assumes the character of a historian must ignore everything of the sort, and often, if their actions demand this, speak good of his enemies and honor them with the highest praises while criticizing and even reproaching roundly his closest friends, should the errors of their conduct impose this duty on him.[35] For just as a living creature which has lost its eyesight is wholly incapacitated, so if History is stripped of her truth all that is left is but an idle tale. We should therefore not shrink from accusing our friends or praising our enemies; nor need we be shy of sometimes praising and sometimes blaming the same people, since it is neither possible that men in the actual business of life should always be in the right, nor is it probable that they should be always mistaken. We must therefore disregard the actors in our narrative and apply to the actions such statements and such judgments as they deserve.

[34] Philinus' bias against the Romans may be a result of their harsh treatment of his city in 261, Fabius' bias against the Carthaginians a result of his nationality.

[35] P. lives up to his demand that the historian has to be impartial in his treatment of the parties in this war, identifying himself with neither. He fails, however, when it comes to his country, Achaea; see n. on 5. 106. 6, also 4. 62. 5; 63. 1; 5. 28. 9.

15. Ὡς δ᾽ ἔστιν ἀληθῆ τὰ νῦν ὑφ᾽ ἡμῶν εἰρημένα σκοπεῖν ἐκ τούτων πάρεστιν. ὁ γὰρ Φιλῖνος ἀρχόμενος ἅμα τῶν πραγμάτων καὶ τῆς δευτέρας βύβλου φησὶ προσκαθῆσθαι τῇ Μεσσήνῃ πολεμοῦντας τούς

2 τε Καρχηδονίους καὶ τοὺς Συρακοσίους, παραγενομένους δὲ τοὺς Ῥωμαίους κατὰ θάλατταν εἰς τὴν πόλιν εὐθὺς ἐξελθεῖν ἐπὶ τοὺς Συρακοσίους· λαβόντας δὲ πολλὰς πληγὰς ἐπανελθεῖν εἰς τὴν Μεσσήνην· αὖθις δ᾽ ἐπὶ τοὺς Καρχηδονίους ἐκπορευθέντας οὐ μόνον πληγὰς λαβεῖν, ἀλλὰ καὶ ζωγρίᾳ τῶν στρατιωτῶν ἱκανοὺς ἀποβαλεῖν. ταῦτα δ᾽ εἰπὼν τὸν μὲν

3 Ἱέρωνά φησι μετὰ τὴν γενομένην συμπλοκὴν οὕτως ἔξω γενέσθαι τοῦ φρονεῖν ὥστε μὴ μόνον παραχρῆμα τὸν χάρακα καὶ τὰς σκηνὰς ἐμπρήσαντα φυγεῖν νυκτὸς εἰς τὰς Συρακούσας, ἀλλὰ καὶ τὰ φρούρια πάντα καταλιπεῖν τὰ κείμενα κατὰ τῆς τῶν Μεσσηνίων χώρας· ὁμοίως δὲ καὶ τοὺς Καρχηδονίους

4 μετὰ τὴν μάχην εὐθέως ἐκλιπόντας τὸν χάρακα διελεῖν σφᾶς εἰς τὰς πόλεις, τῶν δ᾽ ὑπαίθρων οὐδ᾽ ἀντιποιεῖσθαι τολμᾶν ἔτι· διὸ καὶ συνθεωρήσαντας τοὺς ἡγουμένους αὐτῶν ἀποδεδειλιακότας τοὺς ὄχλους

5 βουλεύσασθαι μὴ κρίνειν διὰ μάχης τὰ πράγματα· τοὺς δὲ Ῥωμαίους ἑπομένους αὐτοῖς οὐ μόνον τὴν χώραν πορθεῖν τῶν Καρχηδονίων καὶ Συρακοσίων, ἀλλὰ καὶ τὰς Συρακούσας αὐτὰς προσκαθίσαντας

6 ἐπιβαλέσθαι πολιορκεῖν. ταῦτα δ᾽, ὡς ἐμοὶ δοκεῖ, τῆς πάσης ἐστὶν ἀλογίας πλήρη, καὶ διαστολῆς οὐ προσ-

7 δεῖται τὸ παράπαν. οὓς μὲν γὰρ πολιορκοῦντας τὴν

15. The truth of what I have just said is evident from what follows. Philinus,[36] in commencing his narrative at the outset of his second Book, tells us that the Carthaginians and Syracusans were besieging Messene, that the Romans reaching the city by sea, at once marched out against the Syracusans, but after being severely handled returned to Messene. They next sallied out against the Carthaginians and were not only worsted but lost a considerable number of prisoners. After making these statements he says that Hiero after the engagement so far lost his wits as not only to burn his camp and tents and take flight to Syracuse the same night, but to withdraw all his garrisons from the forts which menaced the territory of Messene. The Carthaginians, likewise, he tells us, after the battle at once quitted their camp and distributed themselves among the towns, not even daring to dispute the open country further: their leaders, he says, seeing how dispirited the ranks were, resolved not to risk a decisive engagement, and the Romans following up the enemy not only laid waste the territory of the Carthaginians and Syracusans, but sat down before Syracuse and undertook its siege. This account is, it seems to me, full of inconsistencies and does not require a lengthy discussion. For those

[36] P. criticizes him for his account of the events narrated in 11–12.

Μεσσήνην καὶ νικῶντας ἐν ταῖς συμπλοκαῖς ὑπέθετο,
τούτους φεύγοντας καὶ τῶν ὑπαίθρων ἐκχωροῦντας
καὶ τέλος πολιορκουμένους καὶ ταῖς ψυχαῖς ἀπο-
8 δεδειλιακότας ἀπέφηνεν· οὓς δ' ἡττωμένους καὶ πολιορκουμένους ὑπεστήσατο, τούτους διώκοντας καὶ
παραχρῆμα κρατοῦντας τῶν ὑπαίθρων καὶ τέλος πο-
9 λιορκοῦντας τὰς Συρακούσας ἀπέδειξε. ταῦτα δὲ συν-
ᾄδειν ἀλλήλοις οὐδαμῶς δύναται· πῶς γάρ; ἀλλ'
ἀναγκαῖον ἢ τὰς ὑποθέσεις εἶναι τὰς πρώτας ψευδεῖς
ἢ τὰς ὑπὲρ τῶν συμβαινόντων ἀποφάσεις. εἰσὶ δ'
10 αὗται μὲν ἀληθεῖς· καὶ γὰρ ἐξεχώρησαν οἱ Καρχηδόνιοι καὶ Συρακόσιοι τῶν ὑπαίθρων, καὶ τὰς Συρακούσας ἐπολιόρκουν οἱ Ῥωμαῖοι κατὰ πόδας, ὡς δ'
οὗτός φησι, καὶ τὴν Ἐχέτλαν, ἐν μέσῃ κειμένην τῇ
11 τῶν Συρακοσίων καὶ Καρχηδονίων ἐπαρχίᾳ. λοιπὸν
ἀνάγκη συγχωρεῖν τὰς ἀρχὰς καὶ τὰς ὑποθέσεις εἶναι
ψευδεῖς, καὶ νικώντων εὐθέως τῶν Ῥωμαίων ἐν ταῖς
περὶ τὴν Μεσσήνην συμπλοκαῖς ἡττημένους αὐτοὺς
ἡμῖν ὑπὸ τοῦ συγγραφέως ἀπηγγέλθαι.

12   Φιλῖνον μὲν οὖν παρ' ὅλην ἄν τις τὴν πραγματείαν
εὕροι τοιοῦτον ὄντα, παραπλησίως δὲ καὶ Φάβιον, ὡς
ἐπ' αὐτῶν δειχθήσεται τῶν καιρῶν. ἡμεῖς δ' ἐπειδὴ
13 τοὺς ἁρμόζοντας πεποιήμεθα λόγους ὑπὲρ τῆς παρ-
εκβάσεως, ἐπανελθόντες ἐπὶ τὰς πράξεις πειρασόμεθα
προστιθέντες ἀεὶ τὸν ἑξῆς λόγον εἰς ἀληθινὰς ἐννοίας
ἄγειν διὰ βραχέων τοὺς ἐντυγχάνοντας ὑπὲρ τοῦ προειρημένου πολέμου.

16. Προσπεσόντων γὰρ εἰς τὴν Ῥώμην ἐκ τῆς

whom he introduced as besieging Messene and victorious in the engagements, he now represents as in flight and abandoning the open country and finally besieged and dispirited, while those whom he represented as defeated and besieged are now stated to be in pursuit of their foes, and at once commanding the open country and finally besieging Syracuse. It is absolutely impossible to reconcile the two assertions, and either his initial statements or his account of what followed must be false. But the latter is true; for as a fact the Carthaginians and Syracusans abandoned the open country, and the Romans at once began to lay siege to Syracuse and, as he says, even to Echetla too, which lies between the Syracusan and Carthaginian provinces. We must therefore concede that Philinus's initial statements are false, and that, while the Romans were victorious in the engagements before Messene, this author announces that they were worsted.

We can trace indeed the same fault throughout the whole work of Philinus and alike through that of Fabius, as I shall show when occasion arises. Now that I have said what is fitting on the subject of this digression, I will return to facts and attempt in a narrative that strictly follows the order of events to guide my readers by a short road to a true notion of this war.

16. When news of the successes of Appius and his le-   263 B.C.

Σικελίας τῶν περὶ τὸν Ἄππιον καὶ τὰ στρατόπεδα
προτερημάτων, καταστήσαντες ὑπάτους Μάνιον Ὀτα-
κίλιον καὶ Μάνιον Οὐαλέριον τάς τε δυνάμεις ἁπάσας
ἐξαπέστελλον καὶ τοὺς στρατηγοὺς ἀμφοτέρους εἰς
2 τὴν Σικελίαν. ἔστι δὲ παρὰ Ῥωμαίοις τὰ πάντα τέτταρα στρατόπεδα Ῥωμαϊκὰ χωρὶς τῶν συμμάχων, ἃ
κατ' ἐνιαυτὸν προχειρίζονται· τούτων ἕκαστον ἀνὰ
3 τετρακισχιλίους πεζούς, ἱππεῖς δὲ τριακοσίους. ὧν
παραγενομένων ἀπό τε τῶν Καρχηδονίων αἱ πλείους
ἀφιστάμεναι πόλεις προσετίθεντο τοῖς Ῥωμαίοις ἀπό
4 τε τῶν Συρακοσίων. ὁ δ' Ἱέρων θεωρῶν τὴν διατροπὴν
καὶ κατάπληξιν τῶν Σικελιωτῶν, ἅμα δὲ τὸ πλῆθος
καὶ τὸ βάρος τῶν Ῥωμαϊκῶν στρατοπέδων, ἐκ πάντων
συνελογίζετο τούτων ἐπικυδεστέρας εἶναι τὰς τῶν
5 Ῥωμαίων ἢ τὰς τῶν Καρχηδονίων ἐλπίδας. διόπερ ἐπὶ
τοῦτο τὸ μέρος ὁρμήσας τοῖς λογισμοῖς διεπέμπετο
πρὸς τοὺς στρατηγούς, ὑπὲρ εἰρήνης καὶ φιλίας ποι-
6 ούμενος τοὺς λόγους. οἱ δὲ Ῥωμαῖοι προσεδέξαντο,
7 καὶ μάλιστα διὰ τὰς χορηγίας· θαλαττοκρατούντων
γὰρ τῶν Καρχηδονίων εὐλαβοῦντο μὴ πανταχόθεν
ἀποκλεισθῶσι τῶν ἀναγκαίων, διὰ τὸ καὶ περὶ τὰ πρὸ
τοῦ διαβάντα στρατόπεδα πολλὴν ἔνδειαν γεγονέναι
8 τῶν ἐπιτηδείων. διόπερ ὑπολαβόντες τὸν Ἱέρωνα
μεγάλην εἰς τοῦτο τὸ μέρος αὐτοῖς παρέξεσθαι χρείαν
9 ἀσμένως προσεδέξαντο τὴν φιλίαν. ποιησάμενοι δὲ
συνθήκας ἐφ' ᾧ τὰ μὲν αἰχμάλωτα χωρὶς λύτρων
ἀποδοῦναι τὸν βασιλέα Ῥωμαίοις, ἀργυρίου δὲ προσ-
θεῖναι τάλαντα τούτοις ἑκατόν, λοιπὸν ἤδη Ῥωμαῖοι

gions reached Rome, they elected Manius Otacilius and Manius Valerius Consuls, and dispatched their whole armed force and both commanders to Sicily. The Romans have four legions of Roman citizens in all apart from the allies. These they enroll annually, each legion comprising four thousand foot and three hundred horse. On their arrival in Sicily most of the cities revolted from the Carthaginians and Syracusans and joined the Romans. Hiero, observing both the confusion and consternation of the Sicilians, and at the same time the numbers and powerful nature of the Roman forces, reached from all this the conclusion that the prospects of the Romans were more brilliant than those of the Carthaginians. His conviction therefore impelling him to side with the Romans, he sent several messages to the Consuls with proposals for peace and friendship. The Romans accepted his overtures, especially for the sake of their supplies; for since the Carthaginians commanded the sea they were apprehensive lest they should be cut off on all sides from the necessities of life, in view of the fact that the armies which had previously crossed to Sicily had run very short of provisions. Therefore, supposing that Hiero would be of great service to them in this respect, they readily accepted his friendly advances. Having made a treaty[37] by which the king bound himself to give up his prisoners to the Romans without ransom, and in addition to this to pay them a hundred talents,

[37] For the treaty of the Romans with Hiero, see *StV* 479.

μὲν ὡς φίλοις καὶ συμμάχοις ἐχρῶντο τοῖς Συρακο-
10 σίοις. ὁ δὲ βασιλεὺς Ἱέρων ὑποστείλας ἑαυτὸν ὑπὸ
τὴν Ῥωμαίων σκέπην, καὶ χορηγῶν ἀεὶ τούτοις εἰς τὰ
κατεπείγοντα τῶν πραγμάτων, ἀδεῶς ἐβασίλευε τῶν
Συρακοσίων τὸν μετὰ ταῦτα χρόνον, φιλοστεφανῶν
11 καὶ φιλοδοξῶν εἰς τοὺς Ἕλληνας. ἐπιφανέστατος γὰρ
δὴ πάντων οὗτος δοκεῖ καὶ πλεῖστον χρόνον ἀπο-
λελαυκέναι τῆς ἰδίας εὐβουλίας ἔν τε τοῖς κατὰ μέρος
καὶ τοῖς καθόλου πράγμασιν.

17. Ἐπανενεχθεισῶν δὲ τῶν συνθηκῶν εἰς τὴν Ῥώμην, καὶ προσδεξαμένου τοῦ δήμου καὶ κυρώσαντος
τὰς πρὸς Ἱέρωνα διαλύσεις, λοιπὸν οὐκέτι πάσας
ἔκρινον ἐξαποστέλλειν οἱ Ῥωμαῖοι τὰς δυνάμεις,
2 ἀλλὰ δύο μόνον στρατόπεδα, νομίζοντες ἅμα μὲν
κεκουφίσθαι τὸν πόλεμον αὐτοῖς προσκεχωρηκότος
τοῦ βασιλέως, ἅμα δὲ μᾶλλον ὑπολαμβάνοντες οὕτως
3 εὐπορήσειν τὰς δυνάμεις τοῖς ἀναγκαίοις. οἱ δὲ Καρχηδόνιοι, θεωροῦντες τὸν μὲν Ἱέρωνα πολέμιον αὐτοῖς
γεγονότα, τοὺς δὲ Ῥωμαίους ὁλοσχερέστερον ἐμπλε-
κομένους εἰς τὰ κατὰ τὴν Σικελίαν, ὑπέλαβον βαρυ-
τέρας προσδεῖσθαι παρασκευῆς, δι' ἧς ἀντοφθαλμεῖν
δυνήσονται τοῖς πολεμίοις καὶ συνέχειν τὰ κατὰ τὴν
4 Σικελίαν. διὸ καὶ ξενολογήσαντες ἐκ τῆς ἀντιπέρας
χώρας πολλοὺς μὲν Λιγυστίνους καὶ Κελτούς, ἔτι δὲ
πλείους τούτων Ἴβηρας, ἅπαντας εἰς τὴν Σικελίαν
5 ἀπέστειλαν. ὁρῶντες δὲ τὴν τῶν Ἀκραγαντίνων πόλιν
εὐφυεστάτην οὖσαν πρὸς τὰς παρασκευὰς καὶ βαρυ-

the Romans henceforth treated the Syracusans as allies and friends. King Hiero[38] having placed himself under the protection of the Romans, continued to furnish them with the resources of which they stood in urgent need, and ruled over Syracuse henceforth in security, treating the Greeks in such a way as to win from them crowns and other honors. We may, indeed, regard him as the most illustrious of princes and the one who reaped longest the fruits of his own wisdom in particular cases and in general policy.

17. When the terms of the treaty were referred to Rome, and when the people had accepted and ratified this agreement with Hiero, the Romans decided not to continue to employ all their forces in the expedition, but only two legions, thinking on the one hand that, now the king had joined them, the war had become a lighter task and calculating that their forces would thus be better off for supplies. The Carthaginians, on the contrary, when they saw that Hiero had become their enemy, and that the Romans were becoming more deeply involved in the enterprise in Sicily, considered that they themselves required stronger forces in order to be able to confront their enemies and control Sicilian affairs. They therefore enlisted foreign mercenaries from the opposite coasts, many of them Ligurians, Celts, and still more Iberians, and dispatched them all to Sicily. Perceiving that the city of Agrigentum[39] had the greatest natural advantages for making

[38] See K. W. Welwei, *Könige und Königtum im Urteil des Polybios* (Diss. Cologne 1963), 91–99.

[39] Once second only to Syracuse in Sicily, the city was destroyed by the Carthaginians in 406, repopulated in the later fourth century, and after 275 controlled by Carthage once again.

τάτην ἅμα τῆς αὐτῶν ἐπαρχίας, εἰς ταύτην συνήθροι-
σαν τά τε χορήγια καὶ τὰς δυνάμεις, ὁρμητηρίῳ
6 κρίνοντες χρῆσθαι ταύτῃ τῇ πόλει πρὸς τὸν πόλεμον.

Τῶν δὲ Ῥωμαίων οἱ μὲν πρὸς τὸν Ἱέρωνα ποιησάμενοι στρατηγοὶ τὰς συνθήκας ἀνακεχωρήκεισαν·
οἱ δὲ μετὰ τούτους κατασταθέντες Λεύκιος Ποστούμιος καὶ Κόιντος Μαμίλιος ἧκον εἰς τὴν Σικελίαν μετὰ
7 τῶν στρατοπέδων. θεωροῦντες δὲ τὴν τῶν Καρχηδονίων ἐπιβολὴν καὶ τὰς περὶ τὸν Ἀκράγαντα παρασκευὰς ἔγνωσαν τολμηρότερον ἐγχειρεῖν τοῖς πρά-
8 γμασι· διὸ καὶ τὰ μὲν ἄλλα μέρη τοῦ πολέμου παρῆ-
καν, φέροντες δὲ παντὶ τῷ στρατεύματι πρὸς αὐτὸν
Ἀκράγαντα προσήρεισαν· καὶ στρατοπεδεύσαντες ἐν
ὀκτὼ σταδίοις ἀπὸ τῆς πόλεως συνέκλεισαν ἐντὸς
9 τειχῶν τοὺς Καρχηδονίους. ἀκμαζούσης δὲ τῆς τοῦ
σίτου συναγωγῆς, καὶ προφαινομένης χρονίου πολιορκίας, ὥρμησαν ἐκθυμότερον τοῦ δέοντος οἱ στρατι-
10 ῶται πρὸς τὸ σιτολογεῖν. οἱ δὲ Καρχηδόνιοι κατιδόντες τοὺς πολεμίους ἐσκεδασμένους κατὰ τῆς χώρας,
ἐξελθόντες ἐπέθεντο τοῖς σιτολογοῦσι. τρεψάμενοι δὲ
τούτους ῥᾳδίως οἱ μὲν ἐπὶ τὴν τοῦ χάρακος ἁρπαγὴν
11 ὥρμησαν, οἱ δ' ἐπὶ τὰς ἐφεδρείας. ἀλλ' ἡ τῶν ἐθισμῶν
διαφορὰ καὶ τότε καὶ πολλάκις ἤδη σέσωκε τὰ Ῥωμαίων πράγματα. τὸ γὰρ πρόστιμον παρ' αὐτοῖς
θάνατός ἐστι τῷ προεμένῳ τὸν τόπον καὶ φυγόντι τὸ
12 παράπαν ἐξ ἐφεδρείας. διὸ καὶ τότε πολλαπλασίους
ὄντας τοὺς ὑπεναντίους ὑποστάντες γενναίως πολλοὺς
μὲν τῶν ἰδίων ἀπέβαλον, ἔτι δὲ πλείους τῶν ἐχθρῶν

48

their preparations, it being also the most important city in their province, they collected their troops and supplies there and decided to use it as a base in the war.

Meanwhile the Roman Consuls who had made the 262 B.C. treaty with Hiero had left, and their successors, Lucius Postumius and Quintus Mamilius, had arrived in Sicily with their legions. On taking note of the plan of the Carthaginians, and their activity at Agrigentum, they decided on a bolder initiative. Abandoning therefore other operations they brought all their forces to bear on Agrigentum itself, and encamping at a distance of eight stades from the city, shut the Carthaginians up within the walls. It was the height of the harvest, and as a long siege was foreseen, the soldiers began gathering corn with more venturesomeness than was advisable. The Carthaginians, observing that the enemy were dispersed about the country, made a sortie and attacked the foragers. Having easily put these to flight, some of them pressed on to plunder the fortified camp while others advanced on the covering force. But on this occasion and often on previous ones it is the excellence of their institutions which has saved the situation for the Romans; for with them death is the penalty[40] incurred by a man who deserts the post or takes flight in any way from such a supporting force. Therefore on this occasion as on others they gallantly faced opponents who largely outnumbered them, and, though they suffered heavy loss, killed

[40] See Mommsen, *Strafr.* 562 with n. 1.

13 ἀπέκτειναν. τέλος δὲ κυκλώσαντες τοὺς πολεμίους
ὅσον οὔπω διασπῶντας τὸν χάρακα, τοὺς μὲν αὐτῶν
διέφθειραν, τοὺς δὲ λοιποὺς ἐπικείμενοι καὶ φονεύ-
οντες συνεδίωξαν εἰς τὴν πόλιν.

18. Μετὰ δὲ ταῦτα συνέβη τοὺς μὲν Καρχηδονίους
εὐλαβέστερον διακεῖσθαι πρὸς τὰς ἐπιθέσεις, τοὺς δὲ
2 Ῥωμαίους φυλακτικώτερον χρῆσθαι ταῖς προνομαῖς.
ἐπεὶ δ᾽ οὐκ ἀντεξῄεσαν οἱ Καρχηδόνιοι πλὴν ἕως
ἀκροβολισμοῦ, διελόντες οἱ στρατηγοὶ τῶν Ῥωμαίων
εἰς δύο μέρη τὴν δύναμιν τῷ μὲν ἑνὶ περὶ τὸ πρὸ τῆς
πόλεως Ἀσκληπιεῖον ἔμενον, θατέρῳ δὲ κατεστρατοπέδευσαν ἐν τοῖς πρὸς Ἡράκλειαν κεκλιμένοις μέ-
3 ρεσι τῆς πόλεως. τὰ δὲ μεταξὺ τῶν στρατοπέδων ἐξ
ἑκατέρου τοῦ μέρους τῆς πόλεως ὠχυρώσαντο, καὶ τὴν
μὲν ἐντὸς αὐτῶν τάφρον προυβάλοντο χάριν τῆς πρὸς
τοὺς ἐξιόντας ἐκ τῆς πόλεως ἀσφαλείας, τὴν δ᾽ ἐκτὸς
αὐτῶν περιεβάλοντο, φυλακὴν ποιούμενοι τῶν ἔξωθεν
ἐπιθέσεων καὶ τῶν παρεισάγεσθαι καὶ παρεισπίπτειν
4 εἰωθότων εἰς τὰς πολιορκουμένας πόλεις. τὰ δὲ μεταξὺ
τῶν τάφρων καὶ τῶν στρατοπέδων διαστήματα φυλακαῖς διέλαβον, ὀχυροποιησάμενοι τοὺς εὐκαίρους τῶν
5 τόπων ἐν διαστάσει. τὰ δὲ χορήγια καὶ τὴν ἄλλην
παρασκευὴν οἱ μὲν ἄλλοι σύμμαχοι πάντες ἤθροιζον
αὐτοῖς καὶ παρῆγον εἰς Ἑρβησόν, αὐτοὶ δ᾽ ἐκ ταύτης
τῆς πόλεως οὐ μακρὰν ὑπαρχούσης ἄγοντες καὶ φέροντες συνεχῶς τὰς ἀγορὰς δαψιλῆ τἀναγκαῖα σφίσι
6 παρεσκεύαζον. πέντε μὲν οὖν ἴσως μῆνας ἐπὶ τῶν
αὐτῶν διέμενον, οὐδὲν ὁλοσχερὲς προτέρημα δυνάμε-

still more of the enemy. Finally surrounding them as they were on the point of tearing up the palisade, they dispatched some on the spot and pressing hard on the rest pursued them with slaughter to the city.

18. After this the Carthaginians were more inclined to be cautious in taking the offensive, while the Romans were more on their guard in foraging. As the Carthaginians did not advance beyond skirmishing range, the Roman generals divided their force into two bodies, remaining with one near the temple of Asclepius outside the walls and encamping with the other on that side of the city that is turned toward Heraclea. They fortified the ground between their camps on each side of the city, protecting themselves by the inner trench from sallies from within and encircling themselves with an outer one to guard against attacks from outside, and to prevent that secret introduction of supplies and men which is usual in the case of beleaguered cities. On the spaces between the trenches and their camps they placed pickets, fortifying suitable places at some distance from each other. Their supplies and other material were collected for them by all the other members of the alliance, and brought to Herbesus, and they themselves constantly fetching in live stock and provisions from this city which was at no great distance, kept themselves abundantly supplied with what they required. So for five months or so matters were at a standstill, neither side being able to score any decisive advantage, nothing

THE HISTORIES OF POLYBIUS

νοι λαβεῖν κατ᾽ ἀλλήλων πλὴν τῶν ἐν αὐτοῖς τοῖς
7 ἀκροβολισμοῖς συμβαινόντων. συναγομένων δὲ τῷ
λιμῷ τῶν Καρχηδονίων διὰ τὸ πλῆθος τῶν ἐν τῇ πόλει
συγκεκλεισμένων ἀνδρῶν, οὐ γὰρ ἐλάττους πέντε μυ-
ριάδων ὑπῆρχον, δυσχρηστούμενος Ἀννίβας ἤδη τοῖς
πράγμασιν, ὁ τεταγμένος ἐπὶ τῶν πολιορκουμένων
δυνάμεων, διεπέμπετο συνεχῶς εἰς τὴν Καρχηδόνα
8 τήν τε περίστασιν διασαφῶν καὶ βοηθεῖν παρακαλῶν.
οἱ δ᾽ ἐν τῇ Καρχηδόνι τῶν ἐπισυνηγμένων στρατιωτῶν καὶ θηρίων γεμίσαντες τὰς ναῦς ἐξέπεμψαν εἰς
9 τὴν Σικελίαν πρὸς Ἄννωνα τὸν ἕτερον στρατηγόν. ὃς
συναγαγὼν τὰς παρασκευὰς καὶ δυνάμεις εἰς Ἡράκλειαν, πρῶτον μὲν πραξικοπήσας κατέσχε τὴν τῶν
Ἐρβησέων πόλιν, καὶ παρείλετο τὰς ἀγορὰς καὶ
τὴν τῶν ἀναγκαίων χορηγίαν τοῖς τῶν ὑπεναντίων
10 στρατοπέδοις. ἐξ οὗ συνέβη τοὺς Ῥωμαίους ἐπ᾽ ἴσου
πολιορκεῖν καὶ πολιορκεῖσθαι τοῖς πράγμασιν. εἰς
γὰρ τοῦτο συνήγοντο τῇ σιτοδείᾳ καὶ σπάνει τῶν
ἀναγκαίων ὥστε πολλάκις βουλεύεσθαι περὶ τοῦ
11 λύειν τὴν πολιορκίαν. ὃ δὴ καὶ τέλος ἂν ἐποίησαν, εἰ
μὴ πᾶσαν σπουδὴν καὶ μηχανὴν προσφερόμενος Ἱέρων τὰ μέτρια καὶ τἀναγκαῖα σφίσι παρεσκεύαζε τῶν
χορηγίων.

19. μετὰ δὲ ταῦτα θεωρῶν ὁ προειρημένος ἀνὴρ
τοὺς μὲν Ῥωμαίους ὑπό τε τῆς νόσου καὶ τῆς ἐνδείας
ἀσθενῶς διακειμένους διὰ τὸ λοιμικὴν εἶναι παρ᾽ αὐτοῖς κατάστασιν, τὰ δὲ σφέτερα στρατόπεδα νομίζων
ἀξιόχρεα πρὸς μάχην ὑπάρχειν, ἀναλαβὼν τά τε

in fact beyond incidental success in their skirmishes; but when the Carthaginians began to be pressed by famine owing to the number of people cooped up in the city—fifty thousand at least in number—Hannibal, the commander of the besieged forces, found himself in a difficult situation and sent constant messages to Carthage explaining his position and begging for reinforcements. The Carthaginian government shipped the troops they had collected and their elephants and sent them to Sicily to Hanno their other general. Hanno concentrated his troops and material of war at Heraclea and in the first place surprised and occupied Herbesus, cutting off the enemy's camps and their provisions and necessary supplies. The result of this was that the Romans were as a fact both besieged and besiegers at the same time; for they were so hard pressed by want of food and scarcity of the necessities of life, that they often contemplated raising the siege, and would in the end have done so, had not Hiero, by using every effort and every device, provided them with a moderate amount of strictly necessary supplies.

19. In the next place Hanno, perceiving that the Romans were weakened by disease and privation, owing to an epidemic having broken out among them, and thinking that his own troops were in fit fighting condition, took with him

2 θηρία περὶ πεντήκοντα τὸν ἀριθμὸν ὄντα καὶ τὴν
λοιπὴν δύναμιν ἅπασαν προῆγε κατὰ σπουδὴν ἐκ τῆς
Ἡρακλείας, παραγγείλας τοῖς Νομαδικοῖς ἱππεῦσι
προπορεύεσθαι, καὶ συνεγγίσασι τῷ χάρακι τῶν
ἐναντίων ἐρεθίζειν καὶ πειρᾶσθαι τοὺς ἱππεῖς αὐτῶν
ἐκκαλεῖσθαι, κἄπειτα πάλιν ἐκκλίνασιν ἀποχωρεῖν,
ἕως ἂν αὐτῷ συμμίξωσι. πραξάντων δὲ τὸ συνταχθὲν
3 τῶν Νομάδων καὶ προσμιξάντων θατέρῳ τῶν στρατοπέδων, εὐθὺς οἱ τῶν Ῥωμαίων ἱππεῖς ἐξεχέοντο καὶ
4 θρασέως ἐπέκειντο τοῖς Νομάσιν. οἱ δὲ Λίβυες ὑπεχώρουν κατὰ τὸ παράγγελμα, μέχρι συνέμιξαν τοῖς περὶ
τὸν Ἄννωνα· λοιπόν τ᾽ ἐκ μεταβολῆς περιχυθέντες
ἐπέκειντο τοῖς πολεμίοις, καὶ πολλοὺς μὲν αὐτῶν
ἀπέκτειναν, τοὺς δὲ λοιποὺς ἕως εἰς τὸν χάρακα
5 συνεδίωξαν. γενομένων δὲ τούτων ἐπεστρατοπέδευσαν
οἱ περὶ τὸν Ἄννωνα τοῖς Ῥωμαίοις, καταλαβόμενοι
τὸν λόφον τὸν καλούμενον Τόρον, ὡς δέκα σταδίους
6 ἀπέχοντες τῶν ὑπεναντίων. καὶ δύο μὲν μῆνας ἔμενον
ἐπὶ τῶν ὑποκειμένων, οὐδὲν ὁλοσχερὲς πράττοντες
7 πλὴν ἀκροβολιζόμενοι καθ᾽ ἑκάστην ἡμέραν. τοῦ δ᾽
Ἀννίβου διαπυρσευομένου καὶ διαπεμπομένου συνεχῶς ἐκ τῆς πόλεως πρὸς τὸν Ἄννωνα, καὶ δηλοῦντος
ὅτι τὰ πλήθη τὸν λιμὸν οὐχ ὑπομένει, πολλοὶ δὲ καὶ
πρὸς τοὺς πολεμίους αὐτομολοῦσι διὰ τὴν ἔνδειαν,
ἔγνω διακινδυνεύειν ὁ τῶν Καρχηδονίων στρατηγός,
οὐχ ἧττον ἐπὶ τοῦτο φερομένων καὶ τῶν Ῥωμαίων διὰ
8 τὰς προειρημένας αἰτίας. διόπερ ἐξαγαγόντες ἀμφότεροι τὰς δυνάμεις εἰς τὸν μεταξὺ τόπον τῶν

all his elephants, about fifty in number, and all the rest of his force, and advanced rapidly from Heraclea. He had ordered the Numidian horse to precede him, and approaching the enemy's fortified camp to provoke him and attempt to draw his cavalry out, after which they were to give away and retire until they rejoined himself. The Numidians acting on these orders advanced up to one of the camps, and the Roman cavalry at once issued forth and boldly attacked them. The Libyans retreated as they had been ordered until they joined Hanno's army and then, wheeling round and encircling the enemy, they attacked them, killing many and pursuing the rest as far as the camp. After this Hanno encamped opposite the Romans, occupying the hill called Torus, at a distance of about ten stades from the enemy. For two months they remained stationary, without any action more decisive than shooting at each other every day; but as Hannibal kept on announcing to Hanno by fire signals and messengers from the city that the population could not support the famine, and that deserters to the enemy were numerous owing to privation, the Carthaginian general decided to risk battle, the Romans being no less eager for this owing to the reasons I stated above. Both therefore led out their forces to the space between the

9 στρατοπέδων συνέβαλλον ἀλλήλοις. ἐπὶ πολὺν δὲ
χρόνον γενομένης τῆς μάχης τέλος ἐτρέψαντο τοὺς
προκινδυνεύσαντας μισθοφόρους τῶν Καρχηδονίων
10 οἱ Ῥωμαῖοι. τούτων δὲ πεσόντων εἰς τὰ θηρία καὶ τὰς
λοιπὰς τάξεις τὰς ἐφεστηκυίας συνέβη πᾶν συν-
11 ταραχθῆναι τὸ τῶν Φοινίκων στρατόπεδον. γενομένου
δ᾽ ἐγκλίματος ὁλοσχεροῦς οἱ μὲν πλεῖστοι διεφθάρησαν αὐτῶν, τινὲς δ᾽ εἰς Ἡράκλειαν ἀπεχώρησαν· οἱ δὲ
Ῥωμαῖοι τῶν τε πλείστων ἐκυρίευσαν θηρίων καὶ τῆς
12 ἐπισκευῆς ἁπάσης. ἐπιγενομένης δὲ τῆς νυκτός, καὶ
διὰ τὴν ἐκ τῶν κατορθωμάτων χαρὰν καὶ διὰ τὸν
κόπον ῥᾳθυμότερον ταῖς φυλακαῖς αὐτῶν χρησα-
μένων, ἀπελπίσας Ἀννίβας τὰ πράγματα, καὶ νομίσας ἔχειν εὐφυῆ καιρὸν πρὸς σωτηρίαν διὰ τὰς προειρημένας αἰτίας, ὥρμησε περὶ μέσας νύκτας ἐκ τῆς
13 πόλεως, ἔχων τὰς ξενικὰς δυνάμεις. χώσας δὲ φορ-
μοῖς ἀχύρων σεσαγμένοις τὰς τάφρους ἔλαθε τοὺς
πολεμίους ἀπαγαγὼν ἀσφαλῶς τὴν δύναμιν. οἱ δὲ
14 Ῥωμαῖοι τῆς ἡμέρας ἐπελθούσης συνέντες τὸ γεγονός, καὶ τῆς οὐραγίας τῆς τῶν περὶ τὸν Ἀννίβαν ἐπὶ
βραχὺ καθαψάμενοι, μετὰ ταῦτα πάντες ὥρμησαν
15 πρὸς τὰς πύλας. οὐδενὸς δ᾽ ἐμποδὼν αὐτοῖς ἱσταμένου
παρεισπεσόντες διήρπασαν τὴν πόλιν, καὶ πολλῶν
μὲν σωμάτων, πολλῆς δὲ καὶ παντοδαπῆς ἐγένοντο
κατασκευῆς ἐγκρατεῖς.

20. Τῆς δ᾽ ἀγγελίας ἀφικομένης εἰς τὴν σύγκλητον
τῶν Ῥωμαίων ὑπὲρ τῶν κατὰ τὸν Ἀκράγαντα, περιχαρεῖς γενόμενοι καὶ ταῖς διανοίαις ἐπαρθέντες οὐκ

camps and engaged. The battle lasted for long, but at the end the Romans put to flight the advanced line of Carthaginian mercenaries, and as the latter fell back on the elephants and the other divisions in their rear, the whole Phoenician army was thrown into disorder. A complete rout ensued, and most of them were put to the sword, some escaping to Heraclea. The Romans captured most of the elephants and all the baggage. But after nightfall, while the Romans, partly from joy at their success and partly from fatigue, had relaxed the vigilance of their watch, Hannibal, regarding his situation as desperate, and thinking for the above reasons that this was a fine opportunity for saving himself, broke out of the city about midnight with his mercenaries. By filling up the trenches with baskets packed tightly with straw he managed to withdraw his force in safety unperceived by the enemy. When day broke the Romans became aware of what had happened, and, after slightly molesting Hannibal's rear guard, advanced with their whole force to the gates. Finding nobody to oppose them they entered the city and plundered it, possessing themselves of many slaves[41] and a quantity of booty of every description.

20. When the news of what had occurred at Agrigentum reached the Roman Senate, in their joy and elation they no longer confined themselves to their original de-

[41] The entire population was sold into slavery; see n. on 14. 4.

ἔμενον ἐπὶ τῶν ἐξ ἀρχῆς λογισμῶν, οὐδ' ἠρκοῦντο
σεσωκέναι τοὺς Μαμερτίνους οὐδὲ ταῖς ἐξ αὐτοῦ τοῦ
2 πολέμου γενομέναις ὠφελείαις, ἐλπίσαντες δὲ καθόλου δυνατὸν εἶναι τοὺς Καρχηδονίους ἐκβαλεῖν ἐκ τῆς
νήσου, τούτου δὲ γενομένου μεγάλην ἐπίδοσιν αὐτῶν
λήψεσθαι τσὰ πράγματα, πρὸς τούτοις ἦσαν τοῖς
3 λογισμοῖς καὶ ταῖς περὶ τοῦτο τὸ μέρος ἐπινοίαις. τὰ
μὲν οὖν περὶ τὰς πεζικὰς δυνάμεις ἑώρων κατὰ λόγον
4 σφίσι προχωροῦντα· μετὰ γὰρ τοὺς τὸν Ἀκράγαντα
πολιορκήσαντας οἱ κατασταθέντες στρατηγοὶ Λεύκιος Οὐαλέριος καὶ Τίτος Ὀτακίλιος ἐδόκουν ἐνδεχομέ-
5 νως χειρίζειν τὰ κατὰ τὴν Σικελίαν. τῆς δὲ θαλάττης
ἀκονιτὶ τῶν Καρχηδονίων ἐπικρατούντων ἐζυγοστα-
6 τεῖτ' αὐτοῖς ὁ πόλεμος· ἐν γὰρ τοῖς ἑξῆς χρόνοις,
κατεχόντων αὐτῶν ἤδη τὸν Ἀκράγαντα, πολλαὶ μὲν
πόλεις προσετίθεντο τῶν μεσογαίων τοῖς Ῥωμαίοις,
ἀγωνιῶσαι τὰς πεζικὰς δυνάμεις, ἔτι δὲ πλείους ἀφίσταντο τῶν παραθαλαττίων, καταπεπληγμέναι τὸν
7 τῶν Καρχηδονίων στόλον. ὅθεν ὁρῶντες αἰεὶ καὶ μᾶλλον εἰς ἑκάτερα τὰ μέρη ῥοπὰς λαμβάνοντα τὸν πόλεμον διὰ τὰς προειρημένας αἰτίας, ἔτι δὲ τὴν μὲν
Ἰταλίαν πορθουμένην πολλάκις ὑπὸ τῆς ναυτικῆς
δυνάμεως, τὴν δὲ Λιβύην εἰς τέλος ἀβλαβῆ διαμένου-
σαν, ὥρμησαν ἐπὶ τὸ συνεμβαίνειν τοῖς Καρχηδονί-
8 οις εἰς τὴν θάλατταν. διὸ καὶ τοῦτο τὸ μέρος οὐχ
ἥκιστά με παρώρμησε ποιήσασθαι μνήμην ἐπὶ πλεῖον τοῦ προειρημένου πολέμου, χάριν τοῦ μηδὲ ταύτην

signs and were no longer satisfied with having saved the Mamertines and with what they had gained in the war itself, but, hoping that it would be possible to drive the Carthaginians entirely out of the island and that if this were done their own power would be much augmented, they directed their attention to this project and to plans that would serve their purpose. As regards their land force at least they noted that all progressed satisfactorily; for the Consuls appointed after those who had reduced Agrigentum, Lucius Valerius Flaccus and Titus Otacilius Crassus, seemed to be managing Sicilian affairs as well as possible; but as the Carthaginians maintained without any trouble the command of the sea, the fortunes of the war continued to hang in the balance. For in the period that followed, 261 B.C. now that Agrigentum was in their hands, while many inland cities joined the Romans from dread of their land forces, still more seaboard cities deserted their cause in terror of the Carthaginian fleet. Hence when they saw that the balance of the war tended more and more to shift to this side or that for the above reasons, and that while Italy was frequently ravaged by naval forces, Libya remained entirely free from damage, they took urgent steps to get on the sea[42] like the Carthaginians. And one of the reasons which induced me to narrate the history of the war named above at some length is just this, that my readers should, in

[42] Rome takes the first steps toward becoming a sea power.

ἀγνοεῖσθαι τὴν ἀρχήν, πῶς καὶ πότε καὶ δι' ἃς αἰτίας
πρῶτον ἐνέβησαν εἰς θάλατταν Ῥωμαῖοι.

9   Θεωροῦντες δὲ τὸν πόλεμον αὐτοῖς τριβὴν λαμβάνοντα, τότε πρῶτον ἐπεβάλοντο ναυπηγεῖσθαι σκάφη,
10 πεντηρικὰ μὲν ἑκατόν, εἴκοσι δὲ τριήρεις. τῶν δὲ
ναυπηγῶν εἰς τέλος ἀπείρων ὄντων τῆς περὶ τὰς
πεντήρεις ναυπηγίας διὰ τὸ μηδένα τότε τῶν κατὰ τὴν
Ἰταλίαν κεχρῆσθαι τοιούτοις σκάφεσι, πολλὴν αὐ-
11 τοῖς παρεῖχε τοῦτο τὸ μέρος δυσχέρειαν. ἐξ ὧν καὶ
μάλιστα συνίδοι τις ἂν τὸ μεγαλόψυχον καὶ παράβο-
12 λον τῆς Ῥωμαίων αἱρέσεως. οὐ γὰρ οἷον εὐλόγους
ἀφορμὰς ἔχοντες, ἀλλ' οὐδ' ἀφορμὰς καθάπαξ, οὐδ'
ἐπίνοιαν οὐδέποτε ποιησάμενοι τῆς θαλάττης, τότε δὴ
πρῶτον ἐν νῷ λαμβάνοντες οὕτως τολμηρῶς ἐνεχείρησαν ὥστε πρὶν ἢ πειραθῆναι τοῦ πράγματος, εὐθὺς
ἐπιβαλέσθαι Καρχηδονίοις ναυμαχεῖν τοῖς ἐκ προγό-
13 νων ἔχουσι τὴν κατὰ θάλατταν ἡγεμονίαν ἀδήριτον.
μαρτυρίῳ δ' ἄν τις χρήσαιτο πρὸς τὴν ἀλήθειαν τῶν
νῦν ὑπ' ἐμοῦ λεγομένων καὶ πρὸς τὸ παράδοξον αὐτῶν
τῆς τόλμης. ὅτε γὰρ τὸ πρῶτον ἐπεχείρησαν δια-
βιβάζειν εἰς τὴν Μεσσήνην τὰς δυνάμεις, οὐχ οἷον
κατάφρακτος αὐτοῖς ὑπῆρχε ναῦς, ἀλλ' οὐδὲ καθόλου
14 μακρὸν πλοῖον οὐδὲ λέμβος οὐδ' εἷς, ἀλλὰ παρὰ
Ταραντίνων καὶ Λοκρῶν ἔτι δ' Ἐλεατῶν καὶ Νεαπο-
λιτῶν συγχρησάμενοι πεντηκοντόρους καὶ τριήρεις
15 ἐπὶ τούτων παραβόλως διεκόμισαν τοὺς ἄνδρας. ἐν ᾧ
δὴ καιρῷ τῶν Καρχηδονίων κατὰ τὸν πορθμὸν ἐπ-
αναχθέντων αὐτοῖς, καὶ μιᾶς νεὼς καταφράκτου διὰ

this case too, not be kept in ignorance of the beginning—how, when, and for what reasons the Romans first took to the sea.

When they saw that the war was dragging on, they undertook for the first time to build ships, a hundred quinqueremes and twenty triremes. As their shipwrights were absolutely inexperienced in building quinqueremes, such ships never having been in use in Italy, the matter caused them much difficulty, and this fact shows us better than anything else how spirited and daring the Romans are when they are determined to do a thing. It was not that they had fairly good resources for it, but they had none whatever, nor had they ever given a thought to the sea; yet when they once had conceived the project, they took it in hand so boldly, that before gaining any experience in the matter they at once engaged the Carthaginians who had held for generations undisputed command of the sea. Evidence of the truth of what I am saying and of their incredible pluck is this. When they first undertook to send their forces across to Messene not only had they not any decked ships, but no long warships at all, not even a single boat, and borrowing fifty-oared boats and triremes from the Tarentines and Locrians, and also from the people of Elea and Naples they took their troops across in these at great hazard. On this occasion the Carthaginians put to sea to attack them as they were crossing the straits, and one of their decked ships advanced too far in its eagerness to

τὴν προθυμίαν προπεσούσης, ὥστ' ἐποκείλασαν γενέσθαι τοῖς Ῥωμαίοις ὑποχείριον, ταύτῃ παραδείγματι
χρώμενοι τότε πρὸς ταύτην ἐποιοῦντο τὴν τοῦ παντὸς

16 στόλου ναυπηγίαν, ὡς εἰ μὴ τοῦτο συνέβη γενέσθαι,
δῆλον ὡς διὰ τὴν ἀπειρίαν εἰς τέλος ἂν ἐκωλύθησαν
τῆς ἐπιβολῆς.

21. οὐ μὴν ἀλλ' οἷς μὲν ἐπιμελὲς ἦν τῆς ναυπηγίας,
ἐγίνοντο περὶ τὴν τῶν πλοίων κατασκευήν, οἱ δὲ τὰ
πληρώματα συναθροίσαντες ἐδίδασκον ἐν τῇ γῇ

2 κωπηλατεῖν τὸν τρόπον τοῦτον. καθίσαντες ἐπὶ τῶν
εἰρεσιῶν ἐν τῇ χέρσῳ τοὺς ἄνδρας τὴν αὐτὴν ἔχοντας
τάξιν ταῖς ἐπ' αὐτῶν τῶν πλοίων καθέδραις, μέσον δ'
ἐν αὐτοῖς στήσαντες τὸν κελευστήν, ἅμα πάντας ἀνα-
πίπτειν ἐφ' αὑτοὺς ἄγοντας τὰς χεῖρας, καὶ πάλιν
προνεύειν ἐξωθοῦντας ταύτας συνείθιζον ἄρχεσθαί τε
καὶ λήγειν τῶν κινήσεων πρὸς τὰ τοῦ κελευστοῦ

3 παραγγέλματα. προκατασκευασθέντων δὲ τούτων
ἅμα τῷ συντελεσθῆναι τὰς ναῦς καθελκύσαντες, καὶ
βραχὺν χρόνον ἐπ' αὐτῆς τῆς ἀληθείας ἐν θαλάττῃ
πειραθέντες, ἔπλεον παρὰ τὴν Ἰταλίαν κατὰ τὸ πρόσ-

4 ταγμα τοῦ στρατηγοῦ. ὁ γὰρ ἐπὶ τῆς ναυτικῆς
δυνάμεως τεταγμένος τοῖς Ῥωμαίοις Γνάιος Κορνήλιος, ὀλίγαις ἡμέραις πρότερον, συντάξας τοῖς ναυάρ-
χοις, ἐπειδὰν καταρτίσωσι τὸν στόλον, πλεῖν ὡς ἐπὶ
τὸν πορθμόν, αὐτὸς ἀναχθεὶς μετὰ νεῶν ἑπτακαίδεκα
προκατέπλευσεν ἐπὶ τὴν Μεσσήνην, σπουδάζων τὰ
κατεπείγοντα πρὸς τὴν χρείαν παρασκευάσαι τῷ στό-

5 λῳ. προσπεσούσης δ' αὐτῷ πράξεως ἐκεῖ περὶ τῆς τῶν

overtake them and running aground fell into the hands of the Romans. This ship they now used as a model, and built their whole fleet on its pattern; so that it is evident that if this had not occurred they would have been entirely prevented from carrying out their design by lack of practical knowledge.

21. Now, however, those to whom the construction of the ships was committed were busy in getting them ready, and those who had collected the crews were teaching them to row on shore in the following fashion. Making the men sit on rowers' benches on dry land, in the same order as on the benches of the ships themselves, and stationing the boatswain in the middle, they accustomed them to fall back all at once bringing their hands up to them, and again to come forward pushing out their hands, and to begin and finish these movements at the word of command of the fugle man. When the crews had been trained, they launched the ships as soon as they were completed, and having practiced for a brief time actual rowing at sea, they sailed along the coast of Italy as their commander had ordered. For the Consul appointed by the Romans to the command of their naval force, Gnaeus Cornelius Scipio, had a few days previously given orders to the captains to sail in the direction of the Straits whenever the fleet was ready, while he himself, putting to sea with seventeen ships, preceded them to Messene, being anxious to provide for all the urgent needs of the fleet. When an opportunity there occurred to obtain

200 B.C.

Λιπαραίων πόλεως, δεξάμενος τὴν ἐλπίδα προχειρότερον τοῦ δέοντος ἔπλει ταῖς προειρημέναις ναυσὶ
6 καὶ καθωρμίσθη πρὸς τὴν πόλιν. ὁ δὲ τῶν Καρχηδονίων στρατηγὸς Ἀννίβας, ἀκούσας ἐν τῷ Πανόρμῳ
τὸ γεγονός, ἐξαποστέλλει Βοώδη τῆς γερουσίας
7 ὑπάρχοντα, ναῦς εἴκοσι δούς. ὃς ἐπιπλεύσας νυκτὸς ἐν
τῷ λιμένι συνέκλεισε τοὺς περὶ τὸν Γνάιον. ἡμέρας δ'
ἐπιγενομένης τὰ μὲν πληρώματα πρὸς φυγὴν ὥρμησεν εἰς τὴν γῆν, ὁ δὲ Γνάιος ἐκπλαγὴς γενόμενος καὶ
ποιεῖν ἔχων οὐδὲν τέλος παρέδωκεν αὑτὸν τοῖς πολε-
8 μίοις. οἱ δὲ Καρχηδόνιοι τάς τε ναῦς καὶ τὸν στρατηγὸν τῶν ὑπεναντίων ὑποχείριον ἔχοντες παραχρῆμα
9 πρὸς τὸν Ἀννίβαν ἀπῆραν. μετ' οὐ πολλὰς δ' ἡμέρας,
οὕτως ἐναργοῦς ὄντος καὶ προσφάτου τοῦ περὶ τὸν
Γνάιον ἀτυχήματος, παρ' ὀλίγον αὐτὸς Ἀννίβας εἰς τὸ
10 παραπλήσιον ἁμάρτημα προφανῶς ἐνέπεσεν. ἀκούσας γὰρ τὸν τῶν Ῥωμαίων στόλον κομιζόμενον παρὰ
τὴν Ἰταλίαν σύνεγγυς εἶναι, κατιδεῖν βουλόμενος τό
τε πλῆθος καὶ τὴν ὅλην σύνταξιν τῶν ὑπεναντίων,
11 λαβὼν πεντήκοντα ναῦς ἐπιπλεῖ. κάμπτων δὲ περὶ τὸ
τῆς Ἰταλίας ἀκρωτήριον ἐμπίπτει τοῖς πολεμίοις ἐν
κόσμῳ καὶ τάξει ποιουμένοις τὸν πλοῦν, καὶ τὰς μὲν
πλείους ἀπέβαλε τῶν νεῶν, αὐτὸς δὲ μετὰ τῶν ὑπο-
λειφθεισῶν ἀνελπίστως καὶ παραδόξως διέφυγεν.
22. Οἱ δὲ Ῥωμαῖοι μετὰ ταῦτα συνεγγίσαντες τοῖς
κατὰ τὴν Σικελίαν τόποις, καὶ συνέντες τὸ γεγονὸς
σύμπτωμα περὶ τὸν Γνάιον, παραυτίκα μὲν διεπέμποντο πρὸς Γάιον Βίλιον τὸν ἡγούμενον τῆς πεζῆς

the city of Lipara[43] by treachery, and embracing the prospect with undue eagerness he sailed with the above-mentioned ships and anchored off the town. The Carthaginian general Hannibal, hearing at Panormus what had happened, sent off Boödes, a member of the Senate,[44] giving him twenty ships. Boödes sailed up to Lipara at night and shut up Gnaeus in the harbor. When day dawned the Roman crews hastily took refuge on land, and Gnaeus, falling into a state of terror and being unable to do anything, finally surrendered to the enemy. The Carthaginians now set off at once to rejoin Hannibal with the captured ships and commander of the enemy. But a few days later, though Gnaeus' disaster was so signal and recent, Hannibal himself came very near falling into the same error with his eyes open. For hearing that the Roman fleet which was sailing along the coast of Italy was near at hand, and wishing to get a glimpse of the numbers and general disposition of the enemy, he sailed toward them with fifty ships. As he was rounding the Cape of Italy he came upon the enemy sailing in good order and trim. He lost most of his ships and escaped himself with the remainder, which was more than he expected or hoped.

22. After this the Romans approached the coast of Sicily and learning of the disaster that had befallen Gnaeus, at once communicated with Gaius Duilius, the commander

[43] The largest of the Aeolian Islands with a town of that name on the east coast.

[44] O. Meltzer, *Geschichte der Karthager* 2 (Berlin 1896) 36–48; W. Huss, *Geschichte der Karthager* (Munich c. 1985) 462–463.

2 δυνάμεως, καὶ τοῦτον ἀνέμενον, ἅμα δ᾽ ἀκούοντες οὐ
μακρὰν εἶναι τὸν τῶν πολεμίων στόλον, ἐγίνοντο πρὸς
παρασκευὴν τοῦ ναυμαχεῖν. ὄντων δὲ τῶν πλοίων

3 φαύλων ταῖς κατασκευαῖς καὶ δυσκινήτων, ὑποτίθεταί
τις αὐτοῖς βοήθημα πρὸς τὴν μάχην τοὺς ἐπικληθέν-
τας μετὰ ταῦτα κόρακας ὧν συνέβαινε τὴν κατασκευ-

4 ὴν εἶναι τοιαύτην. στῦλος ἐν πρώρρᾳ στρογγύλος
εἱστήκει, μῆκος μὲν ὀργυιῶν τεττάρων, κατὰ δὲ τὸ

5 πλάτος τριῶν παλαιστῶν ἔχων τὴν διάμετρον. οὗτος
αὐτὸς μὲν ἐπὶ τῆς κορυφῆς τροχιλίαν εἶχε, περιετίθετο
δ᾽ αὐτῷ κλῖμαξ ἐπικαρσίαις σανίσι καθηλωμένη,

6 πλάτος μὲν ποδῶν τεττάρων, τὸ δὲ μῆκος ἓξ ὀργυιῶν.
τὸ δὲ τρῆμα τοῦ σανιδώματος ἦν παράμηκες καὶ
περιέβαινε περὶ τὸν στῦλον μετὰ τὰς πρώτας εὐθέως
τῆς κλίμακος δύ᾽ ὀργυιάς. εἶχε δὲ καὶ δρύφακτον αὕτη
παρ᾽ ἑκατέραν τὴν ἐπιμήκη πλευρὰν εἰς γόνυ τὸ

7 βάθος. ἐπὶ δὲ τοῦ πέρατος αὐτοῦ προσήρμοστο σιδη-
ροῦν οἷον ὕπερον ἀπωξυσμένον, ἔχον δακτύλιον ἐπὶ
τῆς κορυφῆς, ὡς τὸ ὅλον φαίνεσθαι παραπλήσιον

8 ταῖς σιτοποιικαῖς μηχανήσεσιν. εἰς δὲ τοῦτον τὸν
δακτύλιον ἐνεδέδετο κάλως, ᾧ κατὰ τὰς ἐμβολὰς τῶν
πλοίων ἐξαίροντες τοὺς κόρακας διὰ τῆς ἐν τῷ στύλῳ
τροχιλίας ἀφίεσαν ἐπὶ τὸ κατάστρωμα τῆς ἀλλοτρίας
νεὼς ποτὲ μὲν κατὰ πρῶρραν, ποτὲ δ᾽ ἀντιπεριάγοντες
⟨εἰς⟩ τὰς ἐκ τῶν πλαγίων προσπιπτούσας ἐμβολάς.

9 ὅτε δὲ ταῖς σανίσι τῶν καταστρωμάτων ἐμπαγέντες οἱ
κόρακες ὁμοῦ συνδήσαιεν τὰς ναῦς, εἰ μὲν πλάγιαι
παραβάλοιεν ἀλλήλαις, πανταχόθεν ἐπεπήδων, εἰ δὲ

of the land forces, and awaited his arrival. At the same time, hearing that the enemy's fleet was not far distant, they began to get ready for sea battle. As their ships were ill-built and slow in their movements, someone suggested to them as a help in fighting the engines which afterward came to be called "ravens."[45] They were constructed as follows: On the prow stood a round pole four fathoms in height and three palms in diameter. This pole had a pulley at the summit and round it was put a gangway made of cross planks attached by nails, four feet in width and six fathoms in length. In this gangway was an oblong hole, and it went round the pole at a distance of two fathoms from its near end. The gangway also had a railing on each of its long sides as high as a man's knee. At its extremity was fastened an iron object like a pestle pointed at one end and with a ring at the other end, so that the whole looked like the machine for pounding corn. To this ring was attached a rope with which, when the ship charged an enemy, they raised the ravens by means of the pulley on the pole and let them down on the enemy's deck, sometimes from the prow and sometimes bringing them round when the ships collided broadsides. Once the ravens were fixed in the planks of the enemy's deck and grappled the ships together, if they were broadside on, they boarded from all directions but if they

---

[45] See the discussion of WC 1. 77–78, with bibliography on this much discussed weapon.

κατὰ πρῶρραν, δι' αὐτοῦ τοῦ κόρακος ἐπὶ δύο συν-
10 εχεῖς ἐποιοῦντο τὴν ἔφοδον· ὧν οἱ μὲν ἡγούμενοι τὴν
κατὰ πρόσωπον ἐπιφάνειαν ἐσκέπαζον ταῖς τῶν θυ-
ρεῶν προβολαῖς, οἱ δ' ἑπόμενοι τὰς ἐκ τῶν πλαγίων
ἠσφάλιζον πλευρὰς ὑπὲρ τὸν δρύφακτον ὑπερτιθέ-
11 μενοι τὰς ἴτυς τῶν ὅπλων. οὗτοι μὲν οὖν τοιαύτῃ
κεχρημένοι παρασκευῇ καιρὸν ἐπετήρουν πρὸς ναυμαχίαν.
23. Ὁ δὲ Γάιος Βίλιος ὡς θᾶττον ἔγνω τὴν περιπέτειαν τοῦ τῆς ναυτικῆς δυνάμεως ἡγουμένου, παραδοὺς τὰ πεζικὰ στρατόπεδα τοῖς χιλιάρχοις αὐτὸς
2 διεκομίσθη πρὸς τὸν στόλον. πυθόμενος δὲ τοὺς πολεμίους πορθεῖν τὴν Μυλαῖτιν χώραν, ἐπιπλεῖ στόλῳ
3 παντί. συνιδόντες δ' οἱ Καρχηδόνιοι μετὰ χαρᾶς καὶ
σπουδῆς ἀνήγοντο ναυσὶν ἑκατὸν καὶ τριάκοντα,
καταφρονοῦντες τῆς ἀπειρίας τῶν Ῥωμαίων, καὶ
πάντες ἔπλεον ἀντίπρωρροι τοῖς πολεμίοις, οὐδὲ
τάξεως καταξιώσαντες τὸν κίνδυνον, ἀλλ' ὡς ἐπὶ λείαν
4 τινὰ πρόδηλον. ἡγεῖτο δ' Ἀννίβας αὐτῶν—οὗτος δ' ἦν
ὁ τὰς δυνάμεις ἐκκλέψας νυκτὸς ἐκ τῆς τῶν Ἀκραγαντίνων πόλεως—ἔχων ἑπτήρη τὴν γενομένην Πύρ-
5 ρου τοῦ βασιλέως. ἅμα δὲ τῷ πλησιάζειν συνθεω-
ροῦντες ἀνανενευκότας τοὺς κόρακας ἐν ταῖς ἑκάστων
πρώρραις, ἐπὶ ποσὸν μὲν ἠπόρουν οἱ Καρχηδόνιοι,
ξενιζόμενοι ταῖς τῶν ὀργάνων κατασκευαῖς· οὐ μὴν
ἀλλὰ τελέως κατεγνωκότες τῶν ἐναντίων ἐνέβαλον οἱ
6 πρῶτοι πλέοντες τετολμηκότως. τῶν δὲ συμπλεκομένων σκαφῶν ἀεὶ δεδεμένων τοῖς ὀργάνοις, καὶ τῶν

charged with the prow, they attacked by passing over the gangway of the raven itself two abreast. The leading pair protected the front by holding up their shields, and those who followed secured the two flanks by resting the rims of their shields on the top of the railing. Having, then, adopted this device, they awaited an opportunity for going into action.

23. As for Gaius Duilius, no sooner had he learnt of the disaster which had befallen the commander of the naval forces than handing over his legions to the military tribunes he proceeded to the fleet. Learning that the enemy were ravaging the territory of Mylae,[46] he sailed against them with his whole force. The Carthaginians on sighting him put to sea with a hundred and thirty sail, quite overjoyed and eager, as they despised the inexperience of the Romans. They all sailed straight on the enemy, not even thinking it worth while to maintain order in the attack, but just as if they were falling on a prey that was obviously theirs. They were commanded by Hannibal—the same who stole out of Agrigentum by night with his army—in the seven-banked galley that was formerly King Pyrrhus'.[47] On approaching and seeing the ravens nodding aloft on the prow of each ship, the Carthaginians were at first nonplussed, being surprised at the construction of the engines. However, as they entirely gave the enemy up for lost, the front ships attacked daringly. But when the ships that came into collision were in every case held fast by the

[46] West of Messina on the north coast.
[47] Hannibal's flagship had been taken from the king in a naval battle.

ἀνδρῶν εὐθὺς ἐπιπορευομένων δι᾽ αὐτοῦ τοῦ κόρακος
καὶ συμπλεκομένων ἐπὶ τοῖς καταστρώμασιν, οἱ μὲν
ἐφονεύοντο τῶν Καρχηδονίων, οἱ δὲ παρεδίδοσαν ἑαυτοὺς ἐκπληττόμενοι τὸ γινόμενον· παραπλήσιον γὰρ

7 πεζομαχίας συνέβαινε τὸν κίνδυνον ἀποτελεῖσθαι. διὸ
καὶ τριάκοντα μὲν τὰς πρώτας συμβαλούσας ναῦς
αὐτάνδρους ἀπέβαλον, σὺν αἷς ἐγένετ᾽ αἰχμάλωτον
καὶ τὸ τοῦ στρατηγοῦ πλοῖον· Ἀννίβας δ᾽ ἀνελπίστως

8 καὶ παραβόλως αὐτὸς ἐν τῇ σκάφῃ διέφυγε. τὸ δὲ
λοιπὸν πλῆθος τῶν Καρχηδονίων ἐποιεῖτο μὲν τὸν
ἐπίπλουν ὡς εἰς ἐμβολήν, ἐν δὲ τῷ συνεγγίζειν θεωροῦντες τὸ συμβεβηκὸς περὶ τὰς προπλεούσας ναῦς,

9 ἐξέκλινον καὶ διένευον τὰς τῶν ὀργάνων ἐπιβολάς.
πιστεύοντες δὲ τῷ ταχυναυτεῖν, οἱ μὲν ἐκ πλαγίων, οἱ
δὲ κατὰ πρύμναν ἐκπεριπλέοντες ἀσφαλῶς ἤλπιζον
ποιήσασθαι τὰς ἐμβολάς. πάντη δὲ καὶ πάντως ἀντι-

10 περισταμένων καὶ συνδιανευόντων τῶν ὀργάνων
οὕτως ὥστε κατ᾽ ἀνάγκην τοὺς ἐγγίσαντας συνδε-
δέσθαι, τέλος ἐγκλίναντες ἔφυγον οἱ Καρχηδόνιοι,
καταπλαγέντες τὴν καινοτομίαν τοῦ συμβαίνοντος,
πεντήκοντα ναῦς ἀποβαλόντες.

24. Οἱ δὲ Ῥωμαῖοι παραδόξως ἀντιπεποιημένοι τῆς
κατὰ θάλατταν ἐλπίδος, διπλασίως ἐπερρώσθησαν

2 ταῖς ὁρμαῖς πρὸς τὸν πόλεμον. τότε μὲν οὖν προσσχόντες τῇ Σικελίᾳ τήν τ᾽ Αἰγεσταίων ἔλυσαν πολιορκίαν, ἐσχάτως αὐτῶν ἤδη διακειμένων, κατά τε τὴν ἐκ
τῆς Αἰγέστης ἀναχώρησιν Μάκελλαν πόλιν κατὰ
κράτος εἷλον.

machines, and the Roman crews boarded by means of the ravens and attacked them hand to hand on deck, some of the Carthaginians were cut down and others surrendered from dismay at what was happening, the battle having become just like a fight on land. So the first thirty ships that engaged were taken with all their crews, including the commander's galley, Hannibal himself managing to escape beyond his hopes by a miracle in the jolly boat. The rest of the Carthaginian force was bearing up as if to charge the enemy, but seeing, as they approached, the fate of the advanced ships they turned aside and avoided the blows of the engines. Trusting in their swiftness, they veered round the enemy in the hope of being able to strike him in safety either on the broadside or on the stern, but when the ravens swung round and plunged down in all directions and in all manner of ways so that those who approached them were of necessity grappled, they finally gave way and took to flight, terror-stricken by this novel experience and with the loss of fifty ships.

24. When the Romans had thus, contrary to all expectation, gained the prospect of success at sea their determination to prosecute the war became twice as strong. On this occasion they put in on the coast of Sicily, raised the siege of Segesta which was in the last stage of distress, and in leaving Segesta took the city of Macella by assault.[48]

48 Duilius celebrated the first Roman naval triumph; he was honored with a *columna rostrata*, whose inscription survives and also mentions the rescue of Segesta and the capture of Macella; see *MRR* 1. 205.

3   Μετὰ δὲ τὴν ναυμαχίαν Ἀμίλκας ὁ τῶν Καρχηδονίων στρατηγὸς ὁ τεταγμένος ἐπὶ τῶν πεζικῶν
δυνάμεων, διατρίβων περὶ Πάνορμον, γνοὺς ἐν τοῖς
Ῥωμαϊκοῖς στρατοπέδοις στασιάζοντας τοὺς συμμάχους πρὸς τοὺς Ῥωμαίους περὶ τῶν ἐν ταῖς μάχαις
4   πρωτείων, καὶ πυνθανόμενος στρατοπεδεύειν αὐτοὺς
καθ᾽ ἑαυτοὺς τοὺς συμμάχους μεταξὺ τοῦ Παρώπου
καὶ τῶν Θερμῶν τῶν Ἱμεραίων, ἐπιπεσὼν αὐτοῖς
αἰφνιδίως ἀναστρατοπεδεύουσι μετὰ πάσης τῆς δυνά-
5   μεως σχεδὸν εἰς τετρακισχιλίους ἀπέκτεινε. μετὰ δὲ
ταύτην τὴν πρᾶξιν ὁ μὲν Ἀννίβας ἔχων τὰς δια-
σωθείσας ναῦς ἀπέπλευσεν εἰς τὴν Καρχηδόνα, μετ᾽
οὐ πολὺ δ᾽ ἐκεῖθεν εἰς Σαρδόνα διῆρε, προσλαβὼν
6   ναῦς καί τινας τῶν ἐνδόξων τριηράρχων. χρόνοις δ᾽ οὐ
πολλοῖς κατόπιν ἐν τῇ Σαρδόνι συγκλεισθεὶς ὑπὸ
Ῥωμαίων ἔν τινι λιμένι καὶ πολλὰς ἀποβαλὼν τῶν
νεῶν, παραυτίκα συλληφθεὶς ὑπὸ τῶν διασωθέντων
7   Καρχηδονίων ἀνεσταυρώθη. Ῥωμαῖοι γὰρ ἅμα τῆς
θαλάττης ἥψαντο καὶ τῶν κατὰ Σαρδόνα πραγμάτων
εὐθέως ἀντείχοντο.

8   Τὰ δ᾽ ἐν τῇ Σικελίᾳ στρατόπεδα τῶν Ῥωμαίων
κατὰ μὲν τὸν ἑξῆς ἐνιαυτὸν οὐδὲν ἄξιον ἔπραξαν
9   λόγου, τότε δὲ προσδεξάμενοι τοὺς ἐπικαθεσταμένους
ἄρχοντας Αὖλον Ἀτίλιον καὶ Γάιον Σουλπίκιον ὥρμησαν ἐπὶ τὸν Πάνορμον διὰ τὸ τὰς τῶν Καρχηδονίων
10 δυνάμεις ἐκεῖ παραχειμάζειν. οἱ δὲ στρατηγοὶ συνεγγίσαντες τῇ πόλει μετὰ πάσης τῆς δυνάμεως παρετάξαντο. τῶν δὲ πολεμίων οὐκ ἀντεξιόντων, πάλιν

After the battle at sea Hamilcar,[49] the Carthaginian commander of their land forces, who was quartered in the neighborhood of Panormus, heard that in the Roman camp the allies and the Romans were at variance as to which had most distinguished themselves in the battles, and that the allies were encamped by themselves between Paropus and the Hot Springs of Himera. Suddenly falling on them with his whole force as they were breaking up their camp he killed about four thousand. After this action Hannibal with the ships that escaped sailed away to Carthage and shortly after crossed from there to Sardinia, taking with him additional ships and some of the most celebrated naval officers. Not long afterward he was blockaded in one of the harbors of Sardinia by the Romans and after losing many of his ships was summarily arrested by the surviving Carthaginians and crucified. The Romans, I should explain, from the moment they concerned themselves with the sea, began to entertain designs on Sardinia.

The Roman troops in Sicily did nothing worthy of note during the following year; but at its close when they had received their new commanders the Consuls of next year, 258 B.C. Aulus Atilius and Gaius Sulpicius, they started to attack Panormus, because the Carthaginian forces were wintering there. The Consuls, when they got close up to the city, offered battle with their whole forces, but as the enemy did not come out to meet them they left Panormus and

49 Not "Barcas."

ἐντεῦθεν ἐποιήσαντο τὴν ὁρμὴν ἐπὶ πόλιν Ἱππάναν,
11 καὶ ταύτην μὲν ἐξ ἐφόδου κατὰ κράτος ἔλαβον, εἷλον
δὲ καὶ τὸ Μυττίστρατον, πολλοὺς χρόνους ὑπομεμενη-
12 κὸς τὴν πολιορκίαν διὰ τὴν ὀχυρότητα τοῦ τόπου. τὴν
δὲ Καμαριναίων πόλιν, μικρῷ πρότερον ἀπ' αὐτῶν
ἀποστᾶσαν, τότε προσενέγκαντες ἔργα καὶ κατα-
βαλόντες τὰ τείχη κατέσχον· ὁμοίως δὲ καὶ τὴν Ἔν-
13 ναν καὶ ἕτερα πλείω πολισμάτια τῶν Καρχηδονίων.
ἀπὸ δὲ τούτων γενόμενοι Λιπαραίους ἐπεχείρησαν
πολιορκεῖν.

25. Τῷ δ' ἑξῆς ἐνιαυτῷ Γάιος Ἀτίλιος ὁ στρατηγὸς
τῶν Ῥωμαίων πρὸς Τυνδαρίδα καθορμισθείς, καὶ
συνθεασάμενος ἀτάκτως παραπλέοντα τὸν τῶν Καρχηδονίων στόλον, παραγγείλας τοῖς ἰδίοις πληρώμασιν ἔπεσθαι τοῖς ἡγουμένοις, αὐτὸς ὥρμησε πρὸ
2 τῶν ἄλλων, ἔχων δέκα ναῦς ὁμοπλοούσας. οἱ δὲ Καρχηδόνιοι, συνιδόντες τῶν ὑπεναντίων τοὺς μὲν ἀκμὴν
ἐμβαίνοντας, τοὺς δ' ἀναγομένους, τοὺς δὲ πρώτους
πολὺ προειληφότας τῶν ἄλλων, ἐπιστρέψαντες αὐτοῖς
3 ἀπήντων. καὶ κυκλώσαντες τὰς μὲν ἄλλας διέφθειραν,
τὴν δὲ τοῦ στρατηγοῦ ναῦν παρ' ὀλίγον αὔτανδρον
ἔλαβον. οὐ μὴν ἀλλ' αὕτη μὲν ταῖς ὑπηρεσίαις ἐξηρ-
τυμένη καὶ ταχυναυτοῦσα διέφυγε παραδόξως τὸν
4 κίνδυνον, αἱ δὲ λοιπαὶ τῶν Ῥωμαίων ἐπιπλέουσαι
κατὰ βραχὺ συνηθροίζοντο. γενόμεναι δ' ἐν μετώπῳ
συνέβαλον τοῖς πολεμίοις, καὶ δέκα μὲν αὐτάνδρους

went off to attack Hippana. This city they took by assault and they also took Myttistratum which withstood the siege for long owing to its strong situation. They then occupied Camarina which had lately deserted their cause, bringing up a siege battery and making a breach in the wall. They similarly took Enna and several other small places belonging to the Carthaginians, and when they had finished with these operations they undertook the siege of Lipara.

25. Next year Gaius Atilius Regulus the Roman Consul, 257 B.C. while anchored off Tyndaris, caught sight of the Carthaginian fleet sailing past in disorder. Ordering his crews to follow the leaders, he dashed out before the rest with ten ships sailing together. The Carthaginians, observing that some of the enemy were still embarking, and some just getting under weigh, while those in the van had much outstripped the others, turned and met them. Surrounding them they sunk the rest of the ten, and came very near to taking the admiral's ship with its crew. However, as it was well manned and swift, it foiled their expectation and got out of danger. The rest of the Roman fleet sailed up and gradually got into close order. As soon as they faced the enemy, they bore down on them and took ten ships with their

ναῦς ἔλαβον, ὀκτὼ δὲ κατέδυσαν. αἱ δὲ λοιπαὶ τῶν
Καρχηδονίων ἀπεχώρησαν εἰς τὰς Λιπαραίας καλουμένας νήσους.

5 Ἐκ δὲ ταύτης τῆς ναυμαχίας ἀμφότεροι νομίζοντες
ἐφάμιλλον πεποιῆσθαι τὸν κίνδυνον, ὥρμησαν ὁλοσχερέστερον ἐπὶ τὸ συνίστασθαι ναυτικὰς δυνάμεις
6 καὶ τῶν κατὰ θάλατταν ἀντέχεσθαι πραγμάτων. αἱ δὲ
πεζικαὶ δυνάμεις ἐν τοῖς κατὰ ταῦτα καιροῖς οὐδὲν
ἔπραξαν ἄξιον μνήμης, ἀλλὰ περὶ μικρὰς καὶ τὰς
7 τυχούσας πράξεις κατέτριψαν τοὺς χρόνους. διὸ
παρασκευασάμενοι, καθάπερ εἶπον, εἰς τὴν ἐπιφερο-
μένην θερείαν ἀνήχθησαν Ῥωμαῖοι μὲν τριάκοντα καὶ
τριακοσίαις μακραῖς ναυσὶ καταφράκτοις, καὶ κατ-
8 έσχον εἰς Μεσσήνην. ὅθεν ἀναχθέντες ἔπλεον δεξιὰν
ἔχοντες τὴν Σικελίαν, κάμψαντες δὲ τὸν Πάχυνον
ὑπερῆραν εἰς Ἔκνομον διὰ τὸ καὶ τὸ πεζὸν στράτευμα
9 περὶ τούτους αὐτοὺς εἶναι τοὺς τόπους. Καρχηδόνιοι
δὲ πεντήκοντα καὶ τριακοσίαις ναυσὶ καταφράκτοις
ἀναπλεύσαντες Λιλυβαίῳ προσέσχον, ἐντεῦθεν δὲ
πρὸς Ἡράκλειαν τὴν Μινῴαν καθωρμίσθησαν.

26. ἦν δὲ τῶν μὲν Ῥωμαίων πρόθεσις εἰς τὴν
Λιβύην πλεῖν καὶ τὸν πόλεμον ἐκεῖ περισπᾶν, ἵνα τοῖς
Καρχηδονίοις μὴ περὶ Σικελίας, ἀλλὰ περὶ σφῶν
2 αὐτῶν καὶ τῆς ἰδίας χώρας ὁ κίνδυνος γίνηται. τοῖς δὲ
Καρχηδονίοις τἀναντία τούτων ἐδόκει· συνιδόντες γὰρ
ὡς εὐέφοδός ἐστιν ἡ Λιβύη καὶ πᾶς ὁ κατὰ τὴν χώραν
λαὸς εὐχείρωτος τοῖς ἅπαξ εἰς αὐτὴν ἐμβαλοῦσιν, οὐχ
3 οἷοί τ᾽ ἦσαν ἐπιτρέπειν, ἀλλὰ διακινδυνεύειν καὶ ναυ-

crews, sinking eight. The rest of the Carthaginian fleet withdrew to the islands known as Liparaean.

The result of this battle was that both sides thought that they had fought now on equal terms, and both threw themselves more thoroughly into the task of organizing naval forces and disputing the command of the sea, while in the mean time the land forces accomplished nothing worthy of mention, but spent their time in minor operations of no significance. The Romans, therefore, after making prepa- 256 B.C. rations, as I said, for the coming summer, set to sea with a fleet of three hundred and thirty decked ships of war and put in to Messene. Starting again from there they sailed with Sicily on their right hand, and doubling Cape Pachynus[50] they came round to Ecnomus, because their land forces too happened to be just in that neighborhood. The Carthaginians, setting sail with three hundred and fifty decked vessels, touched at Lilybaeum, and proceeding thence came to anchor off Heraclea Minoa.

26. The plan of the Romans was to sail to Libya and deflect the war to that country, so that the Carthaginians might find no longer Sicily but themselves and their own territory in danger. The Carthaginians were resolved on just the opposite course, for, aware as they were that Africa is easily accessible, and that all the people in the country would be easily subdued by anyone who had once invaded it, they were unable to allow this, and were anxious to run

[50] At the southeastern point of Sicily (Cape Pessero). For the battle of Ecnomus (25. 8–28. 8) see WC 1. 85–86 (with map based on Kromayer). The participants' intentions were to force or to prevent, respectively, a crossing to Africa (26. 3).

μαχεῖν ἔσπευδον. ὄντων δὲ τῶν μὲν πρὸς τὸ κωλύειν,
τῶν δὲ πρὸς τὸ βιάζεσθαι, προφανὴς ἦν ὁ μέλλων
4 ἀγὼν ἐκ τῆς ἑκατέρων συνίστασθαι φιλοτιμίας. οἱ μὲν
οὖν Ῥωμαῖοι πρὸς ἀμφότερα τὴν παρασκευὴν ἁρμόζουσαν ἐποιοῦντο, πρός τε τὴν κατὰ θάλατταν χρείαν
5 καὶ πρὸς τὴν ἀπόβασιν τὴν εἰς τὴν πολεμίαν. διόπερ
ἐπιλέξαντες ἐκ τῶν πεζικῶν στρατοπέδων τὰς ἀρίστας
χεῖρας διεῖλον τὴν πᾶσαν δύναμιν, ἣν ἤμελλον ἀνα-
6 λαμβάνειν, εἰς τέτταρα μέρη. Τὸ δὲ μέρος ἕκαστον
διττὰς εἶχε προσηγορίας· πρῶτον μὲν γὰρ ἐκαλεῖτο
στρατόπεδον καὶ πρῶτος στόλος, καὶ τὰ λοιπὰ κατὰ
λόγον. τὸ δὲ τέταρτον καὶ τρίτην ἐπωνυμίαν ἔτι προσ-
7 ειλήφει· τριάριοι γὰρ ὠνομάζοντο κατὰ τὴν ἐν τοῖς
πεζικοῖς στρατοπέδοις συνήθειαν. καὶ τὸ μὲν σύμπαν
ἦν στράτευμα τούτων τῆς ναυτικῆς δυνάμεως περὶ
τέτταρας καὶ δέκα μυριάδας, ὡς ἂν ἑκάστης νεὼς
8 λαμβανούσης ἐρέτας μὲν τριακοσίους, ἐπιβάτας δ'
ἑκατὸν εἴκοσιν. οἱ δὲ Καρχηδόνιοι τὸ μὲν πλεῖον καὶ
τὸ πᾶν ἡρμόζοντο πρὸς τὸν κατὰ θάλατταν κίνδυνον·
τό γε μὴν πλῆθος αὐτῶν ἦν ὑπὲρ πεντεκαίδεκα μυρι-
9 άδας κατὰ τὸν τῶν νεῶν λόγον. ἐφ' οἷς οὐχ οἷον ἄν τις
παρὼν καὶ θεώμενος ὑπὸ τὴν ὄψιν, ἀλλὰ κἂν ἀκούων
καταπλαγείη τὸ τοῦ κινδύνου μέγεθος καὶ τὴν τῶν
πολιτευμάτων ἀμφοτέρων μεγαλομερίαν καὶ δύναμιν,
στοχαζόμενος ἔκ τε τοῦ τῶν ἀνδρῶν καὶ τοῦ τῶν νεῶν
πλήθους.

10 Οἱ δὲ Ῥωμαῖοι συλλογιζόμενοι διότι τὸν μὲν πλοῦν
εἶναι συμβαίνει πελάγιον, τοὺς δὲ πολεμίους ταχυ-

the risk of a sea battle. The object of the one side being to prevent and that of the other to force a crossing, it was clear that their rival aims would result in the struggle which followed. The Romans had made suitable preparations for both contingencies—for an action at sea and for a landing in the enemy's country. For the latter purpose, selecting the best men from their land forces, they divided into four corps the total force they were about to embark. Each corps had two names; it was called with the First Legion or the First Squadron, and the others accordingly. The fourth had a third name in addition; they were called *triarii* after the usage in the land forces. The whole body embarked on the ships numbered about a hundred and forty thousand, each ship holding three hundred rowers and a hundred and twenty marines. The Carthaginians were chiefly or solely adapting their preparations to a maritime war, their numbers being, to reckon by the number of ships, actually above one hundred and fifty thousand. These are figures calculated to strike not only one present and with the forces under his eyes but even a hearer with amazement at the magnitude of the struggle and at that lavish outlay and vast power of the two states, if he estimates them from the number of men and ships.

The Romans taking into consideration that the voyage was across the open sea and that the enemy were their

ναυτεῖν, πανταχόθεν ἐπειρῶντο ποιεῖσθαι τὴν τάξιν
11 ἀσφαλῆ καὶ δυσπρόσοδον. τὰς μὲν οὖν ἐξήρεις δύ'
οὔσας, ἐφ' ὧν ἔπλεον οἱ στρατηγοὶ Μάρκος Ἀτίλιος
καὶ Λεύκιος Μάλιος, πρώτας ἐν μετώπῳ παραλλήλους
12 ἔταξαν. τούτων δ' ἑκατέρᾳ συνεχεῖς κατὰ μίαν ναῦν
ἐπιτάττοντες τῇ μὲν τὸν πρῶτον, τῇ δὲ τὸν δεύτερον
στόλον ἐπέστησαν, ἀεὶ καθ' ἑκάστην ναῦν ἑκατέρου
τοῦ στόλου μεῖζον τὸ μεταξὺ ποιοῦντες διάστημα.
13 ταῖς δὲ πρώρραις ἔξω νεύοντα τὰ σκάφη τὴν ἐπίστασιν ἐπ' ἀλλήλοις εἶχεν. ἐπειδὴ δὲ τὸν πρῶτον καὶ
δεύτερον στόλον ἁπλῶς εἰς ἔμβολον ἔταξαν, ἐπέβαλον τούτοις ἐπὶ μίαν ναῦν ἐν μετώπῳ τὸ τρίτον στρα-
14 τόπεδον· ὧν ἐπιστάντων ἀπετελέσθη τρίγωνον τὸ πᾶν
εἶδος τῆς τάξεως. ἐπὶ δὲ τούτοις ἐπέστησαν τὰς ἱππη-
γούς, ῥύματα δόντες ἐξ αὐτῶν ταῖς τοῦ τρίτου στόλου
15 ναυσί. ταύταις δὲ κατόπιν ἐπέβαλον τὸν τέταρτον
στόλον, τοὺς τριαρίους κληθέντας, ἐπὶ μίαν παρεκτεί-
ναντες ναῦν, ὡς ὑπερτείνειν ἐξ ἑκατέρου τοῦ μέρους
16 τοὺς πρὸ ἑαυτῶν. καὶ συναρμοσθέντων πάντων κατὰ
τὸν εἰρημένον τρόπον, τὸ μὲν ὅλον ἀπετελέσθη σχῆμα
τῆς τάξεως ἔμβολον, οὗ τὸ μὲν ἐπὶ τὴν κορυφὴν μέρος
ἦν κοῖλον, τὸ δὲ πρὸς τῇ βάσει στερεόν, τὸ δὲ σύμπαν
ἐνεργὸν καὶ πρακτικόν, ἅμα δὲ καὶ δυσδιάλυτον.
    27. Οἱ δὲ τῶν Καρχηδονίων στρατηγοὶ κατὰ τὸν
αὐτὸν καιρὸν παρακαλέσαντες τὰ πλήθη διὰ βραχέων, καὶ συνυποδείξαντες αὐτοῖς ὅτι νικήσαντες μὲν
τῇ ναυμαχίᾳ περὶ Σικελίας ποιήσονται τὸν πόλεμον,
ἡττηθέντες δὲ περὶ τῆς σφετέρας πατρίδος κινδυνεύ-

superiors in speed, tried by every means to range their fleet in an order which would render it secure and difficult to attack. Accordingly, they stationed their two hexereis,[51] on which the commanders, Marcus Atilius Regulus and Lucius Manlius, were sailing, in front and side by side with each other. Behind each of these they placed ships in single file, the first squadron behind the one galley, the second behind the other, so arranging them that the distance between each pair of ships in the two squadrons grew ever greater. The ships were stationed in column with their prows directed outwards. Having thus arranged the first and second squadrons in the form of a simple wedge, they stationed the third in a single line at the base, so that when these ships had taken their places the resulting form of the whole was a triangle. Behind these ships at the base they stationed the horse transports, attaching them by towing lines to the vessels of the third squadron. Finally, behind these they stationed the fourth squadron, known as *triarii*, making a single long line of ships so extended that the line overlapped that in front of it at each extremity. When all had been put together in the manner I have described, the whole arrangement had the form of a wedge, the apex of which was open, the base compact, and the whole effective and practical, while also difficult to break up.

27. About the same time the Carthaginian commanders briefly addressed their forces. They pointed out to them that in the event of victory in the battle they would be fighting afterward for Sicily, but that if defeated they would have to fight for their own country and their homes,

[51] Ships with six banks of oars.

2 σουσι καὶ τῶν ἀναγκαίων, οὕτως αὐτοῖς παρήγγειλαν
ἐμβαίνειν εἰς τὰς ναῦς. προθύμως δὲ πάντων ποιούν-
των τὸ παραγγελλόμενον διὰ τὸ προορᾶσθαι τὸ μέλλον ἐκ τῶν εἰρημένων, εὐθαρσῶς ἀνήγοντο καὶ κατα-
3 πληκτικῶς. θεωροῦντες δὲ τὴν τῶν πολεμίων τάξιν οἱ
στρατηγοί, καὶ πρὸς ταύτην ἁρμοζόμενοι, τὰ μὲν τρία
μέρη τῆς αὐτῶν δυνάμεως ἐπὶ μίαν ἔταττον ναῦν, πρὸς
τὸ πέλαγος ἀνατείναντες τὸ δεξιὸν κέρας, ὡς κυκλώ-
σοντες τοὺς ὑπεναντίους, πάσας ἱστάντες ἀντιπρώρ-
ρους τὰς ναῦς τοῖς πολεμίοις. τὸ δὲ τέταρτον εὐώνυμον
4 τῆς ὅλης τάξεως ἐποίουν, ἐν ἐπικαμπίῳ νεῦον πρὸς
5 τὴν γῆν. ἡγοῦντο δὲ τῶν Καρχηδονίων, τοῦ μὲν δεξιοῦ
κέρως, ἔχων ἐπίπλους καὶ πεντήρεις τὰς μάλιστα
ταχυναυτούσας πρὸς τὴν ὑπερκέρασιν, Ἄννων ὁ περὶ
6 τὸν Ἀκράγαντα λειφθεὶς τῇ παρατάξει· τῶν δ' εὐωνύμων εἶχε τὴν ἐπιμέλειαν Ἀμίλκας ὁ περὶ τὴν Τυνδαρίδα ναυμαχήσας· ὃς τότε κατὰ μέσην τὴν τάξιν
7 ποιούμενος τὸν κίνδυνον ἐχρήσατό τινι στρατηγήματι
κατὰ τὸν ἀγῶνα τοιῷδε. τῶν γὰρ Ῥωμαίων συνθεασα-
μένων ἐπὶ λεπτὸν ἐκτεταμένους τοὺς Καρχηδονίους,
καὶ ποιησαμένων τὴν ὁρμὴν ἐπὶ μέσους, τὴν μὲν
8 ἀρχὴν ὁ κίνδυνος ἔλαβε τοιαύτην. ταχὺ δὲ τῶν περὶ
τὰ μέσα Καρχηδονίων ἐκ παραγγέλματος κλινάντων
πρὸς φυγὴν χάριν τοῦ διασπάσαι τὴν τῶν Ῥωμαίων
τάξιν, οὗτοι μὲν ὑπεχώρουν μετὰ σπουδῆς, οἱ δὲ Ῥω-
9 μαῖοι κατόπιν ἠκολούθουν ἐκθύμως. ὁ μὲν οὖν πρῶτος
καὶ δεύτερος στόλος ἐπέκειτο τοῖς φεύγουσι, τὸ δὲ
τρίτον καὶ τὸ τέταρτον στρατόπεδον ἀπεσπᾶτο, τῶν

and bade them take this to heart and embark. When all readily did as they were ordered, as their general's words had made clear to them the issues at stake, they set to sea in a confident and menacing spirit. The commanders when they saw the enemy's order adapted their own to it. Three-quarters of their force they drew up in a single line, extending their right wing to the open sea for the purpose of encircling the enemy and with all their ships facing the Romans. The remaining quarter of their force formed the left wing of their whole line, and reached shoreward at an angle with the rest. Their right wing was under the command of the same Hanno who had been worsted in the engagement near Agrigentum. He had vessels for charging and also the swiftest quinqueremes for the outflanking movement. The left wing was in charge of Hamilcar, the one who commanded in the sea battle at Tyndaris, and he, fighting as he was in the center of the line, used in the fray the following stratagem. The battle was begun by the Romans who, noticing that the Carthaginian line was thin owing to its great extent, delivered an attack on the center. The Carthaginian center had received Hamilcar's orders to fall back at once with the view of breaking the order of the Romans, and, as they hastily retreated, the Romans pursued them vigorously. While the first and second squadrons thus pressed on the flying enemy, the third and fourth were separated from them, the third squadron towing the

10 μὲν ῥυμουλκούντων τὰς ἱππηγοὺς ναῦς, τῶν δὲ τριαρίων συμμενόντων καὶ συνεφεδρευόντων τούτοις. ἐπεὶ
δὲ τὸν πρῶτον καὶ δεύτερον στόλον ἱκανὸν τῶν ἄλλων
ἐδόκουν ἀπεσπακέναι τόπον οἱ Καρχηδόνιοι, συνθή-
ματος ἀρθέντος ἐκ τῆς Ἀμίλκου νεὼς μετεβάλοντο
11 πάντες ἅμα καὶ συνέβαλον τοῖς ἐπικειμένοις. ἀγῶνος
δὲ συστάντος καρτεροῦ, τῷ μὲν ταχυναυτεῖν ἐκπεριπλέοντες καὶ ῥᾳδίως μὲν προσιόντες, ὀξέως δ' ἀποχω-
12 ροῦντες, πολὺ περιῆσαν οἱ Καρχηδόνιοι, τῷ δὲ βιαιο-
μαχεῖν κατὰ τὰς συμπλοκὰς καὶ συνδεῖν τοῖς κόραξι
τοὺς ἅπαξ ἐγγίσαντας, ἅμα δὲ καὶ τῷ συναγωνιζομέ-
νων ἀμφοτέρων τῶν στρατηγῶν ἐν ὄψει τῶν ἡγουμένων ποιεῖσθαι τὸν κίνδυνον, οὐχ ἧττον ἐπικυδεστέρας
εἶχον οἱ Ῥωμαῖοι τῶν Καρχηδονίων τὰς ἐλπίδας. ἡ
13 μὲν οὖν κατὰ τούτους μάχη τοιαύτην εἶχε διάθεσιν.
    28. κατὰ δὲ τὸν αὐτὸν καιρὸν τὸ μὲν δεξιὸν κέρας
ἔχων Ἄννων, τὸ μεῖναν ἐν ἀποστάσει κατὰ τὴν πρώτην συμβολήν, τό τε πέλαγος ὑπεράρας ἐνέβαλε ταῖς
τῶν τριαρίων ναυσὶ καὶ πολλὴν ἀπορίαν παρεῖχε καὶ
2 δυσχρηστίαν αὐτοῖς. οἱ δὲ παρὰ τὴν γῆν τεταγμένοι
τῶν Καρχηδονίων, παραγεγονότες εἰς μέτωπον ἐκ τῆς
προϋπαρχούσης τάξεως, καὶ ποιήσαντες ἀντιπρώρ-
ρους τὰς ναῦς, ἐνέβαλον τοῖς ῥυμουλκοῦσι τὰς ἱππη-
γούς· οἱ δ' ἀφέμενοι τὰ ῥύματα συνεπλέκοντο καὶ
3 διηγωνίζοντο τοῖς πολεμίοις. ἦν δὲ τρία μέρη τῆς
ὅλης συμπλοκῆς καὶ τρεῖς ναυμαχίαι συνέστησαν
4 πολὺ κεχωρισμέναι τοῖς τόποις ἀλλήλων· τῷ δ' ἑκατέρων πάρισα τὰ μέρη γενέσθαι κατὰ τὸν ἐξ ἀρχῆς

84

horse transports, and the *triarii* remaining with them as a supporting force. When the Carthaginians thought they had drawn off the first and second squadrons far enough from the others, they all, on receiving a signal from Hamilcar's ship, turned simultaneously and attacked their pursuers. The engagement that followed was a very hot one, the superior speed of the Carthaginians enabling them to move round the enemy's flank as well as to approach easily and retire rapidly, while the Romans, relying on their sheer strength when they closed with the enemy, grappling with the ravens every ship as soon as it approached, fighting also, as they were, under the very eyes of both the Consuls, who were personally taking part in the combat, had no less high hopes of success. Such then was the state of the battle in this quarter.

28. At one and the same time Hanno with the right wing, which had held its distance in the first attack, sailed across the open sea and fell upon the ships of the *triarii*, causing them great embarrassment and distress. Meanwhile that part of the Carthaginian force which was posted near the shore, changing their former formation and deploying into line with their prows facing the enemy, attacked the vessels which were towing the horse transports. Letting go their tow lines this squadron met and engaged the enemy. Thus the whole conflict consisted of three parts, and three sea battles were going on at a wide distance from each other. As the respective forces were in each case of equal strength owing to their disposition at

THE HISTORIES OF POLYBIUS

χειρισμὸν ἐφάμιλλον εἶναι συνέβαινε καὶ τὸν κίνδυ-
5   νον. οὐ μὴν ἀλλὰ τὸ κατὰ λόγον ἐν ἑκάστοις ἐπετελεῖ-
το περὶ τὴν μάχην, ὅπερ εἰκὸς ὅταν ᾖ παραπλήσια
6   πάντα τὰ τῶν ἀγωνιζομένων. οἱ γὰρ πρῶτοι <κινδυ-
νεύσαντες πρῶτοι> καὶ διεκρίθησαν· τέλος γὰρ ἐκ-
7   βιασθέντες οἱ περὶ τὸν Ἀμίλκαν εἰς φυγὴν ὥρμησαν.
ὁ μὲν οὖν Λεύκιος ἀνεδεῖτο τὰς αἰχμαλώτους ναῦς· ὁ
δὲ Μάρκος, συνορῶν τὸν περὶ τοὺς τριαρίους καὶ τὰς
ἱππηγοὺς ἀγῶνα, κατὰ σπουδὴν ἐβοήθει τούτοις,
8   ἔχων τοῦ δευτέρου στόλου τὰς ἀκεραίους ναῦς. συνάψαντος δὲ καὶ προσμίξαντος αὐτοῦ τοῖς περὶ τὸν
Ἄννωνα, ταχέως ἀναθαρρήσαντες οἱ τριάριοι, καίπερ
ἤδη κακῶς ἀπαλλάττοντες, πάλιν ἐπερρώσθησαν
9   πρὸς τὸν κίνδυνον. οἱ δὲ Καρχηδόνιοι, τῶν μὲν κατὰ
πρόσωπον αὐτοῖς προσμαχομένων, τῶν δὲ κατὰ νώτου
προσπιπτόντων, δυσχρηστούμενοι, καὶ παραδόξως
ὑπὸ τῶν βοηθησάντων κυκλούμενοι, κλίναντες πελα-
10   γίαν ἐποιοῦντο τὴν ὑποχώρησιν. κατὰ δὲ τὸν αὐτὸν
καιρὸν ὅ τε Λεύκιος, ἐπαναπλέων ἤδη καὶ θεωρῶν
συγκεκλεισμένον πρὸς τῇ γῇ τὸν τρίτον στόλον ὑπὸ
τοῦ τῶν Καρχηδονίων εὐωνύμου κέρατος, ὅ τε Μάρκος, ἐν ἀσφαλεῖ καταλιπὼν τὰς ἱππηγοὺς καὶ τοὺς
τριαρίους, ὥρμησαν ἀμφότεροι βοηθεῖν τοῖς κινδυνεύ-
11   ουσι. παραπλήσιον γὰρ ἦν ἤδη τὸ γινόμενον πολιορ-
κίᾳ· καὶ πάντες ἂν ἀπολώλεισαν οὗτοί γε προφανῶς,
εἰ μὴ δεδιότες τοὺς κόρακας οἱ Καρχηδόνιοι περι-
φράξαντες μὲν αὐτοὺς πρὸς τῇ γῇ συνεῖχον, πρὸς δὲ
τὰς ἐμβολὰς διὰ τὴν συμπλοκὴν εὐλαβῶς ἔχοντες οὐ

the outset, the battle also was fought on equal terms. However, in each case things fell out as one would expect, when the forces engaged are so equally matched. Those who had commenced the battle were also the first to bring the matter to a conclusion, for Hamilcar's division was finally forced back and took to flight. Lucius was now occupied in taking the prizes in tow, and Marcus, observing the struggle in which the *triarii* and horse transports were involved, hastened to their assistance with such of the ships of the second squadron as were undamaged. When he reached Hanno's division and came into conflict with it, the *triarii* at once took heart, though they had had much the worst of it, and recovered their fighting spirit. The Carthaginians, attacked both in front and in the rear, were in difficulties, finding themselves surrounded, to their surprise, by the relieving force, and giving way, they began to retreat out to sea. Meanwhile both Lucius, who was by this time sailing up and observed that the third squadron was shut in close to the shore by the Carthaginian left wing, and Marcus, who had now left the horse transports and *triarii* in safety, hastened together to the relief of this force which was in grave peril; for the state of matters now was just like a siege, and they all would evidently have been lost if the Carthaginians had not been afraid of the ravens and simply hedged them in and held them close to the land instead of charging, apprehensive as they were of coming to close

12 προσῄεσαν. ταχέως δ᾽ ἐπιγενόμενοι καὶ κυκλώσαντες
οἱ στρατηγοὶ τοὺς Καρχηδονίους αὐτάνδρους μὲν
ἔλαβον πεντήκοντα ναῦς τῶν πολεμίων, ὀλίγαι δέ
13 τινες παρὰ τὴν γῆν ἐξελίξασαι διέφυγον. ὁ μὲν οὖν
κατὰ μέρος κίνδυνος τοιαύτην ἔσχε τὴν διάθεσιν, τὸ
δὲ τέλος τῆς συμπάσης ναυμαχίας ἐγένετο κατὰ τοὺς
14 Ῥωμαίους. διεφθάρη δὲ τούτων μὲν εἴκοσι καὶ τέτταρα σκάφη, τῶν δὲ Καρχηδονίων ὑπὲρ τριάκοντα.
ναῦς δὲ τῶν μὲν Ῥωμαίων αὔτανδρος οὐδεμία τοῖς
πολεμίοις ἐγένεθ᾽ ὑποχείριος, τῶν δὲ Καρχηδονίων
ἑξήκοντα καὶ τέτταρες.

29. Μετὰ δὲ ταῦτα πάλιν οἱ Ῥωμαῖοι προσεπισι-
τισάμενοι καὶ τὰς αἰχμαλώτους ναῦς καταρτίσαντες,
ἔτι δὲ τὴν ἁρμόζουσαν τοῖς προτερήμασιν ἐπιμέλειαν
ποιησάμενοι τῶν πληρωμάτων, ἀνήγοντο ποιούμενοι
2 τὸν πλοῦν ὡς ἐπὶ τὴν Λιβύην. προσσχόντες δὲ ταῖς
πρώταις πλεούσαις ναυσὶν ὑπὸ τὴν ἄκραν τὴν Ἑρμαίαν ἐπονομαζομένην, ἣ πρὸ παντὸς τοῦ περὶ τὴν Καρχηδόνα κόλπου κειμένη προτείνει πελάγιος ὡς πρὸς
τὴν Σικελίαν, καὶ προσδεξάμενοι τὰς ἐπιπλεούσας
ἐνταῦθα ναῦς, καὶ πάντα συναθροίσαντες τὸν στόλον,
ἔπλεον παρὰ τὴν χώραν, ἕως ἐπὶ τὴν Ἀσπίδα καλου-
3 μένην πόλιν ἀφίκοντο. ποιησάμενοι δὲ τὴν ἀπόβασιν
ἐνταῦθα καὶ νεωλκήσαντες, ἔτι δὲ τάφρῳ καὶ χάρακι
περιλαβόντες τὰς ναῦς, ἐγίνοντο πρὸς τὸ πολιορκεῖν
αὐτήν, οὐ βουλομένων ἑκουσίως σφίσι προσχωρῆσαι
4 τῶν κατεχόντων τὴν πόλιν. οἱ δὲ διαφυγόντες ἐκ τοῦ
κατὰ τὴν ναυμαχίαν κινδύνου τῶν Καρχηδονίων

quarters. The Consuls, coming up rapidly and surrounding the Carthaginians, captured fifty ships with their crews, a few managing to slip out along shore and escape. The separate encounters fell out as I have described, and the final result of the whole battle was in favor of the Romans. The latter lost twenty-four sail sunk and the Carthaginians more than thirty. Not a single Roman ship with its crew fell into the enemy's hands, but sixty-four Carthaginian ships were so captured.

29. After this the Romans, laying in a further supply of provisions, repairing the captured ships, and bestowing on their men the attention which their success deserved, put to sea and sailed toward Libya, reaching the shore with their advanced ships under the promontory known as the Hermaeum[52] which lies in front of the whole Gulf of Carthage and stretches out to sea in the direction of Sicily. Having waited there until their other ships came up, and having united their whole fleet, they sailed along the coast till they reached the city of Aspis.[53] Landing there and beaching their ships, which they surrounded with a trench and palisade, they set themselves to lay siege to the town, the garrison of which refused to surrender voluntarily. Those Carthaginians who made good their escape from

[52] The victory at sea opened the way to Africa; Regulus landed at modern Cape Bon.

[53] (Aspis = "Shield"): The Roman name is Clupea, south of Hermaeum. Gaius Scribonius Curio landed there in 49, Caesar in 47.

καταπλεύσαντες, καὶ πεπεισμένοι τοὺς ὑπεναντίους ἐκ
τοῦ γεγονότος προτερήματος ἐπαρθέντας εὐθέως ποι-
ήσεσθαι τὸν ἐπίπλουν ἐπ' αὐτὴν τὴν Καρχηδόνα,
παρετήρουν ταῖς πεζικαῖς καὶ ναυτικαῖς δυνάμεσι
5   τοὺς προκειμένους τῆς πόλεως τόπους. ἐπιγνόντες δὲ
τοὺς Ῥωμαίους ἀσφαλῶς ἀποβεβηκότας καὶ πολιορκοῦντας τὴν Ἀσπίδα, τοῦ μὲν παραφυλάττειν τὸν
ἐπίπλουν ἀπέγνωσαν, συνήθροιζον δὲ τὰς δυνάμεις
καὶ περὶ φυλακὴν ἐγίνοντο τῆς τε πόλεως καὶ τῆς
6   χώρας. οἱ δὲ Ῥωμαῖοι κυριεύσαντες τῆς Ἀσπίδος καὶ
φυλακὴν ἀπολιπόντες τῆς πόλεως καὶ χώρας, ἔτι δὲ
πρεσβευτὰς εἰς τὴν Ῥώμην πέμψαντες τοὺς ἀπαγ-
γελοῦντας μὲν περὶ τῶν γεγονότων, ἐρησομένους δὲ
περὶ τῶν μελλόντων, τί δεῖ ποιεῖν καὶ πῶς χρῆσθαι
τοῖς πράγμασι, μετὰ δὲ ταῦτα πάσῃ τῇ δυνάμει κατὰ
7   σπουδὴν ἀναζεύξαντες, ὥρμησαν ἐπὶ τὸ πορθεῖν τὴν
χώραν. οὐδενὸς δ' ἐμποδὼν ἱσταμένου, πολλὰς μὲν
οἰκήσεις περιττῶς κατεσκευασμένας διέφθειραν, πολὺ
δὲ πλῆθος τῆς τετραπόδου λείας περιεβάλοντο· σώ-
8   ματα δὲ πλείω τῶν δισμυρίων ἐπὶ τὰς ναῦς ἀνήγαγον.
ἐν δὲ τούτῳ τῷ καιρῷ παρῆσαν ἐκ τῆς Ῥώμης οἱ
διασαφοῦντες ὅτι δεῖ τὸν μὲν ἕνα τῶν στρατηγῶν
μένειν ἔχοντα δυνάμεις τὰς ἀρκούσας, τὸν δ' ἕτερον
9   ἀποκομίζειν εἰς τὴν Ῥώμην τὸν στόλον. ὁ μὲν οὖν
Μάρκος ἔμενεν, ὑπολειπόμενος ναῦς τετταράκοντα καὶ
πεζοὺς μυρίους καὶ πεντακισχιλίους, ἱππεῖς δὲ πεντα-
10   κοσίους· ὁ δὲ Λεύκιος ἀναλαβὼν τὰ πληρώματα καὶ

the naval battle sailed home, and being convinced that the enemy, elated by their recent success, would at once attack Carthage itself from the sea, kept watch at different points over the approaches to the city with their land and sea forces. But when they learnt that the Romans had safely landed and were laying siege to Aspis, they abandoned the measures taken to guard against an attack from the sea, and uniting their forces devoted themselves to the protection of the capital and its environs. The Romans, after making themselves masters of Aspis, where they left a garrison to hold the town and district, sent a mission to Rome[54] to report on recent events, and to inquire what they should do in future and how they were to deal with the whole situation. They then hastily advanced with their whole force and set about plundering the country. As nobody tried to prevent them, they destroyed a number of handsome and luxuriously furnished dwelling houses, possessed themselves of a quantity of cattle, and captured more than twenty thousand slaves, taking them back to their ships. Messengers from Rome now arrived with instructions for one of the Consuls to remain on the spot with an adequate force and for the other to bring the fleet back to Rome. Marcus Regulus, therefore, remained, retaining forty ships and a force of fifteen thousand infantry and five hundred horse, while Lucius, taking with him the

[54] The consuls landed in Africa without a plan!

τὸ τῶν αἰχμαλώτων πλῆθος, καὶ κομισθεὶς παρὰ τὴν
Σικελίαν ἀσφαλῶς, ἧκεν εἰς τὴν Ῥώμην.

30. Οἱ δὲ Καρχηδόνιοι θεωροῦντες τὴν τῶν πολεμίων παρασκευὴν χρονιωτέραν οὖσαν, πρῶτον μὲν
στρατηγοὺς ἑαυτῶν εἵλοντο δύο, τόν τ᾽ Ἄννωνος
Ἀσδρούβαν καὶ Βώσταρον, μετὰ δὲ ταῦτα πρὸς τὸν
Ἀμίλκαν ἔπεμπον εἰς τὴν Ἡράκλειαν, καλοῦντες κατὰ
2 τάχος αὐτόν. ὁ δ᾽ ἀναλαβὼν ἱππεῖς πεντακοσίους καὶ
πεζοὺς πεντακισχιλίους παρῆν εἰς τὴν Καρχηδόνα·
καὶ κατασταθεὶς στρατηγὸς τρίτος, ἐβουλεύετο μετὰ
τῶν περὶ τὸν Ἀσδρούβαν πῶς δεῖ χρῆσθαι τοῖς παρ-
3 οῦσιν. ἔδοξεν οὖν αὐτοῖς βοηθεῖν τῇ χώρᾳ καὶ μὴ
4 περιορᾶν αὐτὴν ἀδεῶς πορθουμένην. ὁ δὲ Μάρκος
μετά τινας ἡμέρας ἐπεπορεύετο, τὰ μὲν ἀτείχιστα τῶν
ἐρυμάτων ἐξ ἐφόδου διαρπάζων, τὰ δὲ τετειχισμένα
5 πολιορκῶν. ἀφικόμενος δὲ πρὸς πόλιν Ἀδὺν ἀξιόχρεω,
περιστρατοπεδεύσας ταύτην συνίστατο μετὰ σπουδῆς
6 ἔργα καὶ πολιορκίαν. οἱ δὲ Καρχηδόνιοι τῇ τε πόλει
σπουδάζοντες βοηθῆσαι καὶ τῶν ὑπαίθρων ἀντιποι-
7 εῖσθαι κρίνοντες ἐξῆγον τὴν δύναμιν. καὶ καταλαβόμενοι λόφον ὑπερδέξιον μὲν τῶν πολεμίων, ἀφυῆ δὲ
ταῖς ἑαυτῶν δυνάμεσιν, ἐν τούτῳ κατεστρατοπέδευ-
8 σαν. Λοιπὸν ἔχοντες μὲν τὰς πλείστας ἐλπίδας ἐν τοῖς
ἱππεῦσι καὶ τοῖς θηρίοις, ἀφέμενοι δὲ τῶν ἐπιπέδων
χωρίων καὶ συγκλείσαντες σφᾶς αὐτοὺς εἰς τόπους
ἐρυμνοὺς καὶ δυσβάτους, ἔμελλον διδάξειν τοὺς πολεμίους ὃ δέον ἦν πράττειν κατ᾽ αὐτῶν. ὃ δὴ καὶ συνέβη
9 γενέσθαι. συννοήσαντες γὰρ οἱ τῶν Ῥωμαίων ἡγε-

ship's crews and all the prisoners, passed safely along the coast of Sicily and reached Rome.

30. The Carthaginians, observing that the Romans were preparing for a long occupation, in the first place elected two generals from among themselves, Hasdrubal, the son of Hanno, and Bostar, and next sent to Heraclea[55] to Hamilcar, ordering him to return instantly. Taking with him five hundred horse and five thousand foot, he came to Carthage where, being appointed third general, he held a consultation with Hasdrubal and his staff as to what steps should be taken. They decided on marching to the assistance of the country and no longer looking on while it was plundered with immunity. A few days later Regulus had begun to advance, taking by assault and pillaging the unwalled places and laying siege to those which had walls. On reaching Adys, a town of some importance, he encamped about it and busied himself with raising works to besiege it. The Carthaginians, being anxious to relieve the town, and having decided to attempt to regain the command of the open country, led out their forces. They took possession of a hill which, while overlooking the enemy, was not a favorable position for their own army; and there they encamped. In this manner, though their best hope lay in their cavalry and elephants, yet by quitting the level country and shutting themselves up in a precipitous place, difficult of access, they were sure to make it plain to their adversaries how best to attack them, and this is exactly what did happen. For the Roman commanders, perceiving from their

256 B.C.

55 Referring back to 25. 9.

μόνες ἐμπείρως ὅτι τὸ πρακτικώτατον καὶ φοβερώτατον τῆς τῶν ὑπεναντίων δυνάμεως ἠχρείωται διὰ
τοὺς τόπους, οὐκ ἀνέμειναν ἕως ἐκεῖνοι καταβάντες εἰς
10 τὰ πεδία παρετάξαντο, χρώμενοι δὲ τοῖς ἰδίοις καιροῖς
ἅμα τῷ φωτὶ προσέβαινον ἐξ ἑκατέρου τοῦ μέρους
11 πρὸς τὸν λόφον. οἱ μὲν οὖν ἱππεῖς καὶ τὰ θηρία τοῖς
Καρχηδονίοις ἦν ἄχρηστα τελέως· οἱ δὲ μισθοφόροι
πάνυ γενναίως καὶ προθύμως ἐκβοηθήσαντες τὸ μὲν
12 πρῶτον στρατόπεδον ἠνάγκασαν ἐκκλῖναι καὶ φυγεῖν·
ἐπεὶ δὲ προπεσόντες καὶ κυκλωθέντες ὑπὸ τῶν ἐκ
θατέρου μέρους προσβαινόντων ἐτράπησαν, μετὰ
13 ταῦτα πάντες εὐθὺς ἐκ τῆς στρατοπεδείας ἐξέπεσον.
τὰ μὲν οὖν θηρία μετὰ τῶν ἱππέων, ἐπεὶ τάχιστα τῶν
ὁμαλῶν ἥψατο, μετ᾽ ἀσφαλείας ἐποιοῦντο τὴν ἀπο-
14 χώρησιν· οἱ δὲ Ῥωμαῖοι τοὺς πεζοὺς βραχὺν ἐπι-
διώξαντες τόπον καὶ τὸν χάρακα διαρπάσαντες, μετὰ
δὲ ταῦτα πᾶσαν ἐπιπορευόμενοι τὴν χώραν καὶ τὰς
15 πόλεις ἀδεῶς ἐπόρθουν. γενόμενοι δὲ τῆς προσαγο-
ρευομένης πόλεως Τύνητος ἐγκρατεῖς, εὐφυοῦς ὑπαρχούσης πρὸς τὰς προκειμένας ἐπιβολάς, ἔτι δὲ κειμένης εὐκαίρως κατά τε τῆς πόλεως καὶ τῆς σύνεγγυς
ταύτῃ χώρας, κατεστρατοπέδευσαν εἰς αὐτήν.

31. Οἱ δὲ Καρχηδόνιοι μικρῷ μὲν πρότερον κατὰ
θάλατταν, τότε δὲ κατὰ γῆν ἐπταικότες, οὐ διὰ τὴν τῶν
πολλῶν ἀνανδρίαν, ἀλλὰ διὰ τὴν τῶν ἡγουμένων
ἀβουλίαν, κατὰ πάντα τρόπον ἐνεπεπτώκεισαν εἰς
2 δυσχερῆ διάθεσιν. ἅμα γὰρ τοῖς προειρημένοις καὶ τὸ
τῶν Νομάδων ἔθνος συνεπιτιθέμενον αὐτοῖς οὐκ ἐλάτ-

experience of war that the most efficient and formidable part of the enemy's force was rendered unserviceable by their position, did not wait for the Carthaginians to come down and offer battle on the plain, but, seizing on their own opportunity, advanced at daybreak on the hill from both sides. And so their elephants and cavalry were absolutely useless to the Carthaginians, but their mercenaries sallying out with great gallantry and dash compelled the first legion to give way and take to flight; but on their advancing too far and being surrounded and driven back by the force that was attacking on the other side, the whole Carthaginian army were at once dislodged from their camp. The elephants and cavalry, as soon as they reached level ground, effected their retreat in safety, and the Romans, after pursuing the infantry for a short distance and destroying the camp, henceforth overran and plundered the country and its towns unmolested. Having made themselves masters of the town named Tunis,[56] which was a suitable base for these raids, and also well situated for operations against the capital and its immediate environs, they established themselves there.

31. The Carthaginians, having thus been twice defeated, shortly before at sea and now on land, in both cases owing to no lack of bravery in their troops, but owing to the incompetence of their commanders, had now fallen into a thoroughly difficult position. For, in addition to the misfortunes I have mentioned, the Numidians, attacking them at

[56] Less than 20 kilometers southeast of Carthage.

τω, πλείω δὲ τῶν Ῥωμαίων εἰργάζετο κακὰ τὴν χώ-
3 ραν. ἐξ ὧν διὰ τὸν φόβον συμφευγόντων εἰς τὴν πόλιν
τῶν ἀπὸ τῆς χώρας δυσθυμία καὶ λιμὸς ἦν ὁλοσχε-
ρής, τὰ μὲν διὰ τὸ πλῆθος, τὰ δὲ διὰ τὴν προσδοκίαν
4 τῆς πολιορκίας. ὁ δὲ Μάρκος ὁρῶν τοὺς Καρχηδονίους καὶ κατὰ γῆν καὶ κατὰ θάλατταν ἐσφαλμένους,
καὶ νομίζων ὅσον οὔπω κρατήσειν τῆς πόλεως, ἀγωνι-
ῶν δὲ μὴ συμβῇ τὸν ἐπιπαραγινόμενον στρατηγὸν ἐκ
τῆς Ῥώμης φθάσαντα τὴν ἐπιγραφὴν τῶν πραγμάτων
λαβεῖν, προυκαλεῖτο τοὺς Καρχηδονίους εἰς διαλύ-
5 σεις. οἱ δ' ἀσμένως ἀκούσαντες ἐξέπεμψαν αὐτῶν τοὺς
πρώτους ἄνδρας· οἳ καὶ συμμίξαντες αὐτῷ τοσοῦτον
ἀπέσχον τοῦ ῥέπειν ταῖς γνώμαις ἐπὶ τὸ ποιεῖν τι τῶν
λεγομένων ὥστ' οὐδ' ἀκούοντες ὑπομένειν ἐδύναντο τὸ
6 βάρος τῶν ἐπιταγμάτων. ὁ μὲν γὰρ Μάρκος, ὡς ἤδη
κεκρατηκὼς τῶν ὅλων, ὅ τι ποτὲ συνεχώρει, πᾶν ᾤετο
7 δεῖν αὐτοὺς ἐν χάριτι καὶ δωρεᾷ λαμβάνειν· οἱ δὲ
Καρχηδόνιοι θεωροῦντες ὅτι καὶ γενομένοις αὐτοῖς
ὑποχειρίοις οὐδὲν ἂν συνεξακολουθῆσαι βαρύτερον
τῶν τότε προσταγμάτων, οὐ μόνον δυσαρεστήσαντες
τοῖς προτεινομένοις ἐπανῆλθον, ἀλλὰ καὶ προσκόψαν-
8 τες τῇ βαρύτητι τοῦ Μάρκου. τὸ δὲ συνέδριον τῶν
Καρχηδονίων διακοῦσαν τὰ προτεινόμενα παρὰ τοῦ
στρατηγοῦ τῶν Ῥωμαίων, καίπερ σχεδὸν ἀπεγνωκὸς
τὰς τῆς σωτηρίας ἐλπίδας, ὅμως οὕτως ἀνδρωδῶς
ἔστη καὶ γενναίως ὥστε πᾶν ὑπομένειν εἵλετο καὶ
παντὸς ἔργου καὶ καιροῦ πεῖραν λαμβάνειν, ἐφ' ᾧ

the same time as the Romans, inflicted not less but even more damage on the country than the latter. The terror-stricken inhabitants took refuge in the city of Carthage where utter despondency and extreme famine prevailed, the latter owing to overcrowding and the former owing to the expectation of a siege. Regulus, perceiving that the Carthaginians were utterly worsted both by land and sea and expecting to capture the city in a very short time, was yet apprehensive lest his successor in the Consulate should arrive from Rome before Carthage fell and receive the credit of the success, and he therefore invited the enemy to enter into negotiations.[57] The Carthaginians gave a ready ear to these advances, and sent out an embassy of their leading citizens. On meeting Regulus, however, the envoys were so far from being inclined to yield to the conditions he proposed that they could not even bear listening to the severity of his demands. For, imagining himself to be complete master of the situation, he considered they ought to regard any concessions on his part as gifts and acts of grace. As it was evident to the Carthaginians that even if they became subject to the Romans, they could be in no worse case than if they yielded to the present demands, they returned not only dissatisfied with the conditions proposed but offended by Regulus's harshness. The attitude of the Carthaginian Senate on hearing the Roman general's proposals was, although they had almost abandoned all hope of safety, yet one of such manly dignity that rather than submit to anything ignoble or unworthy of their past

[57] In the winter of 256/5; details in *StV* 483.

μηδὲν ἀγεννὲς μηδ' ἀνάξιον τῶν πρὸ τοῦ πράξεων
ὑπομεῖναι.

32. Περὶ δὲ τοὺς καιροὺς τούτους καταπλεῖ τις εἰς
τὴν Καρχηδόνα ξενολόγος τῶν ἀπεσταλμένων εἰς τὴν
Ἑλλάδα πρότερον [εἰς τὴν Καρχηδονίων], ἄγων
στρατιώτας πλείστους, ἐν οἷς καὶ Ξάνθιππόν τινα
Λακεδαιμόνιον, ἄνδρα τῆς Λακωνικῆς ἀγωγῆς μετ-
εσχηκότα καὶ τριβὴν ἐν τοῖς πολεμικοῖς ἔχοντα σύμ-
2 μετρον. ὃς διακούσας τὸ γεγονὸς ἐλάττωμα καὶ πῶς
καὶ τίνι τρόπῳ γέγονε, καὶ συνθεωρήσας τάς τε λοιπὰς παρασκευὰς τῶν Καρχηδονίων καὶ τὸ πλῆθος τῶν
ἱππέων καὶ τῶν ἐλεφάντων, παραυτίκα συνελογίσατο
καὶ πρὸς τοὺς φίλους ἐνεφάνισε διότι συμβαίνει τοὺς
Καρχηδονίους οὐχ ὑπὸ Ῥωμαίων, αὐτοὺς δ' ὑφ' αὑτῶν
3 ἡττᾶσθαι διὰ τὴν ἀπειρίαν τῶν ἡγουμένων. ταχὺ δὲ
διὰ τὴν περίστασιν τῶν τοῦ Ξανθίππου λόγων δια-
δοθέντων εἰς τὰ πλήθη καὶ τοὺς στρατηγούς, ἔγνωσαν
οἱ προεστῶτες ἀνακαλεῖσθαι καὶ πεῖραν αὐτοῦ λαμ-
4 βάνειν. ὁ δὲ παραγενόμενος εἰς τὰς χεῖρας ἔφερε τοῖς
ἄρχουσι τοὺς ἀπολογισμοὺς καὶ παρὰ τί νῦν σφα-
λεῖησαν, καὶ διότι πεισθέντες αὐτῷ καὶ χρησάμενοι
τοῖς ἐπιπέδοις τῶν τόπων ἔν τε ταῖς πορείαις καὶ
στρατοπεδείαις καὶ παρατάξεσιν εὐχερῶς ἑαυτοῖς τε
τὴν ἀσφάλειαν δυνήσονται παρασκευάζειν καὶ τοὺς
5 ὑπεναντίους νικᾶν. οἱ δὲ στρατηγοὶ δεξάμενοι τὰ λεγόμενα καὶ πεισθέντες αὐτῷ παραχρῆμα τὰς δυνάμεις
6 ἐνεχείρισαν. ἦν μὲν οὖν καὶ κατὰ ταύτην τὴν παρὰ τοῦ
Ξανθίππου διαδιδομένην φωνὴν ὁ θροῦς καὶ λαλιά τις

they were willing to suffer anything and to face every exertion and every extremity.

32. Just about this time there arrived at Carthage one of the recruiting officers they had formerly dispatched to Greece, bringing a considerable number of soldiers and among them a certain Xanthippus of Lacedaemon,[58] a man who had been brought up in the Spartan discipline, and had had a fair amount of military experience.[59] On hearing of the recent reverse and how and in what way it occurred, and on taking a comprehensive view of the remaining resources of the Carthaginians and their strength in cavalry and elephants, he at once reached the conclusion and communicated it to friends that the Carthaginians owed their defeat not to the Romans but to themselves, through the inexperience of their generals. Owing to the critical situation Xanthippus's remarks soon got abroad and reached the ears of the generals, whereupon the government decided to summon him before them and examine him. He presented himself before them and communicated to them his estimate of the situation, pointing out why they were now being worsted, and urging that if they would take his advice and avail themselves of the level country for marching, encamping and offering battle they could easily not only secure their own safety, but defeat the enemy. The generals, accepting what he said and resolving to follow his advice, at once entrusted their forces to him. Now even when the original utterance of Xanthippus got abroad, it had caused considerable rumor and more or less sanguine

[58] *RE* Xanthippos 1348–1351 (H. Schaefer).
[59] Probably acquired in the war against Pyrrhus in 273 and in the Chremonidean War of the 260s.

7 εὔελπις παρὰ τοῖς πολλοῖς· ὡς δ᾽ ἐξαγαγὼν πρὸ τῆς
πόλεως τὴν δύναμιν ἐν κόσμῳ παρενέβαλε καί τι καὶ
κινεῖν τῶν μερῶν ἐν τάξει καὶ παραγγέλλειν κατὰ
νόμους ἤρξατο, τηλικαύτην ἐποίει διαφορὰν παρὰ τὴν
τῶν πρότερον στρατηγῶν ἀπειρίαν ὥστε μετὰ κραυγῆς ἐπισημαίνεσθαι τοὺς πολλοὺς καὶ σπεύδειν ὡς
τάχιστα συμβαλεῖν τοῖς πολεμίοις, πεπεισμένους μη-
8 δὲν ἂν παθεῖν δεινὸν ἡγουμένου Ξανθίππου. τούτων δὲ
γινομένων οἱ στρατηγοὶ συνιδόντες τοὺς ὄχλους ἀνα-
τεθαρρηκότας παραδόξως ταῖς ψυχαῖς, παρακαλέσαντες αὐτοὺς τὰ πρέποντα τῷ καιρῷ, μετ᾽ ὀλίγας ἡμέρας
9 ὥρμησαν ἀναλαβόντες τὴν δύναμιν. αὕτη δ᾽ ἦν πεζοὶ
μὲν εἰς μυρίους καὶ δισχιλίους, ἱππεῖς δὲ τετρακισχίλιοι, τὸ δὲ τῶν ἐλεφάντων πλῆθος ἔγγιστά που τῶν
ἑκατόν.

33. Οἱ δὲ Ῥωμαῖοι θεωροῦντες τοὺς Καρχηδονίους
τάς τε πορείας ποιουμένους διὰ τῶν ὁμαλῶν τόπων καὶ
τὰς στρατοπεδείας τιθέντας ἐν τοῖς ἐπιπέδοις τῶν
χωρίων, κατ᾽ αὐτὸ μὲν τοῦτο ξενιζόμενοι διετρέποντο,
2 τοῖς γε μὴν ὅλοις ἔσπευδον ἐγγίσαι τοῖς πολεμίοις.
συνάψαντες δὲ τὴν μὲν πρώτην ἡμέραν κατεστρατοπέδευσαν ὡς δέκα σταδίους ἀποσχόντες τῶν ὑπ-
3 εναντίων. τῇ δὲ κατὰ πόδας οἱ μὲν προεστῶτες τῶν
Καρχηδονίων ἐβουλεύοντο πῶς καὶ τί πρακτέον εἴη
4 κατὰ τὸ παρόν· οἱ δὲ πολλοὶ προθύμως ἔχοντες πρὸς
τὸν κίνδυνον, συστρεφόμενοι κατὰ μέρη καὶ κατ᾽ ὄνομα τὸν Ξάνθιππον ἀναβοῶντες ἐξάγειν σφᾶς ᾤοντο
5 δεῖν τὴν ταχίστην. οἱ δὲ στρατηγοὶ τήν τε τῶν ὄχλων

talk among the populace, but on his leading the army out and drawing it up in good order before the city and even beginning to manœuvre some portions of it correctly and give the word of command in the orthodox military terms, the contrast to the incompetency of the former generals was so striking that the soldiery expressed their approval by cheers and were eager to engage the enemy, feeling sure that if Xanthippus was in command no disaster could befall them. Upon this the generals, seeing the extraordinary recovery of courage among the troops, addressed them in words suitable to the occasion and after a few days took the field with their forces. These consisted of twelve thousand foot, four thousand horse and very nearly a hundred elephants.

33. When the Romans saw that the Carthaginians were marching through the flat country and pitching their camps on level ground, they were surprised indeed and somewhat disturbed by this in particular, but yet were anxious on the whole to get into contact with the enemy. On coming into touch they encamped on the first day at a distance of about ten stades from him. On the following day the Carthaginian government held a council to discuss what should be done for the present and the means thereto. But the troops, eager as they were for a battle, collecting in groups and calling on Xanthippus by name, clearly indicated their opinion that he should lead them forward at once. The generals when they saw the enthusi-

ὁρμὴν καὶ προθυμίαν θεωροῦντες, ἅμα δὲ καὶ τοῦ
Ξανθίππου διαμαρτυρομένου μὴ παριέναι τὸν καιρόν,
παρήγγειλαν τῷ μὲν πλήθει διασκευάζεσθαι, τῷ δὲ
Ξανθίππῳ χρῆσθαι τοῖς πράγμασιν ἐπέτρεψαν ὡς
6 ποτ' αὐτῷ δοκεῖ συμφέρειν. ὁ δὲ λαβὼν τὴν ἐξουσίαν,
τοὺς μὲν ἐλέφαντας ἐξαγαγὼν ἐφ' ἕνα πρὸ πάσης τῆς
δυνάμεως ἐν μετώπῳ κατέστησε, τὴν δὲ φάλαγγα τῶν
Καρχηδονίων ἐν ἀποστήματι συμμέτρῳ τούτοις κατό-
7 πιν ἐπέστησε. τῶν δὲ μισθοφόρων τοὺς μὲν ἐπὶ τὸ
δεξιὸν κέρας παρενέβαλε, τοὺς δ' εὐκινητοτάτους ὁμοῦ
8 τοῖς ἱππεῦσιν ἑκατέρου τοῦ κέρατος προέστησεν. οἱ δὲ
Ῥωμαῖοι συνιδόντες παραταττομένους τοὺς ὑπεναν-
9 τίους ἀντεξῇσαν ἑτοίμως. καταπληττόμενοι δὲ καὶ
προορώμενοι τὴν τῶν ἐλεφάντων ἔφοδον, προθέμενοι
τοὺς γροσφομάχους πολλὰς ἐπ' ἀλλήλαις κατόπιν
ἵστασαν σημείας, τοὺς δ' ἱππεῖς ἐμέρισαν ἐφ' ἑκάτε-
10 ρον τὸ κέρας. τὴν δὲ σύμπασαν τάξιν βραχυτέραν μὲν
ἢ πρόσθεν, βαθυτέραν δὲ ποιήσαντες, τῆς μὲν πρὸς
τὰ θηρία μάχης δεόντως ἦσαν ἐστοχασμένοι, τῆς δὲ
πρὸς τοὺς ἱππεῖς, πολλαπλασίους ὄντας τῶν παρ'
11 αὐτοῖς, ὁλοσχερῶς ἡστόχησαν. ἐπεὶ δ' ἀμφότεροι
κατὰ τὰς ἑαυτῶν προαιρέσεις καὶ καθόλου καὶ κατὰ
μέρος ἑκάστους ἔθηκαν εἰς τὰς ἁρμοζούσας τάξεις,
ἔμενον ἐν κόσμῳ, καραδοκοῦντες τὸν καιρὸν τῆς ἀλλήλων ἐπιθέσεως

34. ἅμα δὲ τῷ τὸν Ξάνθιππον τοῖς μὲν ἐπὶ τῶν
θηρίων παραγγεῖλαι προάγειν καὶ διασπᾶν τὰς τῶν
ὑπεναντίων τάξεις, τοῖς δ' ἱππεῦσιν ἐφ' ἑκατέρου τοῦ

asm and keenness of the soldiers, Xanthippus at the same
time imploring them not to let the opportunity slip, ordered the troops to get ready and gave Xanthippus authority to conduct operations as he himself thought most advantageous. Acting on this authority he sent the elephants
forward and drew them up in a single line in front of the
whole force, placing the Carthaginian phalanx at a suitable
distance behind them. Some of the mercenaries he stationed on the right wing, while the most active he placed
together with the cavalry in front of both wings. The Romans, seeing the enemy drawn up to offer battle, issued
forth to meet them with alacrity. Alarmed at the prospect
of the elephants' charge, they stationed the *velites* in the
van and behind them the legions many maniples deep, di-
viding the cavalry between the two wings. In thus making
their whole line shorter and deeper than before they had
been correct enough in so far as concerned the coming encounter with the elephants, but as to that with the cavalry,
which largely outnumbered theirs, they were very wide of
the mark. When both sides had made that general and detailed disposition of their forces that best suited their plan,
they remained drawn up in order, each awaiting a favorable opportunity to attack.

34. No sooner had Xanthippus ordered the elephant
drivers to advance[60] and break the enemy's line and the
cavalry on each wing to execute a turning movement and

[60] The battle, ending in a severe defeat of the Romans, was
fought in the vicinity of Tunis and Carthage (Meltzer [21. 6], 302–
303).

2 κέρατος κυκλοῦν καὶ προσβάλλειν τοῖς πολεμίοις,
τότε δὴ καὶ τὸ τῶν Ῥωμαίων στρατόπεδον κατὰ τὰ
παρ᾽ αὐτοῖς ἔθη συνεψόφησαν τοῖς ὅπλοις καὶ συν-
3 αλαλάξαντες ὥρμησαν ἐπὶ τοὺς πολεμίους. οἱ μὲν οὖν
ἱππεῖς τῶν Ῥωμαίων ταχέως ἀφ᾽ ἑκατέρων τῶν
κεράτων ἔφυγον, διὰ τὸ πολλαπλασίους εἶναι τοὺς
4 Καρχηδονίους. τῶν δὲ πεζῶν οἱ ταχθέντες ἐπὶ τοῦ
λαιοῦ κέρως, ἅμα μὲν ἐκκλίνοντες τὴν τῶν θηρίων
ἔφοδον, ἅμα δὲ καταφρονοῦντες τῶν μισθοφόρων,
ὥρμησαν ἐπὶ τὸ δεξιὸν κέρας τῶν Καρχηδονίων· τρεψάμενοι δὲ τούτους ἐπέκειντο καὶ κατεδίωκον αὐτοὺς
5 ἕως εἰς τὸν χάρακα. τῶν δὲ κατὰ τοὺς ἐλέφαντας
ταχθέντων οἱ μὲν πρῶτοι συμπεσόντες ὑπὸ τῆς βίας
τῶν ζῴων ἐξωθούμενοι καὶ καταπατούμενοι σωρηδὸν
ἐν χειρῶν νόμῳ διεφθείροντο, τῆς γε μὴν ὅλης τάξεως
τὸ σύστημα διὰ τὸ βάθος τῶν ἐφεστώτων ἕως τινὸς
6 ἀδιάσπαστον ἔμεινεν. ἐπεὶ δ᾽ οἱ μὲν τὰς ἐσχάτας
ἔχοντες τάξεις κυκλούμενοι πανταχόθεν ὑπὸ τῶν ἱππέων ἠναγκάζοντο πρὸς τούτους στρεφόμενοι κινδυνεύειν, οἱ δὲ διὰ μέσων τῶν ἐλεφάντων εἰς τὸ
πρόσθεν ἐκβιαζόμενοι καὶ κατὰ νώτου παριστάμενοι
τῶν θηρίων εἰς ἀκέραιον καὶ συντεταγμένην ἐμ-
πίπτοντες τὴν τῶν Καρχηδονίων φάλαγγα διεφθεί-
7 ροντο, τότε δὴ πανταχόθεν πονοῦντες, οἱ μὲν πλεῖστοι
τῶν Ῥωμαίων συνεπατήθησαν ὑπὸ τῆς ὑπερφυοῦς
βίας τῶν ζῴων, οἱ δὲ λοιποὶ συνηκοντίσθησαν ὑπὸ
τοῦ πλήθους τῶν ἱππέων ἐν αὐτῷ τῷ τῆς παρατάξεως
8 τόπῳ, τελέως δέ τινες ὀλίγοι πρὸς φυγὴν ὥρμησαν.

charge, than the Roman army, clashing their shields and swords together, as is their custom and uttering their battle cry, advanced against the foe. As for the Roman cavalry on both wings it was speedily put to flight owing to the superior numbers of the Carthaginians; while of the infantry, the left wing, partly to avoid the onset of the elephants, and partly owing to the contempt they felt for the mercenary force, fell upon the Carthaginian right wing, and having broken it, pressed on and pursued it as far as the camp. But the first ranks of those who were stationed opposite the elephants, pushed back when they encountered them and trodden under foot by the strength of the animals, fell in heaps in the *mêlée*, while the formation of the main body, owing to the depths of the ranks behind, remained for a time unbroken. At length, however, those in the rear were surrounded on all sides by the cavalry and obliged to face round and fight them, while those who had managed to force a passage through the elephants and collect in the rear of those beasts, encountered the Carthaginian phalanx quite fresh and in good order and were cut to pieces. Henceforth the Romans were in sore straits on all sides, the greater number were trampled to death by the vast weight of the elephants, while the remainder were shot down by the numerous cavalry in their ranks as they stood. Only quite a small body tried to effect their escape, and of

οὐσῶν δὲ πεδινῶν τῶν ὑποχωρήσεων, καὶ τούτων οἱ
μὲν ὑπὸ τῶν θηρίων καὶ τῶν ἱππέων ἀπώλλυντο,
πεντακόσιοι δ᾽ ἴσως οἱ μετὰ Μάρκου τοῦ στρατηγοῦ
φυγόντες μετ᾽ ὀλίγον ὑποχείριοι γενόμενοι σὺν αὐτῷ
9 ᾿κείνῳ πάντες ἐζωγρήθησαν. τῶν μὲν οὖν παρὰ τοῖς
Καρχηδονίοις μισθοφόρων ἔπεσον εἰς ὀκτακοσίους
οἱ κατὰ τὸ λαιὸν τῶν Ῥωμαίων ταχθέντες, τῶν δὲ
Ῥωμαίων ἐσώθησαν μὲν εἰς δισχιλίους οἱ κατὰ τὸ
δίωγμα τῶν προειρημένων ἐκτὸς γενόμενοι τοῦ κιν-
10 δύνου, τὸ δὲ λοιπὸν πλῆθος διεφθάρη πλὴν Μάρκου
11 τοῦ στρατηγοῦ καὶ τῶν ἅμα τούτῳ φυγόντων. αἱ μὲν
οὖν σημαῖαι τῶν Ῥωμαίων αἱ σωθεῖσαι διέπεσον εἰς
12 τὴν Ἀσπίδα παραδόξως· οἱ δὲ Καρχηδόνιοι τοὺς
νεκροὺς σκυλεύσαντες καὶ τὸν στρατηγὸν ἅμα μετὰ
τῶν αἰχμαλώτων ἄγοντες ἐπανῆλθον περιχαρεῖς τοῖς
παροῦσιν εἰς τὴν πόλιν.

35. Ἐν ᾧ καιρῷ πολλά τις ἂν ὀρθῶς ἐπισημαι-
νόμενος εὕροι πρὸς ἐπανόρθωσιν τοῦ τῶν ἀνθρώπων
2 βίου συντελεσθέντα. καὶ γὰρ τὸ διαπιστεῖν τῇ τύχῃ,
καὶ μάλιστα κατὰ τὰς εὐπραγίας, ἐναργέστατον
3 ἐφάνη πᾶσι τότε διὰ τῶν Μάρκου συμπτωμάτων· ὁ
γὰρ μικρῷ πρότερον οὐ διδοὺς ἔλεον οὐδὲ συγγνώμην
τοῖς πταίουσι παρὰ πόδας αὐτὸς ἤγετο δεησόμενος
4 τούτων περὶ τῆς ἑαυτοῦ σωτηρίας. καὶ μὴν τὸ παρ᾽
Εὐριπίδῃ πάλαι καλῶς εἰρῆσθαι δοκοῦν ὡς "ἓν σοφὸν
βούλευμα τὰς πολλὰς χέρας νικᾷ" τότε δι᾽ αὐτῶν τῶν
5 ἔργων ἔλαβε τὴν πίστιν. εἷς γὰρ ἄνθρωπος καὶ μία
γνώμη τὰ μὲν ἀήττητα πλήθη καὶ πραγματικὰ δο-

these, as their line of retreat was over level ground, some were dispatched by the elephants and cavalry, and about five hundred who got away with their general Regulus shortly afterward fell into the enemy's hands and were made prisoners, himself included. It resulted that in this battle the Carthaginians lost about eight hundred of the mercenaries, who had faced the Roman left wing, while of the Romans there were saved but about two thousand,[61] whom the pursuit of the mercenaries I mentioned above carried out of the main battle. All the rest perished with the exception of the general Regulus and those who took to flight together with him. The maniples which escaped got through by extraordinary luck to Aspis. The Carthaginians stripped the dead, and taking with them the general and the other captives, returned to the city in high glee at the turn of affairs.

35. In these events there will be found by one who notes them aright much to contribute to the better conduct of human life. For the precept to distrust Fortune,[62] and especially when we are enjoying success, was most clearly enforced on all by Regulus's misfortunes. He who so short a time previously had refused to pity or take mercy on those in distress was now, almost immediately afterward, being led captive to implore pity and mercy in order to save his own life. And again Euripides' words, so long recognized as just, that "one wise counsel conquers many hands" were then confirmed by the actual facts. For one man and one brain laid low that host which seemed so in-

---

61 Of an army of fifteen thousand (29. 9).
62 Regulus' error was that he trusted *Tyche*; cf. 4. 1.

κοῦντ᾽ εἶναι καθεῖλε, τὸ δὲ προφανῶς πεπτωκὸς ἄρδην
πολίτευμα καὶ τὰς ἀπηλγηκυίας ψυχὰς τῶν δυνάμεων
6 ἐπὶ τὸ κρεῖττον ἤγαγεν. ἐγὼ δὲ τούτων ἐπεμνήσθην
χάριν τῆς τῶν ἐντυγχανόντων τοῖς ὑπομνήμασι διορ-
7 θώσεως. δυεῖν γὰρ ὄντων τρόπων πᾶσιν ἀνθρώποις
τῆς ἐπὶ τὸ βέλτιον μεταθέσεως, τοῦ τε διὰ τῶν ἰδίων
συμπτωμάτων καὶ τοῦ διὰ τῶν ἀλλοτρίων, ἐναργέστε-
ρον μὲν εἶναι συμβαίνει τὸν διὰ τῶν οἰκείων περιπετειῶν, ἀβλαβέστερον δὲ τὸν διὰ τῶν ἀλλοτρίων. διὸ
8 τὸν μὲν οὐδέποθ᾽ ἑκουσίως αἱρετέον, ἐπεὶ μετὰ μεγά-
λων πόνων καὶ κινδύνων ποιεῖ τὴν διόρθωσιν, τὸν δ᾽
ἀεὶ θηρευτέον, ἐπεὶ χωρὶς βλάβης ἔστι συνιδεῖν ἐν
9 αὐτῷ τὸ βέλτιον. ἐξ ὧν συνιδόντι καλλίστην παιδείαν
ἡγητέον πρὸς ἀληθινὸν βίον τὴν ἐκ τῆς πραγματικῆς
10 ἱστορίας περιγινομένην ἐμπειρίαν· μόνη γὰρ αὕτη
χωρὶς βλάβης ἐπὶ παντὸς καιροῦ καὶ περιστάσεως
κριτὰς ἀληθινοὺς ἀποτελεῖ τοῦ βελτίονος. ταῦτα μὲν
οὖν ἡμῖν ἐπὶ τοσοῦτον εἰρήσθω.

36. Καρχηδόνιοι δέ, κατὰ νοῦν ἁπάντων σφίσι
κεχωρηκότων, ὑπερβολὴν χαρᾶς οὐκ ἀπέλιπον διά τε
τῆς πρὸς τὸν θεὸν εὐχαριστίας καὶ διὰ τῆς μετ᾽
2 ἀλλήλων φιλοφροσύνης. Ξάνθιππος δὲ τηλικαύτην
ἐπίδοσιν καὶ ῥοπὴν ποιήσας τοῖς Καρχηδονίων
πράγμασι μετ᾽ οὐ πολὺν χρόνον ἀπέπλευσε πάλιν,
3 φρονίμως καὶ συνετῶς βουλευσάμενος. αἱ γὰρ ἐπι-
φανεῖς καὶ παράδοξοι πράξεις βαρεῖς μὲν τοὺς φθό-
νους, ὀξείας δὲ τὰς διαβολὰς γεννῶσιν· ἃς οἱ μὲν
ἐγχώριοι διά τε τὰς συγγενείας καὶ τὸ τῶν φίλων

vincible and efficient, and restored the fortunes of a state which in the eyes of all was utterly fallen and the deadened spirit of its soldiers. This I mention for the sake of the improvement of the readers of this history. For there are two ways by which all men can reform themselves, the one through their own mischances, the other through those of others, and of these the former is the more impressive, but the latter the less hurtful. Therefore we should never choose the first method if we can help it, as it corrects by means of great pain and peril, but ever pursue the other, since by it we can discern what is best without suffering hurt. Reflecting on this we should regard as the best discipline for actual life the experience that accrues from serious history; for this alone makes us, without inflicting any harm on us, the most competent judges of what is best at every time and in every circumstance. Well, on this subject I have said enough.

36. All having now fallen out with the Carthaginians as they could best desire, there was no extravagance of rejoicing in which they did not indulge, paying thank-offerings to the gods and giving congratulatory entertainments. But Xanthippus, to whom this revolution and notable advance in the fortunes of Carthage, was due, after a little time sailed again for home, and this was a very prudent and sensible decision on his part; for brilliant and exceptional achievements are wont to breed the deepest jealously and most bitter slander. Natives of a place, supported as they are by their kinsmen and having many friends, may possi-

πλῆθος οἷοί τ᾽ ἂν <εἶεν ἐπὶ πολὺν χρόνον> ἀναφέρειν,
οἱ δὲ ξένοι ταχέως ὑφ᾽ ἑκατέρων τούτων ἡττῶνται καὶ
4 κινδυνεύουσι. λέγεται δὲ καὶ ἕτερος ὑπὲρ τῆς ἀπαλ-
λαγῆς τῆς Ξανθίππου λόγος, ὃν πειρασόμεθα διασαφεῖν οἰκειότερον λαβόντες τοῦ παρόντος καιρόν.

5 Ῥωμαῖοι δέ, προσπεσόντων σφίσι παρ᾽ ἐλπίδα τῶν
ἐν Λιβύῃ συμβεβηκότων, εὐθέως ἐγίνοντο πρὸς τὸ
καταρτίζειν τὸν στόλον καὶ τοὺς ἄνδρας ἐξαιρεῖσθαι
6 τοὺς ἐν τῇ Λιβύῃ διασεσωσμένους. οἱ δὲ Καρχηδόνιοι
μετὰ ταῦτα στρατοπεδεύσαντες ἐπολιόρκουν τὴν
Ἀσπίδα, σπουδάζοντες ἐγκρατεῖς γενέσθαι τῶν ἐκ τῆς
7 μάχης διαφυγόντων. διὰ δὲ τὴν γενναιότητα καὶ τόλμαν τῶν ἀνδρῶν οὐδαμῶς ἑλεῖν δυνάμενοι τέλος ἀπ-
8 έστησαν τῆς πολιορκίας. προσπεσόντος δ᾽ αὐτοῖς
ἐξαρτύειν τὸν στόλον τοὺς Ῥωμαίους, καὶ μέλλειν
αὖθις ἐπὶ τὴν Λιβύην ποιεῖσθαι τὸν πλοῦν, τὰ μὲν
ἐπεσκεύαζον σκάφη, τὰ δ᾽ ἐκ καταβολῆς ἐναυπη-
9 γοῦντο. ταχὺ δὲ συμπληρώσαντες ναῦς διακοσίας
ἀνήχθησαν καὶ παρεφύλαττον τὸν ἐπίπλουν τῶν ὑπεναντίων.

10 Οἱ δὲ Ῥωμαῖοι τῆς θερείας ἀρχομένης καθελκύσαντες τριακόσια καὶ πεντήκοντα σκάφη, καὶ στρατηγοὺς ἐπιστήσαντες Μάρκον Αἰμίλιον καὶ Σερούιον
Φόλουιον ἐξαπέστελλον. οἱ δ᾽ ἀναχθέντες ἔπλεον
11 παρὰ τὴν Σικελίαν ὡς ἐπὶ τῆς Λιβύης. συμμίξαντες δὲ
περὶ τὴν Ἑρμαίαν τῷ τῶν Καρχηδονίων στόλῳ, τούτους μὲν ἐξ ἐφόδου καὶ ῥᾳδίως τρεψάμενοι ναῦς

bly be able to hold their own against those for some time, but foreigners when exposed to either speedily succumb and find themselves in peril. There is another account[63] given of Xanthippus's departure which I will endeavor to set forth on an occasion more suitable than the present.

The Romans, who had never expected to receive such bad news from Libya, at once directed their efforts to fitting out their fleet and rescuing their surviving troops there. The Carthaginians after the battle encamped before Aspis and laid siege to it with the object of capturing these survivors, but as they had no success owing to the gallantry and daring of the defenders they at length abandoned the siege. When news reached them that the Romans were preparing their fleet and were about to sail again for Libya, they set to repairing the ships they had and building other entirely new ones, and having soon manned a fleet of two hundred[64] sail, they put to sea and remained on the watch for an attack by the enemy.

In the early summer the Romans, having launched three hundred and fifty ships, sent them off under the command of Marcus Aemilius and Servius Fulvius, who proceeded along the coast of Sicily making for Libya. Encountering the Carthaginian fleet near the Hermaeum they fell on them and easily routed them, capturing one

255 B.C.

---

[63] Not preserved. For Droysen's suggestion that Xanthippus continued his career a decade later in the service of Ptolemy III, see n. in WC 1. 94.   [64] See 36. 10 (three hundred and fifty): These figures have their difficulties (see WC 1. 95), but it is clear that first the Carthaginians lost a large number of ships in battle, and then the Romans a much larger number in the storm near Camarina (37. 2).

12 ἔλαβον αὐτάνδρους ἑκατὸν δεκατέτταρας· τοὺς δ' ἐν
Λιβύῃ διαμείναντας νεανίσκους ἀναλαβόντες ἐκ τῆς
Ἀσπίδος ἔπλεον αὖθις ἐπὶ τῆς Σικελίας.

37. διάραντες δὲ τὸν πόρον ἀσφαλῶς καὶ προσ-
μίξαντες τῇ τῶν Καμαριναίων χώρᾳ, τηλικούτῳ περιέπεσον χειμῶνι καὶ τηλικαύταις συμφοραῖς ὥστε μηδ'
ἂν εἰπεῖν ἀξίως δύνασθαι διὰ τὴν ὑπερβολὴν τοῦ
2 συμβάντος. τῶν γὰρ ἑξήκοντα καὶ τεττάρων πρὸς ταῖς
τριακοσίαις ναυσὶν ὀγδοήκοντα μόνον συνέβη περι-
λειφθῆναι σκάφη, τῶν δὲ λοιπῶν τὰ μὲν ὑποβρύχια
γενέσθαι, τὰ δ' ὑπὸ τῆς ῥαχίας πρὸς ταῖς σπιλάσι καὶ
τοῖς ἀκρωτηρίοις καταγνύμενα πλήρη ποιῆσαι σω-
3 μάτων τὴν παραλίαν καὶ ναυαγίων. ταύτης δὲ μείζω
περιπέτειαν ἐν ἑνὶ καιρῷ κατὰ θάλατταν οὐδ' ἱστορῆ-
4 σθαι συμβέβηκεν. ἧς τὴν αἰτίαν οὐχ οὕτως εἰς τὴν
τύχην ὡς εἰς τοὺς ἡγεμόνας ἐπανοιστέον· πολλὰ γὰρ
τῶν κυβερνητῶν διαμαρτυραμένων μὴ πλεῖν παρὰ τὴν
ἔξω πλευρὰν τῆς Σικελίας τὴν πρὸς τὸ Λιβυκὸν πέλαγος ἐστραμμένην, διὰ τὸ τραχεῖαν εἶναι καὶ δυσ-
προσόρμιστον, ἅμα δὲ καὶ τὴν μὲν οὐδέπω κατα-
λήγειν ἐπισημασίαν, τὴν δ' ἐπιφέρεσθαι· μεταξὺ γὰρ
5 ἐποιοῦντο τὸν πλοῦν τῆς Ὠρίωνος καὶ κυνὸς ἐπιτολῆς·
οὐθενὶ προσσχόντες τῶν λεγομένων ἔπλεον ἔξω πελά-
γιοι, σπουδάζοντές τινας τῶν ἐν τῷ παράπλῳ πόλεις
6 τῇ τοῦ γεγονότος εὐτυχήματος φαντασίᾳ καταπληξάμενοι προσλαβέσθαι. πλὴν οὗτοι μὲν μικρῶν ἐλπίδων ἕνεκα μεγάλοις περιτυχόντες ἀτυχήμασι τότε τὴν

hundred and fourteen ships with their crews. Then having taken on board at Aspis[65] the soldiers who remained in Libya they set sail again for Sicily.

37. They had crossed the strait in safety and were off the territory of Camarina when they were overtaken by so fierce a storm and so terrible a disaster that it is difficult adequately to describe it owing to its surpassing magnitude. For of their three hundred and sixty-four ships only eighty were saved; the rest either foundered or were dashed by the waves against the rocks and headlands and broken to pieces, covering the shore with corpses and wreckage. History tells of no greater catastrophe at sea taking place at one time. The blame must be laid not so much on ill fortune as on the commanders; for the captains had repeatedly urged them not to sail along the outer coast of Sicily, that turned toward the Libyan sea, as it was very rugged and had few safe anchorages: they also warned them that one of the dangerous astral periods was not over and another just approaching (for it was between the rising of Orion and that of Sirius[66] that they undertook the voyage) The commanders, however, paid no attention to a single word they said, they took the outer course and there, in the open sea, they thought to strike terror into some of the cities they passed by the brilliancy of their recent success and thus win them over. But now, all for the sake of such meagre expectations, they exposed themselves to this great disaster, and were obliged to acknowledge their lack

[65] Fragment 51 of the poet Gnaeus Naevius (*FPL* 3rd edition, ed. J. Blänsdorf 1995) may refer to these Roman survivors of the battle. Naevius participated in the war, then described it.

[66] The dates are, approximately, July 4 and July 28 (of 255).

7 αὐτῶν ἀβουλίαν ἔγνωσαν. καθόλου δὲ Ῥωμαῖοι πρὸς
πάντα χρώμενοι τῇ βίᾳ, καὶ τὸ προτεθὲν οἰόμενοι δεῖν
κατ' ἀνάγκην ἐπιτελεῖν καὶ μηδὲν ἀδύνατον εἶναι
σφίσι τῶν ἅπαξ δοξάντων, ἐν πολλοῖς μὲν κατορθοῦσι διὰ τὴν τοιαύτην ὁρμήν, ἐν τισὶ δὲ προφανῶς

8 σφάλλονται, καὶ μάλιστ' ἐν τοῖς κατὰ θάλατταν. ἐπὶ
μὲν γὰρ τῆς γῆς πρὸς ἀνθρώπους καὶ τὰ τούτων ἔργα
ποιούμενοι τὰς ἐπιβολὰς τὰ μὲν πολλὰ κατορθοῦσι
διὰ τὸ πρὸς παραπλησίους δυνάμεις χρῆσθαι τῇ βίᾳ,

9 ποτὲ δὲ καὶ σπανίως ἀποτυγχάνουσι· πρὸς δὲ τὴν
θάλατταν καὶ πρὸς τὸ περιέχον ὅταν παραβάλλωνται
καὶ βιαιομαχῶσι, μεγάλοις ἐλαττώμασι περιπίπτου-

10 σιν. ὃ καὶ τότε καὶ πλεονάκις αὐτοῖς ἤδη συνέβη καὶ
συμβήσεται πάσχειν, ἕως ἄν ποτε διορθώσωνται τὴν
τοιαύτην τόλμαν καὶ βίαν, καθ' ἣν οἴονται δεῖν αὐτοῖς
πάντα καιρὸν εἶναι πλωτὸν καὶ πορευτόν.

38. Οἱ δὲ Καρχηδόνιοι, συνέντες τὸν γεγονότα
φθόρον τοῦ τῶν Ῥωμαίων στόλου, καὶ νομίσαντες
κατὰ μὲν γῆν ἀξιόχρεως σφᾶς εἶναι διὰ τὸ προ-
γεγονὸς εὐτύχημα, κατὰ δὲ θάλατταν διὰ τὴν εἰρη-
μένην τῶν Ῥωμαίων περιπέτειαν, ὥρμησαν προθυ-

2 μότερον ἐπί τε τὰς ναυτικὰς καὶ πεζικὰς παρασκευάς.
καὶ τὸν μὲν Ἀσδρούβαν εὐθὺς ἐξαπέστελλον εἰς τὴν
Σικελίαν, δόντες αὐτῷ τούς τε προϋπάρχοντας καὶ
τοὺς ἐκ τῆς Ἡρακλείας παραγεγονότας στρατιώτας,

3 ἅμα δὲ τούτοις ἐλέφαντας ἑκατὸν καὶ τετταράκοντα.
τοῦτον δ' ἐκπέμψαντες διακοσίας κατεσκευάζοντο

4 ναῦς καὶ τἆλλα τὰ πρὸς τὸν πλοῦν ἡτοίμαζον. ὁ δ'

114

of judgment. The Romans, to speak generally, rely on force in all their enterprises, and think it is incumbent on them to carry out their projects in spite of all, and that nothing is impossible when they have once decided on it. They owe their success in many cases to this spirit, but sometimes they conspicuously fail by reason of it and especially at sea. For on land they are attacking men and the works of man and are usually successful, as there they are employing force against forces of the same nature, although even here they have in some rare instances failed. But when they come to encounter the sea and the atmosphere and choose to fight them by force they meet with signal defeats. It was so on this occasion and on many others, and it will always continue to be so, until they correct this fault of daring and violence which makes them think they can sail and travel where they will at no matter what season.

38. The Carthaginians, on hearing of the destruction of the Roman fleet, conceiving themselves to be now a match for the Romans both on land owing to their recent success and at sea owing to this disaster, were encouraged to make more extensive military and naval preparations. They at once dispatched Hasdrubal to Sicily, giving him the troops they previously had and a force which had joined them from Heraclea, together with a hundred and forty elephants. After dispatching him they began to get ready for sea two hundred ships and to make all other preparations for a naval expedition. Hasdrubal having crossed in safety

Ἀσδρούβας διακομισθεὶς εἰς τὸ Λιλύβαιον ἀσφαλῶς
τά τε θηρία καὶ τὰς δυνάμεις ἐγύμναζε, καὶ δῆλος ἦν
5 ἀντιποιησόμενος τῶν ὑπαίθρων.

Ῥωμαῖοι δὲ τῶν ἐκ τῆς ναυαγίας ἀνακομισθέντων
διακούσαντες τὸ κατὰ μέρος, βαρέως μὲν ἤνεγκαν τὸ
γεγονός· οὐ βουλόμενοι δὲ καθάπαξ εἴκειν, αὖθις
ἔγνωσαν ἐκ δρυόχων εἴκοσι καὶ διακόσια ναυπη-
6 γεῖσθαι σκάφη. τούτων δὲ τὴν συντέλειαν ἐν τριμήνῳ
λαβόντων, ὅπερ οὐδὲ πιστεῦσαι ῥᾴδιον, εὐθέως οἱ
κατασταθέντες ἄρχοντες Αὖλος Ἀτίλιος καὶ Γνάιος
7 Κορνήλιος καταρτίσαντες τὸν στόλον ἀνήχθησαν,
καὶ πλεύσαντες διὰ πορθμοῦ προσέλαβον ἐκ τῆς
Μεσσήνης τὰ διασωθέντα τῶν πλοίων ἐκ τῆς ναυαγίας, καὶ κατάραντες εἰς Πάνορμον τῆς Σικελίας
τριακοσίαις ναυσίν, ἥπερ ἦν βαρυτάτη πόλις τῆς
8 Καρχηδονίων ἐπαρχίας, ἐνεχείρησαν αὐτὴν πολιορκεῖν. συστησάμενοι δὲ κατὰ διττοὺς τόπους ἔργα καὶ
9 τἆλλα παρασκευασάμενοι, προσήγαγον τὰς μηχανάς.
ῥᾳδίως δὲ τοῦ παρὰ θάλατταν πύργου πεσόντος, καὶ
βιασαμένων ταύτῃ τῶν στρατιωτῶν, ἡ μὲν καλουμένη
Νέα πόλις ἑαλώκει κατὰ κράτος· ἡ δὲ Παλαιὰ προσ-
10 αγορευομένη τούτου συμβάντος ἐκινδύνευσε. διὸ καὶ
ταχέως ἐνέδωκαν αὐτὴν οἱ κατοικοῦντες, γενόμενοι δ᾽
ἐγκρατεῖς οὗτοι μὲν ἀπέπλευσαν εἰς τὴν Ῥώμην, ἀπολιπόντες φυλακὴν τῆς πόλεως.

39. Μετὰ δὲ ταῦτα τῆς θερείας ἐπιγενομένης οἱ
κατασταθέντες ἄρχοντες Γνάιος Σερουίλιος καὶ Γάιος
Σεμπρώνιος ἀνέπλευσαν παντὶ τῷ στόλῳ, καὶ διάραν-

to Lilybaeum occupied himself in drilling unopposed his elephants and the rest of his force, and plainly intended to dispute the possession of the open country.

The Romans, on receiving full information about the disaster from the survivors of the shipwreck, were deeply grieved, but being resolved on no account to give in, they decided to put on the stocks a fresh fleet of two hundred and twenty ships. In three months they were completed—a thing difficult to believe—and the new Consuls, Aulus Atilius and Gnaeus Cornelius,[67] having fitted out the fleet, at once put to sea, and passing the straits picked up at Messene the ships that had escaped shipwreck. Descending with their total fleet of three hundred sail on Panormus,[68] the most important city in the Carthaginian province, they undertook its siege. They threw up works in two places and after making the other necessary preparations brought up their battering rams. The tower on the sea shore was easily knocked down, and, the soldiers pressing in through this breach, the so called New Town was stormed, and the part known as the Old Town being now in imminent danger, its inhabitants soon surrendered it. Having taken possession of it the Consuls sailed back to Rome leaving a garrison in the town.   254 B.C.

39. Their successors, Gnaeus Servilius and Gaius Sempronius, put to sea with their whole fleet as soon as it was   253 B.C.

[67] Atilius had been consul in 258 (24. 9), Cornelius in 260 (21. 4), neither successfully; Cornelius was even captured and probably exchanged.

[68] The New Town was stormed, the Old Town surrendered to the Romans.

2 τες εἰς τὴν Σικελίαν ἀφώρμησαν ἐντεῦθεν εἰς τὴν
Λιβύην. κομιζόμενοι δὲ παρὰ τὴν χώραν ἐποιοῦντο
καὶ πλείστας ἀποβάσεις. ἐν αἷς οὐδὲν ἀξιόλογον
πράττοντες παρεγίνοντο πρὸς τὴν τῶν Λωτοφάγων
νῆσον, ἣ καλεῖται μὲν Μῆνιγξ, οὐ μακρὰν δ' ἀπέχει
3 τῆς μικρᾶς Σύρτεως. ἐν ᾗ προσπεσόντες εἴς τινα
βραχέα διὰ τὴν ἀπειρίαν, γενομένης ἀμπώτεως καὶ
4 καθισάντων τῶν πλοίων εἰς πᾶσαν ἦλθον ἀπορίαν. οὐ
μὴν ἀλλὰ πάλιν ἀνελπίστως μετά τινα χρόνον ἐπ-
ενεχθείσης τῆς θαλάττης, ἐκρύψαντες ἐκ τῶν πλοίων
5 πάντα τὰ βάρη μόλις ἐκούφισαν τὰς ναῦς. οὗ γενομένου φυγῇ παραπλήσιον ἐποιήσαντο τὸν ἀπόπλουν.
6 ἁψάμενοι δὲ τῆς Σικελίας καὶ κάμψαντες τὸ Λιλύβαιον
καθωρμίσθησαν εἰς Πάνορμον. ἐντεῦθεν δὲ ποιούμενοι
παραβόλως καὶ διὰ πόρου τὸν πλοῦν εἰς τὴν Ῥώμην
πάλιν περιέπεσον χειμῶνι τηλικούτῳ τὸ μέγεθος ὥστε
πλείω τῶν ἑκατὸν καὶ πεντήκοντα πλοίων ἀποβαλεῖν.

7 Οἱ δ' ἐν τῇ Ῥώμῃ τούτων συμβάντων, καίπερ ὄντες
ἐν παντὶ φιλότιμοι διαφερόντως, ὅμως τότε διὰ τὸ
μέγεθος καὶ τὸ πλῆθος τῶν συμπτωμάτων τοῦ μὲν ἔτι
στόλον ἀθροίζειν ἀναγκασθέντες ὑπὸ τῶν πραγμάτων
8 ἀπέστησαν, ἐν δὲ ταῖς πεζικαῖς δυνάμεσι τὰς ὑπολοί-
πους ἔχοντες ἐλπίδας, τοὺς μὲν στρατηγοὺς ἀπέστελ-
λον Λεύκιον Καικέλιον καὶ Γάιον Φούριον καὶ στρατόπεδα μετὰ τούτων εἰς τὴν Σικελίαν, ἑξήκοντα δὲ μόνον
ἐπλήρωσαν ναῦς χάριν τοῦ τὰς ἀγορὰς κομίζειν τοῖς
9 στρατοπέδοις. ἐκ δὲ τῶν εἰρημένων περιπετειῶν συνέβη πάλιν ἐπικυδέστερα γενέσθαι τὰ τῶν Καρχηδο-

summer and after crossing to Sicily proceeded thence to Libya, and sailing along the coast, made a number of descents in which they accomplished nothing of importance, and finally reached the isle of the Lotus-eaters,[69] which is called Meninx and is not far distant from the lesser Syrtis. Here, owing to their ignorance of these seas, they ran on to some shoals, and, on the tide retreating and the ships grounding fast, they were in a most difficult position. However, as the tide unexpectedly rose again after some time, they managed with difficulty to lighten their ships by throwing overboard all heavy objects. Their departure now was so hasty as to resemble a flight, and having made Sicily and rounded Cape Lilybaeum they anchored at Panormus. As they were rashly crossing the open sea on the way hence to Rome they again encountered such a terrific storm that they lost more than a hundred and fifty ships.

The Roman Government upon this, although in all matters they are exceedingly ambitious of success, still on the present occasion, owing to the magnitude and frequency of the disasters they met with, were obliged by the force of circumstances to renounce[70] the project of getting another fleet together. Relying now solely on their land forces, they dispatched to Sicily with some legions the Consuls[71] Lucius Caecilius and Gaius Furius and only manned sixty ships to revictual the legions. The above disasters resulted in the prospects of the Carthaginians

251 B.C.

69 The island of Djerba; RE Lotophagen 1508 e (H. Lamer) and Lotophagitis 1515 (M. Schwabe).

70 Introduces the absence of a Roman fleet for two years (see 39. 12).

71 Of 251, those of 252 having been omitted.

10 νίων πράγματα. τῆς μὲν γὰρ θαλάττης ἀδεῶς ἐπε-
κράτουν ἐκκεχωρηκότων τῶν Ῥωμαίων, ἐν δὲ ταῖς
11 πεζικαῖς δυνάμεσι μεγάλας εἶχον ἐλπίδας· καὶ τοῦτ
ἔπασχον οὐκ ἀλόγως· οἱ γὰρ Ῥωμαῖοι, διαδοθείσης
φήμης περὶ τῆς ἐν τῇ Λιβύῃ μάχης ὅτι τὰ θηρία τάς
τε τάξεις αὐτῶν διασπάσαι καὶ τοὺς πλείστους δια-
12 φθεῖραι τῶν ἀνδρῶν, οὕτως ἦσαν κατάφοβοι τοὺς
ἐλέφαντας ὡς ἐπὶ δύ' ἐνιαυτοὺς τοὺς ἑξῆς τῶν προειρημένων καιρῶν πολλάκις μὲν ἐν τῇ Λιλυβαίτιδι
χώρᾳ, πολλάκις δ' ἐν τῇ Σελινουντίᾳ παραταττόμενοι
τοῖς πολεμίοις ἐν ἓξ καὶ πέντε σταδίοις οὐκ ἐθάρ-
ρησαν οὐδέποτε κατάρξαι τῆς μάχης οὐδ' εἰς τοὺς
ὁμαλοὺς καθόλου συγκαταβῆναι τόπους, δεδιότες τὴν
13 τῶν ἐλεφάντων ἔφοδον. Θέρμαν δὲ μόνον καὶ Λιπάραν
ἐξεπολιόρκησαν ἐν τούτοις τοῖς καιροῖς, ἀντεχόμενοι
14 τῶν ὀρεινῶν καὶ δυσδιαβάτων τόπων. διὸ καὶ θεωροῦντες οἱ Ῥωμαῖοι τὴν ἐν τοῖς πεζικοῖς στρατοπέδοις
πτοίαν καὶ δυσελπιστίαν, αὖθις ἔγνωσαν ἐκ μετα-
15 μελείας ἀντιλαμβάνεσθαι τῆς θαλάττης. καὶ καταστήσαντες στρατηγοὺς Γάιον Ἀτίλιον καὶ Λεύκιον
Μάλιον ναυπηγοῦνται πεντήκοντα σκάφη, καὶ κατέγραφον καὶ συνήθροιζον στόλον ἐνεργῶς.
40. Ὁ δὲ προεστὼς τῶν Καρχηδονίων Ἀσδρούβας,
ὁρῶν ἀποδειλιῶντας τοὺς Ῥωμαίους ἐν ταῖς προγεγε-
νημέναις παρατάξεσι, πυθόμενος τὸν μὲν ἕνα τῶν
στρατηγῶν μετὰ τῆς ἡμισείας δυνάμεως εἰς τὴν Ἰτα-

---

72 The Romans return to the sea.

becoming once more brighter; for they had now undisturbed command of the sea, the Romans having retired from it, and they had great hopes of their army. These hopes were not unjustified, for the Romans, when the report circulated regarding the battle in Libya that the elephants had broken the Romans' ranks and killed most of their men, grew so afraid of the beasts that for the two years following this period, though often both in the district of Lilybaeum and in that of Selinus they were drawn up at a distance of five or six stades from the enemy, they never dared to begin a battle, and in fact never would come down at all to meet the enemy on flat ground, so much did they dread a charge of the elephants. During this period all they accomplished was the reduction by siege of Therma and Lipara, keeping as they did to mountainous and difficult country. Consequently the Government, observing the timidity and despondency that prevailed in their land forces, changed their minds and decided to try their fortunes at sea again.[72] Having elected Gaius Atilius and Lucius Manlius to the consulship,[73] they proceeded to build fifty ships and actively enroll sailors and get a fleet together.

250 B.C.

40. The Carthaginian commander-in-chief, Hasdrubal,[74] had noted the lack of courage which the Romans exhibited, on the occasions when they were in presence of the enemy, and when he learnt that while one of the

[73] Both men had served as consuls before, Atilius in 257, Manlius in 256.

[74] See 38. 1–4. Philinus now becomes P.'s main source: instead of the regular naming of consuls there are now references to the "year of the war."

λίαν ἀπηλλάχθαι, τὸν δὲ Καικέλιον ἐν τῷ Πανόρμῳ
διατρίβειν τὸ λοιπὸν μέρος ἔχοντα τῆς στρατιᾶς,
2 βουλόμενον ἐφεδρεῦσαι τοῖς τῶν συμμάχων καρποῖς,
ἀκμαζούσης τῆς συγκομιδῆς, ἀναλαβὼν ἐκ τοῦ Λιλυβαίου τὴν δύναμιν ὥρμησε καὶ κατεστρατοπέδευσε
πρὸς τοῖς ὅροις τῆς χώρας τῆς Πανορμίτιδος. ὁ δὲ
3 Καικέλιος, θεωρῶν αὐτὸν κατατεθαρρηκότα, καὶ
σπουδάζων ἐκκαλεῖσθαι τὴν ὁρμὴν αὐτοῦ, συνεῖχε
4 τοὺς στρατιώτας ἐντὸς τῶν πυλῶν. οἷς ἐπαιρόμενος
Ἀσδρούβας, ὡς οὐ τολμῶντος ἀντεξιέναι τοῦ Καικε-
λίου, θρασέως ὁρμήσας παντὶ τῷ στρατεύματι κατῆρε
5 διὰ τῶν στενῶν εἰς τὴν Πανορμῖτιν. φθείροντος δὲ
τοὺς καρποὺς αὐτοῦ μέχρι τῆς πόλεως, ἔμενεν ἐπὶ τῆς
ὑποκειμένης γνώμης ὁ Καικέλιος, ἕως αὐτὸν ἐξεκα-
6 λέσατο διαβῆναι τὸν πρὸ τῆς πόλεως ποταμόν. ἐπεὶ δὲ
τὰ θηρία διεβίβασαν οἱ Καρχηδόνιοι καὶ τὴν δύναμιν, τὸ τηνικαῦτα δὲ τοὺς εὐζώνους ἐξαποστέλλων
ἠρέθιζε, μέχρι πᾶν αὐτοὺς ἐκτάξαι τὸ στρατόπεδον
7 ἠνάγκασε. συνθεασάμενος δὲ γινόμενον ὃ προύθετο,
τινὰς μὲν τῶν εὐκινήτων πρὸ τοῦ τείχους καὶ τάφρου
παρενέβαλε, προστάξας, ἂν ἐγγίζῃ τὰ θηρία πρὸς
8 αὐτούς, χρῆσθαι τοῖς βέλεσιν ἀφθόνως, ὅταν δ' ἐκπιέ-
ζωνται, καταφεύγειν εἰς τὴν τάφρον, καὶ πάλιν ἐκ
ταύτης ὁρμωμένους εἰσακοντίζειν εἰς τὰ προσπίπτον-
9 τα τῶν ζῴων· τοῖς δ' ἐκ τῆς ἀγορᾶς βαναύσοις φέρειν
προσέταξε τὰ βέλη, καὶ παραβάλλειν ἔξω παρὰ τὸν
10 θεμέλιον τοῦ τείχους. αὐτὸς δὲ τὰς σημείας ἔχων ἐπὶ
τῆς κατὰ τὸ λαιὸν κέρας τῶν ὑπεναντίων κειμένης

Consuls with half the whole force had left for Italy, Caecilius and the rest of the army remained at Panormus with the object of protecting the corn of the allies—it now being the height of the harvest—removed his forces from Lilybaeum and encamped on the frontier of the territory of Panormus. Caecilius, observing Hasdrubal's aggressive spirit and wishing to provoke him to attack, kept his own soldiers within the gates. Hasdrubal gained fresh confidence from this, thinking that Caecilius did not venture to come out, and boldly advancing with his whole force, descended through the pass on the territory of Panormus. Caecilius,[75] adhering to his original plan, let him ravage the crops up to the walls, until he had led him on to cross the river that runs in front of the town. Once the Carthaginians had got their elephants and other forces across, he kept sending out light-armed troops to molest them, until he had compelled them to deploy their whole force. When he saw that what he had designed was taking place he stationed some of his light troops before the wall and the trench, ordering them, if the elephants approached, not to spare their missiles, and when driven from their position, they were to take refuge in the trench and sallying from it again shoot at those elephants which charged at them. Ordering the lower classes of the civil population to bring the missiles and arrange them outside at the foot of the wall, he himself with his maniples took up his position at the gate which faced the enemy's left wing and kept send-

[75] His superior strategy wins a battle over the land forces of Hasdrubal and captures more than one hundred elephants. The *gens Caecilia* henceforth displayed an elephant on some of their coins (*MRR* III 36).

THE HISTORIES OF POLYBIUS

11 πύλης ἐφειστήκει, πλείους ἀεὶ καὶ πλείους ἐπαποστέλλων τοῖς ἀκροβολιζομένοις. ἅμα δὲ τῷ τούτων ὁλοσχερεστέραν γενέσθαι τὴν συμπλοκὴν ἀντιφιλοδοξοῦντες οἱ τῶν ἐλεφάντων ἐπιστάται πρὸς τὸν Ἀσδρούβαν, καὶ βουλόμενοι δι᾽ αὐτῶν ποιῆσαι τὸ προτέρημα, πάντες ὥρμησαν ἐπὶ τοὺς προκινδυνεύοντας· τρεψάμενοι δὲ τούτους ῥᾳδίως συνεδίωξαν εἰς

12 τὴν τάφρον. προσπεσόντων δὲ τῶν θηρίων, καὶ τιτρωσκομένων μὲν ὑπὸ τῶν ἐκ τοῦ τείχους τοξευόντων, συνακοντιζομένων δ᾽ ἐνεργοῖς καὶ πυκνοῖς τοῖς ὑσσοῖς καὶ τοῖς γρόσφοις ὑπ᾽ ἀκεραίων τῶν πρὸ τῆς

13 τάφρου διατεταγμένων, συμβελῆ γινόμενα καὶ κατατραυματιζόμενα ταχέως διεταράχθη, καὶ στραφέντα κατὰ τῶν ἰδίων ἐφέρετο, τοὺς μὲν ἄνδρας καταπατοῦντα καὶ διαφθείροντα, τὰς δὲ τάξεις συγχέοντα καὶ

14 κατασπῶντα τὰς αὐτῶν. ἃ καὶ κατιδὼν ὁ Καικέλιος ἐξῆγε τὴν δύναμιν ἐνεργῶς· καὶ συμπεσὼν ἐκ πλαγίου κατὰ κέρας τεταραγμένοις τοῖς πολεμίοις, ἀκεραίους ἔχων καὶ συντεταγμένους, τροπὴν ἐποίει τῶν ὑπεναντίων ἰσχυράν, καὶ πολλοὺς μὲν αὐτῶν ἀπέκτεινε, τοὺς

15 δὲ λοιποὺς ἠνάγκασε φεύγειν προτροπάδην. θηρία δὲ σὺν αὐτοῖς μὲν Ἰνδοῖς ἔλαβε δέκα, τῶν δὲ λοιπῶν τοὺς Ἰνδοὺς ἀπερριφότων, μετὰ τὴν μάχην περιελα-

16 σάμενος ἐκυρίευσε πάντων. ταῦτα δ᾽ ἐπιτελεσάμενος ὁμολογουμένως αἴτιος ἐδόκει γεγονέναι τοῖς Ῥωμαίων πράγμασι τοῦ πάλιν ἀναθαρρῆσαι τὰς πεζικὰς δυνάμεις καὶ κρατῆσαι τῶν ὑπαίθρων.

41. Τοῦ δὲ προτερήματος τούτου προσπεσόντος εἰς

ing constant reinforcements to those engaged in shooting. When this latter force more generally engaged with the enemy, the drivers of the elephants, anxious to exhibit their prowess to Hasdrubal and wishing the victory to be due to themselves, all charged those of the enemy who were in advance and putting them easily to flight pursued them to the trench. When the elephants charged the trench and began to be wounded by those who were shooting from the wall, while at the same time a rapid shower of javelins and spears fell on them from the fresh troops drawn up before the trench, they very soon, finding themselves hit and hurt in many places, were thrown into confusion and turned on their own troops, trampling down and killing the men and disturbing and breaking the ranks. Caecilius, on seeing this, made a vigorous sally and falling on the flank of the enemy, who were now in disorder, with his own fresh and well-ordered troops caused a severe rout among them, killing many and compelling the rest to quit the field in headlong flight. He took ten elephants with their mahouts, and after the battle, having penned up the others who had thrown their mahouts, he captured them all. By this exploit he was universally acknowledged to have caused the Roman land forces to pluck up courage again and gain the command of the open country.

41. When news of this success reached Rome it caused

τὴν Ῥώμην, περιχαρεῖς ἦσαν οὐχ οὕτως ἐπὶ τῷ τοὺς
πολεμίους ἠλαττῶσθαι τῶν θηρίων ἐστερημένους, ὡς
ἐπὶ τῷ τοὺς ἰδίους τεθαρρηκέναι τῶν ἐλεφάντων κε-
2 κρατηκότας. διὸ καὶ πάλιν ἐπερρώσθησαν διὰ ταῦτα
κατὰ τὴν ἐξ ἀρχῆς πρόθεσιν εἰς τὸ μετὰ στόλου καὶ
ναυτικῆς δυνάμεως τοὺς στρατηγοὺς ἐπὶ τὰς πράξεις
ἐκπέμπειν, σπουδάζοντες εἰς δύναμιν πέρας ἐπιθεῖναι
3 τῷ πολέμῳ. παρασκευασθέντων δὲ τῶν ἐπιτηδείων
πρὸς τὴν ἐξαποστολὴν ἔπλεον οἱ στρατηγοὶ διακο-
4 σίαις ναυσὶν ὡς ἐπὶ τῆς Σικελίας. ἔτος δ' ἦν τῷ
πολέμῳ τετταρεσκαιδέκατον. καθορμισθέντες δὲ πρὸς
τὸ Λιλύβαιον, ἅμα καὶ τῶν πεζικῶν ἐκεῖ στρατοπέδων
αὐτοῖς ἀπηντηκότων, ἐνεχείρουν πολιορκεῖν, ὅτι κρατήσαντες ταύτης ῥᾳδίως μεταβιβάσουσι τὸν πόλεμον
5 εἰς τὴν Λιβύην. σχεδὸν δὲ περί γε τούτου τοῦ μέρους
καὶ τῶν Καρχηδονίων οἱ προεστῶτες ὡμοδόξουν καὶ
6 τοὺς αὐτοὺς εἶχον λογισμοὺς τοῖς Ῥωμαίοις. διὸ καὶ
τἆλλα πάρεργα ποιησάμενοι περὶ τὸ βοηθεῖν ἐγίνοντο
καὶ παραβάλλεσθαι καὶ πᾶν ὑπομένειν ὑπὲρ τῆς προειρημένης πόλεως διὰ τὸ μηδεμίαν ἀφορμὴν κατα-
λείπεσθαί σφισι, πάσης δὲ τῆς ἄλλης Σικελίας ἐπι-
κρατεῖν Ῥωμαίους πλὴν Δρεπάνων.

Ἵνα δὲ μὴ τοῖς ἀγνοοῦσι τοὺς τόπους ἀσαφῆ τὰ
λεγόμενα γίνηται, πειρασόμεθα διὰ βραχέων ἀγαγεῖν
εἰς ἔννοιαν τῆς εὐκαιρίας καὶ θέσεως αὐτῶν τοὺς
ἐντυγχάνοντας.

42. τὴν μὲν οὖν σύμπασαν Σικελίαν τῇ θέσει
τετάχθαι συμβαίνει πρὸς τὴν Ἰταλίαν καὶ τἀκείνης

great rejoicing, not so much because of the enemy being weakened by the loss of their elephants as because of the confidence which the capture of these gave to their own troops. They were consequently encouraged to revert to their original plan of sending out the Consuls to the campaign with a fleet and naval force; for they were eager by all means in their power to put an end to the war. When all that was required for the expedition was ready, the Consuls set sail for Sicily with two hundred ships. This was in the fourteenth year of the war.[76] Anchoring off Lilybaeum, 250 B.C. where they were joined by their land forces, they undertook its siege, thinking that if it fell into their possession it would be easy for them to transfer the war to Libya. On this matter at least the Carthaginian Government agreed more or less with the Romans, sharing their estimate of the place's value; so that, shelving all other projects, they devoted their whole attention to the relief of this city and were ready to undertake every risk and burden for this purpose; for if it fell, no base was left for them, as the Romans were masters of all the rest of Sicily except Drepana.[77]

To prevent my narrative from being obscure to readers owing to their ignorance of the geography, I will try to convey briefly to them an idea of the natural advantages and exact position of the places referred to.

42. Sicily, then, as a whole occupies the same position with regard to Italy and its extremity that the Peloponnese

[76] See the note in WC 103–104. The following chapters through 54. 8 deal with Roman operations against Lilybaeum and Drepana designed to remove the last Carthaginian bases in Sicily.

[77] Modern Trapani, some 30 kilometers north of Lilybaeum.

πέρατα παραπλησίως τῇ τῆς Πελοποννήσου θέσει

2 πρὸς τὴν λοιπὴν Ἑλλάδα καὶ τὰ ταύτης ἄκρα, τούτῳ δ᾽ αὐτῷ διαφέρειν ἀλλήλων, ᾗ ᾽κείνη μὲν χερρόνησός ⟨ἐστιν, αὕτη δὲ νῆσος⟩· ἧς μὲν γὰρ ὁ μεταξὺ τόπος

3 ἐστὶ πορευτός, ἧς δὲ πλωτός. τὸ δὲ σχῆμα τῆς Σικελίας ἐστὶ μὲν τρίγωνον, αἱ δὲ κορυφαὶ τῶν γωνιῶν

4 ἑκάστης ἀκρωτηρίων λαμβάνουσι τάξεις, ὧν τὸ μὲν πρὸς μεσημβρίαν νεῦον, εἰς δὲ τὸ Σικελικὸν πέλαγος

5 ἀνατεῖνον, Πάχυνος καλεῖται, τὸ δ᾽ εἰς τὰς ἄρκτους κεκλιμένον ὁρίζει μὲν τοῦ πορθμοῦ τὸ πρὸς δύσεις μέρος, ἀπέχει δὲ τῆς Ἰταλίας ὡς δεκαδύο στάδια,

6 προσαγορεύεται δὲ Πελωριάς. τὸ δὲ τρίτον τέτραπται μὲν εἰς αὐτὴν τὴν Λιβύην, ἐπίκειται δὲ τοῖς προκειμένοις τῆς Καρχηδόνος ἀκρωτηρίοις εὐκαίρως, διέχον ὡς χιλίους σταδίους, νεύει δ᾽ εἰς χειμερινὰς δύσεις, διαιρεῖ δὲ τὸ Λιβυκὸν καὶ τὸ Σαρδῷον πέ-

7 λαγος, προσαγορεύεται δὲ Λιλύβαιον. ἐπὶ δὲ τούτῳ πόλις ὁμώνυμος κεῖται τῷ τόπῳ, περὶ ἣν τότε συνέβαινε τοὺς Ῥωμαίους συνίστασθαι τὴν πολιορκίαν, τείχεσί τε διαφερόντως ἠσφαλισμένην καὶ πέριξ τάφρῳ βαθείᾳ καὶ τενάγεσιν ἐκ θαλάττης, δι᾽ ὧν ἐστιν εἰς τοὺς λιμένας εἴσπλους πολλῆς δεόμενος ἐμπειρίας καὶ συνηθείας.

8 Ταύτῃ δὲ προσστρατοπεδεύσαντες ἐξ ἑκατέρου μέρους οἱ Ῥωμαῖοι, καὶ τὰ μεταξὺ τῶν στρατοπέδων τάφρῳ καὶ χάρακι καὶ τείχει διαλαβόντες, ἤρξαντο προσάγειν ἔργα κατὰ τὸν ἔγγιστα κείμενον τῆς

9 θαλάττης πύργον ὡς πρὸς τὸ Λιβυκὸν πέλαγος.

occupies with regard to the rest of Greece and its extremity, the difference lying in this, that the Peloponnese is a peninsula whereas Sicily is an island, the communication being in the one case by land and in the other by sea. Sicily is triangular in shape, the apices of all three angles being formed by capes. The cape that looks to the south and stretches out into the Sicilian Sea is called Pachynus, that on the north forms the extremity of the western coast of the Strait; it is about twelve stades distant from Italy and is called Pelorias. The third looks toward Libya itself, and is favorably situated as a base for attacking the promontories in front of Carthage, from which it is distant about one thousand stades. It is turned to the southwest, separating the Libyan from the Sardinian Sea, and its name is Lilybaeum. On the cape stands the city of the same name, of which the Romans were now opening the siege. It is excellently defended both by walls and by a deep moat all round, and on the side facing the sea by shoaly water, the passage through which into the harbor requires great skill and practice.

The Romans encamped by this city on either side, fortifying the space between their camps with a trench, a stockade, and a wall. They then began to throw up works against the tower that lay nearest the sea on the Libyan side, and,

προσκατασκευάζοντες δ' ἀεὶ τοῖς ὑποκειμένοις καὶ
παρεκτείνοντες τῶν ἔργων τὰς κατασκευάς, τέλος ἐξ
10 πύργους τοὺς συνεχεῖς τῷ προειρημένῳ κατέβαλον,
τοὺς δὲ λοιποὺς πάντας ἅμα κριοκοπεῖν ἐνεχείρησαν.
γινομένης δ' ἐνεργοῦ καὶ καταπληκτικῆς τῆς πολιορκίας, καὶ τῶν πύργων τῶν μὲν πονούντων ἀν' ἑκάστην
ἡμέραν, τῶν δ' ἐρειπομένων, ἅμα δὲ καὶ τῶν ἔργων
11 ἐπιβαινόντων ἀεὶ καὶ μᾶλλον ἐντὸς τῆς πόλεως, ἦν
ἰσχυρὰ διατροπὴ καὶ κατάπληξις παρὰ τοῖς πολιορκουμένοις, καίπερ ὄντων ἐν τῇ πόλει χωρὶς τοῦ πολι-
12 τικοῦ πλήθους αὐτῶν τῶν μισθοφόρων εἰς μυρίους. οὐ
μὴν ἀλλ' ὅ γε στρατηγὸς αὐτῶν Ἰμίλκων οὐδὲν παρ-
έλειπε τῶν δυνατῶν, ἀλλὰ τὰ μὲν ἀντοικοδομῶν, τὰ δ'
ἀντιμεταλλεύων οὐ τὴν τυχοῦσαν ἀπορίαν παρεῖχε
13 τοῖς ὑπεναντίοις. ἔτι δὲ καθ' ἑκάστην ἡμέραν ἐπιπορευόμενος καὶ τοῖς ἔργοις ἐγχειρῶν, εἴ πως δύναιτο
πῦρ ἐμβαλεῖν, πολλοὺς ὑπὲρ τούτου τοῦ μέρους καὶ
παραβόλους ἀγῶνας δὴ συνίστατο καὶ μεθ' ἡμέραν
καὶ νύκτωρ, ὥστε πλείους ἐνίοτε γίνεσθαι νεκροὺς ἐν
ταῖς τοιαύταις συμπλοκαῖς τῶν εἰωθότων πίπτειν ἐν
ταῖς παρατάξεσι.

43. Κατὰ δὲ τοὺς καιροὺς τούτους τῶν ἡγεμόνων
τινὲς τῶν τὰς μεγίστας χώρας ἐχόντων ἐν τοῖς μισθοφόροις, συλλαλήσαντες ἑαυτοῖς ὑπὲρ τοῦ τὴν πόλιν
ἐνδοῦναι τοῖς Ῥωμαίοις καὶ πεπεισμένοι πειθαρχή-
σειν σφίσι τοὺς ὑποτεταγμένους, ἐξεπήδησαν νυκτὸς
ἐκ τῆς πόλεως ἐπὶ τὸ στρατόπεδον, καὶ διελέγοντο τῷ
2 τῶν Ῥωμαίων στρατηγῷ περὶ τούτων. ὁ δ' Ἀχαιὸς

constantly adding something to what had already been constructed and extending their works, they succeeded at last in knocking down the six adjacent towers, and attacked all the others at once with battering rams. The siege was now so vigorously pursued and so terrifying, each day seeing some of the towers shaken or demolished and the enemy's works advancing further and further into the city, that the besieged were thrown into a state of utter confusion and panic, although, besides the civil population, there were about ten thousand mercenaries in the town. Their general, Himilco, however, omitted no means of resistance in his power, and by counterbuilding and countermining caused the enemy no little difficulty. Every day he would advance and make attempts on the siege works, trying to succeed in setting them on fire, and with this object was indeed engaged by night and day in combats of so desperate a character, that at times more men fell in these encounters than usually fall in a pitched battle.

43. About this time some of the superior officers in the mercenary force, after talking the matter over among themselves and in the full conviction that their subordinates would obey them, sallied from the town by night to the Roman camp and made proposals to the Consul for the surrender of the city. But the Achaean Alexon,[78] who had

[78] A compatriot of P., mentioned for his acts of bravery (43. 3–8).

Ἀλέξων, ὁ καὶ τοῖς Ἀκραγαντίνοις κατὰ τοὺς ἐπάνω
χρόνους αἴτιος γενόμενος τῆς σωτηρίας, καθ' ὃν καιρὸν ἐπεβάλοντο παρασπονδεῖν αὐτοὺς οἱ τῶν Συρακοσίων μισθοφόροι, καὶ τότε πρῶτος συνεὶς τὴν πρᾶξιν
3 ἀνήγγειλε τῷ στρατηγῷ τῶν Καρχηδονίων. ὁ δὲ διακούσας παραχρῆμα συνῆγε τοὺς καταλειπομένους
τῶν ἡγεμόνων, καὶ παρεκάλει μετὰ δεήσεως, μεγάλας
δωρεὰς καὶ χάριτας ὑπισχνούμενος, ἐὰν ἐμμείνωσι τῇ
πρὸς αὐτὸν πίστει καὶ μὴ κοινωνήσωσι τοῖς ἐξελη-
4 λυθόσι τῆς ἐπιβολῆς. δεχομένων δὲ προθύμως τοὺς
λόγους, εὐθέως μετ' αὐτῶν ἀπέστειλε πρὸς μὲν τοὺς
Κελτοὺς Ἀννίβαν τὸν υἱὸν τὸν Ἀννίβου τοῦ μεταλλάξαντος ἐν Σαρδόνι διὰ τὴν προγεγενημένην ἐν τῇ
στρατείᾳ πρὸς αὐτοὺς συνήθειαν, ἐπὶ δὲ τοὺς ἄλλους
μισθοφόρους Ἀλέξωνα διὰ τὴν παρ' ἐκείνοις ἀποδο-
5 χὴν αὐτοῦ καὶ πίστιν· οἳ καὶ συναγαγόντες τὰ πλήθη
καὶ παρακαλέσαντες, ἔτι δὲ πιστωσάμενοι τὰς προτει-
νομένας ἑκάστοις δωρεὰς ὑπὸ τοῦ στρατηγοῦ, ῥᾳδίως
6 ἔπεισαν αὐτοὺς μένειν ἐπὶ τῶν ὑποκειμένων. διὸ καὶ
μετὰ ταῦτα, τῶν ἐκπηδησάντων ⟨ἐκ τοῦ προφανοῦς
ἐρχομένων⟩ πρὸς τὰ τείχη, καὶ βουλομένων παρακαλεῖν καὶ λέγειν τι περὶ τῆς τῶν Ῥωμαίων ἐπαγγελίας,
οὐχ οἷον προσεῖχον αὐτοῖς, ἀλλ' ἁπλῶς οὐδ' ἀκούειν
ἠξίουν, βάλλοντες δὲ τοῖς λίθοις καὶ συνακοντίζοντες
7 ἀπεδίωξαν ἀπὸ τοῦ τείχους. Καρχηδόνιοι μὲν οὖν διὰ
τὰς προειρημένας αἰτίας παρὰ μικρὸν ἦλθον ἀπολέ-
σαι τὰ πράγματα, παρασπονδηθέντες ὑπὸ τῶν μισθο-
8 φόρων· Ἀλέξων δὲ πρότερον Ἀκραγαντίνοις ἔσωσε

on a former occasion saved the Agrigentines, when the Syracusan mercenaries had formed a project of breaking faith with them, was now too the first to get wind of what was going on and informed the Carthaginian general. Himilco on hearing of it at once summoned the remaining officers and urgently implored their aid, promising them lavish gifts and favors if they remained loyal to him and refused to participate in the plot of those who had left the city. On their readily consenting, he bade them return at once to their troops, sending with them to the Celts Hannibal, the son of that Hannibal who died in Sardinia, as they had served under him and were well acquainted with him, while to the other mercenaries he sent Alexon, owing to his popularity and credit with them. They called a meeting of the soldiery and partly by entreating them, partly moreover by assuring them that each man would receive the bounty the general had offered, easily persuaded them to bide by their engagements. So, afterward, when the officers who had quitted the city advanced openly to the walls and attempted to entreat them and tell them of the promises made by the Romans, not only did they pay no attention but would not lend ear to them at all, and chased them away from the wall with stones and other missiles. The Carthaginians, then, for the above reasons very narrowly escaped a complete disaster due to the treachery of their mercenaries, and Alexon, who had previously saved

διὰ τὴν πίστιν οὐ μόνον τὴν πόλιν καὶ τὴν χώραν,
ἀλλὰ καὶ τοὺς νόμους καὶ τὴν ἐλευθερίαν, τότε δὲ
Καρχηδονίοις αἴτιος ἐγένετο τοῦ μὴ σφαλῆναι τοῖς
ὅλοις.

44. Οἱ δ᾽ ἐν τῇ Καρχηδόνι τούτων μὲν οὐδὲν εἰδό-
τες, συλλογιζόμενοι δὲ τὰς ἐν ταῖς πολιορκίαις χρείας, πληρώσαντες στρατιωτῶν πεντήκοντα ναῦς, καὶ
παρακαλέσαντες τοῖς ἁρμόζουσι λόγοις τῆς πράξεως,
τὸν ἐπὶ τούτοις τεταγμένον Ἀννίβαν, ὃς ἦν Ἀμίλκου
μὲν υἱός, τριήραρχος δὲ καὶ φίλος Ἀτάρβου πρῶτος,
ἐξαπέστειλαν κατὰ σπουδήν, ἐντειλάμενοι μὴ κατα-
μελλῆσαι, χρησάμενον δὲ σὺν καιρῷ τῇ τόλμῃ
2 βοηθῆσαι τοῖς πολιορκουμένοις. ὁ δ᾽ ἀναχθεὶς μετὰ
μυρίων στρατιωτῶν, καὶ καθορμισθεὶς ἐν ταῖς καλου-
μέναις Αἰγούσσαις, μεταξὺ δὲ κειμέναις Λιλυβαίου
3 καὶ Καρχηδόνος, ἐπετήρει τὸν πλοῦν. λαβὼν δ᾽ οὔριον
καὶ λαμπρὸν ἄνεμον, ἐκπετάσας πᾶσι τοῖς ἀρμένοις
καὶ κατορώσας ἐπ᾽ αὐτὸ τὸ στόμα τοῦ λιμένος ἐποιεῖτο τὸν πλοῦν, ἔχων καθωπλισμένους καὶ πρὸς μά-
4 χην ἑτοίμους τοὺς ἄνδρας ἐπὶ τῶν καταστρωμάτων. οἱ
δὲ Ῥωμαῖοι, τὰ μὲν αἰφνιδίου γενομένης τῆς ἐπι-
φανείας, τὰ δὲ φοβούμενοι μὴ σὺν τοῖς πολεμίοις ὑπὸ
τῆς βίας τοῦ πνεύματος συγκατενεχθῶσιν εἰς τὸν
λιμένα τῶν ὑπεναντίων, τὸ μὲν διακωλύειν τὸν ἐπίπλουν τῆς βοηθείας ἀπέγνωσαν, ἐπὶ δὲ τῆς θαλάττης
5 ἔστησαν καταπεπληγμένοι τὴν τῶν πολεμίων τόλμαν.
τὸ δ᾽ ἐκ τῆς πόλεως πλῆθος ἠθροισμένον ἐπὶ τὰ τείχη
πᾶν ἅμα μὲν ἠγωνία τὸ συμβησόμενον, ἅμα δ᾽ ἐπὶ τῷ

by his loyalty not only the city and district but the laws and liberties of Agrigentum, now was the cause of the Carthaginians being saved from total ruin.

44. The Carthaginian government knew nothing of all this, but calculating the requirements of a besieged town, they filled fifty ships with troops. After addressing the soldiers in terms befitting the enterprise, they sent them off at once under the command of Hannibal, the son of Hamilcar, trierarch and most intimate friend of Adherbal,[79] with orders not to delay, but at the first opportunity to make a bold attempt to relieve the besieged. Setting sail with ten thousand troops on board, he came to anchor off the islands called Aegusae, which lie between Lilybaeum and Carthage, and there awaited favorable weather. As soon as he had a fine stern breeze he hoisted all sail and running before the wind sailed straight for the mouth of the harbor, his men drawn up on deck armed ready for action. The Romans, partly owing to the suddenness of the fleet's appearance and partly because they feared being carried into the hostile harbor by the force of the wind together with their enemies, made no effort to prevent the entrance of the relieving force, but stood out at sea amazed at the audacity of the Carthaginians. The whole population had assembled on the walls in an agony of suspense on the one hand as to what would happen, and at the same time so overjoyed at the unexpected prospect of succor that they

[79] The commander at Drepana, as 46. 1 makes clear.

παραδόξῳ τῆς ἐλπίδος ὑπερχαρὲς ὑπάρχον μετὰ κρό-
6 του καὶ κραυγῆς παρεκάλει τοὺς εἰσπλέοντας. Ἀννίβας δὲ παραβόλως καὶ τεθαρρηκότως εἰσδραμὼν καὶ
καθορμισθεὶς εἰς τὸν λιμένα μετ' ἀσφαλείας ἀπεβί-
7 βασε τοὺς στρατιώτας. οἱ δ' ἐν τῇ πόλει πάντες οὐχ
οὕτως ἦσαν ἐπὶ τῇ τῆς βοηθείας παρουσίᾳ περιχαρεῖς, καίπερ μεγάλην ἐλπίδα καὶ χεῖρα προσει-
ληφότες, ὡς ἐπὶ τῷ μὴ τετολμηκέναι τοὺς Ῥωμαίους
κωλῦσαι τὸν ἐπίπλουν τῶν Καρχηδονίων.

45. Ἰμίλκων δ' ὁ τεταγμένος ἐπὶ τῆς πόλεως στρατηγός, θεωρῶν τὴν ὁρμὴν καὶ προθυμίαν τῶν μὲν ἐν
τῇ πόλει διὰ τὴν παρουσίαν τῆς βοηθείας, τῶν δὲ
παραγεγονότων διὰ τὴν ἀπειρίαν τῶν περιεστώτων
2 κακῶν, βουλόμενος ἀκεραίοις ἀποχρήσασθαι ταῖς
ἑκατέρων ὁρμαῖς πρὸς τὴν διὰ τοῦ πυρὸς ἐπίθεσιν
3 τοῖς ἔργοις, συνῆγε πάντας εἰς ἐκκλησίαν· παρακαλέσας δὲ τῷ καιρῷ τὰ πρέποντα διὰ πλειόνων, καὶ
παραστήσας ὁρμὴν ὑπερβάλλουσαν διά τε τὸ μέγεθος τῶν ἐπαγγελιῶν τοῖς κατ' ἰδίαν ἀνδραγαθήσασι
καὶ τὰς κατὰ κοινὸν ἐσομένας χάριτας αὐτοῖς καὶ
4 δωρεὰς παρὰ Καρχηδονίων, ὁμοθυμαδὸν ἐπισημαινο-
μένων καὶ βοώντων μὴ μέλλειν, ἀλλ' ἄγειν αὐτούς,
τότε μὲν ἐπαινέσας καὶ δεξάμενος τὴν προθυμίαν
ἀφῆκε, παραγγείλας ἀναπαύεσθαι καθ' ὥραν καὶ πει-
5 θαρχεῖν τοῖς ἡγουμένοις· μετ' οὐ πολὺ δὲ συγκαλέσας
τοὺς προεστῶτας αὐτῶν διένειμε τοὺς ἁρμόζοντας
πρὸς τὴν ἐπίθεσιν ἑκάστοις τόπους, καὶ τὸ σύνθημα
καὶ τὸν καιρὸν τῆς ἐπιθέσεως ἐδήλωσε, καὶ παρήγ-

kept on encouraging the fleet as it sailed in by cheers and clapping of hands. Hannibal, having entered the harbor in this hazardous and daring manner, anchored and disembarked his troops in security. All those in the city were delighted not so much at the arrival of the relief, although their prospects were much improved and their force increased thereby, as at the fact that the Romans had not ventured to try to prevent the Carthaginians from sailing in.

45. Himilco, the commander of the garrison, seeing that all were full of spirit and confidence, the original garrison owing to the arrival of relief, and the newcomers owing to their ignorance as yet of the perilous situation, desired to avail himself of this fresh spirit in both parties and make another attempt to fire the enemy's works. He therefore summoned the soldiers to a general assembly, and addressing them at some length in words suitable to the occasion, roused them to great enthusiasm by his lavish promises of reward to those who distinguished themselves personally, and his assurance that the force as a whole would be duly recompensed by the Government. On their all applauding him and shouting to him not to delay but to lead them on at once, he dismissed them for the present after praising them and expressing his pleasure at their eagerness, ordering them to retire to rest early and obey their officers. Soon afterward he summoned the commanding officers and assigned to each his proper place in the assault, giving them the watchword and informing them of

γειλε τοῖς ἡγεμόσι μετὰ πάντων τῶν ὑποτεταγμένων
6 ἐπὶ τοῖς τόποις ἑωθινῆς εἶναι φυλακῆς. τῶν δὲ πειθαρ-
χησάντων, ἐξαγαγὼν τὴν δύναμιν ἅμα τῷ φωτὶ κατὰ
7 πλείους τόπους ἐνεχείρει τοῖς ἔργοις. οἱ δὲ Ῥωμαῖοι
διὰ τὸ προορᾶσθαι τὸ μέλλον οὐκ ἀργῶς οὐδ᾽ ἀπαρα-
σκεύως εἶχον, ἀλλ᾽ ἑτοίμως ἐβοήθουν πρὸς τὸ δεόμε-
8 νον καὶ διεμάχοντο τοῖς πολεμίοις ἐρρωμένως. πάντων
δ᾽ ἐν βραχεῖ χρόνῳ συμπεσόντων ἀλλήλοις ἦν ἀγὼν
παράβολος πέριξ τοῦ τείχους· οἱ μὲν γὰρ ἐκ τῆς
πόλεως ἦσαν οὐκ ἐλάττους δισμυρίων, οἱ δ᾽ ἔξωθεν ἔτι
9 πλείους τούτων. ὅσῳ δὲ συνέβαινε τοὺς ἄνδρας ἐκτὸς
τάξεως ποιεῖσθαι τὴν μάχην ἀναμὶξ κατὰ τὰς αὐτῶν
προαιρέσεις, τοσούτῳ λαμπρότερος ἦν ὁ κίνδυνος, ὡς
ἂν ἐκ τοσούτου πλήθους κατ᾽ ἄνδρα καὶ κατὰ ζυγὸν
οἷον εἰ μονομαχικῆς συνεστώσης περὶ τοὺς ἀγωνιζο-
10 μένους τῆς φιλοτιμίας. οὐ μὴν ἀλλ᾽ ἥ τε κραυγὴ καὶ
11 τὸ σύστρεμμα διαφέρον ἦν πρὸς αὐτοῖς τοῖς ἔργοις.
οἱ γὰρ ἀρχῆθεν ἐπ᾽ αὐτῷ τούτῳ παρ᾽ ἀμφοῖν ταχθέντες, οἱ μὲν ἐπὶ τῷ τρέψασθαι τοὺς ἐπὶ τῶν ἔργων, οἱ δ᾽
ἐπὶ τῷ μὴ προέσθαι ταῦτα, τηλικαύτην ἐποιοῦντο
φιλοτιμίαν καὶ σπουδήν, οἱ μὲν ἐξῶσαι σπεύδοντες, οἱ
δ᾽ οὐδαμῶς εἶξαι τούτοις τολμῶντες, ⟨ὥστε⟩ διὰ τὴν
12 προθυμίαν τέλος ἐν αὐταῖς μένοντες ταῖς ἐξ ἀρχῆς
χώραις ἀπέθνησκον. οἵ γε μὴν ἅμα τούτοις ἀναμε-
μιγμένοι, δᾷδα καὶ στυππίον καὶ πῦρ ἔχοντες, οὕτω
τολμηρῶς καὶ πανταχόθεν ἅμα προσπίπτοντες ἐνέβαλλον ταῖς μηχαναῖς ὥστε τοὺς Ῥωμαίους εἰς τὸν
ἔσχατον παραγενέσθαι κίνδυνον, μὴ δυναμένους

138

the hour. He ordered all the commanders with the whole of their forces to be on the spot at the morning watch, and his orders having been executed, he led the whole force out as it was getting light and attacked the works in several places. The Romans, who had foreseen what was coming, were not idle or unprepared, but promptly ran to defend the threatened points and opposed a vigorous resistance to the enemy. Soon the whole of both forces were engaged, and a desperate fight was going on all round the walls, the salliers numbering not less than twenty thousand and the force outside being rather more numerous. Inasmuch as they were fighting confusedly and in no order, each man as he thought best, the battle was all the more fierce, such a large force being engaged man to man and company to company, so that there was something of the keenness of single combat in the whole contest. It was, however, particularly at the siege works themselves that there was most shouting and pressure. For those on both sides whose task from the outset was on the one hand to drive the defenders from the works, and on the other not to abandon them, exhibited such emulation and resolution, the assailants doing their very best to turn the Romans out, and the latter refusing to give way, that at last owing to this resolute spirit the men remained and fell on the spot where they had first stood. Yet, in spite of all, the bearers of pinebrands, tow, and fire intermingled with the combatants, attacked the engines from every side, hurling the burning matter at them with such pluck that the Romans were in the utmost

13 κατακρατῆσαι τῆς τῶν ἐναντίων ἐπιβολῆς. ὁ δὲ τῶν
Καρχηδονίων στρατηγός, θεωρῶν ἐν μὲν τῷ κινδύνῳ
πολλοὺς ἀποθνήσκοντας, οὗ δ' ἕνεκα ταῦτ' ἔπραττεν,
14 οὐ δυναμένους κρατῆσαι τῶν ἔργων, ἀνακαλεῖσθαι
τοὺς ἑαυτοῦ παρήγγειλε τοῖς σαλπισταῖς. οἱ δὲ Ῥωμαῖοι παρ' οὐδὲν ἐλθόντες τοῦ πάσας ἀποβαλεῖν τὰς
παρασκευάς, τέλος ἐκράτησαν τῶν ἔργων καὶ πάντα
διετήρησαν ἀσφαλῶς.

46. ὁ μὲν οὖν Ἀννίβας μετὰ τὴν χρείαν ταύτην
ἐξέπλευσε νύκτωρ ἔτι μετὰ τῶν νεῶν λαθὼν τοὺς
πολεμίους εἰς τὰ Δρέπανα πρὸς Ἀτάρβαν τὸν τῶν
2 Καρχηδονίων στρατηγόν. διὰ γὰρ τὴν εὐκαιρίαν τοῦ
τόπου καὶ τὸ κάλλος τοῦ περὶ τὰ Δρέπανα λιμένος ἀεὶ
μεγάλην ἐποιοῦντο σπουδὴν οἱ Καρχηδόνιοι περὶ τὴν
3 φυλακὴν αὐτοῦ. Συμβαίνει δὲ τοῦ Λιλυβαίου τοῦτον
ἀπέχειν τὸν τόπον ὡς ἂν ἑκατὸν καὶ εἴκοσι στάδια.

4 Τοῖς δ' ἐν τῇ Καρχηδόνι βουλομένοις μὲν εἰδέναι
τὰ περὶ τὸ Λιλύβαιον, οὐ δυναμένοις δὲ διὰ τὸ τοὺς
μὲν συγκεκλεῖσθαι, τοὺς δὲ παραφυλάττεσθαι φιλοτίμως, ἐπηγγείλατό τις ἀνὴρ τῶν ἐνδόξων, Ἀννίβας
ἐπικαλούμενος Ῥόδιος, εἰσπλεύσας εἰς τὸ Λιλύβαιον
5 καὶ γενόμενος αὐτόπτης ἅπαντα διασαφήσειν. οἱ δὲ
τῆς ἐπαγγελίας μὲν ἀσμένως ἤκουσαν, οὐ μὴν ἐπί-
στευόν γε διὰ τὸ τῷ στόλῳ τοὺς Ῥωμαίους ἐπὶ τοῦ κατὰ
6 τὸν εἴσπλουν στόματος ἐφορμεῖν. ὁ δὲ καταρτίσας
τὴν ἰδίαν ναῦν ἀνήχθη. καὶ διάρας εἴς τινα τῶν πρὸ
τοῦ Λιλυβαίου κειμένων νήσων, τῇ κατὰ πόδας ἡμέρᾳ
λαβὼν εὐκαίρως ἄνεμον οὔριον περὶ τετάρτην ὥραν

peril, being unable to master the onset of the enemy. But the Carthaginian general, observing that many were falling in the battle, and that his object of taking the works was not being attained, ordered his trumpeters to sound the retreat. Thus the Romans who had come very near losing all their siege material, at length were masters of their works, and remained in secure possession of them.

46. As for Hannibal he sailed out with his ships after the affair while it was still night, unobserved by the enemy, and proceeded to Drepana to meet the Carthaginian commander there, Adherbal. Owing to the convenient situation of Drepana and the excellency of its harbor, the Carthaginians had always given great attention to its protection. The place lies at a distance of about a hundred and twenty stades from Lilybaeum.

The Carthaginians at home wishing to know what was happening at Lilybaeum, but being unable to do so as their own forces were shut up in the town and the Romans were active in their vigilance, one of their leading citizens, Hannibal, surnamed the Rhodian,[80] offered to sail into Lilybaeum and make a full report from personal observation. They listened to his offer eagerly, but did not believe he could do this, as the Romans were anchored outside the mouth of the port. But after fitting out his own ship, he set sail, and crossed to one of the islands that lie before Lilybaeum, and next day finding the wind happily favorable, sailed in at about ten o'clock in the morning in full

[80] The individual whose audacity kept communications between Carthage and the besieged open for some time (46. 4–47. 10); see further 59. 8 and W. Ameling, *Karthago: Studien zu Militär, Staat und Gesellschaft* (Munich 1993) 134–137.

ἀπάντων τῶν πολεμίων ὁρώντων καὶ καταπεπληγμέ-

7 νων τὴν τόλμαν εἰσέπλευσε. καὶ τὴν κατόπιν εὐθέως

8 ἐγίνετο περὶ ἀναγωγήν. ὁ δὲ τῶν Ῥωμαίων στρατηγὸς
βουλόμενος ἐπιμελέστερον τὸν κατὰ τὸν εἴσπλουν
τόπον τηρεῖν, ἐξηρτυκὼς ἐν τῇ νυκτὶ δέκα ναῦς τὰς
ἄριστα πλεούσας, αὐτὸς μὲν ἐπὶ τοῦ λιμένος ἑστὼς
ἐθεώρει τὸ συμβαῖνον, ὁμοίως δὲ καὶ πᾶν τὸ στρα-

9 τόπεδον. αἱ δὲ νῆες τοῦ στόματος ἐξ ἀμφοῖν τοῖν
μεροῖν, ἐφ' ὅσον ἦν δυνατὸν ἔγγιστα τοῖς τενάγεσι
προσάγειν, ἐπεῖχον, ἐπτερωκυῖαι πρὸς τὴν ἐμβολὴν

10 καὶ σύλληψιν τῆς ἐκπλεῖν μελλούσης νεώς. ὁ δὲ Ῥόδιος ἐκ τοῦ προφανοῦς τὴν ἀναγωγὴν ποιησάμενος
οὕτως κατανέστη τῶν πολεμίων τῇ τε τόλμῃ καὶ τῷ
ταχυναυτεῖν ὥστ' οὐ μόνον ἄτρωτον ἐξέπλευσε τὴν
ναῦν ἔχων καὶ τοὺς ἄνδρας, οἷον ἑστῶτα παραδραμὼν

11 τὰ σκάφη τῶν ὑπεναντίων, ἀλλὰ καὶ βραχὺ προ-
πλεύσας ἐπέστη πτερώσας τὴν ναῦν, ὡς ἂν εἰ προκα-

12 λούμενος τοὺς πολεμίους. οὐδενὸς δὲ τολμῶντος ἐπ'
αὐτὸν ἀντανάγεσθαι διὰ τὸ τάχος τῆς εἰρεσίας,
ἀπέπλευσε καταναστὰς μιᾷ νηὶ παντὸς τοῦ τῶν ἐναν-

13 τίων στόλου. καὶ τὸ λοιπὸν ἤδη πλεονάκις ποιῶν
ταὐτὸ τοῦτο μεγάλην χρείαν παρείχετο, τοῖς μὲν Καρχηδονίοις ἀεὶ τὰ κατεπείγοντα διασαφῶν, τοὺς δὲ
πολιορκουμένους εὐθαρσεῖς παρασκευάζων, τοὺς δὲ
Ῥωμαίους καταπληττόμενος τῷ παραβόλῳ.

47. μέγιστα δὲ συνεβάλλετο πρὸς τὴν τόλμαν
αὐτοῦ τὸ διὰ τῶν προβραχέων ἐκ τῆς ἐμπειρίας ἀκρι-

2 βῶς σεσημειῶσθαι τὸν εἴσπλουν. ὑπεράρας γὰρ καὶ

sight of the enemy who were thunderstruck by his audacity. Next day he at once made preparations for departure, but the Roman general, with the view of guarding the entrance more carefully, had fitted out in the night ten of his fastest ships, and now he himself and his whole army stood by the harbor waiting to see what would happen. The ships were waiting on either side of the entrance as near as the shoals would allow them to approach, their oars out and ready to charge and capture, the ship that was about to sail out. But the "Rhodian," getting under weigh in the sight of all, so far outbraved the Romans by his audacity and speed that not only did he bring his ship and her whole crew out unhurt, passing the enemy's ships just as if they were motionless, but after sailing on a short way, he pulled up without shipping his oars as if to challenge the enemy, and no one venturing to come out against him owing to the speed of his rowing, he sailed off, after thus having with one ship successfully defied the whole Roman fleet. After this he several times performed the same feat and was of great service by continuing to report at Carthage the news of most urgent importance, while at the same time he kept up the spirits of the besieged and struck terror into the Romans by his venturesomeness.

47. What tended most to give him confidence was that from experience he had accurately noted the course to be followed through the shoals in entering. For as soon as he

φαινόμενος ἔπειτ᾽ ἂν ἀπὸ τῶν κατὰ τὴν Ἰταλίαν
μερῶν ἐλάμβανε τὸν ἐπὶ τῆς θαλάττης πύργον κατὰ
πρῶρραν οὕτως ὥστε τοῖς πρὸς τὴν Λιβύην τετραμ-
μένοις πύργοις τῆς πόλεως ἐπιπροσθεῖν ἅπασι. δι᾽ οὗ
τρόπου μόνως ἐστὶ δυνατὸν ἐξ οὐρίας τοῦ κατὰ τὸν
3 εἴσπλουν στόματος εὐστοχεῖν. τῇ δὲ τοῦ Ῥοδίου τόλμῃ πιστεύσαντες καὶ πλείους ἀπεθάρρησαν τῶν εἰδό-
των τοὺς τόπους τὸ παραπλήσιον ποιεῖν. ἐξ ὧν οἱ
Ῥωμαῖοι δυσχρηστούμενοι τῷ συμβαίνοντι χωννύειν
4 τὸ στόμα τοῦ λιμένος ἐπεχείρησαν. κατὰ μὲν οὖν τὸ
πλεῖστον μέρος τῆς ἐπιβολῆς οὐδὲν ἤνυον διὰ τὸ
βάθος τῆς θαλάττης καὶ διὰ τὸ μηθὲν δύνασθαι τῶν
ἐμβαλλομένων στῆναι μηδὲ συμμεῖναι τὸ παράπαν,
ἀλλ᾽ ὑπό τε τοῦ κλύδωνος καὶ τῆς τοῦ ῥοῦ βίας τὸ
ῥιπτούμενον εὐθέως ἐν τῇ καταφορᾷ παρωθεῖσθαι καὶ
5 διασκορπίζεσθαι, κατὰ δέ τινα τόπον ἔχοντα βραχέα
συνέστη χῶμα μετὰ πολλῆς ταλαιπωρίας, ἐφ᾽ ᾧ τε-
τρήρης ἐκτρέχουσα νυκτὸς ἐκάθισε καὶ τοῖς πολεμίοις
ὑποχείριος ἐγένετο, διαφέρουσα τῇ κατασκευῇ τῆς
6 ναυπηγίας. ἧς οἱ Ῥωμαῖοι κρατήσαντες καὶ πληρώ-
ματι καταρτίσαντες ἐπιλέκτῳ, πάντας τοὺς εἰσπλέ-
7 οντας, μάλιστα δὲ τὸν Ῥόδιον, ἐπετήρουν. ὁ δὲ κατὰ
τύχην εἰσπλεύσας νυκτὸς μετὰ ταῦτα πάλιν ἀνήγετο
φανερῶς. θεωρῶν δ᾽ ἐκ καταβολῆς αὐτῷ τὴν τετρήρη
8 συνεξορμήσασαν, γνοὺς τὴν ναῦν διετράπη. τὸ μὲν
οὖν πρῶτον ὥρμησεν ὡς καταταχήσων· τῇ δὲ τοῦ
πληρώματος παρασκευῇ καταλαμβανόμενος, τέλος
9 ἐπιστρέψας ἠναγκάσθη συμβαλεῖν τοῖς πολεμίοις.

144

had crossed and come into view, he would get the sea
tower on the Italian side on his bows so that it covered the
whole line of towers turned toward Africa; and this is the
only way that a vessel running before the wind can hit the
mouth of the harbor in entering. Several others who had
local knowledge, gaining confidence from the "Rhodian's"
audacity, undertook to do the same, and in consequence
the Romans, to whom this was a great annoyance, tried to
fill up the mouth of the harbor. For the most part indeed
their attempt was resultless, both owing to the depth of the
sea, and because none of the stuff that they threw in would
remain in its place or hold together in the least, but all they
shot in used to be at once shifted and scattered as it was
sinking to the bottom, by the surge and the force of the
current. However, in one place where there were shoals a
solid bank was formed at the cost of infinite pains, and on
this a four-banked ship which was coming out at night
grounded and fell into the hands of the enemy. This ship
was of remarkably fine build, and the Romans, after capturing it and manning it with a select crew, kept watch for
all the blockade runners and especially for the "Rhodian."
It so happened that he had sailed in that very night, and
was afterward sailing out quite openly, but, on seeing from
the start the four-banked vessel putting out to sea again together with himself and recognizing it, he was alarmed. At
first he made a spurt to get away from it, but finding himself overhauled owing to the good oarsmanship of its crew
he had at length to turn and engage the enemy. Being no

καταπροτερούμενος δὲ τοῖς ἐπιβατικοῖς διά τε τὸ
πλῆθος καὶ διὰ τὴν ἐκλογὴν τῶν ἀνδρῶν, ἐγένετο τοῖς
10 ἐχθροῖς ὑποχείριος. οἱ δὲ Ῥωμαῖοι, κυριεύσαντες καὶ
ταύτης τῆς νεὼς εὖ κατεσκευασμένης, καὶ καταρτίσαντες αὐτὴν τοῖς πρὸς τὴν χρείαν, οὕτως ἐκώλυσαν
τοὺς κατατολμῶντας καὶ πλέοντας εἰς τὸ Λιλύβαιον.

48. Τῶν δὲ πολιορκουμένων ταῖς μὲν ἀντοικοδο-
μίαις ἐνεργῶς χρωμένων, τοῦ δὲ λυμαίνεσθαι καὶ
διαφθείρειν τὰς τῶν ὑπεναντίων παρασκευὰς ἀπεγνω-
2 κότων, γίνεταί τις ἀνέμου στάσις ἔχουσα τηλικαύτην
βίαν καὶ φορὰν εἰς αὐτὰς τὰς τῶν μηχανημάτων
προσαγωγὰς ὥστε καὶ τὰς στοὰς διασαλεύειν καὶ
3 τοὺς προκειμένους τούτων πύργους τῇ βίᾳ βαστάζειν.
ἐν ᾧ καιρῷ συννοήσαντές τινες τῶν Ἑλληνικῶν
μισθοφόρων τὴν ἐπιτηδειότητα τῆς περιστάσεως πρὸς
τὴν τῶν ἔργων διαφθορὰν προσφέρουσι τῷ στρατηγῷ
4 τὴν ἐπίνοιαν. τοῦ δὲ δεξαμένου καὶ ταχέως ἑτοιμάσαν-
τος πᾶν τὸ πρὸς τὴν χρείαν ἁρμόζον, συστραφέντες οἱ
νεανίσκοι κατὰ τριττοὺς τόπους ἐνέβαλον πῦρ τοῖς
5 ἔργοις. ὡς δ' ἂν τῶν μὲν κατασκευασμάτων διὰ τὸν
χρόνον εὖ παρεσκευασμένων πρὸς τὸ ῥᾳδίως ἐμπρη-
σθῆναι, τῆς δὲ τοῦ πνεύματος βίας φυσώσης κατ'
αὐτῶν τῶν πύργων καὶ μηχανημάτων, τὴν μὲν νομὴν
τοῦ πυρὸς ἐνεργὸν συνέβαινε γίνεσθαι καὶ πρακτικήν,
τὴν δ' ἐπάρκειαν καὶ βοήθειαν τοῖς Ῥωμαίοις εἰς
6 τέλος ἄπρακτον καὶ δυσχερῆ. τοιαύτην γὰρ ἔκπληξιν
παρίστα τὸ συμβαῖνον τοῖς βοηθοῦσιν ὥστε μήτε
συννοῆσαι μήτε συνιδεῖν δύνασθαι τὸ γινόμενον, ἀλλ'

match for the boarders, who were numerous and all picked men, he fell into the enemy's hands. His ship was, like the other, very well built, and the Romans when they were in possession of her fitted her out too for this special service and so put a stop to all this venturesome blockade running at Lilybaeum.

48. The besieged were still counterbuilding energetically though they had renounced their effort to spoil or destroy the enemy's works, when there arose a steady wind, blowing with such violence and fury on the actual apparatus for advancing the engines, that it shook the protecting penthouses from their foundations and carried away the wooden towers in front of these by its force. During the gale it struck some of the Greek mercenaries that here was an admirable opportunity for destroying the works, and they communicated their notion to the general, who approved it and made all suitable preparations for the enterprise. The soldiers in several bodies threw fire on the works at three separate points. The whole apparatus being old and readily inflammable, and the wind blowing very strongly on the actual towers and engines, the action of the flames as they spread was most effective, whereas the efforts of the Romans to succor and save the works were quite the reverse, the task being most difficult. The defenders were indeed so terrified by the outbreak that they could neither realize nor understand what was happening,

ἀποσκοτουμένους ὑπὸ τῆς εἰς αὐτοὺς φερομένης
λιγνύος καὶ τῶν ψεψαλύγων, ἔτι δὲ τῆς τοῦ καπνοῦ
πολυπληθίας, οὐκ ὀλίγους ἀπόλλυσθαι καὶ πίπτειν,
μὴ δυναμένους ἐγγίσαι πρὸς αὐτὴν τὴν τοῦ πυρὸς

7 βοήθειαν. ὅσῳ δὲ μείζω συνέβαινε γίνεσθαι τὴν
δυσχρηστίαν περὶ τοὺς ὑπεναντίους διὰ τὰς προειρημένας αἰτίας, τοσούτῳ πλείων εὐχρηστία περὶ

8 τοὺς ἐνιέντας ἦν τὸ πῦρ. τὸ μὲν γὰρ ἐπισκοτοῦν καὶ
βλάπτειν δυνάμενον πᾶν ἐξεφυσᾶτο καὶ προωθεῖτο
κατὰ τῶν ὑπεναντίων, τὸ δὲ βαλλόμενον ἢ ῥιπτούμενον ἐπί τε τοὺς βοηθοῦντας καὶ τὴν τῶν ἔργων
διαφθορὰν εὔστοχον μὲν ἐπεγίνετο διὰ τὸ συνορᾶν
τοὺς ἀφιέντας τὸν πρὸ αὐτῶν τόπον, πρακτικὸν δὲ διὰ
τὸ γίνεσθαι σφοδρὰν τὴν πληγήν, συνεργούσης τοῖς

9 βάλλουσι τῆς τοῦ πνεύματος βίας. τὸ δὲ πέρας τοιαύτην συνέβη γενέσθαι τὴν παντέλειαν τῆς καταφθορᾶς ὥστε καὶ τὰς βάσεις τῶν πύργων καὶ τὰ στύπη

10 τῶν κριῶν ὑπὸ τοῦ πυρὸς ἀχρειωθῆναι. τούτων δὲ
συμβάντων, τὸ μὲν ἔτι διὰ τῶν ἔργων πολιορκεῖν
ἀπέγνωσαν οἱ Ῥωμαῖοι· περιταφρεύσαντες δὲ καὶ
χάρακι περιλαβόντες κύκλῳ τὴν πόλιν, ἔτι δὲ τῆς
ἰδίας στρατοπεδείας τεῖχος προβαλόμενοι, τῷ χρόνῳ

11 παρέδοσαν τὴν πρᾶξιν. οἱ δ' ἐν τῷ Λιλυβαίῳ τὸ
πεπτωκὸς ἐξοικοδομησάμενοι τεῖχος εὐθαρσῶς ὑπέμενον ἤδη τὴν πολιορκίαν.

49. Εἰς δὲ τὴν Ῥώμην προσπεσόντων τούτων, καὶ
μετὰ ταῦτα πλειόνων ἀναγγελλόντων διότι συμβαίνει
τῶν ἀπὸ τοῦ στόλου πληρωμάτων τὸ πλεῖστον μέρος

but half blinded by the flames and sparks that flew in their faces and by the dense smoke, many of them succumbed and fell, unable even to get near enough to combat the actual conflagration. The difficulties that the enemy encountered for these various reasons were immense, while the exertions of the incendiaries were correspondingly facilitated. Everything that could blind or injure the enemy was blown into flame and pushed at them, missiles and other objects hurled or discharged to wound the rescuers or to destroy the works being easily aimed because the throwers could see in front of them, while the blows were most effective as the strong wind gave them additional force. At the end the completeness of the destruction was such that the bases of the towers and the beams of the battering rams were rendered useless by the fire. After this the Romans gave up the attempt to conduct the siege by works, and digging a trench and erecting a stockade all round the city, at the same time building a wall round their own encampment, they left the result to time. But the garrison of Lilybaoum rebuilt the fallen portions of the wall and now confidently awaited the issue of the siege.

49. On the news reaching Rome, and on it being reported from various quarters that the greater part of the crews of their fleet had perished in the works or in the

ἔν τε τοῖς ἔργοις καὶ τῇ καθόλου πολιορκίᾳ διεφθάρ-
2 θαι, σπουδῇ κατέγραφον ναύτας, καὶ συναθροίσαντες
3 εἰς μυρίους ἐξέπεμψαν εἰς τὴν Σικελίαν. ὧν διὰ τοῦ
πορθμοῦ περαιωθέντων καὶ πεζῇ παραγενομένων εἰς
τὸ στρατόπεδον, συναγαγὼν τοὺς χιλιάρχους ὁ στρατηγὸς τῶν Ῥωμαίων Πόπλιος Κλαύδιος ἔφη καιρὸν
4 εἶναι πλεῖν ἐπὶ τὰ Δρέπανα παντὶ τῷ στόλῳ. τὸν γὰρ
στρατηγὸν τῶν Καρχηδονίων Ἀτάρβαν τὸν τεταγμένον ἐπ᾽ αὐτῶν ἀπαράσκευον εἶναι πρὸς τὸ μέλλον,
ἀγνοοῦντα μὲν τὴν παρουσίαν τῶν πληρωμάτων, πε-
πεισμένον δὲ μὴ δύνασθαι πλεῖν τὸν αὐτῶν στόλον
διὰ τὴν γεγενημένην ἐν τῇ πολιορκίᾳ καταφθορὰν τῶν
5 ἀνδρῶν. προχείρως δ᾽ αὐτῶν συγκατατιθεμένων, εὐθέως ἐνεβίβαζε τά τε προϋπάρχοντα καὶ τὰ προσ-
φάτως παραγεγονότα πληρώματα, τοὺς δ᾽ ἐπιβάτας
ἐκ παντὸς ἐπέλεξε τοῦ στρατεύματος ἐθελοντὴν τοὺς
ἀρίστους, ἅτε δὴ τοῦ μὲν πλοῦ σύνεγγυς ὄντος, τῆς δ᾽
6 ὠφελείας ἑτοίμου προφαινομένης. ταῦτα δὲ παρασκευασάμενος ἀνήχθη περὶ μέσας νύκτας, λαθὼν
τοὺς πολεμίους. καὶ τὰς μὲν ἀρχὰς ἄθρους ἔπλει,
7 δεξιὰν ἔχων τὴν γῆν. ἅμα δὲ τῷ φωτὶ τῶν πρώτων ἐπὶ
τὰ Δρέπανα νεῶν ἐπιφαινομένων, κατιδὼν Ἀτάρβας
8 τὸ μὲν πρῶτον ἐξενίσθη διὰ τὸ παράδοξον· ταχὺ δ᾽ ἐν
αὑτῷ γενόμενος, καὶ νοήσας τὸν ἐπίπλουν τῶν ὑπεναντίων, ἔκρινε παντὸς ἔργου πεῖραν λαμβάνειν καὶ πᾶν
ὑπομένειν χάριν τοῦ μὴ περιιδεῖν σφᾶς εἰς πρόδηλον
9 συγκλεισθέντας πολιορκίαν. διόπερ εὐθέως τὰ μὲν
10 πληρώματα συνῆγε πρὸς τὸν αἰγιαλόν, τοὺς δ᾽ ἐκ τῆς

siege operations in general, they set about actively enlist-
ing sailors, and when they had collected about ten thousand dispatched them to Sicily. These reinforcements
were ferried over the Straits and thence proceeded on foot
to the camp, where on their arrival the Roman Consul,
Publius Claudius Pulcher,[81] called a meeting of the Tribunes and told them that now was the time to attack
Drepana with the whole fleet. The Carthaginian general   249 B.C.
Adherbal who commanded there was, he said, unprepared
for such a contingency, as he was ignorant of the arrival of
the crews, and convinced that their fleet was unable to take
the sea owing to the heavy loss of men in the siege. On the
Tribunes readily consenting, he at once embarked the former crews and the new arrivals, and chose for marines the
best men in the whole army, who readily volunteered as
the voyage was but a short one and the prospect of booty
seemed certain. After making these preparations he put to
sea about midnight unobserved by the enemy, and at first
sailed in close order with the land on his right. At daybreak
when the leading ships came into view sailing on Drepana,
Adherbal was at first taken by surprise at the unexpected
sight, but soon recovering his composure and understanding that the enemy had come to attack, he decided to make
every effort and incur every sacrifice rather than expose
himself to the certitude of a blockade. He therefore at
once collected the crews on the beach and summoned by

[81] The Roman attack on Drepana in 249 is followed by naval
defeat at the hands of Adherbal (49. 3–51. 12).

πόλεως μισθοφόρους ἤθροιζε μετὰ κηρύγματος. τῶν
δὲ συλλεχθέντων, ἐπεβάλετο διὰ βραχέων εἰς ἔννοιαν
αὐτοὺς ἄγειν τῆς τε τοῦ νικᾶν ἐλπίδος, ἐὰν τολμήσωσι
11 ναυμαχεῖν, καὶ τῆς ἐν τῇ πολιορκίᾳ δυσχρηστίας, ἐὰν
καταμελλήσωσι προϊδόμενοι τὸν κίνδυνον. ἑτοίμως δ'
αὐτῶν παρορμηθέντων πρὸς τὴν ναυμαχίαν, καὶ
βοώντων ἄγειν καὶ μὴ μέλλειν, ἐπαινέσας καὶ δεξάμε-
12 νος τὴν ὁρμὴν παρήγγειλε κατὰ τάχος ἐμβαίνειν, καὶ
βλέποντας πρὸς τὴν αὐτοῦ ναῦν ἕπεσθαι ταύτῃ κατὰ
πρύμναν. διασαφήσας δὲ τὰ προειρημένα κατὰ σπουδὴν πρῶτος ἐποιεῖτο τὸν ἀνάπλουν, ὑπ' αὐτὰς τὰς
πέτρας ἐπὶ θάτερα μέρη τοῦ λιμένος ἐξάγων τοῦ τῶν
πολεμίων εἴσπλου.

50. Πόπλιος δ' ὁ τῶν Ρωμαίων στρατηγός, θεωρῶν
τοὺς μὲν πολεμίους παρὰ τὴν αὐτοῦ δόξαν οὔτ' εἴκον-
2 τας οὔτε καταπεπληγμένους τὸν ἐπίπλουν, ἀλλὰ πρὸς
τῷ ναυμαχεῖν ὄντας, τῶν δὲ σφετέρων νεῶν τὰς μὲν
ἐντὸς ἤδη τοῦ λιμένος οὔσας, τὰς δ' ἐν αὐτῷ τῷ
3 στόματι, τὰς δὲ φερομένας ἐπὶ τὸν εἴσπλουν, πάσαις
ἀναστρέφειν παρήγγειλε καὶ ποιεῖσθαι τὸν πλοῦν ἔξω
πάλιν. ἔνθα δὴ τῶν μὲν ἐν τῷ λιμένι, τῶν δὲ κατὰ τὸν
εἴσπλουν ἐκ τῆς μεταβολῆς συμπιπτουσῶν, οὐ μόνον
4 θόρυβος ἦν ἐκ τῶν ἀνδρῶν ἄπλετος, ἀλλὰ καὶ τοὺς
ταρσοὺς ἐθραύονθ' αἱ νῆες ἀλλήλαις συγκρούουσαι.
ὅμως δ' οὖν ἀεὶ τοὺς ἀνατρέχοντας ἐκτάττοντες οἱ
τριήραρχοι παρ' αὐτὴν τὴν γῆν ταχέως ἐποίουν ἀντι-
5 πρώρρους τοῖς πολεμίοις. ὁ δὲ Πόπλιος αὐτὸς ἐπέπλει
μὲν ἀρχῆθεν κατόπιν ἐπὶ παντὶ τῷ στόλῳ, τότε δ'

crier the mercenaries from the city. On all being assembled he tried in a few words to impress on their minds the prospect of victory if they risked a battle, and the hardships of a siege should they delay now that they clearly foresaw the danger. Their spirit for the fight was readily aroused, and on their calling on him to lead them on and not delay, he thanked them, praised their zeal, and then ordered them to get on board at once, and keeping their eyes on his ship, to follow in his wake. Having made these orders quite clear to them he quickly got under weigh and took the lead, making his exit close under the rocks on the opposite side of the harbor from that on which the Romans were entering.

50. Publius, the Roman commander, had expected that the enemy would give way and would be intimidated by his attack, but when he saw that on the contrary they intended to fight him, and that his own fleet was partly inside the harbor, partly at the very mouth, and partly still sailing up to enter, he gave orders for them all to put about and sail out again. On the ships already in the harbor fouling those which were entering owing to their sudden turn there was not only great confusion among the men but the ships had the blades of their oars broken as they came into collision. The captains, however, bringing the ships as they cleared the harbor into line, soon drew them up close to the shore with their prows to the enemy. Publius himself from the start had been bringing up the rear of the entire fleet, and

ἐπιστρέψας κατ' αὐτὸν τὸν πλοῦν πρὸς τὸ πέλαγος
6 ἔλαβε τὴν εὐώνυμον τῆς ὅλης δυνάμεως τάξιν. Ἀτάρβας δὲ κατὰ τὸν αὐτὸν καιρὸν ὑπεράρας τὸ λαιὸν τῶν
πολεμίων ['Ρωμαίων], ἔχων πέντε ναῦς ἐπίπλους, ὑπέ-
στησε τὴν ἑαυτοῦ ναῦν ἀντίπρωρον τοῖς πολεμίοις
7 ἀπὸ τοῦ κατὰ τὸ πέλαγος μέρους· ἅμα δὲ καὶ τῶν
ἐπιπλεόντων ἀεὶ τοῖς συνάπτουσι προσεπιταττομένοις
8 ταὐτὸ ποιεῖν παραγγείλας διά τῶν ὑπηρετῶν, κατα-
στάντων δὲ πάντων εἰς μέτωπον σημήνας διὰ τῶν
συνθημάτων, τὰς μὲν ἀρχὰς ἐποιεῖτο τὸν ἐπίπλουν ἐν
9 τάξει, μενόντων πρὸς τῇ γῇ τῶν 'Ρωμαίων διὰ τὸ
προσδέχεσθαι τὰς ἐκ τοῦ λιμένος ἀνατρεχούσας ναῦς.
ἐξ οὗ συνέβαινε μεγάλα τοὺς 'Ρωμαίους ἐλαττωθῆναι
πρὸς αὐτῇ τῇ γῇ ποιησαμένους τὴν συμπλοκήν.

51. ἐπειδὴ δὲ σύνεγγυς αὐτῶν ἦσαν, ἀρθέντων τῶν
συνθημάτων ἐφ' ἑκατέρας τῆς ναυαρχίδος, συνέβαλ-
2 λον ἀλλήλοις. τὸ μὲν οὖν πρῶτον ἰσόρροπος ἦν ὁ
3 κίνδυνος, ὡς ἂν ἀμφοτέρων τοῖς ἀρίστοις ἐκ τῆς
πεζικῆς δυνάμεως ἐπιβάταις χρωμένων· ἀεὶ δὲ μᾶλλον
4 ὑπερεῖχον οἱ Καρχηδόνιοι διὰ τὸ πολλὰ προτερήματα
παρ' ὅλον ἔχειν τὸν ἀγῶνα. τῷ τε γὰρ ταχυναυτεῖν
πολὺ περιῆσαν διὰ τὴν διαφορὰν τῆς ναυπηγίας καὶ
τὴν τῶν πληρωμάτων ἕξιν, ἥ τε χώρα μεγάλα συν-
5 εβάλλετ' αὐτοῖς, ἅτε πεποιημένων τὴν ἔκταξιν ἀπὸ
τῶν κατὰ τὸ πέλαγος τόπων. εἴτε γὰρ πιέζοιντό τινες
ὑπὸ τῶν πολεμίων, κατόπιν ἀνεχώρουν ἀσφαλῶς διὰ τὸ
6 ταχυναυτεῖν εἰς τὸν ἀναπεπταμένον τόπον· κἄπειτ' ἐκ
μεταβολῆς τοῖς προπίπτουσι τῶν διωκόντων, τοτὲ μὲν

now veering out to sea without stopping his course, took up a position on the extreme left. At the same time Adherbal, outflanking the enemy's left with five beaked ships, placed his own ship facing the enemy from the direction of the open sea. As the other ships came up and joined getting into line, he ordered them by his staff officers to place themselves in the same position as his own, and when they all presented a united front he gave the signal to advance that had been agreed upon and at first bore down in line on the Romans, who kept close to the shore awaiting those of their ships that were returning from the harbor. This position close inshore placed them at a great disadvantage in the engagement.

51. When the two fleets approached each other, the signals for battle were raised on both the admirals, and they closed. At first the battle was equally balanced, as the marines in both fleets were the very best men of their land forces; but the Carthaginians gradually began to get the best of it as they had many advantages throughout the whole struggle. They much surpassed the Romans in speed, owing to the superior build of their ships and the better training of the rowers, and their position was very favorable to them, as they had freely developed their line in the open sea. For if any ships found themselves hard pressed by the enemy it was easy for them owing to their speed to retreat safely to the open water and from thence, fetching round on the the foremost of their pursuers, they

περιπλέοντες, τοτὲ δὲ πλάγιοι προσπίπτοντες στρε-
φομένοις καὶ δυσχρηστοῦσι διὰ τὸ βάρος τῶν πλοίων
7 καὶ διὰ τὴν ἀπειρίαν τῶν πληρωμάτων ἐμβολάς τε
συνεχεῖς ἐδίδοσαν καὶ πολλὰ τῶν σκαφῶν ἐβάπτιζον·
εἴτε κινδυνεύοι τις τῶν συμμάχων, ἑτοίμως παρεβοήθουν ἔξω τοῦ δεινοῦ καὶ μετ' ἀσφαλείας, παρὰ τὰς
8 πρύμνας κατὰ τὸ πέλαγος ποιούμενοι τὸν πλοῦν. τοῖς
γε μὴν Ῥωμαίοις τἀναντία τούτων συνέβαινε· τοῖς τε
γὰρ πιεζομένοις οὐκ ἦν εἰς τοὔπισθεν δυνατὸν ἀποχωρεῖν, πρὸς τῇ γῇ ποιουμένοις τὸν κίνδυνον, ἀεὶ δὲ
τὸ θλιβόμενον ὑπὸ τῶν κατὰ πρόσωπον σκάφος ἢ τοῖς
βραχέσι περιπῖπτον ἐκάθιζε κατὰ πρύμναν ἢ πρὸς
9 τὴν γῆν φερόμενον ἐπώκελλε. διεκπλεῖν μὲν οὖν διὰ
τῶν πολεμίων νεῶν καὶ κατόπιν ἐπιφαίνεσθαι τοῖς ἤδη
πρὸς ἑτέρους διαμαχομένοις, ὅπερ ἐν τῷ ναυμαχεῖν
ἐστι πρακτικώτατον, ἀδυνάτως εἶχον, διά τε τὴν βα-
ρύτητα τῶν πλοίων, προσέτι δὲ καὶ τὴν ἀπειρίαν τῶν
10 πληρωμάτων. οὐδὲ μὴν ἐπιβοηθεῖν τοῖς δεομένοις
κατὰ πρύμναν ἐδύναντο διὰ τὸ συγκεκλεῖσθαι πρὸς τῇ
γῇ καὶ μηδὲ μικρὸν ἀπολείπεσθαι τόπον τοῖς βουλο-
11 μένοις ἐπαρκεῖν τῷ δεομένῳ. τοιαύτης δὲ δυσχρηστίας ὑπαρχούσης περὶ τὸν ὅλον ἀγῶνα, καὶ τῶν μὲν
καθιζόντων ἐν τοῖς βραχέσι, τῶν δ' ἐκπιπτόντων σκαφῶν, κατιδὼν ὁ στρατηγὸς τῶν Ῥωμαίων τὸ συμβαῖνον, ὥρμησε πρὸς φυγήν, ἀπὸ τῶν εὐωνύμων παρὰ
τὴν γῆν ἐξελίξας, καὶ σὺν αὐτῷ περὶ τριάκοντα νῆες,
12 αἵπερ ἔτυχον ἐγγὺς οὖσαι. τῶν δὲ λοιπῶν σκαφῶν,
ὄντων ἐνενήκοντα καὶ τριῶν, ἐκυρίευσαν οἱ Καρχηδό-

either got in their rear or attacked them on the flank, and as the enemy then had to turn round and found themselves in difficulty owing to the weight of the hulls and the poor oarsmanship of the crews, they rammed them repeatedly and sunk many. Again if any other of their own ships were in peril they were ready to render assistance with perfect security to themselves, as they were out of immediate danger and could sail in open water past the sterns of their own line. It was, however, just the opposite with the Romans. Those in distress could not retire backward, as they were fighting close to the land, and the ships, hard pressed by the enemy in front, either ran on the shallows stern foremost or made for the shore and grounded. To sail on the one hand through the enemy's line and then appear on the stern of such of his ships as were engaged with others (one of the most effective manœuvres in naval warfare) was impossible owing to the weight of the vessels and their crews' lack of skill. Nor again could they give assistance where it was required from astern, as they were hemmed in close to the shore, and there was not even a small space left for those who wished to come to the rescue of their comrades in distress. Such being their difficult position in every part of the battle, and some of the ships grounding on the shallows while others ran ashore, the Roman commander, when he saw what was happening, took to flight, slipping out on the left along shore, accompanied by about thirty of the ships nearest to him. The remainder, ninety-three in number, were captured by the Carthaginians, including

νιοι, καὶ τῶν πληρωμάτων, ὅσοι μὴ τῶν ἀνδρῶν τὰς
ναῦς εἰς τὴν γῆν ἐκβαλόντες ἀπεχώρησαν.

52. Γενομένης δὲ τῆς ναυμαχίας τοιαύτης, Ἀτάρβας μὲν εὐδοκίμει παρὰ τοῖς Καρχηδονίοις, ὡς δι᾽
αὑτὸν καὶ διὰ τὴν ἰδίαν πρόνοιαν καὶ τόλμαν κατωρ-
2 θωκώς, Πόπλιος δὲ παρὰ τοῖς Ῥωμαίοις ἠδόξει καὶ
διεβέβλητο μεγάλως, ὡς εἰκῇ κἀλογίστως τοῖς πράγμασι κεχρημένος, καὶ τὸ καθ᾽ αὑτὸν οὐ μικροῖς
3 ἐλαττώμασι περιβεβληκὼς τὴν Ῥώμην· διὸ καὶ μετὰ
ταῦτα μεγάλαις ζημίαις καὶ κινδύνοις κριθεὶς περι-
έπεσεν.

4 Οὐ μὴν οἵ γε Ῥωμαῖοι, καίπερ τοιούτων συμβεβηκότων, διὰ τὴν ὑπὲρ τῶν ὅλων φιλοτιμίαν οὐδὲν ἀπέλειπον τῶν ἐνδεχομένων, ἀλλ᾽ εἴχοντο τῶν ἑξῆς
5 πραγμάτων. διὸ καὶ συνάψαντος τοῦ κατὰ τὰς ἀρχαι-
ρεσίας χρόνου, στρατηγοὺς ὑπάτους καταστήσαντες
παραυτίκα τὸν ἕτερον αὐτῶν ἐξέπεμπον Λεύκιον Ἰού-
νιον, τάς τε σιταρχίας παρακομίζοντα τοῖς τὸ Λιλύβαιον πολιορκοῦσι καὶ τὰς ἄλλας ἀγορὰς καὶ
χορηγίας τῷ στρατοπέδῳ· πρὸς δὲ καὶ παραπομποὺς
6 τούτοις ἐπλήρωσαν ἑξήκοντα ναῦς· ὁ δ᾽ Ἰούνιος ἀφικόμενος εἰς τὴν Μεσσήνην, καὶ προσλαβὼν τὰ συν-
ηντηκότα τῶν πλοίων ἀπό τε τοῦ στρατοπέδου καὶ τῆς
ἄλλης Σικελίας, παρεκομίσθη κατὰ σπουδὴν εἰς τὰς
Συρακούσας, ἔχων ἑκατὸν εἴκοσι σκάφη καὶ τὴν ἀγο-
7 ρὰν σχεδὸν ἐν ὀκτακοσίαις ναυσὶ φορτηγοῖς. ἐντεῦθεν
δὲ παραδοὺς τοῖς ταμίαις τὰς ἡμισείας φορτηγοὺς καί
τινα τῶν μακρῶν πλοίων ἐξαπέστειλε, διακομισθῆναι

their crews, with the exception of those men who ran their ships ashore and made off.

52. The battle having resulted so, Adherbal gained a high reputation at Carthage, the success being regarded as due to his foresight and boldness. Publius, on the contrary, fell into ill repute among the Romans, and there was a great outcry against him for having acted rashly and inconsiderately and done all a single man could to bring a great disaster on Rome. He was accordingly brought to trial afterward, condemned to a heavy fine, and narrowly escaped with his life.

Yet so determined were the Romans to bring the whole struggle to a successful issue, that, notwithstanding this reverse, they left undone nothing that was in their power, and prepared to continue the campaign. The time for the elections was now at hand, and accordingly when the new Consuls were appointed they dispatched one of them, Lucius Junius Pullus,[82] with corn for the besiegers of Lilybaeum and such other provisions and supplies as the army required, manning sixty ships to act as a convoy to him. Junius, on arriving at Messene and being joined by the ships from Lilybaeum and the rest of Sicily, coasted along with all speed to Syracuse, having now a hundred and twenty ships and the supplies in about eight hundred transports. There he entrusted half the transports and a few of the warships to the Quaestors and sent them on, as

[82] He was, in fact, consul the previous year; see WC 1. 115.

8 σπουδάζων τῷ στρατοπέδῳ τὰ πρὸς τὴν χρείαν. αὐτὸς
δ' ἐν ταῖς Συρακούσαις ὑπέμενε, τούς τε κατὰ πλοῦν
ἀφυστεροῦντας ἐκ τῆς Μεσσήνης ἀναδεχόμενος καὶ
παρὰ τῶν ἐκ τῆς μεσογαίου συμμάχων σῖτον προσ-
αναλαμβάνων.

53. Κατὰ δὲ τοὺς αὐτοὺς καιροὺς Ἀτάρβας μὲν
ἄνδρας τοὺς ἐν τῇ ναυμαχίᾳ ληφθέντας καὶ τὰς αἰχμ-
2 αλώτους νῆας ἐξαπέστειλεν εἰς τὴν Καρχηδόνα, Καρθάλωνα δὲ τὸν συνάρχοντα δοὺς τριάκοντα ναῦς
ἐξέπεμψε πρὸς αἷς ἔχων αὐτὸς ἑβδομήκοντα κατ-
3 έπλευσε, προστάξας ἄφνω προσπεσόντα ταῖς ὁρμού-
σαις παρὰ τὸ Λιλύβαιον τῶν πολεμίων ναυσίν, ὧν μὲν
ἂν δυνατὸς ᾖ κυριεῦσαι, ταῖς δὲ λοιπαῖς πῦρ ἐμβα-
4 λεῖν. πεισθέντος δὲ τοῦ Καρθάλωνος καὶ ποιησαμένου
τὸν ἐπίπλουν ὑπὸ τὴν ἑωθινήν, καὶ τὰ μὲν ἐμπιπρῶν-
τος, τὰ δ' ἀποσπῶντος τῶν πλοίων, μεγάλην συνέπεσε
γενέσθαι ταραχὴν περὶ τὸ τῶν Ῥωμαίων στρατό-
5 πεδον. προσβοηθούντων γὰρ αὐτῶν ἐπὶ τὰς ναῦς καὶ
γινομένης κραυγῆς, συννοήσας Ἰμίλκων ὁ τὸ Λιλύβαιον τηρῶν, καὶ θεωρῶν ἤδη τῆς ἡμέρας ὑποφαινού-
σης τὸ συμβαῖνον, ἐπαποστέλλει τοὺς ἐκ τῆς πόλεως
6 μισθοφόρους. οἱ δὲ Ῥωμαῖοι, τοῦ δεινοῦ πανταχόθεν
αὐτοὺς περιστάντος, οὐκ εἰς μικρὰν οὐδ' εἰς τὴν τυ-
7 χοῦσαν ἦλθον διατροπήν. ὁ δὲ τῶν Καρχηδονίων
ναύαρχος, ὀλίγα τῶν σκαφῶν τὰ μὲν ἀποσπάσας, τὰ
δὲ συντρίψας, μετὰ ταῦτα μικρὸν ἀπὸ τοῦ Λιλυβαίου
παρακομισθεὶς ὡς ἐφ' Ἡρακλείας ἐτήρει, βουλόμενος
8 διακωλύειν τοὺς ἐπὶ τὸ στρατόπεδον πλέοντας. προσ-

he was anxious to have what the troops required conveyed to them at once. He himself remained in Syracuse waiting for the ships that were left behind on the voyage from Messene and procuring additional supplies and corn from the allies in the interior.

53. At about the same time Adherbal sent the prisoners from the naval battle and the captured ships to Carthage, and giving Carthalo his colleague thirty vessels in addition to the seventy with which he had arrived, dispatched him with orders to make a sudden descent on the enemy's ships that were moored near Lilybaeum, capture all he could and set fire to the rest. When Carthalo acting on these orders made the attack at dawn and began to burn some of the ships and carry off others, there was a great commotion in the Roman camp. For as they rushed to rescue the ships with loud cries, Himilco, on the watch at Lilybaeum, heard them, and as day was just beginning to break, he saw what was happening, and sent out the mercenaries from the town to attack the Romans also. The Romans were now in danger from all sides and in no little or ordinary distress. The Carthaginian admiral, satisfied at having either towed off or broken up some few of the vessels, shortly afterward left Lilybaeum, and after coasting along for some distance in the direction of Heraclea remained on the watch, as his design was to intercept the ships that were on their way to join the army. When his lookout men reported that a con-

αγγειλάντων δὲ τῶν σκοπῶν πλῆθος ἱκανὸν πλοίων
προσφέρεσθαι παντοδαπῶν καὶ συνεγγίζειν, ἀναχθεὶς
ἔπλει, συμμῖξαι σπεύδων διὰ τὸ καταφρονεῖν τῶν

9 Ῥωμαίων ἐκ τοῦ προγεγενημένου προτερήματος.
ὁμοίως δὲ καὶ τοῖς ἐκ τῶν Συρακουσῶν προαπεσταλ-
μένοις ταμίαις ἀνήγγειλαν οἱ προπλεῖν εἰθισμένοι

10 λέμβοι τὸν ἐπίπλουν τῶν ὑπεναντίων. οἱ δὲ νομίσαντες οὐκ ἀξιόχρεως σφᾶς αὐτοὺς εἶναι πρὸς ναυμαχίαν, καθωρμίσθησαν πρός τι πολισμάτιον τῶν ὑπ᾽
αὐτοὺς ταττομένων, ἀλίμενον μέν, σάλους δ᾽ ἔχον καὶ

11 προβολὰς περικλειούσας ἐκ τῆς γῆς εὐφυεῖς. οὗ ποιησάμενοι τὴν ἀπόβασιν, καὶ τούς τε καταπέλτας καὶ
τοὺς πετροβόλους τοὺς ἐκ τῆς πόλεως ἐπιστήσαντες,

12 προσεδόκων τὸν ἐπίπλουν τῶν ὑπεναντίων. οἱ δὲ Καρχηδόνιοι συνεγγίσαντες τὸ μὲν πρῶτον ἐπεβάλοντο
πολιορκεῖν τούτους, ὑπολαβόντες τοὺς μὲν ἄνδρας
καταπλαγέντας εἰς τὸ πολισμάτιον ἀποχωρήσειν, τῶν

13 δὲ πλοίων ἀσφαλῶς κυριεύσειν· οὐ προχωρούσης δὲ
τῆς ἐλπίδος, ἀλλὰ τοὐναντίον ἀμυνομένων γενναίως,
καὶ τοῦ τόπου πολλὰς ἔχοντος καὶ παντοδαπὰς δυσχρηστίας, ὀλίγα τῶν τὰς ἀγορὰς ἐχόντων πλοίων
ἀποσπάσαντες ἀπέπλευσαν πρός τινα ποταμόν, ἐν ᾧ
καθορμισθέντες ἐπετήρουν τὸν ἀνάπλουν αὐτῶν.

54. Ὁ δ᾽ ἐν ταῖς Συρακούσαις ὑπολειφθεὶς στρατηγός, ἐπεὶ τὰ κατὰ τὴν πρόθεσιν ἐπετέλεσε, κάμψας τὸν
Πάχυνον ἐποιεῖτο τὸν πλοῦν ὡς ἐπὶ τὸ Λιλύβαιον,
οὐδὲν εἰδὼς τῶν περὶ τοὺς προπλέοντας συμβεβη-

siderable number of ships of every variety were approaching and at no great distance,[83] he got under weigh and sailed toward them eager to engage them, as after the recent success he had great contempt for the Romans. The approach of the enemy was also announced by the light boats that usually sail in front of a fleet to the Quaestors who had been sent on in advance from Syracuse. Considering themselves not strong enough to accept a battle, they anchored off a certain small fortified town subject to the Romans, which had indeed no harbor, but a roadstead shut in by headlands projecting from the land in a manner that made it a more or less secure anchorage. Here they disembarked, and setting up the catapults and mangonels procured from the fortress, awaited the enemy's attack. The Carthaginians on their approach at first thought of besieging them, supposing that the crews would be afraid and retreat to the city, and that they would then easily possess themselves of the ships; but when their hopes were not realized, the enemy on the contrary making a gallant defense, and the situation of the place presenting many difficulties of every kind, they carried off a few of the ships laden with provisions and sailed away to a certain river where they anchored, and waited for the Romans to put out to sea again.

54. The Consul, who had remained in Syracuse, when he had concluded his business there, rounded Cape Pachynus and sailed in the direction of Lilybaeum in entire ignorance of what had befallen the advance force. The

[83] A second Roman fleet, having avoided battle, is lost in a storm (through 54. 8). Once again, the Romans relinquish the sea (55. 2).

2 κότων. ὁ δὲ τῶν Καρχηδονίων ναύαρχος, σημηνάντων
τῶν σκοπῶν αὐτῷ πάλιν τὴν ἐπιφάνειαν τῶν ὑπεναντίων, ἀναχθεὶς ἔπλει μετὰ σπουδῆς, βουλόμενος αὐτοῖς ὡς πλεῖστον ἀπέχουσι τῶν οἰκείων νεῶν συμ-
3 βαλεῖν. ὁ δ' Ἰούνιος κατιδὼν ἐκ πολλοῦ τὸν στόλον
τὸν τῶν Καρχηδονίων καὶ τὸ πλῆθος τῶν σκαφῶν,
οὔτε συμβαλεῖν τολμῶν οὔτ' ἐκφυγεῖν ἔτι δυνατὸς ὢν
διὰ τὸ σύνεγγυς εἶναι τοὺς πολεμίους, ἐγκλίνας εἰς
τόπους τραχεῖς καὶ κατὰ πάντα τρόπον ἐπισφαλεῖς
4 καθωρμίσθη, κρίνων αἱρετώτερον ὑπάρχειν ὅ τι δέοι
παθεῖν μᾶλλον ἢ τοῖς πολεμίοις αὔτανδρον τὸ σφέτε-
5 ρον στρατόπεδον ὑποχείριον ποιῆσαι. συνιδὼν δὲ καὶ
τὸ περὶ τούτου γεγονὸς ὁ τῶν Καρχηδονίων ναύαρχος,
τὸ μὲν παραβάλλεσθαι καὶ προσάγειν τοιούτοις τόποις ἀπεδοκίμασε, λαβὼν δ' ἄκραν τινὰ καὶ προσορ-
μισθεὶς ταύτῃ, μεταξὺ τῶν στόλων ἐτήρει καὶ προσ-
6 εἶχε τὸν νοῦν ἀμφοτέροις. ἐπιγενομένου δὲ χειμῶνος
καὶ περιστάσεως προφαινομένης ἐκ τοῦ πελάγους
ὁλοσχερεστέρας, οἱ μὲν τῶν Καρχηδονίων κυβερνῆ-
ται διά τε τὴν τῶν τόπων καὶ τὴν τοῦ πράγματος
ἐμπειρίαν προορώμενοι τὸ μέλλον καὶ προλέγοντες τὸ
συμβησόμενον, ἔπεισαν τὸν Καρθάλωνα φυγεῖν τὸν
7 χειμῶνα καὶ κάμψαι τὴν ἄκραν τοῦ Παχύνου. πεισθέντος δὲ νουνεχῶς, οὗτοι μὲν πολλὰ μοχθήσαντες καὶ
μόλις ὑπεράραντες τὴν ἄκραν ἐν ἀσφαλεῖ καθωρ-
8 μίσθησαν, οἱ δὲ τῶν Ῥωμαίων στόλοι, τοῦ χειμῶνος
ἐπιγενομένου καὶ τῶν τόπων εἰς τέλος ὑπαρχόντων
ἀλιμένων, οὕτως διεφθάρησαν ὥστε μηδὲ τῶν ναυαγί-

Carthaginian admiral, when his lookouts again reported that the enemy were in sight, put to sea and sailed with all haste, as he wished to engage them at as great a distance as possible from their own ships. Junius had sighted the Carthaginian fleet for some time, and noticed the number of their ships, but he neither dared to engage them nor could he now escape them, as they were so near. He therefore diverted his course to a rugged and in every way perilous part of the coast and anchored there, thinking that, no matter what happened to him, it would be preferable to his whole force of ships and men falling into the hands of the enemy. The Carthaginian admiral, on seeing what Junius had done, decided not to incur the risk of approaching such a dangerous shore, but, gaining a certain cape and anchoring off it, remained on the alert between the two fleets, keeping his eye on both. When the weather now became stormy, and they were threatened with a heavy gale from the open sea, the Carthaginian captains who were acquainted with the locality and with the weather signs, and foresaw and prophesied what was about to happen, persuaded Carthalo to escape the tempest by rounding Cape Pachynus. He very wisely consented, and with great labor they just managed to get round the cape and anchor in a safe position. But the two Roman fleets, caught by the tempest, and the coast affording no shelter at all, were so completely destroyed that not even the wrecks were good for

ων μηδὲν γενέσθαι χρήσιμον, ἀλλ᾽ ἀμφοτέρους αὐτοὺς ἄρδην καὶ παραλόγως ἀχρειωθῆναι.

55. Τούτου δὲ συμβάντος, τὰ μὲν τῶν Καρχηδονίων αὖθις ἀνέκυψε καὶ πάλιν ἐπιρρεπεστέρας εἶχε
2 τὰς ἐλπίδας, οἱ δὲ Ῥωμαῖοι, πρότερον μὲν ἐπὶ ποσὸν
ἠτυχηκότες, τότε δ᾽ ὁλοσχερῶς, ἐκ μὲν τῆς θαλάττης
ἐξέβησαν, τῶν δ᾽ ὑπαίθρων ἐπεκράτουν· Καρχηδόνιοι
δὲ τῆς μὲν θαλάττης ἐκυρίευον, τῆς δὲ γῆς οὐχ ὅλως
3 ἀπήλπιζον. μετὰ δὲ ταῦτα πάντες ἐπὶ μὲν τοῖς ὅλοις
ἐσχετλίαζον, οἵ τ᾽ ἐν τῇ Ῥώμῃ καὶ τὰ περὶ τὸ Λιλύ-
4 βαιον στρατόπεδα, διὰ τὰ προειρημένα συμπτώματα·
τῆς γε μὴν προθέσεως οὐκ ἀφίσταντο τῆς κατὰ τὴν
πολιορκίαν, ἀλλ᾽ οἱ μὲν ἐχορήγουν κατὰ γῆν ἀπροφασίστως, οἱ δὲ προσεκαρτέρουν ταύτῃ κατὰ τὸ δυνα-
5 τόν. ὁ δ᾽ Ἰούνιος, ἀνακομισθεὶς ἐπὶ τὸ στρατόπεδον ἐκ
τῆς ναυαγίας καὶ περιπαθὴς ὤν, ἐγένετο πρὸς τὸ
καινοτομῆσαί τι καὶ πρᾶξαι τῶν δεόντων, σπουδάζων
6 ἀναμαχέσασθαι τὴν γεγενημένην περιπέτειαν. διὸ καὶ
βραχείας αὐτῷ παραπεσούσης ἀφορμῆς, καταλαμβάνει πραξικοπήσας τὸν Ἔρυκα, καὶ γίνεται τοῦ τε
7 τῆς Ἀφροδίτης ἱεροῦ καὶ τῆς πόλεως ἐγκρατής. ὁ δ᾽
Ἔρυξ ἔστι μὲν ὄρος παρὰ θάλατταν τῆς Σικελίας ἐν
τῇ παρὰ τὴν Ἰταλίαν κειμένῃ πλευρᾷ μεταξὺ Δρεπάνων καὶ Πανόρμου, μᾶλλον δ᾽ ὅμορον καὶ συνάπτον
πρὸς τὰ Δρέπανα, μεγέθει δὲ παρὰ πολὺ διαφέρον τῶν
8 κατὰ τὴν Σικελίαν ὀρῶν πλὴν τῆς Αἴτνης. τούτου δ᾽
ἐπ᾽ αὐτῆς μὲν τῆς κορυφῆς, οὔσης ἐπιπέδου, κεῖται τὸ
τῆς Ἀφροδίτης τῆς Ἐρυκίνης ἱερόν, ὅπερ ὁμολογου-

anything. In this unlooked for manner, then, the Romans had both their fleets disabled.

55. Owing to this occurrence the hopes of the Carthaginians rose again, and it seemed to them that the fortune of war was inclining in their favor, while the Romans, on the contrary, who had been previously to a certain extent unlucky but never had met with so complete a disaster, relinquished the sea, while continuing to maintain their hold on the country. The Carthaginians were now masters of the sea and were not hopeless of regaining their position on land. Subsequently, though all, both at Rome and in the army of Lilybaeum, continued to lament their whole situation after these recent defeats, yet they did not abandon their purpose of pursuing the siege, the government not hesitating to send supplies over land, the besiegers thereby keeping up the investment as well as they could. Junius, returning to the army after the shipwreck in a state of great affliction, set himself to devise some novel and original step that would be of service, being most anxious to make good the loss inflicted by the disaster. Therefore on some slight pretext offering itself, he surprised and occupied Eryx,[84] possessing himself both of the temple of Venus and of the town. Eryx is a mountain near the sea on that side of Sicily which looks toward Italy. It is situated between Drepana and Panormus, or rather it is adjacent to Drepana, on the borders, and is much the biggest mountain in Sicily after Etna.[85] On its summit, which is flat, stands the temple of Venus Erycina, which is indisputably

[84] Roman occupation of Eryx (today Mt. San Giuliano) leads in 247 (56. 2) to a protracted struggle with Hamilcar Barcas.

[85] Not true, but generally believed in antiquity.

μένως ἐπιφανέστατόν ἐστι τῷ τε πλούτῳ καὶ τῇ λοιπῇ
9 προστασίᾳ τῶν κατὰ τὴν Σικελίαν ἱερῶν· ἡ δὲ πόλις
ὑπ᾽ αὐτὴν τὴν κορυφὴν τέταται, πάνυ μακρὰν ἔχουσα
10 καὶ προσάντη πανταχόθεν τὴν ἀνάβασιν. ἐπί τε δὴ
τὴν κορυφὴν ἐπιστήσας φυλακήν, ὁμοίως δὲ καὶ τὴν
ἀπὸ Δρεπάνων πρόσβασιν, ἐτήρει φιλοτίμως ἀμφοτέρους τοὺς τόπους, καὶ μᾶλλον ἔτι τὸν τῆς ἀναβολῆς,
πεπεισμένος οὕτως καὶ τὴν πόλιν ἀσφαλῶς καὶ τὸ
σύμπαν ὄρος ὑφ᾽ αὑτὸν ἕξειν.

56. Οἱ δὲ Καρχηδόνιοι μετὰ ταῦτα στρατηγὸν
καταστήσαντες αὑτῶν Ἀμίλκαν τὸν Βάρκαν ἐπικα-
2 λούμενον, τούτῳ τὰ κατὰ τὸν στόλον ἐνεχείρισαν· ὃς
παραλαβὼν τὰς ναυτικὰς δυνάμεις ὥρμησε πορθή-
σων τὴν Ἰταλίαν. ἔτος δ᾽ ἦν ὀκτωκαιδέκατον τῷ πολέ-
3 μῳ. κατασύρας δὲ τὴν Λοκρίδα καὶ τὴν Βρεττιανὴν
χώραν, ἀποπλέων ἐντεῦθεν κατῆρε παντὶ τῷ στόλῳ
πρὸς τὴν Πανορμῖτιν, καὶ καταλαμβάνει τὸν ἐπὶ τῆς
Εἵρκτης λεγόμενον τόπον, ὃς κεῖται μὲν Ἔρυκος καὶ
Πανόρμου μεταξὺ πρὸς θαλάττῃ, πολὺ δέ τι τῶν
ἄλλων δοκεῖ διαφέρειν τόπων ἐπιτηδειότητι πρὸς
4 ἀσφάλειαν στρατοπέδων καὶ χρονισμόν. ἔστι γὰρ
ὄρος περίτομον ἐξανεστηκὸς ἐκ τῆς περικειμένης χώρας εἰς ὕψος ἱκανόν. τούτου δ᾽ ἡ περίμετρος τῆς ἄνω
στεφάνης οὐ λείπει τῶν ἑκατὸν σταδίων, ὑφ᾽ ἧς ὁ
περιεχόμενος τόπος εὔβοτος ὑπάρχει καὶ γεωργήσι-
μος, πρὸς μὲν τὰς πελαγίους πνοιὰς εὐφυῶς κείμενος,
5 θανασίμων δὲ θηρίων εἰς τέλος ἄμοιρος. περιέχεται δὲ
κρημνοῖς ἀπροσίτοις ἔκ τε τοῦ κατὰ θάλατταν μέρους

the first in wealth and general magnificence of all the Sicilian holy places. The city extends along the hill under the actual summit, the ascent to it being very long and steep on all sides. He garrisoned the summit and also the approach from Drepana, and jealously guarded both these positions, especially the latter, in the conviction that by this means he would securely hold the city and the whole mountain.

56. The Carthaginians shortly afterward appointed Hamilcar surnamed Barcas to the command and entrusted naval operations to him. He started with the fleet to ravage the Italian coast (this, I should say, was in the eighteenth year of the war) and after laying waste Locris and the Bruttii quitted those parts and descended with his whole fleet on the territory of Panormus. Here he seized on a place called Hercte lying near the sea between Eryx and Panormus, and thought to possess peculiar advantages for the safe and prolonged stay of an army. It is an abrupt hill rising to a considerable height from the surrounding flat country. The circumference of its brow is not less than a hundred stades and the plateau within affords good pasturage and is suitable for cultivation, lying well protected against the sharp sea breezes and quite free of animals dangerous to life. On the side looking to the sea and on that

καὶ τοῦ παρὰ τὴν μεσόγαιαν παρήκοντος, τὰ δὲ μεταξὺ τούτων ἐστὶν ὀλίγης καὶ βραχείας δεόμενα κατα-
6 σκευῆς. ἔχει δ' ἐν αὐτῷ καὶ μαστόν, ὃς ἅμα μὲν
ἀκροπόλεως, ἅμα δὲ σκοπῆς εὐφυοῦς λαμβάνει τάξιν
7 κατὰ τῆς ὑποκειμένης χώρας. κρατεῖ δὲ καὶ λιμένος
εὐκαίρου πρὸς τὸν ἀπὸ Δρεπάνων καὶ Λιλυβαίου δρό-
μον ἐπὶ τὴν Ἰταλίαν, ἐν ᾧ πλῆθος ὕδατος ἄφθονον
8 ὑπάρχει. προσόδους δὲ τὰς πάσας ἔχει τριττὰς δυσ-
χερεῖς, δύο μὲν ἀπὸ τῆς χώρας, μίαν δ' ἀπὸ τῆς
9 θαλάττης. ἐν ᾧ καταστρατοπεδεύσας παραβόλως
Ἀμίλκας, ὡς ἂν μήτε πόλεως οἰκείας μήτ' ἄλλης
ἐλπίδος μηδεμιᾶς ἀντεχόμενος, εἰς μέσους δὲ τοὺς
πολεμίους ἑαυτὸν δεδωκώς, ὅμως οὐ μικροὺς οὐδὲ τοὺς
τυχόντας Ῥωμαίοις ἀγῶνας καὶ κινδύνους παρεσκεύ-
10 ασε. πρῶτον μὲν γὰρ ἐντεῦθεν ὁρμώμενος κατὰ θάλατταν τὴν παραλίαν τῆς Ἰταλίας ἐπόρθει μέχρι τῆς
11 Κυμαίων χώρας, δεύτερον δὲ κατὰ γῆν παραστρα-
τοπεδευσάντων αὐτῷ Ῥωμαίων πρὸ τῆς Πανορμιτῶν
πόλεως ἐν ἴσως πέντε σταδίοις, πολλοὺς καὶ ποικίλους ἀγῶνας συνεστήσατο κατὰ γῆν σχεδὸν ἐπὶ τρεῖς
ἐνιαυτούς.

57. περὶ ὧν οὐχ οἷόν τε διὰ τῆς γραφῆς τὸν κατὰ
μέρος ἀποδοῦναι λόγον· καθάπερ γὰρ ἐπὶ τῶν διαφερόντων πυκτῶν καὶ ταῖς γενναιότησι καὶ ταῖς εὐεξί-
αις, ὅταν εἰς τὸν ὑπὲρ αὐτοῦ τοῦ στεφάνου συγκατα-
στάντες καιρὸν διαμάχωνται πληγὴν ἐπὶ πληγῇ
τιθέντες ἀδιαπαύστως, λόγον μὲν ἢ πρόνοιαν ἔχειν
ὑπὲρ ἑκάστης ἐπιβολῆς καὶ πληγῆς οὔτε τοῖς ἀγωνι-

which faces the interior of the island, this plateau is surrounded by inaccessible cliffs, while the parts between require only a little slight strengthening. There is also a knoll on it which serves for an acropolis as well as for an excellent post of observation over the country at the foot of the hill. Besides this Hercte commands a harbor very well situated for ships making the voyage from Drepana and Lilybaeum to Italy to put in at, and with an abundant supply of water. The hill has only three approaches, all difficult, two on the land side and one from the sea. Here Hamilcar established his quarters, at great risk indeed, since he had neither the support of any of their own towns nor any prospect of support from elsewhere, but had thrown himself into the midst of the enemy. Notwithstanding this, the peril to which he put the Romans, and the combats to which he forced them, were by no means slight or insignificant. For in the first place he would sally out with his fleet from this place, and devastate the coast of Italy as far as Cumae, and next, after the Romans had taken up a position on land in front of the city of Panormus and at a distance of about five stades from his own camp, he harassed them by delivering during almost three years constant and variously contrived attacks by land. These combats I am unable to describe in detail here.

57. For as in a boxing match when two champions, both distinguished for pluck and both in perfect training, meet in the decisive contest for the prize, continually delivering blow for blow, neither the combatants themselves nor the spectators can note or anticipate every attack or every

2 ζομένοις οὔτε τοῖς θεωμένοις ἐστὶ δυνατόν, ἐκ δὲ τῆς
καθόλου τῶν ἀνδρῶν ἐνεργείας καὶ τῆς ἑκατέρου
φιλοτιμίας ἔστι καὶ τῆς ἐμπειρίας αὐτῶν καὶ τῆς
δυνάμεως, πρὸς δὲ καὶ τῆς εὐψυχίας, ἱκανὴν ἔννοιαν
λαβεῖν, οὕτως δὲ καὶ περὶ τῶν νῦν λεγομένων στρατη-
3 γῶν. τὰς μὲν γὰρ αἰτίας ἢ τοὺς τρόπους, δι’ ὧν ἀν’
ἑκάστην ἡμέραν ἐποιοῦντο κατ’ ἀλλήλων ἐνέδρας,
ἀντενέδρας, ἐπιθέσεις, προσβολάς, οὔτ’ ἂν ὁ γράφων
ἐξαριθμούμενος ἐφίκοιτο, τοῖς τ’ ἀκούουσιν ἀπέραντος
ἅμα δ’ ἀνωφελὴς ἂν ἐκ τῆς ἀναγνώσεως γίνοιτο
4 χρεία· ἐκ δὲ τῆς καθολικῆς ἀποφάσεως περὶ αὐτῶν καὶ
τοῦ τέλους τῆς φιλοτιμίας μᾶλλον ἄν τις εἰς ἔννοιαν
5 ἔλθοι τῶν προειρημένων. οὔτε γὰρ τῶν ἐξ ἱστορίας
στρατηγημάτων οὔτε τῶν ἐκ τοῦ καιροῦ καὶ τῆς ὑποκειμένης περιστάσεως ἐπινοημάτων οὔτε τῶν εἰς
παράβολον καὶ βίαιον ἀνηκόντων τόλμαν οὐδὲν παρ-
6 ελείφθη. κρίσιν γε μὴν ὁλοσχερῆ γενέσθαι διὰ πλείους αἰτίας οὐχ οἷόν τ’ ἦν· αἵ τε γὰρ δυνάμεις ἀμφοτέρων ἦσαν ἐφάμιλλοι, τά τε κατὰ τοὺς χάρακας
ὁμοίως ἀπρόσιτα διὰ τὴν ὀχυρότητα, τό τε διάστημα
7 τῶν στρατοπέδων βραχὺ παντελῶς. ὅπερ αἴτιον ἦν
μάλιστα τοῦ τὰς μὲν κατὰ μέρος συμπτώσεις ἀπαύ-
στους γίνεσθαι καθ’ ἡμέραν, ὁλοσχερὲς δὲ συντελεῖ-
8 σθαι μηδέν. τούτους γὰρ αὐτοὺς ἀεὶ συνέβαινε δια-
φθείρεσθαι κατὰ τὰς συμπλοκάς, τοὺς ἐν χειρῶν νόμῳ
περιπεσόντας· οἱ δ’ ἅπαξ ἐγκλίναντες εὐθέως ἐκτὸς
τοῦ δεινοῦ πάντες ἦσαν ὑπὸ ταῖς αὐτῶν ἀσφαλείαις,
καὶ πάλιν ἐκ μεταβολῆς ἐκινδύνευον.

blow, but it is possible from the general action of each, and the determination that each displays, to get a fair idea of their respective skill, strength, and courage, so it was with these two generals. The causes or the modes of their daily ambuscades, counterambuscades, attempts, and assaults were so numerous that no writer could properly describe them, while at the same time the narrative would be most tedious as well as unprofitable to the reader. It is rather by a general pronouncement about the two men and the result of their rival efforts that a notion of the facts can be conveyed. Nothing was neglected; neither traditional tactics nor plans suggested by the occasion and by actual pressure of circumstances, nor those strokes which depend on a bold and strong initiative. Yet there were several reasons why no decisive success could be obtained. For the forces on each side were evenly matched; their trenches were so strong as to be equally unapproachable, and they lay at a quite small distance from each other, this being the chief reason why there were daily conflicts at certain points, but no decisive engagement. The losses in these combats consisted only of those who fell in the hand-to-hand fighting, while the side which once gave way used to get out of danger at once behind their defenses, from whence they would issue again and resume the fight.

58. Οὐ μὴν ἀλλ᾽ ὥσπερ ἀγαθὸς βραβευτὴς ἡ τύχη μεταβιβάσασα παραβόλως αὐτοὺς ἐκ τοῦ προειρημένου τόπου καὶ τοῦ προϋπάρχοντος ἀθλήματος εἰς παραβολώτερον ἀγώνισμα καὶ τόπον ἐλάττω συν-

2 έκλεισεν. ὁ γὰρ Ἀμίλκας, τῶν Ῥωμαίων τὸν Ἔρυκα τηρούντων ἐπί τε τῆς κορυφῆς καὶ παρὰ τὴν ῥίζαν, καθάπερ εἴπομεν, κατελάβετο τὴν πόλιν τῶν Ἐρυκίνων, ἥτις ἦν μεταξὺ τῆς τε κορυφῆς καὶ τῶν πρὸς τῇ

3 ῥίζῃ στρατοπεδευσάντων. ἐξ οὗ συνέβαινε παραβόλως μὲν ὑπομένειν καὶ διακινδυνεύειν πολιορκουμένους τοὺς τὴν κορυφὴν κατέχοντας τῶν Ῥωμαίων, ἀπίστως δὲ τοὺς Καρχηδονίους ἀντέχειν, τῶν τε πολεμίων πανταχόθεν προσκειμένων καὶ τῶν χορηγιῶν οὐ ῥᾳδίως αὐτοῖς παρακομιζομένων, ὡς ἂν τῆς θαλάττης καθ᾽ ἕνα τόπον καὶ μίαν πρόσοδον ἀντεχομένοις. οὐ μὴν ἀλλὰ πάλιν ἐνταῦθα πάσαις μὲν ἀμφότεροι ταῖς

4 πολιορκητικαῖς ἐπινοίαις καὶ βίαις χρησάμενοι κατ᾽ ἀλλήλων, πᾶν δὲ γένος ἐνδείας ἀνασχόμενοι, πάσης

5 δ᾽ ἐπιθέσεως καὶ μάχης πεῖραν λαβόντες, τέλος οὐχ, ὡς Φάβιός φησιν, ἐξαδυνατοῦντες καὶ περικακοῦντες, ἀλλ᾽ ὡς ἂν ἀπαθεῖς κἀήττητοί τινες ἄνδρες, ἱερὸν

6 ἐποίησαν τὸν στέφανον. πρότερον γὰρ ἢ ᾽κείνους ἀλλήλων ἐπικρατῆσαι, καίπερ δύ᾽ ἔτη πάλιν ἐν τούτῳ τῷ τόπῳ διαγωνισαμένους, δι᾽ ἄλλου τρόπου συνέβη λαβεῖν τὸν πόλεμον τὴν κρίσιν.

7 Τὰ μὲν οὖν περὶ τὸν Ἔρυκα καὶ τὰς πεζικὰς δυνάμεις τοιαύτην ἔσχε διάθεσιν. τὰ δὲ πολιτεύματ᾽ ἦν ἀμφοτέρων παραπλήσια τοῖς ψυχομαχοῦσι τῶν

58. But Fortune, however, like a good umpire, shifted the scene in a remarkable manner and changed the nature of the contest, confining both in a narrower field, where the struggle grew even more desperate. The Romans, as I said, had garrisons at Eryx on the summit of the mountain and at the foot. Hamilcar now seized the town which lies between the summit and the spot at the foot where the garrison was. The consequence of this was that the 244 B.C. Romans on the summit had to endure a siege which they supported with extraordinary hardihood and adventurous daring, and that the Carthaginians, though it is scarcely credible, maintained their position though the enemy were pressing on them from all sides and the conveyance of supplies was not easy, as they only held one place on the sea and one single road connecting with it. However, here again both sides employed every device and effort that the siege demanded: both endured every kind of privation and both essayed every means of attack and every variety of action. At length not, as Fabius Pictor says, owing to their exhaustion and sufferings, but like two uninjured and invincible champions, they left the contest drawn.[86] For before either could get the better of the other, though the struggle in this place had lasted for another two years, it came about that the war was decided by other means. 243–242

Such then was the condition of affairs at Eryx and as far B.C. as regarded the land forces. We may compare the spirit displayed by both states to that of game cocks engaged in a

[86] The meaning has been explained by W. Dittenberger, *IVO*, p. 115–116; see also Robert, *OMS* 5. 383–384.

8 εὐγενῶν ὀρνίθων. ἐκεῖνοί τε γὰρ πολλάκις ἀπολωλε-
κότες τὰς πτέρυγας διὰ τὴν ἀδυναμίαν, αὐτῇ δὲ τῇ
ψυχῇ μένοντες ἐκβάλλουσι τὰς πληγάς, ἕως ἂν αὐτομάτως ποτὲ περιπεσόντες αὐτοῖς καιρίως ἀλλήλων
διαδράξωνται, κἄπειτα τούτου γενομένου συμβῇ τὸν
9 ἕτερον αὐτῶν προπεσεῖν· οἵ τε Ῥωμαῖοι καὶ Καρχηδόνιοι κάμνοντες ἤδη τοῖς πόνοις διὰ τὴν συνέχειαν
τῶν κινδύνων εἰς τέλος ἀπήλγουν, τήν τε δύναμιν
παρελέλυντο καὶ παρεῖντο διὰ τὰς πολυχρονίους
εἰσφορὰς καὶ δαπάνας.

59. ὁμοίως δὲ Ῥωμαῖοι ψυχομαχοῦντες, καίπερ ἔτη
σχεδὸν ἤδη πέντε τῶν κατὰ θάλατταν πραγμάτων
ὁλοσχερῶς ἀφεστηκότες διά τε τὰς περιπετείας καὶ
διὰ τὸ πεπεῖσθαι δι᾿ αὐτῶν τῶν πεζικῶν δυνάμεων
2 κρινεῖν τὸν πόλεμον, τότε συνορῶντες οὐ προχωροῦν
αὐτοῖς τοὔργον κατὰ τοὺς ἐκλογισμοὺς καὶ μάλιστα
διὰ τὴν τόλμαν τοῦ τῶν Καρχηδονίων ἡγεμόνος, ἔκριναν τὸ τρίτον ἀντιποιήσασθαι τῶν ἐν ταῖς ναυτικαῖς
3 δυνάμεσιν ἐλπίδων, ὑπολαμβάνοντες διὰ τῆς ἐπινοίας
ταύτης, εἰ καιρίως ἅψαιντο τῆς ἐπιβολῆς, μόνως ἂν
οὕτως πέρας ἐπιθεῖναι τῷ πολέμῳ συμφέρον. ὃ καὶ
4 τέλος ἐποίησαν. τὸ μὲν γὰρ πρῶτον ἐξεχώρησαν τῆς
θαλάττης εἴξαντες τοῖς ἐκ τῆς τύχης συμπτώμασι, τὸ
δὲ δεύτερον ἐλαττωθέντες τῇ περὶ τὰ Δρέπανα ναυ-
5 μαχίᾳ· τότε δὲ τρίτην ἐποιοῦντο ταύτην τὴν ἐπιβολήν,
δι᾿ ἧς νικήσαντες καὶ τὰ περὶ τὸν Ἔρυκα στρατόπεδα
τῶν Καρχηδονίων ἀποκλείσαντες τῆς κατὰ θάλατταν
6 χορηγίας τέλος ἐπέθηκαν τοῖς ὅλοις. ἦν δὲ τῆς ἐπι-

death struggle. For we often see that when these birds have lost the use of their wings from exhaustion, their courage remains as high as ever and they continue to strike blow upon blow, until closing by chance they get a deadly hold of each other, and as soon as this happens one or other of the two will soon fall dead. So the Romans and Carthaginians, worn out by their exertions owing to the continual fighting, at length began to be despairing, their strength paralysed and their resources exhausted by protracted taxation and expense.

59. Similarly, in spite of all, the Romans, fighting on by sheer willpower, although they had for nearly five years utterly withdrawn from the sea owing to their disasters and their belief that they would be able to decide the war by the aid of their land forces alone, now, when they saw that chiefly owing to the bold action of the Carthaginian general they were not making the progress on which they had reckoned, decided for the third time to court the prospect of using sea forces. They thought that this course, if they could but strike a deadly blow, was the only way of bringing the war to a favorable conclusion. And this they finally accomplished. It was yielding to the blows of Fortune that they had retired from the sea on the first occasion; the second time it was owing to their defeat at Drepana, but now they made this third attempt, and through it, by gaining a victory and cutting off the supplies from the sea of the Carthaginian army at Eryx, they put an end to the whole war. In this undertaking sheer resolution was the major

βολῆς τὸ πλεῖον ψυχομαχία. χορηγία μὲν γὰρ οὐχ
ὑπῆρχε πρὸς τὴν πρόθεσιν ἐν τοῖς κοινοῖς· οὐ μὴν
ἀλλὰ διὰ τὴν τῶν προεστώτων ἀνδρῶν εἰς τὰ κοινὰ
φιλοτιμίαν καὶ γενναιότητα προσευρέθη πρὸς τὴν
7   συντέλειαν. κατὰ γὰρ τὰς τῶν βίων εὐκαιρίας καθ᾽
ἕνα καὶ δύο καὶ τρεῖς ὑφίσταντο παρέξειν πεντήρη
κατηρτισμένην, ἐφ᾽ ᾧ τὴν δαπάνην κομιοῦνται, κατὰ
8   λόγον τῶν πραγμάτων προχωρησάντων. τῷ δὲ τοιούτῳ τρόπῳ ταχέως ἑτοιμασθέντων διακοσίων πλοίων
πεντηρικῶν, ὧν ἐποιήσαντο τὴν ναυπηγίαν πρὸς
[παράδειγμα] τὴν τοῦ Ῥοδίου ναῦν, μετὰ ταῦτα στρατηγὸν καταστήσαντες Γάϊον Λυτάτιον ἐξέπεμψαν ἀρ-
9   χομένης τῆς θερείας. ὃς καὶ παραδόξως ἐπιφανεὶς τοῖς
κατὰ τὴν Σικελίαν τόποις τόν τε περὶ τὰ Δρέπανα
λιμένα κατέσχε καὶ τοὺς περὶ τὸ Λιλύβαιον ὅρμους,
παντὸς ἀνακεχωρηκότος εἰς τὴν οἰκείαν τοῦ τῶν Καρ-
10   χηδονίων ναυτικοῦ. συστησάμενος δὲ περὶ τὴν ἐν τοῖς
Δρεπάνοις πόλιν ἔργα καὶ τἆλλα πρὸς τὴν πολιορκίαν
παρασκευασάμενος, ἅμα μὲν ταύτῃ προσεκαρτέρει τὰ
11   δυνατὰ ποιῶν, ἅμα δὲ προορώμενος τὴν παρουσίαν
τοῦ Καρχηδονίων στόλου, καὶ μνημονεύων τῆς ἐξ
ἀρχῆς προθέσεως ὅτι μόνως δύναται διὰ τοῦ κατὰ
θάλατταν κινδύνου κρίσεως τὰ ὅλα τυχεῖν, οὐκ ἀχρεῖ-
12   ον οὐδ᾽ ἀργὸν εἴα γίνεσθαι τὸν χρόνον, ἀλλ᾽ ἀν᾽
ἑκάστην ἡμέραν ἀναπείρας καὶ μελέτας ποιῶν τοῖς
πληρώμασιν οἰκείως τῆς ἐπιβολῆς, τῇ τε λοιπῇ τῇ
κατὰ τὴν δίαιταν ἐπιμελείᾳ προσκαρτερῶν, ἀθλητὰς

element in the struggle. For there were no funds in the public treasury for this purpose; but yet, owing to the patriotic and generous spirit of the leading citizens, enough was found to carry out the project; as either one, two, or three of them, according to their means, undertook to provide a quinquereme fully equipped on the understanding that they would be repaid if all went well. In this way a fleet of two hundred quinqueremes was rapidly got ready, all built on the model of the "Rhodian's" ship. They then appointed Gaius Lutatius[87] to the command and dispatched him at the beginning of summer. Suddenly appearing off the coast of Sicily, he seized on the harbor of Drepana and the roadsteads near Lilybaeum, the whole Carthaginian navy having retired to their own country. First of all he constructed works round the city of Drepana and made all preparations for its siege, but while continuing to prosecute this by every means in his power, he foresaw that the Carthaginian fleet would arrive, and was not forgetful of the original motive of the expedition, the belief that it was only by a sea battle that the war could be decisively finished. He did not, then, allow the time to pass uselessly and idly, but every day was spent in exercising and practicing the crews properly for this purpose. He also paid unremitting attention to the matter of good food and drink, so

242 B.C.

[87] His naval victory at the island of Aegusa (60. 4) in 241 ends the war.

ἀπετέλεσε πρὸς τὸ προκείμενον ἐν πάνυ βραχεῖ χρόνῳ τοὺς ναύτας.

60. Οἱ δὲ Καρχηδόνιοι, παρὰ τὴν ὑπόνοιαν προσπεσόντος αὐτοῖς τοῦ πεπλευκέναι στόλῳ τοὺς Ῥωμαίους καὶ πάλιν ἀντιποιεῖσθαι τῆς θαλάττης, παραυτίκα
2 κατήρτιζον τὰς ναῦς, καὶ πληρώσαντες σίτου καὶ τῶν
ἄλλων ἐπιτηδείων, ἐξέπεμπον τὸν στόλον, βουλόμενοι
μηδὲν ἐλλείπειν τὰ περὶ τὸν Ἔρυκα στρατόπεδα τῶν
3 ἀναγκαίων. κατέστησαν δὲ καὶ στρατηγὸν ἐπὶ τῆς
ναυτικῆς δυνάμεως Ἄννωνα· ὃς ἀναχθεὶς καὶ κατάρας
ἐπὶ τὴν Ἱερὰν καλουμένην νῆσον ἔσπευδε τοὺς πολεμίους λαθὼν διακομισθῆναι πρὸς τὸν Ἔρυκα, καὶ τὰς
μὲν ἀγορὰς ἀποθέσθαι καὶ κουφίσαι τὰς ναῦς, προσλαβὼν δ' ἐπιβάτας ἐκ τῶν μισθοφόρων τοὺς ἐπιτηδεί-
ους καὶ Βάρκαν μετ' αὐτῶν, οὕτως συμμίσγειν τοῖς
4 ὑπεναντίοις. ὁ δὲ Λυτάτιος συνεὶς τὴν παρουσίαν τῶν
περὶ τὸν Ἄννωνα, καὶ συλλογισάμενος τὴν ἐπίνοιαν
αὐτῶν, ἀναλαβὼν ἀπὸ τοῦ πεζοῦ στρατεύματος τοὺς
ἀρίστους ἄνδρας ἔπλευσε πρὸς τὴν Αἰγοῦσσαν νῆσον
5 τὴν πρὸ τοῦ Λιλυβαίου κειμένην. κἀνταῦθα παρακαλέσας τὰ πρέποντα τῷ καιρῷ τὰς δυνάμεις διεσάφει
τοῖς κυβερνήταις ὡς ἐσομένης εἰς τὴν αὔριον ναυμα-
6 χίας. ὑπὸ δὲ τὴν ἑωθινήν, ἤδη τῆς ἡμέρας ὑποφαι-
νούσης, ὁρῶν τοῖς μὲν ἐναντίοις φορὸν ἄνεμον καταρ-
ρέοντα καὶ λαμπρόν, σφίσι δὲ δυσχερῆ γινόμενον τὸν
ἀνάπλουν πρὸς ἀντίον τὸ πνεῦμα, κοίλης καὶ τραχείας
οὔσης τῆς θαλάττης, τὸ μὲν πρῶτον διηπόρει τί δεῖ
7 χρῆσθαι τοῖς παροῦσι. συλλογιζόμενος δ' ὡς ἐὰν μὲν

that in a very short time he got his sailors into perfect condition for the anticipated battle.

60. When the unexpected news reached Carthage that the Romans were at sea with a fleet and were again disputing the naval supremacy, they at once got their ships ready, and filling them with corn and other provisions, dispatched their fleet on its errand, desiring that the troops at Eryx should be in no need of necessary supplies. Hanno, whom they had appointed to command the naval force, set sail and reached the so-called Holy Isle from whence he designed to cross as soon as possible to Eryx, unobserved by the enemy, and, after lightening the ships by disembarking the supplies, to take on board as marines the best qualified mercenaries together with Barcas himself and then engage the enemy. Lutatius, learning of Hanno's arrival and divining his intentions, took on board a picked force from the army and sailed to the island of Aegusa which lies off Lilybaeum. There, after exhorting his troops as became the occasion, he informed the captains that the battle would take place next day. In the early morning, just as day was breaking, he saw that a brisk breeze was coming down favorable to the enemy, but that it had become difficult for himself to sail up against the wind, the sea too being heavy and rough. At first he hesitated much what to do under the circumstances, but reflected that if he risked an attack now

241 B.C.

παραβάλληται χειμῶνος ὄντος, πρὸς Ἄννωνα ποιήσεται τὸν ἀγῶνα καὶ πρὸς αὐτὰς τὰς ναυτικὰς δυνάμεις
8 καὶ πρὸς ἔτι γέμοντα τὰ σκάφη, ἐὰν δὲ τηρῶν εὐδίαν
καὶ καταμέλλων ἐάσῃ διᾶραι καὶ συμμῖξαι τοῖς στρατοπέδοις τοὺς πολεμίους, πρός τε τὰς ναῦς εὐκινήτους
καὶ κεκουφισμένας ἀγωνιεῖται πρός τε τοὺς ἀρίστους
ἄνδρας τῶν ἐκ τοῦ πεζοῦ στρατευμάτων, τὸ δὲ μέγιστον πρὸς τὴν Ἀμίλκου τόλμαν, ἧς οὐδὲν ἦν τότε
9 φοβερώτερον· διόπερ ἔκρινε μὴ παρεῖναι τὸν ἐνεστῶτα καιρόν· συνιδὼν δὲ τὰς τῶν πολεμίων ναῦς
ἱστιοδρομούσας, ἀνήγετο μετὰ σπουδῆς. τῶν δὲ πληρωμάτων εὐχερῶς ἀναφερόντων τὸν κλύδωνα ταῖς εὐ-
εξίαις, ταχέως ἐπὶ μίαν ἐκτείνας ναῦν ἀντίπρωρρον
κατέστησε τοῖς πολεμίοις τὸν στόλον.

61. Οἱ δὲ Καρχηδόνιοι κατιδόντες τὸν διάπλουν
αὐτῶν προκατέχοντας τοὺς Ῥωμαίους, καθελόμενοι
τοὺς ἱστοὺς καὶ παρακαλέσαντες κατὰ ναῦν σφᾶς
2 αὐτούς, συνέβαλλον τοῖς ὑπεναντίοις. τῆς δ' ἑκατέρων
παρασκευῆς τὴν ἐναντίαν ἐχούσης διάθεσιν τῇ περὶ
τὰ Δρέπανα γενομένῃ ναυμαχίᾳ, καὶ τὸ τέλος ἑκα-
3 τέροις τῆς μάχης εἰκότως ἐναντίον ἀπέβη. οἱ Ῥωμαῖοι
μὲν γὰρ τήν τε ναυπηγίαν μετειλήφεσαν, καὶ τὰ βάρη
πάντα χωρὶς τῶν πρὸς τὴν ναυμαχίαν ἐπιτηδείων
ἐξετέθειντο· τά τε πληρώματα συγκεκροτημένα διαφέρουσαν αὐτοῖς τὴν χρείαν παρείχετο, τούς τ' ἐπιβάτας
κατ' ἐκλογὴν ἄνδρας ἀπαραχωρήτους ἐκ τῶν πεζικῶν
4 στρατοπέδων εἶχον. περὶ δὲ τοὺς Καρχηδονίους
τἀναντία τούτοις ὑπῆρχεν. αἱ μὲν γὰρ νῆες γέμουσαι

that the weather was stormy, he would be fighting against
Hanno and the naval forces alone and also against heavily
laden ships, whereas if he waited for calm weather and by
his delay allowed the enemy to cross and join the army, he
would have to face ships now lightened and manageable as
well as the pick of the land forces and above all the bravery
of Hamilcar which was what they dreaded most at that
time. He therefore decided not to let the present opportunity slip. When he saw the Carthaginian ships under full
sail he at once got under weigh. As his crews easily mastered the waves owing to their good training, he soon
brought his fleet into a single line with their prows to the
enemy.

61. The Carthaginians, seeing that the Romans were intercepting their crossing, lowered their masts and cheer-
ing each other on in each ship closed with the enemy. As
the outfit of each force was just the reverse of what it had
been at the battle of Drepana, the result also was naturally
the reverse for each. The Romans had reformed their system of shipbuilding and had also put ashore all heavy material except what was required for the battle; their crews
rendered excellent service, as their training had got them
well together, and the marines they had were men selected
from the army for their steadfastness. With the Carthaginians it was just the opposite. Their ships, being loaded,

δυσχρήστως διέκειντο πρὸς τὸν κίνδυνον, τὰ δὲ πληρώματα τελέως ἦν ἀνάσκητα καὶ πρὸς καιρὸν ἐμβε-
βλημένα, τὰ δ᾽ ἐπιβατικὰ νεοσύλλογα καὶ πρωτό-
5 πειρα πάσης κακοπαθείας καὶ παντὸς δεινοῦ. διὰ γὰρ
τὸ μηδέποτ᾽ ἂν ἔτι τοὺς Ῥωμαίους ἐλπίσαι τῆς θαλάττης ἀντιποιήσασθαι καταφρονήσαντες ὠλιγώρουν
6 τῶν ναυτικῶν δυνάμεων. τοιγαροῦν ἅμα τῷ συμβαλεῖν
κατὰ πολλὰ μέρη τῆς μάχης ἐλαττούμενοι ταχέως
ἐλείφθησαν, καὶ πεντήκοντα μὲν αὐτῶν ναῦς κατέδυ-
7 σαν, ἑβδομήκοντα δ᾽ ἑάλωσαν αὔτανδροι· τὸ δὲ λοιπὸν πλῆθος ἐπαράμενον τοὺς ἱστοὺς καὶ κατουρῶσαν
αὖθις ἀπεχώρει πρὸς τὴν Ἱερὰν νῆσον, εὐτυχῶς καὶ
παραδόξως ἐκ μεταβολῆς αὐτοῖς πρὸς τὸν δέοντα
8 καιρὸν τοῦ πνεύματος συνεργήσαντος. ὁ μὲν οὖν Ῥωμαίων στρατηγὸς ἀποπλεύσας πρὸς τὸ Λιλύβαιον καὶ
τὰ στρατόπεδα περὶ τὴν τῶν αἰχμαλώτων πλοίων καὶ
τῶν σωμάτων οἰκονομίαν ἐγίνετο, μεγάλην οὖσαν· οὐ
γὰρ πολὺ τῶν μυρίων ἔλειπε σωμάτων τὰ ληφθέντα
ζωγρίᾳ κατὰ τὸν κίνδυνον.

62. Οἱ δὲ Καρχηδόνιοι, προσπεσούσης αὐτοῖς
ἀπροσδοκήτως τῆς ἥττης, ταῖς μὲν ὁρμαῖς καὶ ταῖς
φιλοτιμίαις ἀκμὴν ἕτοιμοι πολεμεῖν ἦσαν, τοῖς δὲ
2 λογισμοῖς ἐξηπόρουν. οὔτε γὰρ χορηγεῖν ἔτι ταῖς ἐν
τῇ Σικελίᾳ δυνάμεσιν οἷοί τ᾽ ἦσαν, κρατούντων τῆς
θαλάττης τῶν ὑπεναντίων· ἀπογνόντες δὲ ταύτας, καὶ
προδόται τρόπον τινὰ γενόμενοι, ποίαις χερσὶν ἢ
3 ποίοις ἡγεμόσι πολεμήσειαν οὐκ εἶχον. διόπερ ὀξέως
διαπεμψάμενοι πρὸς τὸν Βάρκαν ἐπέτρεψαν ἐκείνῳ

were not in a serviceable condition for battle, while the crews were quite untrained, and had been put on board for the emergency, and their marines were recent levies whose first experience of the least hardship and danger this was. The fact is that, owing to their never having expected the Romans to dispute the sea with them again, they had, in contempt for them, neglected their naval force. So that immediately on engaging they had the worst in many parts of the battle and were soon routed, fifty ships being sunk and seventy captured with their crews. The remainder raising their masts and finding a fair wind got back to Holy Isle, very fortunate in the wind having unexpectedly gone round and helping them just when they required it. As for the Roman Consul he sailed away to Lilybaeum and the legions, and there occupied himself with the disposal of the captured ships and men, a business of some magnitude, as the prisoners made in the battle numbered very nearly ten thousand.

62. Even on hearing of this unexpected defeat the Carthaginians, as far as resolution of mind and will to conquer went, would readily have continued the war, but when it came to a matter of cool calculation they were quite at a loss. For one thing they were no longer able to send supplies to their forces in Sicily as the enemy commanded the sea, and if they abandoned and in a manner betrayed them, they had neither other men nor other leaders with whom to pursue the war. They therefore at once sent a message to Barcas giving him full powers to deal with the situa-

περὶ τῶν ὅλων. ὁ δὲ καὶ λίαν ἐποίησεν ἔργον ἡγεμόνος
4 ἀγαθοῦ καὶ φρονίμου. μέχρι μὲν γὰρ ἐκ τῶν κατὰ
λόγον ἦν τις ἐλπὶς ἐν τοῖς ὑποκειμένοις, οὐδὲν τῶν
παραβόλων ἢ δεινῶν δοκούντων εἶναι παρέλιπεν,
ἀλλὰ πάσας τὰς τοῦ νικᾶν ἐν τῷ πολεμεῖν ἐλπίδας, εἰ
5 καί τις ἄλλος ἡγεμόνων, ἐξήλεγξεν. ἐπειδὴ δὲ περι-
έστη τὰ πράγματα, καὶ τῶν κατὰ λόγον οὐδὲν ἔτι
κατελείπετο πρὸς τὸ σῴζειν τοὺς ὑποταττομένους,
πάνυ νουνεχῶς καὶ πραγματικῶς εἴξας τοῖς παροῦσιν
ὑπὲρ σπονδῶν καὶ διαλύσεων ἐξαπέστελλε πρεσβευ-
6 τάς. τοῦ γὰρ αὐτοῦ νομιστέον ἡγεμόνος εἶναι τὸ
7 δύνασθαι βλέπειν τόν τε τοῦ νικᾶν, ὁμοίως δὲ καὶ τὸν
τοῦ λείπεσθαι καιρόν. τοῦ δὲ Λυτατίου προθύμως
δεξαμένου τὰ παρακαλούμενα διὰ τὸ συνειδέναι τοῖς
σφετέροις πράγμασι τετρυμένοις καὶ κάμνουσιν ἤδη
τῷ πολέμῳ, συνέβη τέλος ἐπιθεῖναι τῇ διαφορᾷ τοιού-
8 των τινῶν συνθηκῶν διαγραφεισῶν· "ἐπὶ τοῖσδε φιλίαν εἶναι Καρχηδονίοις καὶ Ῥωμαίοις, ἐὰν καὶ τῷ
δήμῳ τῶν Ῥωμαίων συνδοκῇ. ἐκχωρεῖν Σικελίας
ἁπάσης Καρχηδονίους καὶ μὴ πολεμεῖν Ἱέρωνι μηδ'
ἐπιφέρειν ὅπλα Συρακοσίοις μηδὲ τῶν Συρακοσίων
9 συμμάχοις. ἀποδοῦναι Καρχηδονίους Ῥωμαίοις χωρὶς λύτρων ἅπαντας τοὺς αἰχμαλώτους. ἀργυρίου κατ-
ενεγκεῖν Καρχηδονίους Ῥωμαίοις ἐν ἔτεσιν εἴκοσι
δισχίλια καὶ διακόσια τάλαντ' Εὐβοϊκά."

63. τούτων δ' ἐπανενεχθέντων εἰς τὴν Ῥώμην, οὐ
προσεδέξατο τὰς συνθήκας ὁ δῆμος, ἀλλ' ἐξαπέστειλεν ἄνδρας δέκα τοὺς ἐπισκεψομένους ὑπὲρ τῶν πρα-

tion. Hamilcar acted thoroughly like the good and prudent leader he was. As long as there had been some reasonable hope in the situation he had left no means, however perilous and venturesome it seemed, unemployed, and if there ever was a general who put to proof in a war every chance of success, it was he. But now that fortunes were reversed and there was no reasonable prospect left of saving the troops under his command, he showed his practical good sense in yielding to circumstance and sending an embassy to treat for peace. For our opinion should be that a general ought to be qualified to discern both when he is victorious and when he is beaten. Lutatius readily consented to negotiate, conscious as he was that the Romans were by this time worn out and enfeebled by the war, and he succeeded in putting an end to the contest by a treaty[88] more or less as follows. "There shall be friendship between the Carthaginians and Romans on the following terms if approved by the Roman people. The Carthaginians to evacuate the whole of Sicily[89] and not to make war on Hiero or bear arms against the Syracusans or the allies of the Syracusans. The Carthaginians to give up to the Romans all prisoners without ransom. The Carthaginians to pay to the Romans by instalments in twenty years two thousand two hundred Euboean talents."

63. But when these terms were referred to Rome, the people did not accept the treaty, but sent ten commission-

[88] *StV* 493.

[89] The entire island, with the exception of Hiero's realm, now becomes the first Roman province, *Sicilia*.

2 γμάτων. οἳ καὶ παραγενόμενοι τῶν μὲν ὅλων οὐδὲν ἔτι
μετέθηκαν, βραχέα δὲ προσεπέτειναν τοὺς Καρχη-
3 δονίους. τόν τε γὰρ χρόνον τῶν φόρων ἐποίησαν
ἥμισυν, χίλια τάλαντα προσθέντες, τῶν τε νήσων
ἐκχωρεῖν Καρχηδονίους προσεπέταξαν, ὅσαι μεταξὺ
τῆς Ἰταλίας κεῖνται καὶ τῆς Σικελίας.
4 Ὁ μὲν οὖν Ῥωμαίοις καὶ Καρχηδονίοις συστὰς
περὶ Σικελίας πόλεμος ἐπὶ τοιούτοις καὶ τοιοῦτον ἔσχε
τὸ τέλος, ἔτη πολεμηθεὶς εἴκοσι καὶ τέτταρα συνεχῶς,
πόλεμος ὢν ἡμεῖς ἴσμεν ἀκοῇ μαθόντες πολυχρονιώ-
5 τατος καὶ συνεχέστατος καὶ μέγιστος. ἐν ᾧ χωρὶς τῶν
λοιπῶν ἀγώνων καὶ παρασκευῶν, καθάπερ εἴπομεν
ἀνώτερον, ἅπαξ μὲν οἱ συνάμφω πλείοσιν ἢ πεντακο-
σίοις, πάλιν δὲ μικρῷ λείπουσιν ἑπτακοσίοις σκάφεσι
6 πεντηρικοῖς ἐναυμάχησαν πρὸς ἀλλήλους. ἀπέβαλόν
γε μὴν Ῥωμαῖοι μὲν ἐν τῷ πολέμῳ τούτῳ πεντήρεις
μετὰ τῶν ἐν ταῖς ναυαγίαις διαφθαρεισῶν εἰς ἑπτακο-
7 σίας, Καρχηδόνιοι δ' εἰς πεντακοσίας. ὥστε τοὺς
θαυμάζοντας τὰς Ἀντιγόνου καὶ Πτολεμαίου καὶ Δημητρίου ναυμαχίας καὶ τοὺς στόλους εἰκότως ἂν περὶ
τούτων ἱστορήσαντας ἐκπεπλῆχθαι τὴν ὑπερβολὴν
8 τῶν πράξεων. εἰ δέ τις βουληθείη συλλογίσασθαι τὴν
διαφορὰν τῶν πεντηρικῶν πλοίων πρὸς τὰς τριήρεις,
αἷς οἵ τε Πέρσαι πρὸς τοὺς Ἕλληνας καὶ πάλιν
Ἀθηναῖοι καὶ Λακεδαιμόνιοι πρὸς ἀλλήλους ἐναυ-
μάχουν, οὐδ' ἂν καθόλου δυνηθείη τηλικαύτας δυνά-
9 μεις εὑρεῖν ἐν θαλάττῃ διηγωνισμένας. ἐξ ὧν δῆλον τὸ
προτεθὲν ἡμῖν ἐξ ἀρχῆς ὡς οὐ τύχῃ Ῥωμαῖοι, καθά-

ers[90] to examine the matter. On their arrival they made no substantial changes in the terms, but only slight modifications rendering them more severe for Carthage: for they reduced the term of payment by one half, added a thousand talents to the indemnity, and demanded the evacuation by the Carthaginians of all islands lying between Sicily and Italy.

Such then was the end of the war between the Romans and Carthaginians for the possession of Sicily, and such were the terms of peace. It had lasted without a break for twenty-four years and is the longest, most unintermittent, and greatest war we know of. Apart from all the other battles and armaments, the total naval forces engaged were, as I mentioned above, on one occasion more than five hundred quinqueremes and on another one very nearly seven hundred. Moreover the Romans lost in this war about seven hundred quinqueremes, inclusive of those that perished in the shipwrecks, and the Carthaginians about five hundred. So that those who marvel at the great sea battles and great fleets of an Antigonus, a Ptolemy, or a Demetrius would, if I mistake not, on inquiring into the history of this war, be much astonished at the huge scale of the operations. Again, if we take into consideration the difference between quinqueremes and the triremes in which the Persians fought against the Greeks and the Athenians and Lacedaemonians against each other, we shall find that no forces of such magnitude ever met at sea. This confirms the assertion I ventured to make at the outset that the progress of the Romans was not due to chance and was not

[90] This practice, which will become common, is attested here for the first time.

περ ἔνιοι δοκοῦσι τῶν Ἑλλήνων, οὐδ' αὐτομάτως,
ἀλλὰ καὶ λίαν εἰκότως ἐν τοιούτοις καὶ τηλικούτοις
πράγμασιν ἐνασκήσαντες οὐ μόνον ἐπεβάλοντο τῇ
τῶν ὅλων ἡγεμονίᾳ καὶ δυναστείᾳ τολμηρῶς, ἀλλὰ
καὶ καθίκοντο τῆς προθέσεως.

64. καὶ τί δήποτ' ἔστι τὸ αἴτιον, ἀπορήσαι τις ἄν,
ὅτι κεκρατηκότες τῶν ὅλων καὶ πολλαπλασίαν ἔχοντες ὑπεροχὴν νῦν ἢ πρόσθεν οὔτ' ἂν πληρῶσαι τοσαύ-
τας ναῦς οὔτ' ἀναπλεῦσαι τηλικούτοις στόλοις δυνη-
2 θεῖεν; οὐ μὴν ἀλλὰ περὶ μὲν ταύτης τῆς ἀπορίας
σαφῶς ἐξέσται τὰς αἰτίας κατανοεῖν, ὅταν ἐπὶ τὴν
ἐξήγησιν αὐτῶν τῆς πολιτείας ἔλθωμεν· ὑπὲρ ἧς οὔθ'
ἡμῖν ἐν παρέργῳ ῥητέον οὔτε τοῖς ἀκούουσιν ἀργῶς
3 προσεκτέον. τὸ μὲν γὰρ θέαμα καλόν, σχεδὸν δ' ὡς
ἔπος εἰπεῖν ἄγνωστον ἕως τοῦ νῦν, χάριν τῶν περὶ
4 αὐτῆς συγγεγραφότων. οἱ μὲν γὰρ ἠγνοήκασιν, οἱ δ'
5 ἀσαφῆ καὶ τελέως ἀνωφελῆ πεποίηνται τὴν ἐξήγησιν.
πλὴν ἔν γε τῷ προειρημένῳ πολέμῳ τὰς μὲν τῶν
πολιτευμάτων ἀμφοτέρων προαιρέσεις ἐφαμίλλους εὕροι τις ἂν γεγενημένας, οὐ μόνον ταῖς ἐπιβολαῖς,
ἀλλὰ καὶ ταῖς μεγαλοψυχίαις, μάλιστα δὲ τῇ περὶ τῶν
6 πρωτείων φιλοτιμίᾳ, τούς γε μὴν ἄνδρας οὐ μικρῷ,
πολλῷ δὲ γενναιοτέρους ἐν παντὶ Ῥωμαίους· ἡγεμόνα
δὲ καὶ γνώμῃ καὶ τόλμῃ θετέον ἄριστον Ἀμίλκαν τῶν
τότε γεγονέναι τὸν Βάρκαν ἐπικαλούμενον, πατέρα δὲ
κατὰ φύσιν Ἀννίβου τοῦ μετὰ ταῦτα πολεμήσαντος
Ῥωμαίοις.

65. Μετὰ δὲ τὰς διαλύσεις ταύτας ἴδιόν τι καὶ

involuntary, as some among the Greeks choose to think, but that by schooling themselves in such vast and perilous enterprises it was perfectly natural that they not only gained the courage to aim at universal dominion, but executed their purpose.

64. Some of my readers will wonder what can be the reason why, now that they are masters of the world and far more puissant than formerly, they could neither man so many ships, nor put to sea with such large fleets. Those, however, who are puzzled by this, will be enabled to understand the reason clearly when we come to deal with their political institutions,[91] a subject not to be treated incidentally by the writer or followed inattentively by the reader. It offers a noble spectacle and one almost wholly unrevealed hitherto, owing to the incompetence of the authors who have dealt with it, some of whom sinned from lack of knowledge, while the account given by others is wanting in clearness and entirely unprofitable. As regards, however, the war of which we are speaking, one will find its purpose and prosecution on the part of the two states equally characterized on both sides by enterprise, by lofty spirit, and above all by ambition for supremacy. In individual courage indeed the Romans were far superior on the whole, but the general to whom the palm must be given both for daring and for genius is Hamilcar called Barcas, the actual father of that Hannibal who afterward made war on the Romans.

65. Shortly after this treaty it so happened that both

[91] P. announces the discussion that will come in book 6.

2 παραπλήσιον ἀμφοτέροις συνέβη παθεῖν. ἐξεδέξατο
γὰρ πόλεμος ἐμφύλιος Ῥωμαίους μὲν ὁ πρὸς τοὺς
Φαλίσκους καλουμένους, ὃν ταχέως καὶ συμφερόντως
ἐπετέλεσαν, ἐν ὀλίγαις ἡμέραις ἐγκρατεῖς γενόμενοι

3 τῆς πόλεως αὐτῶν, Καρχηδονίους δὲ κατὰ τὸν αὐτὸν
καιρὸν οὐ μικρὸς οὐδ' εὐκαταφρόνητος ὁ πρὸς τοὺς
ξένους καὶ τοὺς Νομάδας καὶ τοὺς ἅμα τούτοις ἀπο-

4 στάντας Λίβυας, ἐν ᾧ πολλοὺς καὶ μεγάλους ὑπομείναντες φόβους τέλος οὐ μόνον ὑπὲρ τῆς χώρας ἐκινδύνευσαν, ἀλλὰ καὶ περὶ σφῶν αὐτῶν καὶ τοῦ τῆς

5 πατρίδος ἐδάφους. ἐπὶ δὲ τὸν πόλεμον τοῦτον ἐπιστῆσαι μὲν ἄξιον διὰ πλείους αἰτίας, ἐπὶ κεφαλαίου δὲ καὶ
διὰ βραχέων αὐτοῦ ποιήσασθαι τὴν ἐξήγησιν κατὰ

6 τὴν ἐξ ἀρχῆς πρόθεσιν. τόν τε γὰρ παρὰ τοῖς πολλοῖς
λεγόμενον ἄσπονδον πόλεμον, τίνα φύσιν ἔχει καὶ
διάθεσιν, μάλιστ' ἄν τις ἐκ τῶν τότε γεγονότων ἐπι-

7 γνοίη, τούς τε χρωμένους μισθοφορικαῖς δυνάμεσι
τίνα δεῖ προορᾶσθαι καὶ φυλάττεσθαι μακρόθεν ἐναρ-
γέστατ' ἂν ἐκ τῆς τότε περιστάσεως συνθεωρήσειε,
πρὸς δὲ τούτοις τί διαφέρει καὶ κατὰ πόσον ἤθη

8 σύμμικτα καὶ βάρβαρα τῶν ἐν παιδείαις καὶ νόμοις
καὶ πολιτικοῖς ἔθεσιν ἐκτεθραμμένων· τὸ δὲ μέγιστον
τὰς αἰτίας ἐκ τῶν ἐν ἐκείνοις τοῖς καιροῖς πεπραγμένων κατανοήσειε, δι' ἃς ὁ κατ' Ἀννίβαν συνέστη

9 Ῥωμαίοις καὶ Καρχηδονίοις πόλεμος. ὑπὲρ οὗ διὰ τὸ
μὴ μόνον παρὰ τοῖς συγγραφεῦσιν, ἀλλὰ καὶ παρὰ

states found themselves placed in circumstances peculi-
arly similar. For at Rome there followed a civil war against
the Falisci,[92] but this they brought to a speedy and favorable conclusion, taking Falerii in a few days. But the war
the Carthaginians had to face[93] was no little or contemptible one, being against their mercenaries, the Numidians
and those Libyans who joined in the revolt. In this war they
encountered many great perils and finally were in danger
of losing not only their territory, but their own liberty and
the soil of their native town. For several reasons I think it
worth my while to dwell on this war, and, according to the
plan I stated at the outset, to give a summary and brief narrative of it. In the first place one could not find a better il-
lustration of the nature and character of what is vulgarly
known as a truceless war than the circumstances of this
one, and secondly one can see very clearly from all that
took place what kind of dangers those who employ mercenary forces should foresee and take early precautions to
avert, as well as in what lies the great difference of character between a confused hord of barbarians and men who
have been brought up in an educated, law-abiding, and
civilized community. But the most important thing is that
from the events of that period one can get an idea of the
causes of the Hannibalic war between the Romans and the
Carthaginians. As it is still a matter of dispute, not only
among historians, but among the combatants, what were

241 B.C.

---

[92] North of Rome in southern Etruria. A war of six days, ending in a treaty, *StV*494.   [93] The remainder of the book
through 88.12 is devoted to the uprising of the mercenaries
against Carthage and to Hamilcar's war against them in the years
241–238 (or 237); for its duration see 88. 7.

τοῖς πεπολεμηκόσιν ἔτι νῦν ἀμφισβητεῖσθαι τὰς αἰτίας, χρήσιμόν ἐστι τὴν ἀληθινωτάτην παραστῆσαι
διάληψιν τοῖς φιλομαθοῦσιν.

66. Ὡς γὰρ θᾶττον ἐπιτελεσθεισῶν τῶν προειρημένων διαλύσεων ἀποκατέστησε τὰς περὶ τὸν Ἔρυκα
δυνάμεις εἰς τὸ Λιλύβαιον ὁ Βάρκας, εὐθέως αὐτὸς μὲν
ἀπέθετο τὴν ἀρχήν, ὁ δ' ἐπὶ τῆς πόλεως στρατηγὸς
Γέσκων ἐγίνετο περὶ τὸ περαιοῦν τοὺς στρατιώτας εἰς
2 τὴν Λιβύην. προϊδόμενος δὲ τὸ μέλλον ἐμφρόνως
ἐνεβίβαζε κατὰ μέρη διαιρῶν αὐτοὺς καὶ διαλείμματα
3 ποιῶν τῆς ἐξαποστολῆς, βουλόμενος ἀναστροφὴν διδόναι τοῖς Καρχηδονίοις εἰς τὸ τοὺς καταπλεύσαντας
καὶ μισθοδοτηθέντας τὰ προσοφειλόμενα τῶν ὀψωνίων φθάνειν ἀπαλλαττομένους ἐκ τῆς Καρχηδόνος
εἰς τὴν οἰκείαν πρὶν ἢ τοὺς ἑξῆς περαιουμένους ἐπι-
4 καταλαβεῖν. ὁ μὲν οὖν Γέσκων ἐχόμενος ταύτης τῆς
5 ἐννοίας οὕτως ἐχείριζε τὰ κατὰ τὴν ἐξαποστολήν. οἱ
δὲ Καρχηδόνιοι τὰ μὲν οὐκ εὐπορούμενοι χρημάτων
διὰ τὰς προγεγενημένας δαπάνας, τὰ δὲ καὶ πεπεισμένοι παραιτήσεσθαι τοὺς μισθοφόρους μέρος τι τῶν
προσοφειλομένων ὀψωνίων, ἐὰν καὶ συναθροίσωσι
καὶ δέξωνται πάντας εἰς τὴν Καρχηδόνα, παρακατεῖ-
χον ἐκεῖ τοὺς καταπλέοντας διὰ ταύτην τὴν ἐλπίδα
6 καὶ συνεῖχον ἐν τῇ πόλει. γινομένων δὲ πλειόνων
ἀδικημάτων καὶ νύκτωρ καὶ μεθ' ἡμέραν, τὸ μὲν πρῶτον ὑπιδόμενοι τὸν ὄχλον καὶ τὴν συμβαίνουσαν
ἀκρασίαν ἠξίωσαν τοὺς ἡγεμόνας, ἕως ἂν ἑτοιμασθῇ
μὲν τὰ κατὰ τὰς σιταρχίας αὐτοῖς, προσδέξωνται δὲ

the actual causes of this latter war, it will be useful to students of history if I lay before them the explanation that is nearest to the truth.

66. It is this. When, at once on the conclusion of the treaty, Barcas had transferred his forces from Eryx to Lilybaeum he immediately resigned his command, and Gesco the commandant there took steps for sending the troops over to Africa. Foreseeing what was likely to happen, he very wisely embarked them in detachments and at certain intervals in order to give the Carthaginians time to pay them their arrears as they arrived and to pack them off to their own countries before the next batch that crossed could catch them up. Such was the idea Gesco had, and he managed to dispatch the troops in this manner, but the Carthaginians partly because, owing to their recent outlay, they were not very well off for money, and partly because they were convinced that the mercenaries would let them off part of their arrears of pay, once they had got them all collected in Carthage, detained them there on their arrival in this hope, confining them to the city. As they committed frequent offenses there both by night and by day, the government in the first place, suspicious of their numbers and their present licentious spirit, asked their commanding officers, until arrangements had been made for paying

τοὺς ἀπολειπομένους, ἀναχωρῆσαι πάντας εἴς τινα
πόλιν τὴν προσαγορευομένην Σίκκαν, λαβόντας εἰς
7 τὰ κατεπείγοντα χρυσοῦν ἕκαστον. προθύμως δὲ συν-
υπακουσάντων πρὸς τὴν ἔξοδον, καὶ βουλομένων
αὐτοῦ καταλιπεῖν τὰς ἀποσκευάς, καθάπερ καὶ τὸν
πρῶτον χρόνον ὑπῆρχον, ὡς θᾶττον ἐσομένης τῆς
8 ἐπανόδου πρὸς τοὺς ὀψωνιασμούς, ἀγωνιῶντες οἱ
Καρχηδόνιοι μήποτε διὰ χρόνου παραγεγονότες, καὶ
τινὲς μὲν τέκνων, ἔνιοι δὲ καὶ γυναικῶν ἱμείροντες, οἱ
μὲν οὐκ ἐκπορευθῶσι τὸ παράπαν, οἱ δ' ἐκπορευθέντες
αὖθις ἀνακάμπτωσι πρὸς ταῦτα, καὶ τῷ τοιούτῳ τρόπῳ μηδὲν ἧττον ἀδίκημα γίνηται κατὰ τὴν πόλιν,
9 ταῦτα προορώμενοι μετὰ πολλῆς ἀπεχθείας οὐδαμῶς
βουλομένους τοὺς ἀνθρώπους ἠνάγκασαν τὰς ἀπο-
10 σκευὰς μεθ' ἑαυτῶν ἀπαγαγεῖν. οἱ δὲ μισθοφόροι
συναναχθέντες εἰς τὴν Σίκκαν, καὶ διὰ πολλοῦ χρόνου
τετευχότες ἀνέσεως καὶ σχολῆς, ὅπερ ἀφυέστατον
ὑπάρχει ξενικαῖς δυνάμεσι, καὶ σχεδὸν ὡς εἰπεῖν
ἀρχηγὸν καὶ μόνον αἴτιον γίνεται στάσεως, διῆγον
11 ἀδεῶς. ἅμα δὲ ῥαθυμοῦντες, τινὲς μὲν αὐτῶν ἐξελογί-
ζοντο τὰ προσοφειλόμενα σφίσι τῶν ὀψωνίων ἐπὶ τὸ
πλεῖον, καὶ συγκεφαλαιούμενοι πολλαπλάσια τῶν
καθηκόντων, ταῦτ' ἔφασαν δεῖν ἀπαιτεῖν τοὺς Καρ-
12 χηδονίους· πάντες δ' ἀναμιμνησκόμενοι τῶν ἐπαγγελιῶν, ὧν οἱ στρατηγοὶ κατὰ τοὺς ἐπισφαλεῖς τῶν
καιρῶν παρακαλοῦντες σφᾶς ἐπεποίηντο, μεγάλας
εἶχον ἐλπίδας καὶ μεγάλην προσδοκίαν τῆς ἐσομένης
περὶ αὐτοὺς ἐπανορθώσεως.

196

them in full and those who were still missing had arrived, to withdraw them all to a town called Sicca,[94] each man receiving a gold stater for pressing expenses. The troops readily consented to leave the capital, but wished to leave their baggage there, as they had formerly done, thinking that they would be soon returning to be paid off. The Carthaginians, however, were afraid lest, longing to be with their wives or children after their recent protracted absence, they might in many cases refuse to leave Carthage, or, if they did, would come back again to their families, so that there would be no decrease of outrages in the city. In anticipation then of this, they compelled the men, much against their will and in a manner calculated to cause much offense, to take their personal possessions with them.[95] The mercenaries, when assembled in Sicca, lived in a free and easy manner, having not enjoyed for a long time relaxation of discipline and leisure, things most prejudicial to a force raised abroad, and nearly always the very arch-instigators and sole causes of mutiny. At the same time, as they had nothing else to do, some of them began reckoning up the total pay due to them, all to their own advantage, and having arrived at a most exorbitant result, submitted that this was the sum they should demand from the Carthaginians. The whole force remembered the promises the generals had made to them in critical situations, and had great hopes and indeed great expectations concerning the gain that was due to come to them.

[94] Some one hundred miles southwest of Carthage, modern El Kef.

[95] For ἀποσκευή see Holleaux, Ét. 3. 15–26.

THE HISTORIES OF POLYBIUS

67. διόπερ ἅμα τῷ συλλεχθῆναι πάντας εἰς τὴν Σίκκαν, καὶ παραγενόμενον Ἄννωνα τὸν ὑπάρχοντα στρατηγὸν ἐν τῇ Λιβύῃ τότε τῶν Καρχηδονίων μὴ οἷον τὰς ἐλπίδας καὶ τὰς ἐπαγγελίας ἐκπληροῦν, ἀλλὰ τοὐναντίον λέγοντα τὸ βάρος τῶν φόρων καὶ τὴν καθόλου στενοχωρίαν τῆς πόλεως ἐγχειρεῖν παραιτεῖσθαι μέρος τι τῶν ἐξ ὁμολόγου προσοφειλομένων

2 ὀψωνίων, εὐθέως διαφορὰ καὶ στάσις ἐγεννᾶτο καὶ συνδρομαὶ συνεχεῖς ἐγίνοντο, ποτὲ μὲν κατὰ γένη,

3 ποτὲ δ' ὁμοῦ πάντων. ὡς δ' ἂν μήθ' ὁμοεθνῶν μήθ' ὁμογλώττων ὑπαρχόντων, ἦν ἀμιξίας καὶ θορύβου καὶ

4 τῆς λεγομένης τύρβης πλῆρες τὸ στρατόπεδον. Καρχηδόνιοι γὰρ ἀεὶ χρώμενοι ποικίλαις καὶ μισθοφορικαῖς δυνάμεσι, πρὸς μὲν τὸ μὴ ταχέως συμφρονήσαντας ἀπειθεῖν μηδὲ δυσκαταπλήκτους εἶναι τοῖς ἡγουμένοις ὀρθῶς στοχάζονται, ποιοῦντες ἐκ πολλῶν

5 γενῶν τὴν δύναμιν, πρὸς δὲ τὸ γενομένης ὀργῆς ἢ διαβολῆς ἢ στάσεως διδάξαι καὶ πραῦναι καὶ μετα-

6 θεῖναι τοὺς ἠγνοηκότας ὁλοσχερῶς ἀστοχοῦσιν. οὐ γὰρ οἷον ἀνθρωπίνῃ χρῆσθαι κακίᾳ συμβαίνει τὰς τοιαύτας δυνάμεις, ὅταν ἅπαξ εἰς ὀργὴν καὶ διαβολὴν ἐμπέσωσι πρός τινας, ἀλλ' ἀποθηριοῦσθαι τὸ τελευ-

7 ταῖον καὶ παραστατικὴν λαμβάνειν διάθεσιν. ὃ καὶ τότε συνέβη γενέσθαι περὶ αὐτούς· ἦσαν γὰρ οἱ μὲν Ἴβηρες, οἱ δὲ Κελτοί, τινὲς δὲ Λιγυστῖνοι καὶ Βαλιαρεῖς, οὐκ ὀλίγοι δὲ μιξέλληνες, ὧν οἱ πλείους αὐτό-

8 μολοι καὶ δοῦλοι· τὸ δὲ μέγιστον μέρος αὐτῶν ἦν Λίβυες. διόπερ οὔτ' ἐκκλησιάσαι συναθροίσαντα πάν-

67. The consequence was that when the total force was assembled at Sicca, and when Hanno, who was then commander-in-chief in Africa, came there and not only said that it was impossible to meet their claims and fulfil their hopes, but on the contrary tried by dwelling on the present heavy taxation and general distress of Carthage to induce them to renounce some of their stipulated wage, it produced at once a spirit of dissension and sedition, and the soldiers began to hold constant meetings, sometimes of particular nations and sometimes general. As they were neither all of the same nationality nor spoke the same language, the camp was full of confusion and tumult and what is known as τύρβη or turbulence. For the Carthaginian practice of employing hired troops of various nationalities is indeed well calculated to prevent them from combining rapidly in acts of insubordination or disrespect to their officers, but in cases of an outburst of anger or of slanderous rumors or disaffection it is most prejudicial to all efforts to convey the truth to them, to calm their passions, or to show the ignorant their error. Indeed, such forces, when once their anger is aroused against anyone, or slander spreads among them, are not content with mere human wickedness, but end by becoming like wild beasts or men deranged, as happened in the present case. Some of these troops were Iberians, some Celts, some Ligurians, and some from the Balearic islands; there were a good many Greek halfbreeds, mostly deserters and slaves, but the largest portion consisted of Libyans. It was therefore im-

τας ὁμοῦ δυνατὸν ἦν οὔτ᾽ ἄλλην οὐδεμίαν εὑρέσθαι

9 πρὸς τοῦτο μηχανήν. πῶς γὰρ οἷόν τε; τὸν μὲν γὰρ στρατηγὸν εἰδέναι τὰς ἑκάστων διαλέκτους ἀδύνατον· διὰ πλειόνων δ᾽ ἑρμηνέων ἐκκλησιάζειν, ἅμα τετράκις καὶ πεντάκις περὶ ταὐτοῦ λέγοντα πράγματος, σχεδὸν

10 ὡς εἰπεῖν ἔτι τοῦ πρόσθεν ἀδυνατώτερον. λοιπὸν ἦν διὰ τῶν ἡγεμόνων ποιεῖσθαι τὰς ἀξιώσεις καὶ παρα-

11 κλήσεις· ὅπερ ἐπειρᾶτο τότε συνεχῶς ποιεῖν ὁ Ἄννων. ἀκμὴν δὲ καὶ τούτους συνέβαινεν ἃ μὲν οὐκ αἰσθάνε- σθαι τῶν λεγομένων, ἃ δὲ καὶ συναινέσαντας ἐνίοτε τῷ στρατηγῷ τἀναντία πρὸς τοὺς πολλοὺς ἀναγγέλ- λειν, τοὺς μὲν δι᾽ ἄγνοιαν, τοὺς δὲ διὰ κακίαν· ἐξ ὧν ἦν

12 ἀσαφείας, ἀπιστίας, ἀμιξίας, ἅπαντα πλήρη. πρὸς γὰρ τοῖς ἄλλοις ᾤοντο καὶ τοὺς Καρχηδονίους ἐπίτη- δες τοὺς μὲν εἰδότας στρατηγοὺς τὰς γεγενημένας χρείας κατὰ Σικελίαν ἐξ αὐτῶν, καὶ πεποιημένους σφίσι τὰς ἐπαγγελίας, οὐκ ἐξαποστέλλειν ὡς αὐτούς, τὸν δὲ μηδενὶ τούτων παρηκολουθηκότα τοῦτον ἐκπε-

13 πομφέναι. τέλος δ᾽ οὖν ἀπαξιώσαντες μὲν τὸν Ἄννω- να, διαπιστήσαντες δὲ τοῖς κατὰ μέρος ἡγεμόσιν, ἐξοργισθέντες δὲ πρὸς τοὺς Καρχηδονίους, ὥρμησαν πρὸς τὴν πόλιν· καὶ κατεστρατοπέδευσαν ἀπέχοντες ὡς ἂν ἑκατὸν καὶ εἴκοσι στάδια τῆς Καρχηδόνος ἐπὶ τῷ καλουμένῳ Τύνητι, πλείους ὄντες τῶν δισμυρίων.

68. Οἱ δὲ Καρχηδόνιοι τότε πρὸ ὀφθαλμῶν ἐλάμ-

2 βανον τὴν αὑτῶν ἄγνοιαν, ὅτ᾽ ἦν οὐδὲν ὄφελος. μεγάλα μὲν γὰρ ἥμαρτον, εἰς ἕνα τόπον ἀθροίσαντες τοσοῦτο πλῆθος μισθοφόρων, ἔχοντες οὐδεμίαν ἐλπί-

possible to assemble them and address them as a body or to do so by any other means; for how could the general be expected to know all their languages? And again to address them through several interpreters, repeating the same thing four or five times, was, if anything, more impracticable. The only means was to make demands or entreaties through their officers, as Hanno continued to attempt on the present occasion, and even these did not understand all that was told them, or at times, after seeming to agree with the general, addressed their troops in just the opposite sense either from ignorance or from malice. The consequence was that everything was in a state of uncertainty, mistrust and confusion. For one thing, they thought the Carthaginians had acted purposely in not communicating with them through the generals who were acquainted with their performances in Sicily and who had made them the promises of bounties, but in sending one who had not been present on any of those occasions. At length, then, refusing to treat with Hanno, thoroughly distrusting their divisional officers, and highly indignant with the Carthaginians, they marched on the capital and encamped at a distance of about one hundred and twenty stades from Carthage at the place called Tunis. They were more than twenty thousand in number.

68. Now, when there was no mending, it was brought home to the Carthaginians how blind they had been. For they had committed two great mistakes. The first was in collecting at one place so large a body of mercenaries while

3 δα πολεμικῆς χρείας ἐν ταῖς πολιτικαῖς δυνάμεσι,
τούτου δὲ μεῖζον ἔτι, προέμενοι τὰ τέκνα καὶ τὰς
γυναῖκας καὶ σὺν τούτοις τὰς ἀποσκευάς. οἷς ἐξῆν
ὁμήροις χρησαμένους ἀσφαλέστερον μὲν αὐτοὺς βουλεύσασθαι περὶ τῶν ὑποπιπτόντων, εὐπειθεστέροις δ'
4 ἐκείνοις χρῆσθαι πρὸς τὸ παρακαλούμενον, οὐ μὴν
ἀλλὰ καὶ καταπλαγέντες τὴν στρατοπεδείαν πᾶν ὑπέ-
5 μενον, σπουδάζοντες ἐξιλάσασθαι τὴν ὀργὴν αὐτῶν,
καὶ τάς τε τῶν ἐπιτηδείων ἀγορὰς ἐκπέμποντες δαψι-
λεῖς ἐπώλουν, καθὼς ἐκεῖνοι βούλοιντο καὶ τάττοιεν
τὰς τιμάς, τῶν τε τῆς γερουσίας ἀεί τινας ἐξαπέστελλον πρέσβεις, ὑπισχνούμενοι ποιήσειν πᾶν ὅ, τι ποτ'
6 ἂν αὐτοὺς ἀξιώσαιεν εἰ κατὰ δύναμιν. ἦν δὲ πολὺ τὸ
καθ' ἑκάστην ἡμέραν παρὰ τοῖς μισθοφόροις ἐπινοού-
μενον, ἅτε δὴ κατατεθαρρηκότων μὲν καὶ συντεθεωρη-
7 κότων τὴν κατάπληξιν καὶ πτοίαν τῶν Καρχηδονίων,
πεφρονηματισμένων δὲ καὶ πεπεισμένων διὰ τοὺς
προγεγονότας αὐτοῖς ἐν Σικελίᾳ πρὸς τὰ Ῥωμαϊκὰ
στρατόπεδα κινδύνους μὴ οἷον Καρχηδονίους ἀντο-
φθαλμῆσαί ποτ' ἂν πρὸς αὐτοὺς ἐν τοῖς ὅπλοις, ἀλλὰ
8 μηδὲ τῶν λοιπῶν ἀνθρώπων μηδένα ῥᾳδίως. διόπερ
ἅμα τῷ συγχωρῆσαι τὰ περὶ τῶν ὀψωνίων αὐτοῖς τοὺς
Καρχηδονίους εὐθέως ἐπέβαινον, καὶ τῶν τεθνεώτων
9 ἵππων ἀπήτουν τὰς ἀξίας. προσδεξαμένων δὲ καὶ
τοῦτο, πάλιν τῆς προσοφειλομένης σιτομετρίας ἐκ
πλείονος χρόνου τὴν μεγίστην γεγονυῖαν ἐν τῷ πολέ-
10 μῳ τιμὴν ἔφασκον αὐτοὺς δεῖν κομίζεσθαι. καθόλου δ'
ἀεί τι νέον καὶ καινὸν προσεξεύρισκον, εἰς ἀδύνατον

themselves they could hope for nothing from the fighting power of their civic force. Their second error was even more serious, to let out of their hands the women and children of the mercenaries as well as their movables, all which would have served as hostages, giving themselves greater security in their deliberations about the circumstances and ensuring a more favorable reception for their demands. Still now, in their alarm at the troops encamping so near, they were ready to put up with anything in their eagerness to propitiate them, sending out lavish supplies of provisions which they sold to them at any price they chose to pay and constantly dispatching envoys from the Senate, promising to meet all their demands as far as it was in their power. These increased daily, the mercenaries continuing to invent new claims, gaining confidence as they witnessed the terror and cowardice of the Carthaginians, and being convinced in their arrogance, owing to their success in Sicily against the Roman legions, that not only the Carthaginians, but any other people in the world would not readily face them in arms. When, therefore, the Carthaginians had agreed to their claims for pay, they went a step further and asked for the value of the horses they had lost. This also was conceded, whereupon they maintained that they ought to get the value of the rations of corn due to them for a considerable time at the highest price corn had stood at during the war. In short they always went on devising some new claim, putting matters off so as to make it

ἐκβάλλοντες τὴν διάλυσιν, διὰ τὸ πολλοὺς καχέκτας
11 καὶ στασιώδεις ἐν αὐτοῖς ὑπάρχειν. οὐ μὴν ἀλλὰ πᾶν
τὸ δυνατὸν ὑπισχνουμένων τῶν Καρχηδονίων, κατ-
ένευσαν ἐπιτρέψειν περὶ τῶν ἀμφισβητουμένων ἑνὶ
12 τῶν ἐν Σικελίᾳ γεγονότων στρατηγῶν. πρὸς μὲν οὖν
Ἀμίλκαν τὸν Βάρκαν, μεθ᾽ οὗ συγκεκινδυνεύκεσαν ἐν
τῇ Σικελίᾳ, δυσχερῶς εἶχον, δοκοῦντες οὐχ ἥκιστα δι᾽
ἐκεῖνον ὀλιγωρεῖσθαι, τῷ μήτε πρεσβεύειν πρὸς αὐτοὺς τήν τε στρατηγίαν ἑκουσίως δοκεῖν ἀποτεθεῖ-
13 σθαι· πρὸς δὲ Γέσκωνα πάνυ διέκειντο φιλανθρώπως,
ὃς ἐγεγόνει μὲν ἐν Σικελίᾳ στρατηγός, ἐπεποίητο δ᾽
αὐτῶν πρόνοιαν τὴν ἐνδεχομένην ἔν τε τοῖς ἄλλοις καὶ
μάλιστα περὶ τὴν ἀνακομιδήν. διόπερ ἐπέτρεψαν τούτῳ περὶ τῶν ἀμφισβητουμένων.

69. ὃς παραγενόμενος κατὰ θάλατταν μετὰ τῶν
χρημάτων, καὶ προσπλεύσας πρὸς τὸν Τύνητα, τὸ μὲν
πρῶτον λαμβάνων τοὺς ἡγεμόνας, μετὰ δὲ ταῦτα
2 συναθροίζων κατὰ γένη τοὺς πολλούς, ἃ μὲν ἐπετίμα
περὶ τῶν γεγονότων, ἃ δὲ διδάσκειν ἐπειρᾶτο περὶ τῶν
παρόντων· τὸ δὲ πλεῖον παρεκάλει πρὸς τὸ μέλλον,
ἀξιῶν αὐτοὺς εὔνους ὑπάρχειν τοῖς ἐξ ἀρχῆς μισθο-
3 δόταις. τέλος δ᾽ ὥρμησε πρὸς τὸ διαλύειν τὰ προσοφειλόμενα τῶν ὀψωνίων, κατὰ γένη ποιούμενος τὴν
4 μισθοδοσίαν. ἦν δέ τις Καμπανὸς ηὐτομοληκὼς παρὰ
τῶν Ῥωμαίων δοῦλος, ἔχων σωματικὴν δύναμιν καὶ
τόλμαν ἐν τοῖς πολεμικοῖς παράβολον, ὄνομα Σπέν-
5 διος. οὗτος εὐλαβούμενος μὴ παραγενόμενος αὐτὸν ὁ
δεσπότης κομίσηται, καὶ κατὰ τοὺς Ῥωμαίων νόμους

204

impossible to come to terms, a great many of them being disaffected and mutinous. However, on the Carthaginians promising to concede everything in their power, they agreed to refer the disputed points to one of the generals who had been present in Sicily. Now to Hamilcar Barcas, with whom they had served there, they were ill disposed, thinking that it was largely his fault that they had been slighted, since he never came himself as an envoy to them and was believed to have resigned his command voluntarily. But being very favorably inclined to Gesco, who had been general in Sicily and had been full of attention to them in other matters and in that of their transport, they submitted the points in dispute to him.

69. Gesco, on reaching Tunis by sea bringing the money, at first conferred privately with the officers, and subsequently held meetings of the troops according to their nationalities. He rebuked them for their past conduct, attempted to enlighten them about the present, but most of all dwelt on the future, begging them to show themselves well disposed to those in whose pay they had been from the outset. Finally he proceeded to discharge their arrears, paying off each nationality separately. There was a certain Campanian, a runaway Roman slave, called Spendius, a man of great physical strength and remarkable courage in war. He was afraid of his master coming to claim him, when, if given up, he would by Roman law be tortured

αἰκισθεὶς διαφθαρῇ, πᾶν ἐτόλμα καὶ λέγειν καὶ πράττειν, σπουδάζων διακόψαι τὰς διαλύσεις τὰς πρὸς
6 Καρχηδονίους. ἅμα δὲ τούτῳ καὶ Λίβυς τις Μάθως, ὃς
ἦν μὲν ἐλεύθερος καὶ τῶν συνεστρατευμένων, πλεῖστα
δὲ κεκινηκὼς κατὰ τὰς προειρημένας ταραχάς. ἀγω-
νιῶν οὖν μὴ τίσῃ καὶ τὴν ὑπὲρ τῶν λοιπῶν δίκην, ἐπὶ
7 τῆς αὐτῆς ἐγένετο γνώμης τοῖς περὶ τὸν Σπένδιον. καὶ
λαμβάνων τοὺς Λίβυας ὑπεδείκνυε διότι μετὰ τὸν
ὀψωνιασμὸν χωρισθέντων τῶν ἄλλων γενῶν εἰς τὰς
πατρίδας ἀπερείσονται καὶ τὴν ὑπὲρ ἐκείνων ὀργὴν
εἰς αὐτοὺς οἱ Καρχηδόνιοι, καὶ βουλήσονται διὰ τῆς
εἰς σφᾶς τιμωρίας ἅπαντας καταπλήξασθαι τοὺς ἐν
8 τῇ Λιβύῃ. ταχὺ δὲ προσανασεισθέντες οἱ πολλοὶ τοῖς
τοιούτοις λόγοις, καὶ λαμβανόμενοι βραχείας ἀφορμῆς ἐκ τοῦ τὸν Γέσκωνα τὰ μὲν ὀψώνια διαλύειν, τὰς
δὲ τιμὰς τοῦ τε σίτου καὶ τῶν ἵππων ὑπερτίθεσθαι,
9 συνέτρεχον εὐθέως εἰς ἐκκλησίαν. καὶ τοῦ μὲν Σπενδίου καὶ τοῦ Μάθω διαβαλλόντων καὶ κατηγορούντων
τοῦ τε Γέσκωνος καὶ τῶν Καρχηδονίων ἤκουον, καὶ
10 προσεῖχον ἐπιμελῶς τὸν νοῦν τοῖς λεγομένοις. εἰ δέ
τις ἕτερος προπορευθείη συμβουλεύσων, οὐδ᾽ αὐτὸ
τοῦτο περιμείναντες ἕως τοῦ γνῶναι πότερον ἀντερῶν
ἢ συνηγορήσων πάρεστι τοῖς περὶ τὸν Σπένδιον,
11 παραχρῆμα βάλλοντες τοῖς λίθοις ἀπέκτεινον. καὶ
πολλοὺς δὴ τῷ τοιούτῳ τρόπῳ κατὰ τὰς συνδρομὰς
12 καὶ τῶν ἡγεμόνων καὶ τῶν ἰδιωτῶν διέφθειρον. καὶ
μόνον τὸ ῥῆμα τοῦτο κοινῇ συνίεσαν τὸ βάλλε διὰ τὸ
συνεχῶς αὐτὸ πράττειν. μάλιστα δὲ τοῦτ᾽ ἐποίουν,

and put to death. He therefore hesitated at nothing in his
endeavor both by speech and action to break off the negotiations with the Carthaginians. He was supported by a
Libyan called Mathos, who was indeed a freeman and a
member of the force, but had taken a leading part in the
late disturbances. Consequently he stood in great fear of
being singled out to bear the whole penalty and therefore
was of one mind with Spendius. Taking the Libyans aside,
he pointed out to them that when the other nations de-
parted to their own countries after being paid off, they
would be left to bear the whole weight of the wrath of the
Carthaginians, whose object it would be by the punishment they inflicted on them to terrorize all their Libyan
subjects. The men were soon stirred by such arguments,
and availing themselves of the slender pretext that Gesco
while discharging their pay postponed the compensation
for the horses and corn, they at once held a meeting. When
Spendius and Mathos began to traduce and accuse Gesco
and the Carthaginians, they were all ears, and listened with
great attention, but if anyone else came forward to offer an
opinion, they did not even wait to find out if he were going
to speak in favor of Spendius or against him, but at once
stoned him to death. Numbers both of the officers and pri-
vates perished thus in the different meetings, and in fact
this phrase "Stone him" was the only one that became intelligible to all the different nations, owing to the frequency of the act. They used to behave thus mostly when

13 ὁπότε μεθυσθέντες ἀπὸ τῶν ἀρίστων συνδράμοιεν.
διόπερ ὅτε τις ἄρξαιτο βάλλε λέγειν, οὕτως ἐγίνετο
πανταχόθεν ἅμα καὶ ταχέως ὥστε μηδένα δύνασθαι
14 διαφυγεῖν τῶν ἅπαξ προελθόντων. πλὴν οὐδενὸς ἔτι
τολμῶντος συμβουλεύειν διὰ ταύτην τὴν αἰτίαν, κατέστησαν αὐτῶν στρατηγοὺς Μάθω καὶ Σπένδιον.

70. ὁ δὲ Γέσκων ἑώρα μὲν τὴν ὅλην ἀκαταστασίαν
καὶ ταραχήν, περὶ πλείστου δὲ ποιούμενος τὸ τῇ
πατρίδι συμφέρον, καὶ θεωρῶν ὅτι τούτων ἀποθη-
ριωθέντων κινδυνεύουσι προφανῶς οἱ Καρχηδόνιοι
2 τοῖς ὅλοις πράγμασι, παρεβάλλετο καὶ προσεκαρτέρει, ποτὲ μὲν τοὺς προεστῶτας αὐτῶν εἰς τὰς χεῖρας
3 λαμβάνων, ποτὲ δὲ κατὰ γένη συναθροίζων καὶ παρακαλῶν. οὐ μὴν ἀλλὰ τῶν Λιβύων οὐδέπω κεκομισμέ-
νων τὰς σιταρχίας, οἰομένων δὲ δεῖν ἀποδεδόσθαι
σφίσι, καὶ προσιόντων θρασέως, βουλόμενος ὁ
Γέσκων ἐπιπλῆξαι τὴν προπέτειαν αὐτῶν, Μάθω τὸν
στρατηγὸν ἀπαιτεῖν ἐκέλευσεν. οἱ δ᾽ ἐπὶ τοσοῦτον διωρ-
4 γίσθησαν ὥστ᾽ οὐδὲ τὸν τυχόντα χρόνον ἀναστροφὴν
δόντες ὥρμησαν τὸ μὲν πρῶτον ἐπὶ τὸ διαρπάζειν τὰ
πρόχειρα τῶν χρημάτων, μετὰ δὲ ταῦτα συλλαμ-
βάνειν τόν τε Γέσκωνα καὶ τοὺς μετ᾽ αὐτοῦ Καρ-
5 χηδονίους. οἱ δὲ περὶ τὸν Μάθω καὶ τὸν Σπένδιον
ὑπολαμβάνοντες τάχιστ᾽ ἂν οὕτως ἐκκαυθῆναι τὸν
πόλεμον, εἰ παράνομόν τι πράξειαν καὶ παράσπονδον,
συνήργουν ταῖς τῶν ὄχλων ἀπονοίαις, καὶ τὴν μὲν
ἀποσκευὴν τῶν Καρχηδονίων ἅμα τοῖς χρήμασι διήρ-
παζον, τὸν δὲ Γέσκωνα καὶ τοὺς σὺν αὐτῷ δήσαντες

they held meetings after their midday meal in a drunken condition, so that the moment anyone called out "Stone him," the stones flew from all sides and so quickly that it was impossible for anyone who once came forward to address them to escape. As, for this reason no one dared any longer to express an opinion, they appointed Mathos and Spendius Generals.

70. Gesco saw how complete was the disorganization and disturbance, but valuing more than anything the interest of his country and foreseeing that if these troops became utterly deaf to all considerations of humanity, Carthage would evidently be in the gravest danger, he persisted, at great personal risk, in his conciliatory efforts, sometimes conferring privately with their officers, and at other times summoning and addressing meetings of the separate nations. The Libyans, however, had not yet received their pay,[96] and considering it overdue, came to him to demand it in a very insolent manner, when Gesco, thinking to rebuke their presumption, told them to go and ask Mathos their "General" for it. This aroused their anger to such a pitch, that without a moment's delay they, first of all, seized on what money they could lay their hands on and next arrested Gesco and the Carthaginians who were with him. As for Mathos and Spendius, thinking that the most expeditious means of setting war ablaze would be to commit some violation of law or good faith, they cooperated in the excesses of the soldiery, plundering the personal effects as well as the money chests of the Carthaginians, and after subjecting Gesco and those with him to the outrage of

96 A possible alternative is "their ration allowance."

6 ὑβριστικῶς εἰς φυλακὴν παρεδίδοσαν. καὶ τὸ λοιπὸν
ἐπολέμουν ἤδη φανερῶς πρὸς τοὺς Καρχηδονίους,
συνωμοσίας ἀσεβεῖς καὶ παρὰ τὰ κοινὰ τῶν ἀνθρώπων ἔθη ποιησάμενοι.

7 Ὁ μὲν οὖν πρὸς τοὺς ξένους καὶ Λιβυκὸς ἐπικλη-
θεὶς πόλεμος διὰ ταῦτα καὶ τοιαύτην ἔλαβε τὴν

8 ἀρχήν. οἱ δὲ περὶ τὸν Μάθω συντελεσάμενοι τὰ προειρημένα παραυτίκα μὲν ἐξαπέστελλον πρέσβεις ἐπὶ
τὰς κατὰ τὴν Λιβύην πόλεις, παρακαλοῦντες ἐπὶ τὴν
ἐλευθερίαν καὶ δεόμενοι σφίσι βοηθεῖν καὶ συνεπι-

9 λαμβάνεσθαι τῶν πραγμάτων. μετὰ δὲ ταῦτα πάντων
σχεδὸν τῶν κατὰ τὴν Λιβύην ἑτοίμως συνυπακου-
σάντων αὐτοῖς πρὸς τὴν ἀπὸ τῶν Καρχηδονίων ἀπόστασιν, καὶ τάς τε χορηγίας καὶ τὰς βοηθείας προθύμως ἐξαποστελλόντων, διελόντες σφᾶς πολιορκεῖν
ἐνεχείρησαν οἱ μὲν τὴν Ἰτύκην, οἱ δὲ τοὺς Ἱππακρίτας, διὰ τὸ ταύτας τὰς πόλεις μὴ βούλεσθαι μετασχεῖν αὐτοῖς τῆς ἀποστάσεως.

71. Καρχηδόνιοι δὲ τοὺς μὲν κατ᾽ ἰδίαν βίους ἀεὶ
διεξαγαγόντες ἀπὸ τῶν ἐκ τῆς χώρας γεννημάτων,
τὰς δὲ κοινὰς παρασκευὰς καὶ χορηγίας ἀθροίζοντες
ἐκ τῶν κατὰ τὴν Λιβύην προσόδων, ἔτι δὲ πολεμεῖν

2 εἰθισμένοι ξενικαῖς δυνάμεσι, τότε πάντων ἅμα τούτων οὐ μόνον ἐστερημένοι παραλόγως, ἀλλὰ καὶ καθ᾽
αὐτῶν ὁρῶντες ἕκαστα τῶν προειρημένων ἐπιστρέ-
φοντα, τελέως ἐν μεγάλῃ δυσθυμίᾳ καὶ δυσελπιστίᾳ
καθέστασαν, ἅτε παρὰ τὴν προσδοκίαν αὐτοῖς τῶν

3 πραγμάτων ἀποβεβηκότων. τετρυμένοι γὰρ ἐν τῷ

putting them in fetters, gave them into custody. From this time forward they were at open war with Carthage, having bound themselves by certain impious oaths contrary to the principles recognized by all mankind.

Such then was the origin and beginning of the war 240 B.C. against the mercenaries, generally known as the Libyan war. Mathos, having so far carried out his purpose, at once sent envoys to the Libyan towns urging them to strike a blow for liberty and imploring their support and practical assistance. Hereupon, when nearly all the Libyans had agreed to join in the revolt against Carthage and willingly contributed troops and supplies, they divided their forces into two and undertook the sieges of Utica and Hippou Acra,[97] since these cities had refused to participate in the rebellion.

71. The Carthaginians had ever been accustomed to support their lives individually from the produce of the country, their public expenses for armaments and commissariat had been met by the revenue they derived from Libya, and they had always been in the habit of employing hired soldiers. At the present moment not only did they find themselves deprived of all these resources at one blow, but actually saw them turned against themselves. Consequently they fell into a state of utter depression and despondency, things having turned out quite otherwise than they expected. For they had been much worn by

[97] Modern Bizerta.

περὶ Σικελίας πολέμῳ συνεχῶς, ἤλπιζον ἐπιτελεσθεισῶν τῶν διαλύσεων ἀναπνοῆς τινος τεύξεσθαι καὶ
4 καταστάσεως εὐδοκουμένης. συνέβαινε δ᾽ αὐτοῖς
τἀναντία· μείζονος γὰρ ἐνίστατο πολέμου καταρχὴ
5 καὶ φοβερωτέρου. πρόσθεν μὲν γὰρ ὑπὲρ Σικελίας
ἠμφισβήτουν Ῥωμαίοις, τότε δὲ περὶ σφῶν αὐτῶν καὶ
τῆς πατρίδος ἔμελλον κινδυνεύσειν, πόλεμον ἀναλαμ-
6 βάνοντες ἐμφύλιον. πρὸς δὲ τούτοις οὐχ ὅπλων πλῆθος, οὐ ναυτικὴ δύναμις, οὐ πλοίων κατασκευὴ παρ᾽
αὐτοῖς ἦν, ὡς ἂν τοσαύταις ναυμαχίαις περιπεπτω-
κότων· καὶ μὴν οὐδὲ χορηγιῶν διάθεσις οὐδὲ φίλων
οὐδὲ συμμάχων τῶν βοηθησόντων ἔξωθεν ἐλπὶς οὐδ᾽
7 ἡτισοῦν ὑπῆρχε. διὸ καὶ τότε σαφῶς ἔγνωσαν ἡλίκην
ἔχει διαφορὰν ξενικὸς καὶ διαπόντιος πόλεμος ἐμφυ-
8 λίου στάσεως καὶ ταραχῆς. Οὐχ ἥκιστα δ᾽ αὐτοὶ
σφίσι τῶν τοιούτων καὶ τηλικούτων κακῶν ἐγεγό-
νεισαν αἴτιοι.

72. κατὰ γὰρ τὸν προγεγονότα πόλεμον εὐλόγους
ἀφορμὰς ἔχειν ὑπολαμβάνοντες, πικρῶς ἐπεστάτη-
2 σαν τῶν κατὰ τὴν Λιβύην ἀνθρώπων, παραιρούμενοι
μὲν τῶν ἄλλων πάντων τῶν καρπῶν τοὺς ἡμίσεις,
διπλασίους δὲ ταῖς πόλεσι τοὺς φόρους ἢ πρὶν ἐπιτάττοντες, συγγνώμην δὲ τοῖς ἀπόροις ἢ συμπεριφορὰν οὐδ᾽
3 ἡντινοῦν ἐπ᾽ οὐδενὶ τῶν πραττομένων διδόντες, θαυ-
μάζοντες δὲ καὶ τιμῶντες τῶν στρατηγῶν οὐ τοὺς
πρᾴως καὶ φιλανθρώπως τῷ πλήθει χρωμένους, ἀλλὰ
τοὺς αὑτοῖς μὲν ἑτοιάζοντας πλείστας χορηγίας κἀπι-
4 σκευάς, τοῖς δὲ κατὰ τὴν χώραν πικρότατα χρωμένους,

the long continued war for Sicily, and had hoped that the peace would procure them some rest and a grateful period of tranquillity, and what happened was just the reverse, as they were now threatened by the outbreak of a greater and more formidable war. In the former case they were disputing the dominion of Sicily with the Romans, but now, with a civil war on their hands, they were about to fight a domestic war for their own existence and that of their native city. Besides neither had they a sufficient supply of arms, nor sailors, nor any supply of ships, so many had been the battles in which they had been engaged at sea. They had not even the means of providing supplies and not a single hope of external assistance from friends or allies. So it was now that they thoroughly realized how great is the difference between a war against a foreign state carried on over sea and civil discord and disturbance. They had chiefly themselves to thank for all these grievous mischances.

72. During the former war they had thought themselves reasonably justified in making their government of the Libyans very harsh. They had exacted from the peasantry, without exception, half of their crops, and had doubled the taxation of the townsmen without allowing exemption from any tax or even a partial abatement to the poor. They had applauded and honored not those governors who treated the people with gentleness and humanity, but those who procured for Carthage the largest amount of supplies and stores and used the country people most

ὧν εἷς ἦν Ἄννων. τοιγαροῦν οἱ μὲν ἄνδρες οὐχ οἷον
5 παρακλήσεως πρὸς τὴν ἀπόστασιν, ἀλλ' ἀγγέλου
μόνον ἐδεήθησαν· αἱ δὲ γυναῖκες αἱ τὸν πρὸ τοῦ
χρόνον ἀπαγομένους περιορῶσαι τοὺς σφετέρους ἄνδρας καὶ γονεῖς πρὸς τὰς εἰσφοράς, τότε συνομνύ-
ουσαι κατὰ πόλεις ἐφ' ᾧ μηδὲν κρύψειν τῶν ὑπαρχόντων αὐταῖς, ἀφαιρούμεναι τὸν κόσμον εἰσέφερον
6 ἀπροφασίστως εἰς τοὺς ὀψωνιασμούς. καὶ τοιαύτην
παρεσκεύασαν εὐπορίαν τοῖς περὶ τὸν Μάθω καὶ
Σπένδιον ὥστε μὴ μόνον διαλῦσαι τὰ προσοφειλόμενα τῶν ὀψωνίων τοῖς μισθοφόροις κατὰ τὰς ἐπαγγελίας, ἃς ἐποιήσαντο πρὸς τὴν ἀπόστασιν, ἀλλὰ καὶ
7 πρὸς τὸ συνεχὲς εὐπορῆσαι χορηγίας. οὕτως οὐδέποτε
δεῖ πρὸς τὸ παρὸν μόνον, ἔτι δὲ μᾶλλον πρὸς τὸ
μέλλον ἀποβλέπειν ἀεὶ τοὺς ὀρθῶς βουλευομένους.

73. Οὐ μὴν ἀλλὰ καίπερ ἐν τοιούτοις κακοῖς ὄντες
οἱ Καρχηδόνιοι, προστησάμενοι τὸν Ἄννωνα στρατηγὸν διὰ τὸ δοκεῖν τοῦτον καὶ πρότερον αὐτοῖς τὰ
κατὰ τὴν Ἑκατοντάπυλον τῆς Λιβύης καταστρέψα-
σθαι, συνήθροιζον μὲν μισθοφόρους, καθώπλιζον δὲ
2 τοὺς ἐν ταῖς ἡλικίαις τῶν πολιτῶν· ἐγύμναζον δὲ καὶ
συνέταττον τοὺς πολιτικοὺς ἱππεῖς· παρεσκεύαζον δὲ
καὶ τὰ περιλιπῆ τῶν πλοίων, τριήρεις καὶ πεντη-
3 κοντόρους καὶ τὰ μέγιστα τῶν ἀκατίων. οἱ δὲ περὶ τὸν
Μάθω, παραγενομένων αὐτοῖς εἰς ἑπτὰ μυριάδας Λιβύων, ἐπιδιελόντες τούτους ἀσφαλῶς ἐπολιόρκουν
τοὺς Ἰτυκαίους καὶ τοὺς Ἱππακρίτας, βεβαίως δὲ τὴν
ἐν τῷ Τύνητι στρατοπεδείαν κατεῖχον, ἀποκεκλείκε-

harshly—Hanno for example. The consequence was that the male population required no incitement to revolt—a mere messenger was sufficient—while the women, who had constantly witnessed the arrest of their husbands and fathers for nonpayment of taxes, solemnly bound themselves by oath in each city to conceal none of their belongings, and stripping themselves of their jewels contributed them ungrudgingly to the war fund. Mathos and Spendius were thus so well off that not only could they pay the soldiers their arrears, as they had promised in inciting them to mutiny, but found themselves furnished with ample means for a protracted war. This teaches us that it is the right policy not only to look to the present, but to look forward still more attentively to the future.

73. Yet, although the Carthaginians were in such straits, they first of all appointed Hanno to the command, as he had, they thought, on a former occasion brought matters concerning Hecatompylus in Libya[98] to a satisfactory conclusion; they next busied themselves with enrolling mercenaries and arming the citizens of military age. They also mustered and drilled their civic cavalry and got ready what ships they had left, consisting of triremes, ships with fifty oars and the largest of their light craft. Meanwhile Mathos, when about seventy thousand Libyans had joined him, divided them into several forces with which he maintained unmolested the sieges of Utica and Hippou Acra, secured his main camp at Tunis and thus shut out the Carthaginians

[98] Roman Theveste, modern Tebessa in Numidia. P. here presupposes what will be told by Diodorus 24. 10. 2: its capture during the First Punic War.

σαν δὲ τοὺς Καρχηδονίους ἁπάσης τῆς ἐκτὸς Λιβύης.

4 ἡ γὰρ Καρχηδὼν αὐτὴ μὲν ἐν κόλπῳ κεῖται, προτεί-
νουσα καὶ χερρονησίζουσα τῇ θέσει, τὸ μὲν τῇ θαλάττῃ, τὸ δέ τι καὶ λίμνῃ περιεχομένη κατὰ τὸ πλεῖστον·

5 ὁ δὲ συνάπτων ἰσθμὸς αὐτὴν τῇ Λιβύῃ τὸ πλάτος ὡς
εἴκοσι καὶ πέντε σταδίων ἐστί. τούτου δ' ἐπὶ μὲν τοῦ
πρὸς τὸ πέλαγος νεύοντος μέρους οὐ μακρὰν ἡ τῶν
Ἰτυκαίων κεῖται πόλις, ἐπὶ δὲ θατέρου παρὰ τὴν

6 λίμνην ὁ Τύνης. ἐφ' ὧν ἑκατέρων τότε στρατοπεδεύσαντες οἱ μισθοφόροι, καὶ διακλείσαντες ἀπὸ τῆς
χώρας τοὺς Καρχηδονίους, λοιπὸν ἐπεβούλευον αὐτῇ

7 τῇ πόλει, καὶ ποτὲ μὲν ἡμέρας, ποτὲ δὲ καὶ νύκτωρ
παραγινόμενοι πρὸς τὸ τεῖχος, εἰς φόβους καὶ θορύ-
βους ὁλοσχερεῖς ἐνέβαλλον τοὺς ἔνδον.

74. Ἄννων δὲ περὶ μὲν τὰς παρασκευὰς ἐνδεχομέ-
νως ἐγίνετο· καὶ γὰρ ἦν πρὸς τοῦτο τὸ μέρος εὐφυής·

2 ἐξορμήσας δὲ μετὰ τῆς δυνάμεως ἕτερος ἦν· καὶ γὰρ
τοῖς καιροῖς ἀστόχως ἐχρῆτο καὶ τοῖς ὅλοις πράγμα-

3 σιν ἀπείρως καὶ νωθρῶς. διὸ καὶ τὸ μὲν πρῶτον εἰς
Ἰτύκην παραβοηθήσας τοῖς πολιορκουμένοις καὶ
καταπληξάμενος τοὺς ὑπεναντίους τῷ πλήθει τῶν θη-
ρίων· εἶχε γὰρ οὐκ ἐλάττους ἑκατὸν ἐλεφάντων· καὶ
μετὰ ταῦτα λαβὼν προτερήματος ἀρχὴν ὁλοσχεροῦς
οὕτως ἐχρήσατο κακῶς ὥστε κινδυνεῦσαι προσαπο-

4 λέσαι καὶ τοὺς πολιορκουμένους. κομίσας γὰρ ἐκ τῆς
πόλεως τοὺς καταπέλτας καὶ τὰ βέλη καὶ συλλήβδην
ἁπάσας τὰς πρὸς τὴν πολιορκίαν παρασκευάς, καὶ
στρατοπεδεύσας πρὸ τῆς πόλεως, ἐνεχείρησε προσ-

from all outer Libya. Carthage, I should explain, lies in a gulf, on a promontory or peninsula surrounded mostly by the sea and in part by a lake. The isthmus which connects it with Libya is about twenty-five stades in width and on the side of this isthmus which faces the sea, at no great distance from the capital, lies Utica, while Tunis is on the other side by the lake. So that the mutineers, encamped now as they were before both of these towns and thus shutting off Carthage from the land, continued to threaten the capital itself, appearing before the walls sometimes by day and sometimes by night and creating the utmost terror and commotion within.

74. Hanno was doing fairly well in the matter of outfit, his talent lying in that direction, but when it came to taking the field with his forces, he was another man. He had no idea how to avail himself of opportunities and generally showed an entire lack of experience and energy. It was then that, as regards Utica, he began by coming to the help of the besieged and terrifying the enemy by his strong force of elephants, of which he had no less than a hundred; but when, in consequence of this, he had a chance of gaining a decisive success, he made such poor use of his advantage that he very nearly brought a catastrophe on the besieged, as well as on himself. For bringing from Utica[99] catapults, missiles and all requirements for a siege and encamping before the city he undertook the assault of the en-

---

[99] While the text says "from the city," the context makes clear that this is Utica, not Carthage.

5 βάλλειν πρὸς τὸν τῶν ὑπεναντίων χάρακα. τῶν δὲ
θηρίων βιασαμένων εἰς τὴν παρεμβολήν, οὐ δυνάμενοι τὸ βάρος οὐδὲ τὴν ἔφοδον οἱ πολέμιοι μεῖναι,
6 πάντες ἐξέπεσον ἐκ τῆς στρατοπεδείας. καὶ πολλοὶ
μὲν αὐτῶν ἀπέθανον τρωθέντες ὑπὸ τῶν θηρίων, τὸ δὲ
διασῳζόμενον μέρος πρός τινα λόφον ἐρυμνὸν καὶ
σύμφυτον ἔμενε, πιστεῦον ταῖς ἐξ αὐτῶν τῶν τόπων
7 ἀσφαλείαις. ὁ δ' Ἄννων, εἰθισμένος Νομάσι καὶ Λίβυσι πολεμεῖν, οἵτινες ὅταν ἅπαξ ἐγκλίνωσι, ποιοῦνται τὴν φυγὴν ἐπὶ δύ' ἡμέρας καὶ τρεῖς ἐκτοπίζοντες
αὐτούς, ὑπολαβὼν καὶ τότε πέρας ἔχειν τοῦ πολέμου
8 καὶ νενικηκέναι τοῖς ὅλοις, τῶν μὲν στρατιωτῶν ὠλι-
γώρησε καὶ καθόλου τῆς παρεμβολῆς, αὐτὸς δ' εἰσελθὼν εἰς τὴν πόλιν ἐγίνετο περὶ τὴν τοῦ σώματος
9 θεραπείαν. οἱ δὲ συμπεφευγότες τῶν μισθοφόρων εἰς
τὸν λόφον, σύντροφοι μὲν γεγονότες τῆς Βάρκα τόλμης, συνήθεις δ' ἐκ τῶν κατὰ Σικελίαν ἀγώνων πολλάκις τῆς αὐτῆς ἡμέρας ποτὲ μὲν ὑποχωρεῖν, ποτὲ δὲ
10 πάλιν ἐκ μεταβολῆς ἐγχειρεῖν τοῖς πολεμίοις, καὶ τότε
συνιδόντες τὸν μὲν στρατηγὸν ἀπηλλαγμένον εἰς τὴν
πόλιν, τοὺς δὲ πολλοὺς διὰ τὸ προτέρημα ῥαθυμοῦν-
11 τας καὶ διαρρέοντας ἐκ τῆς στρατοπεδείας, συστραφέντες ἐπιτίθενται τῷ χάρακι, καὶ πολλοὺς μὲν αὐτῶν
ἀπέκτειναν, τοὺς δὲ λοιποὺς ἠνάγκασαν φυγεῖν
12 αἰσχρῶς ὑπὸ τὰ τείχη καὶ τὰς πύλας. ἐκυρίευσαν δὲ
τῆς ἀποσκευῆς ἁπάσης καὶ τῆς τῶν πολιορκουμένων
παρασκευῆς· ἣν Ἄννων πρὸς τοῖς ἄλλοις ἐκκομίσας
13 ἐκ τῆς πόλεως ἐποίησε τοῖς ἐχθροῖς ὑποχείριον. οὐ

218

emy's entrenched camp. When the elephants forced their way into the camp, the enemy unable to face the weight of their attack all evacuated it. Many of them were mangled and killed by the elephants, but those who escaped rallied on a steep hill overgrown with brushwood, relying on the natural security of the position. Hanno had been accustomed to fight with Numidians and Libyans, who once they give way continue their flight for two or three days, trying to get as far away as possible. Thinking then, on the present occasion too, that the war was over and he had secured a complete victory he took no precaution for the safety of his army and camp, but entered the city and occupied himself with the care of his person. The mercenaries, who had rallied on the hill, were men schooled in the daring tactics of Barcas and accustomed from their fighting in Sicily to make in one day repeated retirements followed by fresh attacks. At present, on seeing that the general was absent in the city, while the troops were at their ease owing to their success and streaming out of their camp, they drew themselves up and attacked the camp, putting many to the sword and compelling the rest to take refuge ignominiously under the walls and at the gates. They captured all the baggage and all the artillery of the besieged, which Hanno had brought out of the town and added to his own, thus putting it in the enemy's hands. This was not the only

μόνον δὲ περὶ τοῦτον τὸν καιρὸν οὕτως ἀνεστράφη νωθρῶς, ἀλλὰ καὶ μετ᾽ ὀλίγας ἡμέρας περὶ τὴν καλουμένην Γόρζαν ἀντιστρατοπεδευσάντων αὐτῷ τῶν πολεμίων, λαβὼν καιροὺς δὶς μὲν ἐκ παρατάξεως εἰς τὸ

14 νικᾶν, δὶς δ᾽ ἐξ ἐπιθέσεως, ἅτε καὶ στρατοπεδευόντων σύνεγγυς αὐτῷ τῶν ὑπεναντίων, ἀμφοτέρους δοκεῖ τούτους εἰκῇ καὶ παραλόγως προέσθαι.

75. Διόπερ οἱ Καρχηδόνιοι, θεωροῦντες αὐτὸν κακῶς χειρίζοντα τὰς πράξεις, Ἀμίλκαν τὸν ἐπικαλού-

2 μενον Βάρκαν αὖθις προεστήσαντο, καὶ τοῦτον ἐξέπεμπον εἰς τὸν ἐνεστῶτα πόλεμον στρατηγόν, δόντες ἑβδομήκοντα μὲν ἐλέφαντας καὶ τοὺς ἐπισυνηγμένους τῶν μισθοφόρων καὶ τοὺς ηὐτομοληκότας ἀπὸ τῶν πολεμίων, ἅμα δὲ τούτοις πολιτικοὺς ἱππεῖς καὶ πε-

3 ζούς, ὥστε τοὺς σύμπαντας εἰς μυρίους ὑπάρχειν. ὃς κατὰ τὴν πρώτην εὐθέως ἔξοδον καταπληξάμενος τῷ παραδόξῳ τῆς ἐπιβολῆς ἥττησε μὲν τὰς ψυχὰς τῶν ὑπεναντίων, ἔλυσε δὲ τὴν τῆς Ἰτύκης πολιορκίαν, ἐφάνη δ᾽ ἄξιος τῶν προγεγονότων ἔργων καὶ τῆς παρὰ

4 τῷ πλήθει προσδοκίας. τὸ δὲ πραχθὲν ἦν ὑπ᾽ αὐτοῦ περὶ τὴν χρείαν ταύτην τοιοῦτον. τῶν γεωλόφων τῶν ἐπιζευγνύντων τὸν αὐχένα τὸν συνάπτοντα τὴν Καρχηδόνα πρὸς τὴν Λιβύην ὄντων δυσβάτων, καὶ χειροποιήτους ἐχόντων διεκβολὰς ἐπὶ τὴν χώραν, συνέβαινε τοὺς περὶ τὸν Μάθω πάντας τοὺς διὰ τῶν προειρημένων λόφων εὐκαίρως κειμένους τόπους φυ-

5 λακαῖς διειληφέναι, πρὸς δὲ τούτοις τοῦ προσαγορευομένου Μακάρα ποταμοῦ διείργοντος κατά τινας

occasion on which he acted so negligently, but a few days later at a place called Gorza,[100] when the enemy were encamped opposite him and owing to their proximity he had four opportunities of beating them, twice in a pitched battle and twice by a surprise attack, he is said in each case, even with the enemy camped near him, to have thrown them away by his heedlessness and lack of judgment.

75. The Carthaginians, in consequence, seeing that he was mismanaging matters, again appointed Hamilcar Barcas to the command and dispatched him to the war on hand, giving him seventy elephants, all the additional mercenaries they had been able to collect, and the deserters from the enemy, besides their burgher forces, horse and foot, so that in all he had about ten thousand men. Hamilcar, on his very first expedition, struck terror into the enemy by the unexpectedness of the attack, cowing their spirit, raising the siege of Utica, and showing himself worthy of his past exploits and of the high expectations of the populace. What he accomplished in this campaign was as follows. On the neck of land connecting Carthage with Libya is a chain of hills difficult of access and with several passes to the country artificially cut in them. Mathos had posted guards in all those spots which were favorable for the passage of the hills. In addition to this there is a river called Macaras which shuts off in certain places the access

100 Unknown, near Utica.

τόπους παραπλησίως τὴν ἐπὶ τὴν χώραν τοῖς ἐκ τῆς
πόλεως ἔξοδον, καὶ διὰ τὸ πλῆθος τοῦ ῥεύματος ἀβά-
του κατὰ τὸ πλεῖστον ὑπάρχοντος, μιᾶς δ᾽ οὔσης ἐπ᾽
αὐτῷ γεφύρας, καὶ ταύτην τηρεῖν τὴν δίοδον ἀσφα-
6 λῶς, πόλιν ἐπ᾽ αὐτῆς ᾠκοδομηκότας. ἐξ ὧν συνέβαινε
τοὺς Καρχηδονίους μὴ οἷον στρατοπέδῳ τῆς χώρας
ἐπιβαίνειν, ἀλλὰ μηδὲ τοὺς κατ᾽ ἰδίαν θέλοντας δια-
7 πεσεῖν ῥᾳδίως ἂν δύνασθαι λαθεῖν τοὺς ὑπεναντίους.
εἰς ἃ βλέπων Ἀμίλκας, καὶ παντὸς πράγματος καὶ
καιροῦ πεῖραν λαμβάνων διὰ τὸ δυσχρηστεῖν περὶ
8 τὴν ἔξοδον, διενοήθη τι τοιοῦτον. τοῦ προειρημένου
ποταμοῦ κατὰ τὴν εἰς θάλατταν ἐκβολὴν συνθεωρήσας κατά τινας ἀνέμων στάσεις ἀποθινούμενον τὸ
στόμα καὶ τεναγώδη γινομένην τὴν παρ᾽ αὐτὸ τὸ
στόμα πάροδον, ποιήσας εὐτρεπῆ τῷ στρατοπέδῳ τὰ
πρὸς τὴν ἔξοδον, καὶ κρύπτων ἐν αὐτῷ τὴν ἐπιβολήν,
9 ἐτήρει τὸ προειρημένον σύμπτωμα. παραπεσόντος δὲ
τοῦ καιροῦ, νυκτὸς ἐξορμήσας ἔλαθε πάντας ἅμα τῷ
φωτὶ τὸν προειρημένον τόπον διαβιβάσας τὴν δύνα-
10 μιν. παραδόξου δὲ τοῦ πράγματος φανέντος καὶ τοῖς
ἐν τῇ πόλει καὶ τοῖς ὑπεναντίοις, ὁ μὲν Ἀμίλκας
προῆγε διὰ τοῦ πεδίου, ποιούμενος τὴν πορείαν ἐπὶ
τοὺς τὴν γέφυραν φυλάττοντας.

76. οἱ δὲ περὶ τὸν Σπένδιον συνέντες τὸ γεγονὸς
ἀπήντων εἰς τὸ πεδίον καὶ παρεβοήθουν ἀλλήλοις, οἱ
μὲν ἐκ τῆς περὶ τὴν γέφυραν πόλεως ὄντες οὐκ ἐλάττους μυρίων, οἱ δ᾽ ἀπὸ τῆς Ἰτύκης ὑπὲρ τοὺς μυρίους
2 καὶ πεντακισχιλίους. ἐπεὶ δ᾽ εἰς σύνοπτον ἧκον ἀλλή-

from the town to the country. This river is for the most part unfordable owing to the volume of water, and there is only one bridge, which Mathos had also secured, building a town at the bridge head. So that not only was it impossible for the Carthaginians to reach the country with an army, but it was not even an easy matter for single persons wishing to get through to elude the vigilance of the enemy. Hamilcar, seeing all these obstacles, after passing in review every means and every chance of surmounting this difficulty about a passage, thought of the following plan. He had noticed that when the wind blew strongly from certain quarters the mouth of the river got silted up and the passage became shallow just where it falls into the sea. He therefore got his force ready to march out, and keeping his project to himself, waited for this to occur. When the right time came he started from Carthage at night, and without anyone noticing him, had by daybreak got his army across at the place mentioned. Both those in the city[101] and the enemy were taken by surprise, and Hamilcar advanced through the plain making for the guardians of the bridge.

76. Spendius, on learning what had happened, put his two forces in movement to meet in the plain and render mutual assistance to each other, those from the town near the bridge being not less than ten thousand in number and those from Utica over fifteen thousand. When they got

101 Probably Utica.

λοις, νομίσαντες ἐν μέσῳ τοὺς Καρχηδονίους ἀπειληφέναι, σπουδῇ παρηγγύων ἅμα παρακαλοῦντες σφᾶς

3 αὐτοὺς καὶ συνῆπτον τοῖς πολεμίοις. ὁ δ' Ἀμίλκας ἦγε
μὲν τὴν πορείαν πρώτους ἔχων τοὺς ἐλέφαντας, ἐπὶ δὲ
τούτοις τοὺς ἱππεῖς καὶ τοὺς εὐζώνους, τελευταῖα δὲ τὰ

4 βαρέα τῶν ὅπλων. κατιδὼν δὲ προχειρότερον ἐπιφερο-
μένους τοὺς ὑπεναντίους, ἀναστρέφειν παρήγγειλε

5 πᾶσι τοῖς ἑαυτοῦ. καὶ τοὺς μὲν ἀπὸ τῆς πρωτοπορείας
ἀναστρέψαντας σπουδῇ ποιεῖσθαι τὴν ἀποχώρησιν
ἐκέλευσε· τοὺς δ' ἐπὶ τῆς οὐραγίας ἐξ ἀρχῆς ὑπάρχοντας ἐξ ἐπιστροφῆς περισπῶν ἐξέταττε πρὸς τὴν τῶν

6 πολεμίων ἐπιφάνειαν. οἱ δὲ Λίβυες καὶ μισθοφόροι,
νομίσαντες αὐτοὺς καταπεπληγμένους φυγεῖν, λύσαντες τὴν τάξιν ἐπέκειντο καὶ συνῆπτον εἰς τὰς χεῖρας

7 ἐρρωμένως, ἅμα δὲ τῷ τοὺς ἱππεῖς συνεγγίσαντας
τοῖς παρατεταγμένοις ἐκ μεταβολῆς ὑποστῆναι, τὴν
δὲ λοιπὴν δύναμιν ἐπάγειν, ἐκπλαγεῖς γινόμενοι διὰ
τὸ παράδοξον οἱ Λίβυες ἐγκλίναντες εὐθέως ἔφευγον,

8 ὡς ἂν εἰκῇ καὶ σποράδην ἐπικείμενοι. λοιπὸν οἱ μὲν
τοῖς κατόπιν ἐπιφερομένοις περιπίπτοντες ἐσφάλλον-
το, καὶ διέφθειρον αὐτούς τε καὶ τοὺς οἰκείους· οἱ δὲ
πλείους συνεπατήθησαν, ἐκ χειρὸς τῶν ἱππέων ἐπικει-

9 μένων αὐτοῖς καὶ τῶν θηρίων. ἀπώλοντο μὲν οὖν εἰς
ἑξακισχιλίους τῶν Λιβύων καὶ τῶν ξένων, ἑάλωσαν δὲ
περὶ δισχιλίους· οἱ δὲ λοιποὶ διέφυγον, οἱ μὲν εἰς τὴν

10 πρὸς τῇ γεφύρᾳ πόλιν, οἱ δ' ἐπὶ τὴν πρὸς Ἰτύκῃ
παρεμβολήν. Ἀμίλκας δὲ ποιήσας τὸ προτέρημα τὸν
προειρημένον τρόπον, εἴπετο κατὰ πόδας τοῖς πολε-

in sight of each other, thinking that they had caught the
Carthaginians in a trap between them, they eagerly passed
on the word to engage, and exhorting each other joined
battle with the enemy. Hamilcar was advancing in the following order. In front were the elephants, after them the
cavalry and light-armed troops and last of all the heavy-
armed. When he saw that the enemy were attacking him in
such precipitation he ordered his whole force to face
about. He bade those in front, after facing about, retire
with all speed, and reversing the order of those who originally were in the rear he deployed them to await the
onslaught of the enemy. The Libyans and mercenaries,
thinking that the Carthagians were afraid of them and retreating, broke their ranks and closed with them vigorously. But when the cavalry, on approaching the line of
hoplites, wheeled round again and faced the Libyans,
while at the same time the remainder of the Carthaginian
army was coming up, the enemy were so much surprised
that they at once turned and fled panic-stricken, in the
same loose order and confusion in which they had advanced. Consequently some of them came into collision
with their comrades who were advancing in their rear with
disastrous effect, causing the destruction both of themselves and the latter, but the larger number were trampled
to death, the cavalry and elephants attacking them at close
quarters. About six thousand Libyans and mercenaries fell
and nearly two thousand were made prisoners. The rest escaped, some to the town by the bridge and some to the
camp before Utica. Hamilcar, successful in this fashion,
followed closely on the retreating enemy and took by as-

μίοις, καὶ τὴν μὲν ἐπὶ τῆς γεφύρας πόλιν ἐξ ἐφόδου
κατέσχε, προεμένων καὶ φευγόντων εἰς τὸν Τύνητα
τῶν ἐν αὐτῇ πολεμίων, τὴν δὲ λοιπὴν χώραν ἐπιπορευ-
11 όμενος τὰς μὲν προσήγετο, πλείστας δὲ κατὰ κράτος
ἐξῄρει. τοῖς δὲ Καρχηδονίοις βραχύ τι θάρσους ἐνειρ-
γάσατο καὶ τόλμης, ἐπὶ ποσὸν αὐτοὺς ἀπαλλάξας τῆς
προγεγενημένης δυσελπιστίας.

77. Ὁ δὲ Μάθως αὐτὸς μὲν ἐπὶ τῆς τῶν Ἱππακριτῶν πολιορκίας ἔπεμενε, τοῖς δὲ περὶ τὸν Αὐτάριτον
τὸν τῶν Γαλατῶν ἡγεμόνα καὶ Σπένδιον ἔχεσθαι τῶν
2 ὑπεναντίων συνεβούλευε, τὰ μὲν πεδία φεύγοντας διὰ
τὸ πλῆθος τῶν παρὰ τοῖς ὑπεναντίοις ἱππέων καὶ
θηρίων, ταῖς δ' ὑπωρείαις ἀντιπαράγοντας καὶ συν-
3 επιτιθεμένους κατὰ τὰς ὑποπιπτούσας ἀεὶ δυσχερείας.
ἅμα δὲ ταῖς ἐπινοίαις ταύταις καὶ πρὸς τοὺς Νομάδας
καὶ τοὺς Λίβυας ἐξέπεμπε, δεόμενος βοηθεῖν σφίσι
καὶ μὴ καταπροΐεσθαι τοὺς ὑπὲρ τῆς ἐλευθερίας και-
4 ρούς. ὁ δὲ Σπένδιος, προσλαβὼν ἐκ τοῦ Τύνητος ἀφ'
ἑκάστου τῶν γενῶν τοὺς πάντας εἰς ἑξακισχιλίους,
προῆγε, ταῖς ὑπωρείαις ἀντιπαράγων τοῖς Καρχηδονίοις, ἔχων ἅμα τοῖς προειρημένοις καὶ τοὺς μετ'
5 Αὐτάριτου Γαλάτας, ὄντας εἰς δισχιλίους. τὸ γὰρ
λοιπὸν μέρος αὐτῶν τοῦ κατ' ἀρχὰς συστήματος
ηὐτομολήκει πρὸς τοὺς Ῥωμαίους ἐν ταῖς περὶ τὸν
6 Ἔρυκα στρατοπεδείαις. τοῦ δ' Ἀμίλκου παρεμβεβλη-
κότος ἔν τινι πεδίῳ πανταχόθεν ὄρεσι περιεχομένῳ,
συνέβη τὰς παρὰ τῶν Νομάδων καὶ Λιβύων βοηθείας
7 εἰς τὸν καιρὸν τοῦτον συνάψαι τοῖς περὶ τὸν Σπένδιον.

sault the town by the bridge, the enemy in it deserting it and flying to Tunis. He next traversed the rest of the country, winning over some towns and taking others by assault. He thus restored some confidence and courage to the Carthaginians, delivering them in a measure from their previous despondency.

77. Mathos for his own part continued to prosecute the siege of Hippou Acra, advising Autaritus, the leader of the Gauls, and Spendius to harass the enemy, keeping away from the plains owing to the numbers of the cavalry and elephants opposed to them but marching along the foothills parallel to the Carthaginians and descending on them whenever they were on difficult ground. While adopting this plan he at the same time sent messages to the Numidians and Libyans, begging them to come to his assistance and not lose the chance of gaining their freedom. Spendius, taking with him from Tunis a force of about six thousand men in all drawn from all the tribes, advanced along the slopes parallel to the Carthaginians. He had also with him Autaritus and his Gauls numbering only about two thousand, the rest of the original corps having deserted to the Romans when encamped near Eryx. Hamilcar had established his camp in a plain surrounded by mountains, and just at this time Spendius was joined by the Numidian

γενομένης δὲ τοῖς Καρχηδονίοις τῆς μὲν τῶν Λιβύων
ἐπιστρατοπεδείας αἰφνιδίου καὶ κατὰ πρόσωπον, τῆς
δὲ τῶν Νομάδων ἀπ᾿ οὐρᾶς, τῆς δὲ περὶ τὸν Σπένδιον
ἐκ πλαγίου, μεγάλην αὐτοῖς ἀπορίαν συνέβη περι-
στῆναι καὶ δυσέκφευκτον.

78. Κατὰ δὲ τὸν καιρὸν τοῦτον Ναραύας, ὃς ἦν μὲν
Νομὰς τῶν ἐνδοξοτάτων εἷς, ἦν δὲ καὶ πλήρης ὁρμῆς
πολεμικῆς, οὗτος ἀεὶ μὲν οἰκείως διέκειτο πρὸς τοὺς
Καρχηδονίους, πατρικὴν ἔχων σύστασιν, τότε δὲ
μᾶλλον παρωρμήθη διὰ τὴν Ἀμίλκου τοῦ στρατηγοῦ
2 καταξίωσιν. διὸ καὶ νομίσας ἔχειν εὐφυῆ καιρὸν πρὸς
3 ἔντευξιν αὐτῷ καὶ σύστασιν, ἧκεν εἰς τὴν στρατοπεδείαν, ἔχων περὶ αὐτὸν Νομάδας εἰς ἑκατόν. καὶ συν-
εγγίσας τῷ χάρακι τολμηρῶς ἔμενε, κατασείων τῇ
4 χειρί. τοῦ δ᾿ Ἀμίλκου θαυμάσαντος τὴν ἐπιβολήν, καὶ
προπέμψαντός τινα τῶν ἱππέων, εἰς λόγους ἔφη βού-
5 λεσθαι συνελθεῖν τῷ στρατηγῷ. διαπορούντος δ᾿
ἀκμὴν καὶ διαπιστοῦντος τοῦ τῶν Καρχηδονίων
ἡγεμόνος, παραδοὺς ὁ Ναραύας τὸν ἵππον καὶ τὰς
6 λόγχας τοῖς μεθ᾿ αὑτοῦ, παρῆν ἄνοπλος εὐθαρσῶς εἰς
τὴν παρεμβολήν. οἱ δὲ τὰ μὲν ἐθαύμαζον, τὰ δὲ
7 κατεπλήττοντο τὴν τόλμαν· ὅμως δὲ προσεδέξαντο
καὶ συνῆλθον εἰς τὰς χεῖρας. ὁ δὲ παραγενόμενος εἰς
λόγους ἔφη πᾶσι μὲν Καρχηδονίοις εὐνοεῖν, μάλιστα
δ᾿ ἐπιθυμεῖν Βάρκᾳ γενέσθαι φίλος· διὸ καὶ νῦν παρεῖναι συσταθησόμενος αὐτῷ καὶ κοινωνήσων ἀδόλως
8 παντὸς ἔργου καὶ πάσης ἐπιβολῆς. Ἀμίλκας δὲ ταῦτ᾿
ἀκούσας οὕτως ἥσθη μεγάλως ἐπί τε τῷ κατὰ τὴν

and Libyan reinforcements. The Carthaginians, suddenly finding the additional force of Libyans in their front, and that of the Numidians in their rear, while Spendius was on their flank, were in a very difficult situation, from which it was not easy to extricate themselves.

78. There was a certain Naravas,[102] a Numidian of high rank and full of martial spirit. He had always had that attachment to the Carthaginians which was traditional in his family, and it was now strengthened by his admiration for Hamilcar. Thinking that this was a favorable opportunity for meeting Hamilcar and introducing himself, he rode up to the camp escorted by about a hundred Numidians. Coming close to the palisade he remained there quite fearlessly making signals with his hand. Hamilcar wondered what his object could be and sent out a horseman to meet him, when he said that he desired an interview with the general. The Carthaginian leader remaining still much amazed and distrustful, Naravas handed over his horse and his spears to his attendants, and very boldly came into the camp unarmed. The Carthaginians looked on in mingled admiration and amazement at his daring, but they met and received him, and when he was admitted to the interview, he said that he wished all the Carthaginians well but particularly desired the friendship of Barcas, and this was why he had come to join his cause and offer his cordial assistance in all actions and enterprises. Hamilcar, on hearing this, was so delighted at the young man's courage in com-

[102] There is no article on this Numidian chieftain in *RE*; see Meltzer (21. 6), 2. 379.

παρουσίαν θάρσει καὶ τῇ κατὰ τὴν ἔντευξιν ἁπλότητι
τοῦ νεανίσκου, ὡς οὐ μόνον εὐδόκησε κοινωνὸν αὐτὸν
προσλαβέσθαι τῶν πράξεων, ἀλλὰ καὶ τὴν θυγατέρα

9 δώσειν ἐπηγγείλατο μεθ᾽ ὅρκου, διαφυλάξαντος αὐτοῦ
τὴν πρὸς Καρχηδονίους πίστιν.

Γενομένων δὲ τῶν ὁμολογιῶν, ὁ μὲν Ναραύας ἧκε

10 τοὺς ὑφ᾽ αὑτὸν τεταγμένους ἔχων Νομάδας, ὄντας εἰς
δισχιλίους, ὁ δ᾽ Ἀμίλκας, προσγενομένης αὐτῷ τῆς
χειρὸς ταύτης, παρετάξατο τοῖς πολεμίοις. οἱ δὲ περὶ
τὸν Σπένδιον συνάψαντες ἐπὶ ταὐτὸ τοῖς Λίβυσι καὶ
καταβάντες εἰς τὸ πεδίον συνέβαλλον τοῖς Καρχη-

11 δονίοις. γενομένης δὲ μάχης ἰσχυρᾶς, ἐνίκων οἱ περὶ
τὸν Ἀμίλκαν, καλῶς μὲν τῶν θηρίων ἀγωνισαμένων,

12 ἐπιφανεστάτην δὲ τοῦ Ναραύα παρασχομένου χρείαν.
ὁ μὲν οὖν Αὐτάριτος καὶ Σπένδιος διέφυγον, τῶν δὲ

13 λοιπῶν ἔπεσον μὲν εἰς μυρίους, ἑάλωσαν δ᾽ εἰς τετρακισχιλίους. ἐπιτελεσθέντος δὲ τοῦ κατορθώματος,
Ἀμίλκας τοῖς μὲν βουλομένοις τῶν αἰχμαλώτων μεθ᾽
ἑαυτοῦ συστρατεύειν ἐξουσίαν ἔδωκε καὶ καθώπλιζε

14 τοῖς ἀπὸ τῶν πολεμίων σκύλοις, τοὺς δὲ μὴ βουλομένους ἀθροίσας παρεκάλει, φάσκων, ἕως μὲν τοῦ νῦν
συγγνώμην αὐτοῖς ἔχειν τῶν ἡμαρτημένων· διὸ καὶ
συγχωρεῖν τρέπεσθαι κατὰ τὰς ἰδίας ὁρμὰς οὗ ποτ᾽

15 ἂν ἕκαστος αὐτῶν προαιρῆται. μετὰ δὲ ταῦτα διηπει-
λήσατο μηθένα φέρειν ὅπλον πολέμιον κατ᾽ αὐτῶν,
ὡς, ἐὰν ἁλῷ τις, ἀπαραιτήτου τευξόμενον τιμωρίας.

79. Κατὰ δὲ τοὺς αὐτοὺς καιροὺς οἱ τὴν Σαρδόνα
[τὴν νῆσον] παραφυλάττοντες τῶν μισθοφόρων, ζη-

ing to him and his simple frankness at their interview that not only did he consent to associate him in his undertakings but swore to give him his daughter in marriage if he remained loyal to Carthage.

The agreement having thus been made, Naravas came in with the Numidians under his command, about two thousand in number, and Hamilcar, thus reinforced, offered battle to the enemy. Spendius, after effecting a junction with the Libyans, descended into the plain and attacked the Carthaginians. The battle was a stubborn one, but ended in the victory of Hamilcar, the elephants fighting well and Naravas rendering brilliant services. Autaritus and Spendius escaped, but with the loss of about ten thousand killed and four thousand prisoners. After the victory Hamilcar gave permission to those of the prisoners who chose to join his own army, arming them with the spoils of the fallen enemies; those who were unwilling to do so he collected and addressed saying that up to now he pardoned their offenses, and therefore they were free to go their several ways, wherever each man chose, but in future he threatened that if any of them bore arms against Carthage he would if captured meet with inevitable punishment.

79. About the same time the mercenaries who garrisoned Sardinia, emulous of the exploits of Mathos and

2 λώσαντες τοὺς περὶ τὸν Μάθω καὶ Σπένδιον, ἐπιτίθενται τοῖς ἐν τῇ νήσῳ Καρχηδονίοις. καὶ τὸν μὲν τότε
παρ᾿ αὐτοῖς ὄντα βοήθαρχον Βώσταρον συγκλείσαντες εἰς τὴν ἀκρόπολιν μετὰ τῶν ἑαυτοῦ πολιτῶν
3 ἀπέκτειναν. αὖθις δὲ τῶν Καρχηδονίων στρατηγὸν
ἐξαποστειλάντων μετὰ δυνάμεως Ἄννωνα, κἄπειτα
καὶ τούτων τῶν δυνάμεων ἐγκαταλιπουσῶν τὸν Ἄννω-
4 να, καὶ μεταθεμένων πρὸς σφᾶς, γενόμενοι ζωγρίᾳ
κύριοι τοῦ προειρημένου, παραυτίκα τοῦτον μὲν ἀνεσταύρωσαν, μετὰ δὲ ταῦτα παρηλλαγμένας ἐπινο-
οῦντες τιμωρίας, πάντας τοὺς ἐν τῇ νήσῳ Καρχηδονίους στρεβλοῦντες ἀπέκτειναν. καὶ τὸ λοιπὸν ἤδη
ποιησάμενοι τὰς πόλεις ὑφ᾿ ἑαυτοὺς εἶχον ἐγκρατῶς
5 τὴν νῆσον, ἕως οὗ στασιάσαντες πρὸς τοὺς Σαρδο-
6 νίους ἐξέπεσον ὑπ᾿ ἐκείνων εἰς τὴν Ἰταλίαν. ἡ μὲν οὖν
Σαρδὼ τοῦτον τὸν τρόπον ἀπηλλοτριώθη Καρχηδονίων, νῆσος καὶ τῷ μεγέθει καὶ τῇ πολυανθρωπίᾳ καὶ
7 τοῖς γεννήμασι διαφέρουσα. τῷ δὲ πολλοὺς καὶ
πολὺν ὑπὲρ αὐτῆς πεποιῆσθαι λόγον οὐκ ἀναγκαῖον
ἡγούμεθ᾿ εἶναι ταυτολογεῖν ὑπὲρ τῶν ὁμολογουμένων.
8 Μάθως δὲ καὶ Σπένδιος, ἅμα δὲ τούτοις Αὐτάριτος
ὁ Γαλάτης, ὑπιδόμενοι τὴν Ἀμίλκου φιλανθρωπίαν εἰς
τοὺς αἰχμαλώτους, καὶ φοβηθέντες μὴ τῷ τοιούτῳ
τρόπῳ ψυχαγωγηθέντες ὁρμήσωσι πρὸς τὴν ὑπο-
δεικνυμένην ἀσφάλειαν οἵ τε Λίβυες καὶ τὸ τῶν
μισθοφόρων πλῆθος, ἐβουλεύοντο πῶς ἂν καινοτο-
μήσαντές τι τῶν πρὸς ἀσέβειαν εἰς τέλος ἀποθηρι-
9 ώσειαν τὰ πλήθη πρὸς τοὺς Καρχηδονίους. ἔδοξεν

Spendius, attacked the Carthaginians in the island. They began by shutting up in the citadel and putting to death Bostar, the commander of the foreign contingent, and his compatriots. Next, when the Carthaginians sent Hanno over in command of a fresh force, this force deserted him and joined the mutineers, who thereupon took him prisoner and at once crucified him. After this, devising the most exquisite torments, they tortured and murdered all the Carthaginians in the island, and when they had got all the towns into their power continued to hold forcible possession of Sardinia, until they quarrelled with the natives, and were driven out by them to Italy. Thus was Sardinia lost to the Carthaginians, an island of great extent, most thickly populated and most fertile. Many authors have described it at length, and I do not think it necessary to repeat statements which no one disputes.

Mathos and Spendius, as well as the Gaul Autaritus,   239 B.C. were apprehensive of the effect of Hamilcar's leniency to the prisoners, fearing that the Libyans and the greater part of the mercenaries might thus be won over and hasten to avail themselves of the proffered immunity. They therefore set themselves to devise some infamous crime which would make the hatred of the troops for Carthage more

οὖν αὐτοῖς συναθροῖσαι τοὺς πολλούς. γενομένου δὲ
τούτου γραμματοφόρον εἰσήγαγον, ὡς ἀπεσταλμένον
10 ὑπὸ τῶν ἐκ τῆς Σαρδόνος αἱρετιστῶν. ἡ δ' ἐπιστολὴ
διεσάφει τόν τε Γέσκωνα καὶ τοὺς μετ' αὐτοῦ πάντας,
οὓς παρεσπόνδησαν ἐν τῷ Τύνητι, καθάπερ ἐπάνω
προεῖπον, φυλάττειν ἐπιμελῶς, ὡς πραττόντων τινῶν
ἐκ τοῦ στρατοπέδου τοῖς Καρχηδονίοις ὑπὲρ τῆς τού-
11 των σωτηρίας. λαβόμενος δὲ τῆς ἀφορμῆς ταύτης ὁ
Σπένδιος, πρῶτον μὲν παρεκάλει μὴ πιστεύειν τὴν ὑπὸ
τοῦ στρατηγοῦ τοῦ τῶν Καρχηδονίων γεγενημένην
12 φιλανθρωπίαν πρὸς τοὺς αἰχμαλώτους· οὐ γὰρ σῶσαι
προαιρούμενον αὐτὸν ταῦτα βεβουλεῦσθαι περὶ τῶν
ἁλόντων, ἀλλὰ διὰ τῆς ἐκείνων ἀφέσεως ἡμῶν ἐγκρα-
τῆ γενέσθαι σπουδάζοντα, πρὸς τὸ μὴ τινάς, ἀλλὰ
13 πάντας ἡμᾶς ἅμα τιμωρήσασθαι πιστεύσαντας αὐτῷ.
πρὸς δὲ τούτοις φυλάττεσθαι παρῄνει μὴ προέμενοι
τοὺς περὶ τὸν Γέσκωνα καταφρονηθῶσι μὲν ὑπὸ τῶν
ἐχθρῶν, μεγάλα δὲ βλάψωσι τὰς ἰδίας πράξεις, ἄνδρα
τοιοῦτον καὶ στρατηγὸν ἀγαθὸν ἐάσαντες διαφυγεῖν,
14 ὃν εἰκὸς ἐχθρὸν αὐτοῖς ἔσεσθαι φοβερώτατον. ἔτι δὲ
ταῦτα λέγοντος αὐτοῦ παρῆν ἄλλος γραμματοφόρος,
ὡς ἀπὸ τῶν ἐκ τοῦ Τύνητος ἀπεσταλμένος, παραπλήσια τοῖς ἐκ τῆς Σαρδόνος διασαφῶν.

80. ἐφ' ὃν Αὐτάριτος ὁ Γαλάτης ἐπιβαλὼν μίαν
ἔφη σωτηρίαν εἶναι τοῖς ἑαυτῶν πράγμασι τὸ πάσας
2 ἀπογνῶναι τὰς ἐν Καρχηδονίοις ἐλπίδας· ἕως δ' ἂν
ἀντέχηταί τις τῆς ἐκείνων φιλανθρωπίας, οὐ δυνατὸν
3 αὐτοῖς ἀληθινὸν γενέσθαι τὸν τοιοῦτον σύμμαχον.

234

savage. They decided to call a general meeting and at this they introduced a letter-bearer supposed to have been sent by their confederates in Sardinia. The letter advised them to keep careful guard over Gesco and all the others whom they had, as above narrated, treacherously arrested at Tunis, since some persons in the camp were negotiating with the Carthaginians about their release. Spendius, seizing on this pretext, begged them in the first place to have no reliance on the Carthaginian general's reported clemency to the prisoners. "It is not," he said, "with the intention of sparing their lives that he has taken this course regarding his captives, but by releasing them he designs to get us into his power, so that he may take vengeance not on some, but on all of us who trust him." Moreover, he warned them to take care lest by giving up Gesco and the others they incur the contempt of their enemies and seriously damage their own situation by allowing to escape them so able a man and so good a general, who was sure to become their most formidable enemy. He had not finished his speech when in came another post supposed to be from Tunis with a message similar to that from Sardinia.

80. Autaritus the Gaul was the next speaker. He said that the only hope of safety for them was to abandon all reliance on the Carthaginians. Whoever continued to look forward to clemency from them could be no true ally of their own. Therefore he asked them to trust those, to give a

διόπερ ἠξίου τούτοις πιστεύειν, τούτοις ἀκούειν, τοῖς
τοιούτοις προσέχειν τὸν νοῦν, οἵτινες ἂν ἀεί τι τῶν
ἀπεχθεστάτων καὶ πικροτάτων εἰσαγγέλλωσι κατὰ
Καρχηδονίων· τοὺς δ᾽ ἐναντία τούτοις λέγοντας προ-
4 δότας καὶ πολεμίους ἡγεῖσθαι παρῄνει. ταῦτα δ᾽ εἰπὼν
συνεβούλευε τόν τε Γέσκωνα καὶ τοὺς μετ᾽ αὐτοῦ
συλληφθέντας καὶ τοὺς ὕστερον γενομένους αἰχμα-
5 λώτους τῶν Καρχηδονίων αἰκισαμένους ἀποκτεῖναι.
πρακτικώτατος δ᾽ ἦν οὗτος ἐν ταῖς συμβουλίαις διὰ τὸ
6 πολλοὺς τὴν φωνὴν αὐτοῦ συνιέναι. πάλαι γὰρ στρα-
τευόμενος ἤδη διαλέγεσθαι φοινικιστί· ταύτῃ δέ πως
οἱ πλεῖστοι συνεσαίνοντο τῇ διαλέκτῳ διὰ τὸ μῆκος
7 τῆς προγεγενημένης στρατείας. διόπερ ἐπαινέσαντος
αὐτὸν ὁμοθυμαδὸν τοῦ πλήθους, οὗτος μὲν εὐδοκιμῶν
8 ἀνεχώρησε. πολλῶν δὲ προπορευομένων ἀφ᾽ ἑκάστου
γένους ἅμα, καὶ βουλομένων αὐτὴν παραιτεῖσθαι τὴν
αἰκίαν διὰ τὰς γεγενημένας ἐκ τοῦ Γέσκωνος εἰς
αὐτοὺς εὐεργεσίας, οὔτε μὴν τῶν λεγομένων οὐθὲν ἦν
συνετόν, ὡς ἂν ἅμα πολλῶν, ἑκάστου δὲ κατὰ τὴν
9 ἰδίαν διάλεκτον συμβουλεύοντος· ἐπεὶ δὲ καὶ παρ-
εγυμνώθη διότι τὴν τιμωρίαν παραιτοῦνται, καί τις ἐκ
10 τῶν καθημένων εἶπε βάλλε, πάντας ἅμα κατέλευσαν
τοὺς προπορευθέντας. καὶ τούτους μέν, ὥσπερ ὑπὸ
11 θηρίων διεφθαρμένους, ἐξέφερον οἱ προσήκοντες.
τοὺς δὲ περὶ τὸν Γέσκωνα λαβόντες, ὄντας εἰς ἑπτακο-
σίους, ἦγον ἐκ τοῦ χάρακος οἱ περὶ τὸν Σπένδιον· καὶ
προαγαγόντες βραχὺ πρὸ τῆς στρατοπεδείας πρῶτον
12 μὲν ἀπέκοπτον τὰς χεῖρας, ποιούμενοι τὴν ἀρχὴν ἀπὸ

hearing to those, to attend to those only who bring the most hateful and bitterest accusations against the Carthaginians, and to regard speakers on the other side as traitors and enemies. Finally, he recommended them to torture and put to death not only Gesco and those arrested with him, but all the Carthaginians they had subsequently taken prisoners. He was much the most effective speaker in their councils, because a number of them could understand him. He had been a long time in the service and had learned Phoenician, a language which had become more or less agreeable to their ears owing to the length of the previous war. His speech therefore met with universal approbation, and he retired from the platform amid applause. Numerous speakers from each nationality now came forward all together, maintaining that the prisoners should be spared at least the infliction of torture in view of Gesco's previous kindness to them. Nothing, however, they said was intelligible, as they were all speaking together and each stating his views in his own language. But the moment it was disclosed that they were begging for a remission of the sentence someone among the audience called out "Stone them," and they instantly stoned all the speakers to death. These unfortunates, mangled as if by wild beasts, were carried off for burial by their friends. Spendius and his men then led out from the camp Gesco and the other prisoners, in all about seven hundred. Taking them a short distance away, they first of all cut off their

τοῦ Γέσκωνος, ὃν βραχεῖ χρόνῳ πρότερον ἐκ πάντων
Καρχηδονίων προκρίναντες ἀνέδειξαν μὲν εὐεργέτην
13 αὐτῶν, ἐπέτρεψαν δὲ περὶ τῶν ἀμφισβητουμένων.
ἐπειδὴ δὲ τὰς χεῖρας ἀπέκοψαν, ἠκρωτηρίαζον τοὺς
ταλαιπώρους· κολοβώσαντες δὲ καὶ τὰ σκέλη συν-
τρίψαντες ἔτι ζῶντας ἔρριψαν εἴς τινα τάφρον.

81. Οἱ δὲ Καρχηδόνιοι, τοῦ δυστυχήματος αὐτοῖς
ἀναγγελθέντος, ποιεῖν μὲν οὐδὲν εἶχον, ἐσχετλίαζον
δέ, καὶ περιπαθεῖς γινόμενοι τῇ συμφορᾷ πρὸς μὲν
Ἀμίλκαν καὶ τὸν ἕτερον τῶν στρατηγῶν Ἄννωνα
πρεσβευτὰς ἐξέπεμπον, δεόμενοι βοηθεῖν καὶ τιμω-
2 ρεῖν τοῖς ἠτυχηκόσι. πρὸς δὲ τοὺς ἠσεβηκότας κήρυ-
3 κας ἐξαπέστελλον περὶ τῆς τῶν νεκρῶν ἀναιρέσεως. οἱ
δ᾽ οὔτ᾽ ἔδοσαν, προεῖπόν τε τοῖς παροῦσι μήτε κήρυκα
πέμπειν πρὸς σφᾶς μήτε πρεσβευτήν, ὡς τῆς αὐτῆς
κολάσεως ὑπομενούσης τοὺς παραγενομένους ἧς νῦν
4 Γέσκων τέτευχε. πρὸς δὲ τὸ λοιπὸν ἐδογματοποίησαν
καὶ παρῄνεσαν αὐτοῖς, ὃν μὲν ἂν λάβωσι Καρχηδονίων, τιμωρησαμένους ἀποκτείνειν· ὃν δ᾽ ἂν τῶν
συμμαχούντων αὐτοῖς, ἀποκόψαντας τὰς χεῖρας αὖθις
εἰς Καρχηδόν᾽ ἀποπέμπειν. ὃ δὴ καὶ διετέλεσαν ἐπι-
5 μελῶς ποιοῦντες. διόπερ εἰς ταῦτα βλέπων οὐκ ἄν τις
εἰπεῖν ὀκνήσειεν ὡς οὐ μόνον τὰ σώματα τῶν ἀνθρώπων καί τινα τῶν ἐν αὐτοῖς γεννωμένων ἑλκῶν καὶ
φυμάτων ἀποθηριοῦσθαι συμβαίνει καὶ τελέως ἀβοή-
6 θητα γίνεσθαι, πολὺ δὲ μάλιστα τὰς ψυχάς. ἐπί τε
γὰρ τῶν ἑλκῶν, ἐὰν μὲν θεραπείαν τοῖς τοιούτοις
προσάγῃ τις, ὑπ᾽ αὐτῆς ἐνίοτε ταύτης ἐρεθιζόμενα

hands, beginning with Gesco, that very Gesco whom a short time previously they had selected from all the Carthaginians, proclaiming him their benefactor and referring the points in dispute to him. After cutting off their hands they cut off the wretched men's other extremities too, and after thus mutilating them and breaking their legs, threw them still alive into a trench.

81. The Carthaginians, when news came of this unhappy event, could take no action, but their indignation was extreme, and in the heat of it they sent messengers to Hamilcar and their other general Hanno imploring them to come and avenge the unfortunate victims. To the assassins they sent heralds begging that the bodies might be given up to them. Not only was this request refused but the messengers were told to send neither herald nor envoy again, as any who came would meet with the same punishment that had just befallen Gesco. With regard to treatment of prisoners in the future, the mutineers passed a resolution and engaged each other to torture and kill every Carthaginian and send back to the capital with his hands cut off every ally of Carthage, and this practice they continued to observe carefully. No one looking at this would have any hesitation in saying that not only do men's bodies and certain of the ulcers and tumors afflicting them become so to speak savage and brutalized and quite incurable, but that this is true in a much higher degree of their souls. In the case of ulcers, if we treat them, they are sometimes inflamed by the treatment itself and spread more

θᾶττον ποιεῖται τὴν νομήν· ἐὰν δὲ πάλιν ἀφῇ, κατὰ
τὴν ἐξ αὐτῶν φύσιν φθείροντα τὸ συνεχὲς οὐκ ἴσχει
7 παῦλαν, ἕως ἂν ἀφανίσῃ τὸ ὑποκείμενον· ταῖς τε
ψυχαῖς παραπλησίως τοιαῦται πολλάκις ἐπιφύονται
μελανίαι καὶ σηπεδόνες ὥστε μηδὲν ἀσεβέστερον
8 ἀνθρώπου μηδ᾽ ὠμότερον ἀποτελεῖσθαι τῶν ζῴων. οἷς
ἐὰν μὲν συγγνώμην τινὰ προσάγῃς καὶ φιλανθρωπίαν, ἐπιβουλὴν καὶ παραλογισμὸν ἡγούμενοι τὸ
συμβαῖνον ἀπιστότεροι καὶ δυσμενέστεροι γίνονται
9 πρὸς τοὺς φιλανθρωποῦντας· ἐὰν δ᾽ ἀντιτιμωρῇ, δια-
μιλλώμενοι τοῖς θυμοῖς οὐκ ἔστι τι τῶν ἀπειρημένων
ἢ δεινῶν ὁποῖον οὐκ ἀναδέχονται, σὺν καλῷ τιθέμενοι
τὴν τοιαύτην τόλμαν· τέλος δ᾽ ἀποθηριωθέντες ἐξ-
10 έστησαν τῆς ἀνθρωπίνης φύσεως. τῆς δὲ διαθέσεως
ἀρχηγὸν μὲν καὶ μεγίστην μερίδα νομιστέον ἔθη
μοχθηρὰ καὶ τροφὴν ἐκ παίδων κακήν, συνεργὰ δὲ
καὶ πλείω, μέγιστα δὲ τῶν συνεργῶν, τὰς ἀεὶ τῶν
11 προεστώτων ὕβρεις καὶ πλεονεξίας. ἃ δὴ τότε συνέβαινε καὶ περὶ μὲν τὸ σύστημα τῶν μισθοφόρων, ἔτι
δὲ μᾶλλον περὶ τοὺς ἡγεμόνας αὐτῶν ὑπάρχειν.

82. Ἀμίλκας δέ, δυσχρηστούμενος τῇ τῶν πολεμίων ἀπονοίᾳ, τὸν μὲν Ἅννωνα πρὸς ἑαυτὸν ἐκάλει,
πεπεισμένος ἀθροισθέντων ὁμοῦ τῶν στρατοπέδων
2 θᾶττον ἐπιθήσειν τέλος τοῖς ὅλοις. τῶν δὲ πολεμίων
οὕς ποτε κρατήσειε, τοὺς μὲν ἐν χειρῶν νόμῳ διέφθειρε, τοὺς δὲ ζωγρίᾳ πρὸς αὐτὸν εἰσαναχθέντας
ὑπέβαλλε τοῖς θηρίοις, μίαν ὁρῶν λύσιν ταύτην, εἰ
δυνηθείη τοὺς ἐχθροὺς ἄρδην ἀφανίσαι.

rapidly, while again if we neglect them they continue, in virtue of their own nature, to eat into the flesh and never rest until they have utterly destroyed the tissues beneath. Similarly such malignant lividities and putrid ulcers often grow in the human soul, that no beast becomes at the end more wicked or cruel than man. In the case of men in such a state, if we treat the disease by pardon and kindness, they think we are scheming to betray them or deceive them, and become more mistrustful and hostile to their would-be benefactors, but if, on the contrary, we attempt to cure the evil by retaliation they work up their passions to outrival ours, until there is nothing so abominable or so atrocious that they will not consent to do it, imagining all the while that they are displaying a fine courage. Thus at the end they are utterly brutalized and no longer can be called human beings. Of such a condition the origin and most potent cause lies in bad manners and customs and wrong training from childhood, but there are several contributory ones, the chief of which is habitual violence and unscrupulousness on the part of those in authority over them. All these conditions were present in this mercenary force as a whole and especially in their chiefs.

82. This desperation of the enemy made Hamilcar anxious, and he begged Hanno[103] to join him, being convinced that if both armies united, an end would be put sooner to the whole war. Meanwhile he continued to put to the sword those of the enemy who were conquered in the field, while those brought to him captive prisoners he threw to the elephants to be trampled to death, as it was clear to him that the rebellion would never be stamped out until the enemy were utterly exterminated.

[103] Different necessarily from the Hanno in 79. 3.

THE HISTORIES OF POLYBIUS

3   Δοκούντων δὲ τῶν Καρχηδονίων ἐπικυδεστέρας ἐλπίδας ἔχειν ἤδη κατὰ τὸν πόλεμον, γίνεταί τις ὁλοσχερὴς καὶ παράδοξος περὶ αὐτοὺς παλίρροια τῶν
4   πραγμάτων. οἵ τε γὰρ στρατηγοὶ συνελθόντες ἐπὶ
ταὐτὸ διεστασίασαν πρὸς σφᾶς ἐπὶ τοσοῦτον ὥστε μὴ
μόνον τοὺς κατὰ τῶν ἐχθρῶν παραλιπεῖν καιρούς,
ἀλλὰ καὶ κατὰ σφῶν αὐτῶν πολλὰς ἀφορμὰς διδόναι
5   τοῖς ὑπεναντίοις διὰ τὴν πρὸς ἀλλήλους φιλονεικίαν.
ἃ δὴ καὶ συνέντες οἱ Καρχηδόνιοι τῷ μὲν ἑνὶ τῶν
στρατηγῶν ἀπαλλάττεσθαι προσέταξαν, τῷ δ' ἑτέρῳ
6   μένειν, ὃν ἂν αἱ δυνάμεις προκρίνωσιν. ἅμα δὲ τούτοις
καὶ τὰς παρακομιζομένας ἀγορὰς ἐκ τῶν παρ' αὐτοῖς
καλουμένων Ἐμπορίων, ἐφ' αἷς εἶχον τὰς μεγίστας
ἐλπίδας περί τε τῆς τροφῆς καὶ τῶν ἄλλων ἐπιτηδείων,
διαφθαρῆναι συνέβη κατὰ θάλατταν ὁλοσχερῶς ὑπὸ
7   χειμῶνος. τὰ δὲ κατὰ τὴν Σαρδόνα, καθάπερ ἐπάνω
προεῖπον, ἐτύγχανεν ἀπηλλοτριωμένα, μεγάλας αὐτοῖς αἰεί ποτε χρείας παρεχομένης τῆς νήσου ταύτης
8   κατὰ τὰς περιστάσεις. τὸ δὲ μέγιστον ἡ τῶν Ἱππακριτῶν καὶ τῶν Ἰτυκαίων ἀπέστη πόλις, αἵτινες ἐτύγχανον μόναι τῶν κατὰ τὴν Λιβύην οὐ μόνον τὸν
ἐνεστῶτα πόλεμον ἀναδεδεγμέναι γενναίως, ἀλλὰ καὶ
τοὺς κατ' Ἀγαθοκλέα καιροὺς καὶ τὴν Ῥωμαίων ἔφοδον εὐγενῶς ὑπομεμενηκυῖαι, καὶ συλλήβδην οὐδέ-
9   ποτε βεβουλευμέναι Καρχηδονίοις οὐδὲν ὑπεναντίον.
τότε δὲ χωρὶς τῆς ἀλόγου πρὸς τοὺς Λίβυας ἀποστάσεως καὶ διὰ τῆς μεταθέσεως εὐθέως τούτοις μὲν
τὴν μεγίστην οἰκειότητα καὶ πίστιν ἐναπεδείξαντο,

242

The prospects of the Carthaginians in the war now seemed much brighter, but the tide of events suddenly turned completely against them. For when the two generals met, they quarreled so seriously, that this difference caused them not only to neglect many opportunities of striking a blow at the enemy, but to afford many such to the latter. The Carthaginians perceiving this, ordered one of the two to leave his post and the other to remain in sole command, leaving the choice to the troops. In addition to this they suffered the total loss at sea in a storm, of the supplies they were conveying from the place they call Emporia, supplies on which they entirely relied for this commissariat and other needs. And again, as I said above, they had lost Sardinia, an island which had always been of great service to them in difficult circumstances. The severest blow of all, however, was the defection of Hippou Acra and Utica, the only two cities in Libya which had not only bravely faced the present war, but had gallantly held out during the invasion of Agathocles[104] and that of the Romans; indeed they never had on any occasion given the least sign of hostility to Carthage. But now, apart from their unjustifiable defection to the cause of the Libyans, their sympathies so suddenly changed, that they exhibited the greatest friendship and loyalty to the rebels, while be-

[104] He stormed Utica in 307; Meltzer (21. 6), 1, Berlin 1879, 395–396.

πρὸς δὲ τοὺς Καρχηδονίους ἀπαραίτητον ὀργὴν ἐν-
10 εστήσαντο καὶ μῖσος. τοὺς μὲν γὰρ παραβεβοηθη-
κότας αὐτοῖς παρ' ἐκείνων, ὄντας εἰς πεντακοσίους,
καὶ τὸν ἡγεμόνα τούτων ἀποκτείναντες ἅπαντας ἔρριψαν κατὰ τοῦ τείχους, τὴν δὲ πόλιν ἐνεχείρισαν τοῖς
Λίβυσι· τοῖς γε μὴν Καρχηδονίοις οὐδὲ θάψαι συν-
11 εχώρησαν τοὺς ἠτυχηκότας αἰτουμένοις. τούτων δὲ
συμβαινόντων, οἱ μὲν περὶ τὸν Μάθω καὶ Σπένδιον,
ἐπαρθέντες τοῖς συμβεβηκόσι, πολιορκεῖν ἐνεχείρη-
12 σαν αὐτὴν τὴν Καρχηδόνα. Βάρκας δὲ παραλαβὼν
Ἀννίβαν τὸν στρατηγόν—τοῦτον γὰρ ἐξαπέστειλαν
οἱ πολῖται πρὸς τὰς δυνάμεις, ἐπεὶ τὸν Ἄννωνα τὸ
στρατόπεδον ἔκρινε δεῖν ἀπαλλάττεσθαι, κατὰ τὴν
ὑπὸ τῶν Καρχηδονίων αὐτοῖς δοθεῖσαν ἐπιτροπὴν
περὶ τὰς γενομένας τῶν στρατηγῶν στάσεις πρὸς
13 ἀλλήλους—διόπερ Ἀμίλκας, ἔχων τοῦτόν τε καὶ Ναραύαν, ἐπῄει τὴν χώραν, διακλείων τὰς χορηγίας τοῖς
περὶ τὸν Μάθω καὶ Σπένδιον, μεγίστην αὐτῷ παρ-
εχομένου χρείαν περί τε ταῦτα καὶ τἆλλα Ναραύα τοῦ
14 Νομάδος. Τὰ μὲν οὖν περὶ τὰς ὑπαίθρους δυνάμεις ἐν
τούτοις ἦν.

83. Οἱ δὲ Καρχηδόνιοι περικλειόμενοι πανταχόθεν
ἠναγκάζοντο καταφεύγειν ἐπὶ τὰς συμμαχίδων πό-
2 λεων ἐλπίδας. Ἱέρων δ' ἀεὶ μέν ποτε κατὰ τὸν ἐνεστῶτα πόλεμον μεγάλην ἐποιεῖτο σπουδὴν εἰς πᾶν τὸ
3 παρακαλούμενον ὑπ' αὐτῶν, τότε δὲ καὶ μᾶλλον ἐφιλο-
τιμεῖτο, πεπεισμένος συμφέρειν ἑαυτῷ καὶ πρὸς τὴν ἐν

ginning to show every symptom of passionate and determined hatred of Carthage. After butchering the troops the Carthaginians had sent to assist them, about five hundred in number, together with their commander, they threw all the bodies from the wall, and surrendered the city to the Libyans. They would not even give the Carthaginians the permission they requested to bury their unfortunate compatriots. Mathos and Spendius in the meantime, elated by these events, undertook the siege of Carthage itself. Barcas had now been joined in the command by Hannibal, the general whom the citizens had dispatched to the army, on the soldiers voting that Hanno should be the one to retire, when the decision was left in their hands by the Carthaginians at the time the two generals had quarreled. Accompanied then by this Hannibal and by Naravas, Hamilcar scoured the country, intercepting the supplies of Mathos and Spendius, receiving the greatest assistance in this and all other matters from the Numidian Naravas. Such were the positions of the field forces.

83. The Carthaginians, being shut in on all sides, were obliged to resort to an appeal to the states in alliance with them. Hiero during the whole of the present war had been most prompt in meeting their requests, and was now more complaisant than ever, being convinced that it was in his

Σικελίᾳ δυναστείαν καὶ πρὸς τὴν Ῥωμαίων φιλίαν τὸ
σῴζεσθαι Καρχηδονίους, ἵνα μὴ παντάπασιν ἐξῇ τὸ
προτεθὲν ἀκονιτὶ συντελεῖσθαι τοῖς ἰσχύουσι, πάνυ
4 φρονίμως καὶ νουνεχῶς λογιζόμενος. οὐδέποτε γὰρ
χρὴ τὰ τοιαῦτα παρορᾶν, οὐδὲ τηλικαύτην οὐδενὶ
συγκατασκευάζειν δυναστείαν, πρὸς ἣν οὐδὲ περὶ τῶν
5 ὁμολογουμένων ἐξέσται δικαίων ἀμφισβητεῖν. οὐ μὴν
ἀλλὰ καὶ Ῥωμαῖοι τηροῦντες τὰ κατὰ τὰς συνθήκας
6 δίκαια προθυμίας οὐδὲν ἀπέλειπον. ἐν ἀρχαῖς μὲν γὰρ
ἐγένετό τις ἀμφισβήτησις ἐξ ἀμφοῖν διά τινας τοι-
7 αύτας αἰτίας. τῶν Καρχηδονίων τοὺς πλέοντας ἐξ
Ἰταλίας εἰς Λιβύην καὶ χορηγοῦντας τοῖς πολεμίοις
καταγόντων ὡς αὑτούς, καὶ σχεδὸν ἀθροισθέντων τού-
8 των εἰς τὴν φυλακὴν εἰς τοὺς πεντακοσίους, ἠγα-
νάκτησαν οἱ Ῥωμαῖοι. μετὰ δὲ ταῦτα διαπρεσβευσάμενοι, καὶ κομισάμενοι διὰ λόγου πάντας, ἐπὶ
τοσοῦτον εὐδόκησαν ὥστε παραχρῆμα τοῖς Καρχηδονίοις ἀντιδωρήσασθαι τοὺς ὑπολειπομένους παρ'
9 αὑτοῖς αἰχμαλώτους ἐκ τοῦ περὶ Σικελίαν πολέμου.
ἀπὸ δὲ τούτου τοῦ καιροῦ πρὸς ἕκαστα τῶν παρακα-
10 λουμένων ἑτοίμως καὶ φιλανθρώπως ὑπήκουον. διὸ
καὶ πρὸς μὲν τοὺς Καρχηδονίους ἐπέτρεψαν τοῖς
ἐμπόροις ἐξαγαγεῖν αἰεὶ τὸ κατεπεῖγον, πρὸς δὲ τοὺς
11 πολεμίους ἐκώλυσαν. μετὰ δὲ ταῦτα τῶν μὲν ἐν τῇ
Σαρδόνι μισθοφόρων, καθ' ὃν καιρὸν ἀπὸ τῶν Καρχηδονίων ἀπέστησαν, ἐπισπωμένων αὑτοὺς ἐπὶ τὴν νῆσον οὐχ ὑπήκουσαν· τῶν δ' Ἰτυκαίων ἐγχειριζόντων

own interest for securing both his Sicilian dominions and his friendship with the Romans, that Carthage should be preserved, and that the stronger power should not be able to attain its ultimate object entirely without effort. In this he reasoned very wisely and sensibly, for such matters should never be neglected, and we should never contribute to the attainment by one state of a power so preponderant, that none dare dispute with it even for their acknowledged rights. But now the Romans as well as Hiero observed loyally the engagements the treaty imposed on them.[105] At first there had been a slight dispute between the two states for the following reason. The Carthaginians when they captured at sea traders coming from Italy to Libya with supplies for the enemy, brought them into Carthage, and there were now in their prisons as many as five hundred such. The Romans were annoyed at this, but when on sending an embassy, they recovered all the prisoners by diplomatic means, they were so much gratified, that in return they gave back to the Carthaginians all the remaining prisoners from the Sicilian war and henceforth gave prompt and friendly attention to all their requests. They gave permission to their merchants to export all requirements for Carthage, but not for the enemy, and shortly afterward, when the mercenaries in Sardinia on revolting from Carthage invited them to occupy the island, they refused. Again on the citizens of Utica offering

105 P. seems to refer to both the treaty between Rome and Hiero (16. 9) and the peace treaty with Carthage.

σφᾶς, οὐ προσεδέξαντο, τηροῦντες τὰ κατὰ τὰς συνθήκας δίκαια.

12 Καρχηδόνιοι μὲν οὖν τῆς παρὰ τῶν προειρημένων
φίλων τυγχάνοντες ἐπικουρίας ὑπέμενον τὴν πολιορκίαν.

84. Τοῖς δὲ περὶ τὸν Μάθω καὶ Σπένδιον οὐχ ἧττον
2 πολιορκεῖσθαι συνέβαινεν ἢ πολιορκεῖν. εἰς τοιαύτην
γὰρ αὐτοὺς οἱ περὶ τὸν Ἀμίλκαν ἔνδειαν καθίστασαν
τῶν ἐπιτηδείων, ὥστ' ἀναγκασθῆναι τέλος αὐτοὺς δια-
3 λῦσαι τὴν πολιορκίαν. μετὰ δέ τινα χρόνον ἀθροίσαντες τῶν τε μισθοφόρων τοὺς ἀρίστους καὶ Λιβύων,
τοὺς ἅπαντας εἰς πεντακισμυρίους, μεθ' ὧν ἦν καὶ
Ζάρζας ὁ Λίβυς ἔχων τοὺς ὑφ' αὑτὸν ταττομένους,
ὥρμησαν αὖθις ἀντιπαράγειν ἐν τοῖς ὑπαίθροις καὶ
4 τηρεῖν τοὺς περὶ τὸν Ἀμίλκαν. τῶν μὲν οὖν πεδινῶν
τόπων ἀπείχοντο, καταπεπληγμένοι τὰ θηρία καὶ τοὺς
περὶ τὸν Ναραύαν ἱππεῖς, τοὺς δ' ὀρεινοὺς καὶ στενοὺς
5 ἐπειρῶντο προκαταλαμβάνειν. ἐν οἷς καιροῖς συνέβη
ταῖς μὲν ἐπιβολαῖς καὶ τόλμαις μηδὲν αὐτοὺς λείπεσθαι τῶν ὑπεναντίων, διὰ δὲ τὴν ἀπειρίαν πολλάκις
6 ἐλαττοῦσθαι. τότε γὰρ ἦν, ὡς ἔοικε, συνιδεῖν ἐπ' αὐτῆς
τῆς ἀληθείας πηλίκην ἔχει διαφορὰν ἐμπειρία μεθο-
δικὴ καὶ στρατηγικὴ δύναμις ἀπειρίας καὶ τριβῆς
7 ἀλόγου στρατιωτικῆς. πολλοὺς μὲν γὰρ αὐτῶν ἐν ταῖς
κατὰ μέρος χρείαις ἀποτεμνόμενος καὶ συγκλείων
8 ὥσπερ ἀγαθὸς πεττευτής, ἀμαχεὶ διέφθειρε, πολλοὺς
δ' ἐν τοῖς ὁλοσχερέσι κινδύνοις τοὺς μὲν εἰς ἐνέδρας
ἀνυπονοήτους ἐπαγόμενος ἀνῄρει, τοῖς δ' ἀνελπίστως

to surrender to them they did not accept, but held to their treaty engagements.

The Carthaginians, then, on thus obtaining assistance 288 B.C. from their friends continued to withstand the siege.

84. But Mathos and Spendius were just as much in the position of besieged as of besiegers. Hamilcar had reduced them to such straits for supplies that they were finally forced to raise the siege. A short time afterward, collecting a picked force of mercenaries and Libyans to the number of about fifty thousand and including Zarzas the Libyan and those under his command, they tried again their former plan of marching in the open parallel to the enemy and keeping a watch on Hamilcar. They avoided level ground, as they were afraid of the elephants and Naravas' horse, but they kept on trying to anticipate the enemy in occupying positions on the hills and narrow passes. In this campaign they were quite equal to the enemy in terms of assault and enterprise, but were often worsted owing to their want of tactical skill. This was, it seems, an opportunity for seeing by the light of actual fact, how much experience scientifically acquired and the skill of a general, differ from a soldier's inexperience in the art of war and mere unreasoning routine. For in many partial engagements, Hamilcar, like a good draught player, by cutting off and surrounding large numbers of the enemy, destroyed them without their resisting, while in the more general battles he would sometimes inflict large loss by enticing them into unsuspected ambuscades and sometimes throw them into

καὶ παραδόξως ποτὲ μὲν μεθ᾽ ἡμέραν, ποτὲ δὲ νύκτωρ,
ἐπιφαινόμενος ἐξέπληττεν· ὧν ὅσους λάβοι ζωγρίᾳ,
9 πάντας παρέβαλλε τοῖς θηρίοις. τέλος δ᾽ ἐπιστρατο-
πεδεύσας αὐτοῖς ἀνυπονοήτως ἐν τόποις ἀφυέσι μὲν
πρὸς τὴν ἐκείνων χρείαν, εὐφυέσι δὲ πρὸς τὴν ἑαυτοῦ
δύναμιν, εἰς τοῦτ᾽ ἤγαγε περιστάσεως ὥστε μήτε
διακινδυνεύειν τολμῶντας μήτ᾽ ἀποδρᾶναι δυναμένους
διὰ τὸ τάφρῳ καὶ χάρακι περιειλῆφθαι πανταχόθεν
τέλος ὑπὸ τῆς λιμοῦ συναγομένους ἐσθίειν ἀλλήλων
10 ἀναγκασθῆναι, τοῦ δαιμονίου τὴν οἰκείαν ἀμοιβὴν
αὐτοῖς ἐπιφέροντος τῇ πρὸς τοὺς πέλας ἀσεβείᾳ καὶ
11 παρανομίᾳ. πρὸς μὲν γὰρ τὸν κίνδυνον οὐκ ἐτόλμων
ἐξιέναι, προδήλου τῆς ἥττης καὶ τῆς τιμωρίας τοῖς
ἁλισκομένοις ὑπαρχούσης, περὶ δὲ διαλύσεως οὐδ᾽
ὑπενόουν ποιεῖσθαι μνήμην, συνειδότες σφίσι τὰ πε-
12 πραγμένα. προσανέχοντες δ᾽ ἀεὶ ταῖς ἐκ τοῦ Τύνητος
βοηθείαις διὰ τὰς τῶν ἡγουμένων ἐπαγγελίας πᾶν
ὑπέμενον ποιεῖν κατὰ σφῶν αὐτῶν.

85. ἐπεὶ δὲ κατεχρήσαντο μὲν ἀσεβῶς τοὺς αἰχμαλώτους, τροφῇ ταύτῃ χρώμενοι, κατεχρήσαντο δὲ τὰ
δουλικὰ τῶν σωμάτων, ἐβοήθει δ᾽ ἐκ τοῦ Τύνητος
2 οὐδείς, τότε προδήλου τῆς αἰκίας διὰ τὴν περικάκησιν
ἐκ τῶν πολλῶν τοῖς ἡγεμόσιν ὑπαρχούσης, ἔκριναν οἱ
περὶ τὸν Αὐτάριτον καὶ Ζάρζαν καὶ Σπένδιον ἐγχειρί-
ζειν ἑαυτοὺς τοῖς πολεμίοις καὶ διαλαλεῖν περὶ δια-
3 λύσεως Ἀμίλκᾳ. πέμψαντες οὖν κήρυκα καὶ λαβόντες
4 συγχώρημα περὶ πρεσβείας, ἧκον ὄντες δέκα πρὸς
τοὺς Καρχηδονίους. πρὸς οὓς Ἀμίλκας ὁμολογίας

panic by appearing when they least expected it by day or by night. All those he captured were thrown to the elephants. Finally, taking them by surprise and encamping opposite to them in a position unfavorable for action on their part but favoring his own army he brought them to such a pass, that not daring to risk a battle and unable to escape, as they were entirely surrounded by a trench and palisade, they were at last driven by famine to eat each other[106]—a fitting retribution at the hands of Providence for their violation of all law human and divine in their treatment of their neighbors. They did not venture to march out and do battle, as they were faced by the certainty of defeat and condign punishment for all captured, and they did not even think of asking for terms, as they had their evil deeds on their conscience. Always expecting the relief from Tunis that their leaders continued to promise them, there was no crime against themselves that they scrupled to commit.

85. But when they had used up their prisoners in this abominable manner by feeding on them, and had used up their slaves, and no help came from Tunis, and their leaders saw that their persons were in obvious danger owing to the dreadful extremity to which the common soldiers were reduced, Autaritus, Zarzas and Spendius decided to give themselves up to the enemy and discuss terms with Hamilcar. They therefore dispatched a herald, and when they had obtained leave to send envoys, they went, ten in all, to the Carthaginians. The terms Hamilcar made with them

[106] The victims of cannibalism among the mercenaries were first their prisoners and second their slaves (85. 1).

ἐποιήσατο τοιαύτας· ἐξεῖναι Καρχηδονίοις ἐκλέξα-
σθαι τῶν πολεμίων οὓς ἂν αὐτοὶ βούλωνται δέκα· τοὺς
5 δὲ λοιποὺς ἀφιέναι μετὰ χιτῶνος. γενομένων δὲ τούτων, εὐθέως Ἀμίλκας ἔφη τοὺς παρόντας ἐκλέγεσθαι
κατὰ τὰς ὁμολογίας. τῶν μὲν οὖν περὶ τὸν Αὐτάριτον
καὶ Σπένδιον καὶ τῶν ἄλλων τῶν ἐπιφανεστάτων ἡγε-
6 μόνων τοῦτον τὸν τρόπον ἐκυρίευσαν οἱ Καρχηδόνιοι.
τῶν δὲ Λιβύων, ἐπεὶ τὴν σύλληψιν ᾔσθοντο τῶν ἡγεμόνων, νομισάντων αὐτοὺς παρεσπονδῆσθαι διὰ τὸ
τὰς συνθήκας ἀγνοεῖν, καὶ διὰ ταύτην τὴν αἰτίαν
7 ὁρμησάντων ἐπὶ τὰ ὅπλα, περιστήσας αὐτοῖς Ἀμίλκας τά τε θηρία καὶ τὴν λοιπὴν δύναμιν ἅπαντας
διέφθειρε πλείους ὄντας τῶν τετρακισμυρίων περὶ τὸν
τόπον τὸν Πρίονα καλούμενον· ὃν συμβαίνει διὰ τὴν
ὁμοιότητα τοῦ σχήματος πρὸς τὸ νῦν εἰρημένον ὄργα-
νον ταύτης τετευχέναι τῆς προσηγορίας.

86. Πράξας δὲ τὰ προδεδηλωμένα τοῖς μὲν Καρχηδονίοις αὖθις ἐλπίδα παρέστησε μεγάλην πρὸς τὸ
βέλτιον, καίπερ ἀπεγνωκόσιν ἤδη τὴν σωτηρίαν· αὐτὸς δὲ μετὰ Ναραύα καὶ μετ᾿ Ἀννίβου τὴν χώραν
2 ἐπῄει καὶ τὰς πόλεις. προσχωρούντων δὲ καὶ μετατιθε-
μένων πρὸς αὐτοὺς τῶν Λιβύων διὰ τὸ γεγονὸς εὐτύχημα, ποιησάμενοι τὰς πλείστας πόλεις ὑφ᾿ ἑαυτοὺς
ἧκον ἐπὶ τὸν Τύνητα, καὶ πολιορκεῖν ἐνεχείρησαν τοὺς
3 περὶ τὸν Μάθω. κατὰ μὲν οὖν τὴν ἀπὸ Καρχηδόνος
πλευρὰν προσεστρατοπέδευσεν Ἀννίβας, κατὰ δὲ τὴν
4 ἀπέναντι ταύτης Ἀμίλκας. μετὰ δὲ ταῦτα προσαγα-
γόντες πρὸς τὰ τείχη τοὺς περὶ τὸν Σπένδιον αἰχμα-

were, that the Carthaginians might choose from the enemy any ten they wished, the remainder being free to depart with one tunic apiece. These terms having been agreed to, Hamilcar at once said that by virtue of them he chose the ten envoys. By this means the Carthaginians got into their power Autaritus, Spendius, and the other principal leaders. The Libyans, when they learnt of their officers' arrest, thought they had been betrayed, as they were ignorant of the treaty, and rushed to arms, but Hamilcar, surrounding them (more than forty thousand) with his elephants and the rest of his forces, cut them all to pieces. This occurred near the place called the Saw; it got this name from its resemblance to the tool so called.

86. By this achievement Hamilcar again made the Carthaginians very hopeful of better fortune, although by this time they had nearly given up all for lost. In conjunction with Naravas and Hannibal he now raided the country and its towns. The Libyans in general gave in and went over to them owing to the recent victory, and after reducing most of the cities, the Carthaginians reached Tunis and began to besiege Mathos. Hannibal encamped on the side of the town next Carthage and Hamilcar on the opposite side. Their next step was to take Spendius and the other prison-

5 λώτους ἐσταύρωσαν ἐπιφανῶς. οἱ δὲ περὶ τὸν Μάθω,
κατανοήσαντες τὸν Ἀννίβαν ῥᾳθύμως καὶ κατατεθαρρηκότως ἀναστρεφόμενον, ἐπιθέμενοι τῷ χάρακι πολλοὺς μὲν τῶν Καρχηδονίων ἀπέκτειναν, πάντας δ'
ἐξέβαλον ἐκ τῆς στρατοπεδείας, ἐκυρίευσαν δὲ καὶ
τῆς ἀποσκευῆς ἁπάσης, ἔλαβον δὲ καὶ τὸν στρατηγὸν
6 Ἀννίβαν ζωγρίᾳ. τοῦτον μὲν οὖν παραχρῆμα πρὸς τὸν
τοῦ Σπενδίου σταυρὸν ἀγαγόντες καὶ τιμωρησάμενοι
πικρῶς, ἐκεῖνον μὲν καθεῖλον, τοῦτον δ' ἀνέθεσαν
ζῶντα καὶ περικατέσφαξαν τριάκοντα τῶν Καρχηδο-
7 νίων τοὺς ἐπιφανεστάτους περὶ τὸ τοῦ Σπενδίου σῶμα,
τῆς τύχης ὥσπερ ἐπίτηδες ἐκ παραθέσεως ἀμφοτέροις
ἐναλλὰξ διδούσης ἀφορμὰς εἰς ὑπερβολὴν τῆς κατ'
8 ἀλλήλων τιμωρίας· ὁ δὲ Βάρκας ὀψὲ μὲν συνῆκε τὴν
ἐπίθεσιν τῶν ἐκ τῆς πόλεως διὰ τὴν ἀπόστασιν τῶν
στρατοπέδων· οὐδὲ μὴν συνεὶς οὐδ' οὕτως κατετάχει
9 πρὸς τὴν βοήθειαν διὰ τὰς μεταξὺ δυσχωρίας. διόπερ
ἀναζεύξας ἀπὸ τοῦ Τύνητος, καὶ παρελθὼν ἐπὶ τὸν
Μακάραν ποταμόν, κατεστρατοπέδευσε πρὸς τῷ στόματι τοῦ ποταμοῦ καὶ τῇ θαλάττῃ.

87. Οἱ δὲ Καρχηδόνιοι, παραδόξου τῆς περιπετείας
αὐτοῖς φανείσης δυσθύμως καὶ δυσελπίστως εἶχον
πάλιν· ἄρτι γὰρ ἀναθαρροῦντες ταῖς ψυχαῖς παρὰ
2 πόδας ἔπιπτον αὖθις ταῖς ἐλπίσιν. οὐ μὴν ἀφίσταντο
3 τοῦ ποιεῖν τὰ πρὸς τὴν σωτηρίαν. διὸ καὶ τριάκοντα
μὲν τῆς γερουσίας προχειρισάμενοι, καὶ μετὰ τούτων
τὸν πρότερον μὲν ἀπελθόντα στρατηγὸν Ἄννωνα,
(τότε δ' ἐπαναγαγόντα) σὺν δὲ τούτοις τοὺς ὑπολοί-

ers up to the walls and crucify them there in the sight of all.
Mathos noticed that Hannibal was guilty of negligence and
overconfidence, and attacking his camp, put many Carthaginians to the sword and drove them all out of the camp.
All the baggage fell into the rebel's hands and they made
Hannibal himself prisoner. Taking him at once to Spendius' cross they tortured him cruelly there, and then, taking Spendius down from the cross, they crucified Hannibal
alive on it and slew round the body of Spendius thirty
Carthaginians of the highest rank. Thus did Fortune, as if
it were her design to compare them, give both the bellig-
erents in turn cause and opportunity for inflicting on each
other the cruellest punishments. Owing to the distance between the two camps it was some time before Hamilcar
heard of the sortie and attack, and even then he was slow to
give assistance owing to the difficult nature of the inter-
jacent ground. He therefore broke up his camp before
Tunis and on reaching the river Macaras, encamped at its
mouth by the seaside.

87. The suddenness of this reverse took the Carthaginians by surprise, and they became again despondent and
low-spirited. It was only the other day that their spirits had
begun to revive; so they at once fell again. Yet they did not
omit to take steps for their safety. They appointed a com-
mittee of thirty senators and dispatched them to Hamilcar
accompanied by Hanno, the general who had previously
retired from command, but now resumed it, and by all

πους τῶν ἐν ταῖς ἡλικίαις καθοπλίσαντες, οἷον ἐσχά-
την τρέχοντες ταύτην, ἐξαπέστελλον πρὸς τὸν Βάρ-
4 καν, ἐντειλάμενοι πολλὰ τοῖς τῆς γερουσίας κατὰ
πάντα τρόπον διαλῦσαι τοὺς στρατηγοὺς ἐκ τῆς προγεγενημένης διαφορᾶς καὶ συμφρονεῖν σφᾶς ἀναγκά-
5 σαι, βλέψαντας εἰς τὰ παρόντα τῶν πραγμάτων. ὧν
πολλοὺς καὶ ποικίλους διαθεμένων λόγους, ἐπειδὴ
συνήγαγον ὁμόσε τοὺς στρατηγούς, ἠναγκάσθησαν
συγχωρεῖν καὶ πείθεσθαι τοῖς λεγομένοις οἱ περὶ τὸν
6 Ἄννωνα καὶ τὸν Βάρκαν, καὶ τὸ λοιπὸν ἤδη συμφρονήσαντες μιᾷ γνώμῃ πάντα κατὰ νοῦν ἔπραττον τοῖς
7 Καρχηδονίοις, ὥστε τοὺς περὶ τὸν Μάθω, δυσχρη-
στουμένους ἐν τοῖς κατὰ μέρος κινδύνοις, πολλοὺς
γὰρ ἐποιήσαντο περί τε τὴν Λέπτιν προσαγορευομένην καὶ τινας τῶν ἄλλων πόλεων, τέλος ἐπὶ τὸ διὰ
μάχης κρίνειν ὁρμῆσαι τὰ πράγματα, προθύμως
8 ἐχόντων πρὸς τοῦτο τὸ μέρος καὶ τῶν Καρχηδονίων.
διόπερ ἀμφότεροι τοῦτο προθέμενοι παρεκάλουν μὲν
πάντας τοὺς συμμάχους πρὸς τὸν κίνδυνον, συνῆγον
δὲ τὰς φρουρὰς ἐκ τῶν πόλεων, ὡς ἂν μέλλοντες
9 ἐκκυβεύειν ὑπὲρ τῶν ὅλων. ἐπειδὴ δ' ἑκατέροις ἦν τὰ
πρὸς τὴν ἐπιβολὴν ἕτοιμα, παραταξάμενοι συνέβα-
10 λον ἀλλήλοις ἐξ ὁμολόγου. γενομένου δὲ τοῦ νικήμα-
τος κατὰ τοὺς Καρχηδονίους, οἱ μὲν πλεῖστοι τῶν
Λιβύων ἐν αὐτῷ τῷ κινδύνῳ διεφθάρησαν, οἱ δὲ πρός
τινα πόλιν συμφυγόντες μετ' οὐ πολὺ παρέδοσαν
ἑαυτούς, ὁ δὲ Μάθως ὑποχείριος ἐγένετο τοῖς ἐχθροῖς
ζωγρίᾳ.

their remaining citizens of military age, whom they had armed as a sort of forlorn hope. They enjoined these commissioners to put an end by all means in their power to the two generals' long-standing quarrel, and to force them, in view of the circumstances, to be reconciled. The senators, after they had brought the generals together, pressed them with so many and varied arguments, that at length Hanno and Barcas were obliged to yield and do as they requested. After their reconciliation they were of one mind, and consequently everything went as well as the Carthaginians could wish, so that Mathos, unsuccessful in the many partial engagements which took place around the place called Leptis and some other cities, at length resolved to decide matters by a general battle, the Carthaginians being equally anxious for this. Both sides then, with this purpose, called on all their allies to join them for the battle and summoned in the garrisons from the towns, as if about to stake their all on the issue. When they were each ready to attack, they drew up their armies confronting each other and at a preconcerted signal closed. The Carthaginians gained the victory, most of the Libyans falling in the battle, while the rest escaped to a certain city and soon afterward surrendered, but Mathos himself was taken by the enemy.

88. Τὰ μὲν οὖν ἄλλα μέρη τῆς Λιβύης μετὰ τὴν
2 μάχην εὐθέως ὑπήκουσε τοῖς Καρχηδονίοις· ἡ δὲ τῶν
Ἱππακριτῶν καὶ τῶν Ἰτυκαίων πόλις ἔμενον, οὐδεμίαν
ἀφορμὴν ἔχουσαι πρὸς διάλυσιν διὰ τὸ μὴ καταλείπεσθαι σφίσι τόπον ἐλέους μηδὲ συγγνώμης κατὰ
3 τὰς πρώτας ἐπιβολάς. οὕτως καὶ κατὰ ταύτας τὰς
ἁμαρτίας μεγάλην ἔχει διαφορὰν ἡ μετριότης καὶ τὸ
4 μηδὲν ἀνήκεστον ἐπιτηδεύειν ἑκουσίως. οὐ μὴν ἀλλὰ
παραστρατοπεδεύσαντες ᾗ μὲν Ἄννων, ᾗ δὲ Βάρκας,
ταχέως ἠνάγκασαν αὐτοὺς ὁμολογίας ποιήσασθαι
καὶ διαλύσεις εὐδοκουμένας Καρχηδονίοις.

5 Ὁ μὲν οὖν Λιβυκὸς πόλεμος εἰς τοιαύτην ἀγαγὼν
περίστασιν Καρχηδονίους τοιοῦτον ἔσχε τὸ τέλος,
ὥστε μὴ μόνον κυριεῦσαι πάλιν τῆς Λιβύης τοὺς
Καρχηδονίους, ἀλλὰ καὶ τοὺς αἰτίους τῆς ἀποστά-
6 σεως τιμωρήσασθαι καταξίως· τὸ γὰρ πέρας ἀγαγόντες οἱ νέοι τὸν θρίαμβον διὰ τῆς πόλεως πᾶσαν αἰκίαν
7 ἐναπεδείξαντο τοῖς περὶ τὸν Μάθω. τρία μὲν οὖν ἔτη
καὶ τέτταράς που μῆνας ἐπολέμησαν οἱ μισθοφόροι
πρὸς τοὺς Καρχηδονίους πόλεμον ὧν ἡμεῖς ἴσμεν
ἀκοῇ μαθόντες πολύ τι τοὺς ἄλλους ὠμότητι καὶ
8 παρανομίᾳ διενηνοχότα. Ῥωμαῖοι δὲ κατὰ τὸν καιρὸν
τοῦτον ὑπὸ τῶν ἐκ τῆς Σαρδόνος αὐτομολησάντων
μισθοφόρων πρὸς σφᾶς ἐκκληθέντες ἐπεβάλοντο
9 πλεῖν ἐπὶ τὴν προειρημένην νῆσον. τῶν δὲ Καρχηδονίων ἀγανακτούντων, ὡς αὐτοῖς καθηκούσης μᾶλλον
τῆς τῶν Σαρδῴων δυναστείας, καὶ παρασκευαζομένων
μεταπορεύεσθαι τοὺς ἀποστήσαντας αὐτῶν τὴν νῆ-

88. The rest of Libya at once submitted to Carthage after the battle, but Hippou Acra and Utica still held out,[107] feeling they had no reasonable grounds to expect terms in view of their having been so proof to all considerations of mercy and humanity when they first rebelled. This shows us that even in such offenses it is most advantageous to be moderate and abstain from voluntarily committing unpardonable excesses. However, Hanno besieging one town and Barcas the other soon compelled them to accept such conditions and terms as the Carthaginians thought fit to impose.

This Libyan war, that had brought Carthage into such peril, resulted not only in the Carthaginians regaining possession of Libya, but in their being able to inflict exemplary punishment on the authors of the rebellion. The last scene in it was a triumphal procession of the young men leading Mathos through the town and inflicting on him all kinds of torture. This war had lasted for three years and four months, and it far excelled all wars we know of in cruelty and defiance of principle. The Romans about the same time, on the invitation of the mercenaries who had deserted to them from Sardinia, undertook an expedition to that island. When the Carthaginians were angered on the ground that the sovereignty of Sardinia was rather their own than Rome's, and began preparations for punishing

107 See 82. 8–10.

THE HISTORIES OF POLYBIUS

10 σον, λαβόμενοι τῆς ἀφορμῆς ταύτης οἱ Ῥωμαῖοι
πόλεμον ἐψηφίσαντο πρὸς τοὺς Καρχηδονίους, φάσκοντες αὐτοὺς οὐκ ἐπὶ Σαρδονίους, ἀλλ᾽ ἐπὶ σφᾶς
11 ποιεῖσθαι τὴν παρασκευήν. οἱ δὲ παραδόξως διαπε-
φευγότες τὸν προειρημένον πόλεμον, κατὰ πάντα τρόπον ἀφυῶς διακείμενοι κατὰ τὸ παρὸν πρὸς τὸ πάλιν
12 ἀναλαμβάνειν τὴν πρὸς Ῥωμαίους ἀπέχθειαν, εἴξαντες τοῖς καιροῖς οὐ μόνον ἀπέστησαν τῆς Σαρδόνος,
ἀλλὰ καὶ χίλια τάλαντα καὶ διακόσια προσέθηκαν
τοῖς Ῥωμαίοις, ἐφ᾽ ᾧ μὴ κατὰ τὸ παρὸν ἀναδέξασθαι
τὸν πόλεμον. ταῦτα μὲν οὕτως ἐπράχθη.

those who were the cause of its revolt, the Romans made this the pretext of declaring war on them, alleging that the preparations were not against Sardinia, but against themselves. The Carthaginians, who had barely escaped destruction in this last war, were in every respect ill-fitted at this moment to resume hostilities with Rome. Yielding therefore to circumstances,[108] they not only gave up Sardinia, but agreed[109] to pay a further sum of twelve hundred talents to the Romans to avoid going to war for the present. Such then was the nature of these events.

[108] For the details see WC 1. 149–150.

[109] *StV* 497. Sardinia was soon to become the second Roman *provincia*; the circumstances leading to that counted among the causes of the Hannibalic War (see 65. 8–9 and 3. 10. 4).

ΙΣΤΟΡΙΩΝ ΔΕΥΤΕΡΑ

1. Ἐν μὲν τῇ πρὸ ταύτης βύβλῳ διεσαφήσαμεν πότε Ῥωμαῖοι συστησάμενοι τὰ κατὰ τὴν Ἰταλίαν τοῖς ἐκτὸς ἐγχειρεῖν ἤρξαντο πράγμασιν, ἐπὶ δὲ τούτοις πῶς εἰς Σικελίαν διέβησαν καὶ δι' ἃς αἰτίας τὸν περὶ τῆς προειρημένης νήσου συνεστήσαντο πόλεμον

2 πρὸς Καρχηδονίους, μετὰ δὲ ταῦτα πότε πρῶτον συνίστασθαι ναυτικὰς ἤρξαντο δυνάμεις, καὶ τὰ συμβάντα κατὰ τὸν πόλεμον ἑκατέροις ἕως τοῦ τέλους, ἐν ᾧ Καρχηδόνιοι μὲν ἐξεχώρησαν πάσης Σικελίας, Ῥωμαῖοι δ' ἐπεκράτησαν τῆς ὅλης νήσου πλὴν τῶν ὑφ' Ἱέρωνα ταττομένων μερῶν. ἑξῆς δὲ τούτοις ἐπεβαλό-

3 μεθα λέγειν πῶς στασιάσαντες οἱ μισθοφόροι πρὸς τοὺς Καρχηδονίους τὸν προσαγορευθέντα Λιβυκὸν πόλεμον ἐξέκαυσαν, καὶ τὰ συμβάντα κατὰ τοῦτον ἀσεβήματα μέχρι τίνος προύβη καὶ τίνα διέξοδον ἔλαβε τὰ παράλογα τῶν ἔργων, ἕως τοῦ τέλους καὶ

4 τῆς Καρχηδονίων ἐπικρατείας. νυνὶ δὲ τὰ συνεχῆ τούτοις πειρασόμεθα δηλοῦν κεφαλαιωδῶς ἑκάστων ἐπιψαύοντες κατὰ τὴν ἐξ ἀρχῆς πρόθεσιν.

5 Καρχηδόνιοι γὰρ ὡς θᾶττον κατεστήσαντο τὰ κατὰ τὴν Λιβύην, εὐθέως Ἀμίλκαν ἐξαπέστελλον

BOOK II

1. In the preceding book I stated in the first place at what date the Romans having subjected Italy began to concern themselves in enterprises outside the peninsula; next I narrated how they crossed to Sicily and what were their reasons for undertaking the war with Carthage for the possession of that island. After relating when and how they first built naval forces, I pursued the history of the war on both sides until its end, at which the Carthaginians evacuated all Sicily, and the Romans aquired the whole island except the parts which were Hiero's dominions. In the next place I set myself to describe how the mercenaries mutinied against Carthage and set ablaze the so-called Libyan war; I described all the terrible atrocities committed in this war, all its dramatic surprises, and their issues, until it ended in the final triumph of Carthage. I will now attempt to give a summary view, according to my original project, of the events immediately following.

The Carthaginians, as soon as they had set the affairs of Libya in order, dispatched Hamilcar to the land of Spain   238 B.C.

δυνάμεις συστήσαντες εἰς τοὺς κατὰ τὴν Ἰβηρίαν
6 τόπους. ὁ δ᾽ ἀναλαβὼν τὰ στρατόπεδα καὶ τὸν υἱὸν
Ἀννίβαν, ὄντα τότε κατὰ τὴν ἡλικίαν ἐτῶν ἐννέα, καὶ
διαβὰς κατὰ τὰς Ἡρακλέους στήλας ἀνεκτᾶτο τὰ
7 κατὰ τὴν Ἰβηρίαν πράγματα τοῖς Καρχηδονίοις. δια-
τρίψας δ᾽ ἐν τοῖς τόποις τούτοις ἔτη σχεδὸν ἐννέα, καί
πολλοὺς μὲν πολέμῳ, πολλοὺς δὲ πειθοῖ ποιήσας
Ἰβήρων ὑπηκόους Καρχηδόνι, κατέστρεψε τὸν βίον
8 ἀξίως τῶν προγεγενημένων πράξεων. πρὸς γὰρ τοὺς
ἀνδρωδεστάτους καὶ μεγίστην δύναμιν ἔχοντας παρα-
ταττόμενος, καὶ χρώμενος τολμηρῶς καὶ παραβόλως
ἑαυτῷ κατὰ τὸν τοῦ κινδύνου καιρόν, ἐρρωμένως τὸν
9 βίον μετήλλαξε; τὴν δὲ στρατηγίαν οἱ Καρχηδόνιοι
παρέδοσαν Ἀσδρούβᾳ, τῷ ᾽κείνου κηδεστῇ καὶ τριη-
ράρχῳ.

2. Κατὰ δὲ τοὺς καιροὺς τούτους Ῥωμαῖοι τὴν
πρώτην διάβασιν εἰς τὴν Ἰλλυρίδα καὶ ταῦτα τὰ μέρη
τῆς Εὐρώπης ἐπεβάλοντο ποιεῖσθαι μετὰ δυνάμεως.
2 ἅπερ οὐ παρέργως, ἀλλὰ μετ᾽ ἐπιστάσεως θεωρητέον
τοῖς βουλομένοις ἀληθινῶς τήν τε πρόθεσιν τὴν ἡμετέραν συνθεάσασθαι καὶ τὴν αὔξησιν καὶ κατασκευὴν
3 τῆς Ῥωμαίων δυναστείας. ἔγνωσαν δὲ διαβαίνειν διά
4 τινας τοιαύτας αἰτίας. Ἄγρων ὁ τῶν Ἰλλυριῶν βασιλεὺς ἦν μὲν υἱὸς Πλευράτου, δύναμιν δὲ πεζὴν καὶ
ναυτικὴν μεγίστην ἔσχε τῶν πρὸ αὐτοῦ βεβασιλευ-
5 κότων ἐν Ἰλλυριοῖς. οὗτος ὑπὸ Δημητρίου τοῦ Φιλίππου πατρὸς πεισθεὶς χρήμασιν ὑπέσχετο βοηθήσειν
6 Μεδιωνίοις ὑπ᾽ Αἰτωλῶν πολιορκουμένοις. Αἰτωλοὶ

entrusting him with an army. Taking with him his army and his son Hannibal now nine years of age, he crossed the straits of Gibraltar and applied himself to recovering Spain for the Carthaginians. In this country he spent about nine years during which he reduced many Iberian tribes to obedience either by force of arms or by diplomacy, and finally met with an end worthy of his high achievements, dying bravely in a battle against one of the most warlike and powerful tribes, after freely exposing his person to danger on the field. The Carthaginians handed over the command of the army to Hasdrubal his son-in-law and chief naval officer.[1]

238–229 B.C.

2. It was at this period[2] that the Romans first crossed with an army to Illyria and that part of Europe.[3] This is a matter not to be lightly passed over, but deserving the serious attention of those who wish to gain a true view of the purpose of this work and of the formation and growth of the Roman dominion. The circumstances which decided them to cross were as follows: Agron, king of Illyria,[4] was the son of Pleuratus, and was master of stronger land and sea forces than any king of Illyria before him. Demetrius, the father of Philip V, had induced him by a bribe to go to the assistance of the town of Medion which the Aetolians

233–232 B.C.

---

[1] Hasdrubal's story continues in 13. 1.   [2] In 229. For the First Illyrian War (229–228) see P. Derow, "Kleemporos," *Phoenix* 27 (1973) 118–134, who persuasively argues that Appianus' account (*Ill.* 7. 17–22) is superior to that of Polybius.

[3] M. Zahrnt, *Hermes* 113 (2008) 391–414.

[4] For the Illyrian exploits in 231–229 see J. B. Scholten, *The Politics of Plunder. Aetolians and their Koinon in the Early Hellenistic Era, 279–217 B.C.* (Berkeley, 2000) 139–151.

γὰρ οὐδαμῶς δυνάμενοι πεῖσαι Μεδιωνίους μετέχειν
σφίσι τῆς αὐτῆς πολιτείας, ἐπεβάλοντο κατὰ κράτος
7 ἑλεῖν αὐτούς. στρατεύσαντες οὖν πανδημεί, καὶ περι-
στρατοπεδεύσαντες αὐτῶν τὴν πόλιν, κατὰ τὸ συνεχὲς
8 ἐπολιόρκουν, πᾶσαν βίαν προσφέροντες καὶ μηχανήν.
συνάψαντος δὲ τοῦ χρόνου τῶν ἀρχαιρεσίων, καὶ δέον
στρατηγὸν ἕτερον αἱρεῖσθαι, καὶ τῶν πολιορκουμένων
ἤδη κακῶς διακειμένων, καὶ δοκούντων ἀν᾽ ἑκάστην
ἡμέραν ἐνδώσειν ἑαυτούς, ὁ προϋπάρχων στρατηγὸς
9 προσφέρει λόγον τοῖς Αἰτωλοῖς, φάσκων, ἐπειδὴ τὰς
κακοπαθείας καὶ τοὺς κινδύνους αὐτὸς ἀναδέδεκται
τοὺς κατὰ τὴν πολιορκίαν, δίκαιον εἶναι καὶ τὴν οἰκονομίαν τῶν λαφύρων, ἐπὰν κρατήσωσι, καὶ τὴν ἐπι-
10 γραφὴν τῶν ὅπλων ἑαυτῷ συγχωρεῖσθαι. τινῶν δέ,
καὶ μάλιστα τῶν προϊόντων πρὸς τὴν ἀρχήν, ἀμφισ-
βητούντων πρὸς τὰ λεγόμενα καὶ παρακαλούντων τὰ
πλήθη μὴ προδιαλαμβάνειν, ἀλλ᾽ ἀκέραιον ἐᾶν, ᾧ
ποτ᾽ ἂν ἡ τύχη βουληθῇ περιθεῖναι τοῦτον τὸν στέφα-
11 νον, ἔδοξε τοῖς Αἰτωλοῖς, ὃς ἂν ἐπικατασταθεὶς στρατηγὸς κρατήσῃ τῆς πόλεως, κοινὴν ποιεῖν τῷ προ-
ϋπάρχοντι καὶ τὴν οἰκονομίαν τῶν λαφύρων καὶ τὴν
ἐπιγραφὴν τῶν ὅπλων.

3. Δεδογμένων δὲ τούτων, καὶ δέον τῇ κατὰ πόδας
ἡμέρᾳ γενέσθαι τὴν αἵρεσιν καὶ τὴν παράληψιν τῆς
ἀρχῆς, καθάπερ ἔθος ἐστὶν Αἰτωλοῖς, προσπλέουσι
τῆς νυκτὸς ἑκατὸν λέμβοι πρὸς τὴν Μεδιωνίαν, κατὰ
τοὺς ἔγγιστα τόπους τῆς πόλεως, ἐφ᾽ ὧν ἦσαν Ἰλλυ-

were besieging. The Aetolians being unable to persuade
the Medionians to join their league, determined to reduce
them by force. Levying all their forces they encamped
round the city and continuously laid siege to it, employing
every forcible means and every device. The date of the annual elections[5] was now at hand, and they had to choose
another Strategus. As the besieged were in the utmost extremity and were expected to surrender every day, the actual Strategus addressed the Aetolians, maintaining that as
it was he who had supported the dangers and hardships of
the siege, it was only just, that, on the town falling, he
should have the privilege of dealing with the booty and inscribing with his name the shields dedicated in memory of
the victory. Some, more especially the candidates for the
office, disputed this, and begged the people not to decide
the matter in advance, but leave it, as things stood, to Fortune to determine to whom she should award this prize.
The Aetolians hereupon passed a resolution, that if it was
the new Strategus whoever he might be, to whom the city
fell, he should share with the present one the disposition of
the booty and the honor of inscribing the shields.

3. This decree had been passed, and next day the elec-
tion was to be held, and the new Strategus was to enter at
once into office, as is the practice of the Aetolians, when
that night a hundred boats containing a force of five thousand Illyrians arrived at the nearest point on the coast to

[5] At the autumn equinox: G. Busolt - H. Swoboda, *Griechische
Staatskunde* 2 (Munich 1926) 1521–1524.

2 ριοὶ πεντακισχίλιοι. καθορμισθέντες δέ, καὶ τῆς ἡμέρας ἐπιγενομένης ἐνεργὸν καὶ λαθραίαν ποιησάμενοι
τὴν ἀπόβασιν, καὶ χρησάμενοι τῇ παρ' αὐτοῖς εἰ-
θισμένῃ τάξει, προῆγον κατὰ σπείρας ἐπὶ τὴν τῶν
3 Αἰτωλῶν στρατοπεδείαν. οἱ δ' Αἰτωλοί, συνέντες τὸ
γινόμενον, ἐπὶ μὲν τῷ παραδόξῳ καὶ τῇ τόλμῃ τῶν
Ἰλλυριῶν ἦσαν ἐκπλαγεῖς· πεφρονηματισμένοι δ' ἐκ
πολλοῦ χρόνου, καὶ καταπιστεύσαντες ταῖς ἰδίαις
4 δυνάμεσι, κατὰ ποσὸν εὐθαρσῶς εἶχον. τὸ μὲν οὖν
πολὺ μέρος τῶν ὁπλιτῶν καὶ τῶν ἱππέων αὐτοῦ πρὸ
τῆς στρατοπεδείας ἐν τοῖς ἐπιπέδοις παρενέβαλον,
μέρει δέ τινι τῆς ἵππου καὶ τοῖς εὐζώνοις τοὺς ὑπερδεξίους καὶ πρὸ τοῦ χάρακος εὐφυῶς κειμένους τόπους
5 προκατελάμβανον. οἱ δ' Ἰλλυριοὶ τοὺς μὲν ἐλαφροὺς
ἐξ ἐφόδου προσπεσόντες τῷ τε πλήθει καὶ τῷ βάρει
τῆς συντάξεως ἐξέωσαν, τοὺς δὲ μετὰ τούτων ἱππεῖς
συγκινδυνεύοντας ἠνάγκασαν ἀποχωρῆσαι πρὸς τὰ
6 βαρέα τῶν ὅπλων. λοιπὸν ἐξ ὑπερδεξίου ποιούμενοι
τὴν ἔφοδον ἐπὶ τοὺς ἐν τῷ πεδίῳ τεταγμένους, ταχέως
ἐτρέψαντο, συνεπιθεμένων τοῖς Αἰτωλοῖς ἅμα καὶ τῶν
7 Μεδιωνίων ἐκ τῆς πόλεως. καὶ πολλοὺς μὲν αὐτῶν
ἀπέκτειναν, ἔτι δὲ πλείους αἰχμαλώτους ἔλαβον· τῶν
δ' ὅπλων καὶ τῆς ἀποσκευῆς ἐγένοντο πάσης ἐγκρα-
8 τεῖς. οἱ μὲν οὖν Ἰλλυριοὶ πράξαντες τὸ συνταχθὲν ὑπὸ
τοῦ βασιλέως, καὶ διακομίσαντες τὴν ἀποσκευὴν καὶ
τὴν ἄλλην ὠφέλειαν ἐπὶ τοὺς λέμβους εὐθέως ἀνήγοντο, ποιούμενοι τὸν πλοῦν εἰς τὴν οἰκείαν.

4. οἱ δὲ Μεδιώνιοι τετευχότες ἀνελπίστου σωτη-

Medion.[6] Anchoring there they landed, as soon as it was daylight, with promptitude and secrecy, and forming in the order customary in Illyria, advanced by companies on the Aetolian camp. The Aetolians, on becoming aware of it, were taken aback by the unexpected nature and boldness of the attack, but having for many years ranked very high in their own estimation and relying on their strength, they were more or less confident. Stationing the greater part of their hoplites and cavalry on the level ground just in front of their lines, they occupied with a portion of their cavalry and their light-armed infantry certain favorable positions on the heights in front of the camp. The Illyrians, charging the light infantry, drove them from their positions by their superior force and the weight of their formation, compelling the supporting body of cavalry to fall back on the heavy-armed troops. After this, having the advantage of attacking the latter, who were drawn up on the plain, from higher ground, they speedily put them to flight, the Medionians also joining in the attack from the city. They killed many Aetolians and took a still larger number of prisoners, capturing all their arms and baggage. The Illyrians, having thus executed the orders of their king, carried off to their boats the baggage and other booty and at once set sail for home.

4. The Medionians, thus unexpectedly saved, met in as-

[6] City of Acarnania, for some twenty years part of the Epirote kingdom, free again in that kingdom's final crisis (232–231) and immediately attacked by the Aetolians; henceforth a member of the Acarnanian League refounded at this time.

ρίας, ἀθροισθέντες εἰς τὴν ἐκκλησίαν ἐβουλεύοντο
2 περί τε τῶν ἄλλων καὶ περὶ τῆς τῶν ὅπλων ἐπιγραφῆς.
ἔδοξεν οὖν αὐτοῖς κοινὴν ποιήσειν τὴν ἐπιγραφὴν ἀπό
τε τοῦ τὴν ἀρχὴν τῶν Αἰτωλῶν ἔχοντος καὶ τῶν εἰς τὸ
3 μέλλον προπορευομένων κατὰ τὸ τῶν Αἰτωλῶν δόγμα,
τῆς τύχης ὥσπερ ἐπίτηδες καὶ τοῖς ἄλλοις ἀνθρώποις
ἐπὶ τῶν ἐκείνοις συμβαινόντων ἐνδεικνυμένης τὴν αὐ-
4 τῆς δύναμιν. ἃ γὰρ ὑπὸ τῶν ἐχθρῶν αὐτοὶ προσεδόκων ὅσον ἤδη πείσεσθαι, ταῦτα πράττειν αὐτοῖς ἐκείνοις παρέδωκεν ἐν πάνυ βραχεῖ χρόνῳ κατὰ τῶν
5 πολεμίων. Αἰτωλοὶ δὲ τῇ παραδόξῳ χρησάμενοι συμφορᾷ πάντας ἐδίδαξαν μηδέποτε βουλεύεσθαι περὶ
τοῦ μέλλοντος ὡς ἤδη γεγονότος, μηδὲ προκατελ-
πίζειν βεβαιουμένους ὑπὲρ ὧν ἀκμὴν ἐνδεχόμενόν
ἐστιν ἄλλως γενέσθαι, νέμειν δὲ μερίδα τῷ παραδόξῳ
πανταχῇ μὲν ἀνθρώπους ὄντας, μάλιστα δ᾽ ἐν τοῖς
πολεμικοῖς.
6 Ὁ δὲ βασιλεὺς Ἄγρων, ἐπεὶ κατέπλευσαν οἱ λέμβοι, διακούσας τῶν ἡγεμόνων τὰ κατὰ τὸν κίνδυνον,
καὶ περιχαρὴς γενόμενος ἐπὶ τῷ δοκεῖν Αἰτωλοὺς τοὺς
μέγιστον ἔχοντας τὸ φρόνημα νενικηκέναι, πρὸς μέ-
θας καί τινας τοιαύτας ἄλλας εὐωχίας τραπεὶς ἐνέπεσεν εἰς πλευρῖτιν· ἐκ δὲ ταύτης ἐν ὀλίγαις ἡμέραις
7 μετήλλαξε τὸν βίον. τὴν δὲ βασιλείαν ἡ γυνὴ Τεύτα
διαδεξαμένη τὸν κατὰ μέρος χειρισμὸν τῶν πρα-
8 γμάτων ἐποιεῖτο διὰ τῆς τῶν φίλων πίστεως. χρωμένη
δὲ λογισμοῖς γυναικείοις, καὶ πρὸς αὐτὸ τὸ γεγονὸς
εὐτύχημα μόνον ἀποβλέπουσα, τῶν δ᾽ ἐκτὸς οὐδὲν

sembly and discussed, among other matters, that of the proper inscription for the shields. They decided, in parody of the Aetolian decree, to inscribe them[7] as won *from* and not *by* the present Aetolian chief magistrate and the candidates for next year's office. It seemed as if what had befallen this people was designed by Fortune to display her might to men in general. For in so brief a space of time she put it in their power to do to the enemy the very thing which they thought the enemy were just on the point of doing to themselves. The unlooked-for calamity of the Aetolians was a lesson to mankind never to discuss the future as if it were the present, or to have any confident hope about things that may still turn out quite otherwise. We are but men, and should in every matter assign its share to the unexpected, this being especially true of war.

King Agron, when the flotilla returned and his officers gave him an account of the battle, was so overjoyed at the thought of having beaten the Aetolians, then the proudest of peoples, that he took to carousals and other convivial excesses, from which he fell into a pleurisy that ended fatally in a few days. He was succeeded on the throne by his wife Teuta,[8] who left the details of administration to friends on whom she relied. As, with a woman's natural shortness of view, she could see nothing but the recent success and had no eyes for what was going on elsewhere, she in the

231 B.C.

---

[7] A famous example out of many: "The Athenians from the Lacedaemonians at Pylos" in 425: *Agora* 14 (Princeton 1972), 92–93.

[8] She was in fact regent and guardian for Pinnes, the young son of Agron and Triteuta (App. *Ill.* 7. 19).

περισκεπτομένη, πρῶτον μὲν συνεχώρησε τοῖς κατ'
9 ἰδίαν πλέουσι λήζεσθαι τοὺς ἐντυγχάνοντας, δεύτερον
δ' ἀθροίσασα στόλον καὶ δύναμιν οὐκ ἐλάττω τῆς
πρότερον ἐξέπεμψε, πᾶσαν παραλίαν γῆν ἀποδείξασα
πολεμίαν τοῖς ἡγουμένοις.

5. οἱ δ' ἐξαποσταλέντες τὴν μὲν πρώτην ἐπιβολὴν
ἔσχον ἐπὶ τὴν Ἠλείαν καὶ τὴν Μεσσηνίαν. ταύτας
2 γὰρ ἀεὶ τὰς χώρας Ἰλλυριοὶ πορθοῦντες διετέλουν.
διὰ γὰρ τὸ μῆκος τῆς παραλίας καὶ διὰ τὸ μεσογαίους
εἶναι τὰς δυναστευούσας ἐν αὐταῖς πόλεις μακραὶ καὶ
βραδεῖαι λίαν ἐγίνοντο τοῖς προειρημένοις αἱ παρα-
βοήθειαι πρὸς τὰς ἀποβάσεις τῶν Ἰλλυριῶν· ὅθεν
ἀδεῶς ἐπέτρεχον καὶ κατέσυρον ἀεὶ ταύτας τὰς χώ-
3 ρας. οὐ μὴν ἀλλὰ τότε γενόμενοι τῆς Ἠπείρου κατὰ
4 Φοινίκην προσέσχον ἐπισιτισμοῦ χάριν. συμμίξαντες
δὲ τῶν Γαλατῶν τισιν, οἳ μισθοφοροῦντες παρὰ τοῖς
Ἠπειρώταις διέτριβον ἐν τῇ Φοινίκῃ, τὸ πλῆθος ὄντες
εἰς ὀκτακοσίους, καὶ κοινολογηθέντες τούτοις περὶ
προδοσίας τῆς πόλεως ἐξέβησαν, συγκαταθεμένων
σφίσι τῶν προειρημένων, καὶ τῆς πόλεως ἐξ ἐφόδου
καὶ τῶν ἐν αὐτῇ κύριοι κατέστησαν, συνεργησάντων
5 ἔσωθεν αὐτοῖς τῶν Γαλατῶν. οἱ δ' Ἠπειρῶται πυθόμενοι τὸ γεγονὸς ἐβοήθουν πανδημεὶ μετὰ σπουδῆς.
παραγενόμενοι δὲ πρὸς τὴν Φοινίκην, καὶ προβαλόμενοι τὸν παρὰ τὴν πόλιν ῥέοντα ποταμόν, ἐστρατο-
πέδευσαν, τῆς ἐπ' αὐτῷ γεφύρας ἀνασπάσαντες τὰς

first place authorized privateers to pillage any ships they met, and next she collected a fleet and a force of troops as large as the former one and sent it out, ordering the commanders to treat the entire seaboard[9] as belonging to their enemies.

5. The expedition began by making a descent on Elis and Messenia,[10] lands which the Illyrians had always been in the habit of pillaging, because, owing to the extent of their seaboard and owing to the principal cities being in the interior, help against their raids was distant and slow in arriving; so that they could always overrun and plunder those countries unmolested. On this occasion, however, they put in at Phoenice[11] in Epirus for the purpose of provisioning themselves. There they fell in with certain Gaulish soldiers,[12] about eight hundred in number, at present in the employ of the Epirots. They approached these Gauls with a proposal for the betrayal of the city, and on their agreeing, they landed and captured the town and its inhabitants by assault with the help from within of the Gauls. When the Epirots learnt of this they hastened to come to help with their whole force. On reaching Phoenice they encamped with the river that runs past the town on their front, removing the planking of the bridge so

230 B.C.

---

9 Lammert's suggestion παραλίαν, accepted by B-W. An alternative is Bekker's γῆν, "every land."

10 Both allies of the Aetolians.   11 Modern Feniki in Albania, from c. 230 onwards the capital of the new federal state of Epirus, *RE* 20, 1306–1308 (E. Polaschek).

12 In 7. 7–11 it is made clear that these had been mercenaries of Carthage during the First Punic War. Their acts mirror the events at Messana (1. 7. 2–4) and Rhegium (1. 7. 6–8).

6 σανίδας ἀσφαλείας χάριν. προσαγγελθέντος δ' αὐτοῖς Σκερδιλαΐδαν ἔχοντα πεντακισχιλίους Ἰλλυριοὺς
παραγίνεσθαι κατὰ γῆν διὰ τῶν παρ' Ἀντιγόνειαν
στενῶν, μερίσαντες αὐτῶν τινας ἐξαπέστειλαν παρα-
φυλάξοντας τὴν Ἀντιγόνειαν· αὐτοὶ δὲ τά τε λοιπὰ
ῥᾳθύμως διῆγον, ἀπολαύοντες τῶν ἐκ τῆς χώρας ἀν-
έδην, τῶν τε κατὰ τὰς φυλακὰς καὶ προκοιτίας ὠλι-
7 γώρουν. οἱ δ' Ἰλλυριοὶ συνέντες τὸν μερισμὸν αὐτῶν
καὶ τὴν λοιπὴν ῥᾳθυμίαν, ἐκπορεύονται νυκτός· καὶ τῇ
γεφύρᾳ σανίδας ἐπιβαλόντες τόν τε ποταμὸν ἀσφαλῶς διέβησαν καὶ λαβόντες ὀχυρὸν τόπον ἔμειναν τὸ
8 λοιπὸν μέρος τῆς νυκτός. ἐπιγενομένης δὲ τῆς ἡμέρας
καὶ παραταξαμένων ἀμφοτέρων πρὸ τῆς πόλεως, συνέβη λειφθῆναι τοὺς Ἠπειρώτας, καὶ πολλοὺς μὲν
αὐτῶν πεσεῖν, ἔτι δὲ πλείους ἁλῶναι, τοὺς δὲ λοιποὺς
διαφυγεῖν ὡς ἐπ' Ἀτιντάνων.

6. Οὗτοι μὲν οὖν τοιούτοις περιπεσόντες ἀτυχήμασι, καὶ πάσας ἀπολέσαντες τὰς ἐν αὑτοῖς ἐλπίδας,
ἐπρέσβευον πρὸς τοὺς Αἰτωλοὺς καὶ τὸ τῶν Ἀχαιῶν
2 ἔθνος, δεόμενοι μεθ' ἱκετηρίας σφίσι βοηθεῖν. οἱ δὲ
κατελεήσαντες τὰς συμφορὰς αὐτῶν ὑπήκουσαν, καὶ
3 μετὰ ταῦτα παραβοηθοῦντες ἧκον εἰς Ἑλίκρανον. οἱ
δὲ τὴν Φοινίκην κατασχόντες, τὸ μὲν πρῶτον παραγενόμενοι μετὰ Σκερδιλαΐδου πρὸς τὸ χωρίον παρ-
εστρατοπέδευσαν τοῖς βεβοηθηκόσι, βουλόμενοι
4 συμβαλεῖν. δυσχρηστούμενοι δὲ διὰ τὰς δυσχωρίας
τῶν τόπων, ἅμα δὲ καὶ προσπεσόντων παρὰ τῆς
Τεύτας γραμμάτων, δι' ὧν ᾤετο δεῖν αὐτοὺς τὴν ταχί-

as to be in safety. On news reaching them that Scerdilaïdas[13] with five thousand Illyrians was approaching by
land through the pass near Antigonia, they detached a portion of their force to guard Antigonia, but they themselves
henceforth remained at their ease, faring plenteously on
the produce of the country, and quite neglecting night and
day watches. The Illyrians, leaning of the partition of the
Epirot force and of their general remissness, made a night
sortie, and replacing planks on the bridge, crossed the
river in safety and occupied a strong position where they
remained for the rest of the night. When day broke, both
armies drew up their forces in front of the town and engaged. The battle resulted in the defeat of the Epirots,
many of whom were killed and still more taken prisoners,
the rest escaping in the direction of Atintania.

6. The Epirots, having met with this misfortune and lost
all hope in themselves, sent embassies to the Aetolians
and to the Achaean league imploring their succor. Both
leagues took pity on their situation and consented, and
shortly afterward this relieving force reached Helicranum.
The Illyrians holding Phoenice at first united with Scerdilaïdas, and advancing to Helicranum encamped opposite
the Achaeans the Aetolians who had come to the rescue,
and were anxious to give battle. But the ground was very
difficult and unfavorable to them, and just at this time a
dispatch came from Teuta ordering them to return home

13 Probably King Agron's brother.

στην εἰς οἶκον ἀναχωρεῖν διὰ τὸ τινὰς τῶν Ἰλλυριῶν
5 ἀφεστηκέναι πρὸς τοὺς Δαρδανεῖς, οὕτω λεηλατή-
σαντες τὴν Ἤπειρον ἀνοχὰς ἐποιήσαντο πρὸς τοὺς
6 Ἠπειρώτας. ἐν αἷς τὰ μὲν ἐλεύθερα σώματα καὶ τὴν
πόλιν ἀπολυτρώσαντες αὐτοῖς, τὰ δὲ δουλικὰ καὶ τὴν
λοιπὴν σκευὴν ἀναλαβόντες εἰς τοὺς λέμβους, οἱ μὲν
ἀπέπλευσαν, οἱ δὲ περὶ τὸν Σκερδιλαΐδαν πεζῇ πάλιν
7 ἀνεχώρησαν διὰ τῶν παρὰ τὴν Ἀντιγόνειαν στενῶν,
οὐ μικρὰν οὐδὲ τὴν τυχοῦσαν κατάπληξιν καὶ φόβον
ἐνεργασάμενοι τοῖς τὰς παραλίας οἰκοῦσι τῶν Ἑλλή-
8 νων. ἕκαστοι γὰρ θεωροῦντες τὴν ὀχυρωτάτην ἅμα
καὶ δυνατωτάτην πόλιν τῶν ἐν Ἠπείρῳ παραλόγως
οὕτως ἐξηνδραποδισμένην, οὐκέτι περὶ τῶν ἀπὸ τῆς
χώρας ἠγωνίων, καθάπερ ἐν τοῖς ἔμπροσθεν χρόνοις,
ἀλλὰ περὶ σφῶν αὐτῶν καὶ τῶν πόλεων.
9 Οἱ δ' Ἠπειρῶται παραδόξως διασεσωσμένοι, τοσοῦτον ἀπεῖχον τοῦ πειράζειν ἀμύνεσθαι τοὺς ἠδικη-
κότας ἢ χάριν ἀποδιδόναι τοῖς βοηθήσασιν, ὥστε
τοὐναντίον διαπρεσβευσάμενοι πρὸς τὴν Τεύταν συμ-
10 μαχίαν ἔθεντο μετ' Ἀκαρνάνων πρὸς τοὺς Ἰλλυριούς,
καθ' ἣν ἐκείνοις μὲν κατὰ τοὺς ἑξῆς καιροὺς συνήρ-
11 γουν, τοῖς δ' Ἀχαιοῖς καὶ τοῖς Αἰτωλοῖς ἀντέπραττον.
ἐξ ὧν ἐγένοντο καταφανεῖς ἀκρίτως μὲν κεχρημένοι
τότε τοῖς εὐεργέταις, ἀφρόνως δ' ἐξ ἀρχῆς βεβου-
λευμένοι περὶ τῶν καθ' αὑτοὺς πραγμάτων.
7. τὸ μὲν γὰρ ἀνθρώπους ὄντας παραλόγως περιπεσεῖν τινι τῶν δεινῶν οὐ τῶν παθόντων, τῆς τύχης δὲ
2 καὶ τῶν πραξάντων ἐστὶν ἔγκλημα, τὸ δ' ἀκρίτως καὶ

by the quickest route, as some of the Illyrians had revolted
to the Dardanians. They therefore, after plundering Epirus, made a truce with the Epirots. By the terms of this they
gave up to them the city and its free population on payment of a ransom; the slaves and other goods and chattels
they put on board their boats, and while the one force
sailed off home, Scerdilaïdas marched back through the
pass near Antigonia. They had caused the Greek inhabitants of the coast no little consternation and alarm; for, seeing the most strongly situated and most powerful town in
Epirus thus suddenly taken and devastated, they all began
to be anxious not, as in former times, for their agricultural
produce, but for the safety of themselves and their cities.

The Epirots, thus unexpectedly saved, were so far from
attempting to retaliate on the wrongdoers or from thank-
ing those who had come to their relief, that, on the contrary, they sent an embassy to Teuta, and together with the
Acarnanians entered into an alliance with Illyria,[14] engaging in future to cooperate with the Illyrians and work
against the Achaeans and Aetolians. Their whole conduct
showed them not only to have acted now toward their
benefactors without judgment, but to have blundered
from the outset in the management of their own affairs.

7. For we are but men, and to meet with some unexpected blow is not the sufferer's fault, but that of Fortune
and those who inflict it on him; but when we involve our-

14 Epirus (not all of it) and Acarnania are henceforth allies of
the king of Macedon.

προφανῶς περιβαλεῖν αὐτοὺς ταῖς μεγίσταις συμφοραῖς ὁμολογούμενόν ἐστι τῶν πασχόντων ἁμάρ-
3 τημα. διὸ καὶ τοῖς μὲν ἐκ τύχης πταίουσιν ἔλεος
ἕπεται μετὰ συγγνώμης κἀπικουρία, τοῖς δὲ διὰ τὴν
αὐτῶν ἀβουλίαν ὄνειδος κἀπιτίμησις συνεξακολουθεῖ
4 παρὰ τοῖς εὖ φρονοῦσιν. ἃ δὴ καὶ τότε παρὰ τῶν
5 Ἑλλήνων εἰκότως ἂν τοῖς Ἠπειρώταις ἀπηντήθη.
πρῶτον γὰρ τίς οὐκ ἂν τὴν κοινὴν περὶ Γαλατῶν
φήμην ὑπιδόμενος εὐλαβηθείη τούτοις ἐγχειρίσαι πόλιν εὐδαίμονα καὶ πολλὰς ἀφορμὰς ἔχουσαν εἰς
6 παρασπόνδησιν; δεύτερον τίς οὐκ ἂν ἐφυλάξατο τὴν
αὐτοῦ τοῦ συστήματος ἐκείνου προαίρεσιν; οἵ γε τὴν
μὲν ἀρχὴν ἐξέπεσον ἐκ τῆς ἰδίας, συνδραμόντων ἐπ'
αὐτοὺς τῶν ὁμοεθνῶν, διὰ τὸ παρασπονδῆσαι τοὺς
7 αὑτῶν οἰκείους καὶ συγγενεῖς· ὑποδεξαμένων γε μὴν
αὐτοὺς Καρχηδονίων διὰ τὸ κατεπείγεσθαι πολέμῳ,
τὸ μὲν πρῶτον γενομένης τινὸς ἀντιρρήσεως τοῖς
στρατιώταις πρὸς τοὺς στρατηγοὺς ὑπὲρ ὀψωνίων ἐξ
αὐτῆς ἐπεβάλοντο διαρπάζειν τὴν τῶν Ἀκραγαντίνων
πόλιν, φυλακῆς χάριν εἰσαχθέντες εἰς αὐτήν, ὄντες
8 τότε πλείους τῶν τρισχιλίων· μετὰ δὲ ταῦτα παρ-
εισαγαγόντων αὐτοὺς πάλιν εἰς Ἔρυκα τῆς αὐτῆς
χρείας ἕνεκεν, πολιορκούντων τὴν πόλιν Ῥωμαίων,
ἐπεχείρησαν μὲν καὶ τὴν πόλιν καὶ τοὺς συμπολιορ-
9 κουμένους προδοῦναι· τῆς δὲ πράξεως ταύτης ἀποτυχόντες ηὐτομόλησαν πρὸς τοὺς πολεμίους· παρ' οἷς
πιστευθέντες πάλιν ἐσύλησαν τὸ τῆς Ἀφροδίτης τῆς
10 Ἐρυκίνης ἱερόν. διὸ σαφῶς ἐπεγνωκότες Ῥωμαῖοι τὴν

selves by sheer lack of judgment and with our eyes open in the depth of misfortune, everyone acknowledges that we have none to blame but ourselves. It is for this reason that those whom Fortune leads astray meet with pity, pardon and help, but if their failures are due to their own indiscretion, all right-thinking men blame and reproach them. And in this case the Greeks would have been amply justified in their censure of the Epirots. To begin with would not anyone who is aware of the general reputation of the Gauls, think twice before entrusting to them a wealthy city, the betrayal of which was easy and profitable? In the second place who would not have been cautious in the case of a company with such a bad name? First of all they had been expelled from their own country by a general movement of their fellow countrymen owing to their having betrayed their own friends and kinsmen. Again, when the Carthaginians, hard pressed by the war, received them, they first availed themselves of a dispute about pay between the soldiers and generals to pillage the city of Agrigentum of which they formed the garrison, being then above three thousand strong. Afterward, when the Carthaginians sent them on the same service to Eryx, then besieged by the Romans, they attempted to betray the city and those who were suffering siege in their company, and when this plan fell through, they deserted to the Romans. The Romans entrusted them with the guard of the temple of Venus Erycina, which again they pillaged. Therefore, no sooner

ἀσέβειαν αὐτῶν, ἅμα τῷ διαλύσασθαι τὸν πρὸς Καρχηδονίους πόλεμον οὐδὲν ἐποιήσαντο προυργιαίτερον
τοῦ παροπλίσαντας αὐτοὺς ἐμβαλεῖν εἰς πλοῖα καὶ

11 τῆς Ἰταλίας πάσης ἐξορίστους καταστῆσαι. οὓς
Ἠπειρῶται τῆς δημοκρατίας καὶ τῶν νόμων φύλακας
ποιησάμενοι, καὶ τὴν εὐδαιμονεστάτην πόλιν ἐγχει-
ρίσαντες, πῶς οὐκ ἂν εἰκότως φανείησαν αὐτοὶ τῶν
συμπτωμάτων αὐτοῖς αἴτιοι γεγονότες;

12 Περὶ μὲν οὖν τῆς Ἠπειρωτῶν ἀγνοίας, καὶ περὶ τοῦ
μηδέποτε δεῖν τοὺς εὖ φρονοῦντας ἰσχυροτέραν εἰσ-
άγεσθαι φυλακὴν ἄλλως τε καὶ βαρβάρων, ἐπὶ τοσοῦτον ἔκρινον ποιήσασθαι μνήμην.

8. οἱ δ' Ἰλλυριοὶ καὶ κατὰ τοὺς ἀνωτέρω μὲν χρόνους συνεχῶς ἠδίκουν τοὺς πλοϊζομένους ἀπ' Ἰτα-

2 λίας· καθ' οὓς δὲ καιροὺς περὶ τὴν Φοινίκην διέτριβον,
καὶ πλείους ἀπὸ τοῦ στόλου χωριζόμενοι πολλοὺς τῶν
Ἰταλικῶν ἐμπόρων ἔσθ' οὓς μὲν ἐσύλησαν, οὓς δ'
ἀπέσφαξαν, οὐκ ὀλίγους δὲ καὶ ζωγρίᾳ τῶν ἁλισκο-

3 μένων ἀνῆγον. οἱ δὲ Ῥωμαῖοι, παρακούοντες τὸν πρὸ
τοῦ χρόνον τῶν ἐγκαλούντων τοῖς Ἰλλυριοῖς, τότε καὶ
πλειόνων ἐπελθόντων ἐπὶ τὴν σύγκλητον, κατέστησαν
πρεσβευτὰς εἰς τὴν Ἰλλυρίδα τοὺς ἐπίσκεψιν ποιησο-
μένους περὶ τῶν προειρημένων Γάιον καὶ Λεύκιον

4 Κορογκανίους. ἡ δὲ Τεύτα, καταπλευσάντων πρὸς
αὐτὴν τῶν ἐκ τῆς Ἠπείρου λέμβων, καταπλαγεῖσα τὸ
πλῆθος καὶ τὸ κάλλος τῆς ἀγομένης κατασκευῆς,
(πολὺ γὰρ ἡ Φοινίκη διέφερε τότε τῶν κατὰ τὴν

was the war with Carthage over, than the Romans, having clear evidence of their infamous character, took the very first opportunity of disarming them, putting them on board ship and banishing them from the whole of Italy. These were the men whom the Epirots employed to guard their laws and liberties and to whom they entrusted their most flourishing city. How then can they be acquitted of the charge of causing their own misfortunes?

I thought it necessary to speak at some length on this subject in order to show how foolish the Epirots were, and that no people, if wise, should ever admit a garrison stronger than their own forces, especially if composed of barbarians.

8. To return to the Illyrians. For a long time previously they had been in the habit of maltreating vessels sailing from Italy, and now while they were at Phoenice, a number of them detached themselves from the fleet and robbed or killed many Italian traders, capturing and carrying off no small number of prisoners. The Romans[15] had hitherto turned a deaf ear to the complaints made against the Illyrians, but now when a number of persons approached the Senate on the subject, they appointed two envoys, Gaius and Lucius Coruncanius, to proceed to Illyria, and investigate the matter. Teuta, on the return of the flotilla from Epirus, was so struck with admiration by the quantity and beauty of the spoils they brought back (Phoenice being 230 B.C.

[15] In Appianus' account, their action was not caused by the complaints of Italian merchants but by an embassy from Issa requesting help against the Illyrians: see 8. 5 and Derow (above 2. 1), whose case has since been strengthened by new evidence for the name Kleemporus from Issa (*SEG* 31, 594. 596. 602).

Ἤπειρον πόλεων εὐδαιμονίᾳ), διπλασίως ἐπερρώσθη
5 πρὸς τὴν κατὰ τῶν Ἑλλήνων ἀδικίαν. οὐ μὴν ἀλλὰ
τότε μὲν ἐπέσχε διὰ τὰς ἐγχωρίους ταραχάς, κατα-
στησαμένη δὲ ταχέως τὰ κατὰ τοὺς ἀποστάντας
Ἰλλυριοὺς ἐπολιόρκει τὴν Ἴσσαν διὰ τὸ ταύτην ἔτι
6 μόνον ἀπειθεῖν αὐτῇ. κατὰ δὲ τὸν καιρὸν τοῦτον κατέπλευσαν οἱ τῶν Ῥωμαίων πρέσβεις· καὶ δοθέντος
αὐτοῖς καιροῦ πρὸς ἔντευξιν διελέγοντο περὶ τῶν εἰς
7 αὐτοὺς γεγονότων ἀδικημάτων. ἡ δὲ Τεύτα καθόλου
μὲν παρ᾽ ὅλην τὴν κοινολογίαν ἀγερώχως καὶ λίαν
8 ὑπερηφάνως αὐτῶν διήκουε. καταπαυσάντων δὲ τὸν
λόγον, κοινῇ μὲν ἔφη πειρᾶσθαι φροντίζειν ἵνα μηδὲν
ἀδίκημα γίνηται Ῥωμαίοις ἐξ Ἰλλυριῶν· ἰδίᾳ γε μὴν
οὐ νόμιμον εἶναι τοῖς βασιλεῦσι κωλύειν Ἰλλυριοῖς
9 τὰς κατὰ θάλατταν ὠφελείας· ὁ δὲ νεώτερος τῶν πρεσβευτῶν, δυσχεράνας ἐπὶ τοῖς εἰρημένοις, ἐχρήσατο
10 παρρησίᾳ καθηκούσῃ μέν, οὐδαμῶς δὲ πρὸς καιρόν.
εἶπε γὰρ ὅτι Ῥωμαίοις μέν, ὦ Τεύτα, κάλλιστον ἔθος
ἐστὶ τὰ κατ᾽ ἰδίαν ἀδικήματα κοινῇ μεταπορεύεσθαι
11 καὶ βοηθεῖν τοῖς ἀδικουμένοις· πειρασόμεθα δὴ θεοῦ
βουλομένου σφόδρα καὶ ταχέως ἀναγκάσαι σε τὰ
12 βασιλικὰ νόμιμα διορθώσασθαι πρὸς Ἰλλυριούς. ἡ δὲ
γυναικοθύμως κἀλογίστως δεξαμένη τὴν παρρησίαν,
ἐπὶ τοσοῦτον ἐξωργίσθη πρὸς τὸ ῥηθὲν ὡς ὀλιγωρή-
σασα τῶν παρ᾽ ἀνθρώποις ὡρισμένων δικαίων ἀπο-
πλέουσιν αὐτοῖς ἐπαποστεῖλαί τινας τὸν παρρησια-
13 σάμενον τῶν πρέσβεων ἀποκτεῖναι. προσπεσόντος, δὲ
τοῦ γεγονότος εἰς τὴν Ῥώμην, διοργισθέντες ἐπὶ τῇ

then far the wealthiest city there), that she was twice as eager as before to molest the Greeks. For the present, however, she had to defer her projects owing to the disturbance in her own dominions; she had speedily put down the Illyrian revolt, but was engaged in besieging Issa, which alone still refused to submit to her, when the Roman ambassadors arrived by sea. Audience having been granted them,[16] they began to speak of the outrages committed against them. Teuta, during the whole interview, listened to them in a most arrogant and overbearing manner, and when they had finished speaking, she said she would see to it that Rome suffered no public wrong from Illyria, but that, as for private wrongs, it was contrary to the custom of the Illyrian kings to hinder their subjects from winning booty from the sea. The younger of the ambassadors was very indignant at these words of hers, and spoke out with a frankness most proper indeed, but highly inopportune: "O Teuta," he said, "the Romans have an admirable custom, which is to punish publicly the doers of private wrongs and publicly come to the help of the wronged. Be sure that we will try, God willing, by might and main and right soon, to force thee to mend the custom toward the Illyrians of their kings." Giving way to her temper like a woman and heedless of the consequences, she took this frankness ill, and was so enraged at the speech that, defying the law of nations, when the ambassadors were leaving in their ship, she sent emissaries to assassinate the one who had been so bold of speech. On the news reaching Rome,

[16] The whole story through 8. 12 is fiction, the murder of a Roman (8. 12) fact.

παρανομίᾳ τῆς γυναικὸς εὐθέως περὶ παρασκευὴν
ἐγίνοντο, καὶ στρατόπεδα κατέγραφον καὶ στόλον
συνήθροιζον.

9. Ἡ δὲ Τεύτα, τῆς ὥρας ἐπιγενομένης, ἐπισκευ-
άσασα λέμβους πλείους τῶν πρότερον ἐξαπέστειλε
2 πάλιν εἰς τοὺς κατὰ τὴν Ἑλλάδα τόπους. ὧν οἱ μὲν διὰ
πόρου τὸν πλοῦν ἐπὶ τὴν Κέρκυραν ἐποιοῦντο, μέρος
δέ τι προσέσχε τὸν τῶν Ἐπιδαμνίων λιμένα, λόγῳ
μὲν ὑδρείας κἀπισιτισμοῦ χάριν, ἔργῳ δ' ἐπιβουλῆς
3 καὶ πράξεως ἐπὶ τὴν πόλιν. τῶν δ' Ἐπιδαμνίων
ἀκάκως ἅμα καὶ ῥᾳθύμως αὐτοὺς παραδεξαμένων,
εἰσελθόντες ἐν αὐτοῖς τοῖς περιζώμασιν ὡς ὑδρευσό-
μενοι, μαχαίρας ἔχοντες ἐν τοῖς κεραμίοις, οὕτως
κατασφάξαντες τοὺς φυλάττοντας τὴν πύλην ταχέως
4 ἐγκρατεῖς ἐγένοντο τοῦ πυλῶνος. ἐπιγενομένης δὲ
κατὰ τὸ συντεταγμένον ἐνεργῶς τῆς ἀπὸ τῶν πλοίων
βοηθείας, παραδεξάμενοι τούτους ῥᾳδίως κατεῖχον τὰ
5 πλεῖστα τῶν τειχῶν. τῶν δ' ἐκ τῆς πόλεως ἀπαρα-
σκεύως μὲν διὰ τὸ παράδοξον, ἐκθύμως δὲ βοηθούν-
των καὶ διαγωνιζομένων, συνέβη τοὺς Ἰλλυριοὺς ἐπὶ
πολὺν χρόνον ἀντιποιησαμένους τέλος ἐκπεσεῖν ἐκ
6 τῆς πόλεως. Ἐπιδάμνιοι μὲν οὖν ἐν ταύτῃ τῇ πράξει
διὰ μὲν τὴν ὀλιγωρίαν ἐκινδύνευσαν ἀποβαλεῖν τὴν
πατρίδα, διὰ δὲ τὴν εὐψυχίαν ἀβλαβῶς ἐπαιδεύθησαν
7 πρὸς τὸ μέλλον. τῶν δ' Ἰλλυριῶν οἱ προεστῶτες κατὰ
σπουδὴν ἀναχθέντες, καὶ συνάψαντες τοῖς προπλέ-
ουσι, κατῆραν εἰς τὴν Κέρκυραν· καὶ ποιησάμενοι
καταπληκτικὴν τὴν ἀπόβασιν ἐνεχείρησαν πολιορ-

the woman's outrage created great indignation and they at once set themselves to prepare for an expedition, enrolling legions and getting a fleet together.

9. Teuta, when the season came, fitted out a larger number of boats than before and dispatched them to the Greek coasts. Some of them sailed straight across the high sea to Corcyra, while a part put in to the harbor of Epidamnus,[17] professedly to water and provision, but really with the design of surprising and seizing the town. They were received by the Epidamnians without any suspicion or concern, and landing as if for the purpose of watering, lightly clad but with swords concealed in the water jars, they cut down the guards of the gate and at once possessed themselves of the gate tower. A force from the ships was quickly on the spot, as had been arranged, and thus reinforced, they easily occupied the greater part of the walls. The citizens were taken by surprise and quite unprepared, but they rushed to arms and fought with great gallantry, the result being that the Illyrians, after considerable resistance, were driven out of the town. Thus the Epidamnians on this occasion came very near losing their native town by their negligence, but through their courage escaped with a salutary lesson for the future. The Illyrian commanders hastened to get under weigh and catching up the rest of their flotilla bore down on Corcyra. There they landed, to the consternation of the inhabitants, and laid siege to the

229 B.C.

---

[17] The city almost suffered the fate of Messana, Rhegium, and Phoenice.

8 κεῖν τὴν πόλιν. ὧν συμβαινόντων οἱ Κερκυραῖοι, δυσχρηστούμενοι καὶ δυσελπίστως διακείμενοι τοῖς·
ὅλοις, ἐπρεσβεύοντο πρός τε τοὺς Ἀχαιοὺς καὶ τοὺς
Αἰτωλούς, ἅμα δὲ τούτοις Ἀπολλωνιᾶται καὶ Ἐπιδάμνιοι, δεόμενοι σφίσι βοηθεῖν κατὰ σπουδὴν καὶ
μὴ περιιδεῖν σφᾶς αὐτοὺς ἀναστάτους γενομένους
9 ὑπὸ τῶν Ἰλλυριῶν. οἱ δὲ διακούσαντες τῶν πρέσβεων,
καὶ προσδεξάμενοι τοὺς λόγους, ἐπλήρωσαν κοινῇ
τὰς τῶν Ἀχαιῶν δέκα ναῦς καταφράκτους, καταρτίσαντες δ᾽ ἐν ὀλίγαις ἡμέραις ἔπλεον ἐπὶ τῆς Κερκύρας, ἐλπίζοντες λύσειν τὴν πολιορκίαν.

10. οἱ δ᾽ Ἰλλυριοί, συμπαραλαβόντες Ἀκαρνάνων
ναῦς κατὰ τὴν συμμαχίαν οὔσας ἑπτὰ καταφράκτους,
ἀνταναχθέντες συνέβαλον τοῖς τῶν Ἀχαιῶν σκάφεσι
2 περὶ τοὺς καλουμένους Παξούς. οἱ μὲν οὖν Ἀκαρνᾶνες
καὶ τῶν Ἀχαϊκῶν νεῶν αἱ κατὰ τούτους ταχθεῖσαι
πάρισον ἐποίουν τὸν ἀγῶνα καὶ διέμενον ἀκέραιοι
κατὰ τὰς συμπλοκὰς πλὴν τῶν εἰς αὐτοὺς τοὺς ἄνδρας
3 γινομένων τραυμάτων. οἱ δ᾽ Ἰλλυριοὶ ζεύξαντες τοὺς
παρ᾽ αὐτῶν λέμβους ἀνὰ τέτταρας συνεπλέκοντο τοῖς
πολεμίοις. καὶ τῶν μὲν ἰδίων ὠλιγώρουν, καὶ παρα-
βάλλοντες πλαγίους συνήργουν ταῖς ἐμβολαῖς τῶν
4 ὑπεναντίων. ὅτε δὲ τρώσαντα καὶ δεθέντα κατὰ τὰς
ἐμβολὰς δυσχρήστως (διέκειτο πρὸς τὸ παρὸν) τὰ
τῶν ἀντιπάλων σκάφη, προσκρεμαμένων αὐτοῖς περὶ
τοὺς ἐμβόλους τῶν ἐζευγμένων λέμβων, τότ᾽ ἐπιπη-
δῶντες ἐπὶ τὰ καταστρώματα τῶν Ἀχαϊκῶν νεῶν
5 κατεκράτουν διὰ τὸ πλῆθος τῶν ἐπιβατῶν. καὶ τούτῳ

city. Upon this the Corcyreans, in the utmost distress and despondency sent, together with the peoples of Apollonia and Epidamnus, envoys to the Achaeans and Aetolians, imploring them to hasten to their relief and not allow them to be driven from their homes by the Illyrians. The two Leagues, after listening to the envoys, consented to their request, and both joined in manning the ten decked ships belonging to the Achaeans. In a few days they were ready for sea and sailed for Corcyra in the hope of raising the siege.

10. The Illyrians, now reinforced by seven decked ships sent by the Acarnanians in compliance with the terms of their treaty, put to sea and encountered the Achaean ships off the islands called Paxi.[18] The Acarnanians and those Achaean ships which were told off to engage them fought with no advantage on either side, remaining undamaged in their encounter except for the wounds inflicted on some of the crew. The Illyrians lashed their boats together in batches of four and thus engaged the enemy. They sacrificed their own boats, presenting them broadside to their adversaries in a position favoring their charge, but when the enemy's ships had charged and struck them and getting fixed in them, found themselves in difficulties, as in each case the four boats lashed together were hanging on to their beaks, the marines leapt on to the decks of the Achaean ships and overmastered them by their numbers.

[18] Two islands south of Corcyra; map in *RE* Teuta 1147 (M. Fluss).

τῷ τρόπῳ τεττάρων μὲν πλοίων ἐκυρίευσαν τετρη-
ρικῶν, μίαν δὲ πεντήρη σὺν αὐτοῖς τοῖς ἀνδράσιν
ἐβύθισαν, ἐφ᾽ ἧς ἔπλει Μάργος ὁ Καρυνεύς, ἀνὴρ
πάντα τὰ δίκαια τῷ κοινῷ τῶν Ἀχαιῶν πολιτεύματι
6 πεποιηκὼς μέχρι τῆς καταστροφῆς. οἱ δὲ πρὸς τοὺς
Ἀκαρνᾶνας διαγωνιζόμενοι, συνιδόντες τὸ κατὰ τοὺς
Ἰλλυριοὺς προτέρημα, καὶ πιστεύοντες τῷ ταχυναυτεῖν, ἐπουρώσαντες ἀσφαλῶς τὴν ἀποχώρησιν εἰς τὴν
7 οἰκείαν ἐποιήσαντο. τὸ δὲ τῶν Ἰλλυριῶν πλῆθος, φρο-
νηματισθὲν ἐπὶ τῷ προτερήματι, λοιπὸν ἤδη ῥᾳδίως
8 ἐχρήσατο τῇ πολιορκίᾳ καὶ τεθαρρηκότως. οἱ δὲ
Κερκυραῖοι, δυσελπιστήσαντες τοῖς ὅλοις ἐκ τῶν
συμβεβηκότων, βραχὺν ἔτι χρόνον ὑπομείναντες τὴν
πολιορκίαν, συνέθεντο τοῖς Ἰλλυριοῖς, καὶ παρεδέξαν-
το φρουρὰν καὶ μετὰ τῆς φρουρᾶς Δημήτριον τὸν
9 Φάριον. τούτων δὲ πραχθέντων εὐθέως οἱ τῶν Ἰλλυριῶν προεστῶτες ἀνήγοντο· καὶ κατάραντες εἰς τὴν
Ἐπίδαμνον ταύτην πάλιν ἐπεβάλοντο πολιορκεῖν τὴν
πόλιν.

11. Κατὰ δὲ τοὺς αὐτοὺς καιροὺς τῶν τὰς ὑπάτους
ἀρχὰς ἐχόντων Γνάιος μὲν Φουλούιος ἐξέπλει ναυσὶ
διακοσίαις ἐκ τῆς Ῥώμης, Αὖλος δὲ Ποστούμιος τὰς
2 πεζικὰς ἔχων δυνάμεις ἐξώρμα. τὴν μὲν οὖν πρώτην
ἐπιβολὴν ἔσχε πλεῖν ὁ Γνάιος ἐπὶ τῆς Κερκύρας,
ὑπολαμβάνων ἔτι καταλήψεσθαι τὴν πολιορκίαν
3 ἄκριτον· ὑστερήσας δὲ τῶν καιρῶν ὅμως ἐπὶ τὴν
νῆσον ἔπλει, βουλόμενος ἅμα μὲν ἐπιγνῶναι σαφῶς
τὰ γεγονότα περὶ τὴν πόλιν, ἅμα δὲ πεῖραν λαβεῖν

In this way they captured four quadriremes and sunk with all hands a quinquereme, on board of which was Margus of Caryneia,[19] a man who up to the end served the Achaeans most loyally. The ships that were engaged with the Acarnanians, seeing the success of the Illyrians, and trusting to their speed, made sail with a fair wind and escaped home in safety. The Illyrian forces, highly elated by their success, continued the siege with more security and confidence, and the Corcyreans, whose hopes were crushed by the repulse of their allies, after enduring the siege for a short time longer, came to terms with the Illyrians, receiving a garrison under the command of Demetrius of Pharos.[20] After this the Illyrian commanders at once sailed off and coming to anchor at Epidamnus, again set themselves to besiege that city.

11. At about the same time one of the Consuls,[21] Gnaeus Fulvius, sailed out from Rome with the two hundred ships, while the other, Aulus Postumius, left with the land forces. Gnaeus' first intention had been to make for Corcyra, as he supposed he would find the siege still undecided. On discovering that he was too late, he none the less sailed for that island, wishing on the one hand to find out accurately what had happened about the city, and on the other hand to put to a test the sincerity of communications

229 B.C.

<hr />

[19] A leading Achaean; more on him in 41. 14 and 43. 2.

[20] A vassal of Teuta, see A. Coppola, *Demetrio di Faro* (Rome 1993).

[21] Of 229; the First Illyrian War begins. Postumius was in fact Lucius, not Aulus.

THE HISTORIES OF POLYBIUS

4 τῶν παρὰ τοῦ Δημητρίου προσαγγελλομένων. ὁ γὰρ
Δημήτριος ἐν διαβολαῖς ὢν καὶ φοβούμενος τὴν Τεύταν διεπέμπετο πρὸς τοὺς Ῥωμαίους, ἐπαγγελλόμενος
τήν τε πόλιν ἐγχειριεῖν καὶ τὰ λοιπὰ πράγματα παρα-
5 δώσειν, ὧν ἦν αὐτὸς κύριος. οἱ δὲ Κερκυραῖοι τὴν
παρουσίαν τῶν Ῥωμαίων ἀσμένως ἰδόντες, τήν τε
φρουρὰν παρέδοσαν τῶν Ἰλλυριῶν μετὰ τῆς τοῦ Δημητρίου γνώμης, αὐτοί τε σφᾶς ὁμοθυμαδὸν ἔδωκαν
παρακληθέντες εἰς τὴν τῶν Ῥωμαίων πίστιν, μίαν
ταύτην ὑπολαβόντες ἀσφάλειαν αὐτοῖς ὑπάρχειν εἰς
6 τὸν μέλλοντα χρόνον πρὸς τὴν Ἰλλυριῶν παρανομίαν.
Ῥωμαῖοι δὲ προσδεξάμενοι τοὺς Κερκυραίους εἰς τὴν
φιλίαν ἔπλεον ἐπὶ τῆς Ἀπολλωνίας, ἔχοντες εἰς τὰ
7 κατάλοιπα τῶν πραγμάτων ἡγεμόνα τὸν Δημήτριον.
κατὰ δὲ τὸν αὐτὸν καιρὸν καὶ Ποστούμιος τὰς πεζικὰς
διεβίβαζε δυνάμεις ἐκ τοῦ Βρεντεσίου, πεζοὺς μὲν εἰς
8 δισμυρίους, ἱππεῖς δὲ περὶ δισχιλίους. ἅμα δὲ τῷ
προσέχειν ἑκατέρας ὁμοῦ τὰς δυνάμεις πρὸς τὴν
Ἀπολλωνίαν ὁμοίως καὶ τούτων ἀποδεξαμένων καὶ
δόντων ἑαυτοὺς εἰς τὴν ἐπιτροπὴν παραχρῆμα πάλιν
ἀνήχθησαν, ἀκούοντες πολιορκεῖσθαι τὴν Ἐπί-
9 δαμνον. οἱ δ᾽ Ἰλλυριοὶ συνέντες τὴν ἔφοδον τῶν Ῥωμαίων, οὐδενὶ κόσμῳ λύσαντες τὴν πολιορκίαν ἔφυ-
10 γον. Ῥωμαῖοι δὲ καὶ τοὺς Ἐπιδαμνίους παραλαβόντες
εἰς τὴν πίστιν, προῆγον εἰς τοὺς εἴσω τόπους τῆς
11 Ἰλλυρίδος, ἅμα καταστρεφόμενοι τοὺς Ἀρδιαίους.
συμμιξάντων δὲ πρεσβευτῶν αὐτοῖς καὶ πλειόνων, ὧν
οἱ παρὰ τῶν Παρθίνων ἧκον ἐπιτρέποντες τὰ καθ᾽

290

made to him by Demetrius. Accusations had been brought against the latter, and being in fear of Teuta he sent messages to the Romans undertaking to hand over to them the city and whatever else was under his charge. The Corcyreans were much relieved to see the Romans arrive, and they gave up the Illyrian garrison to them with the consent of Demetrius. They unanimously accepted the Romans' invitation to place themselves under their protection,[22] considering this the sole means of assuring for the future their safety from the violence of the Illyrians. The Romans, having admitted the Corcyreans to their friendship, set sail for Apollonia, Demetrius in future acting as their guide. Simultaneously Postumius was bringing across from Brundisium the land forces consisting of about twenty thousand food and two thousand horse. On the two forces uniting at Apollonia and on the people of that city likewise agreeing to put themselves under Roman protection, they at once set off again, hearing that Epidamnus was being besieged. The Illyrians, on hearing of the approach of the Romans, broke off the siege and fled in disorder. The Romans, taking Epidamnus also under their protection, advanced into the interior of Illyria, subduing the Ardiaeans on their way. Many embassies met them, among them one from the Parthini offering unconditional

[22] Corcyra, Apollonia (11. 8), Epidamnus (11. 10), the Parthini and Atintanes (11. 11), and Issa (11. 12) accepted Roman protection, the Ardiaeans were subdued (11. 10). The nature of the Roman "protectorate" is much disputed; see WC and E. Badian, *PBSR* 20 (1952) 72–93.

αὐτούς, δεξάμενοι τούτους εἰς τὴν φιλίαν, παραπλησίως δὲ καὶ τοὺς παρὰ τῶν Ἀτιντάνων προσεληλυθό-
τας προῆγον ὡς ἐπὶ τὴν Ἴσσαν, διὰ τὸ καὶ ταύτην ὑπὸ
12 τῶν Ἰλλυριῶν πολιορκεῖσθαι τὴν πόλιν. ἀφικόμενοι
δὲ καὶ λύσαντες τὴν πολιορκίαν, προσεδέξαντο καὶ
13 τοὺς Ἰσσαίους εἰς τὴν ἑαυτῶν πίστιν. εἷλον δὲ καὶ
πόλεις τινὰς Ἰλλυρίδας ἐν τῷ παράπλῳ κατὰ κράτος·
ἐν αἷς περὶ Νουτρίαν οὐ μόνον τῶν στρατιωτῶν ἀπέβαλον πολλούς, ἀλλὰ καὶ τῶν χιλιάρχων τινὰς καὶ
14 τὸν ταμίαν. ἐκυρίευσαν δὲ καὶ λέμβων εἴκοσι τῶν
15 ἀποκομιζόντων τὴν ἐκ τῆς χώρας ὠφέλειαν. τῶν δὲ
πολιορκούντων τὴν Ἴσσαν οἱ μὲν ἐν τῇ Φάρῳ διὰ τὸν
Δημήτριον ἀβλαβεῖς ἔμειναν, οἱ δ’ ἄλλοι πάντες ἔφυ-
16 γον εἰς τὸν Ἄρβωνα σκεδασθέντες. ἡ δὲ Τεύτα πάνυ
μετ’ ὀλίγων εἰς τὸν Ῥίζονα διεσώθη, πολισμάτιον εὖ
πρὸς ὀχυρότητα κατεσκευασμένον, ἀνακεχωρηκὸς μὲν
ἀπὸ τῆς θαλάττης, ἐπ’ αὐτῷ δὲ κείμενον τῷ Ῥίζονι
17 ποταμῷ. ταῦτα δὲ πράξαντες, καὶ τῷ Δημητρίῳ τοὺς
πλείστους ὑποτάξαντες τῶν Ἰλλυριῶν, καὶ μεγάλην
αὐτῷ περιθέντες δυναστείαν ἀνεχώρησαν εἰς τὴν Ἐπίδαμνον ἅμα τῷ στόλῳ καὶ τῇ πεζικῇ δυνάμει.

12. Γνάιος μὲν οὖν Φουλούιος εἰς τὴν Ῥώμην
ἀπέπλευσε, τὸ πλεῖον ἔχων μέρος τῆς τε ναυτικῆς καὶ
2 πεζικῆς στρατιᾶς. ὁ δὲ Ποστούμιος, ὑπολειπόμενος
τετταράκοντα σκάφη, καὶ στρατόπεδον ἐκ τῶν περι-
κειμένων πόλεων ἀθροίσας, παρεχείμαζε, συνεφεδρεύ-
ων τῷ τε τῶν Ἀρδιαίων ἔθνει καὶ τοῖς ἄλλοις τοῖς
3 δεδωκόσιν ἑαυτοὺς εἰς τὴν πίστιν. ὑπὸ δὲ τὴν ἐαρινὴν

surrender. They admitted this tribe to their friendship as
well as the Atintanes, and advanced toward Issa which was
also being besieged by the Illyrians. On their arrival they
forced the enemy to raise the siege and took the Issaeans
also under their protection. The fleet too took several Illyrian cities by assault as they sailed along the coast, losing,
however, at Nutria not only many soldiers, but some of
their military tribunes and their quaestor. They also captured twenty boats which were conveying the plunder
from the country. Of the besiegers of Issa those now in
Pharos were allowed, through Demetrius' influence, to remain there unhurt, while the others dispersed and took
refuge at Arbo. Teuta, with only a few followers, escaped to
Rhizon, a small place strongly fortified at a distance from
the sea and situated on the river Rhizon. After accomplish-
ing so much and placing the greater part of Illyria under
the rule of Demetrius, thus making him an important po-
tentate, the Consuls returned to Epidamnus with the fleet
and army.

12. Cnaeus Fulvius now sailed for Rome with the
greater part of both forces, and Postumius, with whom
forty ships were left, enrolled a legion from the cities in the
neighborhood and wintered at Epidamnus to guard the
Ardiaeans and the other tribes who had placed themselves
under the protection of Rome. In the early spring Teuta   228 B.C.

ὥραν ἡ Τεύτα διαπρεσβευσαμένη πρὸς τοὺς Ῥωμαίους ποιεῖται συνθήκας, ἐν αἷς εὐδόκησε φόρους τε
τοὺς διαταχθέντας οἴσειν πάσης τ' ἀναχωρήσειν τῆς
Ἰλλυρίδος πλὴν ὀλίγων τόπων, καὶ τὸ συνέχον ὃ
μάλιστα πρὸς τοὺς Ἕλληνας διέτεινε, μὴ πλεύσειν
πλέον ἢ δυσὶ λέμβοις ἔξω τοῦ Λίσσου, καὶ τούτοις
4 ἀνόπλοις. ὧν συντελεσθέντων ὁ Ποστούμιος μετὰ
ταῦτα πρεσβευτὰς ἐξαπέστειλε πρός τε τοὺς Αἰτωλοὺς
καὶ τὸ τῶν Ἀχαιῶν ἔθνος· οἳ καὶ παραγενόμενοι πρῶτον μὲν ἀπελογίσαντο τὰς αἰτίας τοῦ πολέμου καὶ τῆς
διαβάσεως, ἑξῆς δὲ τούτοις τὰ πεπραγμένα διεξῆλ-
θον, καὶ τὰς συνθήκας παρανέγνωσαν, ἃς ἐπεποίηντο
5 πρὸς τοὺς Ἰλλυριούς. τυχόντες δὲ παρ' ἑκατέρου τῶν
ἐθνῶν τῆς καθηκούσης φιλανθρωπίας αὖθις ἀπέπλευ-
6 σαν εἰς τὴν Κέρκυραν, ἱκανοῦ τινος ἀπολελυκότες
φόβου τοὺς Ἕλληνας διὰ τὰς προειρημένας συνθήκας. οὐ γὰρ τισίν, ἀλλὰ πᾶσι, τότε κοινοὺς ἐχθροὺς
εἶναι συνέβαινε τοὺς Ἰλλυριούς.

7   Ἡ μὲν οὖν πρώτη διάβασις Ῥωμαίων μετὰ δυνάμεως εἰς τὴν Ἰλλυρίδα καὶ ταῦτα τὰ μέρη τῆς
Εὐρώπης, ἔτι δ' ἐπιπλοκὴ μετὰ πρεσβείας εἰς τοὺς
κατὰ τὴν Ἑλλάδα τόπους, τοιάδε καὶ διὰ ταύτας
8 ἐγένετο τὰς αἰτίας. ἀπὸ δὲ ταύτης τῆς καταρχῆς
Ῥωμαῖοι μὲν εὐθέως ἄλλους πρεσβευτὰς ἐξαπέστειλαν πρὸς Κορινθίους καὶ πρὸς Ἀθηναίους, ὅτε δὴ καὶ
Κορίνθιοι πρῶτον ἀπεδέξαντο μετέχειν Ῥωμαίους τοῦ
τῶν Ἰσθμίων ἀγῶνος.

13. Ἀσδρούβας δὲ κατὰ τοὺς αὐτοὺς χρόνους, ἐν

sent an embassy to the Romans and made a treaty,[23] by which she consented to pay any tribute they imposed, to relinquish all Illyria except a few places, and, what mostly concerned the Greeks, undertook not to sail beyond Lissus[24] with more than two unarmed vessels. When this treaty had been concluded Postumius sent ambassadors to the Aetolian and Achaean leagues. On their arrival they first explained the causes of the war and their reason for crossing the Adriatic, and next gave an account of what they had accomplished, reading the treaty they had made with the Illyrians. After meeting with all due courtesy from both the leagues, they returned by sea to Corcyra, having by the conclusion of this treaty, delivered the Greeks from no inconsiderable dread; for the Illyrians were then not the enemies of this people or that, but the common enemies of all.

Such were the circumstances and causes of the Romans crossing for the first time with an army to Illyria and those parts of Europe, and of their first coming into relations through an embassy with Greece. But having thus begun, the Romans immediately afterward sent other envoys[25] to Athens and Corinth, on which occasion the Corinthians first admitted them to participation in the Isthmian games.

13. It was at this point that we left affairs in Spain. Dur-

[23] *StV* 500 (spring 228).

[24] Modern Lesch, near the mouth of the river Drin.

[25] Athens had just extricated herself from Macedonian rule; see C. Habicht, *Athènes Hellénistique. Histoire de la cité d'Alexandre à Marc Antoine*[2] (Paris 2006), chapter 7. Corinth was a member of the Achaean League, hostile to Macedonia. No Roman ambassador went to Pella.

γὰρ τούτοις ἀπελίπομεν τὰ κατὰ τὴν Ἰβηρίαν, νουνεχῶς καὶ πραγματικῶς χειρίζων τὰ κατὰ τὴν ἀρχὴν ἔν
τε τοῖς ὅλοις μεγάλην ἐποιεῖτο προκοπὴν τήν τε παρὰ
μὲν τισὶ Καρχηδόνα, παρὰ δὲ τισὶ Καινὴν πόλιν
προσαγορευομένην κατασκευάσας, οὐ μικρά, μεγάλα
2 δὲ συνεβάλλετο Καρχηδονίοις εἰς πραγμάτων λόγον,
καὶ μάλιστα διὰ τὴν εὐκαιρίαν τοῦ τόπου πρός τε τὰ
κατὰ τὴν Ἰβηρίαν πράγματα καὶ πρὸς τὰ κατὰ τὴν
Λιβύην, περὶ ἧς ἡμεῖς εὐφυέστερον καιρὸν λαβόντες
ὑποδείξομεν τὴν θέσιν αὐτῆς καὶ τὴν χρείαν, ἣν
ἀμφοτέραις δύναται παρέχεσθαι ταῖς εἰρημέναις χώ-
3 ραις. ὃν καὶ θεωροῦντες Ῥωμαῖοι μείζω καὶ φοβε-
ρωτέραν ἤδη συνιστάμενον δυναστείαν, ὥρμησαν ἐπὶ
4 τὸ πολυπραγμονεῖν τὰ κατὰ τὴν Ἰβηρίαν. εὑρόντες δὲ
σφᾶς ἐπικεκοιμημένους ἐν τοῖς ἔμπροσθεν χρόνοις
καὶ προειμένους εἰς τὸ μεγάλην χεῖρα κατασκευάσα-
5 σθαι Καρχηδονίους, ἀνατρέχειν ἐπειρῶντο κατὰ δύναμιν. αὐτόθεν μὲν οὖν ἐπιτάττειν ἢ πολεμεῖν οὐ κατ-
ετόλμων τοῖς Καρχηδονίοις διὰ τὸ τὸν ἀπὸ τῶν
Κελτῶν φόβον ἐπικρέμασθαι τοῖς σφετέροις πράγμασι καὶ μόνον οὐ καθ’ ἑκάστην ἡμέραν προσδοκᾶν τὴν
6 ἔφοδον αὐτῶν. καταψήσαντες δὲ καὶ πραΰναντες τὸν
Ἀσδρούβαν οὕτως ἔκριναν ἐγχειρεῖν τοῖς Κελτοῖς καὶ
διακινδυνεύειν πρὸς αὐτούς, οὐδέποτ’ ἂν ὑπολαμβάνοντες οὐχ οἷον δυναστεῦσαι τῶν κατὰ τὴν Ἰταλίαν,
ἀλλ’ οὐδ’ ἀσφαλῶς οἰκῆσαι τὴν ἑαυτῶν πατρίδα τού-
7 τους ἔχοντες ἐφέδρους τοὺς ἄνδρας. διόπερ ἅμα τῷ

ing these years, Hasdrubal[26] had by his wise and practical administration made great general progress, and by the foundation of the city called by some Carthage, and by others the New Town, made a material contribution to the resources of Carthage, especially owing to its favorable position for action in Spain or Libya. On a more suitable occasion[27] we will describe its position and point out the services it can render to both these countries. The Romans, seeing that Hasdrubal was in a fair way to create a larger and more formidable empire than Carthage formerly possessed, resolved to begin to occupy themselves with Spanish affairs. Finding that they had hitherto been asleep and had allowed Carthage to build up and equip a large body of troops, they tried, as far as possible, to make up for lost time. For the present they did not venture to impose orders on Carthage, or to go to war with her, because the threat of a Celtic invasion was hanging over them,[28] the attack being indeed expected from day to day. They decided, then, to smooth down and conciliate Hasdrubal in the first place, and then to attack the Celts and decide the issue by arms, for they thought that as long as they had these Celts threatening their frontier, not only would they never be masters of Italy, but they would not even be safe in Rome itself. Accordingly, after having sent

228 B.C.

26 This continues 1. 9. New Carthage was founded ca. 228.

27 See 10. 10.

28 It was *metus Gallicus* that motivated the Romans to come to terms with Hasdrubal instead of making war against him..

διαπρεσβευσάμενοι πρὸς τὸν Ἀσδρούβαν ποιήσασθαι συνθήκας, ἐν αἷς τὴν μὲν ἄλλην Ἰβηρίαν παρε-
σιώπων, τὸν δὲ καλούμενον Ἴβηρα ποταμὸν οὐκ ἔδει
Καρχηδονίους ἐπὶ πολέμῳ διαβαίνειν, εὐθέως ἐξήνεγ-
καν τὸν πρὸς τοὺς κατὰ τὴν Ἰταλίαν Κελτοὺς πόλεμον.

14. Ὑπὲρ ὧν δοκεῖ μοι χρήσιμον εἶναι κεφαλαιώδη
μὲν ποιήσασθαι τὴν ἐξήγησιν, ἵνα τὸ τῆς προκατασκευῆς οἰκεῖον συσσώσωμεν κατὰ τὴν ἐξ ἀρχῆς πρόθεσιν, ἀναδραμεῖν δὲ τοῖς χρόνοις ἐπὶ τὴν ἀρχήν, ἐξ
2 ὅτου κατέσχον οἱ προειρημένοι τὴν χώραν· ἡγοῦμαι
γὰρ τὴν περὶ αὐτῶν ἱστορίαν οὐ μόνον ἀξίαν εἶναι
γνώσεως καὶ μνήμης, ἀλλὰ καὶ τελέως ἀναγκαίαν,
χάριν τοῦ μαθεῖν τίσι μετὰ ταῦτα πιστεύσας ἀνδράσι
καὶ τόποις Ἀννίβας ἐπεβάλετο καταλύειν τὴν Ῥωμαί-
3 ων δυναστείαν. πρῶτον δὲ περὶ τῆς χώρας ῥητέον
ποία τίς ἐστι καὶ πῶς κεῖται πρὸς τὴν ἄλλην Ἰταλίαν.
οὕτως γὰρ ἔσται καὶ τὰ περὶ τὰς πράξεις διαφέροντα
κατανοεῖν βέλτιον, ὑπογραφέντων τῶν περί τε τοὺς
τόπους καὶ τὴν χώραν ἰδιωμάτων.

4 Τῆς δὴ συμπάσης Ἰταλίας τῷ σχήματι τριγωνο-
ειδοῦς ὑπαρχούσης, τὴν μὲν μίαν ὁρίζει πλευρὰν αὐτῆς τὴν πρὸς τὰς ἀνατολὰς κεκλιμένην ὅ τ' Ἰόνιος
πόρος καὶ κατὰ τὸ συνεχὲς ὁ κατὰ τὸν Ἀδρίαν κόλπος,
τὴν δὲ πρὸς μεσημβρίαν καὶ δυσμὰς τετραμμένην τὸ
5 Σικελικὸν καὶ Τυρρηνικὸν πέλαγος. αὗται δ' αἱ πλευ-
ραὶ συμπίπτουσαι πρὸς ἀλλήλας κορυφὴν ποιοῦσι
τοῦ τριγώνου τὸ προκείμενον ἀκρωτήριον τῆς Ἰταλίας

envoys to Hasdrubal and made a treaty,[29] in which no mention was made of the rest of Spain, but the Carthaginians engaged not to cross the Ebro in arms, they at once entered on the struggle against the Italian Celts.

14. I think it will be of use to give some account of these peoples, which must be indeed but a summary one, in order not to depart from the original plan of this work as defined in the preface. We must, however, go back to the time when they first occupied these districts. I think the story is not only worth knowing and keeping in mind, but quite necessary for my purpose, as it shows us who were the men and what was the country on which Hannibal afterward relied in his attempt to destroy the Roman dominion. I must first describe the nature of the country and its position as regards the rest of Italy. A sketch of its peculiarities, regionally and as a whole land, will help us better to comprehend the more important of the events I have to relate.

Italy[30] as a whole has the shape of a triangle of which the one or eastern side is bounded by the Ionian Strait and then continuously by the Adriatic Gulf, the next side, that turned to the south and west, by the Sicilian and Tyrrhenian Seas. The apex of the triangle, formed by the meeting of these two sides, is the southernmost cape of Italy known

---

[29] The so-called Ebro treaty, *StV* 503 of 226/5. It is widely but not universally assumed, although not attested, that the Romans accepted a similar clause: "not to cross the Ebro in arms;" against this, P. Bender, *Klio* 79 (1997) 89–90. The treaty was apparently not ratified at Carthage, a fact later leading to debate as to whether or not it was binding on the Carthaginian state. Whether the Roman alliance with Saguntum, south of the Ebro, came before or after the treaty, is unclear. "The Saguntine alliance and the Ebro treaty were irreconcilable" (WC).

[30] A digression on the geography of Italy, through 17. 12.

εἰς τὴν μεσημβρίαν, ὃ προσαγορεύεται μὲν Κόκυνθος,
6 διαιρεῖ δὲ τὸν Ἰόνιον πόρον καὶ τὸ Σικελικὸν πέλαγος.
τὴν δὲ λοιπὴν τὴν παρά τε τὰς ἄρκτους καὶ τὴν
μεσόγαιαν παρατείνουσαν ὁρίζει κατὰ τὸ συνεχὲς ἡ
τῶν Ἄλπεων παρώρεια, λαμβάνουσα τὴν μὲν ἀρχὴν
ἀπὸ Μασσαλίας καὶ τῶν ὑπὲρ τὸ Σαρδῷον πέλαγος
τόπων, παρήκουσα δὲ συνεχῶς μέχρι πρὸς τὸν τοῦ
παντὸς Ἀδρίου μυχόν, πλὴν βραχέος, ὃ προκατα-
7 λήγουσα λείπει τοῦ μὴ συνάπτειν αὐτῷ. παρὰ δὲ τὴν
προειρημένην παρώρειαν, ἣν δεῖ νοεῖν ὡς ἂν εἰ βάσιν
τοῦ τριγώνου, παρὰ ταύτην ἀπὸ μεσημβρίας ὑπόκειται πεδία τῆς συμπάσης Ἰταλίας τελευταῖα πρὸς τὰς
ἄρκτους, ὑπὲρ ὧν ὁ νῦν δὴ λόγος, ἀρετῇ καὶ μεγέθει
διαφέροντα τῶν κατὰ τὴν Εὐρώπην, ὅσα πέπτωκεν
8 ὑπὸ τὴν ἡμετέραν ἱστορίαν. ἔστι δὲ τὸ μὲν ὅλον εἶδος
καὶ τῆς ταῦτα τὰ πεδία περιγραφούσης γραμμῆς
τριγωνοειδές. τούτου δὲ τοῦ σχήματος τὴν μὲν κορυφὴν ἥ τε τῶν Ἀπεννίνων καλουμένων ὀρῶν καὶ τῶν
Ἀλπεινῶν σύμπτωσις οὐ μακρὰν ἀπὸ τοῦ Σαρδῴου
9 πελάγους ὑπὲρ Μασσαλίας ἀποτελεῖ. τῶν δὲ πλευρῶν
παρὰ μὲν τὴν ἀπὸ τῶν ἄρκτων, ὡς ἐπάνω προεῖπον,
τὰς Ἄλπεις αὐτὰς ἐπὶ δισχιλίους καὶ διακοσίους στα-
10 δίους παρήκειν συμβαίνει, παρὰ δὲ τὴν ἀπὸ μεσημ-
11 βρίας τὸν Ἀπεννῖνον ἐπὶ τρισχιλίους ἑξακοσίους.
βάσεώς γε μὴν τάξιν λαμβάνει τοῦ παντὸς σχήματος
ἡ παραλία τοῦ κατὰ τὸν Ἀδρίαν κόλπου· τὸ δὲ μέγεθος τῆς βάσεώς ἐστιν ἀπὸ πόλεως Σήνης ἕως ἐπὶ τὸν
μυχὸν ὑπὲρ τοὺς δισχιλίους σταδίους καὶ πεντακο-

as Cocynthus and separating the Ionian Strait from the Sicilian Sea. The remaining side of the triangle bordering on the interior (sc. of Europe) to the north is bounded continuously by the chain of the Alps[31] which beginning at Marseilles and the northern coasts of the Sardinian Sea stretches in an unbroken line almost to the head of the whole Adriatic, only failing to join that sea by stopping at quite a short distance from it. At the foot of this chain, which we should regard as the base of the triangle, on its southern side, lies the last plain of all Italy to the north. It is with this that we are now concerned, a plain surpassing in fertility and size any other in Europe with which we are acquainted. The general shape of the lines that bound this plain is likewise triangular. The apex of the triangle is formed by the meeting of the Apennines and Alps not far from the Sardinian Sea at a point above Marseilles. Its northern side is, as I have said, formed by the Alps themselves and is about two thousand two hundred stades in length, the southern side by the Apennines which extend for a distance of three thousand six hundred stades. The base of the whole triangle is the coast of the Adriatic, its length from the city of Sena[32] to the head of the gulf being more than two thousand five hundred stades; so that

[31] The earliest clear historical reference to them.

[32] *Sena Gallica*, on the coast between Rimini and Ancona; today Sinigaglia.

12 σίους, ὥστε τὴν πᾶσαν περίμετρον τῶν προειρημένων
πεδίων μὴ πολὺ λείπειν τῶν μυρίων σταδίων.

15. περί γε μὴν τῆς ἀρετῆς οὐδ᾽ εἰπεῖν ῥᾴδιον.
σίτου τε γὰρ τοσαύτην ἀφθονίαν ὑπάρχειν συμβαίνει
κατὰ τοὺς τόπους, ὥστ᾽ ἐν τοῖς καθ᾽ ἡμᾶς καιροῖς
πολλάκις τεττάρων ὀβολῶν εἶναι τῶν πυρῶν τὸν Σικελικὸν μέδιμνον, τῶν δὲ κριθῶν δυεῖν, τοῦ δ᾽ οἴνου τὸν

2 μετρητὴν ἰσόκριθον. ἐλύμου γε μὴν καὶ κέγχρου τελέως ὑπερβάλλουσα δαψίλεια γίνεται παρ᾽ αὐτοῖς. τὸ
δὲ τῶν βαλάνων πλῆθος τὸ γινόμενον ἐκ τῶν κατὰ
διάστημα δρυμῶν ἐν τοῖς πεδίοις ἐκ τούτων ἄν τις

3 μάλιστα τεκμήραιτο· πλείστων γὰρ ὑϊκῶν ἱερείων
κοπτομένων ἐν Ἰταλίᾳ διά τε τὰς εἰς τοὺς ἰδίους βίους
καὶ τὰς εἰς τὰ στρατόπεδα παραθέσεις, τὴν ὁλοσχε-
ρεστάτην χορηγίαν ἐκ τούτων συμβαίνει τῶν πεδίων

4 αὐτοῖς ὑπάρχειν. περὶ δὲ τῆς κατὰ μέρος εὐωνίας καὶ
δαψιλείας τῶν πρὸς τὴν τροφὴν ἀνηκόντων οὕτως ἄν

5 τις ἀκριβέστατα κατανοήσειε· ποιοῦνται γὰρ τὰς
καταλύσεις οἱ διοδεύοντες τὴν χώραν ἐν τοῖς παν-
δοκείοις, οὐ συμφωνοῦντες περὶ τῶν κατὰ μέρος ἐπι-

6 τηδείων, ἀλλ᾽ ἐρωτῶντες πόσου τὸν ἄνδρα δέχεται. ὡς
μὲν οὖν ἐπὶ τὸ πολὺ παρίενται τοὺς καταλύτας οἱ
πανδοκεῖς, ὡς ἱκανὰ πάντ᾽ ἔχειν τὰ πρὸς τὴν χρείαν,
ἡμιασσαρίου· τοῦτο δ᾽ ἔστι τέταρτον μέρος ὀβολοῦ·
σπανίως δὲ τοῦθ᾽ ὑπερβαίνουσι. τό γε μὴν πλῆθος

7 τῶν ἀνδρῶν, καὶ τὸ μέγεθος καὶ κάλλος τῶν σωμάτων,
ἔτι δὲ τὴν ἐν τοῖς πολέμοις τόλμαν, ἐξ αὐτῶν τῶν
πράξεων σαφῶς ἔσται καταμαθεῖν.

the whole circumference of this plain is not much less than ten thousand stades.

15. Its fertility is not easy to describe. It produces such an abundance of grain, that often in my time the price of wheat was four obols per Sicilian medimnus and that of barley two obols, a metretes of wine costing the same as the medimnus of barley. Panic and millet are produced in enormous quantities, while the amount of acorns grown in the woods dispersed over the plain can be estimated from the fact that, while the number of swine slaughtered in Italy for private consumption as well as to feed the army is very large, almost the whole of them are supplied by this plain. The cheapness and abundance of all articles of food will be most clearly understood from the following fact. Travelers in this country who put up in inns, do not bargain for each separate article they require, but ask what is the charge per diem for one person. The innkeepers, as a rule, agree to receive guests, providing them with enough of all they require for half an *as* per diem, *i.e.* the fourth part of an obol, the charge being very seldom higher. As for the numbers of the inhabitants, their stature and beauty and their courage in war, the facts of their history will speak.

8   Τῶν δ᾽ Ἄλπεων ἑκατέρας τῆς πλευρᾶς, τῆς ἐπὶ τὸν
Ῥοδανὸν ποταμὸν καὶ τῆς ἐπὶ τὰ προειρημένα πεδία
νευούσης, τοὺς βουνώδεις καὶ γεώδεις τόπους κατοικοῦσι, τοὺς μὲν ἐπὶ τὸν Ῥοδανὸν καὶ τὰς ἄρκτους
ἐστραμμένους Γαλάται Τρανσαλπῖνοι προσαγορευ-
όμενοι, τοὺς δ᾽ ἐπὶ τὰ πεδία Ταυρίσκοι καὶ Ἄγωνες

9 καὶ πλείω γένη βαρβάρων ἕτερα. Τρανσαλπῖνοί γε
μὴν οὐ διὰ τὴν τοῦ γένους, ἀλλὰ διὰ τὴν τοῦ τόπου
διαφορὰν προσαγορεύονται, τὸ γὰρ τρὰνς ἐξερμηνευ-
όμενόν ἐστι πέραν· διὸ τοὺς ἐπέκεινα τῶν Ἄλπεων

10 Τρανσαλπίνους καλοῦσι. τὰ δ᾽ ἄκρα διά τε τὴν τραχύ-
τητα καὶ τὸ πλῆθος τῆς ἐπιμενούσης ἀεὶ χιόνος ἀοί-
κητα τελέως ἐστί.

   16. τὸν δ᾽ Ἀπεννῖνον ἀπὸ μὲν τῆς ἀρχῆς τῆς ὑπὲρ
Μασσαλίαν καὶ τῆς πρὸς τὰς Ἄλπεις συμπτώσεως
Λιγυστῖνοι κατοικοῦσι, καὶ τὴν ἐπὶ τὸ Τυρρηνικὸν
πέλαγος αὐτοῦ πλευρὰν κεκλιμένην καὶ τὴν ἐπὶ τὰ

2 πεδία, παρὰ θάλατταν μὲν μέχρι πόλεως Πίσης, ἡ
πρώτη κεῖται τῆς Τυρρηνίας ὡς πρὸς τὰς δυσμάς,

3 κατὰ δὲ τὴν μεσόγαιαν ἕως τῆς Ἀρρητίνων χώρας.
ἑξῆς δὲ Τυρρηνοί· τούτοις δὲ συνεχεῖς ἑκάτερον τὸ

4 κλίμα νέμονται τῶν προειρημένων ὀρῶν Ὄμβροι.
λοιπὸν ὁ μὲν Ἀπεννῖνος, ἀπέχων τῆς κατὰ τὸν Ἀδρίαν
θαλάττης σταδίους ὡς ἂν εἰ πεντακοσίους, ἀπολείπει
τὰ πεδία, δεξιὸς ἀπονεύων, καὶ διὰ μέσης τῆς λοιπῆς

5 Ἰταλίας διήκων εἰς τὸ Σικελικὸν κατατείνει πέλαγος.
τὸ δ᾽ ἀπολειπόμενον μέρος πεδινὸν τῆς πλευρᾶς ἐπὶ

6 θάλατταν καὶ πόλιν καθήκει Σήνην. ὁ δὲ Πάδος ποτα-

304

The hilly ground with sufficient soil on both slopes of the Alps, that on the north toward the Rhone and that toward the plain I have been describing, is inhabited in the former case by the Transalpine Gauls and in the latter by the Taurisci, Agones and several other barbarous tribes. Transalpine is not a national name but a local one, *trans* meaning "beyond," and those beyond the Alps being so called. The summits of the Alps are quite uninhabited owing to their ruggedness and the quantity of snow which always covers them.

16. The Apennines, from their junction with the Alps above Marseilles, are inhabited on both slopes, that looking to the Tyrrhenian sea and that turned to the plain, by the Ligurians whose territory reaches on the seaboard side as far as Pisa, the first city of western Etruria, and on the land side as far as Arretium.[33] Next come the Etruscans, and after them both slopes are inhabited by the Umbrians. After this the Apennines, at a distance of about five hundred stades from the Adriatic, quit the plain and, turning to the right, pass along the center of the rest of Italy as far as the Sicilian sea, the remaining flat part of this side of the triangle continuing to the sea and the city of Sena. The

---

[33] Arezzo.

μός, ὑπὸ δὲ τῶν ποιητῶν Ἠριδανὸς θρυλούμενος, ἔχει
μὲν τὰς πηγὰς ἀπὸ τῶν Ἄλπεων ὡς πρὸς τὴν κορυφὴν
μᾶλλον τοῦ προειρημένου σχήματος, καταφέρεται δ'
εἰς τὰ πεδία, ποιούμενος τὴν ῥύσιν ὡς ἐπὶ μεσημ-
7 βρίαν. ἀφικόμενος δ' εἰς τοὺς ἐπιπέδους τόπους, ἐκ-
κλίνας τῷ ῥεύματι πρὸς ἕω φέρεται δι' αὐτῶν· ποιεῖ δὲ
τὴν ἐκβολὴν δυσὶ στόμασιν εἰς τοὺς κατὰ τὸν Ἀδρίαν
τόπους· τὸ δὲ πλεῖον ἀποτέμνεται μέρος τῆς πεδιάδος
8 χώρας εἰς τὰς Ἄλπεις καὶ τὸν Ἀδριατικὸν μυχόν. ἄγει
δὲ πλῆθος ὕδατος οὐδενὸς ἔλαττον τῶν κατὰ τὴν
Ἰταλίαν ποταμῶν, διὰ τὸ τὰς ῥύσεις τὰς ἐπὶ τὰ πεδία
νευούσας ἀπό τε τῶν Ἄλπεων καὶ τῶν Ἀπεννίνων
9 ὀρῶν εἰς τοῦτον ἐμπίπτειν ἁπάσας καὶ πανταχόθεν.
μεγίστῳ δὲ καὶ καλλίστῳ ῥεύματι φέρεται περὶ κυνὸς
ἐπιτολήν, αὐξόμενος ὑπὸ τοῦ πλήθους τῶν ἀνατη-
10 κομένων χιόνων ἐν τοῖς προειρημένοις ὄρεσιν. ἀνα-
πλεῖται δ' ἐκ θαλάττης κατὰ τὸ στόμα τὸ καλούμενον
11 Ὄλανα σχεδὸν ἐπὶ δισχιλίους σταδίους. τὴν μὲν γὰρ
πρώτην ἐκ τῶν πηγῶν ἔχει ῥύσιν ἁπλῆν, σχίζεται δ'
εἰς δύο μέρη κατὰ τοὺς προσαγορευομένους Τριγα-
βόλους· τούτων δὲ τὸ μὲν ἕτερον στόμα προσονο-
12 μάζεται Παδόα, τὸ δ' ἕτερον Ὄλανα. κεῖται δ' ἐπὶ
τούτῳ λιμήν, οὐδενὸς τῶν κατὰ τὸν Ἀδρίαν ἥττω
παρεχόμενος ἀσφάλειαν τοῖς ἐν αὐτῷ καθορμιζομέ-
νοις. παρά γε μὴν τοῖς ἐγχωρίοις ὁ ποταμὸς προσ-
13 αγορεύεται Βόδεγκος. Τἆλλα δὲ τὰ περὶ τὸν ποταμὸν
τοῦτον ἱστορούμενα παρὰ τοῖς Ἕλλησι, λέγω δὴ τὰ
περὶ Φαέθοντα καὶ τὴν ἐκείνου πτῶσιν, ἔτι δὲ τὰ

river Po,[34] celebrated by poets as the Eridanus, rises in the Alps somewhere near the apex of the triangle and descends to the plain, flowing in a southerly direction. On reaching the flat ground, it takes a turn to the East and flows through the plain, falling into the Adriatic by two mouths. It cuts off the larger half of the plain, which thus lies between it on the south and the Alps and head of the Adriatic on the north. It has a larger volume of water than any other river in Italy, since all the streams that descend into the plain from the Alps and Apennines fall into it from either side, and is highest and finest at the time of the rising of the Dog-star, as it is then swollen by the melting of the snow on those mountains. It is navigable for about two thousand stades from the mouth called Olana; for the stream, which has been a single one from its source, divides at a place called Trigaboli, one of the mouths being called Padua and the other Olana. At the latter there is a harbor, which affords as safe anchorage as any in the Adriatic. The native name of the river is Bodencus. The other tales the Greeks tell about this river, I mean touching Phaëthon and his fall and the weeping poplar trees and the

[34] See *RE* Padus 2178–2202 (H. Philipp) for P.'s "classic description," 16. 6–15.

δάκρυα τῶν αἰγείρων καὶ τοὺς μελανείμονας τοὺς περὶ
τὸν ποταμὸν οἰκοῦντας, οὕς φασι τὰς ἐσθῆτας εἰσέτι
14 νῦν φορεῖν τοιαύτας ἀπὸ τοῦ κατὰ Φαέθοντα πένθους,
καὶ πᾶσαν δὴ τὴν τραγικὴν καὶ ταύτῃ προσεοικυῖαν
ὕλην, ἐπὶ μὲν τοῦ παρόντος ὑπερθησόμεθα, διὰ τὸ μὴ
λίαν καθήκειν τῷ τῆς προκατασκευῆς γένει τὴν περὶ
15 τῶν τοιούτων ἀκριβολογίαν. μεταλαβόντες δὲ καιρὸν
ἁρμόττοντα ποιησόμεθα τὴν καθήκουσαν μνήμην, καὶ
μάλιστα διὰ τὴν Τιμαίου περὶ τοὺς προειρημένους
τόπους ἄγνοιαν.

17. Πλὴν ταῦτά γε τὰ πεδία τὸ παλαιὸν ἐνέμοντο
Τυρρηνοί, καθ' οὓς χρόνους καὶ τὰ Φλεγραῖά ποτε
καλούμενα τὰ περὶ Καπύην καὶ Νώλην· ἃ δὴ καὶ διὰ
τὸ πολλοῖς ἐμποδὼν εἶναι καὶ γνωρίζεσθαι μεγάλην
2 ἐπ' ἀρετῇ δόξαν εἴληφε. διὸ καὶ τοὺς ἱστοροῦντας τὰς
Τυρρηνῶν δυναστείας οὐ χρὴ ποιεῖσθαι τὴν ἀναφορὰν ἐπὶ τὴν νῦν κατεχομένην ὑπ' αὐτῶν χώραν, ἀλλ'
ἐπὶ τὰ προειρημένα πεδία καὶ τὰς ἐκ τούτων τῶν
3 τόπων ἀφορμάς. οἷς ἐπιμιγνύμενοι κατὰ τὴν παράθε-
σιν Κελτοὶ καὶ περὶ τὸ κάλλος τῆς χώρας ὀφθαλμι-
άσαντες, ἐκ μικρᾶς προφάσεως μεγάλῃ στρατιᾷ
παραδόξως ἐπελθόντες ἐξέβαλον ἐκ τῆς περὶ τὸν
Πάδον χώρας Τυρρηνοὺς καὶ κατέσχον αὐτοὶ τὰ
4 πεδία. τὰ μὲν οὖν πρῶτα καὶ περὶ τὰς ἀνατολὰς τοῦ
Πάδου κείμενα Λάοι καὶ Λεβέκιοι, μετὰ δὲ τούτους
Ἴνσομβρες κατῴκησαν, ὃ μέγιστον ἔθνος ἦν αὐτῶν·
5 ἑξῆς δὲ τούτοις παρὰ τὸν ποταμὸν Γονομάνοι. τὰ δὲ
πρὸς τὸν Ἀδρίαν ἤδη προσήκοντα γένος ἄλλο πάνυ

black clothing of the inhabitants near the river, who, they say, still dress thus in mourning for Phaëthon, and all matter of a tragic nature and similar to this legend, may be left aside for the present, detailed treatment of such things not suiting very well the character of my introduction. I will, however, when I find a suitable occasion make proper mention of all this, especially as Timaeus has shown much ignorance concerning the district.

17. The Etruscans were the oldest inhabitants of this plain at the same period that they possessed also that Phlegraean plain in the neighborhood of Capua and Nola, which, accessible and well known as it is to many, has such a reputation for fertility. Those therefore who would know something of the dominion of the Etruscans should not look at the country they now inhabit, but at these plains and the resources they drew thence. The Celts,[35] being close neighbors of the Etruscans and associating much with them, cast covetous eyes on their beautiful country, and on a small protext, suddenly attacked them with a large army and, expelling them from the plain of the Po, occupied it themselves. Those occupying the first districts near the source of the Po, were the Laevi and Lebecii, after them the Insubres, the largest tribe of all, and next these, on the banks of the river, the Cenomani. The part of the plain near the Adriatic had never ceased to be in the pos-

[35] For all the Celtic tribes mentioned here see W. V. Harris, *CAH* (2nd edition) 8 (1989), 107–118 and map 7.

παλαιὸν διακατέσχε· προσαγορεύονται δ᾽ Οὐένετοι,
τοῖς μὲν ἔθεσι καὶ τῷ κόσμῳ βραχὺ διαφέροντες

6 Κελτῶν, γλώττῃ δ᾽ ἀλλοίᾳ χρώμενοι. περὶ ὧν οἱ τραγῳδιογράφοι πολύν τινα πεποίηνται λόγον καὶ πολ-

7 λὴν διατέθεινται τερατείαν. τὰ δὲ πέραν τοῦ Πάδου τὰ
περὶ τὸν Ἀπεννῖνον πρῶτοι μὲν Ἄναρες, μετὰ δὲ
τούτους Βοῖοι κατῴκησαν· ἑξῆς δὲ τούτων ὡς πρὸς τὸν
Ἀδρίαν Λίγγονες, τὰ δὲ τελευταῖα πρὸς θαλάττῃ Σήνωνες.

8   Τὰ μὲν οὖν ἐπιφανέστατα τῶν κατασχόντων τοὺς

9 προειρημένους τόπους ἐθνῶν ταῦθ᾽ ὑπῆρχεν. ᾤκουν δὲ
κατὰ κώμας ἀτειχίστους, τῆς λοιπῆς κατασκευῆς

10 ἄμοιροι καθεστῶτες. διὰ γὰρ τὸ στιβαδοκοιτεῖν καὶ
κρεαφαγεῖν, ἔτι δὲ μηδὲν ἄλλο πλὴν τὰ πολεμικὰ καὶ
τὰ κατὰ γεωργίαν ἀσκεῖν, ἁπλοῦς εἶχον τοὺς βίους,
οὔτ᾽ ἐπιστήμης ἄλλης οὔτε τέχνης παρ᾽ αὐτοῖς τὸ

11 παράπαν γινωσκομένης. ὕπαρξίς γε μὴν ἑκάστοις ἦν
θρέμματα καὶ χρυσὸς διὰ τὸ μόνα ταῦτα κατὰ τὰς
περιστάσεις ῥᾳδίως δύνασθαι πανταχῇ περιαγαγεῖν

12 καὶ μεθιστάναι κατὰ τὰς αὐτῶν προαιρέσεις. περὶ δὲ
τὰς ἑταιρείας μεγίστην σπουδὴν ἐποιοῦντο διὰ τὸ καὶ
φοβερώτατον καὶ δυνατώτατον εἶναι παρ᾽ αὐτοῖς τοῦτον ὃς ἂν πλείστους ἔχειν δοκῇ τοὺς θεραπεύοντας καὶ
συμπεριφερομένους αὐτῷ.

18. Τὰς μὲν οὖν ἀρχὰς οὐ μόνον τῆς χώρας ἐπε-
κράτουν, ἀλλὰ καὶ τῶν σύνεγγυς πολλοὺς ὑπηκόους

2 ἐπεποίηντο, τῇ τόλμῃ καταπεπληγμένους. μετὰ δέ
τινα χρόνον μάχῃ νικήσαντες Ῥωμαίους καὶ τοὺς

session of another very ancient tribe called the Veneti, differing slightly from the Gauls in customs and costume and speaking another language. About this people the tragic poets tell many marvellous stories. On the other bank of the Po, by the Apennines, the first settlers beginning from the west were the Anares and next them the Boii. Next the latter, toward the Adriatic, were the Lingones and lastly, near the sea, the Senones.

These are the names of the principal tribes that settled in the district. They lived in unwalled villages, without any superfluous furniture; for as they slept on beds of leaves and fed on meat and were exclusively occupied with war and agriculture, their lives were very simple, and they had no knowledge whatever of any art or science. Their possessions consisted of cattle and gold, because these were the only things they could carry about with them everywhere according to circumstances and shift where they chose. For them, having followers is of the greatest importance, those among them being the most feared and most powerful who were thought to have the largest number of attendants and associates.

18. On their first invasion they not only conquered this country but reduced to subjection many of the neighboring peoples, striking terror into them by their audacity. Not long afterward[36] they defeated the Romans and their

390 B.C.

36 In 390, although P. makes it 386 (1. 6. 1–2).

μετὰ τούτων παραταξαμένους, ἑπόμενοι τοῖς φεύγουσι
τρισὶ τῆς μάχης ἡμέραις ὕστερον κατέσχον αὐτὴν
3 τὴν Ῥώμην πλὴν τοῦ Καπετωλίου. γενομένου δ᾽ ἀντι-
σπάσματος, καὶ τῶν Οὐενέτων ἐμβαλόντων εἰς τὴν
χώραν αὐτῶν, τότε μὲν ποιησάμενοι συνθήκας πρὸς
Ῥωμαίους καὶ τὴν πόλιν ἀποδόντες, ἐπανῆλθον εἰς
4 τὴν οἰκείαν. μετὰ δὲ ταῦτα τοῖς ἐμφυλίοις συνείχοντο
πολέμοις, ἔνιοι δὲ καὶ τῶν τὰς Ἄλπεις κατοικούντων
ὁρμὰς ἐποιοῦντο, καὶ συνηθροίζοντο πολλάκις ἐπ᾽
αὐτούς, θεωροῦντες ἐκ παραθέσεως τὴν παραγεγε-
5 νημένην αὐτοῖς εὐδαιμονίαν. ἐν ᾧ καιρῷ Ῥωμαῖοι τήν
τε σφετέραν δύναμιν ἀνέλαβον καὶ τὰ κατὰ τοὺς
6 Λατίνους αὖθις πράγματα συνεστήσαντο. παραγενομένων δὲ πάλιν τῶν Κελτῶν εἰς Ἄλβαν στρατεύματι
μεγάλῳ μετὰ τὴν τῆς πόλεως κατάληψιν ἔτει τρια-
κοστῷ, τότε μὲν οὐκ ἐτόλμησαν ἀντεξαγαγεῖν Ῥωμαῖοι τὰ στρατόπεδα, διὰ τὸ παραδόξου γενομένης
τῆς ἐφόδου προκαταληφθῆναι καὶ μὴ καταταχῆσαι
7 τὰς τῶν συμμάχων ἀθροίσαντας δυνάμεις. αὖθις δ᾽ ἐξ
ἐπιβολῆς ἑτέρας ἔτει δωδεκάτῳ μετὰ μεγάλης στρατιᾶς ἐπιπορευομένων, προαισθόμενοι καὶ συναγείραν-
τες τοὺς συμμάχους, μετὰ πολλῆς προθυμίας ἀπήντων, σπεύδοντες συμβαλεῖν καὶ διακινδυνεῦσαι περὶ
8 τῶν ὅλων. οἱ δὲ Γαλάται καταπλαγέντες τὴν ἔφοδον
αὐτῶν καὶ διαστασιάσαντες πρὸς σφᾶς, νυκτὸς ἐπιγενομένης φυγῇ παραπλησίαν ἐποιήσαντο τὴν ἀποχώ-
9 ρησιν εἰς τὴν οἰκείαν. ἀπὸ δὲ τούτου τοῦ φόβου
τριακαίδεκα μὲν ἔτη τὴν ἡσυχίαν ἔσχον, μετὰ δὲ

allies in a pitched battle, and pursuing the fugitives, occupied, three days after the battle, the whole of Rome with the exception of the Capitol, but being diverted by an invasion of their own country by the Veneti, they made on this occasion a treaty with the Romans,[37] and evacuating the city, returned home. After this they were occupied by domestic wars, and certain of the neighboring Alpine tribes, witnessing to what prosperity they had attained in comparison with themselves, frequently gathered to attack them. Meanwhile the Romans reestablished their power and again became masters of Latium. Thirty years after the occupation of Rome,[38] the Celts again appeared before Alba with a large army, and the Romans on this occasion did not venture to meet them in the field, because, owing to the suddenness of the attack, they were taken by surprise and had not had time to anticipate it by collecting the forces of their allies. But when, twelve years later, the Celts again invaded in great strength, they had early word of it, and, assembling their allies, marched eagerly to meet them, wishing for nothing better than a decisive battle. The Gauls, alarmed by the Roman advance and at variance among themselves, waited until nightfall and then set off for home, their retreat resembling a flight. After this panic, they kept quiet for thirteen years, and then, as they saw how rapidly the power of the Romans was growing, they

360 B.C.

348 B.C.

[37] *StV* 245, considered apocryphal.

[38] All dates in this chapter and the following are controversial, except for the battle at Sentinum (19. 6) in 295, in which the consul P. Decius Mus perished in an act of *devotio*, *MRR* 1. 177. See R. M. Errington, *JRS* 57 (1967) 96–108.

ταῦτα συνορῶντες αὐξανομένην τὴν Ῥωμαίων δύναμιν, εἰρήνην ἐποιήσαντο καὶ συνθήκας.

19. ἐν αἷς ἔτη τριάκοντα μείναντες ἐμπεδῶς, αὖθις γενομένου κινήματος ἐκ τῶν Τρανσαλπίνων, δείσαντες μὴ πόλεμος αὐτοῖς ἐγερθῇ βαρύς, ἀπὸ μὲν αὐτῶν ἔτρεψαν τὰς ὁρμὰς τῶν ἐξανισταμένων, δωροφοροῦντες καὶ προτιθέμενοι τὴν συγγένειαν, ἐπὶ δὲ Ῥωμαίους

2 παρώξυναν καὶ μετέσχον αὐτοῖς τῆς στρατείας. ἐν ᾗ τὴν ἔφοδον ποιησάμενοι διὰ Τυρρηνίας, ὁμοῦ συστρατευσαμένων σφίσι Τυρρηνῶν, καὶ περιβαλόμενοι λείας πλῆθος, ἐκ μὲν τῆς Ῥωμαίων ἐπαρχίας ἀσφα-

3 λῶς ἐπανῆλθον. εἰς δὲ τὴν οἰκείαν ἀφικόμενοι, καὶ στασιάσαντες περὶ τὴν τῶν εἰλημμένων πλεονεξίαν, τῆς τε λείας καὶ τῆς αὑτῶν δυνάμεως τὸ πλεῖστον

4 μέρος διέφθειραν. τοῦτο δὲ σύνηθές ἐστι Γαλάταις πράττειν, ἐπειδὰν σφετερίσωνταί τι τῶν πέλας, καὶ μάλιστα διὰ τὰς ἀλόγους οἰνοφλυγίας καὶ πλησμο-

5 νάς. μετὰ δὲ ταῦτα πάλιν ἔτει τετάρτῳ συμφρονήσαντες ἅμα Σαυνῖται καὶ Γαλάται παρετάξαντο Ῥωμαίοις ἐν τῇ Καμερτίων χώρᾳ καὶ πολλοὺς αὐτῶν

6 ἐν τῷ κινδύνῳ διέφθειραν. ἐν ᾧ καιρῷ προσφιλονεικήσαντες πρὸς τὸ γεγονὸς ἐλάττωμ᾽ αὐτοῖς Ῥωμαῖοι μετ᾽ ὀλίγας ἡμέρας ἐξῆλθον, καὶ συμβαλόντες πᾶσι τοῖς στρατοπέδοις ἐν τῇ τῶν Σεντινάτων χώρᾳ πρὸς τοὺς προειρημένους τοὺς μὲν πλείστους ἀπέκτειναν, τοὺς δὲ λοιποὺς ἠνάγκασαν προτροπάδην ἑκάστους

7 εἰς τὴν οἰκείαν φυγεῖν. διαγενομένων δὲ πάλιν ἐτῶν δέκα παρεγένοντο Γαλάται μετὰ μεγάλης στρατιᾶς,

made a formal peace with them, to the terms of which they adhered steadfastly for thirty years.

19. But then, when a fresh movement began among the 334 B.C. Transalpine Gauls, and they feared they would have a big war on their hands, they deflected from themselves the inroad of the migrating tribes by bribery and by pleading their kinship, but they incited them to attack the Romans, and even joined them in the expedition. They advanced 299 B.C. through Etruria, the Etruscans too uniting with them, and, after collecting a quantity of booty, retired quite safely from the Roman territory, but, on reaching home, fell out with each other about division of the spoil and succeeded in destroying the greater part of their own forces and of the booty itself. This is quite a common event among the Gauls, when they have appropriated their neighbor's property, chiefly owing to their inordinate drinking and surfeiting. Four years later the Gauls made a league with the Samnites, and engaging the Romans in the territory of 295 B.C. Camerinum inflicted on them considerable loss; meanwhile the Romans, determined on avenging their reverse, advanced again a few days after with all their legions, and attacking the Gauls and Samnites in the territory of Sentinum, put the greater number of them to the sword and compelled the rest to take precipitate flight each to their separate homes. Again, ten years afterward, the

8 πολιορκήσοντες τὴν Ἀρρητίνων πόλιν. Ῥωμαῖοι δὲ
παραβοηθήσαντες, καὶ συμβαλόντες πρὸ τῆς πόλεως,
ἡττήθησαν. ἐν δὲ τῇ μάχῃ ταύτῃ Λευκίου τοῦ στρατηγοῦ τελευτήσαντος Μάνιον ἐπικατέστησαν τὸν Κό-
9 ριον. οὗ πρεσβευτὰς ἐκπέμψαντος εἰς Γαλατίαν ὑπὲρ
τῶν αἰχμαλώτων, παρασπονδήσαντες ἐπανείλοντο
10 τοὺς πρέσβεις. τῶν δὲ Ῥωμαίων ὑπὸ τὸν θυμὸν ἐκ
χειρὸς ἐπιστρατευσαμένων, ἀπαντήσαντες συνέβα-
11 λον οἱ Σήνωνες καλούμενοι Γαλάται. Ῥωμαῖοι δ' ἐκ
παρατάξεως κρατήσαντες αὐτῶν τοὺς μὲν πλείστους
ἀπέκτειναν, τοὺς δὲ λοιποὺς ἐξέβαλον, τῆς δὲ χώρας
12 ἐγένοντο πάσης ἐγκρατεῖς. εἰς ἣν καὶ πρώτην τῆς
Γαλατίας ἀποικίαν ἔστειλαν τὴν Σήνην προσαγορευομένην πόλιν, ὁμώνυμον οὖσαν τοῖς πρότερον αὐτὴν
13 κατοικοῦσι Γαλάταις, ὑπὲρ ἧς ἀρτίως διεσαφήσαμεν,
φάσκοντες αὐτὴν παρὰ τὸν Ἀδρίαν ἐπὶ τῷ πέρατι
κεῖσθαι τῶν περὶ τὸν Πάδον πεδίων.

20. οἱ δὲ Βοῖοι, θεωροῦντες ἐκπεπτωκότας τοὺς
Σήνωνας, καὶ δείσαντες περὶ σφῶν καὶ τῆς χώρας, μὴ
πάθωσι τὸ παραπλήσιον, ἐξεστράτευσαν πανδημεὶ
2 παρακαλέσαντες Τυρρηνούς. ἀθροισθέντες δὲ περὶ
τὴν Ὀάδμονα προσαγορευομένην λίμνην παρετάξαν-
3 το Ῥωμαίοις. ἐν δὲ τῇ μάχῃ ταύτῃ Τυρρηνῶν μὲν οἱ
πλεῖστοι κατεκόπησαν, τῶν δὲ Βοίων τελέως ὀλίγοι
4 διέφυγον. οὐ μὴν ἀλλὰ τῷ κατὰ πόδας ἐνιαυτῷ συμφρονήσαντες αὖθις οἱ προειρημένοι καὶ τοὺς ἄρτι τῶν
νέων ἡβῶντας καθοπλίσαντες παρετάξαντο πρὸς Ῥω-
5 μαίους. ἡττηθέντες δ' ὁλοσχερῶς τῇ μάχῃ μόλις εἶξαν

Gauls appeared in force and besieged Arretium. The 283 B.C.
Romans, coming to the help of the town, attacked them in
front of it and were defeated. In this battle[39] their Praetor
Lucius Caecilius fell, and they nominated Manius Curius
in his place. When Manius sent legates to Gaul to treat for
the return of the prisoners, they were treacherously slain,
and this made the Romans so indignant that they at once
marched upon Gaul. They were met by the Gauls called
Senones, whom they defeated in a pitched battle,[40] killing
most of them and driving the rest out of their country, the
whole of which they occupied. This was the first part of
Gaul in which they planted a colony, calling it Sena after
the name of the Gauls who formerly inhabited it. This is
the city I mentioned above as lying near the Adriatic at the
extremity of the plain of the Po.

20. Hereupon the Boii, seeing the Senones expelled
from their territory, and fearing a like fate for themselves
and their own land, implored the aid of the Etruscans and
marched out in full force. The united armies gave battle to 282 B.C.
the Romans near Lake Vadimon, and in this battle most of
the Etruscans were cut to pieces while only quite a few of
the Boii escaped. But, notwithstanding, in the very next
year these two peoples once more combined and arming
their young men, even the mere striplings, again encountered the Romans in a pitched battle. They were utterly

[39] The date is disputed, 284 or 283. Caecilius was consul in 284
but may have fallen in 283: WC 1. 188; 3. 760–761; *MRR* 3. 78–79.

[40] Victory of the consul Publius Cornelius Dolabella at Lake
Vadimo.

ταῖς ψυχαῖς, καὶ διαπρεσβευσάμενοι περὶ σπονδῶν
6 καὶ διαλύσεων, συνθήκας ἔθεντο πρὸς Ῥωμαίους. ταῦτα δὲ συνέβαινε γίνεσθαι τῷ τρίτῳ πρότερον ἔτει τῆς
Πύρρου διαβάσεως εἰς τὴν Ἰταλίαν, πέμπτῳ δὲ τῆς
7 Γαλατῶν περὶ Δελφοὺς διαφθορᾶς. ἐν γὰρ τούτοις ἡ
τύχη τοῖς καιροῖς ὡς ἂν εἰ λοιμικήν τινα πολέμου
8 διάθεσιν ἐπέστησε πᾶσι Γαλάταις. ἐκ δὲ τῶν προειρημένων ἀγώνων δύο τὰ κάλλιστα συνεκύρησε Ῥωμαί-
οις· τοῦ γὰρ κατακόπτεσθαι συνήθειαν ἐσχηκότες ὑπὸ
Γαλατῶν οὐδὲν ἠδύναντο δεινότερον ἰδεῖν οὐδὲ προσ-
9 δοκῆσαι τῶν αὐτοῖς ἤδη πεπραγμένων· ἐξ ὧν πρός τε
Πύρρον ἀθληταὶ τέλειοι γεγονότες τῶν κατὰ πόλεμον
10 ἔργων συγκατέστησαν τήν τε Γαλατῶν τόλμαν ἐν
καιρῷ καταπληξάμενοι λοιπὸν ἀπερισπάστως τὸ μὲν
πρῶτον πρὸς Πύρρον περὶ τῆς Ἰταλίας ἐπολέμουν,
μετὰ δὲ ταῦτα πρὸς Καρχηδονίους ὑπὲρ τῆς Σικελιωτῶν ἀρχῆς διηγωνίζοντο.

21. Γαλάται δ᾽ ἐκ τῶν προειρημένων ἐλαττωμάτων
ἔτη μὲν πέντε καὶ τετταράκοντα τὴν ἡσυχίαν ἔσχον,
2 εἰρήνην ἄγοντες πρὸς Ῥωμαίους. ἐπεὶ δ᾽ οἱ μὲν αὐτόπται γεγονότες τῶν δεινῶν ἐκ τοῦ ζῆν ἐξεχώρησαν
διὰ τὸν χρόνον, ἐπεγένοντο δὲ νέοι, θυμοῦ μὲν ἀλο-
γίστου πλήρεις, ἄπειροι δὲ κἀόρατοι παντὸς κακοῦ
3 καὶ πάσης περιστάσεως, αὖθις ἤρξαντο τὰ καθεστῶτα
κινεῖν, ὃ φύσιν ἔχει γίνεσθαι, καὶ τραχύνεσθαι μὲν ἐκ
τῶν τυχόντων πρὸς Ῥωμαίους, ἐπισπᾶσθαι δὲ τοὺς ἐκ
4 τῶν Ἄλπεων Γαλάτας. τὸ μὲν οὖν πρῶτον χωρὶς τοῦ

defeated[41] and it was only now that their courage at length gave way and that they sent an embassy to sue for terms and made a treaty with the Romans.[42] This took place three years before the crossing of Pyrrhus to Italy and five years before the destruction of the Gauls at Delphi; for it really seems that at this time Fortune afflicted all Gauls alike with a sort of epidemic of war. From all these struggles the Romans gained two great advantages. In the first place, having become accustomed to be cut up by Gauls, they could neither undergo nor expect anymore terrible experience, and next, owing to this, when they met Pyrrhus they had become perfectly trained athletes in war, so that they were able to daunt the courage of the Gauls before it was too late, and henceforth could give their whole mind first to the fight with Pyrrhus for Italy and afterward to the maintenance of the contest with Carthage for the possession of Sicily.

21. After these reverses, the Gauls remained quiet and at peace with Rome for forty-five years. But when, as time went on, those who had actually witnessed the terrible struggle were no more, and a younger generation had taken their place, full of unreflecting passion and absolutely without experience of suffering or peril, they began again, as was natural, to disturb the settlement, becoming exasperated against the Romans on the least pretext and inviting the Alpine Gauls to make common cause with

[41] By the consul Quintus Aemilius Papus in 282. Problems of dates and locations remain disputed in chapters 19 and 20. The chronological table in WC 1. 191 might be open to slight revisions.

[42] The synchronisms point to 283 rather than 282 (so, however, WC).

πλήθους δι' αὐτῶν τῶν ἡγουμένων ἐν ἀπορρήτοις
5 ἐπράττετο τὰ προειρημένα. διὸ καὶ παραγενομένων
τῶν Τρανσαλπίνων ἕως Ἀριμίνου μετὰ δυνάμεως, δια-
πιστήσαντα τὰ πλήθη τῶν Βοίων καὶ στασιάσαντα
πρός τε τοὺς ἑαυτῶν προεστῶτας καὶ πρὸς τοὺς παραγεγονότας, ἀνεῖλον μὲν τοὺς ἰδίους βασιλεῖς Ἄτιν καὶ
Γάλατον, κατέκοψαν δ' ἀλλήλους, συμβαλόντες ἐκ
6 παρατάξεων. ὅτε δὴ καὶ Ῥωμαῖοι κατάφοβοι γενόμενοι τὴν ἔφοδον, ἐξῆλθον μετὰ στρατοπέδου· συνέντες δὲ τὴν αὐθαίρετον καταφθορὰν τῶν Γαλατῶν,
7 αὖθις ἀνεχώρησαν εἰς τὴν οἰκείαν. μετὰ δὲ τοῦτον τὸν
φόβον ἔτει πέμπτῳ, Μάρκου Λεπέδου στρατηγοῦντος,
κατεκληρούχησαν ἐν Γαλατίᾳ Ῥωμαῖοι τὴν Πικεν-
τίνην προσαγορευομένην χώραν, ἐξ ἧς νικήσαντες ἐξ-
8 έβαλον τοὺς Σήνωνας προσαγορευομένους Γαλάτας,
Γαΐου Φλαμινίου ταύτην τὴν δημαγωγίαν εἰσηγησα-
μένου καὶ πολιτείαν, ἣν δὴ καὶ Ῥωμαίοις ὡς ἔπος
εἰπεῖν φατέον ἀρχηγὸν μὲν γενέσθαι τῆς ἐπὶ τὸ
χεῖρον τοῦ δήμου διαστροφῆς, αἰτίαν δὲ καὶ τοῦ μετὰ
ταῦτα πολέμου συστάντος αὐτοῖς πρὸς τοὺς προειρη-
9 μένους. πολλοὶ μὲν γὰρ τῶν Γαλατῶν ὑπεδύοντο τὴν
πρᾶξιν, μάλιστα δ' οἱ Βοῖοι, διὰ τὸ συντερμονεῖν τῇ
τῶν Ῥωμαίων χώρᾳ, νομίσαντες οὐχ ὑπὲρ ἡγεμονίας
ἔτι καὶ δυναστείας Ῥωμαίους τὸν πρὸς αὐτοὺς ποιήσασθαι πόλεμον, ἀλλ' ὑπὲρ ὁλοσχεροῦς ἐξαναστά-
σεως καὶ καταφθορᾶς.

22. Διόπερ εὐθέως τὰ μέγιστα τῶν ἐθνῶν, τό τε τῶν
Ἰνσόμβρων καὶ Βοίων, συμφρονήσαντα διεπέμποντο

them. At first these advances were made secretly by their
chiefs without the knowledge of the multitude; so that
when a force of Transalpine Gauls advanced as far as
Ariminum the Boian populace were suspicious of them,
and quarrelling with their own leaders as well as with the
strangers, killed their kings, Atis and Galatus, and had a
pitched battle with the other Gauls in which many fell on
either side. The Romans had been alarmed by the advance
of the Gauls, and a legion was on its way; but, on learning of the Gauls' self-inflicted losses, they returned home.
Five years after this alarm, in the consulship of Marcus
Aemilius Lepidus,[43] the Romans divided among their citizens the territory in Gaul known as Picenum, from which
they had ejected the Senones when they conquered them.
Gaius Flaminius[44] was the originator of this popular policy,
which we must pronounce to have been, one may say, the
first step in the demoralization of the populace, as well as
the cause of the war with the Gauls which followed. For
what prompted many of the Gauls and especially the Boii,
whose territory bordered on that of Rome, to take action
was the conviction that now the Romans no longer made
war on them for the sake of supremacy and sovereignty,
but with a view to their total expulsion and extermination.

22. The two largest tribes, therefore, the Insubres and
Boii, made a league and sent messengers to the Gauls

[43] Consul in 232.

[44] Tribune of the plebs who carried an agrarian law against
the Senate's opposition. He was killed in battle as consul in 217 (3.
84. 6).

πρὸς τοὺς κατὰ τὰς Ἄλπεις καὶ περὶ τὸν Ῥοδανὸν
ποταμὸν κατοικοῦντας Γαλάτας, προσαγορευομένους
δὲ διὰ τὸ μισθοῦ στρατεύειν Γαισάτους· ἡ γὰρ λέξις

2 αὕτη τοῦτο σημαίνει κυρίως. ὧν τοῖς βασιλεῦσι Κογ-
κολιτάνῳ καὶ Ἀνηροέστῳ παραυτίκα μὲν χρυσίου
προτείναντες πλῆθος, εἰς τὸ μέλλον δ' ὑποδεικνύντες
τὸ μέγεθος τῆς Ῥωμαίων εὐδαιμονίας καὶ τὸ πλῆθος
τῶν ὑπαρξόντων αὐτοῖς ἀγαθῶν, ἐὰν κρατήσωσι,
προυτρέποντο καὶ παρώξυνον πρὸς τὴν ἐπὶ Ῥωμαίους

3 στρατείαν. ῥᾳδίως δ' ἔπεισαν, ἅμα τοῖς προειρημένοις
διδόντες μὲν τὰ πιστὰ περὶ τῆς αὑτῶν συμμαχίας,
ἀναμιμνήσκοντες δὲ τῆς τῶν ἰδίων προγόνων πράξεως

4 αὐτούς· ἐν ᾗ 'κεῖνοι στρατεύσαντες οὐ μόνον ἐνίκησαν
μαχόμενοι Ῥωμαίους, ἀλλὰ καὶ μετὰ τὴν μάχην ἐξ

5 ἐφόδου κατέσχον αὐτὴν τὴν Ῥώμην· γενόμενοι δὲ καὶ
τῶν ὑπαρχόντων ἁπάντων ἐγκρατεῖς, καὶ τῆς πόλεως
αὐτῆς ἑπτὰ μῆνας κυριεύσαντες, τέλος ἐθελοντὶ καὶ
μετὰ χάριτος παραδόντες τὴν πόλιν, ἄθραυστοι κἀσι-

6 νεῖς ἔχοντες τὴν ὠφέλειαν εἰς τὴν οἰκείαν ἐπανῆλθον.
ὧν ἀκούοντες οἱ περὶ αὐτοὺς ἡγεμόνες οὕτω παρωρ-
μήθησαν ἐπὶ τὴν στρατείαν ὥστε μηδέποτε μήτε πλείους μήτ' ἐνδοξοτέρους μήτε μαχιμωτέρους ἄνδρας

7 ἐξελθεῖν ἐκ τούτων τῶν τόπων τῆς Γαλατίας. κατὰ δὲ
τοὺς καιροὺς τούτους Ῥωμαῖοι τὰ μὲν ἀκούοντες, τὰ δὲ

8 καταμαντευόμενοι τὸ μέλλον, εἰς φόβους ἐνέπιπτον
συνεχεῖς καὶ ταραχὰς ἐπὶ τοσοῦτον ὥστε ποτὲ μὲν
στρατόπεδα καταγράφειν καὶ σίτου καὶ τῶν ἐπιτηδείων ποιεῖσθαι παρασκευάς, ποτὲ δὲ καὶ τὰς δυνάμεις

dwelling among the Alps and near the Rhone, who are called Gaesatae[45] because they serve for hire, this being the proper meaning of the word. They urged and incited their kings Concolitanus and Aneroëstus to make war on Rome, offering them at present a large sum in gold, and as to the future, pointing out to them the great prosperity of the Romans, and the vast wealth that would be theirs if they were victorious. They had no difficulty in persuading them, as, in addition to all this, they pledged themselves to be loyal allies and reminded them of the achievement of their own ancestors, who had not only overcome the Romans in combat, but, after the battle, had assaulted and taken Rome itself, possessing themselves of all it contained, and, after remaining masters of the city for seven months, had finally given it up of their own free will and as an act of grace, and had returned home with their spoil, unbroken and unscathed. When the kings had been told all this, they became so eager for the expedition that on no occasion has that district of Gaul sent out so large a force or one composed of men so distinguished or so warlike. All this time, the Romans, either hearing what was happening or divining what was coming, were in such a state of constant alarm and unrest, that at times we find them busy enrolling legions and making provision of grain and other

[45] *RE* Gaesati 462–463 (M. Ihm) and Gaesum 463–464 (O. Fiebiger).

ἐξάγειν ἐπὶ τοὺς ὅρους, ὡς ἤδη παρόντων εἰς τὴν χώραν τῶν πολεμίων, οὐδέπω κεκινηκότων ἐκ τῆς

9 οἰκείας τῶν Κελτῶν. οὐκ ἐλάχιστα δὲ συνήργησε καὶ Καρχηδονίοις τοῦτο τὸ κίνημα πρὸς τὸ κατασκευ-

10 άσασθαι τὰ κατὰ τὴν Ἰβηρίαν ἀσφαλῶς. Ῥωμαῖοι γάρ, ὡς καὶ πρόσθεν ἡμῖν εἴρηται, κρίνοντες ἀναγκαι-ότερα ταῦτα διὰ τὸ πρὸς ταῖς πλευραῖς αὐτῶν ὑπάρ-χειν παρορᾶν ἠναγκάζοντο τὰ κατὰ τὴν Ἰβηρίαν, σπουδάζοντες πρότερον ἐν καλῷ θέσθαι τὰ κατὰ τοὺς

11 Κελτούς. διόπερ ἀσφαλισάμενοι τὰ πρὸς τοὺς Καρχη-δονίους διὰ τῶν πρὸς τὸν Ἀσδρούβαν ὁμολογιῶν, ὑπὲρ ὧν ἄρτι δεδηλώκαμεν, ἐνεχείρησαν ὁμοθυμαδὸν ἐν τούτοις τοῖς καιροῖς πρὸς τοὺς κατὰ τὴν Ἰταλίαν πολεμίους, νομίζοντες συμφέρειν σφίσι τὸ διακρι-θῆναι πρὸς τούτους.

23. Οἱ δὲ Γαισάται Γαλάται συστησάμενοι δύνα-μιν πολυτελῆ καὶ βαρεῖαν, ἧκον ὑπεράραντες τὰς Ἄλπεις εἰς τὸν Πάδον ποταμὸν ἔτει μετὰ τὴν τῆς

2 χώρας διάδοσιν ὀγδόῳ. τὸ μὲν οὖν τῶν Ἰνσόμβρων καὶ Βοίων γένος ἔμεινε γενναίως ἐν ταῖς ἐξ ἀρχῆς ἐπιβολαῖς, οἱ δ᾽ Οὐένετοι καὶ Γονομάνοι, διαπρεσβευ-

3 σαμένων Ῥωμαίων, τούτοις εἵλοντο συμμαχεῖν. Διὸ καὶ μέρος τι τῆς δυνάμεως καταλιπεῖν ἠναγκάσθησαν οἱ βασιλεῖς τῶν Κελτῶν φυλακῆς χάριν τῆς χώρας

4 πρὸς τὸν ἀπὸ τούτων φόβον. αὐτοὶ δ᾽ ἐξάραντες παντὶ τῷ στρατεύματι κατατεθαρρηκότως ὥρμησαν, ποιού-μενοι τὴν πορείαν ὡς ἐπὶ Τυρρηνίας, ἔχοντες πεζοὺς μὲν εἰς πεντακισμυρίους, ἱππεῖς δὲ καὶ συνωρίδας εἰς

stores, at times marching to the frontier, as if the enemy had already invaded their territory, while as a fact the Celts had not yet budged from their own country. This movement of the Gauls contributed in no small measure to the rapid and unimpeded subjugation of Spain by the Carthaginians; for the Romans, as I stated above,[46] regarded this matter as of more urgency, since the danger was on their flank, and were compelled to neglect the affairs of Spain until they had dealt with the Gauls. They therefore secured themselves against the Carthaginians by the treaty with Hasdrubal, the terms of which I stated above, and threw their whole effort into the struggle with their enemies in Italy, considering it their main interest to bring this to a decisive conclusion.

23. The Gaesatae, having collected a richly equipped and formidable force, crossed the Alps, and descended into the plain of the Po in the eighth year after the partition[47] of Picenum. The Insubres and Boii held stoutly to 225 B.C. their original purpose; but the Veneti and Cenomani, on the Romans sending an embassy to them, decided to give them their support; so that the Celtic chiefs were obliged to leave part of their forces behind to protect their territory from invasion by these tribes. They themselves marched confidently out with their whole available army, consisting of about fifty thousand foot and twenty thousand horse and chariots, and advanced on Etruria. The

46 13. 5–6.
47 See 21. 7.

5 δισμυρίους. Ῥωμαῖοι δ᾽ ὡς θᾶττον ἤκουσαν τοὺς Κελτοὺς ὑπερβεβληκέναι τὰς Ἄλπεις, Λεύκιον μὲν Αἰμίλιον ὕπατον μετὰ δυνάμεως ἐξαπέστειλαν ὡς ἐπ᾽ Ἀριμίνου, τηρήσοντα ταύτῃ τῶν ἐναντίων τὴν ἔφοδον, ἕνα
6 δὲ τῶν ἐξαπελέκεων εἰς Τυρρηνίαν. ὁ μὲν γὰρ ἕτερος
τῶν ὑπάτων Γάιος Ἀτίλιος προεξεληλυθὼς ἔτυχεν εἰς
7 Σαρδόνα μετὰ τῶν στρατοπέδων, οἱ δ᾽ ἐν τῇ Ῥώμῃ
πάντες περιδεεῖς ἦσαν, μέγαν καὶ φοβερὸν αὐτοῖς
ὑπολαμβάνοντες ἐπιφέρεσθαι κίνδυνον. ἔπασχον δὲ
τοῦτ᾽ εἰκότως, ἔτι περὶ Γαλατῶν ἐγκαθημένου ταῖς
8 ψυχαῖς αὐτῶν τοῦ παλαιοῦ φόβου. διὸ καὶ πρὸς ταύτην ἀναφέροντες τὴν ἔννοιαν τὰ μὲν συνήθροιζον, τὰ
δὲ κατέγραφον στρατόπεδα, τοῖς δ᾽ ἑτοίμοις εἶναι
9 παρήγγελλον τῶν συμμάχων. καθόλου δὲ τοῖς ὑποτε-
ταγμένοις ἀναφέρειν ἐπέταξαν ἀπογραφὰς τῶν ἐν
ταῖς ἡλικίαις, σπουδάζοντες εἰδέναι τὸ σύμπαν πλῆ-
10 θος τῆς ὑπαρχούσης αὐτοῖς δυνάμεως. σίτου δὲ καὶ
βελῶν καὶ τῆς ἄλλης ἐπιτηδειότητος πρὸς πόλεμον
τηλικαύτην ἐποιήσαντο κατασκευὴν ἡλίκην οὐδείς πω
11 μνημονεύει πρότερον. συνηργεῖτο δ᾽ αὐτοῖς πάντα καὶ
12 πανταχόθεν ἑτοίμως. καταπεπληγμένοι γὰρ οἱ τὴν
Ἰταλίαν οἰκοῦντες τὴν τῶν Γαλατῶν ἔφοδον, οὐκέτι
Ῥωμαίοις ἡγοῦντο συμμαχεῖν οὐδὲ περὶ τῆς τούτων
ἡγεμονίας γίνεσθαι τὸν πόλεμον, ἀλλὰ περὶ σφῶν
ἐνόμιζον ἕκαστοι καὶ τῆς ἰδίας πόλεως καὶ χώρας ἐπι-
13 φέρεσθαι τὸν κίνδυνον. διόπερ ἑτοίμως τοῖς παραγ-
γελλομένοις ὑπήκουον.

24. Ἵνα δὲ συμφανὲς ἐπ᾽ αὐτῶν γένηται τῶν ἔργων

Romans, the moment they heard that the Gauls had crossed the Alps, sent Lucius Aemilius, their Consul, with his army to Ariminum to await here the attack of the enemy, and one of their Praetors to Etruria, their other Consul, Gaius Atilius having already gone to Sardinia with his legions. There was great and general alarm in Rome, as they thought they were in imminent and serious peril, and this indeed was but natural, as the terror the old invasion had inspired still dwelt in their minds. No one thought of anything else therefore, they busied themselves mustering and enrolling their own legions and ordered those of the allies to be in readiness. All their subjects in general were commanded to supply lists of men of military age,[48] as they wished to know what their total forces amounted to. Of corn, missiles and other war material they had laid in such a supply as no one could remember to have been collected on any previous occasion. On every side there was a ready disposition to help in every possible way; for the inhabitants of Italy, terror-struck by the invasion of the Gauls, no longer thought of themselves as the allies of Rome or regarded this war as undertaken to establish Roman supremacy, but every man considered that the peril was descending on himself and his own city and country. So there was great alacrity in obeying orders.

24. But, that it may appear from actual facts what a

[48] Those 18 to 46 years inclusive: *RE* Iuniores 959–960 (A. Rosenberg).

ἡλίκοις Ἀννίβας ἐτόλμησε πράγμασιν ἐπιθέσθαι
[μετὰ δὲ ταῦτα] καὶ πρὸς ἡλίκην δυναστείαν παραβόλως ἀντοφθαλμήσας ἐπὶ τοσοῦτο καθίκετο τῆς
προθέσεως ὥστε τοῖς μεγίστοις συμπτώμασι περι-
2 βάλλειν Ῥωμαίους, ῥητέον ἂν εἴη τὴν παρασκευὴν
3 καὶ τὸ πλῆθος τῆς ὑπαρχούσης αὐτοῖς τότε δυνάμεως.
μετὰ μὲν δὴ τῶν ὑπάτων ἐξεληλύθει τέτταρα στρατόπεδα Ῥωμαϊκά, πεντάκις μὲν χιλίους καὶ διακο-
4 σίους πεζικούς, ἱππεῖς δὲ τριακοσίους ἔχον ἕκαστον.
σύμμαχοι δὲ μεθ᾽ ἑκατέρων ἦσαν οἱ συνάμφω πεζοὶ
5 μὲν τρισμύριοι, δισχίλιοι δ᾽ ἱππεῖς. τῶν δ᾽ ἐκ τοῦ
καιροῦ προσβοηθησάντων εἰς τὴν Ῥώμην Σαβίνων
καὶ Τυρρηνῶν ἱππεῖς μὲν ἦσαν εἰς τετρακισχιλίους,
6 πεζοὶ δὲ πλείους τῶν πεντακισμυρίων. τούτους μὲν
ἀθροίσαντες ὡς ἐπὶ Τυρρηνίας προεκάθισαν, ἐξαπ-
7 έλεκυν αὐτοῖς ἡγεμόνα συστήσαντες. οἱ δὲ τὸν Ἀπεννῖνον κατοικοῦντες Ὄμβροι καὶ Σαρσινάτοι συνήχθη-
σαν εἰς δισμυρίους, μετὰ δὲ τούτων Οὐένετοι καὶ
8 Γονομάνοι δισμύριοι. τούτους δ᾽ ἔταξαν ἐπὶ τῶν ὅρων
τῆς Γαλατίας, ἵν᾽ ἐμβαλόντες εἰς τὴν τῶν Βοίων χώραν ἀντιπερισπῶσι τοὺς ἐξεληλυθότας. τὰ μὲν οὖν
9 προκαθήμενα στρατόπεδα τῆς χώρας ταῦτ᾽ ἦν. ἐν δὲ
τῇ Ῥώμῃ διέτριβον ἡτοιμασμένοι χάριν τῶν συμβαινόντων ἐν τοῖς πολέμοις, ἐφεδρείας ἔχοντες τάξιν,
Ῥωμαίων μὲν αὐτῶν πεζοὶ δισμύριοι, μετὰ δὲ τούτων
ἱππεῖς χίλιοι καὶ πεντακόσιοι, τῶν δὲ συμμάχων πεζοὶ
10 μὲν τρισμύριοι, δισχίλιοι δ᾽ ἱππεῖς. καταγραφαὶ δ᾽
ἀνηνέχθησαν Λατίνων μὲν ὀκτακισμύριοι πεζοί, πεν-

great power it was that Hannibal ventured to attack, and how mighty was that empire boldly confronting which he came so near his purpose as to bring great disasters on Rome, I must state what were their resources and the actual number of their forces[49] at this time. The Consuls were in command of four legions of Roman citizens, each consisting of five thousand two hundred foot and three hundred horse. The allied forces in each Consular army numbered thirty thousand foot and two thousand horse. The cavalry of the Sabines and Etruscans, who had come to the temporary assistance of Rome, were four thousand strong, their infantry above fifty thousand. The Romans massed these forces and posted them on the frontier of Etruria under the command of a Praetor. The levy of the Umbrians and Sarsinates inhabiting the Apennines amounted to about twenty thousand, and with these were twenty thousand Veneti and Cenomani. These they stationed on the frontier of Gaul, to invade the territory of the Boii and divert them back from their expedition. These were the armies protecting the Roman territory. In Rome itself there was a reserve force, ready for any war contingency, consisting of twenty thousand foot and fifteen hundred horse, all Roman citizens, and thirty thousand foot and two thousand horse furnished by the allies. The lists of men able to bear arms that had been returned were as follows. Latins eighty thousand foot and five thousand horse,

[49] P's. figures (through 24. 16) go back to official records. Even so, problems abound. For details see WC 1. 196–203 with bibliography and P. A. Brunt, *Italian Manpower, 225 B C.–A.D. 14* (Oxford 1971).

τακισχίλιοι δ' ἱππεῖς, Σαυνιτῶν δὲ πεζοὶ μὲν ἑπτακισ-
11 μύριοι, μετὰ δὲ τούτων ἱππεῖς ἑπτακισχίλιοι, καὶ μὴν
Ἰαπύγων καὶ Μεσσαπίων συνάμφω πεζῶν μὲν πέντε
12 μυριάδες, ἱππεῖς δὲ μύριοι σὺν ἑξακισχιλίοις, Λευκα-
νῶν δὲ πεζοὶ μὲν τρισμύριοι, τρισχίλιοι δ' ἱππεῖς,
Μαρσῶν δὲ καὶ Μαρρουκίνων καὶ Φρεντανῶν, ἔτι δ'
13 Οὐεστίνων, πεζοὶ μὲν δισμύριοι, τετρακισχίλιοι δ'
ἱππεῖς. ἔτι γε μὴν κἂν Σικελίᾳ καὶ Τάραντι στρατόπεδα δύο παρεφήδρευεν, ὧν ἑκάτερον ἦν ἀνὰ τετρακισχιλίους καὶ διακοσίους πεζούς, ἱππεῖς δὲ διακο-
14 σίους. Ῥωμαίων δὲ καὶ Καμπανῶν ἡ πληθὺς πεζῶν
μὲν εἰς εἴκοσι καὶ πέντε κατελέχθησαν μυριάδες,
ἱππέων δ' ἐπὶ ταῖς δύο μυριάσιν ἐπῆσαν ἔτι τρεῖς
15 χιλιάδες. ὥστ' εἶναι τὸ [κεφάλαιον τῶν μὲν προκαθη-
μένων τῆς Ῥώμης δυνάμεων πεζοὶ μὲν ὑπὲρ πεντεκαί-
16 δεκα μυριάδες, ἱππεῖς δὲ πρὸς ἑξακισχιλίους, τὸ δὲ]
σύμπαν πλῆθος τῶν δυναμένων ὅπλα βαστάζειν αὐτῶν τε Ῥωμαίων καὶ τῶν συμμάχων πεζῶν ὑπὲρ τὰς
17 ἑβδομήκοντα μυριάδας, ἱππέων δ' εἰς ἑπτὰ μυριάδας.
ἐφ' οὓς Ἀννίβας ἐλάττους ἔχων δισμυρίων ἐπέβαλεν
εἰς τὴν Ἰταλίαν. περὶ μὲν οὖν τούτων ἐν τοῖς ἑξῆς
σαφέστερον ἐκποιήσει κατανοεῖν.

25. Οἱ δὲ Κελτοὶ κατάραντες εἰς τὴν Τυρρηνίαν
ἐπεπορεύοντο τὴν χώραν, πορθοῦντες ἀδεῶς· οὐδενὸς
δ' αὐτοῖς ἀντιταττομένου, τέλος ἐπ' αὐτὴν ὥρμησαν
2 τὴν Ῥώμην. ἤδη δ' αὐτῶν περὶ πόλιν ὄντων ἣ καλεῖται
μὲν Κλούσιον, ἀπέχει δ' ἡμερῶν τριῶν ὁδὸν ἀπὸ τῆς
Ῥώμης, προσαγγέλλεται διότι κατόπιν αὐτοῖς ἕπον-

Samnites seventy thousand foot and seven thousand horse, Iapygians and Messapians fifty thousand foot and sixteen thousand horse in all, Lucanians thirty thousand foot and three thousand horse, Marsi, Marrucini, Frentani, and Vestini twenty thousand foot and four thousand horse. In Sicily and Tarentum were two reserve legions, each consisting of about four thousand two hundred foot and two hundred horse. Of Romans and Campanians there were on the roll two hundred and fifty thousand and twenty-three thousand horse; so that the total number[50] of Romans and allies able to bear arms was more than seven hundred thousand foot and seventy thousand horse, while Hannibal invaded Italy with an army of less than twenty thousand[51] men. On this matter I shall be able to give my readers more explicit information in the course of this work.

25. The Celts, descending on Etruria, overran the country devastating it without let or hindrance and, as nobody appeared to oppose them, they marched on Rome itself. When they had got as far as Clusium,[52] a city three days' journey from Rome, news reached them that the

[50] The bracketed paragraph is probably a gloss, as most editors assume.

[51] P. here neglects Hannibal's cavalry of 6,000 (for the corrected figure see WC 3. 761).

[52] Modern Chiusi, 160 km north of Rome.

ται καὶ συνάπτουσιν αἱ προκαθήμεναι τῶν Ῥωμαίων

3 ἐν τῇ Τυρρηνίᾳ δυνάμεις. οἱ δ' ἀκούσαντες ἐξ ὑπο-

4 στροφῆς ἀπήντων, σπεύδοντες τούτοις συμβαλεῖν. ἐγγίσαντες δ' ἀλλήλοις ἤδη περὶ δυσμὰς ἡλίου, τότε μὲν ἐν συμμέτρῳ διαστήματι καταστρατοπεδεύσαντες

5 ηὐλίσθησαν ἀμφότεροι. τῆς δὲ νυκτὸς ἐπιγενομένης πῦρ ἀνακαύσαντες οἱ Κελτοὶ τοὺς μὲν ἱππεῖς ἀπέλι- πον, συντάξαντες ἅμα τῷ φωτὶ συμφανεῖς γενομένους

6 τοῖς πολεμίοις ὑποχωρεῖν κατὰ τὸν αὐτὸν στίβον. αὐτοὶ δὲ λαθραίαν ποιησάμενοι τὴν ἀποχώρησιν ὡς ἐπὶ πόλιν Φαισόλαν, αὐτοῦ παρενέβαλον, πρόθεσιν ἔχοντες ἅμα μὲν ἐκδέχεσθαι τοὺς ἑαυτῶν ἱππεῖς, ἅμα

7 δὲ παραδόξως ἐνοχλῆσαι τὴν τῶν ὑπεναντίων ἔφοδον. οἱ δὲ Ῥωμαῖοι τῆς ἡμέρας ἐπιγενομένης συνιδόντες τοὺς ἱππεῖς αὐτούς, καὶ νομίσαντες τοὺς Κελτοὺς ἀποδεδρακέναι, κατὰ σπουδὴν ἠκολούθουν τοῖς ἱπ-

8 πεῦσι κατὰ τὴν ἐκείνων ἀποχώρησιν. ἅμα δὲ τῷ συν- εγγίζειν τοῖς πολεμίοις διαναστάντων τῶν Κελτῶν, καὶ συμπεσόντων αὐτοῖς, ἦν ἀγὼν τὰς ἀρχὰς ἐξ

9 ἀμφοῖν βίαιος. τέλος δὲ καθυπερεχόντων τῶν Κελτῶν τῇ τόλμῃ καὶ τῷ πλήθει, συνέβη διαφθαρῆναι μὲν τῶν Ῥωμαίων οὐκ ἐλάττους ἑξακισχιλίων, τοὺς δὲ λοιποὺς φεύγειν· ὧν οἱ πλείους πρός τινα τόπον ἐρυμνὸν ἀπο-

10 χωρήσαντες ἔμενον. οὓς τὸ μὲν πρῶτον οἱ Κελτοὶ πολιορκεῖν ἐπεβάλοντο· κακῶς δ' ἀπαλλάττοντες ἐκ τῆς προγεγενημένης ἐν τῇ νυκτὶ πορείας καὶ κακο- παθείας καὶ ταλαιπωρίας, ὥρμησαν πρὸς ἀνάπαυσιν καὶ θεραπείαν, φυλακὴν ἀπολιπόντες τῶν ἰδίων ἱπ-

advanced force which the Romans had posted in Etruria was on their heels and approaching. On hearing this, they turned to meet it, eager to engage it. At sunset the two armies were in close proximity, and encamped for the night at no great distance from each other. After nightfall, the Celts lit their campfires, and, leaving orders with their cavalry to wait until daybreak and then, when visible to the enemy, to follow on their track, they themselves secretly retreated to a town called Faesulae and they drew up for battle there, their intention being to wait for their cavalry, and also to put unexpected difficulties in the way of the enemy's attack. At daybreak, the Romans, seeing the cavalry alone and thinking the Celts had taken to flight, followed the cavalry with all speed on the line of the Celts' retreat. On their approaching the enemy, the Celts left their position and attacked them, and a conflict, at first very stubborn, took place, in which finally the numbers and courage of the Celts prevailed, not fewer than six thousand Romans falling and the rest taking to flight. Most of them retreated to a hill of some natural strength where they remained. The Celts at first attempted to take this by storm, but as they were getting the worst of it, fatigued as they were by their long night march and the suffering and hardships it involved, they hastened to rest and refresh themselves, leaving a detachment of their cavalry to keep guard round

11 πέων περὶ τὸν λόφον, πρόθεσιν ἔχοντες κατὰ τὴν
ἐπιοῦσαν πολιορκεῖν τοὺς συμπεφευγότας, ἐὰν μὴ
παραδῶσιν ἑαυτοὺς ἑκουσίως.

26. Κατὰ δὲ τὸν καιρὸν τοῦτον Λεύκιος Αἰμίλιος ὁ
προκαθήμενος ἐπὶ τῶν κατὰ τὸν Ἀδρίαν τόπων ἀκούσας τοὺς Κελτοὺς διὰ Τυρρηνίας ἐμβεβληκότας συνεγγίζειν τῇ Ῥώμῃ, παρῆν βοηθῶν κατὰ σπουδὴν
2 εὐτυχῶς εἰς δέοντα καιρόν. καταστρατοπεδεύσαντος δ᾽
αὐτοῦ σύνεγγυς τῶν πολεμίων, κατιδόντες τὰ πυρὰ
καὶ νοήσαντες τὸ γεγονὸς οἱ συμπεφευγότες ἐπὶ τὸν
λόφον, ταχέως ἀναθαρρήσαντες ἐξαπέστειλαν αὑτῶν
τινας τῆς νυκτὸς ἀνόπλους διὰ τῆς ὕλης ἀναγγε-
3 λοῦντας τῷ στρατηγῷ τὸ συμβεβηκός. ὁ δὲ διακούσας, καὶ θεωρῶν οὐδὲ διαβούλιον αὐτῷ καταλειπόμενον ὑπὲρ τῶν ἐνεστώτων, τοῖς μὲν χιλιάρχοις
ἅμα τῷ φωτὶ παρήγγειλε τοὺς πεζοὺς ἐξάγειν, αὐτὸς
δὲ τοὺς ἱππεῖς ἀναλαβὼν καθηγεῖτο τῆς δυνάμεως,
4 ποιούμενος τὴν πορείαν ἐπὶ τὸν προειρημένον βουνόν.
οἱ δὲ τῶν Γαλατῶν ἡγεμόνες, ἀφορῶντες τὰ πυρὰ τῆς
νυκτὸς καὶ συλλογιζόμενοι τὴν παρουσίαν τῶν πολε-
5 μίων συνήδρευον. οἷς Ἀνηροέστης ὁ βασιλεὺς γνώμην εἰσέφερε λέγων ὅτι δεῖ τοσαύτης λείας ἐγκρατεῖς
γεγονότας, ἦν γάρ, ὡς ἔοικε, καὶ τὸ τῶν σωμάτων καὶ
θρεμμάτων πλῆθος, ἔτι δὲ τῆς ἀποσκευῆς ἧς εἶχον,
6 ἀμύθητον· διόπερ ἔφη δεῖν μὴ κινδυνεύειν ἔτι μηδὲ
παραβάλλεσθαι τοῖς ὅλοις, ἀλλ᾽ εἰς τὴν οἰκείαν ἀδεῶς
ἐπανάγειν· ταῦτα δ᾽ ἀποσκευασαμένους καὶ γενομένους εὐζώνους αὖθις ἐγχειρεῖν ὁλοσχερῶς, ἐὰν δοκῇ,

the hill, intending next day to make an assault on the fugitives, if they did not offer to surrender.

26. At this very time Lucius Aemilius,[53] who was in command of the advanced force near the Adriatic, on hearing that the Celts had invaded Etruria and were approaching Rome, came in haste to help, fortunately arriving in the nick of time. He encamped near the enemy, and the fugitives on the hill, seeing his campfires and understanding what had occurred, immediately plucked up courage and dispatched by night some unarmed messengers through the wood to announce to the commander the plight they were in. On hearing of it and seeing that there was no alternative course under the circumstances, the latter ordered his Tribunes to march out the infantry at daybreak, he himself proceeding in advance with the cavalry toward the hill mentioned above. The leaders of the Gauls, on seeing the campfires at night, surmised that the enemy had arrived and held a council at which the King Aneroëstes expressed the opinion, that having captured so much booty (for it appears that the quantity of prisoners, cattle and miscellaneous spoil was enormous), they should not give battle again nor risk the fortune of the whole enterprise, but return home in safety, and having got rid of all their encumbrances and lightened themselves, return

[53] The consul.

7 τοῖς Ῥωμαίων πράγμασι. δόξαντος δὲ σφίσι κατὰ τὴν
Ἀνηροέστου γνώμην χρήσασθαι τοῖς παροῦσιν, οὗτοι
μὲν τῆς νυκτὸς ταῦτα βουλευσάμενοι, πρὸ φωτὸς
ἀναζεύξαντες προῆγον παρὰ θάλατταν διὰ τῆς Τυρ-
8 ρηνῶν χώρας. ὁ δὲ Λεύκιος, ἀναλαβὼν ἐκ τοῦ βουνοῦ
τὸ διασῳζόμενον τοῦ στρατοπέδου μέρος ἅμα ταῖς
ἰδίαις δυνάμεσι, τὸ μὲν διακινδυνεύειν ἐκ παρατάξεως
οὐδαμῶς ἔκρινε συμφέρειν, ἐπιτηρεῖν δὲ μᾶλλον καιροὺς καὶ τόπους εὐφυεῖς, ἑπόμενος, ἐάν πού τι βλάψαι
τοὺς πολεμίους ἢ τῆς λείας ἀποσπάσαι δυνηθῇ.

27. Κατὰ δὲ τοὺς καιροὺς τούτους ἐκ Σαρδόνος
μετὰ τῶν στρατοπέδων Γάιος Ἀτίλιος ὕπατος εἰς Πίσας καταπεπλευκὼς προῆγε μετὰ τῆς δυνάμεως εἰς
Ῥώμην, ἐναντίαν ποιούμενος τοῖς πολεμίοις τὴν πο-
2 ρείαν. ἤδη δὲ περὶ Τελαμῶνα τῆς Τυρρηνίας τῶν
Κελτῶν ὑπαρχόντων, οἱ προνομεύοντες ἐξ αὐτῶν ἐμπεσόντες εἰς τοὺς παρὰ τοῦ Γαΐου προπορευομένους
3 ἑάλωσαν· καὶ τά τε προγεγονότα διεσάφουν ἀνακρι-
νόμενοι τῷ στρατηγῷ καὶ τὴν παρουσίαν ἀμφοτέρων
τῶν στρατοπέδων ἀνήγγελλον, σημαίνοντες διότι τε-
λείως σύνεγγύς εἰσιν οἱ Κελτοὶ καὶ τούτων κατόπιν οἱ
4 περὶ τὸν Λεύκιον. ὁ δὲ τὰ μὲν ξενισθεὶς ἐπὶ τοῖς
προσπίπτουσι, τὰ δ᾽ εὔελπις γενόμενος ἐπὶ τῷ δοκεῖν
μέσους κατὰ πορείαν ἀπειληφέναι τοὺς Κελτούς, τοῖς
μὲν χιλιάρχοις παρήγγειλε τάττειν τὰ στρατόπεδα,
καὶ βάδην εἰς τοὔμπροσθεν προάγειν, καθ᾽ ὅσον ἂν οἱ
5 τόποι προσδέχωνται τὴν μετωπηδὸν ἔφοδον. Αὐτὸς δὲ
συνθεωρήσας εὐκαίρως λόφον κείμενον ὑπὲρ τὴν

and, if advisable, try issues with the Romans. It was decided under the circumstances to take the course recommended by Aneroëstes, and having come to this resolution
in the night, they broke up their camp before daybreak and
retreated along the sea coast through Etruria. Lucius now
took with him from the hill the survivors of the other army
and united them with his other forces. He thought it by no
means advisable to risk a general battle, but decided to
hang on the enemy's rear and watch for times and places
favorable for inflicting damage on them or wresting some
of the spoil from their hands.

27. Just at this time, Gaius Atilius,[54] the other Consul,
had reached Pisa from Sardinia with his legions and was on
his way to Rome, marching in the opposite direction to the
enemy. When the Celts were near Telamon in Etruria,[55]
their foragers encountered the advance guard of Gaius
and were made prisoners. On being examined by the Consul they narrated all that had recently occurred and told
him of the presence of the two armies, stating that the
Gauls were quite near and Lucius behind them. The news
surprised him but at the same time made him very hopeful, as he thought he had caught the Gauls on the march
between the two armies. He ordered his Tribunes to put
the legions in fighting order and to advance thus at marching pace in so far as the nature of the ground allowed the
attack in line. He himself had happily noticed a hill situ-

[54] By chance, the other consul arrives from Sardinia at Pisa
and marches south, so that the Celts find themselves at Telamon
between two consular armies.

[55] *RE* Telamon no. 4, 192–193 and Suppl. 6, 1169–1171 (H.
Philipp).

337

ὁδόν, ὑφ᾽ ὃν ἔδει παραπορευθῆναι τοὺς Κελτούς, ἀναλαβὼν τοὺς ἱππεῖς, ὥρμησε σπεύδων προκαταλα-
βέσθαι τὴν ἀκρολοφίαν καὶ πρῶτος κατάρξαι τοῦ
κινδύνου, πεπεισμένος τῆς ἐπιγραφῆς τῶν ἐκβαινόν-
6 των πλεῖστον οὕτω κληρονομήσειν. οἱ δὲ Κελτοὶ τὸ
μὲν πρῶτον τὴν παρουσίαν τῶν περὶ τὸν Ἀτίλιον
ἀγνοοῦντες, ἐκ δὲ τοῦ συμβαίνοντος ὑπολαμβάνοντες
τοὺς περὶ τὸν Αἰμίλιον περιπεπορεῦσθαι τὴν νύκτα
τοῖς ἱππεῦσι καὶ προκαταλαμβάνεσθαι τοὺς τόπους,
εὐθέως ἐξαπέστελλον τοὺς παρ᾽ αὑτῶν ἱππεῖς καί
τινας τῶν εὐζώνων, ἀντιποιησομένους τῶν κατὰ τὸν
7 βουνὸν τόπων. ταχὺ δὲ συνέντες τὴν τοῦ Γαΐου παρουσίαν ἔκ τινος τῶν ἀχθέντων αἰχμαλώτων, σπουδῇ
παρενέβαλον τοὺς πεζούς, ποιούμενοι τὴν ἔκταξιν
ἅμα πρὸς ἑκατέραν τὴν ἐπιφάνειαν, καὶ τὴν ἀπ᾽ οὐρᾶς
8 καὶ τὴν κατὰ πρόσωπον· οὓς μὲν γὰρ ᾔδεσαν ἑπομένους αὐτοῖς, οὓς δὲ κατὰ τὸ στόμα προσεδόκων ἀπαν-
τήσειν, ἔκ τε τῶν προσαγγελλομένων τεκμαιρόμενοι
καὶ τῶν κατ᾽ αὐτὸν τὸν καιρὸν συμβαινόντων.

28. οἱ δὲ περὶ τὸν Αἰμίλιον ἀκηκοότες μὲν τὸν εἰς
τὰς Πίσας κατάπλουν τῶν στρατοπέδων, οὔπω δὲ
προσδοκῶντες αὐτὰ συνεγγίζειν, τότε σαφῶς ἐκ τοῦ
περὶ τὸν λόφον ἀγῶνος ἔγνωσαν διότι τελέως ἐγγὺς
2 εἶναι συμβαίνει τὰς οἰκείας αὐτῶν δυνάμεις. διὸ καὶ
τοὺς μὲν ἱππεῖς παραυτίκα βοηθήσοντας ἐξαπέστελλον τοῖς ἐν τῷ λόφῳ διαγωνιζομένοις, αὐτοὶ δὲ κατὰ
τὰς εἰθισμένας τάξεις διακοσμήσαντες τοὺς πεζοὺς
3 προῆγον ἐπὶ τοὺς ὑπεναντίους. οἱ δὲ Κελτοὶ τοὺς μὲν

ated above the road by which the Celts must pass, and taking his cavalry with him, advanced at full speed, being anxious to occupy the crest of the hill before their arrival and be the first to begin the battle, feeling certain that thus he would get the largest share of credit for the result. The Celts at first were ignorant of the arrival of Atilius and imagined from what they saw, that Aemilius' cavalry had got round their flank in the night and were engaged in occupying the position. They therefore at once sent on their own cavalry and some of their light-armed troops to dispute the possession of the hill. But very soon they learnt of Gaius' presence from one of the prisoners brought in, and lost no time in drawing up their infantry, deploying them so that they faced both front and rear, since, both from the intelligence that reached them and from what was happening before their eyes, they knew that the one army was following them, and they expected to meet the other in their front.

28. Aemilius, who had heard of the landing of the legions at Pisa but had not any idea that they were already so near him, now, when he saw the fight going on round the hill, knew that the other Roman army was quite close. Accordingly, sending on his cavalry to help those who were fighting on the hill, he drew up his infantry in the usual order and advanced against the foe. The Celts had drawn

ἐκ τῶν Ἄλπεων Γαισάτους προσαγορευομένους ἔταξαν πρὸς τὴν ἀπ' οὐρᾶς ἐπιφάνειαν ᾗ προσεδόκων
τοὺς περὶ τὸν Αἰμίλιον, ἐπὶ δὲ τούτοις τοὺς Ἴνσομ-
4 βρας· πρὸς δὲ τὴν κατὰ πρόσωπον τοὺς Ταυρίσκους
καὶ τοὺς ἐπὶ τάδε τοῦ Πάδου κατοικοῦντας Βοίους
παρενέβαλον, τὴν ἐναντίαν μὲν στάσιν ἔχοντας τοῖς
προειρημένοις, βλέποντας δὲ πρὸς τὴν τῶν τοῦ Γαΐου
5 στρατοπέδων ἔφοδον. τὰς δ' ἁμάξας καὶ συνωρίδας
ἐκτὸς ἑκατέρου τοῦ κέρατος παρέστησαν, τὴν δὲ λείαν
εἴς τι τῶν παρακειμένων ὀρῶν φυλακὴν περιστήσαν-
6 τες ἤθροιζον. γενομένης δ' ἀμφιστόμου τῆς τῶν Κελτῶν δυνάμεως, οὐ μόνον καταπληκτικήν, ἀλλὰ καὶ
7 πρακτικὴν εἶναι συνέβαινε τὴν τάξιν. οἱ μὲν οὖν
Ἴνσομβρες καὶ Βοῖοι τὰς ἀναξυρίδας ἔχοντες καὶ
8 τοὺς εὐπετεῖς τῶν σάγων περὶ αὐτοὺς ἐξέταξαν. οἱ δὲ
Γαισάται διά τε τὴν φιλοδοξίαν καὶ τὸ θάρσος ταῦτ'
ἀπορρίψαντες γυμνοὶ μετ' αὐτῶν τῶν ὅπλων πρῶτοι
τῆς δυνάμεως κατέστησαν, ὑπολαβόντες οὕτως ἔσεσθαι πρακτικώτατοι, διὰ τό τινας τῶν τόπων βατώδεις
ὄντας ἐμπλέκεσθαι τοῖς ἐφάμμασι καὶ παραποδίζειν
9 τὴν τῶν ὅπλων χρείαν. τὸ μὲν οὖν πρῶτον αὐτὸς ὁ
κατὰ τὸν λόφον ἐνειστήκει κίνδυνος, ἅπασιν ὢν σύν-
οπτος, ὡς ἂν ἅμα τοσούτου πλήθους ἱππέων ἀφ'
ἑκάστου τῶν στρατοπέδων ἀναμὶξ ἀλλήλοις συμπε-
10 πτωκότος. ἐν δὲ τούτῳ τῷ καιρῷ συνέβη Γάιον μὲν τὸν
ὕπατον παραβόλως ἀγωνιζόμενον ἐν χειρῶν νόμῳ
τελευτῆσαι τὸν βίον, τὴν δὲ κεφαλὴν αὐτοῦ πρὸς τοὺς
βασιλέας ἐπανενεχθῆναι τῶν Κελτῶν· τοὺς δὲ τῶν

up facing their rear, from which they expected Aemilius to attack, the Gaesatae from the Alps and behind them the Insubres, and facing in the opposite direction, ready to meet the attack of Gaius' legions, they placed the Taurisci and the Boii from the right bank of the Po. Their wagons and chariots they stationed at the extremity of either wing and collected their booty on one of the neighboring hills with a protecting force round it. This order of the Celtic forces, facing both ways, not only presented a formidable appearance, but was well adapted to the exigencies of the situation. The Insubres and Boii drew up for battle wearing their trousers and light cloaks, but the Gaesatae had discarded these garments owing to their proud confidence in themselves, and stood naked, with nothing but their arms, in front of the whole army, thinking that thus they would be more efficient, as some of the ground was overgrown with brambles which would catch in their clothes and impede the use of their weapons. At first the battle was confined to the hill, all the armies gazing on it, so great were the numbers of cavalry from each host combating there pell-mell. In this action Gaius the Consul fell in the mellay fighting with desperate courage, and his head was brought to the Celtic kings; but the Roman cavalry, after a

THE HISTORIES OF POLYBIUS

Ῥωμαίων ἱππεῖς, κινδυνεύσαντας ἐρρωμένως τέλος
11 ἐπικρατῆσαι τοῦ τόπου καὶ τῶν ὑπεναντίων. μετὰ δὲ
ταῦτα τῶν πεζικῶν στρατοπέδων ἤδη σύνεγγυς ὄντων
ἀλλήλοις ἴδιον ἦν καὶ θαυμαστὸν τὸ συμβαῖνον οὐ
μόνον τοῖς ἐν αὐτῷ τῷ καιρῷ τότε παροῦσιν, ἀλλὰ καὶ
τοῖς ποτε μετὰ ταῦτα δυναμένοις ὑπὸ τὴν ὄψιν λαμβάνειν ἐκ τῶν λεγομένων τὸ γεγονός.
29. πρῶτον μὲν γὰρ ἐκ τριῶν στρατοπέδων τῆς
μάχης συνισταμένης, δῆλον ὡς ξένην καὶ παρηλ-
λαγμένην εἰκὸς καὶ τὴν ἐπιφάνειαν καὶ τὴν χρείαν
2 φαίνεσθαι τοῦ συντεταγμένου. δεύτερον δὲ πῶς οὐκ ἂν
ἀπορῆσαι τις καὶ νῦν καὶ τότε παρ' αὐτὸν ὢν τὸν
καιρὸν πότερον οἱ Κελτοὶ τὴν ἐπισφαλεστάτην εἶχον
χώραν, ἐξ ἀμφοῖν τοῖν μεροῖν ἅμα τῶν πολεμίων
3 ἐπαγόντων αὐτοῖς, ἢ τοὐναντίον τὴν ἐπιτευκτικω-
τάτην, ἅμα μὲν ἀγωνιζόμενοι πρὸς ἀμφοτέρους, ἅμα
δὲ τὴν ἀφ' ἑκατέρων ἀσφάλειαν ἐκ τῶν ὄπισθεν αὐτοῖς
παρασκευάζοντες, τὸ δὲ μέγιστον ἀποκεκλειμένης
πάσης τῆς εἰς τοὔπισθεν ἀναχωρήσεως καὶ τῆς ἐν τῷ
4 λείπεσθαι σωτηρίας; ἡ γὰρ τῆς ἀμφιστόμου τάξεως
5 ἰδιότης τοιαύτην ἔχει τὴν χρείαν. τούς γε μὴν Ῥωμαίους τὰ μὲν εὐθαρσεῖς ἐποίει τὸ μέσους καὶ πάντο-
θεν περιειληφέναι τοὺς πολεμίους, τὰ δὲ πάλιν ὁ
κόσμος αὐτοὺς καὶ θόρυβος ἐξέπληττε τῆς τῶν Κελ-
6 τῶν δυνάμεως. ἀναρίθμητον μὲν γὰρ ἦν τὸ τῶν βυκα-
νητῶν καὶ σαλπιγκτῶν πλῆθος. οἷς ἅμα τοῦ παντὸς
στρατοπέδου συμπαιανίζοντος τηλικαύτην καὶ τοιαύτην συνέβαινε γίνεσθαι κραυγὴν ὥστε μὴ μόνον

342

stubborn struggle, at length overmastered the enemy and gained possession of the hill. The infantry were now close upon each other, and the spectacle was a strange and marvellous one, not only to those actually present at the battle, but to all who could afterward picture it to themselves from the reports.

29. For in the first place, as the battle was between three armies, it is evident that the appearance and the movements of the forces marshaled against each other must have been in the highest degree strange and unusual. Again, it must have been to all present, and still is to us, a matter of doubt whether the Celts, with the enemy advancing on them from both sides, were more dangerously situated, or, on the contrary, more effectively, since at one and the same time they were fighting against both their enemies and were protecting themselves in the rear from both, while, above all, they were absolutely cut off from retreat or any prospect of escape in the case of defeat, this being the peculiarity of this two-faced formation. The Romans, however, were on the one hand encouraged by having caught the enemy between their two armies, but on the other they were terrified by the fine order of the Celtic host and the dreadful din, for there were innumerable horn-blowers and trumpeters, and, as the whole army were shouting their war cries at the same time, there was such a tumult of sound that it seemed that not only the

τὰς σάλπιγγας καὶ τὰς δυνάμεις, ἀλλὰ καὶ τοὺς παρακειμένους τόπους συνηχοῦντας ἐξ αὐτῶν δοκεῖν προΐε-
7 σθαι φωνήν. ἐκπληκτικὴ δ᾽ ἦν καὶ τῶν γυμνῶν προεστώτων ἀνδρῶν ἥ τ᾽ ἐπιφάνεια καὶ κίνησις, ὡς ἂν
8 διαφερόντων ταῖς ἀκμαῖς καὶ τοῖς εἴδεσι. πάντες δ᾽ οἱ
τὰς πρώτας κατέχοντες σπείρας χρυσοῖς μανιάκαις
9 καὶ περιχείροις ἦσαν κατακεκοσμημένοι. Πρὸς ἃ βλέ-
ποντες οἱ Ῥωμαῖοι τὰ μὲν ἐξεπλήττοντο, τὰ δ᾽ ὑπὸ τῆς
τοῦ λυσιτελοῦς ἐλπίδος ἀγόμενοι διπλασίως παρωξύ-
νοντο πρὸς τὸν κίνδυνον.

30. πλὴν ἅμα τῷ τοὺς ἀκοντιστὰς προελθόντας ἐκ
τῶν Ῥωμαϊκῶν στρατοπέδων κατὰ τὸν ἐθισμὸν εἰσακοντίζειν ἐνεργοῖς καὶ πυκνοῖς τοῖς βέλεσι, τοῖς μὲν
ὀπίσω τῶν Κελτῶν πολλὴν εὐχρηστίαν οἱ σάγοι μετὰ
2 τῶν ἀναξυρίδων παρεῖχον· τοῖς δὲ γυμνοῖς προεστῶσι
παρὰ τὴν προσδοκίαν τοῦ πράγματος συμβαίνοντος
τἀναντία πολλὴν ἀπορίαν καὶ δυσχρηστίαν παρεῖχε
3 τὸ γινόμενον. οὐ γὰρ δυναμένου τοῦ Γαλατικοῦ θυρεοῦ
τὸν ἄνδρα περισκέπειν, ὅσῳ γυμνὰ καὶ μείζω τὰ
σώματ᾽ ἦν, τοσούτῳ συνέβαινε μᾶλλον τὰ βέλη
4 πίπτειν ἔνδον. τέλος δ᾽ οὐ δυνάμενοι μὲν ἀμύνασθαι
τοὺς εἰσακοντίζοντας διὰ τὴν ἀπόστασιν καὶ τὸ
πλῆθος τῶν πιπτόντων βελῶν, περικακοῦντες δὲ καὶ
δυσχρηστούμενοι τοῖς παροῦσιν, οἱ μὲν εἰς τοὺς πολεμίους ὑπὸ τοῦ θυμοῦ καὶ τῆς ἀλογιστίας εἰκῆ προ-
πίπτοντες καὶ διδόντες σφᾶς αὐτοὺς ἑκουσίως ἀπέθνησκον, οἱ δ᾽ εἰς τοὺς φίλους ἀναχωροῦντες ἐπὶ
πόδα καὶ προδήλως ἀποδειλιῶντες διέστρεφον τοὺς

trumpets and the soldiers but all the country round had got a voice and caught up the cry. Very terrifying too were the appearance and the gestures of the naked warriors in front, all in the prime of life, and finely built men, and all in the leading companies richly adorned with gold torques and armlets. The sight of them indeed dismayed the Romans, but at the same time the prospect of winning such spoils made them twice as keen for the fight.

30. But when the javelineers advanced, as is their usage, from the ranks of the Roman legions and began to hurl their javelins thick and fast, the Celts in the rear ranks indeed were well protected by their trousers and cloaks, but it fell out far otherwise than they had expected with the naked men in front, and they found themselves in a very difficult and helpless predicament. For the Gaulish shield does not cover the whole body; so that their nakedness was a disadvantage, and the bigger they were the better chance had the missiles of going home. At length, unable to drive off the javelineers owing to the distance and the hail of javelins, and reduced to the utmost distress and perplexity, some of them, in their impotent rage, rushed wildly on the enemy and sacrificed their lives, while others, retreating step by step on the ranks of their comrades, threw them into disorder by their display of faintheartedness. Thus

5 κατόπιν. τὸ μὲν οὖν τῶν Γαισατῶν φρόνημα παρὰ τοῖς
6 ἀκοντισταῖς τούτῳ τῷ τρόπῳ κατελύθη, τὸ δὲ τῶν
Ἰνσόμβρων καὶ Βοίων ἔτι δὲ Ταυρίσκων πλῆθος ἅμα
τῷ τοὺς Ῥωμαίους δεξαμένους τοὺς ἑαυτῶν ἀκοντιστὰς προσβάλλειν σφίσι τὰς σπείρας συμπεσὸν
7 τοῖς πολεμίοις ἐκ χειρὸς ἐποίει μάχην ἐχυράν. δια-
κοπτόμενοι γὰρ ἔμενον ἐπ᾽ ἴσον ταῖς ψυχαῖς, αὐτῷ
τούτῳ καὶ καθόλου καὶ κατ᾽ ἄνδρα λειπόμενοι, ταῖς
8 τῶν ὅπλων κατασκευαῖς. οἱ μὲν οὖν θυρεοὶ πρὸς
ἀσφάλειαν, αἱ δὲ μάχαιραι πρὸς πρᾶξιν μεγάλην
διαφορὰν . . . ἔχειν, τὴν δὲ Γαλατικὴν καταφορὰν
9 ἔχειν μόνον. ἐπεὶ δ᾽ ἐξ ὑπερδεξίων καὶ κατὰ κέρας
οἱ τῶν Ῥωμαίων ἱππεῖς ἐμβαλόντες ἀπὸ τοῦ λόφου
προσέφερον τὰς χεῖρας ἐρρωμένως, τόθ᾽ οἱ μὲν πεζοὶ
τῶν Κελτῶν ἐν αὐτῷ τῷ τῆς παρατάξεως τόπῳ κατεκόπησαν, οἱ δ᾽ ἱππεῖς πρὸς φυγὴν ὥρμησαν.

31. Ἀπέθανον μὲν οὖν τῶν Κελτῶν εἰς τετρακισ-
μυρίους, ἑάλωσαν δ᾽ οὐκ ἐλάττους μυρίων, ἐν οἷς καὶ
2 τῶν βασιλέων Κογκολιτάνος. ὁ δ᾽ ἕτερος αὐτῶν Ἀνη-
ρόεστος εἴς τινα τόπον συμφυγὼν μετ᾽ ὀλίγων προσ-
3 ήνεγκε τὰς χεῖρας αὑτῷ καὶ τοῖς ἀναγκαίοις. ὁ δὲ
στρατηγὸς τῶν Ῥωμαίων τὰ μὲν σκῦλα συναθροίσας
εἰς τὴν Ῥώμην ἀπέστειλε, τὴν δὲ λείαν ἀπέδωκε τοῖς
4 προσήκουσιν. αὐτὸς δ᾽ ἀναλαβὼν τὰ στρατόπεδα καὶ
διελθὼν παρ᾽ αὐτὴν τὴν Λιγυστικὴν εἰς τὴν τῶν Βοίων
ἐνέβαλε χώραν. πληρώσας δὲ τὰς ὁρμὰς τῶν στρατοπέδων τῆς ὠφελείας ἐν ὀλίγαις ἡμέραις ἧκε μετὰ
5 τῶν δυνάμεων εἰς τὴν Ῥώμην. καὶ τὸ μὲν Καπετώλιον

was the spirit of the Gaesatae broken down by the javelineers; but the main body of the Insubres, Boii, and Taurisci, once the javelineers had withdrawn into the ranks and the Roman maniples attacked them, met the enemy and kept up a stubborn hand-to-hand combat. For, though being almost cut to pieces, they held their ground, equal to their foes in courage, and inferior only, as a force and individually, in their arms. The Roman shields, it should be added, were far more serviceable for defense and their swords for attack, the Gaulish sword being only good for a cut and not for a thrust. But finally, attacked from higher ground and on their flank by the Roman cavalry, which rode down the hill and charged them vigorously, the Celtic infantry were cut to pieces where they stood, their cavalry taking to flight.

31. About forty thousand Celts were slain and at least ten thousand taken prisoners, among them the king Concolitanus.[56] The other king, Aneroëstes, escaped with a few followers to a certain place where he put an end to his life and to those of his friends. The Roman Consul collected the spoils and sent them to Rome, returning the booty of the Gauls to the owners. With his legions he traversed Liguria and invaded the territory of the Boii, from whence, after letting his legions pillage to their heart's content, he returned at their head in a few days to Rome. He

[56] This king was killed in battle, the other, Aneroestes, took his own life after the battle was lost.

ἐκόσμησε ταῖς τε σημαίαις καὶ τοῖς μανιάκαις· τοῦτο
δ᾽ ἔστι χρυσοῦν ψέλιον, ὃ φοροῦσι περὶ τὸν τράχηλον
6 οἱ Γαλάται. τοῖς δὲ λοιποῖς σκύλοις καὶ τοῖς αἰχμα-
λώτοις πρὸς τὴν εἴσοδον ἐχρήσατο τὴν ἑαυτοῦ καὶ
πρὸς τὴν τοῦ θριάμβου διακόσμησιν.

7 Ἡ μὲν οὖν βαρυτάτη τῶν Κελτῶν ἔφοδος οὕτω καὶ
τούτῳ τῷ τρόπῳ διεφθάρη, πᾶσι μὲν Ἰταλιώταις,
μάλιστα δὲ Ῥωμαίοις, μέγαν καὶ φοβερὸν ἐπικρε-
8 μάσασα κίνδυνον. ἀπὸ δὲ τοῦ κατορθώματος τούτου
κατελπίσαντες Ῥωμαῖοι δυνήσεσθαι τοὺς Κελτοὺς ἐκ
τῶν τόπων τῶν περὶ τὸν Πάδον ὁλοσχερῶς ἐκβαλεῖν,
τούς τε μετὰ ταῦτα κατασταθέντας ὑπάτους Κόϊντον
Φόλουιον καὶ Τίτον Μάλιον ἀμφοτέρους καὶ τὰς δυνάμεις μετὰ παρασκευῆς μεγάλης ἐξαπέστειλαν ἐπὶ τοὺς
9 Κελτούς. οὗτοι δὲ τοὺς μὲν Βοίους ἐξ ἐφόδου καταπληξάμενοι συνηνάγκασαν εἰς τὴν Ῥωμαίων ἑαυτοὺς
10 δοῦναι πίστιν, τὸν δὲ λοιπὸν χρόνον τῆς στρατείας,
ἐπιγενομένων ὄμβρων ἐξαισίων, ἔτι δὲ λοιμικῆς διαθέσεως ἐμπεσούσης αὐτοῖς, εἰς τέλος ἄπρακτον εἶχον.

32. Μετὰ δὲ τούτους κατασταθέντες Πόπλιος Φού-
ριος καὶ Γάιος Φλαμίνιος αὖθις ἐνέβαλον εἰς τὴν
Κελτικὴν διὰ τῆς τῶν Ἀνάρων χώρας, οἷς συμβαίνει
2 μὴ μακρὰν ἀπὸ Μασσαλίας ἔχειν τὴν οἴκησιν. οὓς εἰς
τὴν φιλίαν προσαγαγόμενοι διέβησαν εἰς τὴν τῶν
Ἰνσόμβρων γῆν κατὰ τὰς συρροίας τοῦ τ᾽ Ἀδόα καὶ
3 Πάδου ποταμοῦ. λαβόντες δὲ πληγὰς περί τε τὴν
διάβασιν καὶ περὶ τὴν στρατοπεδείαν, παραυτίκα μὲν
ἔμειναν, μετὰ δὲ ταῦτα σπεισάμενοι καθ᾽ ὁμολογίαν

sent to ornament the Capitol the standards and necklaces
(the gold necklets worn by the Gauls), but the rest of the
spoil and the prisoners he used for his entry into Rome and
the adornment of his triumph.[57]

Thus were destroyed these Celts during whose invasion, the most serious that had ever occurred, all the Ital-
ians and especially the Romans had been exposed to great
and terrible peril. This success encouraged the Romans to
hope that they would be able entirely to expel the Celts
from the plain of the Po; and both the Consuls of the next
year, Quintus Fulvius and Titus Manlius, were sent against
them with a formidable expeditionary force. They sur-   224 B.C.
prised and terrified the Boii, compelling them to submit to
Rome, but the rest of the campaign had no practical results
whatever, owing to the very heavy rains, and an epidemic
which broke out among them.

32. Next year's Consuls, however, Publius Furius and   223 B.C.
Gaius Flaminius, again invaded the Celtic territory,
throughout the country of the Anares who dwelt not far
from Marseilles. Having admitted this tribe to their friendship, they crossed into the territory of the Insubres, near
the junction of the Po and Adda. Both in crossing and in
encamping on the other side, they suffered some loss, and
at first remained on the spot, but later made a truce and

[57] On March 5, 224 "De Galleis."

349

4 ἀνέλυσαν ἐκ τῶν τόπων. περιελθόντες δὲ πλείους ἡμέρας, καὶ διελθόντες τὸν Κλούσιον ποταμόν, ἦλθον εἰς
τὴν τῶν Γονομάνων χώραν, καὶ προσλαβόντες τούτους, ὄντας συμμάχους, ἐνέβαλον πάλιν ἀπὸ τῶν
κατὰ τὰς Ἄλπεις τόπων εἰς τὰ τῶν Ἰνσόμβρων πεδία
καὶ τήν τε γῆν ἐδῄουν καὶ τὰς κατοικίας αὐτῶν ἐξ-
5 επόρθουν. οἱ δὲ τῶν Ἰνσόμβρων προεστῶτες, θεωροῦντες ἀμετάθετον οὖσαν τὴν ἐπιβολὴν τῶν Ῥωμαίων, ἔκριναν τῆς τύχης λαβεῖν πεῖραν καὶ
6 διακινδυνεῦσαι πρὸς αὐτοὺς ὁλοσχερῶς. συναθροίσαντες οὖν ἁπάσας ⟨τὰς δυνάμεις⟩ ἐπὶ ταὐτόν, καὶ
τὰς χρυσᾶς σημαίας τὰς ἀκινήτους λεγομένας
καθελόντες ἐκ τοῦ τῆς Ἀθηνᾶς ἱεροῦ, καὶ τἆλλα παρασκευασάμενοι δεόντως, μετὰ ταῦτα τεθαρρηκότως καὶ
καταπληκτικῶς ἀντεστρατοπέδευσαν τοῖς πολεμίοις,
7 ὄντες τὸ πλῆθος εἰς πέντε μυριάδας. οἱ δὲ Ῥωμαῖοι, τὰ
μὲν ὁρῶντες σφᾶς ἐλάττους ὄντας παρὰ πολὺ τῶν
ἐναντίων, ἐβούλοντο συγχρῆσθαι ταῖς τῶν συμμα-
8 χούντων αὐτοῖς Κελτῶν δυνάμεσι· τὰ δὲ συλλογισάμενοι τήν τε Γαλατικὴν ἀθεσίαν καὶ διότι πρὸς
ὁμοφύλους τῶν προσλαμβανομένων μέλλουσι ποιεῖσθαι τὸν κίνδυνον, εὐλαβοῦντο τοιούτοις ἀνδράσι τοι-
9 ούτου καιροῦ καὶ πράγματος κοινωνεῖν. τέλος δ᾽ οὖν
αὐτοὶ μὲν ὑπέμειναν ἐντὸς τοῦ ποταμοῦ, τοὺς δὲ τῶν
Κελτῶν σφίσι συνόντας διαβιβάσαντες εἰς τὸ πέραν
ἀνέσπασαν τὰς ἐπὶ τοῦ ῥείθρου γεφύρας, ἅμα μὲν
10 ἀσφαλιζόμενοι τὰ πρὸς ἐκείνους, ἅμα δὲ μίαν ἑαυτοῖς
ἀπολείποντες ἐλπίδα τῆς σωτηρίας τὴν ἐν τῷ νικᾶν,

evacuated the territory under its terms. After a circuitous march of some days, they crossed the river Clusius and reached the country of the Cenomani, who were their allies, and accompanied by them, again invaded from the district at the foot of the Alps the plains of the Insubres and began to lay the country waste and pillage their dwellings. The chieftains of the Insubres, seeing that the Romans adhered to their purpose of attacking them, decided to try their luck in a decisive battle. Collecting all their forces in one place, they took down the golden standards called "immovable" from the temple of Minerva, and having made all other necessary preparations, boldly took up a menacing position opposite the enemy. They were about fifty thousand strong. The Romans, on the one hand, as they saw that the enemy were much more numerous than themselves, were desirous of employing also the forces of their Celtic allies, but on the other hand, taking into consideration Gaulish treachery and the fact that they were going to fight against those of the same nation as these allies, they were shy of asking such men to participate in an action of such vital importance. Finally, remaining themselves on their side of the river, they sent the Celts who were with them across it, and demolished the bridges that crossed the stream, firstly as a precaution against their allies, and secondly to leave themselves no hope of safety except in

διὰ τὸ κατόπιν αὐτοῖς ἄβατον ὄντα παρακεῖσθαι τὸν
11 προειρημένον ποταμόν. πράξαντες δὲ ταῦτα πρὸς τῷ
διακινδυνεύειν ἦσαν.

33. Δοκοῦσι δ' ἐμφρόνως κεχρῆσθαι τῇ μάχῃ ταύτῃ Ῥωμαῖοι, τῶν χιλιάρχων ὑποδειξάντων ὡς δεῖ
2 ποιεῖσθαι τὸν ἀγῶνα κοινῇ καὶ κατ' ἰδίαν ἑκάστους.
συνεωρακότες γὰρ ἐκ τῶν προγεγονότων κινδύνων ὅτι
τοῖς τε θυμοῖς κατὰ τὴν πρώτην ἔφοδον, ἕως ἂν
ἀκέραιον ᾖ, φοβερώτατόν ἐστι πᾶν τὸ Γαλατικὸν
3 φῦλον, αἵ τε μάχαιραι ταῖς κατασκευαῖς, καθάπερ
εἴρηται πρότερον, μίαν ἔχουσι τὴν πρώτην καταφορὰν καιρίαν, ἀπὸ δὲ ταύτης εὐθέως ἀποξυστροῦνται,
καμπτόμεναι κατὰ μῆκος καὶ κατὰ πλάτος ἐπὶ τοσοῦτον ὥστ' ἐὰν μὴ δῷ τις ἀναστροφὴν τοῖς χρωμένοις,
ἐρείσαντας πρὸς τὴν γῆν ἀπευθῦναι τῷ ποδί, τελέως
4 ἄπρακτον εἶναι τὴν δευτέραν πληγὴν αὐτῶν· ἀνα-
δόντες οὖν οἱ χιλίαρχοι τὰ τῶν τριαρίων δόρατα τῶν
κατόπιν ἐφεστώτων ταῖς πρώταις σπείραις, καὶ
παραγγείλαντες ἐκ μεταλήψεως τοῖς ξίφεσι χρῆσθαι,
συνέβαλον ἐκ παρατάξεως κατὰ πρόσωπον τοῖς Κελ-
5 τοῖς. ἅμα δὲ τῷ πρὸς τὰ δόρατα ταῖς πρώταις καταφο-
ραῖς χρωμένων τῶν Γαλατῶν ἀχρειωθῆναι τὰς μαχαίρας συνδραμόντες εἰς τὰς χεῖρας τοὺς μὲν Κελτοὺς
ἀπράκτους ἐποίησαν, ἀφελόμενοι τὴν ἐκ διάρσεως
αὐτῶν μάχην, ὅπερ ἴδιόν ἐστι Γαλατικῆς χρείας, διὰ
6 τὸ μηδαμῶς κέντημα τὸ ξίφος ἔχειν· αὐτοὶ δ' οὐκ ἐκ
καταφορᾶς, ἀλλ' ἐκ διαλήψεως ὀρθαῖς χρώμενοι ταῖς
μαχαίραις, πρακτικοῦ τοῦ κεντήματος περὶ αὐτὰς

victory, the river, which was impassable, lying in their rear. After taking these measures they prepared for battle.

33. The Romans are thought to have managed matters very skillfully in this battle, their tribunes having instructed them how they should fight, both as individuals and collectively. For they had observed from former battles that Gauls in general are most formidable and spirited in their first onslaught, while still fresh, and that, from the way their swords are made, as has been already explained, only the first cut takes effect; after this they at once assume the shape of a strigil, being so much bent both lengthwise and sidewise that unless the men are given leisure to rest them on the ground and set them straight with the foot, the second blow is quite ineffectual. The tribunes therefore distributed amongst the front lines the spears of the triarii who were stationed behind them, ordering them to use their swords instead only after the spears were done with. They then drew up opposite the Celts in order of battle and engaged. Upon the Gauls slashing first at the spears and making their swords unserviceable the Romans came to close quarters, having rendered the enemy helpless by depriving them of the power of raising their hands and cutting, which is the peculiar and only stroke of the Gauls, as their swords have no points. The Romans, on the contrary, instead of slashing, continued to thrust with their swords which did not bend, the points being very effective. Thus,

ὑπάρχοντος, τύπτοντες εἰς τὰ στέρνα καὶ τὰ πρόσωπα
καὶ πληγὴν ἐπὶ πληγῇ φέροντες, διέφθειραν τοὺς
πλείστους τῶν παραταξαμένων διὰ τὴν τῶν χιλι-
7 άρχων πρόνοιαν. ὁ μὲν γὰρ στρατηγὸς Φλαμίνιος οὐκ
ὀρθῶς δοκεῖ κεχρῆσθαι τῷ προειρημένῳ κινδύνῳ. παρ'
αὐτὴν γὰρ τὴν ὀφρὺν τοῦ ποταμοῦ ποιησάμενος τὴν
ἔκταξιν διέφθειρε τὸ τῆς Ῥωμαϊκῆς μάχης ἴδιον, οὐχ
ὑπολειπόμενος τόπον πρὸς τὴν ἐπὶ πόδα ταῖς σπείραις
8 ἀναχώρησιν. εἰ γὰρ συνέβη βραχὺ μόνον πιεσθῆναι
τῇ χώρᾳ τοὺς ἄνδρας κατὰ τὴν μάχην, ῥίπτειν ἂν εἰς
τὸν ποταμὸν αὐτοὺς ἔδει διὰ τὴν ἀστοχίαν τοῦ προ-
9 εστῶτος. οὐ μὴν ἀλλά γε πολλῷ νικήσαντες ταῖς
σφετέραις ἀρεταῖς, καθάπερ εἶπον, καὶ παμπληθοῦς
μὲν λείας, οὐκ ὀλίγων δὲ σκύλων κρατήσαντες, ἐπανῆλθον εἰς τὴν Ῥώμην.
34. Τῷ δ' ἑξῆς ἔτει, διαπρεσβευσαμένων τῶν Κελτῶν ὑπὲρ εἰρήνης καὶ πᾶν ποιήσειν ὑπισχνουμένων,
ἔσπευσαν οἱ κατασταθέντες ὕπατοι Μάρκος Κλαύδιος
καὶ Γνάιος Κορνήλιος τοῦ μὴ συγχωρηθῆναι τὴν
2 εἰρήνην αὐτοῖς. οἱ δ' ἀποτυχόντες, καὶ κρίναντες ἐξ-
ελέγξαι τὰς τελευταίας ἐλπίδας, αὖθις ὥρμησαν ἐπὶ
τὸ μισθοῦσθαι τῶν περὶ τὸν Ῥοδανὸν Γαισάτων
Γαλατῶν εἰς τρισμυρίους· οὓς παραλαβόντες εἶχον ἐν
3 ἑτοίμῳ καὶ προσεδόκων τὴν τῶν πολεμίων ἔφοδον. οἱ
δὲ τῶν Ῥωμαίων στρατηγοί, τῆς ὥρας ἐπιγενομένης,
ἀναλαβόντες τὰς δυνάμεις ἦγον εἰς τὴν τῶν Ἰνσόμ-
4 βρων χώραν. παραγενόμενοι δὲ καὶ περιστρατοπε-

striking one blow after another on the breast or face, they slew the greater part of their adversaries. This was solely due to the foresight of the tribunes, the Consul Flaminius[58] being thought to have mismanaged the battle by deploying his force at the very edge of the riverbank and thus rendering impossible a tactical movement peculiar to the Romans, as he left the maniples no room to fall back gradually. For had the troops been even in the slightest degree pushed back from their ground during the battle, they would have had to throw themselves into the river, all owing to their general's blunder. However, as it was, they gained a decisive victory by their own skill and valor, as I said, and returned to Rome with a quantity of booty and many trophies.

34. Next year the Celts sent ambassadors begging for peace and engaging to accept any conditions, but the new Consuls[59] Marcus Claudius and Gnaeus Cornelius strongly urged that no peace should be granted them. On meeting with a refusal, the Celts decided to resort to their last hope and again appealed to the Gaesatae on the Rhone, and hired a force of about thirty thousand men. When they had these troops they kept them in readiness and awaited the attack of the enemy. The Roman Consuls, when the season came, invaded the territory of the Insubres with their legions. Encamping round a city called

222 B.C.

---

[58] He was out of favor with the Senate (and with P.); see 21. 8. His blunder did not prevent those serving under him to achieve victory.   [59] Marcus Claudius Marcellus was then elected to the consulate four more times and became one of the great warriors of the Hannibalic War. Plutarch wrote his *Life* pairing him with Pelopidas of Thebes.

δεύσαντες πόλιν Ἀχέρρας, ἣ μεταξὺ κεῖται τοῦ Πάδου
5 καὶ τῶν Ἀλπεινῶν ὀρῶν, ἐπολιόρκουν ταύτην. οἱ δ᾽
Ἴνσομβρες, βοηθεῖν μὲν οὐ δυνάμενοι, διὰ τὸ προκαταληφθῆναι τοὺς εὐφυεῖς τόπους, σπεύδοντες δὲ
λῦσαι τὴν πολιορκίαν τῶν Ἀχέρρων, μέρος τι τῆς
δυνάμεως διαβιβάσαντες τὸν Πάδον εἰς τὴν τῶν
Ἀνάρων χώραν ἐπολιόρκουν τὸ προσαγορευόμενον
6 Κλαστίδιον. προσπεσόντος δὲ τοῦ συμβαίνοντος τοῖς
στρατηγοῖς, ἀναλαβὼν τοὺς ἱππεῖς Μάρκος Κλαύδιος
καί τινας τῶν πεζικῶν ἠπείγετο, σπεύδων βοηθῆσαι
7 τοῖς πολιορκουμένοις. οἱ δὲ Κελτοί, πυθόμενοι τὴν
παρουσίαν τῶν ὑπεναντίων, λύσαντες τὴν πολιορκίαν
8 ὑπήντων καὶ παρετάξαντο. τῶν δὲ Ῥωμαίων αὐτοῖς
τοῖς ἱππεῦσιν ἐξ ἐφόδου τολμηρῶς σφίσι προσπεσόντων, τὰς μὲν ἀρχὰς ἀντεῖχον· μετὰ δὲ ταῦτα περι-
ισταμένων καὶ κατὰ νώτου καὶ κατὰ κέρας, δυσχρηστούμενοι τῇ μάχῃ, τέλος ἐτράπησαν ὑπ᾽ αὐτῶν τῶν
9 ἱππέων. καὶ πολλοὶ μὲν εἰς τὸν ποταμὸν ἐμπεσόντες
ὑπὸ τοῦ ῥεύματος διεφθάρησαν, οἱ δὲ πλείους ὑπὸ τῶν
10 πολεμίων κατεκόπησαν. ἔλαβον δὲ καὶ τὰς Ἀχέρρας
οἱ Ῥωμαῖοι σίτου γεμούσας, ἐκχωρησάντων εἰς τὸ
Μεδιόλανον τῶν Γαλατῶν, ὅσπερ ἐστὶ κυριώτατος
11 τόπος τῆς τῶν Ἰνσόμβρων χώρας. οἷς ἐκ ποδὸς ἐπα-
κολουθήσαντος τοῦ Γναΐου, καὶ προσβαλόντος ἄφνω
12 πρὸς τὸ Μεδιόλανον, τὸ μὲν πρῶτον ἡσυχίαν ἔσχον·
ἀπολυομένου δ᾽ αὐτοῦ πάλιν εἰς τὰς Ἀχέρρας, ἐπεξελ-
θόντες καὶ τῆς οὐραγίας ἁψάμενοι θρασέως πολλοὺς
μὲν νεκροὺς ἐποίησαν, μέρος δέ τι καὶ φυγεῖν αὐτῶν

Acerrae lying between the Po and the Alps, they laid siege to it. The Insubres could not come to the assistance of the besieged, as the Romans had occupied all the advantageous positions, but, with the object of making the latter raise the siege, they crossed the Po with part of their forces, and entering the territory of the Anares, laid siege to a town there called Clastidium. On the Consuls learning of this, Marcus Claudius set off in haste with the cavalry and a small body of infantry to relieve the besieged if possible. The Celts, as soon as they were aware of the enemy's arrival, raised the siege and advancing to meet them, drew up in order of battle. When the Romans boldly charged them with their cavalry alone, they at first stood firm, but afterward, being taken both in the rear and on the flank, they found themselves in difficulties and were finally put to rout by the cavalry unaided, many of them throwing themselves into the river and being swept away by the current, while the larger number were cut to pieces by the enemy. The Romans now took Acerrae, which was well stocked with corn, the Gauls retiring to Mediolanum, the chief place in the territory of the Insubres. Gnaeus followed close on their heels, and suddenly appeared before Mediolanum.[60] The Gauls at first did not stir, but, when he was on his way back to Acerrae, they sallied out, and made a bold attack on his rear, in which they killed a considerable number of the Romans and even forced a portion of them

[60] Milan.

THE HISTORIES OF POLYBIUS

13 ἠνάγκασαν, ἕως ὁ Γνάιος ἀνακαλεσάμενος τοὺς ἐκ
τῆς πρωτοπορείας παρώρμησε στῆναι καὶ συμβαλεῖν
14 τοῖς πολεμίοις. οἱ μὲν οὖν Ῥωμαῖοι, πειθαρχήσαντες
τῷ στρατηγῷ, διεμάχοντο πρὸς τοὺς ἐπικειμένους εὐ-
15 ρώστως. οἱ δὲ Κελτοί, διὰ τὸ παρὸν εὐτύχημα μείναντες ἐπὶ ποσὸν εὐθαρσῶς, μετ' οὐ πολὺ τραπέντες
ἔφευγον εἰς τὰς παρωρείας. ὁ δὲ Γνάιος ἐπακολουθή-
σας τήν τε χώραν ἐπόρθει καὶ τὸ Μεδιόλανον εἷλε
κατὰ κράτος.

35. οὗ συμβαίνοντος οἱ προεστῶτες τῶν Ἰνσόμβρων, ἀπογνόντες τὰς τῆς σωτηρίας ἐλπίδας, πάντα
τὰ καθ' αὑτοὺς ἐπέτρεψαν τοῖς Ῥωμαίοις.

2 Ὁ μὲν οὖν πρὸς τοὺς Κελτοὺς πόλεμος τοιοῦτον
ἔσχε τὸ τέλος, κατὰ μὲν τὴν ἀπόνοιαν καὶ τόλμαν τῶν
ἀγωνιζομένων ἀνδρῶν, ἔτι δὲ κατὰ τὰς μάχας καὶ τὸ
πλῆθος τῶν ἐν αὐταῖς ἀπολλυμένων καὶ παραταττο-
3 μένων, οὐδενὸς καταδεέστερος τῶν ἱστορημένων, κατὰ
δὲ τὰς ἐπιβολὰς καὶ τὴν ἀκρισίαν τοῦ κατὰ μέρος
χειρισμοῦ τελέως εὐκαταφρόνητος, διὰ τὸ μὴ τὸ πλεῖον, ἀλλὰ συλλήβδην ἅπαν τὸ γινόμενον ὑπὸ τῶν
4 Γαλατῶν θυμῷ μᾶλλον ἢ λογισμῷ βραβεύεσθαι. περὶ
ὧν ἡμεῖς συνθεωρήσαντες μετ' ὀλίγον χρόνον αὐτοὺς
ἐκ τῶν περὶ τὸν Πάδον πεδίων ἐξωσθέντας, πλὴν
ὀλίγων τόπων τῶν ὑπ' αὐτὰς τὰς Ἄλπεις κειμένων,
οὐκ ᾠήθημεν δεῖν οὔτε τὴν ἐξ ἀρχῆς ἔφοδον αὐτῶν
ἀμνημόνευτον παραλιπεῖν οὔτε τὰς μετὰ ταῦτα πρά-
5 ξεις οὔτε τὴν τελευταίαν ἐξανάστασιν, ὑπολαμβάνοντες οἰκεῖον ἱστορίας ὑπάρχειν τὰ τοιαῦτ' ἐπεισόδια

358

to take to flight, until Gnaeus, calling back the forces in advance, urged the fugitives to rally and withstand the enemy. After this the Romans, on their part obeying their Consul, continued to fight vigorously with their assailants, and the Celts after holding their ground for a time, encouraged as they were by their momentary success, were shortly put to flight and took refuge on the mountains. Gnaeus, following them, laid waste the country and took Mediolanum itself by assault,

35. upon which the chieftains of the Insubres, despairing of safety, put themselves entirely at the mercy of the Romans.

Such was the end of the war against the Celts, a war which, if we look to the desperation and daring of the combatants and the numbers who took part and perished in the battles, is second to no war in history, but is quite contemptible as regards the plan of the campaigns, and the judgment shown in executing it, not most steps but every single step that the Gauls took being commended to them rather by the heat of passion than by cool calculation. As I have witnessed them not long afterward entirely expelled from the plain of the Po, except a few regions close under the Alps, I did not think it right to make no mention either of their original invasion or of their subsequent conduct and their final expulsion; for I think it is the proper task of History to record and hand down to future genera-

τῆς τύχης εἰς μνήμην ἄγειν καὶ παράδοσιν τοῖς ἐπι-
6 γινομένοις, ἵνα μὴ τελέως οἱ μεθ᾽ ἡμᾶς ἀνεννόητοι
τούτων ὑπάρχοντες ἐκπλήττωνται τὰς αἰφνιδίους καὶ
παραλόγους τῶν βαρβάρων ἐφόδους, ἀλλ᾽ ἐπὶ ποσὸν
ἐν νῷ λαμβάνοντες ὡς ὀλιγοχρόνιόν ἐστι καὶ λίαν
εὔφθαρτον ⟨τὸ τοιοῦτον⟩, τὴν ἔφοδον αὐτῶν ὑπο-
μένωσι καὶ πάσας ἐξελέγχωσι τὰς σφετέρας ἐλπίδας
7 πρότερον ἢ παραχωρῆσαί τινος τῶν ἀναγκαίων. καὶ
γὰρ τοὺς τὴν Περσῶν ἔφοδον ἐπὶ τὴν Ἑλλάδα καὶ
Γαλατῶν ἐπὶ Δελφοὺς εἰς μνήμην καὶ παράδοσιν ἡμῖν
ἀγαγόντας οὐ μικρά, μεγάλα δ᾽ οἶμαι συμβεβλῆσθαι πρὸς τοὺς ὑπὲρ τῆς κοινῆς τῶν Ἑλλήνων ἐλευ-
8 θερίας ἀγῶνας. οὔτε γὰρ χορηγιῶν οὔθ᾽ ὅπλων οὔτ᾽
ἀνδρῶν πλῆθος καταπλαγεὶς ἄν τις ἀποσταίη τῆς
τελευταίας ἐλπίδος, τοῦ διαγωνίζεσθαι περὶ τῆς σφετέρας χώρας καὶ πατρίδος, λαμβάνων πρὸ ὀφθαλμῶν
τὸ παράδοξον τῶν τότε γενομένων, καὶ μνημονεύσας
ὅσας μυριάδας καὶ τίνας τόλμας καὶ πηλίκας παρασκευὰς ἡ τῶν σὺν νῷ καὶ μετὰ λογισμοῦ κινδυνευ-
9 όντων αἵρεσις καὶ δύναμις καθεῖλεν. ὁ δ᾽ ἀπὸ Γαλατῶν φόβος οὐ μόνον τὸ παλαιόν, ἀλλὰ καὶ καθ᾽ ἡμᾶς
10 ἤδη πλεονάκις ἐξέπληξε τοὺς Ἕλληνας. διὸ καὶ μᾶλλον ἔγωγε παρωρμήθην ἐπὶ τὸ κεφαλαιώδη μέν,
ἀνέκαθεν δὲ ποιήσασθαι τὴν ὑπὲρ τούτων ἐξήγησιν.

36. Ἀσδρούβας δ᾽ ὁ τῶν Καρχηδονίων στρατηγός,
ἀπὸ γὰρ τούτων παρεξέβημεν τῆς ἐξηγήσεως, ἔτη
χειρίσας ὀκτὼ τὰ κατὰ τὴν Ἰβηρίαν, ἐτελεύτησε

tions such episodes of Fortune, that those who live after us may not, owing to entire ignorance of these incidents, be unduly terrified by sudden and unexpected invasions of barbarians, but that, having a fair comprehension of how short-lived and perishable is the might of such peoples, they may confront the invaders and put every hope of safety to the test, before yielding a jot of anything they value. For indeed I consider that the writers who chronicled and handed down to us the story of the Persian invasion[61] of Greece and the attack of the Gauls on Delphi have made no small contribution to the struggle of the Hellenes for their common liberty. For there is no one whom hosts of men or abundance of arms or vast resources could frighten into abandoning his last hope, that is to fight to the end for his native land, if he kept before his eyes what part the unexpected played in those events, and bore in mind how many myriads of men, what determined courage and what armaments were brought to nought by the resolve and power of those who faced the danger with intelligence and coolness. It is not only in old times but more than once in my own days that the Greeks have been alarmed by the prospect of a Gaulish invasion; and this especially was my motive for giving here an account of the Gauls, summary indeed, but going back to the beginnings.

36. This digression has led us away from the affairs of Spain, where Hasdrubal, after governing the country for

221 B.C.

[61] P. compares this Celtic invasion with the Persian Wars and the attack of Delphi by the Gauls in 279/8. For the latter, the writer whom he has in mind is almost certainly Hieronymus of Cardia: C. Habicht, *Untersuchungen zur politischen Geschichte Athens im 3. Jahrhundert v.Chr.* (Munich 1979) 89 with n. 9.

δολοφονηθεὶς ἐν τοῖς ἑαυτοῦ καταλύμασι νυκτὸς ὑπό
τινος Κελτοῦ τὸ γένος ἰδίων ἕνεκεν ἀδικημάτων, οὐ
2 μικράν, ἀλλὰ μεγάλην ποιήσας ἐπίδοσιν τοῖς Καρχηδονίοις πράγμασιν, οὐχ οὕτω διὰ τῶν πολεμίων ἔργων
3 ὡς διὰ τῆς πρὸς τοὺς δυνάστας ὁμιλίας. τὴν δὲ στρατηγίαν οἱ Καρχηδόνιοι τῶν κατὰ τὴν Ἰβηρίαν Ἀννίβᾳ
περιέθεσαν, ὄντι νέῳ, διὰ τὴν ὑποφαινομένην ἐκ τῶν
4 πράξεων ἀγχίνοιαν αὐτοῦ καὶ τόλμαν. ὃς παραλαβὼν
τὴν ἀρχὴν εὐθέως δῆλος ἦν ἐκ τῶν ἐπινοημάτων
πόλεμον ἐξοίσων Ῥωμαίοις. ὃ δὴ καὶ τέλος ἐποίησε,
5 πάνυ βραχὺν ἐπισχὼν χρόνον. τὰ μὲν οὖν κατὰ Καρχηδονίους καὶ Ῥωμαίους ἀπὸ τούτων ἤδη τῶν καιρῶν
6 ἐν ὑποψίαις ἦν πρὸς ἀλλήλους καὶ παρατριβαῖς. οἱ
μὲν γὰρ ἐπεβούλευον, ἀμύνασθαι σπεύδοντες διὰ τὰς
περὶ Σικελίαν ἐλαττώσεις, οἱ δὲ Ῥωμαῖοι διηπίστουν,
7 θεωροῦντες αὐτῶν τὰς ἐπιβολάς. ἐξ ὧν δῆλον ἦν τοῖς
ὀρθῶς σκοπουμένοις ὅτι μέλλουσι πολεμεῖν ἀλλήλοις
οὐ μετὰ πολὺν χρόνον.

37. Κατὰ δὲ τοὺς αὐτοὺς καιροὺς Ἀχαιοὶ καὶ Φίλιππος ὁ βασιλεὺς ἅμα τοῖς ἄλλοις συμμάχοις συν-
ίσταντο τὸν πρὸς Αἰτωλοὺς πόλεμον τὸν προσαγο-
2 ρευθέντα συμμαχικόν. ἡμεῖς δ' ἐπειδὴ τάς τε περὶ
Σικελίαν καὶ Λιβύην καὶ τὰς ἑξῆς πράξεις διεξιόντες
κατὰ τὸ συνεχὲς τῆς προκατασκευῆς ἥκομεν ἐπὶ τὴν
ἀρχὴν τοῦ τε συμμαχικοῦ καὶ τοῦ δευτέρου συστάντος
μὲν Ῥωμαίοις καὶ Καρχηδονίοις πολέμου, προσαγο-
ρευθέντος δὲ παρὰ τοῖς πλείστοις Ἀννιβιακοῦ, κατὰ
δὲ τὴν ἐξ ἀρχῆς πρόθεσιν ἀπὸ τούτων τῶν καιρῶν

eight years, was assassinated at night in his lodging by a
certain Celt owing to wrongs of a private nature. He had
largely increased the power of Carthage, not so much by
military action as by friendly intercourse with the chiefs.
The Carthaginians appointed Hannibal to the chief command in Spain, although he was still young,[62] owing to the
shrewdness and courage he had evinced in their service.
From the moment that he assumed the command,[63] it was
evident from the measures he took that he intended
to make war on Rome, as indeed he finished by doing,
and that very shortly. The relations between Carthage and
Rome were henceforth characterized by mutual suspicion
and friction. The Carthaginians continued to form designs
against Rome as they were eager to be revenged for their
reverses in Sicily, while the Romans, detecting their projects, mistrusted them profoundly. It was therefore evident
to all competent judges that it would not be long before
war broke out between them.

37. It was about this same time[64] that the Achaeans and
King Philip with their allies began the war against the
Aetolians known as the Social War. I have now given a con-
tinuous sketch, suitable to this preliminary plan of my
book, of events in Sicily, Libya and so forth down to the beginning of the Social War and that second war between the
Romans and Carthaginians usually known as the Hannibalic War. This, as I stated at the outset, is the date at which

[62] He was 25 or 26 at the time (1. 6).   [63] This is the Roman version, refuted by P.'s later statement that for two years
Hannibal avoided provoking the Romans (3. 14. 10).

[64] 220. P. now begins to sketch the affairs of Greece down to
this date (through chapter 70), at which his Introduction ends.

ἐπηγγειλάμεθα ποιήσασθαι τὴν ἀρχὴν τῆς ἑαυτῶν
3 συντάξεως, πρέπον ἂν εἴη τούτων ἀφεμένους ἐπὶ τὰς
κατὰ τὴν Ἑλλάδα μεταβαίνειν πράξεις, ἵνα πανταχόθεν ὁμοίαν ποιησάμενοι τὴν προκατασκευὴν καὶ
τὴν ἔφοδον ἐπὶ τοὺς αὐτοὺς καιροὺς οὕτως ἤδη [τῆς
4 Ἰταλίας καὶ] τῆς ἀποδεικτικῆς ἱστορίας ἀρχώμεθα.
ἐπεὶ γὰρ οὐ τινὰς πράξεις, καθάπερ οἱ πρὸ ἡμῶν, οἷον
τὰς Ἑλληνικὰς ἢ Περσικάς, ὁμοῦ δὲ τὰς ἐν τοῖς
γνωριζομένοις μέρεσι τῆς οἰκουμένης ἀναγράφειν
ἐπικεχειρήκαμεν, διὰ τὸ πρὸς τοῦτο τὸ μέρος τῆς
ὑποθέσεως ἴδιόν τι συμβεβλῆσθαι τοὺς καθ᾽ ἡμᾶς
5 καιρούς, ὑπὲρ ὧν σαφέστερον ἐν ἑτέροις δηλώσομεν,
δέον ἂν εἴη καὶ πρὸ τῆς κατασκευῆς ἐπὶ βραχὺ τῶν
ἐπιφανεστάτων καὶ γνωριζομένων ἐθνῶν καὶ τόπων
6 ἐφάψασθαι τῆς οἰκουμένης. περὶ μὲν οὖν τῶν κατὰ τὴν
Ἀσίαν καὶ τῶν κατὰ τὴν Αἴγυπτον ἀρκούντως ἂν ἔχοι
ποιεῖσθαι τὴν ἀνάμνησιν ἀπὸ τῶν νῦν ῥηθέντων καιρῶν, διὰ τὸ τὴν μὲν ὑπὲρ τῶν προγεγονότων παρ᾽
αὐτοῖς ἱστορίαν ὑπὸ πλειόνων ἐκδεδόσθαι καὶ γνώριμον ὑπάρχειν ἅπασιν, ἐν δὲ τοῖς καθ᾽ ἡμᾶς καιροῖς
μηδὲν αὐτοῖς ἐξηλλαγμένον ἀπηντῆσθαι μηδὲ παρ-
άλογον ὑπὸ τῆς τύχης, ὥστε προσδεῖσθαι τῆς τῶν
7 προγεγονότων ὑπομνήσεως. περὶ δὲ τοῦ τῶν Ἀχαιῶν
ἔθνους καὶ περὶ τῆς Μακεδόνων οἰκίας ἁρμόσει διὰ
8 βραχέων ἀναδραμεῖν τοῖς χρόνοις, ἐπειδὴ περὶ μὲν
ταύτην ὁλοσχερὴς ἐπαναίρεσις, περὶ δὲ τοὺς Ἀχαιούς,
καθάπερ ἐπάνω προεῖπον, παράδοξος αὔξησις καὶ
9 συμφρόνησις ἐν τοῖς καθ᾽ ἡμᾶς καιροῖς γέγονε. πολ-

364

I purpose to begin my general history, and, now bidding goodbye for the present to the West, I must turn to the affairs of Greece, so that everywhere alike I may bring down this preliminary or introductory sketch to the same date, and, having done so, start on my detailed narrative. For as I am not, like former historians, dealing with the history of one nation, such as Greece or Persia, but have undertaken to describe the events occurring in all known parts of the world—my own times having, as I will more clearly explain elsewhere, materially contributed to my purpose—I must, before entering on the main portion of my work, touch briefly on the state of the principal and best known nations and countries of the world. As for Asia and Egypt, it will suffice to mention what took place there after the above date, since their previous history has been written by many[65] and is familiar to all, besides which in our own times Fortune has wrought no such surprising change in these countries as to render any notice of their past necessary. But as regards the Achaean nation and the royal house of Macedon it will be proper to refer briefly to earlier events, since our times[66] have seen, in the case of the latter, its complete destruction, and in the case of the Achaeans, as I said above, a growth of power and a political union in the highest degree remarkable. For while many

[65] Mainly Hieronymus of Cardia (*FGrH* 154), down to 272, also Duris of Samos (*FGrH* 76), to ca. 280, and Phylarchus of Athens (*FGrH* 81) to 221. P. will focus on Greece proper.

[66] A sentence clearly written after 168 and before 146, as was 38. 9.

λῶν γὰρ ἐπιβαλομένων ἐν τοῖς παρεληλυθόσι χρόνοις
ἐπὶ ταὐτὸ συμφέρον ἀγαγεῖν Πελοποννησίους,
οὐδενὸς δὲ καθικέσθαι δυνηθέντος, διὰ τὸ μὴ τῆς
κοινῆς ἐλευθερίας ἕνεκεν, ἀλλὰ τῆς σφετέρας δυνα-
10 στείας χάριν ἑκάστους ποιεῖσθαι τὴν σπουδήν, τοιαύτην καὶ τηλικαύτην ἐν τοῖς καθ᾽ ἡμᾶς καιροῖς ἔσχε
προκοπὴν καὶ συντέλειαν τοῦτο τὸ μέρος ὥστε μὴ
μόνον συμμαχικὴν καὶ φιλικὴν κοινωνίαν γεγονέναι
πραγμάτων περὶ αὐτούς, ἀλλὰ καὶ νόμοις χρῆσθαι
τοῖς αὐτοῖς καὶ σταθμοῖς καὶ μέτροις καὶ νομίσμασι,
11 πρὸς δὲ τούτοις ἄρχουσι, βουλευταῖς, δικασταῖς τοῖς
αὐτοῖς, καθόλου δὲ τούτῳ μόνῳ διαλλάττειν τοῦ μὴ
μιᾶς πόλεως διάθεσιν ἔχειν σχεδὸν τὴν σύμπασαν
Πελοπόννησον τῷ μὴ τὸν αὐτὸν περίβολον ὑπάρχειν
τοῖς κατοικοῦσιν αὐτήν, τἄλλα δ᾽ εἶναι καὶ κοινῇ καὶ
κατὰ πόλεις ἑκάστοις ταὐτὰ καὶ παραπλήσια.

38. Πρῶτον δὲ πῶς ἐπεκράτησε καὶ τίνι τρόπῳ τὸ
τῶν Ἀχαιῶν ὄνομα κατὰ πάντων Πελοποννησίων οὐκ
2 ἄχρηστον μαθεῖν. οὔτε γὰρ χώρας καὶ πόλεων πλήθει
διαφέρουσιν οἱ πάτριον ἐξ ἀρχῆς ἔχοντες τὴν προσηγορίαν ταύτην οὔτε πλούτοις οὔτε ταῖς τῶν ἀνδρῶν
3 ἀρεταῖς. τό τε γὰρ τῶν Ἀρκάδων ἔθνος, ὁμοίως δὲ καὶ
τὸ τῶν Λακώνων, πλήθει μὲν ἀνδρῶν καὶ χώρας οὐδὲ
παρὰ μικρὸν ὑπερέχει· καὶ μὴν οὐδὲ τῶν τῆς ἀνδρα-
γαθίας πρωτείων οὐδενὶ τῶν Ἑλλήνων οἷοί τ᾽ εἰσὶν
4 οὐδέποτε παραχωρεῖν οἱ προειρημένοι. πῶς οὖν καὶ
διὰ τί νῦν εὐδοκοῦσιν οὗτοί τε καὶ τὸ λοιπὸν πλῆθος
τῶν Πελοποννησίων, ἅμα τὴν πολιτείαν τῶν Ἀχαιῶν

have attempted in the past to induce the Peloponnesians to adopt a common policy, no one ever succeeding, as each was working not in the cause of general liberty,[67] but for his own aggrandizement, this object has been so much advanced, and so nearly attained, in my own time that not only have they formed an allied and friendly community, but they have the same laws, weights, measures and coinage, as well as the same magistrates, senate, and courts of justice, and almost the whole Peloponnesus falls short of being a single city only in the fact of its inhabitants not being enclosed by one wall, all other things being, both as regards the whole and as regards each separate town, very nearly identical.

38. In the first place it is of some service to learn how and by what means all the Peloponnesians came to be called Achaeans. For the people whose original and ancestral name this was are distinguished neither by the extent of their territory, nor by the number of their cities, nor by exceptional wealth or the exceptional valor of their citizens. Both the Arcadian and Laconian nations far exceed them, indeed, in population and the size of their countries, and certainly neither of the two could ever bring themselves to yield to any Greek people the palm for military valor. How is it, then, that both these two peoples and the rest of the Peloponnesians have consented to change not only their political institutions for those of the Achaeans,

[67] P.'s praise of the Achaean League culminates in the statement that it granted non-Achaeans equal treatment ($\iota\sigma\acute{o}\tau\eta\varsigma$), and that this was the reason for its success.

5 καὶ τὴν προσηγορίαν μετειληφότες; δῆλον ὡς τύχην
μὲν λέγειν οὐδαμῶς ἂν εἴη πρέπον· φαῦλον γάρ·
αἰτίαν δὲ μᾶλλον ζητεῖν. χωρὶς γὰρ ταύτης οὔτε τῶν
κατὰ λόγον οὔτε τῶν παρὰ λόγον εἶναι δοκούντων
οὐδὲν οἷόν τε συντελεσθῆναι. ἔστι δ᾽ οὖν, ὡς ἐμὴ
6 δόξα, τοιαύτη τις. ἰσηγορίας καὶ παρρησίας καὶ καθόλου δημοκρατίας ἀληθινῆς σύστημα καὶ προαίρεσιν
εἰλικρινεστέραν οὐκ ἂν εὕροι τις τῆς παρὰ τοῖς Ἀχαι-
7 οῖς ὑπαρχούσης. αὕτη τινὰς μὲν ἐθελοντὴν αἱρετιστὰς
εὗρε Πελοποννησίων, πολλοὺς δὲ πειθοῖ καὶ λόγῳ
προσηγάγετο· τινὰς δὲ βιασαμένη σὺν καιρῷ παραχρῆμα πάλιν εὐδοκεῖν ἐποίησεν αὐτῇ τοὺς ἀναγκα-
8 σθέντας. οὐδενὶ γὰρ οὐδὲν ὑπολειπομένη πλεονέκτημα
τῶν ἐξ ἀρχῆς, ἴσα δὲ πάντα ποιοῦσα τοῖς ἀεὶ προσ-
λαμβανομένοις, ταχέως καθικνεῖτο τῆς προκειμένης
9 ἐπιβολῆς, δύο συνεργοῖς χρωμένη τοῖς ἰσχυροτάτοις,
ἰσότητι καὶ φιλανθρωπίᾳ. διὸ ταύτην ἀρχηγὸν καὶ
αἰτίαν ἡγητέον τοῦ συμφρονήσαντας Πελοποννησίους τὴν ὑπάρχουσαν αὐτοῖς εὐδαιμονίαν καταστήσα-
σθαι.

10 Τὰ μὲν οὖν τῆς προαιρέσεως καὶ τὸ τῆς πολιτείας
ἰδίωμα τὸ νῦν εἰρημένον καὶ πρότερον ὑπῆρχε παρὰ
11 τοῖς Ἀχαιοῖς. δῆλον δὲ τοῦτο καὶ δι᾽ ἑτέρων μὲν
πλειόνων, πρὸς δὲ τὸ παρὸν ἀρκέσει πίστεως χάριν ἓν
ἢ καὶ δεύτερον ληφθὲν μαρτύριον.

39. καθ᾽ οὓς γὰρ καιροὺς ἐν τοῖς κατὰ τὴν Ἰταλίαν
τόποις κατὰ τὴν Μεγάλην Ἑλλάδα τότε προσαγορευ-
2 ομένην ἐνεπρήσθη τὰ συνέδρια τῶν Πυθαγορείων,

but even their name? It is evident that we should not say it is the result of chance, for that is a poor explanation. We must rather seek for a cause, for every event whether probable or improbable must have some cause. The cause here, I believe to be more or less the following. One could not find a political system and principle so favorable to equality and freedom of speech, in a word so sincerely democratic, as that of the Achaean league. Owing to this, while some of the Peloponnesians chose to join it of their own free will, it won many others by persuasion and argument, and those whom it forced to adhere to it when the occasion presented itself suddenly underwent a change and became quite reconciled to their position. For by reserving no special privileges for original members, and putting all new adherents exactly on the same footing, it soon attained the aim it had set itself, being aided by two very powerful coadjutors, equality and humanity. We must therefore look upon this as the initiator and cause of that union that has established the present prosperity of the Peloponnese.

These characteristic principles and constitution had existed in Achaea from an early date. There is abundant testimony of this, but for the present it will suffice to cite one or two instances in confirmation of this assertion.

39. When, in the district of Italy, then known as Great Hellas, the clubhouses of the Pythagoreans were burnt

μετὰ ταῦτα γενομένου κινήματος ὁλοσχεροῦς περὶ τὰς
πολιτείας, ὅπερ εἰκός, ὡς ἂν τῶν πρώτων ἀνδρῶν ἐξ
3 ἑκάστης πόλεως οὕτω παραλόγως διαφθαρέντων, συνέβη τὰς κατ᾽ ἐκείνους τοὺς τόπους Ἑλληνικὰς πόλεις
ἀναπλησθῆναι φόνου καὶ στάσεως καὶ παντοδαπῆς
4 ταραχῆς. ἐν οἷς καιροῖς ἀπὸ τῶν πλείστων μερῶν τῆς
Ἑλλάδος πρεσβευόντων ἐπὶ τὰς διαλύσεις, Ἀχαιοῖς
καὶ τῇ τούτων πίστει συνεχρήσαντο πρὸς τὴν τῶν
5 παρόντων κακῶν ἐξαγωγήν. οὐ μόνον δὲ κατὰ τούτους
τοὺς καιροὺς ἀπεδέξαντο τὴν αἵρεσιν τῶν Ἀχαιῶν,
ἀλλὰ καὶ μετά τινας χρόνους ὁλοσχερῶς ὥρμησαν ἐπὶ
6 τὸ μιμηταὶ γενέσθαι τῆς πολιτείας αὐτῶν. παρακαλέσαντες γὰρ σφᾶς καὶ συμφρονήσαντες Κροτωνι-
ᾶται, Συβαρῖται, Καυλωνιᾶται, πρῶτον μὲν ἀπέδειξαν
Διὸς Ἀμαρίου κοινὸν ἱερὸν καὶ τόπον, ἐν ᾧ τάς τε
συνόδους καὶ τὰ διαβούλια συνετέλουν, δεύτερον τοὺς
ἐθισμοὺς καὶ νόμους ἐκλαβόντες τοὺς τῶν Ἀχαιῶν
ἐπεβάλοντο χρῆσθαι καὶ διοικεῖν κατὰ τούτους τὴν
7 πολιτείαν. ὑπὸ δὲ τῆς Διονυσίου Συρακοσίου δυναστείας, ἔτι δὲ τῆς τῶν περιοικούντων βαρβάρων ἐπικρατείας ἐμποδισθέντες, οὐχ ἑκουσίως, ἀλλὰ κατ᾽
8 ἀνάγκην αὐτῶν ἀπέστησαν. μετὰ δὲ ταῦτα Λακεδαιμονίων μὲν παραδόξως πταισάντων περὶ τὴν ἐν

---

68 See *OCD* Pythagoreanism (F. Graf), with bibliography.
Events described in this chapter date mainly to the 5th century.
This and the closely contemporary passage in Pseudo-Scymnus
303–304 are the first occurrences of the expression "Great Hellas"; see D. Marcotte in his edition of Ps.-Scymnus (Paris 2000)

down,[68] there ensued, as was natural, a general revolutionary movement, the leading citizens of each city having thus unexpectedly perished, and in all the Greek towns of the district murder, sedition, and every kind of disturbance were rife. Embassies arrived from most parts of Greece offering their services as peacemakers, but it was the Achaeans on whom these cities placed most reliance and to whom they committed the task of putting an end to their present troubles. And it was not only at this period that they showed their approval of Achaean political principles; but a short time afterward, they resolved to model their own constitution exactly on that of the League. The Crotonians, Sybarites[69] and Caulonians, having called a conference and formed a league, first of all established a common temple and holy place of Zeus Homarius[70] in which to hold their meetings and debates, and next, adopting the customs and laws of the Achaeans, decided to conduct their government according to them. It was only indeed the tyranny of Dionysius of Syracuse[71] and their subjection to the barbarian tribes around them which defeated this purpose and forced them to abandon these institutions, much against their will. Again, subsequently, when the Lacedaemonians were unexpectedly defeated at Leuctra, and the

371 B.C.

61. This work was written between 128/7 and 108/7: B. Bravo, *La chronique d' Apollodore et le Pseudo-Skymnos* (Leuven 2009) XIII-XIV. [69] Both citizens of Achaean colonies. Croton destroyed Sybaris in 510 (later rebuilt at a different location). See note on 7. 1. 1. [70] The federal sanctuary of the Achaean League, near Aegium: *RE* Zeus 270–271 (H. Schwabl). The location of its Italian counterpart is not known.

[71] See 1. 6. 1. The barbarians are the Bruttians.

Λεύκτροις μάχην, Θηβαίων δ᾽ ἀνελπίστως ἀντιποιη-
σαμένων τῆς τῶν Ἑλλήνων ἡγεμονίας, ἦν ἀκρισία
περὶ πάντας μὲν τοὺς Ἕλληνας, μάλιστα δὲ περὶ τοὺς
προειρημένους, ὡς ἂν τῶν μὲν μὴ συγχωρούντων
9 ἡττῆσθαι, τῶν δὲ μὴ πιστευόντων ὅτι νενικήκασιν. οὐ
μὴν ἀλλά γε περὶ τῶν ἀμφισβητουμένων ἐπέτρεψαν
Θηβαῖοι καὶ Λακεδαιμόνιοι μόνοις τῶν Ἑλλήνων
10 Ἀχαιοῖς, οὐ πρὸς τὴν δύναμιν ἀποβλέψαντες· σχεδὸν
γὰρ ἐλαχίστην τότε δὴ τῶν Ἑλλήνων εἶχον· τὸ δὲ
πλεῖον εἰς τὴν πίστιν καὶ τὴν ὅλην καλοκἀγαθίαν.
ὁμολογουμένως γὰρ δὴ τότε ταύτην περὶ αὐτῶν πάντες εἶχον τὴν δόξαν.

11 Τότε μὲν οὖν ψιλῶς αὐτὰ τὰ κατὰ τὴν προαίρεσιν
ὑπῆρχε παρ᾽ αὐτοῖς· ἀποτέλεσμα δ᾽ ἢ πρᾶξις ἀξιόλο-
γος πρὸς αὔξησιν τῶν ἰδίων ἀνήκουσα πραγμάτων
12 οὐκ ἐγίνετο, τῷ μὴ δύνασθαι φῦναι προστάτην ἄξιον
τῆς προαιρέσεως, ἀεὶ δὲ τὸν ὑποδείξαντα ποτὲ μὲν ὑπὸ
τῆς Λακεδαιμονίων ἀρχῆς ἐπισκοτεῖσθαι καὶ κωλύε-
σθαι, ποτὲ δὲ μᾶλλον ὑπὸ τῆς Μακεδόνων.

40. ἐπεὶ δέ ποτε σὺν καιρῷ προστάτας ἀξιόχρεως
εὗρε, ταχέως τὴν αὑτῆς δύναμιν ἐποίησε φανεράν,
ἐπιτελεσαμένη τὸ κάλλιστον ἔργον, τὴν Πελοπον-
2 νησίων ὁμόνοιαν. ἧς ἀρχηγὸν μὲν καὶ καθηγεμόνα
τῆς ὅλης ἐπιβολῆς Ἄρατον νομιστέον τὸν Σικυώνιον,
ἀγωνιστὴν δὲ καὶ τελεσιουργὸν τῆς πράξεως Φιλοποί-
μενα τὸν Μεγαλοπολίτην, βεβαιωτὴν δὲ τοῦ μόνιμον

---

72 This arbitration, mentioned nowhere else, is rather dubi-
ous.

Thebans, as unexpectedly, claimed the hegemony of Greece, great uncertainty prevailed in the whole country and especially among these two peoples, the Lacedaemonians not acknowledging their defeat, and the Thebans not wholly believing in their victory. They, however, referred the points in dispute to the Achaeans[72] alone among all the Greeks, not taking their power into consideration, for they were then almost the weakest state in Greece, but in view of their trustworthiness and high character in every respect. For indeed this opinion of them was at that time, as is generally acknowledged, held by all.

Up to now, these principles of government had merely existed amongst them, but had resulted in no practical steps worthy of mention for the increase of the Achaean power, since the country seemed unable to produce a statesman worthy of these principles, anyone who showed a tendency to act so being thrown into the dark and hampered either by the Lacedaemonian power or still more by that of Macedon.

40. When, however, in due time, they found statesmen capable of enforcing them, their power at once became manifest, and the League achieved the splendid result of uniting all the Peloponnesian states. Aratus of Sicyon[73] should be regarded as the initiator and conceiver of the project; it was Philopoemen of Megalopolis[74] who pro-

[73] See F. W. Walbank, *Aratos* (Cambridge 1933). Aratus' *Memoirs* (*FGrH* 231) contained forty books ending in 220. They are P.'s main source for Peloponnesian affairs.

[74] The leading Achaean statesman after Aratus' death in 213 until his own in 183. P. wrote his biography. R. M. Errington, *Philopoemen* (Oxford 1969). For more see 10. 21. 2 and 5.

αὐτὴν ἐπὶ ποσὸν γενέσθαι Λυκόρταν καὶ τοὺς ταὐτὰ
3 τούτῳ προελομένους ἄνδρας. τίνα δ᾽ ἦν ἑκάστοις τὰ
πραχθέντα καὶ πῶς καὶ κατὰ ποίους καιροὺς πειρασόμεθα δηλοῦν, ἀεὶ κατὰ τὸ πρέπον τῇ γραφῇ ποιού-
4 μενοι τὴν ἐπίστασιν. τῶν μέντοι γ᾽ Ἀράτῳ διῳκημέ-
νων καὶ νῦν καὶ μετὰ ταῦτα πάλιν ἐπικεφαλαιούμενοι
μνησθησόμεθα διὰ τὸ καὶ λίαν ἀληθινοὺς καὶ σαφεῖς
ἐκεῖνον περὶ τῶν ἰδίων συντεταχέναι πράξεων ὑπο-
5 μνηματισμούς, τῶν δὲ τοῖς ἄλλοις ἀκριβεστέραν καὶ
μετὰ διαστολῆς ποιησόμεθα τὴν ἐξήγησιν. ὑπολαμβάνω δὲ ῥάστην ἐμοί τ᾽ ἂν γενέσθαι τὴν διήγησιν καὶ
τοῖς ἐντυγχάνουσιν εὐπαρακολούθητον τὴν μάθησιν,
εἰ ποιησαίμεθα τὴν ἐπίστασιν ἀπὸ τούτων τῶν καιρῶν, ἐν οἷς κατὰ πόλιν διαλυθέντος τοῦ τῶν Ἀχαιῶν
ἔθνους ὑπὸ τῶν ἐκ Μακεδονίας βασιλέων ἀρχὴ πάλιν
6 ἐγένετο καὶ σύννευσις τῶν πόλεων πρὸς ἀλλήλας. ἀφ᾽
ἧς αὐξανόμενον κατὰ τὸ συνεχὲς τὸ ἔθνος εἰς ταύτην
ἦλθε τὴν συντέλειαν, ἐν ᾗ καθ᾽ ἡμᾶς ἦν, ὑπὲρ ἧς κατὰ
μέρος ἀρτίως εἶπον.

41. Ὀλυμπιὰς μὲν ἦν εἰκοστὴ καὶ τετάρτη πρὸς
ταῖς ἑκατόν, ὅτε Πατρεῖς ἤρξαντο συμφρονεῖν καὶ
2 Δυμαῖοι, καιροὶ δὲ καθ᾽ οὓς Πτολεμαῖος ὁ Λάγου καὶ
Λυσίμαχος, ἔτι δὲ Σέλευκος καὶ Πτολεμαῖος ὁ Κεραυ-
νὸς μετήλλαξαν τὸν βίον. πάντες γὰρ οὗτοι περὶ τὴν
3 προειρημένην ὀλυμπιάδα τὸ ζῆν ἐξέλιπον. τοὺς μὲν
οὖν ἀνώτερον τούτων χρόνους τοιαύτη τις ἦν ἡ περὶ τὸ
4 προειρημένον ἔθνος διάθεσις. ἀπὸ γὰρ Τισαμενοῦ
βασιλευθέντες, ὃς ἦν Ὀρέστου μὲν υἱός, κατὰ δὲ τὴν

moted and finally realized it, while Lycortas[75] and his party were those who assured the permanency, for a time, of this union. I will attempt to indicate how and at what date each of the three contributed to the result, insofar as this does not conflict with the scheme of my history. Aratus' government,[76] however, will be dealt with here and in future quite summarily, as he published a truthful and clearly written memoir of his own career; but the achievements of the two others will be narrated in greater detail and at more length. I think it will be easiest for myself to set forth the narrative and for my readers to follow it if I begin from the period when, after the dissolution of the Achaean League by the kings of Macedonia,[77] the cities began again to approach each other with a view to its renewal. Henceforward the League continued to grow until it reached in my own time the state of completion I have just partially described.

41. It was in the 124th Olympiad that Patrae and Dyme took the initiative, by entering into a league, just about the date of the deaths[78] of Ptolemy son of Lagus, Lysimachus, Seleucus, and Ptolemy Ceraunus, which all occurred in this Olympiad. The condition of the Achaean nation before this date had been more or less as follows. Their first king was Tisamenus the son of Orestes,[79] who, when ex-

284–280
B.C.

[75] P.'s father and an influential politician, close to Philopoemen.

[76] P.'s brevity is partially offset by Plutarch's *Life of Aratus*.

[77] A protracted process involving several kings of the late 4th and early 3rd centuries.

[78] These kings all died between 283 and 279.

[79] Mythical times. Ogygus (cf. 4. 1. 5) mentioned only by P.

τῶν Ἡρακλειδῶν κάθοδον ἐκπεσὼν τῆς Σπάρτης κατ-
5 έσχε τοὺς περὶ Ἀχαΐαν τόπους, ἀπὸ τούτου κατὰ τὸ
συνεχὲς καὶ κατὰ τὸ γένος ἕως Ὠγύγου βασιλευθέντες, μετὰ ταῦτα δυσαρεστήσαντες τοῖς τοῦ προειρημένου παισὶν ἐπὶ τῷ μὴ νομίμως, ἀλλὰ δεσποτικῶς
αὐτῶν ἄρχειν, μετέστησαν εἰς δημοκρατίαν τὴν πολι-
6 τείαν. λοιπὸν ἤδη τοὺς ἑξῆς χρόνους μέχρι τῆς
Ἀλεξάνδρου καὶ Φιλίππου δυναστείας ἄλλοτε μὲν
ἄλλως ἐχώρει τὰ πράγματ' αὐτοῖς κατὰ τὰς περιστάσεις, τό γε μὴν κοινὸν πολίτευμα, καθάπερ εἰρή-
7 καμεν, ἐν δημοκρατίᾳ συνέχειν ἐπειρῶντο. τοῦτο δ' ἦν
ἐκ δώδεκα πόλεων, ἃς ἔτι καὶ νῦν συμβαίνει διαμένειν,
πλὴν Ὠλένου καὶ Ἑλίκης τῆς πρὸ τῶν Λευκτρικῶν
8 ὑπὸ τῆς θαλάττης καταποθείσης· αὗται δ' εἰσὶ Πά-
τραι, Δύμη, Φαραί, Τριταία, Λεόντιον, Αἴγιον, Αἴγει-
9 ρα, Πελλήνη, Βοῦρα, Καρύνεια. κατὰ δὲ τοὺς ὑστέ-
ρους μὲν τῶν κατ' Ἀλέξανδρον καιρῶν, προτέρους δὲ
τῆς ἄρτι ῥηθείσης ὀλυμπιάδος, εἰς τοιαύτην διαφορὰν
καὶ καχεξίαν ἐνέπεσον, καὶ μάλιστα διὰ τῶν ἐκ Μακεδονίας βασιλέων, ἐν ᾗ συνέβη πάσας τὰς πόλεις
χωρισθείσας ἀφ' αὑτῶν ἐναντίως τὸ συμφέρον ἄγειν
10 ἀλλήλαις. ἐξ οὗ συνέπεσε τὰς μὲν ἐμφρούρους αὐτῶν
γενέσθαι διά τε Δημητρίου καὶ Κασσάνδρου, καὶ μετὰ
ταῦτα δι' Ἀντιγόνου τοῦ Γονατᾶ, τὰς δὲ καὶ τυραν-
νεῖσθαι· πλείστους γὰρ δὴ μονάρχους οὗτος ἐμφυ-
11 τεῦσαι δοκεῖ τοῖς Ἕλλησι. περὶ δὲ τὴν εἰκοστὴν καὶ
τετάρτην ὀλυμπιάδα πρὸς ταῖς ἑκατόν, καθάπερ ἐπάνω προεῖπον, αὖθις ἤρξαντο μετανοήσαντες συμ-

pelled from Sparta on the return of the Heraclidae, occupied Achaea, and they continued to be ruled by kings of his house down to Ogygus. Being dissatisfied with the rule of Ogygus' sons, which was despotical and not constitutional, they changed their government to a democracy. After this, down to the reigns of Alexander and Philip, their fortunes varied according to circumstances, but they always endeavored, as I said, to keep their League a democracy. This consisted of twelve cities, which still all exist with the exception of Olenus[80] and of Helice[81] which was engulfed by the sea a little before the battle of Leuctra. These cities[82] are Patrae, Dyme, Pharae, Tritaea, Leontium, Aegium, Aegira, Pellene, Bura, and Caryneia. After the time of Alexander and previous to the above Olympiad they fell, chiefly thanks to the kings of Macedon, into such a state of discord and ill feeling that all the cities separated from the League and began to act against each others' interests. The consequence[83] was that some of them were garrisoned by Demetrius and Cassander and afterward by Antigonus Gonatas, and some even had tyrants imposed on them by the latter, who planted more monarchs in Greece than any other king. But, as I said above, about the 125th Olympiad they began to repent and form a fresh league. (This was

---

[80] Small town, abandoned before 281/0: *RE* Olenos 2435–2442 (F. Bölte).   [81] City east of Aegium, destroyed in 373 by a *tsunami* (tidal wave after an earthquake).

[82] All ten participated in the campaign of Cn. Domitius in 122 against the Allobrogi (*ISE* 60); for the date, Th. Schwertfeger, *Der achaiische Bund von 146 bis 27 v. Chr.* (Munich 1974), 27–40. See n. on 3. 39. 8. For these cities see now A. Rizakis, *Achaïe* 3 (Athens 2008), for Patras vol. 2, Athens 1998.

[83] See WC 1. 232–233 for known details.

φρονεῖν. ταῦτα δ᾽ ἦν κατὰ τὴν Πύρρου διάβασιν εἰς
12 Ἰταλίαν. καὶ πρῶτοι μὲν συνέστησαν Δυμαῖοι, Πατρεῖς, Τριταιεῖς, Φαραιεῖς· διόπερ οὐδὲ στήλην ὑπάρχειν συμβαίνει τῶν πόλεων τούτων περὶ τῆς συμπολι-
13 τείας. μετὰ δὲ ταῦτα μάλιστά πως ἔτει πέμπτῳ τὴν
φρουρὰν ἐκβαλόντες Αἰγιεῖς μετέσχον τῆς συμπολι-
14 τείας· ἑξῆς δὲ τούτοις Βούριοι, τὸν τύραννον ἀποκτείναντες. ἅμα δὲ τούτοις Καρυνεῖς ἀποκατέστησαν.
συνιδὼν γὰρ Ἰσέας ὁ τῆς Καρυνείας τότε τυραννεύων
ἐκπεπτωκυῖαν μὲν ἐξ Αἰγίου τὴν φρουράν, ἀπολωλότα
δὲ τὸν ἐν τῇ Βούρᾳ μόναρχον διὰ Μάργου καὶ τῶν
Ἀχαιῶν, ἑαυτὸν δὲ πανταχόθεν ὁρῶν ὅσον οὐκ ἤδη
15 πολεμηθησόμενον, ἀποθέμενος τὴν ἀρχὴν καὶ λαβὼν
τὰ πιστὰ παρὰ τῶν Ἀχαιῶν ὑπὲρ τῆς ἀσφαλείας
προσέθηκε τὴν πόλιν πρὸς τὸ τῶν Ἀχαιῶν σύστημα.

42. Τίνος οὖν χάριν ἐπὶ τοὺς χρόνους τούτους
ἀνέδραμον; ἵνα πρῶτον μὲν γένηται συμφανὲς πῶς
καὶ κατὰ ποίους καιροὺς καὶ τίνες πρῶτοι τῶν ἐξ
ἀρχῆς Ἀχαιῶν αὖθις ἐποιήσαντο τὴν ἐπιβολὴν τῆς
2 νῦν συστάσεως, δεύτερον δ᾽ ἵνα καὶ τὰ τῆς προαιρέσεως μὴ μόνον διὰ τῆς ἡμετέρας ἀποφάσεως,
3 ἀλλὰ καὶ δι᾽ αὐτῶν τῶν πραγμάτων πίστεως τυγχάνῃ,
διότι μία τις ἀεὶ τῶν Ἀχαιῶν αἵρεσις ὑπῆρχε, καθ᾽ ἣν
προτείνοντες μὲν τὴν παρ᾽ αὐτοῖς ἰσηγορίαν καὶ παρρησίαν, πολεμοῦντες δὲ καὶ καταγωνιζόμενοι συνεχῶς
τοὺς ἢ δι᾽ αὐτῶν ἢ διὰ τῶν βασιλέων τὰς σφετέρας
πατρίδας καταδουλουμένους, τούτῳ τῷ τρόπῳ καὶ ταύτῃ τῇ προθέσει τοῦτο τοὔργον ἐπετέλεσαν, τὰ μὲν δι᾽

just about the date of Pyrrhus' crossing to Italy.) The first cities to do so[84] were Dyme, Patrae, Tritaea, and Pharae, and for this reason we do not even find any formal inscribed record of their adherence to the League. About five years afterward the people of Aegium expelled their garrison and joined the League, and the Burians were the next to do so, after putting their tyrant to death. Caryneia joined almost at the same time, for Iseas, its tyrant, when he saw the garrison expelled from Aegium, and the monarch of Bura killed by Margus[85] and the Achaeans, and war just about to be made on himself by all the towns round, abdicated and, on receiving an assurance from the Achaeans that his life would be spared, added his city to the League.

42. Why, the reader will ask, do I go back to these times? It is, firstly, to show which of the original Achaean cities took the first steps to re-form the League and at what dates, and, secondly, that my assertion regarding their political principle may be confirmed by the actual evidence of facts. What I asserted was that the Achaeans always followed one single policy, ever attracting others by the offer of their own equality and liberty and ever making war on and crushing those who either themselves or through the kings attempted to enslave their native cities, and that, in this manner and pursuing this purpose, they accomplished

---

[84] For the gradual development of the League see R. Urban, *Wachstum und Krise des Achäischen Bundes* (Wiesbaden 1979), and the chronological table in WC 1. 234.

[85] His death was reported in 2. 10. 5; he reappears in 43. 2 as the first elected single strategus, in 255/4.

4 αὐτῶν, τὰ δὲ καὶ διὰ τῶν συμμάχων. καὶ γὰρ τὰ δι᾽
ἐκείνων συνεργήματα γεγονότα πρὸς τοῦτο τὸ μέρος
ἐν τοῖς ἑξῆς χρόνοις ἐπὶ τὴν τῶν Ἀχαιῶν προαίρεσιν

5 ἀνοιστέον. πολλοῖς γὰρ κοινωνήσαντες πραγμάτων,
πλείστων δὲ καὶ καλλίστων Ῥωμαίοις, οὐδέποτε τὸ
παράπαν ἐπεθύμησαν ἐκ τῶν κατορθωμάτων οὐδενὸς

6 ἰδίᾳ λυσιτελοῦς, ἀλλ᾽ ἀντὶ πάσης τῆς ἑαυτῶν φιλοτιμίας, ἣν παρείχοντο τοῖς συμμάχοις, ἀντικατηλλάτ-
τοντο τὴν ἑκάστων ἐλευθερίαν καὶ τὴν κοινὴν ὁμόνοι-

7 αν Πελοποννησίων. σαφέστερον δ᾽ ὑπὲρ τούτων ἔσται
διαλαμβάνειν ἐξ αὐτῶν τῶν περὶ τὰς πράξεις ἐνεργη-
μάτων.

43. Εἴκοσι μὲν οὖν ἔτη τὰ πρῶτα καὶ πέντε συν-
επολιτεύσαντο μεθ᾽ ἑαυτῶν αἱ προειρημέναι πόλεις,
γραμματέα κοινὸν ἐκ περιόδου προχειριζόμεναι καὶ

2 δύο στρατηγούς. μετὰ δὲ ταῦτα πάλιν ἔδοξεν αὐτοῖς
ἕνα καθιστάνειν καὶ τούτῳ πιστεύειν ὑπὲρ τῶν ὅλων.
καὶ πρῶτος ἔτυχε τῆς τιμῆς ταύτης Μάργος ὁ Καρυ-

3 νεύς. τετάρτῳ δ᾽ ὕστερον ἔτει τοῦ προειρημένου στρατηγοῦντος Ἄρατος ὁ Σικυώνιος, ἔτη μὲν ἔχων εἴκοσι,
τυραννουμένην δ᾽ ἐλευθερώσας τὴν πατρίδα διὰ τῆς
ἀρετῆς τῆς ἑαυτοῦ καὶ τόλμης, προσένειμε πρὸς τὴν
τῶν Ἀχαιῶν πολιτείαν, ἀρχῆθεν εὐθὺς ἐραστὴς γενό-

4 μενος τῆς προαιρέσεως αὐτῶν. ὀγδόῳ δὲ πάλιν ἔτει
στρατηγὸς αἱρεθεὶς τὸ δεύτερον, καὶ πραξικοπήσας
τὸν Ἀκροκόρινθον, Ἀντιγόνου κυριεύοντος, καὶ γενόμενος ἐγκρατής, μεγάλου μὲν ἀπέλυσε φόβου τοὺς
τὴν Πελοπόννησον κατοικοῦντας, ἐλευθερώσας δὲ Κο-

their task in part unaided and in part with the help of allies. For the Achaean political principle must be credited also with the results furthering their end, to which their allies in subsequent years contributed. Though they took so much part in the enterprises of others, and especially in many of those of the Romans which resulted brilliantly, they never showed the least desire to gain any private profit from their success, but demanded, in exchange for the zealous aid they rendered their allies, nothing beyond the liberty of all states and the union of the Peloponnesians. This will be more clearly evident when we come to see the League in active operation.

43. For twenty-five years, then, these cities enjoyed a common political life, electing in rotation a Secretary of state and two Strategi. After this they decided to elect one Strategus and entrust him with the general direction of their affairs, the first to be nominated to this honorable office being Margus of Caryneia. Four years[86] after Margus' term of office, Aratus of Sicyon, though only twenty years of age, freed his city from its tyrant by his enterprise and courage, and, having always been a passionate admirer of the Achaean polity, made his own city a member of the League. Eight years after this,[87] during his second term of office as Strategus, he laid a plot to rule the citadel of Corinth which was held by Antigonus, thus delivering the Peloponnesians from a great source of fear, and

255 B.C.

243 B.C.

[86] 251/0. More in Plu., *Arat.* 5–9.

[87] In 243/2. The capture of Acrocorinth was Aratus' most famous feat. Only two years earlier, King Antigonus had retaken the citadel, following the death of his rebellious nephew Alexander who had been in control for several years.

ρινθίους προσηγάγετο πρὸς τὴν τῶν Ἀχαιῶν πολι-
5 τείαν. ἐπὶ δὲ τῆς αὐτῆς ἀρχῆς καὶ τὴν τῶν Μεγαρέων
6 πόλιν διαπραξάμενος προσένειμε τοῖς Ἀχαιοῖς. ταῦτά
τ᾽ ἐγίνετο τῷ πρότερον ἔτει τῆς Καρχηδονίων ἥττης,
ἐν ᾗ καθόλου Σικελίας ἐκχωρήσαντες πρῶτον ὑπέμει-
7 ναν τότε φόρους ἐνεγκεῖν Ῥωμαίοις. μεγάλην δὲ προκοπὴν ποιήσας τῆς ἐπιβολῆς ἐν ὀλίγῳ χρόνῳ, λοιπὸν
ἤδη διετέλει προστατῶν μὲν τοῦ τῶν Ἀχαιῶν ἔθνους,
πάσας δὲ τὰς ἐπιβολὰς καὶ πράξεις πρὸς ἓν τέλος
8 ἀναφέρων· τοῦτο δ᾽ ἦν τὸ Μακεδόνας μὲν ἐκβαλεῖν ἐκ
Πελοποννήσου, τὰς δὲ μοναρχίας καταλῦσαι, βεβαι-
9 ῶσαι δ᾽ ἑκάστοις τὴν κοινὴν καὶ πάτριον ἐλευθερίαν.
μέχρι μὲν οὖν ἦν Ἀντίγονος ὁ Γονατᾶς, πρός τε τὴν
ἐκείνου πολυπραγμοσύνην καὶ πρὸς τὴν Αἰτωλῶν
10 πλεονεξίαν ἀντιταττόμενος διετέλει, πραγματικῶς
ἕκαστα χειρίζων, καίπερ εἰς τοῦτο προβάντων ἀμφοτέρων ἀδικίας καὶ τόλμης ὥστε ποιήσασθαι συνθήκας
πρὸς ἀλλήλους ὑπὲρ διαιρέσεως τοῦ τῶν Ἀχαιῶν
ἔθνους.

44. Ἀντιγόνου δὲ μεταλλάξαντος, καὶ συνθεμένων
τῶν Ἀχαιῶν καὶ συμμαχίαν πρὸς Αἰτωλοὺς καὶ μετα-
σχόντων εὐγενῶς σφίσι τοῦ πρὸς Δημήτριον πολέμου, τὰ μὲν τῆς ἀλλοτριότητος καὶ δυσμενείας ἤρθη
κατὰ τὸ παρόν, ὑπεγένετο δὲ κοινωνικὴ καὶ φιλική τις
2 αὐτοῖς διάθεσις. Δημητρίου δὲ βασιλεύσαντος δέκα
μόνον ἔτη, καὶ μεταλλάξαντος τὸν βίον περὶ τὴν
πρώτην διάβασιν εἰς τὴν Ἰλλυρίδα Ῥωμαίων, ἐγένετό
τις εὔροια πραγμάτων πρὸς τὴν ἐξ ἀρχῆς ἐπιβολὴν

induced the city he had liberated to join the League. In the same term of office he obtained the adhesion of Megara to the Achaeans by the same means. These events took place in the year before that defeat of the Carthaginians which forced them to evacuate Sicily and submit for the first time to pay tribute to Rome. Having in so short a space of time thus materially advanced his projects, he continued to govern the Achaean nation, all his schemes and action being directed to one object, the expulsion of the Macedonians from the Peloponnese, the suppression of the tyrants, and the reestablishment on a sure basis of the federal and individual freedom of each state. During the life of Antigonus Gonatus he continued to offer a most effectual opposition both to the meddlesomeness of this king and the lust for plunder of the Aetolians, although the two were so unscrupulous and venturesome that they entered into an arrangement[88] for the purpose of dissolving the Achaean League.

44. But, on the death of Antigonus, the Achaeans even made an alliance with the Aetolians and supported them ungrudgingly in the war against Demetrius,[89] so that, for the time at least, their estrangement and hostility ceased, and a more or less friendly and sociable feeling sprang up between them. Demetrius only reigned for ten years, his death[90] taking place at the time the Romans first crossed to Illyria, and after this the tide of events seemed to flow for a

242–241 B.C.

239 B.C.

229 B.C.

[88] *StV* 490, probably in 243 after Aratus had taken Acrocorinth.
[89] The "Demetrian War," 239–229.
[90] Spring 229.

3 τῶν Ἀχαιῶν, οἱ γὰρ ἐν τῇ Πελοποννήσῳ μόναρχοι,
δυσελπιστήσαντες ἐπὶ τῷ μετηλλαχέναι μὲν τὸν Δημήτριον, ὃς ἦν αὐτοῖς οἷον εἰ χορηγὸς καὶ μισθο-
δότης, ἐπικεῖσθαι δὲ τὸν Ἄρατον, οἰόμενον δεῖν σφᾶς
ἀποτίθεσθαι τὰς τυραννίδας, καὶ τοῖς μὲν πεισθεῖσι
μεγάλας δωρεὰς καὶ τιμὰς προτείνοντα, τοῖς δὲ μὴ
προσέχουσιν ἔτι μείζους ἐπανατεινόμενον φόβους καὶ
4 κινδύνους διὰ τῶν Ἀχαιῶν, ὥρμησαν ἐπὶ τὸ πεισθέντες ἀποθέσθαι μὲν τὰς τυραννίδας, ἐλευθερῶσαι δὲ
5 τὰς ἑαυτῶν πατρίδας, μετασχεῖν δὲ τῆς τῶν Ἀχαιῶν
πολιτείας. Λυδιάδας μὲν οὖν ὁ Μεγαλοπολίτης ἔτι
ζῶντος Δημητρίου, κατὰ τὴν αὐτοῦ προαίρεσιν, πάνυ
πραγματικῶς καὶ φρονίμως προϊδόμενος τὸ μέλλον,
ἀπετέθειτο τὴν τυραννίδα, καὶ μετεσχήκει τῆς ἐθνικῆς
6 συμπολιτείας. Ἀριστόμαχος δ᾽ ὁ τῶν Ἀργείων τύραν-
νος καὶ Ξένων ὁ τῶν Ἑρμιονέων καὶ Κλεώνυμος ὁ τῶν
Φλιασίων τότ᾽ ἀποθέμενοι τὰς μοναρχίας ἐκοινώνη-
σαν τῆς τῶν Ἀχαιῶν δημοκρατίας.

45. Ὁλοσχερεστέρας δὲ γενομένης αὐξήσεως διὰ
ταῦτα καὶ προκοπῆς περὶ τὸ ἔθνος, Αἰτωλοὶ διὰ τὴν
ἔμφυτον ἀδικίαν καὶ πλεονεξίαν φθονήσαντες, τὸ δὲ
πλεῖον ἐλπίσαντες καταδιελέσθαι τὰς πόλεις, καθάπερ καὶ πρότερον τὰς μὲν Ἀκαρνάνων διενείμαντο
πρὸς Ἀλέξανδρον, τὰς δὲ τῶν Ἀχαιῶν ἐπεβάλοντο
2 πρὸς Ἀντίγονον τὸν Γονατᾶν, καὶ τότε παραπλησίαις

91 He brought Megalopolis into the League in 235; see n. on
51. 3.

time in favor of the Achaeans' constant purpose; for the Peloponnesian tyrants were much cast down by the death of Demetrius, who had been, so to speak, their furnisher and paymaster, and equally so by the threatening attitude of Aratus, who demanded that they should depose themselves, offering abundance of gifts and honors to those who consented to do so, and menacing those who turned a deaf ear to him with still more abundant chastisement on the part of the Achaeans. They therefore hurried to accede to his demand, laying down their tyrannies, setting their respective cities free, and joining the Achaean League. Lydiades of Megalopolis[91] had even foreseen what was likely to happen, and with great wisdom and good sense had forestalled the death of Demetrius and of his own free will laid down his tyranny and adhered to the national government. Afterward Aristomachus, tyrant of Argos,[92] Xenon, tyrant of Hermione, and Cleonymus, tyrant of Phlius, also resigned and joined the democratic Achaean League.

45. The League being thus materially increased in extent and power, the Aetolians, owing to that unprincipled passion for aggrandizement which is natural to them, either out of envy or rather in the hope of partitioning the cities, as they had previously partitioned[93] those of Acarnania with Alexander and had proposed to do regarding Achaea with Antigonus Gonatas, went so far as to join

[92] The city joined the League in 229/8, and probably so did Phlius; Hermione only in the early twenties.

[93] The partition gave the Aetolians eastern, and Alexander western Acarnania. Alexander was still alive and in possession of Leucas in 242: *Chiron* 31 (2001) 342–344, no. 5.

ἐλπίσιν ἐπαρθέντες, ἀπετόλμησαν Ἀντιγόνῳ τε τῷ
κατ᾽ ἐκείνους τοὺς καιροὺς προεστῶτι Μακεδόνων,
ἐπιτροπεύοντι δὲ Φιλίππου παιδὸς ὄντος, καὶ Κλεομένει τῷ βασιλεῖ Λακεδαιμονίων κοινωνεῖν, καὶ συμπλέ-
3 κειν ἀμφοτέροις ἅμα τὰς χεῖρας. ὁρῶντες γὰρ τὸν
Ἀντίγονον, κυριεύοντα μὲν τῶν κατὰ Μακεδονίαν
ἀσφαλῶς, ὁμολογούμενον δὲ καὶ πρόδηλον ἐχθρὸν
ὄντα τῶν Ἀχαιῶν διὰ τὸ τὸν Ἀκροκόρινθον πραξι-
4 <κοπήσαντας καταλαβεῖν>. ὑπέλαβον, εἰ τοὺς Λακεδαιμονίους προσλαβόντες ἔτι κοινωνοὺς σφίσι τῆς
ἐπιβολῆς προεμβιβάσαιεν εἰς τὴν πρὸς τὸ ἔθνος ἀπέχθειαν, ῥᾳδίως ἂν καταγωνίσασθαι τοὺς Ἀχαιοὺς ἐν
καιρῷ συνεπιθέμενοι καὶ πανταχόθεν περιστήσαντες
5 αὐτοῖς τὸν πόλεμον. ὃ δὴ καὶ ταχέως ἂν ἐκ τῶν κατὰ
λόγον ἐπετέλεσαν, εἰ μὴ τὸ κυριώτατον παρεῖδον τῆς
προθέσεως, οὐ συλλογισάμενοι διότι ταῖς ἐπιβολαῖς
Ἄρατον ἕξουσιν ἀνταγωνιστήν, ἄνδρα δυνάμενον πά-
6 σης εὐστοχεῖν περιστάσεως. τοιγαροῦν ὁρμήσαντες
ἐπὶ τὸ πολυπραγμονεῖν καὶ χειρῶν ἄρχειν ἀδίκων οὐχ
οἷον ἤνυσάν τι τῶν ἐπινοηθέντων, ἀλλὰ τοὐναντίον
καὶ τὸν Ἄρατον τότε προεστῶτα καὶ τὸ ἔθνος ἐσωμα-
τοποίησαν, πραγματικῶς ἀντιπερισπάσαντος ἐκείνου
7 καὶ λυμηναμένου τὰς ἐπιβολὰς αὐτῶν. ὡς δ᾽ ἐχει-
ρίσθη τὰ ὅλα δῆλον ἔσται διὰ τῶν λέγεσθαι μελλόντων.

46. Θεωρῶν γὰρ τοὺς Αἰτωλοὺς ὁ προειρημένος

---

94 Not true: see J. V. A. Fine, *AJPh* 61 (1940) 129–150.

hands[94] with Antigonus Doson,[95] then regent of Macedonia and guardian to Philip, who was still a child, and Cleomenes, king of Sparta.[96] They saw that Antigonus[97] was undisputed master of Macedonia and at the same time the open and avowed enemy of the Achaeans owing to their seizure by treachery of the Acrocorinthus, and they supposed that if they could get the Lacedaemonians also to join them in their project, exciting first their animosity against the League, they could easily crush the Achaeans by attacking them at the proper time all at once and from all quarters. This indeed they would in all probability soon have done, but for the most important factor which they had overlooked in their plans. They never took into consideration that in this undertaking they would have Aratus[98] as their opponent, a man capable of meeting any emergency. Consequently the result of their intrigues and unjust aggression was that not only did they entirely fail in their designs, but on the contrary consolidated the power of the League, and of Aratus who was then Strategus,[99] as he most adroitly diverted and spoilt all their plans. How he managed all this the following narrative will show.

46. Aratus saw that the Aetolians were ashamed of

[95] Regent in 229, king since 228/7, also guardian to Philip, son of Demetrius II. S. Le Bohec, *Antigone Dôsôn roi de Macédoine* (Nancy 1993).

[96] King 235–222, see Plu., *Cleom.*, and P. Cartledge, in P. Cartledge-A. Spawforth, *Hellenistic and Roman Sparta* (London-New York 1989), 38–58.

[97] Contrary to P.'s statement, hostility existed between the king and the Aetolians.   [98] His *Memoirs* are P.'s source.

[99] 229/8, for the ninth time.

387

ἀνὴρ τὸν μὲν πόλεμον τὸν πρὸς αὐτοὺς αἰσχυνομένους
ἀναλαβεῖν ἐκ τοῦ φανεροῦ διὰ τὸ καὶ λίαν εἶναι
προσφάτους τὰς ἐκ τῶν Ἀχαιῶν εὐεργεσίας περὶ τὸν

2 Δημητριακὸν πόλεμον εἰς αὐτούς, συμβουλευομένους
δὲ τοῖς Λακεδαιμονίοις καὶ φθονοῦντας τοῖς Ἀχαιοῖς
ἐπὶ τοσοῦτον ὥστε Κλεομένους πεπραξικοπηκότος αὐτοὺς καὶ παρῃρημένου Τεγέαν, Μαντίνειαν, Ὀρχομε-
νόν, τὰς Αἰτωλοῖς οὐ μόνον συμμαχίδας ὑπαρχούσας,
ἀλλὰ καὶ συμπολιτευομένας τότε πόλεις, οὐχ οἷον

3 ἀγανακτοῦντας ἐπὶ τούτοις, ἀλλὰ καὶ βεβαιοῦντας
αὐτῷ τὴν παράληψιν, καὶ τοὺς πρότερον κατὰ τῶν
μηδὲν ἀδικούντων πᾶσαν ἱκανὴν ποιουμένους πρό-
φασιν εἰς τὸ πολεμεῖν διὰ τὴν πλεονεξίαν τότε συνορῶν ἑκουσίως παρασπονδουμένους καὶ τὰς μεγίστας
ἀπολλύντας πόλεις ἐθελοντὴν ἐφ᾽ ᾧ μόνον ἰδεῖν ἀξιό-
χρεων γενόμενον ἀνταγωνιστὴν Κλεομένη τοῖς Ἀχαι-

4 οῖς, ἔγνω δεῖν εἰς ταῦτα βλέπων οὗτός τε καὶ πάντες
ὁμοίως οἱ προεστῶτες τοῦ τῶν Ἀχαιῶν πολιτεύματος
πολέμου μὲν πρὸς μηδένα κατάρχειν, ἐνίστασθαι δὲ

5 ταῖς τῶν Λακεδαιμονίων ἐπιβολαῖς. τὸ μὲν οὖν πρῶτον ἐπὶ τούτων ἦσαν τῶν διαλήψεων· θεωροῦντες δὲ
κατὰ τοὺς ἑξῆς χρόνους τὸν Κλεομένη θρασέως ἐποι-
κοδομοῦντα μὲν τὸ καλούμενον Ἀθήναιον ἐν τῇ τῶν
Μεγαλοπολιτῶν χώρα, πρόδηλον δὲ καὶ πικρὸν ἀνα-

6 δεικνύντα σφίσι πολέμιον ἑαυτόν, τότε δὴ συναθροίσαντες τοὺς Ἀχαιοὺς ἔκριναν μετὰ τῆς· βουλῆς ἀναλαμβάνειν φανερῶς τὴν πρὸς τοὺς Λακεδαιμονίους
ἀπέχθειαν.

openly declaring war on them, as it was so very recently
that the Achaeans had helped them[100] in their war against
Demetrius, but that they were so much of one mind with
the Lacedaemonians and so jealous of the Achaeans that
when Cleomenes broke faith with them and possessed
himself of Tegea, Mantinea, and Orchomenus, cities
which were not only allies of the Aetolians, but at the time
members of their league, they not only showed no resent-
ment, but actually set their seal to his occupation. He saw
too that they, who on previous occasions, owing to their
lust of aggrandizement, found any pretext adequate for
making war on those who had done them no wrong, now
allowed themselves to be treacherously attacked and to
suffer the loss of some of their largest cities simply in order
to see Cleomenes become a really formidable antagonist
of the Achaeans. Aratus, therefore, and all the leading men
of the Achaean League decided not to take the initiative in
going to war with anyone, but to resist Spartan aggression.
This at least was their first resolve; but when shortly afterward Cleomenes boldly began to fortify against them the
so-called Athenaeum in the territory of Megalopolis, and
to show himself their avowed and bitter enemy, they called
the Council of the League together and decided on open
war with Sparta.[101]

[100] 2. 6. 1.
[101] Autumn 229 or spring 228 (before May), still in Aratus'
ninth year as general. The war was to last until 222.

7 Ὁ μὲν οὖν Κλεομενικὸς προσαγορευθεὶς πόλεμος τοιαύτην ἔλαβε τὴν ἀρχὴν καὶ κατὰ τούτους τοὺς καιρούς.

47. οἱ δ᾽ Ἀχαιοὶ τὸ μὲν πρῶτον διὰ τῆς ἰδίας δυνάμεως ὥρμησαν ἀντοφθαλμεῖν τοῖς Λακεδαιμονίοις, ἅμα μὲν ὑπολαμβάνοντες κάλλιστον εἶναι τὸ μὴ δι᾽ ἑτέρων σφίσι πορίζεσθαι τὴν σωτηρίαν, ἀλλ᾽

2 αὐτοὺς δι᾽ αὑτῶν σῴζειν τὰς πόλεις καὶ τὴν χώραν, ἅμα δὲ βουλόμενοι καὶ τὴν πρὸς Πτολεμαῖον τηρεῖν φιλίαν διὰ τὰς προγεγενημένας εὐεργεσίας καὶ μὴ

3 φαίνεσθαι πρὸς ἑτέρους ἐκτείνοντες τὰς χεῖρας, ἤδη δ᾽ ἐπὶ ποσὸν τοῦ πολέμου προβαίνοντος, καὶ τοῦ Κλεομένους τό τε πάτριον πολίτευμα καταλύσαντος καὶ τὴν ἔννομον βασιλείαν εἰς τυραννίδα μεταστήσαντος, χρωμένου δὲ καὶ τῷ πολέμῳ πρακτικῶς καὶ παρα-

4 βόλως, προορώμενος Ἄρατος τὸ μέλλον, καὶ δεδιὼς τήν τε τῶν Αἰτωλῶν ἀπόνοιαν καὶ τόλμαν, ἔκρινε πρὸ

5 πολλοῦ λυμαίνεσθαι τὴν ἐπιβολὴν αὐτῶν. κατανοῶν δὲ τὸν Ἀντίγονον καὶ πρᾶξιν ἔχοντα καὶ σύνεσιν καὶ πίστεως ἀντιποιούμενον, τοὺς δὲ βασιλεῖς σαφῶς εἰδὼς φύσει μὲν οὐδένα νομίζοντας οὔτε <σύνε>ργον οὔτε πολέμιον, ταῖς δὲ τοῦ συμφέροντος ψήφοις αἰεὶ

6 μετροῦντας τὰς ἔχθρας καὶ τὰς φιλίας, ἐπεβάλετο λαλεῖν πρὸς τὸν εἰρημένον βασιλέα καὶ συμπλέκειν τὰς χεῖρας, ὑποδεικνύων αὐτῷ τὸ συμβησόμενον ἐκ

7 τῶν πραγμάτων. προδήλως μὲν οὖν αὐτὸ πράττειν ἀσύμφορον ἡγεῖτο διὰ πλείους αἰτίας. τόν τε γὰρ

This was the date at which the war known as the Cleo-   227 B.C.
menic war began; and such was its origin.

47. The Achaeans at first decided to face the Lacedaemonians single-handed, considering it in the first place
most honorable not to owe their safety to others but to protect their cities and country unaided, and also desiring to
maintain their friendship with Ptolemy[102] owing to the ob-
ligations they were under to him, and not to appear to him
to be seeking aid elsewhere. But when the war had lasted
for some time, and Cleomenes, having overthrown the ancient polity at Sparta and changed the constitutional king-
ship into a tyranny,[103] showed great energy and daring in   225 B.C.
the conduct of the campaign, Aratus, foreseeing what was
likely to happen and dreading the reckless audacity of the
Aetolians, determined to be beforehand with them and
spoil their plans. He perceived that Antigonus[104] was a
man of energy and sound sense, and that he claimed to be a
man of honor, but he knew that kings do not regard anyone
as their natural ally or foe, but measure friendship and en-
mity by the sole standard of expediency. He therefore decided to approach that monarch and put himself on con-
fidential terms with him, pointing out to him to what the
present course of affairs would probably lead. Now for several reasons he did not think it expedient to do this overtly.
In the first place he would thus expose himself to being

[102] Ptolemy III Euergetes, 246–221. He continued his father's
policy of sending an annual subvention to the League.

[103] In 23. 11. 5 it is "monarchy"!

[104] Heretofore the archenemy of the League, but now approached to save it from extinction. Aratus had unsuccessfully
appealed for aid to Aetolia, Athens, and Egypt (Plu., *Arat*. 41. 3).

Κλεομένη καὶ τοὺς Αἰτωλοὺς ἀνταγωνιστὰς παρα-
8 σκευάζειν ἤμελλε πρὸς τὴν ἐπιβολήν, τούς τε πολλοὺς
τῶν Ἀχαιῶν διατρέψειν, καταφεύγων ἐπὶ τοὺς ἐχθροὺς
καὶ δοκῶν ὁλοσχερῶς ἀπεγνωκέναι τὰς ἐν αὐτοῖς
9 ἐλπίδας· ὅπερ ἥκιστα φαίνεσθαι πράττων ἐβούλετο.
διόπερ ἔχων τοιαύτην πρόθεσιν ἀδήλως αὐτὰ διενο-
10 εῖτο χειρίζειν. ἐξ οὗ πολλὰ παρὰ τὴν ἑαυτοῦ γνώμην
ἠναγκάζετο καὶ λέγειν καὶ ποιεῖν πρὸς τοὺς ἐκτός, δι'
ὧν ἤμελλε τὴν ἐναντίαν ἔμφασιν ὑποδεικνύων ταύτην
11 ἐπικρύψεσθαι τὴν οἰκονομίαν. ὧν χάριν ἔνια τούτων
οὐδ' ἐν τοῖς ὑπομνήμασι κατέταξεν.

48. Εἰδὼς δὲ τοὺς Μεγαλοπολίτας κακοπαθοῦντας
μὲν τῷ πολέμῳ διὰ τὸ παρακειμένους τῇ Λακεδαίμονι
προπολεμεῖν τῶν ἄλλων, οὐ τυγχάνοντας δὲ τῆς καθηκούσης ἐπικουρίας ὑπὸ τῶν Ἀχαιῶν διὰ τὸ κἀκείνους
2 δυσχρηστεῖσθαι θλιβομένους ὑπὸ τῆς περιστάσεως,
σαφῶς δὲ γινώσκων οἰκείως διακειμένους αὐτοὺς πρὸς
τὴν Μακεδόνων οἰκίαν ἐκ τῶν κατὰ τὸν Ἀμύντου
3 Φίλιππον εὐεργεσιῶν, διειλήφει διότι ταχέως ἂν ὑπὸ
τοῦ Κλεομένους πιεζόμενοι καταφύγοιεν ἐπὶ τὸν Ἀντί-
4 γονον καὶ τὰς Μακεδόνων ἐλπίδας· κοινολογηθεὶς οὖν
δι' ἀπορρήτων περὶ τῆς ὅλης ἐπιβολῆς Νικοφάνει καὶ
Κερκιδᾷ τοῖς Μεγαλοπολίταις, οἵτινες ἦσαν αὐτοῦ

---

105 The king had made the Hellenic League the judge in a dispute between Megalopolis and Sparta and the verdict favored
Megalopolis; see *SIG* 665, lines 19–24 and n. 4: see further n. on
31. 1. 7.

outbidden in his project by Cleomenes and the Aetolians, and next he would damage the spirit of the Achaean troops by thus appealing to an enemy and appearing to have entirely abandoned the hopes he had placed in them—this being the very last thing he wished them to think. Therefore, having formed this plan, he decided to carry it out by covert means. He was consequently compelled in public both to do and to say many things quite contrary to his real intention, so as to keep his design concealed by creating the exactly opposite impression. For this reason there are some of these matters that he does not even refer to in his Memoirs.

48. He knew that the people of Megalopolis were suffering severely from the war as, owing to their being on the Lacedaemonian border, they had to bear the full brunt of it, and could not receive proper assistance from the Achaeans, as the latter were themselves in difficulties and distress. As he also knew for a surety that they were well disposed to the royal house of Macedon ever since the favors[105] received in the time of Philip, son of Amyntas, he felt sure that, hard pressed as they were by Cleomenes, they would be very ready to take refuge in Antigonus and hopes of safety from Macedonia. He therefore communicated his project confidentially to Nicophanes and Cercidas of Megalopolis[106] who were family friends of his own

---

106 Statesman, lawgiver, and poet, author of satirical verses with a social content, *Studi Cercidei [P. Oxy 1082]*, a cura di E. Livrea (Bonn 1986). He reappears as commander of Achaean forces in 222 (2. 65. 3). *RE* Kerkidas no. 2, 294–308 (G. A. Gerhard, with a note by W. Kroll).

5 πατρικοὶ ξένοι καὶ πρὸς τὴν ἐπιβολὴν εὐφυεῖς, ῥᾳδίως
διὰ τούτων ὁρμὴν παρέστησε τοῖς Μεγαλοπολίταις
εἰς τὸ πρεσβεύειν πρὸς τοὺς Ἀχαιοὺς καὶ παρακαλεῖν
6 πρὸς τὸν Ἀντίγονον ὑπὲρ βοηθείας. οἱ μὲν οὖν Μεγαλοπολῖται κατέστησαν αὐτοὺς τοὺς περὶ τὸν Νικοφάνη καὶ τὸν Κερκιδᾶν πρεσβευτὰς πρός τε τοὺς
Ἀχαιοὺς κἀκεῖθεν εὐθέως πρὸς τὸν Ἀντίγονον, ἂν
7 αὐτοῖς συγκατάθηται τὸ ἔθνος. οἱ δ᾽ Ἀχαιοὶ συνεχώ-
8 ρησαν πρεσβεύειν τοῖς Μεγαλοπολίταις. σπουδῇ δὲ
συμμίξαντες οἱ περὶ τὸν Νικοφάνη τῷ βασιλεῖ διελέγοντο περὶ μὲν τῆς ἑαυτῶν πατρίδος αὐτὰ τἀναγκαῖα
διὰ βραχέων καὶ κεφαλαιωδῶς, τὰ δὲ πολλὰ περὶ τῶν
ὅλων κατὰ τὰς ἐντολὰς τὰς Ἀράτου καὶ τὰς ὑποθέσεις.

49. αὗται δ᾽ ἦσαν ὑποδεικνύναι τὴν Αἰτωλῶν καὶ
Κλεομένους κοινοπραγίαν τί δύναται καὶ ποῖ τείνει,
καὶ δηλοῦν ὅτι πρώτοις μὲν αὐτοῖς Ἀχαιοῖς εὐλα-
2 βητέον, ἑξῆς δὲ καὶ μᾶλλον Ἀντιγόνῳ. τοῦτο μὲν γὰρ
ὡς Ἀχαιοὶ τὸν ἐξ ἀμφοῖν πόλεμον οὐκ ἂν ὑπενέγκαιεν
εὐθεώρητον εἶναι πᾶσι, τοῦτο δ᾽ ὡς Αἰτωλοὶ καὶ Κλεομένης κρατήσαντες τούτων οὐκ εὐδοκήσουσιν οὐδὲ μὴ
μείνωσιν ἐπὶ τῶν ὑποκειμένων ἔτι τοῦ πρόσθεν ῥᾷον
3 εἶναι τῷ νοῦν ἔχοντι συνιδεῖν. τήν τε γὰρ Αἰτωλῶν
πλεονεξίαν οὐχ οἷον τοῖς Πελοποννησίων ὅροις εὐδο-
κῆσαί ποτ᾽ ἂν περιληφθεῖσαν, ἀλλ᾽ οὐδὲ τοῖς τῆς
4 Ἑλλάδος, τήν τε Κλεομένους φιλοδοξίαν καὶ τὴν ὅλην
ἐπιβολὴν κατὰ μὲν τὸ παρὸν αὐτῆς ἐφίεσθαι τῆς
Πελοποννησίων ἀρχῆς, τυχόντα δὲ ταύτης τὸν προειρημένον κατὰ πόδας ἀνθέξεσθαι τῆς τῶν Ἑλλήνων

and well suited for the business, and he had no difficulty through them in inciting the Megalopolitans to send an embassy to the Achaeans begging them to appeal to Antigonus for help. Nicophanes and Cercidas themselves were appointed envoys by the Megalopolitans, in the first place to the Achaeans and next, if the League consented, with orders to proceed at once to Antigonus. The Achaeans agreed to allow the Megalopolitans to send an embassy; and with the other ambassadors hastened to meet the king. They said no more than was strictly necessary on the subject of their own city, treating this matter briefly and summarily, but dwelt at length on the general situation, in the sense that Aratus had directed and prompted.

49. He had charged them[107] to point out the importance and the probable consequences of the common action of the Aetolians and Cleomenes, representing that in the first place the Achaeans were imperiled by it and next and in a larger measure Antigonus himself. For it was perfectly evident to all that the Achaeans could not hold out against both adversaries, and it was still more easy for any person of intelligence to see that, if the Aetolians and Cleomenes were successful, they would surely not rest content and be satisfied with their advantage. The Aetolian schemes of territorial aggrandizement would never stop short of the boundaries of the Peloponnese or even those of Greece itself, while Cleomenes' personal ambition, and far-reaching projects, though for the present he aimed only at supremacy in the Peloponnese, would, on his attaining this, at once develop into a claim to be overlord of

107 The whole picture, through 49. 10, is taken from Aratus' *Memoirs* and far from the truth.

5 ἡγεμονίας. ἧς οὐχ οἷόν τε καθικέσθαι μὴ οὐ πρόσθεν
6 καταλύσαντα τὴν Μακεδόνων ἀρχήν. σκοπεῖν οὖν
αὐτὸν ἠξίουν, προορώμενον τὸ μέλλον, πότερον συμ-
φέρει τοῖς σφετέροις πράγμασι μετ' Ἀχαιῶν καὶ Βοιωτῶν ἐν Πελοποννήσῳ πρὸς Κλεομένη πολεμεῖν ὑπὲρ
τῆς τῶν Ἑλλήνων ἡγεμονίας ἢ προέμενον τὸ μέγιστον
ἔθνος διακινδυνεύειν ἐν Θετταλίᾳ πρὸς Αἰτωλοὺς καὶ
Βοιωτούς, ἔτι δ' Ἀχαιοὺς καὶ Λακεδαιμονίους, ὑπὲρ
7 τῆς Μακεδόνων ἀρχῆς. ἐὰν μὲν οὖν Αἰτωλοὶ τὴν ἐκ
τῶν Ἀχαιῶν εἰς αὑτοὺς γεγενημένην εὔνοιαν ἐν τοῖς
κατὰ Δημήτριον καιροῖς ἐντρεπόμενοι τὴν ἡσυχίαν
ἄγειν ὑποκρίνωνται, καθάπερ καὶ νῦν, πολεμήσειν
αὐτοὺς ἔφασαν τοὺς Ἀχαιοὺς πρὸς τὸν Κλεομένη· κἂν
μὲν ἡ τύχη συνεπιλαμβάνηται, μὴ δεῖσθαι χρείας τῶν
8 βοηθησόντων· ἂν δ' ἀντιπίπτῃ τὰ τῆς τύχης, Αἰτωλοὶ
δὲ συνεπιτίθωνται, προσέχειν αὐτὸν παρεκάλουν τοῖς
πράγμασιν, ἵνα μὴ πρόηται τοὺς καιρούς, ἔτι δὲ
9 δυναμένοις σῴζεσθαι Πελοποννησίοις ἐπαρκέσῃ· περὶ
δὲ πίστεως καὶ χάριτος ἀποδόσεως ῥᾳθυμεῖν αὐτὸν
ᾤοντο δεῖν· τῆς γὰρ χρείας ἐπιτελουμένης αὐτὸν εὑ-
ρήσειν τὸν Ἄρατον εὐδοκουμένας ἀμφοτέροις ὑπ-
10 ισχνοῦντο πίστεις. ὁμοίως δ' ἔφασαν καὶ τὸν καιρὸν
τῆς βοηθείας αὐτὸν ὑποδείξειν.

50. Ὁ μὲν οὖν Ἀντίγονος ἀκούσας ταῦτα, καὶ
δόξας ἀληθινῶς καὶ πραγματικῶς ὑποδεικνύναι τὸν
2 Ἄρατον, προσεῖχε τοῖς ἑξῆς πραττομένοις ἐπιμελῶς.

---

108 They moved at this time, 227, away from Aetolia and closer

all Hellas, a thing impossible without his first putting an end to the dominion of Macedon. They implored him then to look to the future and consider which was most in his interest, to fight in the Peloponnese against Cleomenes for the supremacy of Greece with the support of the Achaeans and Boeotians,[108] or to abandon the greatest of the Greek nations to its fate and then do battle in Thessaly for the throne of Macedonia with the Aetolians, Boeotians, Achaeans, and Spartans all at once. Should the Aetolians, owing to the benefits received from the Achaeans in their war with Demetrius, pretend to continue their present inaction, the Achaeans alone, they said, would fight against Cleomenes, and, if Fortune favored them, would require no help; but should they meet with ill success and be attacked by the Aetolians also, they entreated him to take good heed and not let the opportunity slip, but come to the aid of the Peloponnesians while it was still possible to save them. As for conditions of alliance and the return they could offer him for his support, they said he need not concern himself, for once the service they demanded was being actually rendered, they promised him that Aratus would find terms satisfactory to both parties. Aratus himself, they said, would also indicate the date at which they required his aid.

50. Antigonus, having listened to them, felt convinced that Aratus took a true and practical view of the situation, and carefully considered the next steps to be taken, prom-

to Macedon (see 20. 5. 8). An important document of this rapprochement is *SIG* 519, with the commentary by D. Knoepfler in *Les Élites et leurs Facettes*, ed. M. Cebeillac-Gervasoni and L. Lamoine (Rome and Clermont-Ferrand 2003), 85–106.

ἔγραψε δὲ καὶ τοῖς Μεγαλοπολίταις, ἐπαγγελλόμενος
βοηθήσειν, ἐὰν καὶ τοῖς Ἀχαιοῖς τοῦτο βουλομένοις
3 ᾖ. τῶν δὲ περὶ τὸν Νικοφάνη καὶ Κερκιδᾶν ἐπανελ-
θόντων εἰς οἶκον, καὶ τάς τε παρὰ τοῦ βασιλέως
ἐπιστολὰς ἀποδόντων καὶ τὴν λοιπὴν εὔνοιαν αὐτοῦ
4 καὶ προθυμίαν διασαφούντων, μετεωρισθέντες οἱ
Μεγαλοπολῖται προθύμως ἔσχον ἰέναι πρὸς τὴν σύνοδον τῶν Ἀχαιῶν καὶ παρακαλεῖν ἐπισπάσασθαι τὸν
Ἀντίγονον καὶ τὰ πράγματα κατὰ σπουδὴν ἐγχειρί-
5 ζειν αὐτῷ. ὁ δ' Ἄρατος, διακούσας κατ' ἰδίαν τῶν περὶ
τὸν Νικοφάνη τὴν τοῦ βασιλέως αἵρεσιν, ἣν ἔχοι
πρός τε τοὺς Ἀχαιοὺς καὶ πρὸς αὐτόν, περιχαρὴς ἦν
τῷ μὴ διακενῆς πεποιῆσθαι τὴν ἐπίνοιαν μηδ' εὑρῆ-
σθαι κατὰ τὴν τῶν Αἰτωλῶν ἐλπίδα τὸν Ἀντίγονον εἰς
6 τέλος ἀπηλλοτριωμένον ἑαυτοῦ. πάνυ δὲ πρὸς λόγον
ἡγεῖτο γίνεσθαι καὶ τὸ τοὺς Μεγαλοπολίτας προθύ-
μους εἶναι διὰ τῶν Ἀχαιῶν φέρειν ἐπὶ τὸν Ἀντίγονον
7 τὰ πράγματα. μάλιστα μὲν γάρ, ὡς ἐπάνω προεῖπον,
ἔσπευδε μὴ προσδεηθῆναι τῆς βοηθείας· εἰ δ' ἐξ
ἀνάγκης ἐπὶ τοῦτο δέοι καταφεύγειν, οὐ μόνον ἠβού-
λετο δι' αὑτοῦ γενέσθαι τὴν κλῆσιν, ἔτι δὲ μᾶλλον ἐξ
8 ἁπάντων τῶν Ἀχαιῶν. ἠγωνία γάρ, εἰ παραγενόμενος
ὁ βασιλεὺς καὶ κρατήσας τῷ πολέμῳ τοῦ Κλεομένους
καὶ τῶν Λακεδαιμονίων, ἀλλοιότερόν τι βουλεύσοιτο
περὶ τῆς κοινῆς πολιτείας, μήποθ' ὁμολογουμένως τῶν
9 συμβαινόντων αὐτὸς ἀναλάβῃ τὴν αἰτίαν, δόξαντος
δικαίως τοῦτο πράττειν διὰ τὴν ἐξ αὐτοῦ προγεγενημένην ἀδικίαν περὶ τὸν Ἀκροκόρινθον εἰς τὴν Μακεδό-

ising the Megalopolitans by letter to come to their assistance if such was the wish of the Achaeans too. Upon
Nicophanes and Cercidas returning home and delivering
the king's letter, assuring at the same time their people of
his goodwill toward them and readiness to be of service,
the Megalopolitans were much elated and most ready to go
to the meeting of the Achaeans and beg them to invite the
aid of Antigonus and at once put the direction of affairs
in his hands. Aratus had private information from Nicophanes of the king's favorable inclination toward the
League and himself, and was much gratified to find that his
project had not been futile, and that he had not, as the
Aetolians had hoped, found Antigonus entirely alienated
from him. He considered it a great advantage that the
Megalopolitans had readily consented to approach Antigonus through the Achaeans; for, as I said above, what he
chiefly desired was not to be in need of asking for help at
all, but if it became necessary to resort to this, he wished
the appeal to come not only from himself personally, but
from the League as a whole. For he was afraid that if the
king appeared on the scene and, after conquering Cleomenes and the Lacedaemonians, took any measures the reverse of welcome regarding the League, he himself would
be universally blamed for what happened, as the king
would seem to have justice on his side owing to Aratus'
offense[109] against the house of Macedon in the case of the

109 The event (43. 4) had been a breach of the peace.

10 νων οἰκίαν. διόπερ ἅμα τῷ παρελθόντας τοὺς Μεγαλοπολίτας εἰς τὸ κοινὸν βουλευτήριον τά τε γράμματα
τοῖς Ἀχαιοῖς ἐπιδεικνύναι καὶ διασαφεῖν τὴν ὅλην
εὔνοιαν τοῦ βασιλέως, πρὸς δὲ τούτοις ἀξιοῦν ἐπισπάσασθαι τὸν Ἀντίγονον τὴν ταχίστην, εἶναι δὲ καὶ
11 τὸ πλῆθος ἐπὶ τῆς αὐτῆς ὁρμῆς, προελθὼν Ἄρατος,
καὶ τήν τε τοῦ βασιλέως προθυμίαν ἀποδεξάμενος καὶ
τὴν τῶν πολλῶν διάληψιν ἐπαινέσας, παρεκάλει διὰ
πλειόνων μάλιστα μὲν πειρᾶσθαι δι᾽ αὑτῶν σῴζειν καὶ
τὰς πόλεις καὶ τὴν χώραν· οὐδὲν γὰρ εἶναι τούτου
κάλλιον οὐδὲ συμφορώτερον· ἐὰν δ᾽ ἄρα πρὸς τοῦτο τὸ
μέρος ἀντιβαίνῃ τὰ τῆς τύχης, πρότερον ἔφη δεῖν
ἐξελέγξαντας πάσας τὰς ἐν αὑτοῖς ἐλπίδας τότε καταφεύγειν ἐπὶ τὰς τῶν φίλων βοηθείας.

51. ἐπισημηναμένου δὲ τοῦ πλήθους, ἔδοξε μένειν
ἐπὶ τῶν ὑποκειμένων καὶ δι᾽ αὑτῶν ἐπιτελεῖν τὸν
2 ἐνεστῶτα πόλεμον. ἐπεὶ δὲ Πτολεμαῖος ἀπογνοὺς μὲν
τὸ ἔθνος Κλεομένει χορηγεῖν ἐπεβάλετο, βουλόμενος
αὐτὸν ἐπαλείφειν ἐπὶ τὸν Ἀντίγονον διὰ τὸ πλείους
ἐλπίδας ἔχειν ἐν τοῖς Λακεδαιμονίοις ἤπερ ἐν τοῖς
Ἀχαιοῖς τοῦ δύνασθαι διακατέχειν τὰς τῶν ἐν Μακε-
3 δονίᾳ βασιλέων ἐπιβολάς, οἱ δ᾽ Ἀχαιοὶ τὸ μὲν πρῶτον
ἠλαττώθησαν περὶ τὸ Λύκαιον, συμπλακέντες κατὰ
πορείαν τῷ Κλεομένει, τὸ δὲ δεύτερον ἐκ παρατάξεως
ἡττήθησαν ἐν τοῖς Λαδοκείοις καλουμένοις τῆς Μεγα-

---

[110] Because Cleomenes now seemed to be a stronger counter-
weight against Macedonia than the Achaeans; *StV* 505.

Acrocorinthus. Therefore, when the Megalopolitans appeared before the the federal council chamber and, showing the king's letter, assured them of his general friendly sentiments, at the same time begging the Achaeans to ask for his intervention at once, and when Aratus saw that this was the inclination of the Achaeans also, he rose, and after expressing his gratification at the king's readiness to assist them and his approval of the attitude of the meeting, he addressed them at some length, begging them if possible to attempt to save their cities and country by their own efforts, that being the most honorable and advantageous course, but, should adverse fortune prevent this, then, but only when they had no hope left in their own resources, he advised them to resort to an appeal to their friends for aid.

51. The people applauded his speech, and a decree was passed to leave things as they were for the present and conduct the war unaided. But a series of disasters overtook them. In the first place Ptolemy threw over the League[110] and began to give financial support to Cleomenes with a view of setting him on to attack Antigonus, as he hoped to be able to keep in check more effectually the projects of the Macedonian kings with the support of the Lacedaemonians than with that of the Achaeans. Next the Achaeans were worsted[111] by Cleomenes while on the march near the Lycaeum and again in a pitched battle at a place in the territory of Megalopolis called Ladoceia,

111 The first two defeats happened during Aratus' tenth year as general, 227/6. For Lydiadas see 44. 5. New documents on him and his family were recently published by A. Stavrianopoulou, *Tekmeria* 7 (2002) 117–156. The defeat at the Hecatombaeon occurred in 226/5 during the generalship of Hyperbatus.

THE HISTORIES OF POLYBIUS

λοπολίτιδος, ὅτε καὶ Λυδιάδας ἔπεσε, τὸ δὲ τρίτον
ὁλοσχερῶς ἔπταισαν ἐν τῇ Δυμαίᾳ περὶ τὸ καλού-
4 μενον Ἑκατόμβαιον, πανδημεὶ διακινδυνεύοντες, τότ'
ἤδη τῶν πραγμάτων οὐκέτι διδόντων ἀναστροφὴν
ἠνάγκαζε τὰ περιεστῶτα καταφεύγειν ὁμοθυμαδὸν ἐπὶ
5 τὸν Ἀντίγονον. ἐν ᾧ καιρῷ πρεσβευτὴν τὸν υἱὸν
ἐξαποστείλας Ἄρατος πρὸς Ἀντίγονον ἐβεβαιώσατο
6 τὰ περὶ τῆς βοηθείας. παρεῖχε δ' αὐτοῖς ἀπορίαν καὶ
δυσχρηστίαν μεγίστην τὸ μήτε τὸν βασιλέα δοκεῖν
ἂν βοηθῆσαι χωρὶς τοῦ κομίσασθαι τὸν Ἀκροκόρινθον καὶ λαβεῖν ὁρμητήριον πρὸς τὸν ἐνεστῶτα πόλεμον τὴν τῶν Κορινθίων πόλιν, μήτε τοὺς Ἀχαιοὺς ἂν
7 τολμῆσαι Κορινθίους ἄκοντας ἐγχειρίσαι Μακεδόσι.
διὸ καὶ τὸ πρῶτον ὑπέρθεσιν ἔσχε τὸ διαβούλιον
χάριν τῆς περὶ τῶν πίστεων ἐπισκέψεως.

52. Ὁ δὲ Κλεομένης, καταπληξάμενος τοῖς προειρημένοις εὐτυχήμασι, λοιπὸν ἀδεῶς ἐπεπορεύετο τὰς
πόλεις, ἃς μὲν πείθων, αἷς δὲ τὸν φόβον ἀνατει-
2 νόμενος. προσλαβὼν δὲ τῷ τρόπῳ τούτῳ Καφύας,
Πελλήνην, Φενεόν, Ἄργος, Φλιοῦντα, Κλεωνάς, Ἐπί-
δαυρον, Ἑρμιόνα, Τροίζηνα, τελευταῖον Κόρινθον,
αὐτὸς μὲν προσεστρατοπέδευσε τῇ τῶν Σικυωνίων
πόλει, τοὺς δ' Ἀχαιοὺς ἀπέλυσε τοῦ μεγίστου προ-
3 βλήματος. τῶν γὰρ Κορινθίων τῷ μὲν Ἀράτῳ στρατη-
γοῦντι καὶ τοῖς Ἀχαιοῖς παραγγειλάντων ἐκ τῆς
πόλεως ἀπαλλάττεσθαι, πρὸς δὲ τὸν Κλεομένη δια-
πεμπομένων καὶ καλούντων, παρεδόθη τοῖς Ἀχαιοῖς
4 ἀφορμὴ καὶ πρόφασις εὔλογος. ἧς ἐπιλαβόμενος

402

Lydiades falling here, and finally their whole force met with utter defeat at the Hecatombaeum in the territory of Dyme. Circumstances now no longer giving them any respite, they were compelled by their position to appeal with one voice to Antigonus. Aratus in this emergency sent his son[112] as envoy to the king and confirmed the details for assistance.[113] They were, however, in considerable doubt and difficulty about the Acrocorinthus, as it did not seem that Antigonus would come to their assistance unless it were restored to him, so that he could use Corinth as a base for the present war, nor could they go to the length of handing over the Corinthians against their will to Macedon. This even caused at first an adjournment of the deliberations for the consideration of the guarantees he required.

52. Cleomenes, having inspired terror by the victories I mentioned, henceforth made an unimpeded progress[114] through the cities, gaining some by persuasion and others by threats He annexed in this manner Caphyae, Pellene, Pheneus, Argos, Phlius, Cleonae, Epidaurus, Hermione, Troezen, and finally Corinth. He now sat down in front of Sicyon, but he had solved the chief difficulty of the Achaeans; for the Corinthians by ordering Aratus, who was then in command,[115] and the Achaeans to quit Corinth, and by sending to invite Cleomenes, furnished the Achaeans with good and reasonable ground for offering

112 The younger Aratus. He now learned about the price to be paid for the king's assistance: the return of Acrocorinth to him.

113 *StV* 506.

114 Details in Plu., *Cleom.* 17.

115 See WC 1. 252–253.

Ἄρατος καὶ προτείνας Ἀντιγόνῳ τὸν Ἀκροκόρινθον,
κατεχόντων Ἀχαιῶν τότε τὸν τόπον τοῦτον, ἔλυσε μὲν
τὸ γεγονὸς ἔγκλημα πρὸς τὴν οἰκίαν, ἱκανὴν δὲ πίστιν
παρέσχετο τῆς πρὸς τὰ μέλλοντα κοινωνίας, τὸ δὲ
συνέχον, ὁρμητήριον παρεσκεύασεν Ἀντιγόνῳ πρὸς
τὸν κατὰ Λακεδαιμονίων πόλεμον.

5   Ὁ δὲ Κλεομένης, ἐπιγνοὺς τοὺς Ἀχαιοὺς συν-
τιθεμένους τὰ πρὸς τὸν Ἀντίγονον, ἀναζεύξας ἀπὸ τοῦ
Σικυῶνος, κατεστρατοπέδευσε περὶ τὸν Ἰσθμὸν, δια-
λαβὼν χάρακι καὶ τάφρῳ τὸν μεταξὺ τόπον τοῦ τ᾽
Ἀκροκορίνθου καὶ τῶν Ὀνείων καλουμένων ὀρῶν,
πᾶσαν ἤδη βεβαίως περιειληφὼς ταῖς ἐλπίσι τὴν
6 Πελοποννησίων ἀρχήν. Ἀντίγονος δὲ πάλαι μὲν ἦν ἐν
παρασκευῇ, καραδοκῶν τὸ μέλλον κατὰ τὰς ὑποθέσεις
7 τὰς Ἀράτου· τότε δὲ συλλογιζόμενος ἐκ τῶν προσπιπτόντων ὅσον οὔπω παρεῖναι τὸν Κλεομένη μετὰ
τῆς δυνάμεως εἰς Θετταλίαν, διαπεμψάμενος πρός τε
τὸν Ἄρατον καὶ τοὺς Ἀχαιοὺς ὑπὲρ τῶν ὡμολογη-
μένων, ἧκεν ἔχων τὰς δυνάμεις διὰ τῆς Εὐβοίας ἐπὶ
8 τὸν Ἰσθμόν. οἱ γὰρ Αἰτωλοὶ πρὸς τοῖς ἄλλοις καὶ τότε
βουλόμενοι κωλῦσαι τὸν Ἀντίγονον τῆς βοηθείας,
ἀπεῖπον αὐτῷ πορεύεσθαι μετὰ δυνάμεως ἐντὸς Πυ-
λῶν· εἰ δὲ μή, διότι κωλύσουσι μεθ᾽ ὅπλων αὐτοῦ τὴν
δίοδον.

9   Ὁ μὲν οὖν Ἀντίγονος καὶ Κλεομένης ἀντεστρα-
τοπέδευον ἀλλήλοις, ὁ μὲν εἰσελθεῖν σπουδάζων εἰς
Πελοπόννησον, ὁ δὲ Κλεομένης κωλῦσαι τῆς εἰσόδου
τὸν Ἀντίγονον.

to Antigonus[116] the Acrocorinthus then held by them.[117] Availing himself of this, Aratus not only atoned for his former offense to the royal house, but gave sufficient guarantee of future loyalty, further providing Antigonus with a base for the war against the Lacedaemonians.

Cleomenes, when he became aware of the understanding between the Achaeans and Antigonus, left Sicyon and encamped on the Isthmus, uniting by a palisade and trench the area between the Acrocorinthus and the mountain called the Ass's Back, regarding confidently the whole Peloponnese as being henceforth his own domain. Antigonus had been for long making his preparations, awaiting the turn of events, as Aratus had recommended, but now, judging from the progress of events that Cleomenes was on the point of appearing in Thessaly with his army, he communicated with Aratus and the Achaeans reminding them of the terms of their treaty, and passing through Euboea[118] with his forces, reached the Isthmus, the Aetolians having, in addition to other measures they took to prevent his assisting the Achaeans, forbidden him to advance with any army beyond Thermopylae, threatening, if he attempted it, to oppose his passage.

Antigonus and Cleomenes now faced each other, the former bent on penetrating into the Peloponnese and the latter on preventing him.

224 B.C.

116 Spring of 224.
117 Having lost the city, the Achaeans held on to the citadel.
118 Avoiding Thermopylae.

53. οἱ δ᾽ Ἀχαιοί, καίπερ οὐ μετρίως ἠλαττωμένοι τοῖς ὅλοις, ὅμως οὐκ ἀφίσταντο τῆς προθέσεως οὐδ᾽ 2 ἐγκατέλειπον τὰς ἐν αὑτοῖς ἐλπίδας, ἀλλ᾽ ἅμα τῷ τὸν Ἀριστοτέλη τὸν Ἀργεῖον ἐπαναστῆναι τοῖς Κλεομενισταῖς, βοηθήσαντες καὶ παρεισπεσόντες μετὰ Τιμοξένου τοῦ στρατηγοῦ, κατέλαβον τὴν τῶν Ἀργείων 3 πόλιν. ὃ δὴ καὶ νομιστέον αἰτιώτατον γεγονέναι πραγμάτων κατορθώσεως. τὸ γὰρ ἐπιλαβόμενον τῆς ὁρμῆς τοῦ Κλεομένους καὶ προηττῆσαν τὰς ψυχὰς τῶν δυνάμεων τοῦτ᾽ ἦν, ὡς ἐξ αὐτῶν φανερὸν ἐγένετο τῶν 4 πραγμάτων. καὶ γὰρ τόπους εὐφυεστέρους προκατέχων, καὶ χορηγίαις δαψιλεστέραις Ἀντιγόνου χρώμενος, καὶ τόλμῃ καὶ φιλοτιμίᾳ μείζονι παρωρμημέ- 5 νος, ὅμως ἅμα τῷ προσπεσεῖν αὐτῷ διότι κατειλῆφθαι συμβαίνει τὴν τῶν Ἀργείων πόλιν ὑπὸ τῶν Ἀχαιῶν, εὐθὺς ἀνάσπαστος, ἀπολιπὼν τὰ προδεδηλωμένα προτερήματα, φυγῇ παραπλησίαν ἐποιεῖτο τὴν ἀποχώρησιν, δείσας μὴ πανταχόθεν αὐτὸν περιστῶσιν οἱ 6 πολέμιοι. παραπεσὼν δ᾽ εἰς Ἄργος, καὶ κατὰ ποσὸν ἀντιποιησάμενος τῆς πόλεως, μετὰ ταῦτα γενναίως μὲν τῶν Ἀχαιῶν, φιλοτίμως δὲ τῶν Ἀργείων ἐκ μεταμελείας αὐτὸν ἀμυναμένων, ἀποπεσὼν καὶ ταύτης τῆς ἐπιβολῆς, καὶ ποιησάμενος τὴν πορείαν διὰ Μαντινείας, οὕτως ἐπανῆλθεν εἰς τὴν Σπάρτην.

54. Ὁ δ᾽ Ἀντίγονος ἀσφαλῶς εἰς τὴν Πελοπόννησον εἰσελθὼν παρέλαβε τὸν Ἀκροκόρινθον, οὐδένα δὲ χρόνον μείνας εἴχετο τῶν προκειμένων καὶ παρῆν εἰς 2 Ἄργος. ἐπαινέσας δὲ τοὺς Ἀργείους, καὶ καταστη-

53. The Achaeans, although they had suffered such very serious reverses, yet did not abandon their purpose or their self-reliance, but on Aristoteles of Argos revolting against the partisans of Cleomenes, they sent a force to his assistance and entering the city by surprise under the command of their Strategus, Timoxenus,[119] established themselves there. We should look on this achievement as the principal cause of the improvement in their fortunes which ensued. For events clearly showed that it was this which checked Cleomenes' ardor and subdued in advance the spirit of his troops. Though his position was stronger than that of Antigonus, and he was much better off for supplies, as well as animated by greater courage and ambition, no sooner did the news reach him that Argos had been seized by the Achaeans than he instantly took himself off, abandoning all these advantages, and made a precipitate retreat, fearing to be surrounded on all sides by the enemy. Gaining entrance to Argos he possessed himself of part of the city, but, on the Achaeans making a gallant resistance, in which the Argives joined with all the zeal of repentant sinners, this plan broke down too, and, marching by way of Mantinea, he returned to Sparta.

54. Antigonus now safely entered the Peloponnese and took possession of the Acrocorinthus and, without wasting any time there, pushed on and reached Argos. Having thanked the Argives and put matters in the city on a proper

[119] On the structure of command and on chronology see WC 1. 254–255.

σάμενος τὰ κατὰ τὴν πόλιν, αὖθις ἐκ ποδὸς ἐκίνει,
3 ποιούμενος τὴν πορείαν ὡς ἐπ' Ἀρκαδίας. ἐκβαλὼν δὲ
τὰς φρουρὰς ἐκ τῶν ἐποικοδομηθέντων χωρίων ὑπὸ
Κλεομένους κατά τε τὴν Αἰγῦτιν καὶ Βελμινᾶτιν χώραν, καὶ παραδοὺς τὰ φρούρια Μεγαλοπολίταις, ἧκε
4 πρὸς τὴν τῶν Ἀχαιῶν σύνοδον εἰς Αἴγιον. ἀπολογι-
σάμενος δὲ περὶ τῶν καθ' αὑτὸν καὶ χρηματίσας περὶ
τῶν μελλόντων, ἔτι δὲ κατασταθεὶς ἡγεμὼν ἁπάντων
5 τῶν συμμάχων, μετὰ ταῦτα χρόνον μέν τινα παρα-
χειμάζων διέτριβε περὶ Σικυῶνα καὶ Κόρινθον. τῆς δ'
ἐαρινῆς ὥρας ἐνισταμένης ἀναλαβὼν τὰς δυνάμεις
6 προῆγε. καὶ διανύσας τριταῖος πρὸς τὴν τῶν Τεγεατῶν πόλιν, ἀπηντηκότων καὶ τῶν Ἀχαιῶν ἐνταῦθα,
7 περιστρατοπεδεύσας ἤρξατο πολιορκεῖν αὐτήν. τῶν δὲ
Μακεδόνων ἐνεργῶς χρωμένων τῇ τε λοιπῇ πολιορκίᾳ
καὶ τοῖς ὀρύγμασι, ταχέως ἀπελπίσαντες οἱ Τεγεᾶται
8 τὴν σωτηρίαν παρέδοσαν αὐτούς. ὁ δ' Ἀντίγονος,
ἀσφαλισάμενος τὰ κατὰ τὴν πόλιν, εἴχετο κατὰ τὸ
συνεχὲς τῶν ἑξῆς, καὶ προῆγε κατὰ σπουδὴν εἰς τὴν
9 Λακωνικήν. ἐγγίσας δὲ τῷ Κλεομένει προκαθημένῳ
10 τῆς ἑαυτοῦ χώρας κατεπείραζε, καὶ συνίστατό τινας
ἀκροβολισμούς. προσπεσόντος δὲ διὰ τῶν κατασκό-
πων αὐτῷ τοὺς ἐξ Ὀρχομενοῦ στρατιώτας παρα-
βεβοηθηκέναι πρὸς τὸν Κλεομένη, παραυτίκα ποιη-
11 σάμενος ἀναζυγὴν ἠπείγετο. καὶ τὸν μὲν Ὀρχομενὸν
ἐξ ἐφόδου κατὰ κράτος εἷλε· μετὰ δὲ ταῦτα περιστρα-
12 τοπεδεύσας τὴν τῶν Μαντινέων ἐπολιόρκει πόλιν.
ταχὺ δὲ καὶ ταύτην καταπληξαμένων τῶν Μακεδόνων

footing, he moved on again at once, making for Arcadia. After having ejected the garrisons from the forests that Cleomenes had built there to command the country in the territory of Aegys and Belbina, and handed over these forts to the Megalopolitans, he came to Aegium where the meeting of the Achaean League was in session. He gave them an account of the measures he had taken and arranged with them for the future conduct of the war. He was appointed hereupon commander-in-chief of all the allied forces,[120] and after this he retired for a short time to his winter quarters near Sicyon and Corinth. Early in spring[121] he advanced with his army and reached Tegea in three days. Here the Achaeans joined him, and the siege of the city was opened. The Macedonians conducted the siege energetically, especially by mining, and the Tegeans soon gave up all hope of holding out and surrendered. Antigonus, after securing the city, continued to pursue his plan of campaign and advanced rapidly on Laconia. He encountered Cleomenes posted on the frontier to defend Laconia and began to harass him, a few skirmishes taking place; but on learning from his scouts that the troops from Orchomenus had left to come to the aid of Cleomenes, he at once hastily broke up his camp and hurried thither. He surprised Orchomenus, and captured it by assault, and after this he laid siege to Mantinea which likewise the Mace-

223 B.C.

[120] In 224, Antigonus had founded a League of Greek states (*StV* 507) and was already commander of its forces. He probably was elected *hegemon* of the Achaean League, a position previously held by Ptolemy (see WC 1. 256).

[121] For Antigonus' campaign in 223 see Le Bohec (45. 2), 405–410.

καὶ λαβόντων ὑποχείριον, ἀναζεύξας προῆγε τὴν ἐφ᾽

13 Ἡραίας καὶ Τελφούσης. παραλαβὼν δὲ καὶ ταύτας
τὰς πόλεις, ἐθελοντὴν προσχωρησάντων αὐτῷ τῶν
κατοικούντων, οὕτως ἤδη συνάπτοντος τοῦ χειμῶνος

14 παρῆν εἰς Αἴγιον πρὸς τὴν τῶν Ἀχαιῶν σύνοδον. καὶ
τοὺς μὲν Μακεδόνας ἐπ᾽ οἴκου διαφῆκε πάντας εἰς τὴν
χειμασίαν, αὐτὸς δὲ τοῖς Ἀχαιοῖς διελέγετο καὶ συν-
διενοεῖτο περὶ τῶν ἐνεστώτων.

55. Κατὰ δὲ τοὺς καιροὺς τούτους συνθεωρῶν ὁ
Κλεομένης τὰς μὲν δυνάμεις διαφειμένας, τὸν δ᾽ Ἀντίγονον μετὰ τῶν μισθοφόρων ἐν Αἰγίῳ διατρίβοντα,
καὶ τριῶν ἡμερῶν ὁδὸν ἀφεστῶτα τῆς Μεγάλης πό-

2 λεως, τὴν δὲ πόλιν ταύτην εἰδὼς δυσφύλακτον οὖσαν
διὰ τὸ μέγεθος καὶ τὴν ἐρημίαν, τότε δὲ καὶ ῥαθύμως
τηρουμένην διὰ τὴν Ἀντιγόνου παρουσίαν, τὸ δὲ μέγιστον ἀπολωλότας τοὺς πλείστους τῶν ἐν ταῖς ἡλικίαις
ἔν τε τῇ περὶ τὸ Λύκαιον καὶ μετὰ ταῦτα τῇ περὶ
Λαδόκεια μάχῃ, λαβὼν συνεργούς τινας τῶν ἐκ Μεσ-

3 σήνης φυγάδων, οἳ διατρίβοντες ἐτύγχανον ἐν τῇ
Μεγάλῃ πόλει, παρεισῆλθε διὰ τούτων λάθρα νυκτὸς

4 ἐντὸς τῶν τειχῶν. τῆς δ᾽ ἡμέρας ἐπιγενομένης παρ᾽
ὀλίγον ἦλθε τοῦ μὴ μόνον ἐκπεσεῖν, ἀλλὰ καὶ τοῖς
ὅλοις κινδυνεῦσαι διὰ τὴν εὐψυχίαν τῶν Μεγαλοπο-

5 λιτῶν. ὃ δὴ καὶ τρισὶ μησὶ πρότερον αὐτῷ συνέβη
παθεῖν παρεισπεσόντι κατὰ τὸν Κωλαιὸν προσαγο-

6 ρευόμενον τόπον τῆς πόλεως. τότε δὲ τῷ πλήθει τῆς
δυνάμεως καὶ τῷ προκαταλαμβάνεσθαι τοὺς εὐκαίρους τόπους καθίκετο τῆς ἐπιβολῆς, καὶ πέρας ἐκβα-

donians soon frightened into submission and then he advanced on Heraea and Telphusa which the inhabitants surrendered to him of their own accord. The winter was now approaching. Antigonus came to Aegium to be present at the meeting of the Achaean Synod, and dismissing all his Macedonians to their homes for the winter, occupied himself in discussing the present situation with the Achaeans and making joint plans for the future.

55. Cleomenes at this juncture had observed that Antigonus had dismissed his other troops and, keeping only his mercenaries with him, was spending the time at Aegium at a distance of three days' march from Megalopolis. He knew that this latter city was very difficult to defend, owing to its extent and partial desolation, that it was at present very carelessly guarded owing to the presence of Antigonus in the Peloponnese, and above all that it had lost the greater part of its citizens of military age in the battles at the Lycaeum and at Ladoceia. He therefore procured the cooperation of certain Messenian exiles then living in Megalopolis and by their means got inside the walls[122] secretly by night. On day breaking, he came very near not only being driven out, but meeting with complete disaster owing to the bravery of the Megalopolitans, who had indeed expelled and defeated him three months previously when he entered the city by surprise in the quarter called Colaeum. But on this occasion, owing to the strength of his forces, and owing to his having had time to seize on the most advantageous positions, his project succeeded, and

[122] The sack of Megalopolis occurred in autumn 223. A different version, based on Phylarchus, is told in Plu., *Cleom.* 23–25.

7 λῶν τοὺς Μεγαλοπολίτας κατέσχε τὴν πόλιν. γενόμενος δ' ἐγκρατὴς οὕτως αὐτὴν πικρῶς διέφθειρε καὶ
δυσμενῶς ὥστε μηδ' ἐλπίσαι μηδένα διότι δύναιτ' ἂν
8 συνοικισθῆναι πάλιν. τοῦτο δὲ ποιῆσαί μοι δοκεῖ διὰ
τὸ κατὰ τὰς τῶν καιρῶν περιστάσεις παρὰ μόνοις
Μεγαλοπολίταις καὶ Στυμφαλίοις μηδέποτε δυνηθῆ-
ναι μήθ' αἱρετιστὴν καὶ κοινωνὸν τῶν ἰδίων ἐλπίδων
9 μήτε προδότην κατασκευάσασθαι. τὸ μὲν γὰρ Κλειτο-
ρίων φιλελεύθερον καὶ γενναῖον εἰς ἀνὴρ κατῄσχυνε
διὰ τὴν ἑαυτοῦ κακίαν, Θεάρκης· ὃν εἰκότως ἐξαρνοῦν-
ται Κλειτόριοι μὴ φῦναι παρὰ σφίσι, γενέσθαι δ'
ὑποβολιμαῖον ἐξ Ὀρχομενοῦ τῶν ἐπηλύδων τινὸς
στρατιωτῶν.

56. Ἐπεὶ δὲ τῶν κατὰ τοὺς αὐτοὺς καιροὺς Ἀράτῳ
γεγραφότων παρ' ἐνίοις ἀποδοχῆς ἀξιοῦται Φύλαρχος, ἐν πολλοῖς ἀντιδοξῶν καὶ τἀναντία γράφων
2 αὐτῷ, χρήσιμον ἂν εἴη, μᾶλλον δ' ἀναγκαῖον ἡμῖν,
Ἀράτῳ προῃρημένοις κατακολουθεῖν περὶ τῶν Κλεο-
μενικῶν, μὴ παραλιπεῖν ἄσκεπτον τοῦτο τὸ μέρος, ἵνα
μὴ τὸ ψεῦδος ἐν τοῖς συγγράμμασιν ἰσοδυναμοῦν
3 ἀπολείπωμεν πρὸς τὴν ἀλήθειαν. καθόλου μὲν οὖν ὁ
συγγραφεὺς οὗτος πολλὰ παρ' ὅλην τὴν πραγματείαν
4 εἰκῇ καὶ ὡς ἔτυχεν εἴρηκε. πλὴν περὶ μὲν τῶν ἄλλων
ἴσως οὐκ ἀναγκαῖον ἐπιτιμᾶν κατὰ τὸ παρὸν οὐδ'
ἐξακριβοῦν· ὅσα δὲ συνεπιβάλλει τοῖς ὑφ' ἡμῶν γρα-
φομένοις καιροῖς, ταῦτα δ' ἔστι τὰ περὶ τὸν Κλεο-

---

123 The extended criticism of Phylarchus, who favored Cle-

finally he drove out the Megalopolitans and occupied their city. On possessing himself of it, he destroyed it with such systematic cruelty and animosity, that nobody would have thought it possible that it could ever be reinhabited. I believe him to have acted so, because the Megalopolitans and Stymphalians were the only peoples from among whom in all their vicissitudes he could never procure himself a single partisan to share in his projects or a single traitor. For in the case of the Clitorians their noble love of freedom was sullied by the malpractices of one man Thearces whom, as one would expect, they naturally deny to have been a native-born citizen, affirming that he was the son of a foreign soldier and foisted in from Orchomenus.

56. Since, among those authors who were contemporaries of Aratus, Phylarchus,[123] who on many points is at variance and in contradiction with him, is by some received as trustworthy, it will be useful or rather necessary for me, as I have chosen to rely on Aratus' narrative for the history of the Cleomenic war, not to leave the question of their relative credibility undiscussed, so that truth and falsehood in their writings may no longer be of equal authority. In general Phylarchus through his whole work makes many random and careless statements; but while perhaps it is not necessary for me at present to criticize in detail the rest of these, I must minutely examine such as relate to events occurring in the period with which I am

omenes, continues through 63.6. At issue are mainly the treatment of Mantinea (by Aratus) and that of Megalopolis (by Cleomenes). Phylarchus was the source of Plu., *Cleom.* and is partly preserved in *FGrH* 81, F 53–6 and 58. P. is just as biased as he accuses Phylarchus to be.

μενικὸν πόλεμον, ὑπὲρ τούτων ἀναγκαῖόν ἐστιν ἡμῖν
5 διευκρινεῖν. ἔσται δὲ πάντως ἀρκοῦντα ταῦτα πρὸς τὸ
καὶ τὴν ὅλην αὐτοῦ προαίρεσιν καὶ δύναμιν ἐν τῇ
6 πραγματείᾳ καταμαθεῖν. βουλόμενος δὴ διασαφεῖν
τὴν ὠμότητα τὴν Ἀντιγόνου καὶ Μακεδόνων, ἅμα δὲ
τούτοις τὴν Ἀράτου καὶ τῶν Ἀχαιῶν, φησὶ τοὺς Μαντινέας γενομένους ὑποχειρίους μεγάλοις περιπεσεῖν
ἀτυχήμασι, καὶ τὴν ἀρχαιοτάτην καὶ μεγίστην πόλιν
τῶν κατὰ τὴν Ἀρκαδίαν τηλικαύταις παλαῖσαι συμφοραῖς ὥστε πάντας εἰς ἐπίστασιν καὶ δάκρυα τοὺς
7 Ἕλληνας ἀγαγεῖν. σπουδάζων δ' εἰς ἔλεον ἐκκαλεῖσθαι τοὺς ἀναγινώσκοντας καὶ συμπαθεῖς ποιεῖν
τοῖς λεγομένοις, εἰσάγει περιπλοκὰς γυναικῶν καὶ
κόμας διερριμμένας καὶ μαστῶν ἐκβολάς, πρὸς δὲ
τούτοις δάκρυα καὶ θρήνους ἀνδρῶν καὶ γυναικῶν
8 ἀναμὶξ τέκνοις καὶ γονεῦσι γηραιοῖς ἀπαγομένων.
ποιεῖ δὲ τοῦτο παρ' ὅλην τὴν ἱστορίαν, πειρώμενος ἐν
9 ἑκάστοις ἀεὶ πρὸ ὀφθαλμῶν τιθέναι τὰ δεινά. τὸ μὲν
οὖν ἀγεννὲς καὶ γυναικῶδες τῆς αἱρέσεως αὐτοῦ παρ-
είσθω, τὸ δὲ τῆς ἱστορίας οἰκεῖον ἅμα καὶ χρήσιμον
10 ἐξεταζέσθω. δεῖ τοιγαροῦν οὐκ ἐκπλήττειν τὸν συγ-
γραφέα τερατευόμενον διὰ τῆς ἱστορίας τοὺς ἐντυγχάνοντας οὐδὲ τοὺς ἐνδεχομένους λόγους ζητεῖν καὶ
τὰ παρεπόμενα τοῖς ὑποκειμένοις ἐξαριθμεῖσθαι, καθάπερ οἱ τραγῳδιογράφοι, τῶν δὲ πραχθέντων καὶ
ῥηθέντων κατ' ἀλήθειαν αὐτῶν μνημονεύειν πάμπαν,
11 κἂν πάνυ μέτρια τυγχάνωσιν ὄντα. τὸ γὰρ τέλος
ἱστορίας καὶ τραγῳδίας οὐ ταὐτόν, ἀλλὰ τοὐναντίον.

414

now dealing, that of the Cleomenic war. This partial examination will however be quite sufficient to convey an idea of the general purpose and character of his work. Wishing, for instance, to insist on the cruelty of Antigonus and the Macedonians and also on that of Aratus and the Achaeans, he tells us that the Mantineans, when they surrendered, were exposed to terrible sufferings and that such were the misfortunes that overtook this, the most ancient and greatest city in Arcadia, as to impress deeply and move to tears all the Greeks. In his eagerness to arouse the pity and attention of his readers he treats us to a picture of clinging women with their hair disheveled and their breasts bare, or again of crowds of both sexes together with their children and aged parents weeping and lamenting as they are led away to slavery. This sort of thing he keeps up throughout his history, always trying to bring horrors vividly before our eyes. Leaving aside the ignoble and womanish character of such a treatment of his subject, let us consider the nature and use of history. A historical author should not try to thrill his readers by such exaggerated pictures, nor should he, like a tragic poet, try to imagine the probable utterances of his characters or reckon up all the consequences probably incidental to the occurrences with which he deals, but simply record what really happened and what really was said, however commonplace. For the object of tragedy is not the same as that of history but quite

ἐκεῖ μὲν γὰρ δεῖ διὰ τῶν πιθανωτάτων λόγων ἐκ-
πλῆξαι καὶ ψυχαγωγῆσαι κατὰ τὸ παρὸν τοὺς ἀκούοντας, ἐνθάδε δὲ διὰ τῶν ἀληθινῶν ἔργων καὶ λόγων
εἰς τὸν πάντα χρόνον διδάξαι καὶ πεῖσαι τοὺς φιλομα-
12 θοῦντας, ἐπειδήπερ ἐν ἐκείνοις μὲν ἡγεῖται τὸ πιθανόν,
κἂν ᾖ ψεῦδος, διὰ τὴν ἀπάτην τῶν θεωμένων, ἐν δὲ
τούτοις τἀληθὲς διὰ τὴν ὠφέλειαν τῶν φιλομαθούν-
13 των. χωρίς τε τούτων τὰς πλείστας ἡμῖν ἐξηγεῖται τῶν
περιπετειῶν, οὐχ ὑποτιθεὶς αἰτίαν καὶ τρόπον τοῖς
γινομένοις, ὧν χωρὶς οὔτ' ἐλεεῖν εὐλόγως οὔτ' ὀργί-
ζεσθαι καθηκόντως δυνατὸν ἐπ' οὐδενὶ τῶν συμβαι-
14 νόντων. ἐπεὶ τίς ἀνθρώπων οὐ δεινὸν ἡγεῖται τύπτε-
σθαι τοὺς ἐλευθέρους; ἀλλ' ὅμως, ἐὰν μὲν ἄρχων
ἀδίκων χειρῶν πάθῃ τις τοῦτο, δικαίως κρίνεται πε-
πονθέναι· ἐὰν δ' ἐπὶ διορθώσει καὶ μαθήσει ταὐτὸ
τοῦτο γίνηται, προσέτι καὶ τιμῆς καὶ χάριτος οἱ
15 τύπτοντες τοὺς ἐλευθέρους ἀξιοῦνται. καὶ μὴν τό γε
τοὺς πολίτας ἀποκτεινύναι μέγιστον ἀσέβημα τίθεται
καὶ μεγίστων ἄξιον προστίμων· καίτοι γε προφανῶς ὁ
μὲν τὸν κλέπτην ἢ μοιχὸν ἀποκτείνας ἀθῷός ἐστιν, ὁ
δὲ τὸν προδότην ἢ τύραννον τιμῶν καὶ προεδρίας
16 τυγχάνει παρὰ πᾶσιν. οὕτως ἐν παντὶ τὸ τέλος κεῖται
τῆς διαλήψεως ὑπὲρ τούτων οὐκ ἐν τοῖς τελουμένοις,
ἀλλ' ἐν ταῖς αἰτίαις καὶ προαιρέσεσι τῶν πραττόντων
καὶ ταῖς τούτων διαφοραῖς.

57. Μαντινεῖς τοίνυν τὸ μὲν πρῶτον ἐγκαταλι-
πόντες τὴν μετὰ τῶν Ἀχαιῶν πολιτείαν ἐθελοντὴν
Αἰτωλοῖς ἐνεχείρισαν αὑτοὺς καὶ τὴν πατρίδα, μετὰ δὲ

the opposite. The tragic poet should thrill and charm his audience for the moment by the verisimilitude of the words he puts into his characters' mouths, but it is the task of the historian to instruct and convince for all time serious students by the truth of the facts and the speeches he narrates, since in the one case it is the probable that takes precedence, even if it be untrue, the purpose being to create illusion in spectators, in the other it is the truth, the purpose being to confer benefit on learners. Apart from this, Phylarchus simply narrates most of such catastrophes and does not even suggest why things are done or to what end, without which it is impossible in any case to feel either legitimate pity or proper anger. Who, for instance, does not think it an outrage for a free man to be beaten? but if this happen to one who was the first to resort to violence, we consider that he got only his desert, while where it is done for the purpose of correction or discipline, those who strike free men are not only excused but deemed worthy of thanks and praise. Again, to kill a citizen is considered the greatest of crimes and that deserving the highest penalty, but obviously he who kills a thief or adulterer is left untouched, and the slayer of a traitor or tyrant everywhere meets with honor and distinction. So in every such case a final judgment on facts of this kind lies not in what is done, but in the reasons and purposes of the doer and in the differences with those present.

57. Now the Mantineans had, in the first instance, deserted the Achaean League, and of their own free will put themselves and their city into the hands first of the

2 ταῦτα Κλεομένει. γεγονότες δ᾽ ἐπὶ τοιαύτης προαιρέσεως καὶ μετέχοντες τῆς Λακεδαιμονίων πολιτείας
ἔτει τετάρτῳ πρότερον τῆς Ἀντιγόνου παρουσίας ἑά-
3 λωσαν κατὰ κράτος ὑπὸ τῶν Ἀχαιῶν, Ἀράτου πραξι-
κοπήσαντος αὐτῶν τὴν πόλιν. ἐν ᾧ καιρῷ τοσοῦτον
ἀπέσχον τοῦ παθεῖν τι δεινὸν διὰ τὴν προειρημένην
ἁμαρτίαν, ὡς καὶ περιβόητον συνέβη γενέσθαι τὸ
πραχθὲν διὰ τὴν ὀξύτητα τῆς κατὰ τὴν προαίρεσιν
4 ἀμφοτέρων μεταβολῆς. ἅμα γὰρ τῷ κατασχεῖν τὴν
πόλιν Ἄρατος παραυτίκα μὲν τοῖς ὑφ᾽ αὑτὸν ταττο-
μένοις παρήγγελλε μηδένα μηδενὸς ἅπτεσθαι τῶν
5 ἀλλοτρίων, ἑξῆς δὲ τούτοις τοὺς Μαντινέας συναθροίσας παρεκάλεσε θαρρεῖν καὶ μένειν ἐπὶ τῶν ἰδίων·
ὑπάρξειν γὰρ αὐτοῖς τὴν ἀσφάλειαν πολιτευομένοις
6 μετὰ τῶν Ἀχαιῶν. τοῖς δὲ Μαντινεῦσιν ἀνυπονοήτου
καὶ παραδόξου φανείσης τῆς ἐλπίδος, παραυτίκα πάν-
7 τες ἐπὶ τῆς ἐναντίας ἐγένοντο γνώμης. καὶ πρὸς οὓς
μικρῷ πρότερον μαχόμενοι πολλοὺς μὲν τῶν ἀναγκαίων ἐπεῖδον ἀπολλυμένους, οὐκ ὀλίγους δ᾽ αὐτῶν
βιαίοις τραύμασι περιπεσόντας, τούτους εἰς τὰς ἰδίας
οἰκίας εἰσαγόμενοι καὶ ποιησάμενοι σφίσι καὶ τοῖς
ἄλλοις ἀναγκαίοις ὁμεστίους, οὐδὲν ἀπέλειπον τῆς
8 μετ᾽ ἀλλήλων φιλοφροσύνης. καὶ τοῦτ᾽ εἰκότως ἐποί-
ουν· οὐ γὰρ οἶδ᾽ εἴ τινες ἀνθρώπων εὐγνωμονεστέροις
ἐνέτυχον πολεμίοις οὐδ᾽ εἴ τινες ἀβλαβέστερον ἐπά-
λαισαν τοῖς μεγίστοις δοκοῦσιν εἶναι συμπτώμασι
Μαντινέων διὰ τὴν Ἀράτου καὶ τῶν Ἀχαιῶν εἰς αὐτοὺς φιλανθρωπίαν.

Aetolians and then of Cleomenes. They had deliberately ranged themselves on his side and been admitted to Spartan citizenship, when, four years before the invasion of Antigonus, their city was betrayed to Aratus and forcibly occupied by the Achaeans. On this occasion, so far from their being cruelly treated owing to their recent delinquency, the circumstances became celebrated because of the sudden revulsion of sentiments on both sides. For immediately Aratus had the city in his hands, he at once issued orders to his troops to keep their hands off the property of others, and next, calling an assembly of the Mantineans, bade them be of good courage and retain possession of all they had; for if they joined the Achaean League he would assure their perfect security. The prospect of safety thus suddenly revealed to them took the Mantineans completely by surprise, and there was an instantaneous and universal reversal of feeling. The very men at whose hands they had seen, in the fight that had just closed, many of their kinsmen slain and many grievously wounded, were now taken into their houses, and received into their families with whom they lived on the kindest possible terms. This was quite natural, for I never heard of any men meeting with kinder enemies or being less injured by what is considered the greatest of calamities than the Mantineans, all owing to their humane treatment by Aratus and the Achaeans.

58. μετὰ δὲ ταῦτα προορώμενοι τὰς ἐν αὑτοῖς στάσεις καὶ τὰς ὑπ᾽ Αἰτωλῶν καὶ Λακεδαιμονίων ἐπιβουλάς, πρεσβεύσαντες πρὸς τοὺς Ἀχαιοὺς ἠξίωσαν

2 δοῦναι παραφυλακὴν αὑτοῖς. οἱ δὲ πεισθέντες ἀπεκλήρωσαν ἐξ αὑτῶν τριακοσίους ἄνδρας· ὧν οἱ λαχόντες ὥρμησαν ἀπολιπόντες τὰς ἰδίας πατρίδας καὶ τοὺς βίους, καὶ διέτριβον ἐν Μαντινείᾳ, παραφυλάττοντες

3 τὴν ἐκείνων ἐλευθερίαν ἅμα καὶ σωτηρίαν. σὺν δὲ τούτοις καὶ μισθοφόρους διακοσίους ἐξέπεμψαν, οἳ μετὰ τῶν Ἀχαιῶν συνδιετήρουν τὴν ὑποκειμένην αὐ

4 τοῖς κατάστασιν. μετ᾽ οὐ πολὺ δὲ στασιάσαντες πρὸς σφᾶς οἱ Μαντινεῖς, καὶ Λακεδαιμονίους ἐπισπασάμενοι, τήν τε πόλιν ἐνεχείρισαν καὶ τοὺς παρὰ τῶν Ἀχαιῶν διατρίβοντας παρ᾽ αὑτοῖς κατέσφαξαν· οὗ μεῖζον παρασπόνδημα καὶ δεινότερον οὐδ᾽ εἰπεῖν εὐ

5 μαρές. ἐπειδὴ γὰρ ἔδοξε σφίσι καθόλου τὴν πρὸς τὸ ἔθνος χάριν καὶ φιλίαν ἀθετεῖν, τῶν γε προειρημένων ἀνδρῶν ἐχρῆν δήπου φεισαμένους ἐᾶσαι πάντας ὑπο

6 σπόνδους ἀπελθεῖν· τοῦτο γὰρ καὶ τοῖς πολεμίοις ἔθος ἐστὶ συγχωρεῖσθαι κατὰ τοὺς κοινοὺς τῶν ἀνθρώπων

7 νόμους. οἱ δ᾽ ἵνα Κλεομένει καὶ Λακεδαιμονίοις ἱκανὴν παράσχωνται πίστιν πρὸς τὴν ἐνεστῶσαν ἐπιβολήν, τὰ κοινὰ τῶν ἀνθρώπων δίκαια παραβάντες τὸ μέγι

8 στον ἀσέβημα κατὰ προαίρεσιν ἐπετέλεσαν. τὸ γὰρ τούτων αὐτόχειρας γενέσθαι καὶ τιμωροὺς οἵτινες πρότερον μὲν κατὰ κράτος λαβόντες αὐτοὺς ἀθῴους ἀφῆκαν, τότε δὲ τὴν ἐκείνων ἐλευθερίαν καὶ σωτηρίαν

9 ἐφύλαττον, πηλίκης ὀργῆς ἐστιν ἄξιον; τί δ᾽ ἂν πα

58. Subsequently, as they foresaw discord among themselves and plots by the Aetolians and Lacedaemonians, they sent an embassy to the Achaeans asking for a garrison. The Achaeans consented and chose by lot three hundred of their own citizens, who set forth, abandoning their own native cities and possessions, and remained in Mantinea to watch over the liberty and safety of its townsmen. At the same time they sent two hundred hired soldiers, who aided this Achaean force in safeguarding the established government. Very soon however the Mantineans became involved in internal conflicts, and, inviting the Lacedaemonians, put the city into their hands and massacred the garrison the Achaeans had sent them. It is not easy to name any greater or more atrocious act of treachery than this. For in resolving to forswear their friendship and gratitude, they should at least have spared the lives of these men and allowed them all to depart under terms. Such treatment is, by the common law of nations, accorded even to enemies; but the Mantineans, simply in order to give Cleomenes and the Lacedaemonians a satisfactory guarantee of their good faith in this undertaking violated the law recognized by all mankind and deliberately committed the most heinous of crimes. Vengeful murderers of the very men who previously on capturing their city had left them unharmed, and who now were guarding their liberties and lives— against such men, one asks oneself, can any indignation be too strong? What should we consider to be an adequate

THE HISTORIES OF POLYBIUS

θόντες οὗτοι δίκην δόξαιεν ἁρμόζουσαν δεδωκέναι;
τυχὸν ἴσως εἴποι τις ἄν, πραθέντες μετὰ τέκνων καὶ
10 γυναικῶν, ἐπεὶ κατεπολεμήθησαν. ἀλλὰ τοῦτό γε καὶ
τοῖς μηθὲν ἀσεβὲς ἐπιτελεσαμένοις κατὰ τοὺς τοῦ
πολέμου νόμους ὑπόκειται παθεῖν. οὐκοῦν ὁλοσχερεστέρας τινὸς καὶ μείζονος τυχεῖν ἦσαν ἄξιοι τιμω-
11 ρίας, ὥστ᾽ εἴπερ ἔπαθον ἃ Φύλαρχός φησιν, οὐκ ἔλεον
εἰκὸς ἦν συνεξακολουθεῖν αὐτοῖς παρὰ τῶν Ἑλλήνων,
ἔπαινον δὲ καὶ συγκατάθεσιν μᾶλλον τοῖς πράττουσι
12 καὶ μεταπορευομένοις τὴν ἀσέβειαν αὐτῶν. ἀλλ᾽ ὅμως
οὐδενὸς περαιτέρω συνεξακολουθήσαντος Μαντινεῦσι
κατὰ τὴν περιπέτειαν πλὴν τοῦ διαρπαγῆναι τοὺς
βίους καὶ πραθῆναι τοὺς ἐλευθέρους, ὁ συγγραφεὺς
αὐτῆς τῆς τερατείας χάριν οὐ μόνον ψεῦδος εἰσήνεγκε
13 τὸ ὅλον, ἀλλὰ καὶ τὸ ψεῦδος ἀπίθανον, καὶ διὰ τὴν
ὑπερβολὴν τῆς ἀγνοίας οὐδὲ τὸ παρακείμενον ἠδυνή-
θη συνεπιστῆσαι, πῶς οἱ αὐτοὶ κατὰ τοὺς αὐτοὺς
καιροὺς κυριεύσαντες Τεγεατῶν κατὰ κράτος οὐδὲν
14 τῶν ὁμοίων ἔπραξαν. καίτοι γ᾽ εἰ μὲν ἡ τῶν πραττόντων ὠμότης ἦν αἰτία, καὶ τούτους εἰκὸς ἦν πεπονθέναι
15 ταὐτὰ τοῖς ὑπὸ τὸν αὐτὸν ὑποπεπτωκόσι καιρόν. εἰ δὲ
περὶ μόνους γέγονε Μαντινεῖς ἡ διαφορά, φανερὸν ὅτι
καὶ τὴν αἰτίαν τῆς ὀργῆς ἀνάγκη διαφέρουσαν γεγονέναι περὶ τούτους.

59. Πάλιν Ἀριστόμαχον τὸν Ἀργεῖον φησιν ἄνδρα
τῆς ἐπιφανεστάτης οἰκίας ὑπάρχοντα, καὶ τετυραν-
νηκότα μὲν Ἀργείων, πεφυκότα δ᾽ ἐκ τυράννων, ὑποχείριον Ἀντιγόνῳ καὶ τοῖς Ἀχαιοῖς γενόμενον, εἰς

punishment for them? Someone might perhaps say that now when they were crushed by armed force they should have been sold into slavery with their wives and children. But to this fate the usage of war exposes those who have been guilty of no such impious crime. These men therefore were worthy of some far heavier and more extreme penalty; so that had they suffered what Phylarchus alleges, it was not to be expected that they should have met with pity from the Greeks, but rather that approval and assent should have been accorded to those who executed judgment on them for their wickedness. Yet, while nothing more serious befel the Mantineans, in this their hour of calamity, than the pillage of their property, and the enslavement of the free population, Phylarchus, all for the sake of making his narrative sensational, composed a tissue not only of falsehoods, but of improbable falsehoods, and, owing to his gross ignorance, was not even able to compare an analogous case and explain how the same people at the same time, on taking Tegea by force, did not commit any such excesses. For if the cause lay in the barbarity of the perpetrators, the Tegeans should have met with the same treatment as those who were conquered at the same time. If only the Mantineans were thus exceptionally treated, we must evidently infer that there was some exceptional cause for anger against them.

59. Again he tells us that Aristomachus of Argos, a man of most noble birth, having himself been tyrant of Argos and being descended from tyrants, fell into the hands of Antigonus and the Achaeans and that he was led away cap-

Κεγχρεὰς ἀπαχθῆναι καὶ στρεβλούμενον ἀποθανεῖν,
2 ἀδικώτατα καὶ δεινότατα παθόντα πάντων ἀνθρώπων.
τηρῶν δὲ καὶ περὶ ταύτην τὴν πρᾶξιν ὁ συγγραφεὺς
τὸ καθ᾽ αὑτὸν ἰδίωμα, φωνάς τινας πλάττει διὰ τῆς
νυκτὸς αὐτοῦ στρεβλουμένου προσπιπτούσας τοῖς
σύνεγγυς κατοικοῦσιν, ὧν τοὺς μὲν ἐκπληττομένους
τὴν ἀσέβειαν, τοὺς δ᾽ ἀπιστοῦντας, τοὺς δ᾽
ἀγανακτοῦντας ἐπὶ τοῖς γινομένοις προστρέχειν πρὸς
3 τὴν οἰκίαν φησί. περὶ μὲν οὖν τῆς τοιαύτης τερατείας
4 παρείσθω· δεδήλωται γὰρ ἀρκούντως. ἐγὼ δ᾽ Ἀριστόμαχον, εἰ καὶ μηδὲν εἰς τοὺς Ἀχαιοὺς ἕτερον ἥμαρτε,
κατά γε τὴν τοῦ βίου προαίρεσιν καὶ τὴν εἰς πατρίδα
5 παρανομίαν τῆς μεγίστης ἄξιον κρίνω τιμωρίας. καίπερ ὁ συγγραφεύς, βουλόμενος αὔξειν αὐτοῦ τὴν
δόξαν καὶ παραστήσασθαι τοὺς ἀκούοντας εἰς τὸ
μᾶλλον αὐτῷ συναγανακτεῖν ἐφ᾽ οἷς ἔπαθεν, οὐ μόνον
αὐτόν φησι γεγονέναι τύραννον, ἀλλὰ κὰκ τυράννων
6 πεφυκέναι. ταύτης δὲ μείζω κατηγορίαν ἢ πικροτέραν
οὐδ᾽ ἂν εἰπεῖν ῥᾳδίως δύναιτ᾽ οὐδείς. αὐτὸ γὰρ τοὔνομα περιέχει τὴν ἀσεβεστάτην ἔμφασιν καὶ πάσας
7 περιείληφε τὰς ἐν ἀνθρώποις ἀδικίας καὶ παρανομίας.
Ἀριστόμαχος δ᾽ εἰ τὰς δεινοτάτας ὑπέμεινε τιμωρίας,
ὡς οὗτός φησιν, ὅμως οὐχ ἱκανὴν ἔδωκεν δίκην μιᾶς
8 ἡμέρας, ἐν ᾗ παρεισπεσόντος εἰς τὴν πόλιν Ἀράτου
μετὰ τῶν Ἀχαιῶν, καὶ μεγάλους ἀγῶνας καὶ κινδύνους
ὑπομείναντος ὑπὲρ τῆς Ἀργείων ἐλευθερίας, τέλος δ᾽
ἐκπεσόντος διὰ τὸ μηδένα συγκινηθῆναι τῶν ἔσωθεν
9 αὐτῷ ταξαμένων, διὰ τὸν ἀπὸ τοῦ τυράννου φόβον,

tive to Cenchreae and there racked to death, no man deserving less such a terrible fate. Exercising in this case too his peculiar talent, the author gives us a made-up story of his cries when on the rack having reached the ears of the neighbors during the night, some of whom, horrified at the crime, others scarcely crediting their senses and others in hot indignation ran to the house. About Phylarchus' vice of sensationalism I need say no more, for I have given sufficient evidence of it; but as for Aristomachus, even if he had been guilty of no other offense to the Achaeans, I consider that the general tenor of his life and his treason to his own country rendered him worthy of the most severe punishment. Our author, it is true, with the view of magnifying his importance and moving his readers to share his own indignation at his fate, tells us that he "not only had been a tyrant himself but was descended from tyrants." It would be difficult for anyone to bring a graver or more bitter accusation against a man. Why! the very word "tyrant" alone conveys to us the height of impiety and comprises in itself the sum of all human defiance of law and justice. Aristomachus, if it is true that he was subjected to the most terrible punishment, as Phylarchus tells us, did not get his full deserts for the doings of one day; I mean the day on which when Aratus with the Achaeans had gained entrance to the town and fought hard to free the Argives at great risk, but was finally driven out, because none of those inside the city who had agreed to join him ventured to stir owing to their

Ἀριστόμαχος, ἀφορμῇ ταύτῃ καὶ προφάσει χρησάμενος, ὥς τινων συνειδότων τὰ περὶ τὴν εἴσοδον τῶν
Ἀχαιῶν, ὀγδοήκοντα τοὺς πρώτους τῶν πολιτῶν οὐδὲν
ἀδικήσαντας στρεβλώσας ἐναντίον τῶν ἀναγκαίων
10   κατέσφαξε. παρίημι τὰ παρ᾽ ὅλον τὸν βίον αὐτοῦ καὶ
τῶν προγόνων ἀσεβήματα· μακρὸν γάρ.

60. διόπερ οὐκ εἴ τινι τῶν ὁμοίων περιέπεσε δεινὸν
ἡγητέον, πολὺ δὲ δεινότερον, εἰ μηδενὸς τούτων
2   πεῖραν λαβὼν ἀθῷος ἀπέθανεν. οὐδ᾽ Ἀντιγόνῳ
προσαπτέον οὐδ᾽ Ἀράτῳ παρανομίαν, ὅτι λαβόντες
κατὰ πόλεμον ὑποχείριον τύραννον στρεβλώσαντες
ἀπέκτειναν, ὅν γε καὶ κατ᾽ αὐτὴν τὴν εἰρήνην τοῖς
ἀνελοῦσι καὶ τιμωρησαμένοις ἔπαινος καὶ τιμὴ συν-
3   εξηκολούθει παρὰ τοῖς ὀρθῶς λογιζομένοις. ὅτε δὲ
χωρὶς τῶν προειρημένων καὶ τοὺς Ἀχαιοὺς παρεσπόν-
4   δησε, τί παθεῖν ἦν ἄξιος; ἐκεῖνος γὰρ ἀπέθετο μὲν τὴν
τυραννίδα χρόνοις οὐ πολλοῖς πρότερον, ὑπὸ τῶν
καιρῶν συγκλειόμενος διὰ τὸν Δημητρίου θάνατον,
ἀνελπίστως δὲ τῆς ἀσφαλείας ἔτυχε περισταλεὶς ὑπὸ
5   τῆς τῶν Ἀχαιῶν πραότητος καὶ καλοκἀγαθίας· οἵτινες
οὐ μόνον αὐτὸν τῶν ἐκ τῆς τυραννίδος ἀσεβημάτων
ἀζήμιον ἐποίησαν, ἀλλὰ καὶ προσλαβόντες εἰς τὴν
πολιτείαν τὴν μεγίστην τιμὴν περιέθεσαν, ἡγεμόνα
6   καὶ στρατηγὸν καταστήσαντες σφῶν αὐτῶν. ὁ δ᾽
ἐπιλαθόμενος τῶν προειρημένων φιλανθρώπων παρὰ

---

124 P. omits to mention that his hero Aratus was once con-

fear of the tyrant, Aristomachus, availing himself of the
pretext that certain persons were cognisant of the entrance
of the Achaeans, put to death eighty of the leading citizens
who were quite innocent, after torturing them before the
eyes of their relatives. I say nothing of the crimes that he
and his ancestors were guilty of all through their lives: it
would be too long a story.[124]

60. We must not therefore think it shocking if he met
with treatment similar to what he had inflicted: it would
have been much more so had he died in peace, without ex-
periencing any such. Nor should we charge Antigonus and
Aratus with criminal conduct, if having captured him in
war they had tortured and put to death a tyrant, any man
who killed and punished whom even in time of peace
would have been applauded and honored by all right-
thinking people. When I add that in addition to all his
other offenses he broke his faith with the Achaeans, what
fate shall we say was too bad for him? Not many years previously he had laid down his tyranny, finding himself in an
embarrassed position owing to the death of Demetrius,
and quite contrary to his expectation suffered no harm, being protected by the Achaeans, who showed themselves
most lenient and generous; for not only did they inflict no
punishment on him for the crimes he had committed during his tyranny, but receiving him into their League they
invested him with the highest dignity, making him their
Strategus[125] and Commander-in-chief. But instantly dismissing from his mind all these benefits, the moment it

demned by the arbitrating city of Mantinea of having attacked that
family's territory in peacetime (Plu., *Arat*. 25. 5).

[125] For the year 228/7.

πόδας, ἐπεὶ μικρὸν ἐπικυδεστέρας ἔσχε τὰς ἐλπίδας
ὑπὲρ τοῦ μέλλοντος ἐν Κλεομένει, τήν τε πατρίδα καὶ
τὴν ἑαυτοῦ προαίρεσιν ἀποσπάσας ἀπὸ τῶν Ἀχαιῶν
ἐν τοῖς ἀναγκαιοτάτοις καιροῖς προσένειμε τοῖς
7 ἐχθροῖς. ὃν ὑποχείριον γενόμενον οὐκ ἐν Κεγχρεαῖς
ἔδει τὴν νύκτα στρεβλούμενον ἀποθανεῖν, ὡς Φύλαρχός φησι, περιαγόμενον δ᾽ εἰς τὴν Πελοπόννησον καὶ
μετὰ τιμωρίας παραδειγματιζόμενον οὕτως ἐκλιπεῖν
8 τὸ ζῆν. ἀλλ᾽ ὅμως τοιοῦτος ὢν οὐδενὸς ἔτυχε δεινοῦ
πλὴν τοῦ καταποντισθῆναι διὰ τῶν ἐπὶ ταῖς Κεγχρεαῖς τεταγμένων.

61. Χωρίς τε τούτων τὰς μὲν Μαντινέων ἡμῖν
συμφορὰς μετ᾽ αὐξήσεως καὶ διαθέσεως ἐξηγήσατο,
δῆλον ὅτι καθήκειν ὑπολαμβάνων τοῖς συγγραφεῦσι
2 τὰς παρανόμους τῶν πράξεων ἐπισημαίνεσθαι, τῆς δὲ
Μεγαλοπολιτῶν γενναιότητος, ᾗ περὶ τοὺς αὐτοὺς
ἐχρήσαντο καιρούς, οὐδὲ κατὰ ποσὸν ἐποιήσατο μνή-
3 μην, ὥσπερ τὸ τὰς ἁμαρτίας ἐξαριθμεῖσθαι τῶν
πραξάντων οἰκειότερον ὑπάρχον τῆς ἱστορίας τοῦ τὰ
καλὰ καὶ δίκαια τῶν ἔργων ἐπισημαίνεσθαι, ἢ τοὺς
ἐντυγχάνοντας τοῖς ὑπομνήμασιν ἧττόν τι διορθου-
μένους ὑπὸ τῶν σπουδαίων καὶ ζηλωτῶν ἔργων ἤπερ
4 ὑπὸ τῶν παρανόμων καὶ φευκτῶν πράξεων. ὁ δὲ πῶς
μὲν ἔλαβε Κλεομένης τὴν πόλιν καὶ πῶς ἀκέραιον
διαφυλάξας ἐξαπέστειλε παραχρῆμα πρὸς τοὺς
Μεγαλοπολίτας εἰς τὴν Μεσσήνην γραμματοφόρους,
ἀξιῶν αὐτοὺς ἀβλαβῆ κομισαμένους τὴν ἑαυτῶν πατρίδα κοινωνῆσαι τῶν ἰδίων πραγμάτων, ταῦτα μὲν

seemed to him that his prospects would be somewhat more brilliant if he sided with Cleomenes, he broke away from the Achaeans, transferring from them to the enemy at a most critical time his personal support and that of his country. Surely when they got him into their hands, he should not have been racked to death at night in Cenchreae, as Phylarchus says, but should have been led round the whole Peloponnesus and tortured as a spectacle for the public until dead. Yet notwithstanding his abominable character, all the harm he suffered was to be drowned in the sea by the officers in command at Cenchreae.

61. To take another instance, Phylarchus, while narrating with exaggeration and elaboration the calamities of the Mantineans, evidently deeming it a historian's duty to lay stress on criminal acts, does not even make mention of the noble conduct of the Megalopolitans at nearly the same date, as if it were rather the proper function of history to chronicle the commission of sins than to call attention to right and honorable actions, or as if readers of his memoirs would be improved less by account of good conduct which we should emulate than by criminal conduct which we should shun. He tells us how Cleomenes took the city, and before doing any damage to it, sent at once a post to the Megalopolitans at Messene offering to hand back their own native country to them uninjured on condition of their throwing in their lot with him. So much he lets us

THE HISTORIES OF POLYBIUS

ἡμῖν ἐδήλωσε, βουλόμενος ὑποδεῖξαι τὴν Κλεομένους
5 μεγαλο\ψ\ψ\ψψ\χίαν καὶ με\ριότητα πρὸς τοὺς πολεμίους.
ἔτι δὲ πῶς οἱ Μεγαλοπολῖται τῆς ἐπιστολῆς ἀνα-
γινωσκομένης οὐκ ἐάσαιεν εἰς τέλος ἀναγνωσθῆναι,
μικροῦ δὲ καταλεύσαιεν τοὺς γραμματοφόρους, ἕως
6 τούτου διεσάφησε. τὸ δ' ἀκόλουθον καὶ τὸ τῆς ἱστορίας ἴδιον ἀφεῖλε, τὸν ἔπαινον καὶ τὴν ἐπ' ἀγαθῷ
7 μνήμην τῶν ἀξιολόγων προαιρέσεων. καίτοι γ' ἐμποδὼν ἦν. εἰ γὰρ τοὺς λόγῳ καὶ δόγματι μόνον ὑπομεί-
ναντας πόλεμον ὑπὲρ φίλων καὶ συμμάχων ἄνδρας
ἀγαθοὺς νομίζομεν, τοῖς δὲ καὶ χώρας καταφθορὰν
καὶ πολιορκίαν ἀναδεξαμένοις οὐ μόνον ἔπαινον, ἀλ-
8 λὰ καὶ χάριτας καὶ δωρεὰς τὰς μεγίστας ἀπονέμομεν,
τίνα γε χρὴ περὶ Μεγαλοπολιτῶν ἔχειν διάληψιν; ἆρ'
9 οὐχὶ τὴν σεμνοτάτην καὶ βελτίστην; οἳ πρῶτον μὲν
τὴν χώραν Κλεομένει προεῖντο, μετὰ δὲ ταῦτα πάλιν
ὁλοσχερῶς ἔπταισαν τῇ πατρίδι διὰ τὴν πρὸς τοὺς
10 Ἀχαιοὺς αἵρεσιν, τὸ δὲ τελευταῖον, δοθείσης ἀνελπίστως καὶ παραδόξως αὐτοῖς ἐξουσίας ἀβλαβῆ ταύτην ἀπολαβεῖν, προείλαντο στέρεσθαι χώρας, τάφων,
ἱερῶν, πατρίδος, τῶν ὑπαρχόντων, ἁπάντων συλλήβδην τῶν ἐν ἀνθρώποις ἀναγκαιοτάτων, χάριν τοῦ
11 μὴ προδοῦναι τὴν πρὸς τοὺς συμμάχους πίστιν. οὗ τί
κάλλιον ἔργον ἢ γέγονεν ἢ γένοιτ' ἄν ἐπὶ τί δ' ἄν;
μᾶλλον συγγραφεὺς ἐπιστῆσαι τοὺς ἀκούοντας; διὰ
τίνος δ' ἔργου μᾶλλον ἂν παρορμήσαι πρὸς φυλακὴν
πίστεως καὶ πρὸς ἀληθινῶν πραγμάτων καὶ βεβαίων
12 κοινωνίαν; ὧν οὐδεμίαν ἐποιήσατο μνήμην Φύλαρχος,

know, wishing to show the magnanimity of Cleomenes and his moderation to his enemies, and he goes on to tell how when the letter was being read out they would not allow the reader to continue until the end, and how they came very near stoning the letter-bearers. So far he makes everything quite clear to us, but he deprives us of what should follow and what is the special virtue of history, I mean praise and honorable mention of conduct noteworthy for its excellence. And yet he had an opportunity ready to his hand here. For if we consider those men to be good who by speeches and resolutions only expose themselves to war for the sake of their friends and allies, and if we bestow not only praise but lavish thanks and gifts on those who have suffered their country to be laid waste and their city besieged, what should we feel for the Megalopolitans? Surely the deepest reverence and the highest regard. In the first place they left their lands at the mercy of Cleomenes, next they utterly lost their city owing to their support of the Achaeans, and finally, when quite unexpectedly it was put in their power to get it back undamaged, they preferred to lose their land, their tombs, their temples, their homes, and their possessions, all in fact that is dearest to men, rather than break faith with their allies. What more noble conduct has there ever been or could there be? To what could an author with more advantage call the attention of his readers, and how could he better stimulate them to loyalty to their engagements and to thus share in an honorable and firmly established state? But Phylarchus, blind, as it seems to me, to the most noble actions and those most

τυφλώττων, ὥς γ᾽ ἐμοὶ δοκεῖ, περὶ τὰ κάλλιστα καὶ μάλιστα συγγραφεῖ καθήκοντα τῶν ἔργων.

62. Οὐ μὴν ἀλλὰ τούτοις ἑξῆς φησιν ἀπὸ τῶν ἐκ τῆς Μεγάλης πόλεως λαφύρων ἑξακισχίλια τάλαντα τοῖς Λακεδαιμονίοις πεσεῖν, ὧν τὰ δισχίλια Κλεο-

2 μένει δοθῆναι κατὰ τοὺς ἐθισμούς. ἐν δὲ τούτοις πρῶ- τον μὲν τίς οὐκ ἂν θαυμάσειε τὴν ἀπειρίαν καὶ τὴν ἄγνοιαν τῆς κοινῆς ἐννοίας ὑπὲρ τῆς τῶν Ἑλληνικῶν πραγμάτων χορηγίας καὶ δυνάμεως; ἣν μάλιστα δεῖ

3 παρὰ τοῖς ἱστοριογράφοις ὑπάρχειν. ἐγὼ γὰρ οὐ λέγω κατ᾽ ἐκείνους τοὺς χρόνους, ἐν οἷς ὑπό τε τῶν ἐν Μακεδονίᾳ βασιλέων, ἔτι δὲ μᾶλλον ὑπὸ τῆς συν- εχείας τῶν πρὸς ἀλλήλους πολέμων ἄρδην κατέφθαρ-

4 το τὰ Πελοποννησίων, ἀλλ᾽ ἐν τοῖς καθ᾽ ἡμᾶς καιροῖς, ἐν οἷς πάντες ἓν καὶ ταὐτὸ λέγοντες μεγίστην καρ- ποῦσθαι δοκοῦσιν εὐδαιμονίαν, ὅμως ἐκ Πελοποννή- σου πάσης ἐξ αὐτῶν τῶν ἐπίπλων χωρὶς σωμάτων

5 οὐχ οἷόν τε συναχθῆναι τοσοῦτο πλῆθος χρημάτων. καὶ διότι τοῦτο νῦν οὐκ εἰκῆ, λόγῳ δέ τινι μᾶλλον

6 ἀποφαινόμεθα, δῆλον ἐκ τούτων. τίς γὰρ ὑπὲρ Ἀθη- ναίων οὐχ ἱστόρηκε διότι καθ᾽ οὓς καιροὺς μετὰ Θη- βαίων εἰς τὸν πρὸς Λακεδαιμονίους ἐνέβαινον πόλε- μον, καὶ μυρίους μὲν ἐξέπεμπον στρατιώτας, ἑκατὸν δ᾽

7 ἐπλήρουν τριήρεις, ὅτι τότε κρίναντες ἀπὸ τῆς ἀξίας ποιεῖσθαι τὰς εἰς τὸν πόλεμον εἰσφορὰς ἐτιμήσαντο τήν τε χώραν τὴν Ἀττικὴν ἅπασαν καὶ τὰς οἰκίας, ὁμοίως δὲ καὶ τὴν λοιπὴν οὐσίαν· ἀλλ᾽ ὅμως τὸ σύμ- παν τίμημα τῆς ἀξίας ἐνέλιπε τῶν ἑξακισχιλίων δια-

worthy of an author's attention, has not said a single word on the subject.

62. Further he tells us that from the booty of Megalopolis six thousand talents fell to the Lacedaemonians, of which two thousand were given to Cleomenes according to usage. Now in this statement one marvels first at his lack of practical experience and of that general notion of the wealth and power of Greece so essential to a historian. For, not speaking of those times, when the Peloponnese had been utterly ruined by the Macedonian kings and still more by continued intestinal wars, but in our own times, when all are in complete unison and enjoy, it is thought, very great prosperity, I assert that a sale of all the goods and chattels, apart from slaves, in the whole Peloponnese would not bring in such a sum. That I do not make this assertion lightly but after due estimate will be evident from the following consideration.[126] Who has not read that when the Athenians, in conjunction with the Thebans, entered on the war against the Lacedaemonians, sending out a force of ten thousand men and manning a hundred triremes, they decided to meet the war expenses by a property tax and made a valuation for this purpose of the whole of Attica including the houses and other property. This estimate, however, fell short of 6000 talents by 250, from

[126] See WC 1. 268–269.

8 κοσίοις καὶ πεντήκοντα ταλάντοις. ἐξ ὧν οὐκ ἀπεοικὸς
   ἂν φανείη τὸ περὶ Πελοποννησίων ἄρτι ῥηθὲν ὑπ᾽
9 ἐμοῦ. κατὰ δ᾽ ἐκείνους τοὺς καιροὺς ἐξ αὐτῆς τῆς
   Μεγάλης πόλεως ὑπερβολικῶς ἀποφαινόμενος οὐκ ἄν
10 τις εἰπεῖν τολμήσειε πλείω γενέσθαι τριακοσίων, ἐπειδήπερ ὁμολογούμενόν ἐστι διότι καὶ τῶν ἐλευθέρων
   καὶ τῶν δουλικῶν σωμάτων τὰ πλεῖστα συνέβη διαφυγεῖν εἰς τὴν Μεσσήνην. μέγιστον δὲ τῶν προειρη-
11 μένων τεκμήριον· οὐδενὸς γὰρ ὄντες δεύτεροι τῶν
   Ἀρκάδων Μαντινεῖς οὔτε κατὰ τὴν δύναμιν οὔτε κατὰ
   τὴν περιουσίαν, ὡς αὐτὸς οὗτός φησιν, ἐκ πολιορκίας
   δὲ καὶ παραδόσεως ἁλόντες, ὥστε μήτε διαφυγεῖν
12 μηδένα μήτε διακλαπῆναι ῥᾳδίως μηδέν, ὅμως τὸ πᾶν
   λάφυρον ἐποίησαν μετὰ τῶν σωμάτων κατὰ τοὺς αὐτοὺς καιροὺς τάλαντα τριακόσια.

63. Τὸ δὲ συνεχὲς τούτῳ τίς οὐκ ἂν ἔτι μᾶλλον
   θαυμάσειε; ταῦτα γὰρ ἀποφαινόμενος λέγει πρὸ τῆς
   παρατάξεως δέχ᾽ ἡμέραις μάλιστα τὸν παρὰ Πτολεμαίου πρεσβευτὴν ἐλθεῖν ἀγγέλλοντα πρὸς τὸν Κλεομένη διότι Πτολεμαῖος τὸ μὲν χορηγεῖν ἀπολέγει,
2 διαλύεσθαι δὲ παρακαλεῖ πρὸς τὸν Ἀντίγονον. τὸν δ᾽
   ἀκούσαντά φησι κρῖναι διότι δεῖ τὴν ταχίστην ἐκκυβεύειν τοῖς ὅλοις πρὸ τοῦ συνεῖναι τὰ προσπεπτωκότα
   τὰς δυνάμεις, διὰ τὸ μηδεμίαν ὑπάρχειν ἐν τοῖς ἰδίοις
3 πράγμασιν ἐλπίδα τοῦ δύνασθαι μισθοδοτεῖν. ἀλλ᾽
   εἴπερ ἑξακισχιλίων ἐγκρατὴς ἐγεγόνει ταλάντων κατὰ
   τοὺς αὐτοὺς καιρούς, τὸν Πτολεμαῖον αὐτὸν ἠδύνατο
4 ταῖς χορηγίαις ὑπερθέσθαι. πρὸς δὲ τὸν Ἀντίγονον, εἰ

which it would seem that my assertion about the Peloponnese at the present day is not far wide of the mark. But as regards the times of which we are dealing, no one, even if he were exaggerating, would venture to say that more than three hundred talents could be got out of Megalopolis, since it is an acknowledged fact that most of the free population and the slaves had escaped to Messene. But the best proof of what I say is the following: Mantinea, both in wealth and power, was second to no city in Arcadia, as Phylarchus himself says, and it surrendered after a siege, so that it was not easy for anyone to escape or for anything to be stolen, but yet the value of the whole booty together with slaves amounted at this very period to but three hundred talents.

63. What he tells us next is still more astounding; for after this assertion about the booty, he states that just ten days before the battle an envoy from Ptolemy reached Cleomenes informing him that that king withdrew his subvention and requested him to come to terms with Antigonus. He says that Cleomenes on hearing this resolved to stake his all on a battle before it reached the ears of his troops, as he had no hope of being able to meet their pay from his own resources. But if at this very time he had six thousand talents at his command, he could have been more generous than Ptolemy himself in the matter of subventions; and if he could only dispose of three hundred

μόνον τριακοσίων ὑπῆρχε κύριος, καὶ λίαν ἱκανὸς ἦν
5 ἀσφαλῶς ὑπομένων τρίβειν τὸν πόλεμον. τὸ δ' ἅμα
μὲν πάσας ἀποφαίνειν τῷ Κλεομένει τὰς ἐλπίδας ἐν
Πτολεμαίῳ διὰ τὰς χορηγίας, ἅμα δὲ τοσούτων χρημάτων αὐτὸν φάναι κύριον γεγονέναι κατὰ τοὺς αὐτοὺς καιρούς, πῶς οὐ τῆς μεγίστης ἀλογίας, ἔτι δ'
6 ἀσκεψίας ἐστὶ σημεῖον; πολλὰ δὲ καὶ ἕτερα τῷ συγγραφεῖ τοιαῦτα, καὶ κατὰ τοὺς ὑποκειμένους καιροὺς
καὶ παρ' ὅλην τὴν πραγματείαν κατατέτακται, περὶ ὧν
ἀρκεῖν ὑπολαμβάνω κατὰ τὴν ἐξ ἀρχῆς πρόθεσιν καὶ
τὰ νῦν εἰρημένα.

64. Μετὰ δὲ τὴν τῆς Μεγάλης πόλεως ἅλωσιν
Ἀντιγόνου παραχειμάζοντος ἐν τῇ τῶν Ἀργείων πόλει, συναγαγὼν Κλεομένης ἅμα τῷ τὴν ἐαρινὴν ὥραν
ἐνίστασθαι καὶ παρακαλέσας τὰ πρέποντα τοῖς καιροῖς, ἐξαγαγὼν τὴν στρατιὰν ἐνέβαλεν εἰς τὴν τῶν
2 Ἀργείων χώραν, ὡς μὲν τοῖς πολλοῖς ἐδόκει, παραβόλως καὶ τολμηρῶς διὰ τὴν ὀχυρότητα τῶν κατὰ τὰς
εἰσόδους τόπων, ὡς δὲ τοῖς ὀρθῶς λογιζομένοις,
3 ἀσφαλῶς καὶ νουνεχῶς. ὁρῶν γὰρ τὸν Ἀντίγονον
διαφεικότα τὰς δυνάμεις, ἤδει σαφῶς ὡς πρῶτον μὲν
τὴν εἰσβολὴν ἀκινδύνως ποιήσεται, δεύτερον ἔτι τῆς
χώρας καταφθειρομένης ἕως τῶν τειχῶν ἀνάγκη τοὺς
Ἀργείους θεωροῦντας τὸ γινόμενον ἀσχάλλειν καὶ
4 καταμέμφεσθαι τὸν Ἀντίγονον. εἰ μὲν οὖν συμβαίη
μὴ δυνάμενον αὐτὸν ὑποφέρειν τὸν ἐπιρραπισμὸν τῶν
ὄχλων ἐξελθεῖν καὶ διακινδυνεῦσαι τοῖς παροῦσι,
πρόδηλον ἐκ τῶν κατὰ λόγον ἦν αὐτῷ διότι νικήσει

talents it was enough to enable him to continue the war against Antigonus with absolute financial security. But to state in one breath that Cleomenes depended entirely on Ptolemy for money and that at the very same time he was in possession of such a large sum, is a sign of the greatest levity and want of reflection. Phylarchus has made many similar statements not only about this period but all through his work. I think, however, that, in view of the original intention (of this digression), what I have said should suffice.

64. After the capture of Megalopolis, while Antigonus 222 B.C. was still in winter quarters at Argos, Cleomenes at the beginning of spring collected his troops, and after addressing them in terms suitable to the occasion, led them out and invaded Argolis. Most people think that this was rash and hazardous on his part, owing to the strength of the frontier, but if we judge rightly it was really a safe and wise course. For as he saw that Antigonus had dismissed his forces, he knew well that, in the first place, he would be exposed to no danger in invading, and secondly, that, if the country were laid waste up to the walls, the Argives on seeing it would certainly be much vexed and lay the blame on Antigonus. If, therefore, unable to support the reproaches of the people, he marched out and risked a battle with such forces as he had, the probabilities were in favor of Cleomenes gain-

5 ῥαδίως. εἰ δ' ἐμμείνας τοῖς λογισμοῖς ἀφησυχάζοι, καταπληξάμενος τοὺς ὑπεναντίους καὶ ταῖς ἰδίαις δυνάμεσι θάρσος ἐνεργασάμενος ἀσφαλῶς ὑπέλαβε ποιήσασθαι τὴν ἀναχώρησιν εἰς τὴν οἰκείαν. ὃ καὶ 6 συνέβη γενέσθαι. τῆς γὰρ χώρας δῃουμένης οἱ μὲν ὄχλοι συστρεφόμενοι τὸν Ἀντίγονον ἐλοιδόρουν. ὁ δὲ καὶ λίαν ἡγεμονικῶς καὶ βασιλικῶς οὐδὲν περὶ πλείονος ποιούμενος τοῦ κατὰ λόγον ⟨χρήσασθαι τοῖς⟩ 7 πράγμασιν ἦγε τὴν ἡσυχίαν. ὁ δὲ Κλεομένης κατὰ τὴν ἐξ ἀρχῆς πρόθεσιν καταφθείρας μὲν τὴν χώραν, καταπληξάμενος δὲ τοὺς ὑπεναντίους, εὐθαρσεῖς δὲ πεποιηκὼς τὰς ἑαυτοῦ δυνάμεις πρὸς τὸν ἐπιφερόμενον κίνδυνον, ἀσφαλῶς εἰς τὴν οἰκείαν ἐπανῆλθε.

65. Τοῦ δὲ θέρους ἐνισταμένου καὶ συνελθόντων τῶν Μακεδόνων καὶ τῶν Ἀχαιῶν ἐκ τῆς χειμασίας ἀναλαβὼν τὴν στρατιὰν Ἀντίγονος προῆγε μετὰ τῶν 2 συμμάχων εἰς τὴν Λακωνικήν, ἔχων Μακεδόνας μὲν τοὺς εἰς τὴν φάλαγγα μυρίους, πελταστὰς δὲ τρισχιλίους, ἱππεῖς δὲ τριακοσίους, Ἀγριᾶνας δὲ σὺν τούτοις χιλίους καὶ Γαλάτας ἄλλους τοσούτους, μισθοφόρους δὲ τοὺς πάντας πεζοὺς μὲν τρισχιλίους, ἱππεῖς δὲ 3 τριακοσίους, Ἀχαιῶν δ' ἐπιλέκτους πεζοὺς μὲν τρισχιλίους, ἱππεῖς δὲ τριακοσίους, καὶ Μεγαλοπολίτας χιλίους εἰς τὸν Μακεδονικὸν τρόπον καθωπλισμένους, 4 ὧν ἡγεῖτο Κερκιδᾶς Μεγαλοπολίτης, τῶν δὲ συμμάχων Βοιωτῶν μὲν πεζοὺς δισχιλίους, ἱππεῖς δὲ διακοσίους, Ἠπειρωτῶν πεζοὺς χιλίους, ἱππεῖς πεντήκοντα, Ἀκαρνάνων ἄλλους τοσούτους, Ἰλλυριῶν χιλίους ἑξ-

ing an easy victory; but if, adhering to his plan, he remained quiet, he thought he could, after terrifying his enemies and inspiring his own troops with fresh courage, effect a safe retreat to Laconia, as actually happened. For, when the country was being laid waste, the populace held meetings in which they heaped abuse on Antigonus; but he, like a true general and prince, paid no attention to anything but a wise conduct of affairs, and remained quiet, while Cleomenes, having carried out his intention of devastating the country and thus striking terror into the enemy and encouraging his own troops to face the coming danger, retired in safety to his own country.

65. Early in summer, on the Macedonians and Achaeans rejoining from their winter quarters, Antigonus advanced with his own army and the allies into Laconia. His Macedonian forces consisted of ten thousand to form the phalanx, three thousand peltasts, and three hundred horse. He had besides a thousand Agrianians, and a thousand Gauls, while his mercenary force numbered three thousand foot and three hundred horse. The Achaeans furnished three thousand picked infantry and three hundred horse. There were also a thousand Megalopolitans armed in the Macedonian manner under the command of Cercidas of Megalopolis.[127] The allies consisted of two thousand Boeotian foot and two hundred horse, a thousand Epirot foot and fifty horse, the same number of Acarnanians, and one thousand six hundred Illyrians under the

[127] 48. 4. For ἐπίλεκτοι see M. Launey, *Recherches sur les armées hellénistiques*, 2 vols. (Paris 1949–1950), 1049, for *epilektoi* of the Achaeans *IVO* 297, third century.

5 ακοσίους, ἐφ' ὧν ἦν Δημήτριος ὁ Φάριος, ὥστ' εἶναι
πᾶσαν τὴν δύναμιν πεζοὺς μὲν εἰς δισμυρίους ὀκτα-
6 κισχιλίους, ἱππεῖς δὲ χιλίους καὶ διακοσίους. ὁ δὲ
Κλεομένης, προσδοκῶν τὴν ἔφοδον, τὰς μὲν ἄλλας
τὰς εἰς τὴν χώραν εἰσβολὰς ἠσφαλίσατο φυλακαῖς
7 καὶ τάφροις καὶ δένδρων ἐκκοπαῖς, αὐτὸς δὲ κατὰ τὴν
Σελλασίαν καλουμένην μετὰ τῆς δυνάμεως ἐστρατο-
πέδευε, τῆς πάσης ὑπαρχούσης αὐτῷ στρατιᾶς εἰς δύο
μυριάδας, στοχαζόμενος ἐκ τῶν κατὰ λόγον ταύτῃ
8 ποιήσασθαι τοὺς ὑπεναντίους τὴν εἰσβολήν· ὃ καὶ
συνεκύρησε. δύο δὲ λόφων ἐπ' αὐτῆς τῆς εἰσόδου
κειμένων, ὧν τὸν μὲν Εὔαν, τὸν δ' ἕτερον Ὄλυμπον
9 καλεῖσθαι συμβαίνει, τῆς δ' ὁδοῦ μεταξὺ τούτων
παρὰ τὸν Οἰνοῦντα ποταμὸν φερούσης εἰς τὴν Σπάρτην, ὁ μὲν Κλεομένης, τῶν προειρημένων λόφων συνάμφω τάφρον καὶ χάρακα προβαλόμενος, ἐπὶ μὲν
τὸν Εὔαν ἔταξε τοὺς περιοίκους καὶ συμμάχους,
ἐφ' ὧν ἐπέστησε τὸν ἀδελφὸν Εὐκλείδαν, αὐτὸς δὲ
τὸν Ὄλυμπον κατεῖχε μετὰ Λακεδαιμονίων καὶ τῶν
10 μισθοφόρων. ἐν δὲ τοῖς ἐπιπέδοις παρὰ τὸν ποταμὸν
ἐφ' ἑκάτερα τῆς ὁδοῦ τοὺς ἱππεῖς μετὰ μέρους τινὸς
11 τῶν μισθοφόρων παρενέβαλεν. Ἀντίγονος δὲ παραγενόμενος καὶ συνθεωρήσας τήν τε τῶν τόπων ὀχυρότητα καὶ τὸν Κλεομένη πᾶσι τοῖς οἰκείοις μέρεσι τῆς
δυνάμεως οὕτως εὐστόχως προκατειληφότα τὰς εὐκαιρίας ὥστε παραπλήσιον εἶναι τὸ σύμπαν σχῆμα τῆς
12 στρατοπεδείας τῆς τῶν ἀγαθῶν ὁπλομάχων προβολῆς·
οὐδὲν γὰρ ἀπέλειπε τῶν πρὸς ἐπίθεσιν ἅμα καὶ φυλα-

command of Demetrius of Pharos. His total force thus amounted to twenty-eight thousand foot and one thousand two hundred horse. Cleomenes, who expected the invasion, had occupied the other passes into Laconia, placing garrisons in them and fortifying them by means of trenches and barricades of trees, and himself encamped at a place called Sellasia,[128] with a force of twenty thousand men, as he conjectured that the invaders would most likely take this route, as in fact they did. At the actual pass there are two hills, one called Euas and the other Olympus, the road to Sparta running between these along the bank of the river Oenous. Cleomenes, having fortified both of these hills with a trench and palisade, posted on Euas the perioeci and allies under the command of his brother Eucleidas, while he himself held Olympus with the Spartans and mercenaries. On the low ground beside the river on each side of the road he drew up his cavalry and a certain portion of the mercenaries. Antigonus on his arrival observed the great natural strength of the position and how Cleomenes had so cleverly occupied the advantageous points with the portions of his force suitable in each case, that his whole formation resembled a charge. For attack and defense alike nothing was wanting, the position

[128] The battle (65–69. 11) took place in 222. For the location see map in WC 1. 276, based on Kromayer.

κήν, ἀλλ᾽ ἦν ὁμοῦ παράταξις ἐνεργὸς καὶ παρεμβολὴ
δυσπρόσοδος·

66. διὸ καὶ τὸ μὲν ἐξ ἐφόδου καταπειράζειν καὶ
συμπλέκεοθαι προχείρως ἀπέγνω, στρατοπεδεύσας δ᾽
ἐν βραχεῖ διαστήματι, καὶ λαβὼν πρόβλημα τὸν
Γοργύλον καλούμενον ποταμόν, τινὰς μὲν ἡμέρας ἐπι-
μένων συνεθεώρει τάς τε τῶν τόπων ἰδιότητας καὶ τὰς
2 τῶν δυνάμεων διαφοράς, ἅμα δὲ καὶ προδεικνύων
τινὰς ἐπιβολὰς πρὸς τὸ μέλλον ἐξεκαλεῖτο τὰς τῶν
3 ὑπεναντίων ἐπινοίας. Οὐ δυνάμενος δὲ λαβεῖν οὐδὲν
ἀργὸν οὐδ᾽ ἔξοπλον διὰ τὸ πρὸς πᾶν ἑτοίμως ἀντικι-
4 νεῖσθαι τὸν Κλεομένη, τῆς μὲν τοιαύτης ἐπινοίας
ἀπέστη, τέλος δ᾽ ἐξ ὁμολόγου διὰ μάχης ἀμφότεροι
προέθεντο κρίνειν τὰς πράξεις· πάνυ γὰρ εὐφυεῖς καὶ
παραπλησίους ἡγεμόνας ἡ τύχη συνέβαλε τούτους
5 τοὺς ἄνδρας. πρὸς μὲν οὖν τοὺς κατὰ τὸν Εὔαν ὁ
βασιλεὺς ἀντέταξε τῶν τε Μακεδόνων τοὺς χαλκάσπι-
δας καὶ τοὺς Ἰλλυριούς, κατὰ σπείρας ἐναλλὰξ τεταγμένους, Ἀλέξανδρον τὸν Ἀκμήτου καὶ Δημήτριον
6 τὸν Φάριον ἐπιστήσας. ἐπὶ δὲ τούτοις τοὺς Ἀκαρνᾶνας
καὶ Κρῆτας ἐπέβαλε· τούτων δὲ κατόπιν ἦσαν δισχί-
7 λιοι τῶν Ἀχαιῶν, ἐφεδρείας λαμβάνοντες τάξιν. τοὺς
δ᾽ ἱππεῖς περὶ τὸν Οὐνοῦντα ποταμὸν ἀντέθηκε τῷ τῶν
πολεμίων ἱππικῷ, συστήσας αὐτοῖς Ἀλέξανδρον ἡγεμόνα καὶ συμπαραθεὶς πεζοὺς τῶν Ἀχαϊκῶν χιλίους
8 καὶ Μεγαλοπολίτας τοὺς ἴσους. αὐτὸς δὲ τοὺς μισθοφόρους ἔχων καὶ τοὺς Μακεδόνας κατὰ τὸν Ὄλυμπον πρὸς τοὺς περὶ τὸν Κλεομένη διέγνω ποιεῖσθαι

being at one and the same time a fortified camp difficult to approach and a line of battle ready for action.

66. Antigonus therefore decided to make no hasty attempt to force the position and come to blows with the enemy, but encamped at a short distance with the river Gorgylus on his front, and for several days remained there noting the peculiar features of the country and the character of the forces, while at the same time, by threatening certain movements, he attempted to make the enemy show his hand. But being unable to find any weak or unprotected spot, since Cleomenes always checked him at once by a countermovement, he abandoned this project, and finally the kings agreed to try issues in a battle: for they were very gifted and evenly matched, these two generals whom Fortune had thus brought face to face. To confront those on Euas Antigonus drew up the brazen-shielded Macedonians and the Illyrians in alternate companies, placing them under the command of Alexander son of Acmetus,[129] and Demetrius of Pharos. Behind these stood the Acarnanians and Cretans, and in the rear as a reserve were two thousand Achaeans. His cavalry he opposed to that of the enemy by the river Oenous under the command of Alexander and supported by a thousand Achaean and as many Megalopolitan infantry. He himself in person decided to attack Cleomenes on Olympus with the merce-

[129] Honored at Gonnoi in Thessaly by a decree that made known his ethnic (Macedonian from Arcynia) and his correct patronymic: son of Admetos. The decree was decorated with a Macedonian shield: Habicht, *Ancient Macedonia* 1 (1970), 269–273. Recently, Alexander turned up as commander of King Philip V at Euromus in western Asia Minor (*SEG* 43. 706).

9 τὴν μάχην. προτάξας οὖν τοὺς μισθοφόρους ἐπέστησε
διφαλαγγίαν ἐπάλληλον τῶν Μακεδόνων· ἐποίει δὲ
10 τοῦτο διὰ τὴν στενότητα τῶν τόπων. σύνθημα δ' ἦν
τοῖς μὲν Ἰλλυριοῖς τότε ποιεῖσθαι τὴν ἀρχὴν τῆς
πρὸς τὸν λόφον προσβολῆς, ὅταν ἴδωσιν ἀρθεῖσαν
ἀπὸ τῶν κατὰ τὸν Ὄλυμπον τόπων σινδόνα· προσηρ-
τημένοι γὰρ ἦσαν οὗτοι νυκτὸς ἐν τῷ Γοργύλῳ ποτα-
11 μῷ πρὸς αὐτῇ τῇ τοῦ λόφου ῥίζῃ · τοῖς δὲ Μεγαλοπολίταις καὶ τοῖς ἱππεῦσι παραπλησίως, ἐπειδὰν φοινι-
κὶς ἐξαρθῇ παρὰ τοῦ βασιλέως.

67. Ἐπειδὴ δ' ὁ μὲν καιρὸς ἧκε τῆς χρείας, τὸ δὲ
σύνθημα τοῖς Ἰλλυριοῖς ἀπεδόθη, παρήγγειλαν δὲ
ποιεῖν τὸ δέον οἷς ἦν ἐπιμελές, πάντες εὐθέως ἀνα-
δείξαντες αὑτοὺς κατήρχοντο τῆς πρὸς τὸν βουνὸν
2 προσβολῆς. οἱ δὲ μετὰ τῶν Κλεομένους ἱππέων ἐξ
ἀρχῆς ταχθέντες εὔζωνοι, θεωροῦντες τὰς σπείρας
τῶν Ἀχαιῶν ἐρήμους ἐκ τῶν κατόπιν οὔσας, κατ'
οὐρὰν προσπίπτοντες εἰς ὁλοσχερῆ κίνδυνον ἦγον
3 τοὺς πρὸς τὸν λόφον βιαζομένους, ὡς ἂν τῶν μὲν περὶ
τὸν Εὐκλείδαν ἐξ ὑπερδεξίου κατὰ πρόσωπον αὐτοῖς
ἐφεστώτων, τῶν δὲ μισθοφόρων κατόπιν ἐπικειμένων
καὶ προσφερόντων τὰς χεῖρας ἐρρωμένως. ἐν ᾧ καιρῷ
4 συννοήσας τὸ γινόμενον, ἅμα δὲ προορώμενος τὸ
μέλλον, Φιλοποίμην ὁ Μεγαλοπολίτης τὸ μὲν πρῶτον
ὑποδεικνύειν ἐπεβάλλετο τοῖς προεστῶσι τὸ συμβη-
5 σόμενον· οὐδενὸς δὲ προσέχοντος αὐτῷ διὰ τὸ μήτ' ἐφ'
ἡγεμονίας τετάχθαι μηδεπώποτε κομιδῇ τε νέον ὑπάρχειν αὐτόν, παρακαλέσας τοὺς ἑαυτοῦ πολίτας ἐνέβα-

naries and the rest of the Macedonians. Putting the mercenaries in front, he drew up the Macedonians behind them
in two phalanxes with no interval between, the narrowness
of the space rendering this necessary. It was arranged that
the Illyrians were to begin their assault on the hill upon
seeing a flag of linen waved from the neighborhood of
Olympus, for in the night they had succeeded in taking
up a position close under the hill in the bed of the river
Gorgylus. The signal for the Megalopolitans and cavalry
was to be a scarlet flag waved by the king.

67. When the time to begin the action came, the signal was given to the Illyrians, and, the officers calling on
their men to do their duty, they all instantly showed themselves and began the attack on the hill. The light-armed
mercenaries, who had been posted near Cleomenes' cavalry, upon seeing that the rear line was left exposed by
the Achaeans, attacked them from behind, and the whole
force that was pressing on to the hill was thus threatened
with a serious disaster, as Eucleidas' troops were facing
them from above while the mercenaries were vigorously
attacking their rear. At this critical moment Philopoemen
of Megalopolis,[130] who saw what was happening and foresaw what was likely to happen, first attempted to call the
attention of the commanding officers to it, but as no one
paid any attention to him, since he had never held any
command and was quite a young man, he called on his own
fellow citizens to follow him and boldly fell upon the

130 Plu. *Phil*. 6, likewise reports his intervention, from P.'s biography. Philopoemen was thirty years at the time.

6 λε τοῖς πολεμίοις τολμηρῶς. οὗ γενομένου ταχέως οἱ
προσκείμενοι μισθοφόροι κατ᾽ οὐρὰν τοῖς προσβαί
νουσιν, ἀκούσαντες τῆς κραυγῆς καὶ συνιδόντες τὴν
τῶν ἱππέων συμπλοκήν, ἀφέμενοι τῶν προκειμένων
ἀνέτρεχον εἰς τὰς ἐξ ἀρχῆς τάξεις καὶ προσεβοήθουν
7 τοῖς παρ᾽ αὑτῶν ἱππεῦσι. τούτου δὲ συμβάντος, ἀπ
ερίσπαστον γενόμενον τό τε τῶν Ἰλλυριῶν καὶ Μακε
δόνων καὶ τῶν ἅμα τούτοις προσβαινόντων πλῆθος
ἐκθύμως ὥρμησε καὶ τεθαρρηκότως ἐπὶ τοὺς ὑπεναν
8 τίους. ἐξ οὗ καί μετὰ ταῦτα φανερὸν ἐγενήθη διότι τοῦ
κατὰ τὸν Εὐκλείδαν προτερήματος αἴτιος ἐγίνετο Φι
λοποίμην.

68. ὅθεν καὶ τὸν Ἀντίγονόν φασι μετὰ ταῦτα κατα
πειράζοντα πυνθάνεσθαι τοῦ ταχθέντος ἐπὶ τῶν ἱπ
πέων Ἀλεξάνδρου διὰ τί πρὸ τοῦ παραδοθῆναι τὸ
2 σύνθημα τοῦ κινδύνου κατάρξαιτο. τοῦ δ᾽ ἀρνουμένου,
φάσκοντος δὲ μειράκιόν τι Μεγαλοπολιτικὸν προ
εγχειρῆσαι παρὰ τὴν ἑαυτοῦ γνώμην, εἰπεῖν διότι τὸ
μὲν μειράκιον ἡγεμόνος ἔργον ἀγαθοῦ ποιῆσαι, συν
θεασάμενον τὸν καιρόν, ἐκεῖνος δ᾽ ἡγεμὼν ὑπάρχων
μειρακίου τοῦ τυχόντος.

3 Οὐ μὴν ἀλλ᾽ οἵ γε περὶ τὸν Εὐκλείδαν ὁρῶντες
προσβαινούσας τὰς σπείρας, ἀφέμενοι τοῦ χρῆσθαι
4 ταῖς τῶν τόπων εὐκαιρίαις· τοῦτο δ᾽ ἦν ἐκ πολλοῦ
συναντῶντας καὶ προσπίπτοντας τοῖς πολεμίοις τὰ
μὲν ἐκείνων στίφη συνταράττειν καὶ διαλύειν, αὐτοὺς
δ᾽ ὑποχωρεῖν ἐπὶ πόδα καὶ μεθίστασθαι πρὸς τοὺς
5 ὑπερδεξίους ἀεὶ τόπους ἀσφαλῶς· οὕτω γὰρ ἂν προ-

enemy. Upon this the mercenaries who were attacking the assailants of the hill in the rear, hearing the clamor and seeing the cavalry engaged, abandoned what they had in hand and running back to their original position came to the aid of their cavalry. The Illyrians and Macedonians and the rest of this attacking force were now disengaged, and threw themselves with great dash and courage on the enemy. Thus, as became evident afterward, the success of the attack on Eucleidas was due to Philopoemen.

68. Hence it is said that subsequently Antigonus asked Alexander, the commander of the cavalry, to convict him of his shortcomings, why he had begun the battle before the signal was given. On Alexander denying this and saying that a stripling from Megalopolis had begun it contrary to his own judgment, the king said that this stripling in grasping the situation had acted like a good general and Alexander himself, the general, like an ordinary stripling.

To continue our narrative, Eucleidas' troops, on seeing the enemy's lines advancing, cast away the advantage the ground gave them. They should have charged the enemy while still at a distance, thus breaking his ranks and throwing them into disorder, and then retreating slowly, have returned in safety to the higher ground. Thus having in the

λυμηνάμενοι καὶ συγχέαντες τὸ καθοπλισμοῦ καὶ τῆς
συντάξεως ἰδίωμα τῶν ὑπεναντίων ῥᾳδίως αὐτοὺς
6 ἐτρέψαντο διὰ τὴν τῶν τόπων εὐφυΐαν· τούτων μὲν
οὐδὲν ἐποίησαν, καθάπερ δ᾽ ἐξ ἑτοίμου σφίσι τῆς
7 νίκης ὑπαρχούσης τοὐναντίον ἔπραξαν. κατὰ γὰρ τὴν
ἐξ ἀρχῆς στάσιν ἔμενον ἐπὶ τῶν ἄκρων, ὡς ἀνωτάτω
σπεύδοντες λαβεῖν τοὺς ὑπεναντίους, εἰς τὸ τὴν φυγὴν
ἐπὶ πολὺ καταφερῆ καὶ κρημνώδη γενέσθαι τοῖς πολε-
8 μίοις. συνέβη δ᾽, ὅπερ εἰκὸς ἦν, τοὐναντίον· οὐ γὰρ
ἀπολιπόντες αὐτοῖς ἀναχώρησιν, προσδεξάμενοι δ᾽
ἀκεραίους ἅμα καὶ συνεστώσας τὰς σπείρας, εἰς τοῦτο δυσχρηστίας ἦλθον ὥστε δι᾽ αὐτῆς τῆς τοῦ λόφου
9 κορυφῆς διαμάχεσθαι πρὸς τοὺς βιαζομένους. λοιπὸν
ὅσον ἐκ ποδὸς ἐπιέσθησαν τῷ βάρει τοῦ καθοπλισμοῦ
καὶ τῆς συντάξεως, εὐθέως οἱ μὲν Ἰλλυριοὶ τὴν κατάστασιν ἐλάμβανον, οἱ δὲ περὶ τὸν Εὐκλείδαν τὴν ὑπὸ
πόδα, διὰ τὸ μὴ καταλείπεσθαι τόπον εἰς ἀναχώρησιν
10 καὶ μετάστασιν ἑαυτοῖς. ἐξ οὗ ταχέως συνέβη τρα-
πέντας αὐτοὺς ὀλεθρίῳ χρήσασθαι φυγῇ, κρημνώδη
καὶ δύσβατον ἐχόντων ἐπὶ πολὺ τὴν ἀναχώρησιν τῶν
τόπων.
69. Ἅμα δὲ τούτοις ὁ περὶ τοὺς ἱππεῖς συνετελεῖτο
κίνδυνος, ἐκπρεπῆ ποιουμένων τὴν χρείαν τῶν Ἀχαϊκῶν ἱππέων ἁπάντων, μάλιστα δὲ Φιλοποίμενος, διὰ
τὸ περὶ τῆς αὐτῶν ἐλευθερίας συνεστάναι τὸν ὅλον
2 ἀγῶνα. καθ᾽ ὃν καιρὸν τῷ προειρημένῳ συνέβη τὸν
μὲν ἵππον πεσεῖν πληγέντα καιρίως, αὐτὸν δὲ πεζο-
μαχοῦντα περιπεσεῖν τραύματι βιαίῳ δι᾽ ἀμφοῖν τοῖν

448

first instance spoilt and broken up that peculiar serried formation of the enemy so well adapted to their special equipment, they would easily have put them to flight owing to their favorable position. Instead of doing this, they acted as if the victory were already in their hand and did exactly the opposite. They remained, that is, at the summit in their original position with the view of getting their opponents as high up the hill as possible so that the enemy's flight would be for a long distance down the steep and precipitous slope. As might have been expected, the result was just the reverse. They had left themselves no means of retreat and on being charged by the Macedonian cohorts which were still fresh and in good order, they were so hard put to it that they had to fight with the assailants along the very top of the hill. From now onwards, wherever they were forced back by the weight of their adversaries' weapons and formation, the Illyrians at once occupied the place where they had stood, while each backward step Eucleidas' men took was on to lower ground, since they had not left themselves any room for orderly retreat or change of formation. The consequence was that very soon they had to turn and take to a flight which proved disastrous, as, for a long distance, it was over difficult and precipitous ground.

69. At this same time the cavalry action was going on, all the Achaean horsemen, and especially Philopoemen, rendering most distinguished service, as the whole struggle was for their liberty. Philopoemen's horse fell mortally wounded, and he, fighting on foot, received a serious wound through both thighs. Meanwhile the two kings at

3 μηροῖν. οἱ δὲ βασιλεῖς κατὰ τὸν Ὄλυμπον τὸ μὲν
πρῶτον ἐποιοῦντο διὰ τῶν εὐζώνων καὶ μισθοφόρων
τὴν συμπλοκήν, παρ' ἑκατέροις σχεδὸν ὑπαρχόντων
4 τούτων εἰς πεντακισχιλίους. ὧν ποτὲ μὲν κατὰ μέρη,
ποτὲ δ' ὁλοσχερῶς συμπιπτόντων, διαφέρουσαν συνέβαινε γίνεσθαι τὴν ἐξ ἀμφοῖν χρείαν, ὁμοῦ τῶν τε
βασιλέων καὶ τῶν στρατοπέδων ἐν συνόψει ποιου-
5 μένων τὴν μάχην. ἡμιλλῶντο δὲ πρὸς ἑαυτοὺς καὶ κατ'
6 ἄνδρα καὶ κατὰ τάγμα ταῖς εὐψυχίαις. ὁ δὲ Κλεομένης, ὁρῶν τοὺς μὲν περὶ τὸν ἀδελφὸν πεφευγότας,
τοὺς δ' ἐν τοῖς ἐπιπέδοις ἱππεῖς ὅσον οὔπω κλίνοντας,
καταπλαγὴς ὢν μὴ πανταχόθεν προσδέξηται τοὺς
πολεμίους, ἠναγκάζετο διασπᾶν τὰ προτειχίσματα
καὶ πᾶσαν τὴν δύναμιν ἐξάγειν μετωπηδὸν κατὰ μίαν
7 πλευρὰν τῆς στρατοπεδείας. ἀνακληθέντων δὲ τῶν
παρ' ἑκατέροις εὐζώνων ἐκ τοῦ μεταξὺ τόπου διὰ τῆς
σάλπιγγος, συναλαλάξασαι καὶ καταβαλοῦσαι τὰς
8 σαρίσας συνέβαλλον αἱ φάλαγγες ἀλλήλαις. ἀγῶνος
δὲ γενομένου κραταιοῦ, καὶ ποτὲ μὲν ἐπὶ πόδα ποιουμένων τὴν ἀναχώρησιν καὶ πιεζομένων ἐπὶ πολὺ τῶν
Μακεδόνων ὑπὸ τῆς τῶν Λακώνων εὐψυχίας, ποτὲ δὲ
τῶν Λακεδαιμονίων ἐξωθουμένων ὑπὸ τοῦ βάρους τῆς
9 τῶν Μακεδόνων τάξεως, τέλος οἱ περὶ τὸν Ἀντίγονον
συμφράξαντες τὰς σαρίσας, καὶ χρησάμενοι τῷ τῆς
ἐπαλλήλου φάλαγγος ἰδιώματι, βίᾳ προσπεσόντες
10 ἐξέωσαν ἐκ τῶν ὀχυρωμάτων τοὺς Λακεδαιμονίους. τὸ
μὲν οὖν ἄλλο πλῆθος ἔφευγε προτροπάδην φονευόμε-
νον· ὁ δὲ Κλεομένης ἱππεῖς τινας ἔχων περὶ ἑαυτὸν

Olympus opened the battle with their light-armed troops
and mercenaries, of which each had about five thousand.
These, now attacking each other in detachments and now
along the whole line, exhibited the greatest gallantry on
both sides, all the more so as they were fighting under the
eyes of the kings and their armies. Man therefore vied with
man and regiment with regiment in a display of courage.
Cleomenes, seeing his brother's troops in flight and the
cavalry on the level ground on the point of giving way, was
afraid of being charged from all sides and was compelled to
pull down part of his defenses and to lead out his whole
force in line from one side of the camp. Each side now re-
called by bugle their light-armed troops from the space between them, and shouting their war cry and lowering their
lances, the two phalanxes met. A stubborn struggle followed. At one time the Macedonians gradually fell back
facing the enemy, giving way for a long distance before the
courage of the Lacedaemonians, at another the latter were
pushed from their ground by the weight of the Macedonian phalanx, until Antigonus' men, closing up their pikes
and taking advantage of the peculiar formation of the
double phalanx, delivered a charge which finally forced
the Lacedaemonians from their stronghold. The whole
Spartan army now fled in rout, followed and cut down by
the enemy; but Cleomenes with a few horsemen reached

11 ἀπεχώρησε μετὰ τούτων ἀσφαλῶς εἰς τὴν Σπάρτην.
ἐπιγενομένης δὲ τῆς νυκτὸς καταβὰς εἰς Γύθιον, ἡτοι-
μασμένων αὐτῷ τῶν πρὸς τὸν πλοῦν ἐκ πλείονος
χρόνου πρὸς τὸ συμβαῖνον, ἀπῆρε μετὰ τῶν φίλων εἰς
Ἀλεξάνδρειαν.

70. Ἀντίγονος δ' ἐγκρατὴς γενόμενος ἐξ ἐφόδου
τῆς Σπάρτης, τά τε λοιπὰ μεγαλοψύχως καὶ φιλανθρώπως ἐχρήσατο τοῖς Λακεδαιμονίοις, τό τε πολίτευμα τὸ πάτριον αὐτοῖς ἀποκαταστήσας ἐν ὀλίγαις
ἡμέραις ἀνέζευξε μετὰ τῶν δυνάμεων ἐκ τῆς πόλεως,
προσαγγελθέντος αὐτῷ τοὺς Ἰλλυριοὺς εἰσβεβληκό-
2 τας εἰς Μακεδονίαν πορθεῖν τὴν χώραν. οὕτως ἀεί
ποθ' ἡ τύχη τὰ μέγιστα τῶν πραγμάτων παρὰ λόγον
3 εἴωθε κρίνειν. καὶ γὰρ τότε Κλεομένης, εἴτε τὰ κατὰ
τὸν κίνδυνον παρείλκυσε τελέως ὀλίγας ἡμέρας, εἴτ'
ἀναχωρήσας ἀπὸ τῆς μάχης εἰς τὴν πόλιν ἐπὶ βραχὺ
τῶν καιρῶν ἀντεποιήσατο, διακατέσχεν ἂν τὴν ἀρχήν.
4 Οὐ μὴν ἀλλ' ὅ γ' Ἀντίγονος παραγενόμενος εἰς
Τεγέαν, καὶ τούτοις ἀποδοὺς τὴν πάτριον πολιτείαν,
δευτεραῖος ἐντεῦθεν εἰς Ἄργος ἐπ' αὐτὴν ἦλθε τὴν τῶν
5 Νεμέων πανήγυριν. ἐν ᾗ τυχὼν πάντων τῶν πρὸς
ἀθάνατον δόξαν καὶ τιμὴν ἀνηκόντων ὑπό τε τοῦ
κοινοῦ τῶν Ἀχαιῶν καὶ κατ' ἰδίαν ἑκάστης τῶν πόλε-
6 ων, ὥρμησε κατὰ σπουδὴν εἰς Μακεδονίαν. καταλα-
βὼν δὲ τοὺς Ἰλλυριοὺς ἐν τῇ χώρᾳ καὶ συμβαλὼν ἐκ
παρατάξεως, τῇ μὲν μάχῃ κατώρθωσε, τῇ δὲ παρα-

---

131 The main port of Laconia, south of Sparta.

Sparta in safety. At nightfall he went down to Gythion,[131] where all had been prepared some time previously for the voyage in view of contingencies, and set sail with his friends for Alexandria.[132]

70. Antigonus having attacked and taken Sparta,[133] treated the Lacedaemonians in all respects with great generosity and humanity, and, after restoring the ancient form of government,[134] left the city in a few days with his whole army, as he had received news that the Illyrians had invaded Macedonia and were ravaging the country. Thus ever is it the way of Fortune to decide the most weighty issues against rule and reason. For on this occasion Cleomenes, had he deferred giving battle for merely a few days, or had he, on returning to Sparta after the battle, waited ever so short a time to avail himself of the turn of events, would have saved his crown.

Antigonus however, on reaching Tegea, restored the old form of government there also, and two days later arrived at Argos just in time for the Nemean festival,[135] at which the Achaean League and each several city heaped on him every honor they could think of to immortalize his memory.[136] He then hastily left for Macedonia, where he found the Illyrians. Engaging them in a pitched battle, he was victorious, but in the course of the fight he strained

[132] For Cleomenes in Egypt see 5. 35–39.

[133] The city was taken by an enemy for the first time.

[134] The reforms of Cleomenes were abolished, the ephors reinstated.   [135] Obviously postponed from 223. After 229 (as occasionally before) it was held at Argos, no longer at Nemea.

[136] For the various honors bestowed on the king, by the Achaeans and others, see Le Bohec (45. 2), 454–465.

κλήσει καὶ κραυγῇ τῇ κατ᾽ αὐτὸν τὸν κίνδυνον ἐκθύμως χρησάμενος εἰς αἵματος ἀναγωγὴν καί τινα τοιαύτην διάθεσιν ἐμπεσὼν μετ᾽ οὐ πολὺ νόσῳ τὸν βίον
7 μετήλλαξε, καλὰς ἐλπίδας ὑποδείξας ἐν αὑτῷ πᾶσι
τοῖς Ἕλλησιν, οὐ μόνον κατὰ τὴν ἐν τοῖς ὑπαίθροις
χρείαν, ἔτι δὲ μᾶλλον κατὰ τὴν ὅλην αἵρεσιν καὶ
8 καλοκἀγαθίαν. τὴν δὲ Μακεδόνων βασιλείαν ἀπέλιπε
Φιλίππῳ τῷ Δημητρίου.

71. Τίνος δὲ χάριν ἐποιησάμεθα τὴν ἐπὶ πλεῖον
2 ὑπὲρ τοῦ προειρημένου πολέμου μνήμην; διότι τῶν
καιρῶν τούτων συναπτόντων τοῖς ὑφ᾽ ἡμῶν ἱστορεῖσθαι μέλλουσι χρήσιμον ἐδόκει, μᾶλλον δ᾽ ἀναγκαῖον
εἶναι κατὰ τὴν ἐξ ἀρχῆς πρόθεσιν τὸ ποιῆσαι πᾶσιν
ἐναργῆ καὶ γνώριμον τὴν ὑπάρχουσαν περὶ Μακε-
3 δόνας καὶ τοὺς Ἕλληνας τότε κατάστασιν. περὶ δὲ
τοὺς αὐτοὺς καιροὺς καὶ Πτολεμαίου νόσῳ τὸν βίον
μεταλλάξαντος Πτολεμαῖος ὁ κληθεὶς Φιλοπάτωρ διε-
4 δέξατο τὴν βασιλείαν. μετήλλαξε δὲ καὶ Σέλευκος ὁ
Σελεύκου τοῦ Καλλινίκου καὶ Πώγωνος ἐπικληθέντος·
5 Ἀντίοχος δὲ διεδέξατο τὴν ἐν Συρίᾳ βασιλείαν, ἀδελ-
φὸς ὢν αὐτοῦ. παραπλήσιον γὰρ δή τι συνέβη τούτοις
καὶ τοῖς πρώτοις μετὰ τὴν Ἀλεξάνδρου τελευτὴν
κατασχοῦσι τὰς ἀρχὰς ταύτας, λέγω δὲ Σελεύκῳ,
6 Πτολεμαίῳ, Λυσιμάχῳ. ἐκεῖνοί τε γὰρ πάντες περὶ
τὴν εἰκοστὴν καὶ τετάρτην πρὸς ταῖς ἑκατὸν ὀλυμπιάδα μετήλλαξαν, καθάπερ ἐπάνω προεῖπον, οὗτοί τε
περὶ τὴν ἐνάτην καὶ τριακοστήν.

7   Ἡμεῖς δ᾽ ἐπειδὴ τὴν ἐπίστασιν καὶ προκατασκευὴν

himself so much by shouting to his troops to cheer them on that he took to vomiting blood and, falling into the morbid condition which accompanies this, died soon afterward.[137] He had aroused high hopes of himself throughout Greece, not so much by his support in the field as by his general high principles and excellence. He was succeeded on the throne of Macedon by Philip son of Demetrius.

220 B.C.

71. Now to explain why I have dealt with this war at such length. As this period immediately precedes those times, the history of which I am about to write, I thought it would be of service, or rather that the original plan of this work made it necessary for me, to make clearly known to everyone the state of affairs in Macedonia and Greece at this time. Just about the same time Ptolemy Euergetes fell sick and died, being succeeded by Ptolemy surnamed Philopator. Seleucus, the son of the Seleucus surnamed Callinicus or Pogon, also died at this time,[138] his brother Antiochus succeeding him in the kingdom of Syria. The same thing in fact occurred in the case of these three kings, as in that of the first successors of Alexander in the three kingdoms, Seleucus, Ptolemy, and Lysimachus, who all, as I stated above,[139] died in the 124th Olympiad, while these kings died in the 139th.

284–280 B.C.

224–220 B.C.

I have thus completed this Introduction or preliminary

[137] Not immediately, for he appointed guardians for Philip (V), the son of Demetrius II, who was to succeed him.

[138] The deaths of Ptolemy III in 221 and of Seleucus III (in 223 or 222) were almost contemporary with Antigonus' death.

[139] 41. 2.

τῆς ὅλης ἱστορίας διεληλύθαμεν, δι' ἧς ὑποδέδεικται
πότε καὶ πῶς καὶ δι' ἃς αἰτίας τῶν κατὰ τὴν Ἰταλίαν
κρατήσαντες Ῥωμαῖοι πρῶτον ἐγχειρεῖν ἤρξαντο τοῖς
ἔξω πράγμασι, καὶ πρῶτον ἐτόλμησαν ἀμφισβητεῖν
8 Καρχηδονίοις τῆς θαλάττης, ἅμα δὲ τούτοις καὶ τὴν
περὶ τοὺς Ἕλληνας καὶ Μακεδόνας, ὁμοίως δὲ καὶ
περὶ Καρχηδονίους ὑπάρχουσαν τότε κατάστασιν δε-
9 δηλώκαμεν, καθῆκον ἂν εἴη παραγεγονότας ἐπὶ τοὺς
καιροὺς τούτους κατὰ τὴν ἐξ ἀρχῆς πρόθεσιν, ἐν οἷς
ἔμελλον οἱ μὲν Ἕλληνες τὸν συμμαχικόν, Ῥωμαῖοι δὲ
τὸν Ἀννιβιακόν, οἱ δὲ κατὰ τὴν Ἀσίαν βασιλεῖς τὸν
10 περὶ Κοίλης Συρίας ἐνίστασθαι πόλεμον, καὶ τὴν
βύβλον ταύτην ἀφορίζειν ἀκολούθως τῇ τε τῶν προγεγονότων πραγμάτων περιγραφῇ καὶ τῇ τῶν κεχει-
ρικότων τὰ πρὸ τοῦ δυναστῶν καταστροφῇ.

part of my History. In it I have shown in the first place when, how, and why the Romans, having mastered Italy, first entered on enterprises outside that land and disputed the command of the sea with the Carthaginians, and next I have dealt with the state of Greece and Macedonia and with that of Carthage as this existed then. So having, as was my original purpose, reached the date at which the Greeks[140] were on the eve of the Social War, the Romans on the eve of the Hannibalic War, and the kings of Asia about to enter on the war for Coele-Syria, I must now bring this Book to its close, which coincides with the final events preceding these wars and the death of the three kings who had up to now directed affairs.

[140] "Hellenes" was the official name of the members of the League founded by Antigonus Doson in 224; see 54.4.

INDEX

ACARNANIA, Acarnanians
  2:6.10.45.65.66
Acerrae 2:34
Achaea, Achaeans 1:3.
  2:6.9.10.12.37–61.65–67
Acrocorinthus 2:45.50 52
Adherbal 1:44.46.49.50.52.53
Admetus 2:66
Adriatic region 1:2. 2:19.26
Adriatic sea 2:12.14.16.17
Adda, river 2:32
Adys 1:30
Aegira 2:41
Aegium: 2:41.54
Aegospotami, battle of 1:6
Aegusae, islands 1:44.60
Aegys 2:54
L. Aemilius Papus, cos. 225,
  2:23.26–28.31
M. Aemilius Lepidus, cos. 282,
  2:21
M. Aemilius Paullus, cos. 255,
  1:36
Aetna 1:55
Aetolia, Aetolians 1:3. 2:2–
  4.6.9.12.37.43–47.49.50.57.58
Africa, Africans, see Libya, Lib-
  yans
Agathocles 1:7.82

Agones 2:15
Agrianians 2:65
Agrigentum 1:17.18.20.27.43.
  2:7
Agron (Illyria) 2:2.4
Alba 2:18
Alexander, son of Admetus 2:66
Alexander of Epirus 2:45
Alexander the Great 2:41.71
Alexander 2:68
Alexandria (Egypt) 2:69
Alexon, Achaean 1:43
Alps 2.14–16.23.32.34.35
Anares 2:17.32.34
Aneroestus 2:22.26.31
Antalcidas, peace of 1:6
Antigonia 2:5.6
Antigonus 1 1:63
Antigonus Gonatas 2:41.43–45
Antigonus Doson 2:45.47–
  57.60.63–70
Antiochus III 1:3 2:71
Apennines, mountains
  2:14.16.17
Apollonia 2:9.11
Aratus, of Sicyon, senior 1:3
  2:40.43–52.56.57.59.60
Aratus, junior 2:51
Arbo 2:11

INDEX

Arcadia, Arcadians
   2:38.54.56.62
Ardiaeans 2:11.12
Argolis 2:64
Argos, Argives 2:44.52–
   54.59.64.70
Ariminum 2:21.23
Aristomachus of Argos
   2:44.54.60
Aristoteles of Argos 2:53
Arretium 2:16
Artemidorus 1:8
Asclepius, 1:18
Asia 1:2.3. 2:37
Aspis 1:29.34.36
Atarbes, see Adherbal
Athens,Athenians, Attica 1:63.
   2:12.62
Athenaeum 2:46
A. Atilius Calatinus, cos. 258
   and 254, 1:24.38
C. Atilius, cos. 250, 1:39
C. Atilius Regulus, cos. 257.
   250, 1:25.39
C. Atilius Regulus, cos. 225,
   2:23.27.28
M. Atilius Regulus, cos. 267.
   256, 1:26.28–31.34
Atintania 2:11
Atis 2:21
Attica 2:62
Autaritus 1:77–80.85

Balearic islands 1:67
Belbina 2:54
Bodencus, river 2:16
Boeotians 2:49.65
Boii 2:17.20–24.28.30.31
Boödes: Carthaginian 1;21

Bostar 1:30.79
Brundisium 2:11
Bruttii 1:56
Bura 2:41

L. Caecilius Metellus, cos.
   251. 247, 1:39.40
L. Caecilius Metellus, cos. 284,
   Praetor 283, 2:19
Camarina 1:24.37
Camerinum 2:19
Campanians, in Messana,
   1:7.8.9. 2:24
Caphyae 2:52
Capua 2:17
Carthage, Carthaginians
   1:3.7.8.10–12.15.17–88.
   2:1.7.13.20.22.36.43.71
Carthage, New 2:13
Carthalo 1:53.4
Caryneia 2:10.41
Cassander 2:41
Caulonians 2:39
Celtiberia 2:13
Celts 1:13.17.43.67.77.
   2:5.13.17.24–34
Cenchreae 2:59
Cenomani 2:17.23.24.32
Centuripa 1:9
Cercidas of Megalopolis
   2:48.50.65
Chalcidian mountain 1:11
Clastidium 2:34
A. Claudius Caudex, cos. 264,
   1:11.12.16
M. Claudius Marcellus, cos.
   222, 2:34
P. Claudius Pulcher, cos. 249,
   1:49.50.52

Cleomenes of Sparta: 1:13. 2:45–58.60–67.69.70
Cleonae 2:52
Cleonymus, Tyrant of Phlius 2:44
Clitorians 2:55
Clusium 2:25
Clusius, river 2:32
Cocynthus 2:14
Coele-Syria 1:3. 2:71
Colaeum 2:55
Concolitanus, king of the Boii 2:22.31
Corcyra 2:9–12
Corinth, Corinthians 2:12.43.51.52.54
Cn. Cornelius Scipio, cos. 260. 254, 1:21.22.38
Cn. Cornelius Scipio Calvus, cos. 222, 2:34
Coruncanius, C. and L., in Illyria, 2:8
Crete, Cretans 2:66
Crotonians 2:39
Cumae 1:56
M'. Curius 2:19
Cyamosorus, river 1:9

Danube (Ister), river 1:2
Dardanians 2:6
Decius of Campania 1:7
Delphi 1:6. 2:20.35
Demetrius I Poliorcetes 1:63. 2:41
Demetrius II, son of Antigonus Gonatas 1:3. 2:2.44.46.49.60.70
Demetrius of Pharos 2:10.11.65

Dionysius, senior, tyrant of Syracuse 1:6. 2:39
Drepana 1:41.46.49.55.56.59.61
C. Duilius, cos. 260, victor at Mylae 1:22.23
Dyme 2:41.51

Ebro 2:14
Echetla 1:15
Ecnomus, Roman victory 1:25
Egypt 2:37
Elea 1:20
Elis 2:5
Elleporus, battle of the 1:6
Emporia 1:82
Enna 1:24
Epidamnus, Epidamnians 2:9–12
Epidaurus 2:52
Epirus, Epirots 2:5–7.65
Eridanos (Po) 2:16
Eryx, Mount 1:55–60. 66.77. 2:7
Eryx, town 1:55
Etruria, Etruscans 1:6. 2:16.17.19.20.23–27
Euas 2.65.66
Euboea 2:52
Euclidas 2:65–69
Euripides, the poet 1:35
Europe 1:2. 2:12.14

Q. Fabius Pictor 1:14.15.58
Faesulae (Fiesole) 2:25
Falerii 1:65
Falisci 1:65
C. Flaminius, cos. 223 and 217, 2:21,32,33
Frentani 2:24

Cn. Fulvius Centumalus, cos. 229, 2:11.12
Q. Fulvius, cos. 224, 2:31
Servius Fulvius, cos. 255, 1:36
C. Furius Pacilus, cos. 251, 1:39
P. Furius, cos. 223, 2:32

GAESATAE, GAESATI 2:22.23.28.30.34
Galatus 2:21
Gauls (see also Celts) 1:6. 2:7.17.19.65
Gauls, Alpine 2:21
Gauls, Transalpine 2:15.19.21
Gauls (Celts), take Rome 1:6
Gesco, Gisco 1:66.68–77.79–81
Gorgylus, river 2:66
Gorza 1:74
Greece, Greeks 1:3.32. 2:37.49.71
Gythion (Gythaeum) 2:69

HAMILCAR, at Panormus, at Tyndaris and Ecnomus 1:25.27.28.30
Hamilcar Barcas 1:13.56.58.60.61.64.68– 78.81.82.84.85–88. 2:1
Hamilcar, father of Hannibal 1:44
Hannibal, Hamilcar Barcas's son 1:64. 2:1.14.24.36
Hannibal, son of Hamilcar 1:44.46
Hannibal, Carthaginian General at Panormus 1:21.24
Hannibal, Carthaginian General at Agrigentum 1:18.19.23
Hannibal, son of the above 1:43

Hannibal 1:82.86
Hannibal, surnamed the Rhodian 1.46.47.59
Hannibalic war (2nd Punic War) 1:3.65 2:37.71
Hanno 1:67.72– 74.77.81.82.87.88
Hanno, general in Sicily at Agrigentum 1:18.19.27.28.60
Hasdrubal, son of Hanno 1:30.38.40
Hasdrubal, son-in-law of Hamilcar Barcas 1:13. 2:1.13.22.36
Hecatompylus 1.73. 2:51
Helice 2:41
Helicranum 2:6
Heraclea 1:18.19.25.30.38.52
Heraclidae 2:41
Heraea 2:54
Herbesus 1:18
Hercte 1:56
Hercules' pillars 2:1
Hermaeum 1:29.36
Hermione 2:44.52
Hiero of Syracuse 1:8.11.15– 18.62.83. 2:1
Himera 1:24
Himilco 1:42.43.45.53
Hippana 1:24
Hippou Acra ("Hippacritae") 1:70.73.77.82.88
Holy Isle 1:61

IAPYGIANS 2:24
Iberians 1:17.67 2:1
Iberus, see Ebro
Illyria, Illyrians 1:13. 2:3.5–12. 2:44.65–68.70

Indian mahouts 1:40
Insubres 2:22.23.28.30.32.34.35
Ionian sea 2:14
Iseas 2:41
Issa 2:11
Ister, see Danube
Isthmian games 2:12
Isthmus of Corinth 2:52
Italy 1:3.20 2:13.14
L. Iunius Pullus, cos. 249,
    1:52.54.55

LACEDAEMON, Sparta, Laconia,
    Lacedaemonians, Spartans
    1:2.6.63. 2:38.39.41.45.46.
    47.49–52.54.57.58.62.64.65.
    69.70
Lai or Laevi 2:17
Ladoceia 2.51.55
Latins 1.6 2:18.24
Lebecii 2:17
Leontium, in Achaea 2:41
Leptines 1:9
Leptis 1:87
Leuctra, battle of 1:6. 2:39.41
Libya, Libyans, cf. also
    Numidians
    1:2.3.10.13.19.20.26.29.36.39.
    41.42.67–88
Libyan War 1:67–88. 2:1
Liguria, Ligurians 1:17.67.
    2:16.31
Lilybaeum, promontory 1:39.42
Lilybaeum, town 1:25.39–
    48.52–56.59–61.66
Lingones 2:17
Lipara 1:21.24.39
Liparaean islands 1:25
Lissus 2:12

Locrians 1:20
Locris 1:56
Longanus, river 1:9
Lotus-eaters 1:39
Lucanians 2:24
C. Lutatius Catulus, cos. 242,
    victor at Aegatian Isles
    1:59.60.62
Lycaeum 2:55
Lycortas 2:40
Lydiadas 2:44.51
Lysimachus of Thrace 2:41.71

MACARAS, river 1:86
Macedonia, Macedonians 1:2.
    2:37.39.40.43.45.48–
    50.54.56.65–71
Macella, taken by Romans
    1:24
Magna Graecia 2:39
Mamertines 1:7–11.20
Q. Mamilius, cos. 262, 1:17
L. Manlius Vulso Longus,
    cos.256 and 250,
    1:26.28.29.39
T. Manlius Torquatus, cos.224,
    2:31
Mantineans 2:46.53–58.61.62
Margus of Caryneia 2:10.41.43
Marrucini 2:24
Marsi 2:24
Massilia 2:14.16.32
Mathos 1:69.50.72.73.77.79.82–
    88
Mediolanum 2:34
Medion or Medeon 2:2–4
Megalopolis, Megalopolitans
    2:44.48.50.51.54.55.61.62.64–
    66

INDEX

Megara 2:43

Meninx 1:39

Mercenaries' war, see Libyan War

Mergane 1:8

Messapians 2:24

Messene (Messana) in Italy 1:7.8.10.11.15.20.21.25.52

Messene, Messenia, in Greece 2:5.59.61.62

Minerva (Athena) 2:39

Mylae 1:23

Mylaean plain 1:9

Myttistratum 1:24

NARAVAS 1:78.82.84.86

Naples 1:20

Nemean festival 2:70

New Carthage: 2:13

Nicophanes 2:48.50

Nola 2:17

Numidians 1:19.31.74.77

Nutria 2:11

OENOUS 2:65.66

Ogygus 2:41

Olana, one of the two mouths of the Po 2:16

Olenus 2:41

Olympus, in Laconia 2:65.66.69

Onei (ass's back) mountains 2:52

Orchomenus in Arcadia 2:46.54.55

Orestes 2:41

Orion 1:37

M'. Otacilius, cos. 263, 1:16

T. Otacilius, cos. 261, 1:20

PACHYNUS 1:25.42.54

Padua 2:16

Padus, river, see Po,

Panormus, in Sicily 1:21.24.38.39.40.55.56

Paropus 1:24

Parthini 2:11

Patrae 2:41

Paxi, islands 2:10

Pellene, in Achaea 2:41.52

Peloponnesus, Peloponnesians 1:42. 2:37.38.43.49.52.54.55.62

Pelorias, Cape 1:11.42

Persians 1:2.63. 2:35.37

Perseus 1:3

Phäeton 2:16

Pharae, in Achaea 2:41

Pharos 2:11

Pheneus 2:52

Philinus, historian 1:14

Philip II , son of Amyntas 2:41.48

Philip V, king of Macedon, son of Demetrius, father of Perseus 1:3. 2:37.45.70

Philopoemen 2:40.67–69

Phlegraean plain 2:17

Phlius 2:44.52

Phoenice, in Epirus 2:5.8

Phylarchus, historian 2:56–63

Picenum 2:21.23

Pisa 2:16.27.28

Pleuratus 2:2

Po (Eridanus): 2:16.17.19.23.28.31.32.34.35

L Postumius, cos. 229, 2:11.12

L. Postumius Albinus, cos. 262, 1:17

Prion, mountain in Africa 1:85
Ptolemy I, son of Lagus 1:63.
  2:41.71
Ptolemy Ceraunus, king of
  Macedon 2:41
Ptolemy III, Euergetes
  2:47.51.63.71
Ptolemy IV, Philopator 1:3. 2:71
Pyrrhus 1:6.7.23. 2:20.41
Pythagoreans 2:39

RHEGIUM 1:6–8.10
Rhizon 2:11
Rhone 2:15.22.34
Roman dominion 1:1.2
Romans 1 passim.
  2:7.8.11.12.21.22.24.25–31.71
Rome 1.7.10.17.29
  2:.13.18.23.25.31.36

SABINES 2.24
Samnites 1:6. 2:19.24
Sardinia
  1:2.10.24.43.79.82.83.88.
  2:23.27
Sardinian sea 1:42. 2:14
Sarsinates 2:24
Saw, a place 1:85
Scerdilaïdas 2:5.6
Segesta 1:24
Seleucus I, Nicator 2:41.71
Seleucus II, Callinicus 2:71
Seleucus III, Ceraunus 2:71
Selinus 1:39
Sellasia, battle of 2:65
C. Sempronius Blaesus, cos.
  253, 1:39
Sena 2:14.16
Senones 2:17.20

Sentinum 2:19
Cn. Servilius Caepio, cos. 253,
  1:39
Sicca 1:66.67
Sicily 1:2.5.10.13.16.42.62.63.
  2:1.24.36.37.43
Sicilian sea 1:42. 2:14.16
Sicyon 2:42.52.54
Sirius 1:37
Social War 1:3
Spain, Spaniards 1:10.13.
  2:1.13.22.36
Sparta, Spartans, see Laconia,
  Lacedaemonians
Spendius 1:69–72.77–82.84–86
Stymphalians 2:55
C. Sulpicus Paterculus, cos.
  259, 1:24
Sunes 1:11
Sybarites 2:39
Syracuse, Syracusans
  1:8.9.11.15.16.43.52.53.62
Syrtis minor 1:39

TARENTUM, Tarentines 1:6.20.
  2:24
Taurisci 2:15.28.30
Tegea 2:4.6.54.58.70
Telamon 2:27
Telphusa 2:54
Teuta, regent of Illyria
  2:4.6.8.9.11.12
Thearces 2:55
Thebans 2:39.62
Therma 1:39
Thermopylae 2:52
Thessaly 2:49.52
Timaeus, historian 1.5
Timoxenus 2:53

INDEX

Tisamenus 2:41
Torus, hill 1:19
Trigaboli, place at the Po 2:16
Tritaea 2:41
Troezen 2:52
Tunis
   1:30.67.69.73.76.77.79.84–86
Tyndaris 1:25
Tyrrhenian sea 1:20. 2:14.16

Umbrians 2:16.24
Utica, Uticans 1:70.73.74–
   76.82.83.88

Vadimon, Lake 2:20
L. Valerius Flaccus, cos. 261,
   1:20

M'. Valerius Maximus, cos. 263,
   1:16
Veneti 2:17.18.23.24
Venus Erycina 1:55. 2:7
Vestini 2: 24

Xanthippus of Sparta
   1:32.33.36
Xeno 2:44

Zarzas 1:84.85
Zeus Amarius 2:39